11th Edition

Every Tenant's
Legal Guide

Attorneys Ann O'Connell and Janet Portman

NOLO
LAW for ALL

ELEVENTH EDITION   MAY 2024

Cover Design   SUSAN PUTNEY

Book Design   SUSAN PUTNEY

Proofreading   IRENE BARNARD

Index   VICTORIA BAKER

Printing   SHERIDAN

Names: Portman, Janet, author. | O'Connell, Ann, author.
Title: Every tenant's legal guide / Attorney Ann O'Connell, Attorney Janet
    Portman.
Description: 11th Edition. | El Segundo : Nolo, 2024. | Includes index.
Identifiers: LCCN 2023033936 | ISBN 9781413331721 (paperback) | ISBN
    9781413331738 (ebook)
Subjects: LCSH: Landlord and tenant--United States--Popular works.
Classification: LCC KF590.Z9 P67 2024 | DDC 346.7304/34--dc23
LC record available at https://lccn.loc.gov/2023033936

Please note

Accurate, plain-English legal information can help you solve many of
your own legal problems. But this text is not a substitute for personalized
advice from a knowledgeable lawyer. If you want the help of a trained
professional—and we'll always point out situations in which we think
that's a good idea—consult an attorney licensed to practice in your state.

MH Sub I, LLC dba Nolo, 909 N. Pacific Coast Hwy, 11th Fl, El Segundo, CA 90245

About the Authors

Ann O'Connell is a legal editor at Nolo specializing in landlord-tenant and real estate law. She is a coauthor of *Nolo's Essential Guide to Buying Your First Home* and *Every Landlord's Legal Guide*. Before joining Nolo, Ann was a freelance writer for other publications and law firms. She is a member of the bar in California, Nevada, and Colorado, where she is both an active attorney and a real estate broker. Ann has practiced in California and Colorado, and had her own firm in Colorado, where she focused on real estate, landlord-tenant, and small business law. Ann earned her B.A. from Boston College and her J.D. from UC Berkeley Law.

Janet Portman, an attorney and Nolo's Executive Editor, received undergraduate and graduate degrees from Stanford and a law degree from Santa Clara University. She is an expert on landlord-tenant law and the coauthor of *Every Landlord's Legal Guide, The California Landlord's Law Book: Rights & Responsibilities, California Tenants' Rights, Renters' Rights*, and *Leases & Rental Agreements*. As a practicing attorney, she specialized in criminal defense before joining Nolo.

Table of Contents

Appendixes

Your Tenant Companion

Dealing with your landlord or property manager can be challenging, to say the least. The goal of this book is to make your life as a tenant easier: Not only will you learn the legal knowledge you need to be a responsible renter, but you'll also learn when it's time to take a stand and defend your rights.

Because the law varies from state to state, this book includes state-specific information about landlord-tenant laws that are most important to renters. At the back of the book, you'll find detailed charts on everything from state security deposit rules to state laws prohibiting landlord retaliation.

Sometimes, if you're dealing with a large, corporate landlord, you might not even know who your landlord is! We'll explain how to determine the contact information for your landlord, and why, when, and how to approach your landlord about your rental concerns and requests.

This book also includes dozens of practical forms, sample letters, notices, and checklists to help you through the entire rental process. Each form is easy to customize for your particular situation. We provide filled-in samples in the text, and you'll find the forms on the companion page for this book on the Nolo website (see below for details).

But let's face it—even conscientious and knowledgeable tenants don't always get good results. Some landlords are stingy, petty, and obnoxious, bent on extracting the last dollar from their tenants at the least possible cost to themselves.

Trying to deal with them reasonably just doesn't work. The information and tips in this book are your legal weapons to fight back and protect your rights.

Even when the law is 110% on your side, though, avoiding conflict sometimes is wiser than engaging in a drawn-out, costly, and risky legal dispute with your landlord. This book discusses how to evaluate your options when you're in a dispute with your landlord—and how to make the call to walk away rather than fight.

We hope that by reading this book, you'll find the information you need to handle conflicts with your landlord, and that you'll learn strategies that will help you avoid these conflicts in the first place.

CAUTION
Who shouldn't use this book? Don't use this book if you are renting commercial property or space in a mobile home park, hotel, or marina. Also, if you are a tenant in government-subsidized or -owned housing (including the "Section 8" program), your lease might contain terms required by the government, which neither you nor your landlord can change.

Get Forms and More at This Book's Companion Page on Nolo.com

This book includes many forms, such as a rental application and a demand for the return of a security deposit. You can download the forms and worksheets in this book at

www.nolo.com/back-of-book/EVTEN.html

See Appendix B, "How to Use the Downloadable Forms on the Nolo Website" for a list of forms available on Nolo.com. For guidance on finding legal (and other) assistance, understanding the law, and asserting your rights, see Nolo's Legal Resources for Tenants (on Nolo's home page, choose Legal Articles, then Tenants).

Finding a Place to Rent

A good apartment or house should provide more than shelter, warmth, and a place to lay your head; it should be a true home. Yet many renters make bad choices—they spend too much in rent, pick the wrong location, or settle for a place that doesn't truly meet their needs. Although you might not be able to afford your dream rental in a tight rental market, you can take steps to find a solid apartment or house that meets your needs and budget.

Perhaps the most important bit of advice is to take your time. One of the worst—and most costly—mistakes you can make is to sign a lease or put down a hefty deposit at the end of a long, frustrating day of apartment-hunting, only to realize later that the place is completely unsuitable. Consider staying with friends or family for a few weeks or finding a short-term rental to give yourself more time to examine what's out there. Never, ever, send a deposit to a landlord you haven't met for a rental you haven't seen (almost always, you're being scammed).

Whether you're looking for your first or tenth rental, living by yourself or with others, this chapter shows you how to:

- set clear priorities before you start your search
- use a variety of resources to tap into available rentals, and
- beat the competition by pulling together the information landlords want to see—good references and credit information—before you visit prospective rentals.

This chapter also explains your legal rights and responsibilities regarding the rental application process, credit reports, credit-check fees, and holding deposits. (For details on antidiscrimination laws that limit what landlords can say and do in the tenant selection process, see Chapter 5.)

RELATED TOPIC

Preparing for a move. If you're moving from one rental to another, be sure you understand all the legal and practical rules for ending a tenancy, getting your deposit returned, and moving out. See Chapters 15 and 16 for details.

Check Your Credit Rating Before You Start Your Housing Search

Your credit report contains a wealth of information that landlords use to evaluate you as a potential tenant. For example, many reports list bankruptcy filings, uncollected child support, and unpaid debts that have been reported to the credit reporting agency. The report will also reflect favorable information, such as your ability to pay your card balances and other debts on time. To make sure your credit report is accurate—or to give yourself time to clean it up if there are problems or errors—get a copy of your report before you start looking. "Rental Applications and Credit Reports," below, provides complete details.

Setting Your Rental Priorities

Most people start their housing search with some general idea of how much they can afford to pay, where they want to live, how big a place they need, and whether the style of the unit (older and classic, or simple and modern) is important. To find the best rental for your needs though, go further: Set guidelines in advance, being realistic about your budget and what's available for rent.

Here's our approach to finding a rental house or apartment you can afford and will enjoy living in:

Step 1: Establish priorities. Know your maximum rent, desired location, and ideal number of bedrooms before you start looking. If you're renting with one or more other people, make sure you agree on the basics. The list "Rental Priorities," below, suggests factors to consider.

Step 2: Rate your priorities with a Rental Priorities Worksheet. Once you've identified your priorities, rank them. Designate your "must-haves," and be realistic about what would be "nice to have." To make this simple, we've prepared a Rental Priorities Worksheet, shown below. There's space for you to write down the "must-haves," "nice-to-haves," and your absolute deal killers. Don't limit yourself too much: try to have only one or two "must-haves."

 FORM

The Nolo website includes a downloadable copy of the Rental Priorities Worksheet. See Appendix B for the link to the forms in this book.

Step 3: Prepare (and don't forget to review) your Rental Priorities Worksheet. Once you complete the priorities section of the Worksheet, save it to your phone or tablet, or make several copies for use when looking at apartments or rental houses.

Step 4: View potential rentals. Complete a Worksheet for each rental unit you're seriously considering, as follows:

- Enter the address, contact person, phone number, email, rent, deposit, term (month-to-month or year lease), and other key information on the top of the form.
- As you walk around the rental unit and talk with the landlord or manager, indicate the pluses and minuses and how it stacks up against your mandatory and secondary priorities (as well any deal-killers) that apply.

- Note whether you think some factor of the rental can be adjusted to better accommodate your needs—for example, "Rent is high, but there's enough space for an extra (rent-paying) roommate."
- Jot down additional features in the section for Other Comments, such as "Neighbors seem very friendly" or "Tiny yard for kids to play, but great park is just a block away."

Step 5: Evaluate your options. Ideally, you'll have found at least one option that meets your must-haves. Make sure that these must-haves aren't canceled out by any deal-killers, though. Settling for a rental with a true deal-killer could have you wanting to move out as soon as you move in. Especially if you're renting in a tight market, focus on avoiding your deal-killers rather than capturing all of your must- or nice-to-haves. For example, if a high-crime neighborhood is a deal-killer for you, you're probably going to be happier living in a smaller apartment in a safe, walkable neighborhood than you would be if you prioritize your "must-have" of a spacious apartment.

Check Out the Lease or Rental Agreement Before Deciding

Leases and rental agreements cover many issues, such as the amount of rent and deposits, length of the tenancy, number of tenants, and pets. In addition, some rental agreements might include provisions that you find unacceptable—for example, restrictions on how long guests can stay or a ban on using the apartment for your home business. Ask for a copy of the lease or rental agreement early on so you can weigh the pros and cons of the agreement itself before you mentally commit to a place. Be sure to read Chapter 2 for details on leases and rental agreements and how to negotiate terms before you sign on the dotted line.

Rental Priorities

When you're making your list of priorities, consider these issues:

Rent

Figure out the maximum monthly amount you can afford to pay. Include additional costs, such as utilities, internet, and parking. As a general rule, it's best to not spend more than 25% to 35% of your monthly take-home pay on housing costs. This range varies, though, depending on your other life expenses and whether you live in an area with a high cost of living.

Deposits

Depending on state law and landlord practices, you might be required to pay as much as two months' rent as a security deposit. If you have limited cash to pay deposits and other up-front fees, include the maximum you can pay in the "Mandatory Priorities" list on your worksheet. You'll also want to find out if the landlord offers any alternatives to traditional lump-sum security deposits, such as a fee-in-lieu of the deposit, a bond, or a security deposit payment plan. (Chapter 4 covers security deposits in general and these potential security deposit alternatives.)

Location and Neighborhood

Where you live is often more important than the size and amenities of the unit you rent. If you know the exact area you want, list it. If you don't, think about what attributes your ideal neighborhood would have. For example, if being able to walk to restaurants is important, don't rent an apartment in a car-dependent suburb.

Schools

If you have school-age children, the proximity and quality of local schools are very important considerations. If you're new to the area, try contacting your state department of education or the local school district to find out to what extent your address determines which schools your children can attend—every school district has different rules. It should be able to provide data for individual schools and districts, including academic test scores, enrollment figures, racial and ethnic information, and even dropout rates. Your next step is to research (and visit, if possible) local schools and school districts to learn about class size, class offerings, instructional practices, and services. Finally, check out resources such as the local school board's meeting minutes, PTA meeting minutes, and online ranking and review sites. Look online for a local parents' network ("[your city] parents' network"), which might be a goldmine of information (and opinions!).

Work or School Commute

If you commute to work or school, note the maximum times or distance you're willing to travel each day. If you'll rely on public transit, note it.

Ability to Run a Business From Home

If you're planning to run a business from home, make sure local law or landlord policies don't prohibit your home-based business. See Chapter 2 for more information on this topic.

Pets

If you have a pet, you'll need to make sure the landlord allows pets. (See Chapter 2 for suggestions on how to negotiate with landlords who don't normally allow pets.)

Number of Tenants

If you will have roommates, find out what the occupancy limit is for each rental you consider. (Chapter 5 discusses occupancy standards many landlords set, limiting the number of tenants in a particular rental unit.)

Rental Term

Do you want the flexibility of a short-term rental agreement, or the security of a long-term lease? (Chapter 2 discusses the pros and cons of leases and rental agreements. Also, Chapter 15 discusses sublets, which might be a short-term rental option.)

Move-In Date

If you need a place immediately, write "Must be available now" in your priority list. But don't be too quick to pass up a great place that's not available for several weeks. It might be worth it to get a short-term rental for the interim. Also, if a fantastic apartment is available now, but you have to give 30 days' notice on your

Rental Priorities (continued)

current place, it might be worth paying double rent for a while so you don't have to pass on a terrific apartment.

Number and Type of Rooms

How many bedrooms, baths, or other rooms do you need? Do you need suitable space for your home office? Is a finished basement important? Is a modern kitchen with lots of counter space and good light ideal? How about a large living room for entertaining? Be realistic about what you can't live without.

Furnishings

If you want something completely furnished, make this a priority. Furnished rentals can be difficult to find and pricey, though—keep in mind that you can always rent furniture yourself if you can't find a furnished apartment. You can find prices and even package deals on the websites of most major furniture rental companies.

Other Interior Needs

Other priorities might include good space separation for roommates, a fireplace, lots of closets, air-conditioning, or in-unit laundry. Check the services available within the unit—for example, does your phone have good reception? What type of internet service is available? If you have a disability or have special needs, and want a rental that is already compatible with your needs, mark these as priorities. (For more on rights of the disabled, see Chapter 5.)

Security

For many people, a top-notch security system for the building, rental unit, and parking area is important—for example, bars on all windows, a doorman or a front gate security system with intercom that allows you to screen visitors before they actually get to the front door of your apartment.

Quiet

If you can't stand the idea of living on a busy street with lots of traffic or in an apartment with paper-thin walls, make this a priority.

Yard and Outdoor Space

If you have a dog or want room for a garden or for kids to play, a fenced-in yard will be important. Or maybe a deck, patio, or balcony ranks high on your wish list.

Parking

Parking can be critical, especially if you live in an urban area. Write down how many vehicles you have and whether you need garage parking or easy street parking with no restrictions. Don't forget your other modes of transportation, either—where do you want to be able to keep your bicycle or e-bike?

Other Tenants

You might prefer a building with certain types of tenants, such as students or families. Landlords can't legally choose (or refuse) tenants who are members of a protected class (see Chapter 5 for a discussion of discriminatory housing practices), but there's no law prohibiting tenants from choosing properties that tend to be populated by distinct groups. For example, affordable housing near a college will be filled with students, and pricey buildings in spruced-up business or financial areas are likely to be peopled with older, professional types.

Landlord and Manager

Who your landlord is can have a major impact on your overall satisfaction with the rental, as well as how often you see the landlord. Maybe you're okay with a landlord who lives next door in the duplex, or maybe you'd prefer the relative anonymity of a massive complex with a professional on-site manager. Your past experiences with either type of landlord might determine your preferences, but keep in mind that each type can be good or bad, depending on how that person or entity does business. For any rental you visit, try to ask residents about how the property is managed.

Smoking Policies

If you're a smoker and want to be able to smoke in your rental and in common areas, make sure that it's allowed in your unit. Conversely, if you want to live in a place that's free of odors, smoke stains, and secondhand smoke, make it a priority.

Purchase Potential

If you want to move into a rental you can eventually buy, investigate this from the start. This book does not cover rent-to-own contracts, so you'll need to do additional research for advice on these agreements.

Rental Priorities Worksheet

Address: 178 Park St., #4F, Springsteen, New Jersey 00000

Contact: Emily Greenwood (Owner)   Email: emily@greenwood.com   Phone: (609) 555-1212

Rent: $3,200/month   Deposit: $3,200   Other fees: _____

Term: one year lease   Date seen: February 15, 20xx   Date available: March 1, 20xx

Brief description of rental unit and building: Sunny three-bedroom apt. in four-story brownstone. Recently remodeled kitchen. One and one-half baths. Lots of charm. Great location!

Mandatory Priorities:

- ☑ Close to university (a 10-minute walk!)
- ☐ Maximum $3,000 rent (over our limit, but high-speed internet and electricity are included)
- ☑ Modern kitchen
- ☑ Lots of light
- ☑ Three bedrooms
- ☑ Two bathrooms
- ☐ _____

Secondary Priorities:

- ☑ Hardwood floors
- ☑ Small building
- ☐ Allows pets
- ☐ Fireplace
- ☐ _____
- ☐ _____

Absolute No Ways:

- ☐ High-crime area
- ☐ Run-down area
- ☐ _____
- ☐ _____
- ☐ _____
- ☐ _____

Other Comments: Neighbors seem very friendly. Noisy dog next door. Train station a few blocks away. Last vacancy was two years ago.

How to Find Available Rentals

As you begin your search, you'll need to be realistic about your time and financial constraints and how they will influence your search. For example, the housing search of a well-paid couple who wants to move to a bigger apartment sometime in the next six months will look very different from that of a graduate student on a limited budget who has only a few weeks to find a place before school starts.

How you go about finding available rentals will also depend on other factors, most importantly where you want to live and whether you want a lease for a year or more or prefer a month-to-month rental agreement. In some cities, Craigslist is your best resource (though be aware of rampant rental scams—more on that later). In others, you might want to work with a real estate broker. In all areas, it always makes sense to assertively and creatively use your own personal contacts and networks. Of course, the tighter the rental market you face, the more important it will be to pursue as many search options as possible. Here's a rundown of your choices.

Personal Contacts

If you know people who live or work near where you want to live, ask them for leads. Using personal contacts as housing scouts can be quite effective, because when people plan to move, friends, neighbors, and business associates almost always know about it before a for-rent sign goes up.

Prepare a brief description of exactly what you want (your rental priorities). Send this to friends, coworkers, and your social media networks. Don't forget local businesspeople with whom you have a friendly relationship—doctors, shopkeepers, tradesmen, and insurance brokers might all have good leads for available rentals. If your company has an internal online employee portal, get the word out this way. Let as many people know of your housing search as possible. You never know who might come through with the perfect apartment.

Online Apartment and Rental Listings

For many tenants, Craigslist.org will be the best place to find an apartment or rental housing. It's free for both landlords and tenants.

Local online services might also be available. Some services focus on large metro areas. If you're looking for a rental in a major city, ask around to see what websites are most commonly used.

Many websites offer national listings for small and large towns alike, including:

- Zillow (Zillow.com)
- Hotpads (a Zillow company; Hotpads.com)
- Zumper (Zumper.com)
- Apartments.com
- Apartment List (Apartmentlist.com)
- ForRent.com, and
- Rent.com.

Many of these sites provide more than apartment listings, offering information and links covering renters' insurance, moving tips, and more. Useful phone apps are also free for some of these sites.

Another online option is to see if the area you're looking in has a presence on social media. Many communities have designated Facebook groups for rentals. You might also check out Nextdoor.com to see if any owners in the area have posted their property for rent (real estate agents are not allowed to post on Nextdoor.com but can place paid ads).

 CAUTION
Before you use any online apartment rental service, make sure it's reputable. Check how long the company has been in business, who owns it, how they handle problems with apartment listings, and look for consumer complaints (start with your state's consumer protection agency's website).

If you respond to any online listings (especially those on Craigslist), be on the lookout for scams. In all cases, be cautious about giving out personal identifying information, such as your Social Security number and even your phone number, before you're reasonably sure that there's no shady business going on.

While the majority of advertisers are legit, a few use online listing services for scams and worse. Common scams to look out for include:

- A person posing online as the owner or landlord who wants you to put down a deposit to hold the property (sight unseen).
- Fake listings where the scammer has stolen photos from an old rental listing or a current listing of a property for sale.
- A scammer has rented a short-term rental property and is listing it (and possibly even showing it) as a long-term rental that they own.
- Properties that are priced well below market—if it sounds too good to be true, it is. The scammer is looking to either get valuable personal information from you or to collect a deposit to hold the property.

The number one way to avoid a rental scam is to insist on seeing the property in person. Most scammers aren't willing to take the scam as far as to meet you in person (and allow you to put an actual face to their criminal activity). In the vast majority of scams, the scammer won't actually be able to give you access to the property. (Some scammers do go so far as to steal keys, break in, or otherwise gain access, and these ruses are more difficult to see through. Search the internet for the rental address and make sure it's not offered somewhere else as either a short-term rental or a property for sale.) Trust your gut, and don't give out personal information until you're confident the rental is the real deal.

Pound the Pavement

In some neighborhoods, landlords simply post "Apartment For Rent" signs in front of the building or in one of the windows. Others put notices on neighborhood bulletin boards, such as the local recreation center, laundromat or coffee shop.

Many tenants find great apartments or houses to rent by posting their own "Apartment Wanted" signs (sometimes offering a finder's fee) in local stores or businesses, such as a dance studio, a health club, or even an auto repair shop.

If you want to live in a particular apartment building or complex, but there's no sign listed, stop by anyway and talk to the manager. If there's no onsite manager, look near the building's entrance for signage with contact information. Also, try to talk with some of the other tenants. You might get a lead on someone who's planning to move soon.

Classified Ads

Some landlords in smaller cities (or areas with cool or stagnant rental markets) still advertise their rental units in the newspaper real estate classified ads. The largest section usually runs in the Sunday paper. The classifieds are usually organized by city or neighborhood and include basic information such as rent, location, number of bedrooms and baths, and any special features such as a fireplace or view.

Get early editions of papers (for example, Sunday papers are available late Friday night in some areas) and start calling as soon as possible to get a jump on the competition. Better yet, go online. Many papers post their classifieds before the information hits the streets.

 RELATED TOPIC
Illegal ads. Classified ads run by landlords should never mention sex, race, religion, disability, or age (unless the rental is really legally sanctioned senior citizens housing). Chapter 5 discusses the topic of discriminatory advertising.

Advertising Yourself to Landlords

While the internet is full of websites that landlords use to post rentals, only a few offer the opposite service: Letting people who are searching for a rental describe themselves, their needs, and their price range, hoping that a landlord in the area will see their post and contact them.

Craigslist offers this service ("housing wanted"), and their pages are chock-full of posts that run the gamut from sophisticated to self-defeating. If you decide to place an ad for yourself in this manner, follow the tips below. They're geared to these twin goals:

- giving a potential landlord relevant information about your needs and nature, so that the landlord doesn't waste time calling someone who isn't suited for the rental—and you don't waste time taking these calls, and
- painting an accurate picture of yourself that fits every landlord's search for tenants who are stable, clean, and honest.

With these goals in mind, design your ad as follows:

- Describe what you're looking for, but resist listing all of your "must-haves." You're likely to appear as a demanding tenant (a landlord's worst nightmare).
- Describe your job, your interests, and how you spend your free time carefully. Any activities that spell "property damage" or "party animal" might backfire.
- Don't play the sympathy card. You might be down on your luck, but don't expect landlords to choose you because they feel sorry for you. Instead, emphasize the positive—your respect for your neighbors, longevity at your current rental, and so on.

Use a new and dedicated email account for your posting. That way, you will avoid having your main inbox flooded with spam.

CAUTION

Be aware of your online presence. More than one applicant has been sunk by the results of a prospective landlord's Google search, which turned up disturbing information about the applicant's honesty or living habits. If you can, delete compromising information and photos.

What the Words Really Mean

With online ads, as with print ads, you need to watch for misleading statements or just plain puffery. We took a look at ads for rentals in the Bay Area and came up with this gem for a Marin County apartment:

Closest train: Bay Area Rapid Transit (BART)

Distance to train: More than 5-minute drive.

Nearest highway: 101 Freeway

Distance to nearest highway: Less than 5-minute drive.

The real story: The closest BART station is in the next county, over a bridge that has poor public transit—more like an hour's trip on the bus. The freeway is, indeed, less than five minutes away— it's directly across the street!

TIP

Looking for a pet-friendly rental? Go to a local park or veterinarian's office and talk to people with animals. They might have some good leads. Also, check out www.humanesociety.org (search "renting with pets"). They provide helpful advice on how to put your best paw forward, with links to sites listing animal-friendly apartments.

Real Estate Brokers

Some local real estate offices, especially in large cities, also handle rental properties. If you're moving into a new area, especially someplace like New

York City, or have limited time to apartment-hunt, real estate brokers can be very useful. A good broker should do lots of legwork for you. The more prepared you are (by setting priorities as we discuss above), the more helpful a broker can be.

As with apartment-finding services, choose your broker carefully:

- **Get full information about all fees, which can be quite hefty.** In New York City, for example, real estate brokers often charge either a fee that is tied to the rent (for example, two months' rent or 15% of the first year's rent). Sometimes the property owner covers the real estate broker's fee, but typically the tenant pays.
- **Ask about the type and exclusivity of the broker's listings.** Why pay a hefty fee if you can find the same place through Craigslist, or for a lower price through an apartment-finding service? And don't waste your time with a broker whose properties don't meet your needs as to neighborhood, type of unit, or budget.
- **Choose a broker with lots of experience and a good reputation.** The best way to do this is through recommendations from people who have used the broker in the last few years and whose judgment you trust. Interview a few brokers and ask a lot of questions about their services, how long they've been in business, and their knowledge of the area. Be sure to check online reviews and see if any complaints are on file with the Better Business Bureau.

CAUTION
Avoid brokers who try to pressure you into paying their fee before you sign a lease or rental agreement. Don't pay until the deal is final.

Management Companies

Property management companies often contract with landlords to rent units and manage all aspects of the rental property. In many areas, a handful of management companies control a significant number of rental properties. You can find the names of the bigger companies just by driving around and looking at signs posted outside apartment buildings. Or, search online for property managers in the area.

You can usually approach management companies directly. Ask for a list of their currently available or upcoming rentals.

TIP
Beat the competition by getting on a waiting list. If you want to rent in a particular big complex and you have a little time, ask the property manager if you can get prequalified or be placed on a waiting list.

University, Alumni, and Corporate Housing Offices

College housing offices can be an excellent source of rentals. If you want a short-term rental, you can often find places that never appear on Craigslist—for example, the home of a professor who's going on sabbatical for six months. If you're not affiliated with a university, try to find someone who is. The same holds true for housing offices available to employees of local corporations. And don't forget to check out your college alumni association. It might also provide information on rentals in the area (or you can contact fellow alumni for leads).

If you'll be renting in a college town, look for periodicals published by the school, aimed at alumni, students, and visiting professors. These publications often have "For Rent" sections in their classified ads. While you might not be an alum, a student, or a visiting professor, you might still be a desirable tenant. Along the same lines, look at magazines aimed at particular groups, like cyclists, runners, chefs. If your town has sizeable numbers of these folks, the periodical might have listings posted by their subscribers, which might not show up in other places.

Renting a Place When You're New in Town

If you're completely unfamiliar with the area you're moving to, you might not have enough local knowledge to find a good place in a congenial location at a fair price.

Your HR office at work or college housing office are good places to start. Also, check online community resources and websites such as StreetAdvisor (StreetAdvisor.com) and City-Data (City-Data.com) for street, neighborhood, and city reviews.

But there's no substitute for your own legwork. Ask your friends and colleagues, walk and drive around neighborhoods, talk to local residents and shop owners, read local newspapers, check the library's community resources file, visit the local planning department and chamber of commerce, and do whatever else will help you get a better sense of a neighborhood or city.

If you're in a hurry to move, one sensible alternative is to leave your furniture in storage and stay in a hotel or take a short-term furnished rental. Check out Airbnb, VRBO, and similar services for good leads.

While finding a temporary rental means moving twice, it's far better than settling on an apartment or area that's not to your taste.

Visiting Prospective Rentals

Everyone needs a home-hunting strategy—whether you make an appointment to see an apartment by yourself or attend an open house with dozens of others. Here are some basic tips:

Visit promising rentals as soon as they come on the market. Especially in college towns and popular neighborhoods, apartments and rental houses move fast. If a place sounds good, schedule a visit as soon as it's listed.

Be prepared. Carrying some basic tools will help you figure out if the place is right for you. Bring a tape measure to make sure your furniture will fit, a notebook or other way to take notes, and a camera or your phone to capture photos and videos of each place. (Ask the landlord if it's okay to take pictures.) And, bring your Rental Priorities Worksheet as discussed above.

Finally, don't forget your checkbook. Some landlords might accept electronic deposit payments on the spot, but many will still want an old-fashioned check to hold a rental.

Show up with everything you need to fill out a rental application, including references and credit information. (See "Rental Applications and Credit Reports," below, for more on these issues.)

Be on your best "good tenant" behavior. While you're looking at a rental unit, the landlord or manager will be looking at and evaluating you. Show up on time for any appointment and present yourself as being both conscientious and agreeable. Realize that landlords live in fear of demanding and fussy tenants who complain about trivial things. So while we recommend checking out the rental unit's condition (see below) and making sure significant defects are being remedied, it's usually a mistake to ask for a long list of upgrades and repairs before you're even offered the place. Better to save your requests until the landlord makes you an offer. But make sure you do your essential negotiating before you sign a lease or rental agreement.

Look around carefully for signs of problems in the rental unit and building. While you don't want to come across as a nit-picking housing inspector with white gloves, do keep your eyes open. Don't broadcast your concerns (subtlety is a strong point here), but try to check as many of the following things as possible:

- Look for obvious damage, such as loose steps, torn carpet, or shaky handrails.
- Check for dirt, mildew, and signs of insects or rodents. (But try to overlook the sloppiness of a current tenant. Piles of dishes in the sink and mounds of clothes on the floor are only temporary.)
- Flush the toilet and run water in the shower and sinks. Check the water temperature and pressure.

- Make sure the windows and doors are in good shape, open and close easily, and have secure locks.
- Walk around the building, checking out any elevators and common areas such as stairs, laundry rooms, and lobbies, as well as the parking area, garage, and yard. Again, check for general cleanliness and repair. Good lighting is especially important in common areas.
- Ask about building and neighborhood security, especially if you have concerns about the area. Get neighborhood crime stats from the local police department. If criminal incidents have occurred on the property, find out what kind and when, and what steps have been taken to provide reasonable safety to tenants and guests. If you learn later that the answers were not accurate, you might have grounds for getting out of your lease or rental agreement. Chapter 14 gives more information on your rights to a safe place to live.

At this point, you're just trying to get a general sense of the place. Ask yourself: Does this feel safe and comfortable? Clean and in good repair? If you decide you want the rental unit, and before you actually sign a lease or rental agreement, you will want to do a more detailed inventory of the condition of the rental unit, completing the Landlord-Tenant Checklist we recommend in Chapter 6. (You want your landlord to acknowledge any existing defects so they can't blame you later for causing them.)

If there are some minor problems, or improvements you want—for example, a new coat of paint in the living room—you might be able to negotiate before you move in. (Chapter 2 shows how.) Major problems, such as lack of heat, might be the landlord's legal responsibility to fix. (For details on housing standards and landlords' responsibility to provide habitable housing, see Chapter 8.) Also, see Chapter 2 for information on disclosures landlords must make to prospective tenants, such as the presence of lead-based paint in the rental unit.

Think of creative ways to use space. You might need to compromise on the number and type of rooms in exchange for a great location or lower rent. Use your imagination or check out home design books, magazines, and websites such as Apartment Therapy for ideas on how to make the most of your living space. For example, you might be able to carve out a study at the end of an extra-large living room, using bookcases or screens to divide the space. Rolling carts with butcher block tops can add instant space to a kitchen with limited counters.

Walk, drive, and/or bike around the neighborhood. If you're not familiar with the area, check out restaurants, shops, local businesses and schools, and bus, subway, and train stations. Do this at night (ideally, by car and with a friend) as well as the daytime.

Checking Out the Landlord and Manager

Your prospective landlord will probably check you out pretty thoroughly. Make sure you return the favor: Do the homework necessary to find out what it's really like to live in your landlord's building.

Ask Current Tenants

Visit the building after work. If you can, ask residents about pros and cons of living in the building. Inquire about security and noise in the building or neighborhood and if there are any problems regarding repairs and basic services such as heat and hot water. See if you can get a sense of the landlord's personality and style of operating. An excellent indicator of whether you can expect smooth sailing is to find out how often there are vacancies in the building and, in particular, how often your prospective landlord has had to evict tenants. A low rate of turnovers and evictions suggests that tenants like living there and that the landlord has chosen considerate, law-abiding renters who will be good neighbors.

Ask Neighbors in Nearby Buildings

Other people and businesses in the neighborhood might know something about the reputation of the building, landlord, or manager. Ask if tenants seem to stay more than a year—if so, that's the mark of a well-run building. By speaking with neighbors, you can confirm the truthfulness of the landlord's or property manager's representations, such as a claim that there have been no recent incidents requiring a police response.

Check Out ApartmentRatings.com

This comprehensive website has hundreds of thousands of renter reviews of individual apartments and property managers nationwide. It includes other information useful to new tenants, such as noise and safety ratings of each rental.

Google the Property

Don't let your interest in a particular rental go too far without running a Google search on the:

- owner's name (if you have it)
- property manager's/landlord's name, and
- property address.

You won't want to rent from a manager who has received a lot of bad online reviews. And even if searching the address doesn't tell you anything about the management, it might reveal information such as crimes that have happened on the property, notorious bad neighbors, or even ongoing challenges with the location (for example, if the intersection nearest the rental regularly floods when it rains, you might find someone griping about it online).

Check for Any Notices of Default

If you're concerned about the landlord's financial stability, find out whether the property you're considering is the subject of a notice of default (the first public step toward foreclosure). Banks and other lenders must file these notices, in the courthouse of the county in which the property is located, when the owner has failed to make payments on a loan or mortgage for a specified number of months (two is common). Obviously, renting a property that's liable to be foreclosed upon during your tenancy is not a good idea—even if you get to stay, you might end up with an owner (especially if it's the bank itself) who will not be a conscientious landlord.

Checking Out Other Tenants and the Neighbors

Not surprisingly, many tenants are as concerned about who their potential neighbors will be as they are about the physical aspects of the prospective rental. Anyone who has lived in close proximity to others knows that a law-abiding, considerate neighbor is every bit as important as a view, a second bathroom, or a parking spot.

If you visited the rental and had a chance to talk with other residents, you might already have a rough impression of your prospective neighbors. But you might want to learn more. In particular, you might want reassurance that the tenant next door doesn't have a dangerous criminal background. How much information can you expect to learn from your landlord and from law enforcement? In general, here's what you can expect.

First, no law requires your landlord to investigate tenants' criminal history. Of course, many landlords do inquire or run back- ground checks, and most will avoid renting to those with violent criminal backgrounds. But if you ask and are told, "I have no idea," you have no legal basis to press your landlord for more. And even if the landlord does know about a tenant's unsavory past, no law requires disclosure (though the landlord might be held liable if you are later injured by this tenant, as the example below illustrates).

EXAMPLE: Nancy and her daughter rented an apartment from Martin. When Nancy applied for the apartment, she told Martin that she was not home in the afternoon and that her daughter would be on her own until Nancy came home from work. Nancy was concerned for her daughter's safety and asked Martin if any of the other tenants had criminal histories or had done anything to suggest that they would act inappropriately with children.

Martin told Nancy she had nothing to worry about from the neighbors. In fact, however, Martin knew that a downstairs tenant had a conviction, albeit an old one, for child molestation. Tragically, this neighbor molested Nancy's daughter. Nancy sued the offender and Martin, on the grounds that he knew about and failed to disclose a dangerous condition—namely, the presence of a known molester. Martin's insurance company settled the case in Nancy's favor for a large sum.

Although you cannot count on your landlord for a full answer to your questions, you might be able look online for help. Every state has a version of "Megan's Law," a federal law passed in 1996 and named after a young girl who was killed by a convicted child molester who lived in her neighborhood. The original law charged the FBI with keeping a nationwide database of persons convicted of sexual offenses against minors and violent sexual offenses against anyone (42 U.S.C. §§ 14701 and following). The state versions typically require certain convicted sexual offenders to register with local law enforcement officials, who keep a database on their whereabouts.

If you are concerned about whether prospective neighbors are registered sex offenders, you can search for the rental's address and find out if any registered offenders live within a certain distance of the address.

To find out how to access your state's sex offender registry, contact your local law enforcement agency, call the Parents for Megan's Law Hotline at 888-ASK-PFML, or find the state's sex offender registry website at www.fbi.gov/scams-and-safety/sex-offender-registry. Keep in mind that a database search might not give you accurate information. In many states, the databases are not current, or have mistaken information, which might result in both false positives and false negatives.

TIP

Concerned about too many Airbnb guests in the rental property? Many tenants rent out their apartments on a short-term basis through websites such as Airbnb. While that might be fine with you (maybe you even hope to do the same), you might not want to live someplace where lots of different people (whom your landlord has not screened) are coming and going. At any rate, be sure you know your landlord's policies on Airbnb and how other tenants in your building are handling their short-term rentals (if any). See "Tenant Rights to Use Airbnb and Similar Vacation Rental Services" in Chapter 1 for more on the subject.

Report Deceptive Advertising

If a rental unit is unavailable, inferior, or rents for more than advertised, contact the consumer fraud division of the local district attorney's office. Such deceptive advertising is illegal, and many property owners have been prosecuted for such practices.

Rental Applications and Credit Reports

Once you find a place you like, it's time to ask the landlord what the next steps are. Most of the time, you'll be asked to fill out a rental application. The goal of the application is to collect the information necessary for the landlord to determine whether you're likely to pay the rent on time, keep the rental in good condition, and not cause problems.

When a landlord insists on receiving a fully completed application, checking your references, and reviewing your credit report, it's a good thing: You'll probably have fewer problems with other tenants in the building if the landlord is strict about screening. Who wants to move into a great building where tenants are causing trouble that the landlord could have averted by proper screening?

Rental Applications

On most rental applications, you must provide information about your employment, income, credit history (including any bankruptcies), and rental housing history (including evictions). If you are self-employed, the landlord might require the last few years' tax returns and other documentation of income.

It's legal to ask for your Social Security number, driver's license number, or other identifying information (such as an Individual Taxpayer Identification Number, or ITIN). Except in California, Colorado, and New York City, landlords may also ask for proof of an applicant's right to be in the United States under U.S. immigration laws.

Under federal fair housing laws, landlords who ask for such immigration information must ask all tenants, not just those whom they suspect might be in the country illegally. It is, however, illegal to discriminate on the basis of national origin. (See Chapter 5.)

A sample Rental Application is shown below, so that you can get an idea of the information you will need. It's a good idea to complete this rental

application and take it with you when you see a potential rental unit—that way, you can either present it to the landlord or use the information you've entered to fill out the landlord's own rental application.

Most careful landlords will make a few calls to confirm that the information you've supplied on the Rental Application is correct. Current and past landlords, credit sources, and employers will normally request permission from you before they'll talk to a prospective landlord. Along with the Application, you'll want to give your landlord a Consent to Background and Reference Check, which supplies this permission.

This consent form carefully limits the information that sources are authorized to give. In other words, you aren't giving the landlord carte blanche to inquire about topics that don't relate to your qualifications as a tenant, such as "Where is this fellow from?" or "Do you think there is a boyfriend in the picture?" Questions such as these are often illegal (because they tend to violate fair housing laws), and, even if they're legal, they seek information that's none of the landlord's business. Hopefully, the wording on the form will remind (or instruct) both the reference and the inquiring landlord that only information directly related to the applicant's qualifications as a tenant should be exchanged.

The landlord can make copies of the consent form and mail, email, or fax them to the references. A sample Consent to Background and Reference Check is shown below; note how the applicant has filled in her own information but left blank the lines for the prospective landlord's name, the date, and her signature.

Keep in mind that even with your consent to a reference check, you cannot force a prior landlord or an employer to provide information.

Rental Application

A separate application is required from each applicant age 18 or older.

Date and time received by Landlord _____

THIS SECTION TO BE COMPLETED BY LANDLORD

Address of property to be rented: _____178 Park St., Apt. 4F, Springsteen, NJ 00000_____

Rental term: ☐ month-to-month ☑ lease from _____March 1, 20xx_____ to _____February 28, 20xx_____

Amounts Due Prior to Occupancy

First month's rent	$ _____3,200_____
Security deposit	$ _____3,200_____
Credit-check fee	$ _____40_____
Other (specify): _____	$ _____
TOTAL..	$ _____6,440_____

Applicant

Full Name—include all names you use or have used in the past: _____Hannah Silver_____

Home phone: ___609-555-3789___ Work phone: ___609-555-4567___ Cell phone: ___609-555-6543___

Email: _____hannah@coldmail.com_____

Social Security number: ___123-00-4567___ Driver's license number/State: ___D123456/New Jersey___

Other identifying information: _____

Vehicle make: ___Toyota___ Model: ___Corolla___ Color: ___White___ Year: _2019_

License plate number/State: ___NJ1234567/New Jersey___

Additional Occupants

List everyone, including minor children, who will live with you:

Full Name	Relationship to Applicant
Dennis Olson	Husband

Rental History

FIRST-TIME RENTERS: INSTEAD ATTACH A DESCRIPTION OF YOUR HOUSING SITUATION FOR THE PAST FIVE YEARS.

Current address: ___39 Maple St., Princeton, NJ 00000___

Dates lived at address: ___May 2020–present___ Rent: $ ___2,000___ Security deposit: $ ___4,000___

Landlord/Manager: ___Jane Tucker___ Landlord/manager's phone: ___609-555-7523___

Reason for leaving: ___New job in northern New Jersey___

Previous address: _1215 Middlebrook Lane, Princeton, NJ 00000_

Dates lived at address: _June 2018–May 2020_ Rent: $ _1,800_ Security deposit: $ _1,800_

Landlord/Manager: _Ed Palermo_ Landlord/Manager's phone: _609-555-3711_

Reason for leaving: _Better apartment_

Previous address: _1527 Highland Dr., New Brunswick, NJ 00000_

Dates lived at address: _Jan. 2017–June 2018_ Rent: $ _1,800_ Security deposit: $ _1,800_

Landlord/Manager: _Millie & Joe Lewis_ Landlord/Manager's phone: _609-555-9999_

Reason for leaving: _Wanted to live closer to work_

Employment History

EMPLOYEES: ATTACH TAX RETURNS FROM THE MOST RECENT TWO YEARS, PLUS PAY STUBS FROM THE PAST SIX MONTHS. SELF-EMPLOYED APPLICANTS: INSTEAD ATTACH TAX RETURNS FOR THE PAST TWO YEARS.

Name and address of current employer: _Argonworks, 54 Nassau St., Princeton, NJ 00000_

Phone: _609-555-2333_

Name of supervisor: _Tom Schmidt_ Supervisor's phone: _609-555-2333_

Dates employed at this job: _2018–date_ Position or title: _Marketing Associate_

Name and address of previous employer: _Princeton Times_
13 Junction Rd., Princeton, NJ 00000 Phone: _609-555-1111_

Name of supervisor: _Dory Krossber_ Supervisor's phone: _609-555-2366_

Dates employed at this job: _June 2017–Feb. 2018_ Position or title: _Marketing Associate_

Income

1. Your gross monthly employment income (before deductions): $ _8,000_

2. Average monthly amounts of other income (specify sources): $ _____
   Note: This does not include my husband's income. See his application. $ _____
   $ _____

   TOTAL: $ _8,000_

Bank/Financial Accounts

	Account Number	Bank/Institution	Branch
Savings account:	1222345	N.J. Federal	Trenton, NJ
Checking account:	789101	Princeton S&L	Princeton, NJ
Money market or similar account:	234789	City Bank	Princeton, NJ

Credit Card Accounts

Major credit card: ☑Visa ☐Mastercard ☐Discover ☐American Express ☐Other: _____

Issuer: ___City Bank_____ Account no.: __1234 5555 6666 7777___

Balance: $__1,000_____ Average monthly payment: $__1,000_____

Major credit card: ☐Visa ☐Mastercard ☐Discover ☐American Express ☑Other: __Dept. Store___

Issuer: ___City Bank_____ Account no.: __2345 0000 9999 8888___

Balance: $_500_____ Average monthly payment: $_500_____

Loans

Type of loan (mortgage, car, student loan, etc.)	Name of creditor	Account number	Amount owed	Monthly payment

Other Major Obligations (such as child support, alimony, tax liens, etc.)

Type	Payee	Amount owed	Monthly payment

Pets

Type: _____ Breed: _____ Sex: _____

Neutered/Spayed: _____ Age: _____ Weight: _____ Years owned: _____

Miscellaneous

Describe water-filled furniture you want to have in the rental property: ___None_____
_____

Do you smoke? ☐yes ☑no

Have you ever: Filed for bankruptcy?   ☐yes ☑no   How many times? _____

               Been sued?   ☐yes ☑no   How many times? _____

               Sued someone else?   ☐yes ☑no   How many times? _____

               Been evicted?   ☐yes ☑no   How many times? _____

Explain (include dates) any "yes" listed above: _____
_____
_____

References and Emergency Contact

Personal reference: _Joan Stanley_   Relationship: _Friend, coworker_

Address: _785 Spruce St., Princeton, NJ 00000_

Email: _joan.stanley@email.com_   Phone: _609-555-4578_

Personal reference: _Marnie Swatt_   Relationship: _Friend_

Address: _82 East 59th St., #12B, NYC, NY 00000_

Email: _marnie.swatt@email.com_   Phone: _212-555-8765_

Contact in emergency: _Connie & Martin Silver_   Relationship: _Parents_

Address: _7852 Pierce St., Somerset, NJ 00000_

Email: _connie.silver@email.com_   Phone: _609-555-7878_

Source

Where did you learn of this vacancy? _Craigslist_

I certify that all the information given above is true and correct and understand that my lease or rental agreement may be terminated if I have made any material false or incomplete statements in this application. I authorize verification of the information provided in this application from my credit sources, credit bureaus, current and previous landlords and employers, and personal references. This permission will survive the expiration of my tenancy. I give permission for the landlord or its agent to obtain a consumer report about me for the purpose of this application, to ensure that I can continue to meet the terms of the tenancy, for the collection and recovery of any financial obligations relating to my tenancy, or for any other permissible purpose.

Hannah Silver   _February 15, 20xx_
Applicant   Date

Landlord's/Manager's notes: _____

How to Impress Prospective Landlords

Bringing the following information when you first meet prospective landlords will give you a competitive edge over other applicants:

- a completed rental application
- written references from landlords, employers, friends, and colleagues, and
- a current copy of your credit report.

FORM

The Nolo website includes a downloadable copy of the Rental Application and the Consent to Background and Reference Check forms. See Appendix B for a link to the forms in this book.

Consent to Background and Reference Check

I authorize _____ to obtain information about me from my credit sources, current and previous landlords, employers, and personal references, to enable _____ to evaluate my rental application. I authorize my credit sources, credit bureaus, current and previous landlords, current and previous employers, and personal references to disclose to _____ information about me that is relevant to _____'s evaluation of me as a prospective tenant.

_____
Applicant's Signature

Hannah Silver
Printed name

39 Maple Street. Princeton, NJ 00000
Address

609-555-3789
Phone Number

_____
Date

TIP

Fill out applications only when you're truly interested. Don't waste your time (or money, if the landlord charges a credit-check fee) filling out a rental application unless you really want a place. If you are interested, but still want to keep your options open, go ahead and fill out an application. Don't worry that this will lock you into taking a place—only signing a lease or rental agreement does so.

Landlord References

Landlords usually want references from your current and previous landlords, and details of your rental history. In talking with your past landlord or manager, prospective landlords will ask the following types of questions:

- Did you pay rent on time?
- Were you considerate of neighbors (no loud parties; you cleaned up after your dog)?
- Did you make any unreasonable demands or complaints?
- Did you take good care of the rental property?
- In general, were you a good tenant?

If you are leaving a current rental because the neighbors, the landlord, or the manager was awful, prepare your defense in advance—by mounting a preemptive offense. Explain the difficulty and offer evidence to bolster your version, such as a letter from other dissatisfied tenants, police reports chronicling disturbances at the property, a list of the times the former landlord was hauled before the local rent board for violations, or, if problems rose to the point of litigation, a copy of a court judgment in your favor. No matter how righteous your position, however, be advised that it won't count for much unless you can show that, aside from your use of legal tenant remedies such as rent withholding, you always paid the rent on time, left voluntarily, and left a clean and undamaged apartment or house.

Do You Need References for Your Dog (or Cat)?

If you have a dog or cat, don't be surprised if the landlord wants to meet your pet, to make sure it's well-groomed and well-behaved, before making a final decision. Here are some ideas for how to make the best case for your pet:

- Get written references from current and previous landlords and neighbors saying how sweet and well-mannered your pet is.
- Bring a cat or dog résumé, describing your pet, favorite activities, and health (include vaccination history). If you search online for "sample pet resume," you'll find some good examples.
- Pull together any materials that support your pet's good behavior, such as paperwork that shows your dog passed obedience training classes.

See the "Pets" section in Chapter 2 for more advice on negotiating with landlords on pets. Also, see the discussion of tenant rights when it comes to service and support animals in Chapter 5.

Employer References

Conscientious landlords will usually want to speak with your current employer to verify your income and length of employment and to get a better sense of your character—for example, to see if you're a responsible person.

Your employer might not talk with a prospective landlord without your written permission. Use the Consent to Background and Reference Check, explained above.

Character References

Some landlords also want character references from people (nonrelatives) who know you well. Below is an example of the type of letter that will help you beat the competition.

Sample Character Reference

February, 20xx

To Whom It May Concern:

I am writing to recommend Hannah Silver for the rental unit you have available. I have known Hannah for ten years and I cannot recommend her too highly. You won't find a better tenant.

I know Hannah as both a close personal friend and a colleague. We first met in 2019 when I started work as a technical writer at Argonworks in Princeton. Hannah has been the marketing director at Argonworks since 2018.

Hannah is extremely reliable and responsible. She's not the type of person who will pay her rent late (or come up with excuses why she needs a few extra days), bother you about small things, annoy other tenants with loud music, or generally cause you problems. I have been to her apartment many times, and she is a meticulous housekeeper and very organized. She will take excellent care of your rental property.

Hannah is trustworthy, and she keeps her commitments. She has always worked 100% plus on marketing Argonworks products, consistently meets her deadlines, and gives her best. She is a wonderful person to work with, a talented businesswoman, and a cooperative team player. I am confident that Hannah will be one of your best tenants.

All in all, Hannah is a fantastic person who will be greatly missed when she moves out of the area.

I will be happy to provide further information about Hannah. If you have any questions, please feel free to call me at work (609-555-1232) or home (609-555-4578), or email me at Joan @Joan.com.

Sincerely,

Joan Stanley

Joan Stanley
785 Spruce St.
Princeton, NJ 00000

> **TIP**
>
> **Alert references.** Make sure that all of your references know to expect a call or email from a potential landlord. Even better, get written references first. And obviously, only give out the names of people who know you well and who have positive things to say about you—anticipate the crafty landlord who asks for four references and calls only the fourth one on the list.

> **CAUTION**
>
> **Complete all rental applications truthfully.** Prospective landlords will be able to verify much of the information you give by ordering a credit report. Nothing will hurt your chances of getting a place more than lying, whether it be by failing to reveal a previous eviction, providing the name of a friend as a landlord reference, or overstating your income.

The Importance of Your Credit History

Many landlords find it essential to check a prospective tenant's credit history with at least one credit reporting agency, to see how responsible you are at managing money and whether you will be a reliable tenant who pays rent on time. This credit check can be the most important part of the rental application process.

A landlord can find out your credit history over the past 7 to 10 years, including whether you have ever been:

- late or delinquent in paying rent or bills, including student or car loans
- the subject of a "charge-off" (when a store declares an overdue account uncollectible)
- contacted by a collections agency, demanding a debt that resulted from your being evicted, or
- involved in another type of lawsuit, such as a personal injury claim.

A credit report will also state whether you have filed for bankruptcy in the past 10 years.

If a landlord doesn't rent to you because of negative information in your credit report, or charges you a higher rent because of such information, the landlord is legally required (under the federal Fair Credit Reporting Act, 15 U.S.C. §§ 1681 and following) to give you the name and address of the agency that reported the negative information. Landlords must tell you that you have a right to obtain a free copy of your file from the agency that reported the negative information. You must request it within 60 days of being rejected by the landlord. Landlords must also tell you that the credit reporting agency did not make the rejection decision and cannot explain it, and that if you dispute the information in the report, you can provide a consumer statement setting forth your position.

How Far Can Credit Reporting Agencies Go?

Some landlords—especially those who rent luxury units or insist on long-term leases—go beyond a routine credit report and ask a screening agency to pull together detailed information about your character, general reputation, personal characteristics, or mode of living.

Almost all such checks are considered "investigative consumer reports" under federal law (15 U.S.C. §§ 1681 and following, as amended by the Fair and Accurate Credit Transactions Act of 2003). Legally, a landlord does not need your permission before asking for one; however, a landlord who requests a background check on a prospective tenant must tell you within three days of requesting the report that the report might be made and that it will concern your character, personal characteristics, and criminal history. This gives you an opportunity to withdraw your rental application if you don't want the credit reporting agency to proceed with the report. The landlord must also tell you that more information about the nature and scope of the report will be provided upon your written request. The landlord must provide this added information within five days of your request.

If you are turned down wholly or in part based on information contained in the investigative report, the landlord must tell you this and give you the name and address of the agency that prepared the report.

Credit-Check Fees

It is legal for a prospective landlord to charge you a fee for the cost of the credit report itself and the landlord's time and trouble. Some states regulate the exact amount of the fee by statute; others require landlords to charge a reasonable fee. Any credit-check fee should be reasonably related to the cost of the credit check—$30 or $50 is common. California sets a maximum screening fee and requires landlords to provide an itemized receipt when accepting a credit check fee. If you think you're being charged too high a fee, call your city or district attorney's office for advice. (Find your agency at USA.gov/state-consumer.)

Be sure you understand the purpose of any fee you are charged and whether it provides any guarantee that you will get the rental unit. Don't confuse the fee with a holding deposit, which is normally a separate charge.

Giving Landlords Access to Your Credit Report

The big credit bureaus don't make it easy for landlords to order individual credit reports (ostensibly in order to curb identity theft). To provide a service, however, some of the bureaus have created alternative pathways. Experian offers "Experian Connect," which allows the tenant/consumer to order the report and give access directly from the service to the landlord. Experian also provides a "VantageScore," which is a credit score similar to the FICO score.

TransUnion provides a similar service, initiated by the landlord. Landlords create an account ("Smart-Move") and invite tenants to supply information that results in a credit report generated for the landlord. Landlords also get a "ResidentScore," which purports to digest the relevant information in the credit report and generate a numerical rating of the suitability of the applicant.

 CAUTION

Watch out for fraudulent credit-check fees. Some landlords have been known to take credit-check fees from several prospective tenants and never run the credit checks, illegally pocketing the money instead. You can easily find out if this has happened to you by contacting a credit reporting agency as soon as you've been rejected by a landlord. As discussed above, you're entitled to a free copy of your credit report if a landlord rejects you because of information in it, which should indicate who's requested your report recently. Problems can also develop if the landlord takes a long time to check a tenant's credit and the tenant, not knowing whether the rental will be approved, rents another place. To avoid these and other possible areas of dispute, it is wise to sign a brief agreement with a landlord, clarifying the purpose of any up-front fee and whether it will be refunded if you don't get the place. (See the discussion of holding deposits below.) If you have any problems, contact your city or district attorney's office or a tenants' rights group for advice.

Check Your Credit Rating and Clean Up Your File

Because your credit report is so important, you should always check it before you start your housing search. This will give you the opportunity to correct or clear up any mistakes, such as out-of-date or just plain wrong information. It's all too common for credit bureaus to confuse names, addresses, Social Security numbers, or employers.

Especially if you have a common name, chances are good you'll find information in your credit file on other people with the same name. Obviously, you don't want this incorrect information given to prospective landlords, especially if the person you're being confused with is in worse financial shape than you are.

The three largest credit bureaus, with offices throughout the United States, are Experian, Equifax, and TransUnion. As mentioned above, you are entitled to a free copy of your report when you are denied credit (including a place to live) because of information in your credit report. You can also get a free copy once every 12 months. Go to AnnualCreditReport.com to place your request.

Once you get your report, if you find errors, check your files at the other two agencies. You have the right to insist that the credit bureau verify anything that's wrong, inaccurate, or out of date. Information that can't be verified must be removed. All three of the major credit reporting agencies— Experian, Equifax, and TransUnion—allow you to dispute inaccurate information by going online. To start the online dispute process, go to:

- Equifax: www.equifax.com/disputes
- Experian: www.experian.com/disputes, and
- TransUnion: www.transunion.com/disputes.

You can also submit your dispute by calling the agency or sending a letter in the mail. If you send a letter, list each incorrect item and explain why it's wrong. Under federal law, the credit bureau must investigate within 30 days (under some states' laws, it's sooner). If the investigation confirms that you are right (or if the creditor who provided the information can no longer verify it), the bureau must delete the information from your file.

If the credit reporting agency fails to remove inaccurate or outdated information, lists a debt you refused to pay because of a legitimate dispute with the creditor, or reports a bogus lawsuit against you that was abandoned, you have the right to place

a 100-word statement in your file, giving your version of the situation. Do so immediately.

If the credit bureau fails to cooperate, and the information is really wrong, contact the creditor that reported the information for help in getting it out. If that doesn't work, you have several options:

- Contact the Federal Trade Commission (FTC) for advice. Check their website (FTC.gov) or call the national office at 877-FTC-HELP.
- Threaten to sue the credit reporting agency in small claims court. (Chapter 19 discusses small claims suits.)
- Complain to your Congressional representative, who might be able to put pressure on the FTC to fix your problem.

Keep in mind that if one credit bureau has inaccurate information on you, it's likely that others do, too. If you find errors in your one bureau's report, be sure to check your files from the other two.

 TIP

Bring copies of your recent credit report with you when you apply for a rental. If you're submitting multiple applications, the credit check fees will mount up. Most landlords insist on running the check themselves, because they're afraid that applicants will doctor their reports, but you might be able to persuade some to accept yours. For example, in Wisconsin, a landlord cannot charge you for a report if, before the landlord requests a consumer report, you offer a report that's less than 30 days old from a consumer reporting agency. (Wis. Admin. Code § ATCP 134.05(4)(b).) And in Washington, landlords must advise tenants whether they will accept a comprehensive and reusable screening report done by a consumer reporting agency. (Even if the landlord is willing to accept a reusable report, the landlord may order its own screening report, but may not charge the tenant a fee for doing so. The landlord also can't charge for a report if it fails to provide the information about whether it will accept a reusable report.) Landlords who maintain a website that advertises residential rentals must include this information on the home page. (Wash. Rev. Code § 59.18.257.)

How to Deal With Problems in Your Credit Report

If your credit file shows negative but accurate information, or you have no credit history because you're a first-time renter and have never borrowed money or used a credit card, you can take steps to look better to prospective landlords:

- Get a creditworthy person to cosign the lease or rental agreement. (See Chapter 2 for details on cosigners.)
- Pay a large deposit, or offer to prepay rent for several months. (Chapter 4 discusses security deposits and state limits.)
- Show proof of steps you've taken to improve bad credit—for example, your enrollment in a debt counseling group, your recent history of making and paying for purchases on credit and maintaining a checking or savings account.
- Get more positive references from friends, colleagues, employers, and previous landlords.

RESOURCE

For more information on obtaining your credit file, getting out of debt, and rebuilding your credit, see *Solve Your Money Troubles: Strategies to Get Out of Debt and Stay That Way* and *Credit Repair,* both by Amy Loftsgordon and Cara O'Neill (Nolo). For useful articles or consumer credit and credit reports, see the Debt Management and Personal Finance sections of Nolo.com.

Beyond the Credit Report: Tenant Screening Services

All three of the credit bureaus also offer tenant screening services (as do many property management websites, such as Avail (Avail.co), and TurboTenant (TurboTenant.com)). Tenant screening services purport to gather applicants' information on a number of fronts (like prior bankruptcies, criminal history, involvements in lawsuits, skipped payments, and so on), analyze the information, and generate a recommendation. You must give consent for your landlord to use a tenant screening service.

The good news is that the information provided by screening services is geared to the rental housing context (whereas a credit score was designed to predict whether the applicant would repay a loan). The method also protects your credit score, because the report counts only as a "soft inquiry" to your file (multiple requests for credit reports can significantly lower a credit score). Importantly, SSNs are not revealed to the landlord. Either the landlord or the applicant can pay for the service.

Applicants initiate the screening process by filling out an application to generate a report. The report contains a recommendation on whether to rent to this applicant. (Note that some states and cities limit how and when landlords can consider applicants' criminal histories.) For a bit more money, landlords can ask for a credit score, too.

Consumer Relief After the Coronavirus Pandemic

Although the coronavirus pandemic seems to be in our rearview mirror, fallout continues to be felt by some renters. Specifically, suppose your ability to pay rent was affected by the coronavirus, and you asked your landlord to defer your rent payment or even lower it. The landlord agreed—but should your lower payments or skipped payments show up on your credit report? No.

The federal Coronavirus Aid, Relief, and Economic Security (CARES) Act prohibited creditors, including landlords, from adverse credit reporting during the COVID-19 crisis under certain circumstances. If your landlord agreed to defer payments or modify the rent, the landlord should not have reported your account as delinquent to the credit reporting agencies, so long as you weren't already behind on your rent payments. If such a notation shows up on your report, file a dispute and submit a statement of your own (consumers can write a 100-word statement disputing the contents of a report).

For information on the current status of coronavirus-related aid for renters, visit the "Help for Renters" page on the federal Consumer Financial Protection Bureau's website (www. consumerfinance.gov/coronavirus/mortgage-and-housing-assistance/renter-protections).

How Landlords Reject Tenants

Federal and state antidiscrimination laws limit what landlords can say and do in the tenant selection process. (See Chapter 5.) Basically, a landlord is legally free to choose among prospective tenants as long as all tenants are evaluated more or less equally. For example, a landlord can refuse to rent to a smoker, as long as this no-smoking policy applies to all tenants—not just tenants who are members of a protected class.

Permissible Reasons for Rejecting Tenants

A landlord is entitled to reject you for any of the following reasons:

- poor credit history, which leads the landlord to believe that you will be unable to pay rent
- income that the landlord reasonably regards as insufficient to pay the rent
- negative references from previous landlords indicating relevant problems—such as property damage or consistent late rent payments
- previous eviction lawsuits
- convictions for criminal offenses, unless the conviction was for past drug use (see Chapter 5 for a discussion of illegal discrimination on the basis of disability)
- current illegal behavior, such as dealing drugs
- your inability to meet terms of the lease or rental agreement—for example, if you want to keep a pet and the landlord's policy is no pets (assuming you do not have a disability, as discussed in Chapter 5)

- more people than the landlord wants to live in the unit—assuming that the limit on the number of tenants is clearly tied to health and safety or legitimate business needs (Chapter 5 discusses occupancy limits), or
- untruthful and material responses on the rental application.

What Landlords Must Tell You

You are entitled to certain information from a landlord who turns you down based on information in your credit report, even when other factors also played a role in the rejection. Known as an "adverse action report," the landlord must tell you the name and address of the agency that supplied the report, as well as that:

- you may request a copy of your report from the agency that reported the negative information, by asking within the next 60 days (or one year after receiving your last free annual credit report)
- the agency didn't make the decision not to rent to you and cannot explain the reason for the rejection, and
- you can dispute the accuracy of the information in the report and attach your own consumer statement (Fair Credit Reporting Act, as amended by the Fair and Accurate Credit Transactions Act of 2003, 15 U.S.C. §§ 1681 and following).

Landlords must also supply an adverse action report when they offer to rent to an applicant, but only if the applicant will agree to additional conditions, such as paying a higher rent or larger security deposit, or bringing a cosigner onto the lease. If the landlord rejects you or demands tougher terms based on information the landlord learned independent of the credit report or a background screening report, the landlord need not give you the adverse action report.

Illegal Discrimination

Antidiscrimination laws specify clearly illegal reasons to refuse to rent to a tenant. The federal Fair Housing Acts (42 U.S.C. §§ 3601–3619) prohibit discrimination on the basis of race, color, religion, national origin, sex (including gender identity and sexual orientation), familial status (children), or physical or mental disability (including alcoholism and past drug addiction). Many states and cities also prohibit discrimination based on marital status or source of income. (Chapter 5 discusses illegal discrimination and how to file a complaint with a fair housing agency.)

Also, landlords risk violating the law if they screen certain categories of applicants more stringently than others—for example, requiring credit reports or a higher income level only from racial minorities.

Finder's Fees and Holding Deposits

Almost every landlord requires tenants to give a substantial security deposit. The laws concerning how much can be charged and when deposits must be returned are discussed in Chapters 4 and 16. Here we discuss some other fees and deposits that are occasionally required.

Finder's Fees

Real estate brokers may legitimately charge a fee for their services. And there's nothing wrong with a landlord charging you for the actual cost of performing a credit check.

Less legitimate, however, is landlords' practice of collecting "finder's fees" just for renting the place to a tenant. Unlike brokers, which actually do some work for their money, a finder's fee charged by a landlord just for the privilege of being offered a rental is nothing short of a rip-off. You should suspect this ploy if you're told to pay a finder's fee directly to the landlord or management company to get a particular unit. You should also be suspicious if you're directed to pay a finder's fee to an apartment locator "service" set up by the landlord as a front to collect the fee (as opposed to really being in the business of locating apartments).

What can you do about this blatant nonsense? If the rental is a good one and the fee something you can afford without too much pain, perhaps it's in your best interests to shut up and pay up. However, if you want to challenge this "pay me for nothing" fee, consider the following avenues.

Read your state's security deposit statutes and the cases that have interpreted them. (The citations are found in the "State Security Deposit Rules" chart in Appendix A; Chapter 20 explains how to find cases that explain statutes.) If your state prohibits nonrefundable security deposits (security deposits are explained at length in Chapter 4), look for a case where the judge ruled that the term "security deposit" includes a finder's fee. Because the fee is kept by the landlord, a landlord who collects a finder's fee violates the statute. This theory was used successfully by a group of tenants in California. (*People v. Sangiacomo,* 129 Cal.App.3d 364 (1982).)

Sue in small claims court. You might argue that you're being forced to pay for a nonexistent service—in legalese, it's a case of fraud. You could also point out that it's a matter of bait-and-switch: Charging a finder's fee is the same as charging a higher rent for the first month, which your landlord probably has not made clear in ads for the unit. (Chapter 19 gives advice on using small claims court.)

Contact your city attorney or district attorney's office (consumer fraud unit) for advice, or your local rent control board. Especially in areas with rent control, finder's fees might be illegal by statute or court decision.

Receipt and Holding Deposit Agreement

This will acknowledge receipt of the sum of $__500__ ("Holding Deposit") by _____Jim Chow_____ _____ ("Landlord") from __Hannah Silver__ _____ ("Applicant") as a holding deposit to hold vacant the rental property at __178 Park St., #4F, Springsteen, NJ 00000__ _____ ("Property"), until _____February 20, 20xx_____ at _____5 P.M._____ ("Hold Date"). The Property will be rented to Applicant on a _____one-year_____ basis at a rent of $__3,200__ per month, if Applicant signs Landlord's written _____lease_____ and pays Landlord the first month's rent and a $_____3,200_____ security deposit on or before the Hold Date, in which event the Holding Deposit will be applied to the first month's rent.

This Agreement depends upon Landlord receiving a satisfactory report of Applicant's references and credit history. Landlord and Applicant agree that if Applicant fails to sign the lease or rental agreement and pay the remaining rent and security deposit, Landlord may retain of this Holding Deposit a sum equal to the prorated daily rent of $_____106_____ per day, until a new tenant begins paying rent, and/or a sum equal to any actual damages Landlord suffers, such as the costs of rerenting.

Hannah Silver _____ _February 16, 20xx_
Applicant   Date

Jim Chow _____ _February 16, 20xx_
Landlord/Manager   Date

Holding Deposits

Sometimes, if you make a deal with a landlord but don't actually sign a lease or rental agreement, the landlord will want some type of cash deposit, then and there, to hold the rental unit. This might happen when the landlord wants time to do a credit check or call your references. Or it can happen if you need to borrow money (or wait for a paycheck) to come up with enough to cover the rent and security deposit. For example, a landlord might ask for $500 cash to hold the place for you until you bring your first month's rent and any deposits you agreed on, pending the results of a credit check.

If you give a landlord a holding deposit and later decide not to take the place, there is a good chance you won't get most or all of your deposit back. So be sure you really want the place before making this kind of deposit. The laws of most states are unclear as to what portion of a holding deposit landlords can keep when would-be tenants change their minds about renting the property, or when the tenants' credit doesn't check out to the landlord's satisfaction. And even if the law does limit landlords to keeping a "reasonable" amount (often based on how long the unit was kept off the market), you might have to go to small claims court to force the landlord to actually return your money.

In California, for example, the basic rule is that a landlord can keep an amount that bears a "reasonable" relation to the landlord's costs—for example, for more advertising and for prorated rent during the time the property was held vacant. A California landlord who keeps a larger amount can be sued for breach of contract. A few states require landlords to provide a receipt for any holding deposit and a written statement of the conditions under which the fee or deposit is refundable.

Most states, however, don't have specific laws on holding deposits. So, whatever you and a landlord agree on, such as your right to get half of the holding deposit back if you decide not to take the place within a certain number of days, be sure to write it down. Include:

- the amount of the deposit
- the dates the landlord will hold the rental property vacant, and
- the conditions for returning the deposit or applying it to the security deposit.

Also, be sure you and the landlord understand what will happen to the deposit when you take the place. Usually, it will be applied to the first month's rent. To make this clear, have the landlord give you a receipt for the deposit that includes a statement of what will happen to the deposit when you come back with the rent.

A sample Receipt and Holding Deposit Agreement that you might want to adapt to your own situation is shown above.

 FORM
The Nolo website includes a downloadable copy of the Receipt and Holding Deposit Agreement. See Appendix B for the link to the forms in this book.

Choosing Roommates

The greatest place in the world won't make up for an obnoxious, inconsiderate, or financially irresponsible roommate. Make sure you're compatible with everyone you live with, particularly with respect to issues such as neatness and privacy needs.

How to Find a Roommate

Craigslist and university housing offices are just two of the many sources for finding roommates. You might also want to check out roommate sites such as Roomster (Roomster.com) or Roommates.com. Many services will screen and match compatible roommates, based on detailed questionnaires you fill out. Some groups—senior or religious organizations, for example—might also keep lists of people looking for roommates or help you to find a compatible person.

Whether you're filling out an application with an agency that matches roommates, or responding to a "Roommate Wanted" notice, be honest and try to make sure you're getting clear answers from prospective roommates. It might sound excessive, but checking references is always a good idea. Talk to former landlords and other roommates, following our advice above on how landlords screen tenants.

Before you move in with roommates, it's always a good idea to make a written roommate agreement addressing important issues, including:

- neatness and cleaning standards
- financial responsibility
- privacy
- noise
- amount of entertaining, including overnight guests
- pets
- food tastes and sharing
- political preferences or strong personal beliefs
- children, and
- smoking.

No, this isn't overkill—after all, you routinely sign an agreement with the landlord, whom you won't see a fraction as often as a roommate. Roommate referral services often have form agreements, or you can use the sample roommate agreement in Chapter 7.

CAUTION

Always know your legal status when you move into an existing rental with roommates. Are you a full-fledged cotenant (having signed the lease or rental agreement) or a subtenant (responsible to the other tenant, not the landlord)? You have very different legal rights and responsibilities depending on your status. (See the detailed discussion of roommates in Chapter 7.)

Leases and Rental Agreements

The lease or rental agreement you and your landlord sign defines your legal relationship. It is a contract in which:

- you agree to pay rent and abide by other terms (such as no pets and no additional roommates), and
- your landlord agrees to provide you with a place to live, often with listed amenities.

If you don't pay rent, or you violate another contract provision, the landlord will have grounds to end your tenancy. If your landlord violates a lease or rental agreement term, you also have certain rights. Depending on the situation, you might have the right to break the lease or sue the landlord for damages.

There's no official state or national lease or rental agreement that landlords and tenants must use. Because each contract differs, you won't be able to find a one-size-fits-all explanation of the agreement your landlord presents to you. It's up to you to read and understand what's in the document before you sign it.

This chapter discusses provisions typically included in leases and rental agreements, and explains the differences between these two documents. It also points out terms that are unfair to tenants and provides tips on how to bargain for better provisions when you start a tenancy. Once you've read this chapter, you'll recognize when it's wise to turn down an agreement altogether.

 RELATED TOPIC

Other chapters in this book go into greater detail on topics covered in leases and rental agreements, including:

- Rules involving rent, including late fees, grace periods, and rent control: Chapter 3.
- Use and return of security deposits: Chapters 4 and 16.
- Occupancy limits and policies: Chapter 5.
- Tenants, cotenants, sublets, and assignments: Chapters 7 and 15.
- Landlord's repair and maintenance responsibilities, and how to enforce your rights: Chapters 8, 9, and 10.
- Landlord's right to enter rental property and tenant privacy rights: Chapter 11.

- Notice and procedures for changing a lease or rental agreement after you have begun your tenancy: Chapter 15.
- Impact of a rental property sale or foreclosure on a tenant's lease: Chapter 15.
- How to break a lease as painlessly as possible: Chapter 15.
- Grounds and procedures for terminating tenancies: Chapters 17 and 18.

Appendix A includes details on state laws regarding many of the topics covered in this chapter, such as security deposit limits and landlord access rules.

How Leases and Rental Agreements Differ

Both leases and rental agreements cover the important details of a tenancy, such as the amount of rent and deposits you must pay and the number of people who can live in the rental unit.

Although many landlords and tenants refer to all contracts for rentals as "leases," the differences between a lease and a rental agreement are important:

- A **rental agreement** is a contract that typically lasts only a short term, such as a month, and renews automatically unless the landlord or tenant serves notice on the other that it won't renew.
- A **lease** covers a longer, fixed term. Leases don't renew automatically unless specifically noted in the lease itself.

These differences affect not only how long you can stay in the rental but also—perhaps more importantly—the strength of your bargaining position if you and your landlord get into a dispute.

Month-to-Month Rental Agreement

A written rental agreement provides the tenant with the right to stay in the rental for a short period of time, usually one month. The law refers to these agreements as periodic or month-to-month tenancies, landlords may use rental agreements for tenancies of other durations—for example, if the rent were due every two weeks.

A month-to-month rental agreement auto-matically renews each month unless you or your landlord gives the other the proper amount of written notice (typically 30 days) to terminate the agreement.

Landlords can raise the rent or change other terms of the month-to-month rental agreement with proper written notice. (Chapter 15 discusses these changes.)

If you live in an urban area with a tight rental market, where new tenants are easy to find, you might be offered a rental agreement. Landlords sometimes prefer to use a rental agreement because it:

- gives them the right to raise the rent as often as they wish (unless an applicable law, such as a rent control ordinance, provides otherwise), and
- usually allows them to easily get rid of problem tenants without the need to give a reason, because in most places, rental agreements can be terminated for no reason.

But of course, not all landlords think this way. Some wisely prefer to find and keep good long-term tenants and avoid the hassles of new tenants coming and going—even if it means less flexibility in terms of increasing rent or terminating the tenancy.

Fixed-Term Lease

A lease is a contract that obligates both you and the landlord for a set period of time, usually a year. With a lease, your landlord can't raise the rent or change other terms of the tenancy until the lease runs out, unless the lease itself provides for an increase (landlords and tenants can always agree to make changes, however).

Many landlords prefer the stability of renting to long-term tenants. As a result, landlords who use leases will probably take an extra measure of care when choosing tenants who will be around for a while.

Sometimes external factors influence the landlord's choice. If you live in an area with a high vacancy rate or where it is difficult to find tenants for a particular season of the year—for example, a college town, where most students are gone during the summer—landlords often insist on a fixed-term lease, usually for one year. Single-family houses are likely to come with leases, because the landlord will want to minimize the number of times the house must be prepared for new tenants. Preparing an apartment, by contrast, is not as big a job.

A lease has a definite beginning and ending date. Your landlord can't force you to move out before the lease term expires unless you fail to pay the rent or violate another significant term of the lease or state law, such as repeatedly making too much noise, damaging the rental unit, or selling drugs on (or even near) the property. (Chapter 18 discusses evictions for lease violations.)

What happens when a lease expires? At the end of the lease term, your landlord can decline to renew the lease (unless a local or state law requires a good reason, or "just cause," for deciding not to renew); or might opt to negotiate with you to sign a new lease with the same or different terms. If you and the landlord do nothing, but you stay and keep paying monthly rent, most states will consider you a month-to-month tenant renting under an oral lease. (Chapter 15 discusses what happens at the end of a lease period.)

Tenants Who Enlist or Enter Active Duty May Break a Lease

The War and National Defense Servicemembers' Civil Relief Act helps active duty military personnel handle legal affairs. (50 U.S.C. § 3901 and following.) Among its provisions, it allows tenants who enter active military service after signing a lease or rental agreement to break the lease or agreement. Chapter 15, How Tenancies End or Change, gives details.

Lease or Rental Agreement: What's Better for You?

Although you might not have the bargaining power to insist on one arrangement over the other, you'll want to recognize situations in which a rental agreement or lease is a clear necessity or a definite problem.

Nolo's Tenant-Friendly Leases and Rental Agreements

Nolo has developed standard lease and rental agreement forms that are clearly written, fair to both landlords and tenants, and good in all 50 states. If your landlord does not give you a written lease or rental agreement, or hands you one that is clearly unfair, you might suggest using Nolo's forms.

Our forms are available online and with *Every Landlord's Legal Guide* and *Leases & Rental Agreements*, both by Ann O'Connell and Janet Portman. Nolo also publishes an online, interactive state-specific lease and rental agreement. For more information on these products, go to Nolo.com.

For example, if you might want to move again soon, you'll prefer the flexibility of a rental agreement. But if you plan to stay put for the foreseeable future, it's often better to have a lease, because of the security it provides. If you ask for needed repairs or protest unreasonable landlord conduct (for example, entering your home without notice when there isn't an emergency), the landlord can't respond by giving you a 30-day notice to move—something that's generally allowed if you have a month-to-month tenancy. (If your state protects you against landlord retaliation, you can fight a spiteful landlord, but it will cost you time and money.) Even if your landlord decides to sell the property halfway into the lease, the new owner usually must honor existing leases.

If you feel nervous about seeing your future (or at least one year of it) set in concrete by virtue of a lease, you can relax. Most leases don't lock you in nearly as much as you might think. If you need to break your lease before the term ends, you can often avoid or substantially limit your financial obligation. In most states, the landlord must try to find another suitable tenant as soon as is reasonably possible in order to "mitigate" (minimize) the loss suffered as a result of a broken lease. If the landlord rerents the unit fairly quickly, your financial exposure might not be that great.

 RENT CONTROL

Rent control gives you many of the protections of a lease. If your unit is covered by a state or local rent control law that limits the landlord's ability to raise rent or terminate the tenancy without a good reason, your need for the protection a lease provides is lessened. On the other hand, many rent control ordinances do allow some rent increases—for example, when the landlord's operating costs, such as taxes and major capital improvements, have risen. Also, rent control ordinances usually allow landlords to evict tenants in order to move themselves or a relative in, or to make certain repairs. A lease normally protects you against these dangers. (Chapter 3 discusses rent control.)

Oral Leases and Rental Agreements

Oral leases or rental agreements are perfectly legal for month-to-month tenancies and, in most states, for leases of a year or less. If you have an oral lease for a term exceeding one year, it becomes an oral month-to-month agreement after the first year is up.

With an oral monthly tenancy, the period between rent payments typically determines how much notice your landlord must give you before increasing the rent or terminating your tenancy. For example, if you pay monthly, you are entitled to 30 days' notice.

Lease With Option to Purchase

If you want to buy a single-family rental, especially in a rising market, and you expect to stay in the area and have more money soon, consider a lease-option. Lease options work when your landlord wants to sell you the rental house, and you're in general agreement about the price and terms but can't come up with the necessary financing now. Here are the basics.

Under a lease-option contract, you lease a house for a set period of time—usually from one to five years—and you obtain the right (option) to buy the house at a specified future time for a price already established.

The rent you pay might increase during the contract term. In addition to paying rent, you'll pay in some form for the option: Most often either a lump-sum payment at the start of the contract, or in the form of higher-than-market rent.

The total cost of tying up the property with the option could range from a few hundred dollars to thousands of dollars. Unless your contract says otherwise, you are not entitled to a refund of what you paid to secure the option or any refund in rent if you do not exercise the option.

Depending on the terms of the contract, you can exercise the option to buy the property:

- at any time during the lease period
- at a date specified in the contract, or
- when another prospective buyer makes an offer on the house. The owner must give you a chance to match the offered price.

In some states, leasing a home with an option to purchase triggers the owners' duty to disclose important information about the property, just as they must do when selling the home. For this reason, and because it's so important to get the terms and conditions right, you should work with an experienced real estate lawyer if you plan on signing a lease-option.

Should You Use an Oral Rental Agreement?

Although an oral agreement is legal and enforceable, it's usually unwise to rely on one. Oral agreements often lead to disputes. As time passes, people's memories (even yours) become unreliable. Promises are forgotten and other important issues—such as your landlord's policies on returning security deposits—are often not discussed at all. If you and your landlord disagree about a particular policy or procedure, you will not be able to settle it by referring to your written agreement. Instead, you are likely to end up in court arguing over who said what to whom, when, and in what context. Follow the suggestion below if you can't get the landlord to agree to a full, written agreement, but want the security of having at least the key terms of the rental written down.

How to Make Oral Understandings Binding: The Letter of Understanding

An effective way to lock in your landlord's oral promises is to write a letter of understanding, in which you relate your understanding of what was discussed and agreed to, and invite a response if the landlord feels that you have misrepresented the conversation and conclusion. Whether you hand-deliver the letter to the landlord, mail it return-receipt requested, or mail it first class, the laws in most states will presume that your landlord received the letter and agrees with your version unless you promptly hear otherwise. If your landlord doesn't respond to your letter and ultimately fails to make good on a promise, your letter should help you prove your version of the facts in court if needed. It's almost as good as getting the promise into a lease or rental agreement. (See the Sample Letter of Understanding, below.)

Sample Letter of Understanding

777 Walnut Street

San Gimo, Arizona 00000

(414) 552-4567

January 20, 20xx

Manny Money

125 Capitol Mall

San Gimo, Arizona 00000

Dear Mr. Money,

Thank you for showing me Apartment #3 today at your apartment complex, Willow Run. As I'm sure you remember, we discussed the poor condition of the living room carpet, which you said you were planning to replace within two months. Since every other aspect of the apartment and the building seems like a good fit for me, I signed a lease, based on your promise that the carpet will be replaced within two months of my starting date of February 1, 20xx.

Please let me know immediately if your understanding of your promise regarding the living room rug differs from mine. As I mentioned today, I would not want to live with that stained carpet for more than two months, and would consider the lease to be breached if the carpet were not replaced by April 1, 20xx. I have every hope that you will take care of the matter as promised and that I will fully enjoy my tenancy at Willow Run.

Yours truly,

Sally Smart

Sally Smart

Typical Provisions in Leases and Rental Agreements

Here are the most important provisions found in most leases and rental agreements. Unfortunately, these are often buried in legalese and paragraph-long sentences. Hang in there and follow along with the lease your prospective landlord has given you. We'll strip pretentious phrases and verbose clauses down to their (usually) simple legal meanings.

If you run across terms or whole clauses not discussed here, get more information before you sign. Tenants' rights groups, which exist in many areas, will be able to answer your questions. Or, if you're signing a long-term lease for a valuable property, you might even want to see a lawyer. (See Chapter 20 for how to find and work with an attorney and do your own legal research, including online resources for doing so.)

RENT CONTROL

If you are protected by rent control, you'll see additional information in your lease or rental agreement, such as the name and address of the rent control board, a citation to the law itself, and sometimes basic information on how to enforce your rights. (Chapter 3 provides details on rent control.)

Identification of Landlord and Tenant

Every lease or rental agreement must identify the "parties" to the agreement. Your role in the agreement is clear: You are the renter/tenant (or the "lessee"). Who exactly is the other party to the contract (the "landlord" or "lessor") can be a bit trickier, especially when the property is owned by an entity or managed by someone other than the owner. In the most straightforward situation, the owner is also the landlord and will be named in the contract. Commonly, though, the property will be owned by one person (or a trust or corporate entity) and managed by a third-party individual or company. In this situation, the lease or rental agreement might not indicate who the owner is—it might only identify the manager as being the landlord. In nearly all situations, it won't affect you to not know the true owner of the property—you only need to know whom to contact to pay rent and report issues

Any competent adult—at least 18 years of age—can be a party to a lease or rental agreement. A teenager who is under 18 and has achieved legal adult status through a court order (called emancipation), military service, or marriage, can also be a party to a lease in most states.

Landlords typically want all adults who will live in the premises, including both members of a couple, to sign the lease or rental agreement. Doing this makes the individual signers each fully responsible for all terms, including the full amount of the rent.

To remind tenants of this rule, many leases and rental agreements state that all tenants are "jointly and severally" liable for paying rent and abiding by terms of the agreement. This bit of legalese means that each tenant is legally responsible for the whole rent (how you divide up the rent among tenants is up to you), and that the misdeeds of one tenant— for example, keeping a pet in violation of a no-pets clause—will allow the landlord to evict all of you.

Identification of the Premises

Your lease or rental agreement will state the address of the property being rented (often called "the premises") and should provide details on any other spaces you might have access to, such as a parking space, storage areas, or common areas. If your rental is furnished, the furnishings might be included in the definition of "the premises," or your landlord might require you to sign a separate inventory of the included furnishings, as discussed in Chapter 6.

Some leases and rental agreements also specify that you will use the premises as your "primary residence." This condition would exclude, for example, the tenant who lives primarily with his girlfriend but still wants to keep his own place; or the businessperson who travels to the same city a few times a month and needs a regular home away from home. From a landlord's point of view, the primary residence requirement makes sense because landlords worry that:

- You won't pay the rent on time if you are re-sponsible for rent or house payments elsewhere.
- A home that is infrequently occupied will not be kept up with the same care as you would give a steady residence.
- A vacant unit will be an easy mark for a burglary.

- Your real intention is to advertise your rental unit on Airbnb or a similar online service (see "Tenant Rights to Use Airbnb and Similar Vacation Rental Services" in Chapter 7, for more on this).

If your rented home will *not* be your primary residence, you'll need to think about how to deal with this issue. If the landlord lives at a distance and you are sure that you can always pay the rent on time, you might decide to take a chance and remain mum. But if your landlord or manager lives nearby or is often on-site, your absence will be noticed. As long as you always pay rent on time, every time, your tenancy probably won't be terminated—especially if you let the landlord know when you will be out of town for extended periods of time. In fact, this type of notification might even be a lease requirement or a state law. (See "Extended Absences by Tenant," below.)

Suppose now that your landlord lets you stay, knowing full well that you're in violation of the "primary residence" provision. If the landlord decides to terminate your tenancy on this ground many months down the line, it might be too late. If you fight an eviction action you might be able to convince a judge that your landlord waived the right to enforce the primary residence provision by knowingly allowing you to stay.

Restrictions on Home Businesses

If you are one of the millions of Americans who work from home or run a business from your house or apartment, make sure your lease or rental agreement doesn't specify that the premises are "for residential purposes only." If you're working alone or your job primarily consists of making phone calls or using your computer, you've probably got nothing to worry about.

On the other hand, if you meet with clients or have an unusual number of packages coming and going from your apartment, you'll want to discuss the issue with your prospective landlord. That's be-cause the landlord is likely to be concerned if there's a potential that your business will inconvenience your neighbors.

Where will your visitors park, for example? Will your piano students disturb other residents?

A landlord who does allow you to run a business from your rental might require you to maintain certain types of liability insurance. The additional insurance would cushion the landlord from liability if someone related to your business is injured at the rental property—for example, a customer who trips and falls on the front steps.

Also, be aware that if you use your residence as a commercial site, the property might need to meet the accessibility requirements of the federal Americans with Disabilities Act (ADA). For more information on the ADA, visit ADA.gov.

Child Care Operations

If you want to operate a child care or day care business in your rental, you might be entitled to do so—even if your landlord has a general policy against rental-based businesses. In California and New York, legislators and the courts have declared a strong public policy in favor of home-based child care, and have limited a landlord's ability to say no. (Cal. Health & Safety Code §§ 1597.40 and following; *Haberman v. Gotbaum*, 698 N.Y.S.2d 406 (N.Y. City Civ. Ct., 1999).) Local laws might address this situation as well. If you intend to do regular child care, check with your state's office of consumer protection to find out whether your state has laws that cover in-home child care in residential rentals.

Zoning Laws

Finally, even if it's okay with your landlord, your home-based business might violate local zoning laws restricting the type of businesses allowed (if any) in your residential neighborhood. Although many ordinances vaguely allow "traditional home-based businesses," in residential areas, they often:

- restrict the amount of car and truck traffic the business can generate

- bar outside signs
- prohibit nonresident employees or at least limit their number, and
- set a limit on the percentage of the floor space that can be devoted to the business.

In some cities, for example, dentists, physicians (except for psychiatrists), and unlicensed massage therapists may not operate home offices. In others, photo labs and recording studios are banned.

Homeowners' Association Rules

If your rental unit is in a planned unit or condominium development, be sure to ask your landlord to confirm that home businesses are allowed by the homeowners' association's covenants, conditions, and restrictions (CC&Rs).

Limits on Occupants

When you visited the rental, your landlord probably informed you of the unit's occupancy limit (the maximum number of people who can live there). The occupancy limit is probably also mentioned in your lease or rental agreement, along with a reminder that you cannot bring in additional roommates without permission.

Occupancy limits are legal as long as they are tied to health and safety needs, such as the size and number of bedrooms, or the landlord's legitimate business needs, such as limitations of the plumbing or electrical systems. They are not legal if based on the age or sex of the occupant or the whim of the landlord. For example, a restriction limiting a spacious two-bedroom flat to one occupant just because the landlord prefers to have fewer people living at the property would be illegal.

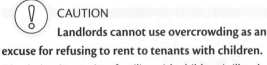

CAUTION

Landlords cannot use overcrowding as an excuse for refusing to rent to tenants with children. Discrimination against families with children is illegal, except in housing reserved for senior citizens only. (Chapter 5 discusses antidiscrimination laws.)

Guest Policies

Most landlords don't want tenants who haven't signed the lease or rental agreement (and haven't been screened and approved) living in the rental, for several reasons:

- More people means more wear and tear on the rental.
- It's harder for landlords to get unauthorized occupants to pay for rent or repairs.
- Unapproved guests, especially if they are frequent and short-term, might annoy other tenants in the building who don't like the idea of strangers coming and going.
- Unapproved residents can create legal hassles in the event of an eviction.

To deal with these potential problems, some landlords set a time limit for guest stays, such as no more than 10 days in any 6-month period, and require written approval for longer stays. This type of provision can be annoying because it allows your landlord to nose into your private affairs.

If you plan on having regular guests—for example, your college roommate stays with you two weekends a month when she's in town on business, or your boyfriend sleeps over a few nights a week—you'll need to think about how to handle this issue. If your landlord lives far away and doesn't have a resident manager, you might decide to take a chance that you'll never be found out. You might get away with it if you're always current with the rent and have no hassles with other residents.

But if the landlord lives onsite or nearby, it's best to request a revision of this clause. If the landlord resists, consider looking for another rental.

Term of the Tenancy

Your agreement will state whether it's a month-to-month tenancy or a fixed-term lease. "How Leases and Rental Agreements Differ," above, discusses the differences between these two approaches to renting.

Watch Out for Termination Fees

Occasionally, a lease includes a termination fee—what lawyers quaintly call a "liquidated damages" clause. This means if you move out before the lease expires, you are supposed to pay the landlord a predetermined amount of money (damages) to make up for the rent the landlord will lose due to your early departure.

Unless the amount of liquidated damages is close to the damages a landlord actually suffers, this approach is unfair and likely to be ruled illegal. (In Florida and Oregon however, landlords may use liquidated damages clauses under certain conditions.)

If you move out before your lease expires, under the law of most states you are legally responsible to pay the landlord only for the actual losses you cause. If you provide a suitable new tenant to move in immediately, the landlord might lose little or nothing. (And in most states, the landlord is legally obligated to minimize losses by trying to find a new tenant to replace you as soon as is reasonably possible.) In short, landlords who didn't lose any money when you moved out aren't entitled to a liquidated damages windfall.

Courts don't look kindly on liquidated damages clauses, especially if the amount far exceeds the amount the landlord really lost. Of course, should the issue ever come up, it takes time and trouble to go to court and get a judge to throw out a liquidated damages clause. If possible, try to get a clause like this deleted before you sign a lease or rental agreement.

Lease Provision

A lease obligates both you and the landlord for a specific term, typically one year. It sets a definite date for the beginning and expiration of the lease. It might also cover:

- **What happens at the end of the lease.** For example, it might have a built-in option to extend the lease at the same or a higher rent.

- **Monetary consequences for failing to leave when the lease ends ("holding over").** For example, the monthly rent might increase if you stay without permission. These clauses are not always legal. (See the discussion on penalties for holding over in Chapter 15.)
- **Periodic rent increases.** Without this type of built-in rent increase, your landlord cannot increase the rent until the lease ends. Periodic rent increases might be set at specific dollar amounts or tied to a consumer price index. Avoid agreeing to increases that are pegged to the landlord's increased operating expenses—you might have a hard time arguing that the increased expenses were necessary or accurate.
- **Rent increases allowed by law.** Landlords in rent control cities might build-in the rent board's annual allowable increase.
- **Financial penalties if you break the lease.** Most of these penalties (called liquidated damages) are illegal, although states are increasingly allowing landlords to set consequences in advance for breaking leases. See "Watch Out for Termination Fees," above.

Rental Agreement Provision

Rental agreements usually provide for a month-to-month tenancy. They also specify how much written notice your landlord must give to change or end the tenancy—most commonly, 30 days. See Chapter 15 for details.

Rent, Late Fees, and Grace Periods

Your lease or rental agreement will specify the amount of rent, when it's due (typically the first of the month), and where it's to be paid (via mail to the landlord's office or home is common). Your agreement might also include details on how rent is to be paid, such as by personal check or electronic funds. Many landlords spell out their policies on late fees (if rent is not paid on time) and bounced checks. Most states have legal limits on the amount that can be charged for late fees. (See Chapter 3.)

A grace period is a promise by the landlord to not terminate your tenancy until you are a certain number of days late with the rent. Except for a few states that impose mandatory grace periods, you'll almost never encounter a grace period spelled out in a rental agreement. You might see something like a "late fee after five days" clause, but this is not the same thing as a grace period—with a clause like this, your landlord can immediately take steps to terminate your tenancy if you don't pay rent on the due date (but won't charge you late fees until after five days).

Deposits and Fees

All states allow landlords to collect a deposit when a tenant moves in and hold it until the tenant leaves. Landlords might call this a security deposit, cleaning deposit, or last month's rent. The general purpose of a deposit is insurance: It's a financial cushion for the landlord should you fail to pay the rent when it is due or leave the rental unit filthy or in poor repair.

State laws typically control the amount landlords can charge, how deposits may be used, when they must be returned, and what type of itemization a landlord must provide to a tenant when deductions are made. In addition, some states allow landlords to charge nonrefundable fees for items such as cleaning and pets, while others specifically prohibit nonrefundable fees. Several cities and states require landlords to put deposits in a separate bank account and pay tenants interest on them.

If your lease or rental agreement is a good one, it might provide lots of helpful details on deposits—for example, where they will be held, interest payments, and the conditions under which the security deposit will be returned or withheld. A few states require specific information like this to be included in leases and rental agreements, but most don't, so most agreements simply state the dollar amount of the deposit.

To avoid confusion and legal hassles about your security deposit, be sure you get all the information you need before you sign a lease or rental agreement. You'll need to know:

- what deductions the landlord can make
- how the landlord expects you to clean the rental unit when you leave
- the deadline for the landlord to return the deposit, and
- whether the deposit can be used for last month's rent.

If this information isn't spelled out in the lease or rental agreement, ask your landlord to add it.

CAUTION

Watch out for automatic lien provisions. Your lease might have a clause that gives the landlord an "automatic lien" on your possessions if you fail to pay the rent or damage the unit. The purpose of this clause is to give your landlord the right to seize and sell your property without first going to court to prove the debt and give you a chance to hang on to certain property that is protected by state law. If you are presented with a lease that has an automatic lien provision (sometimes called a "distraint" or "distress" power), you should be concerned. Reputable landlords don't attempt to use them. While you might ultimately prevail in a lawsuit to compensate you for your seized possessions, that's little comfort when you return home to find your computer or other personal items missing.

Utilities

Your lease or rental agreement might specify who pays for the utilities. Normally, landlords pay for garbage and sometimes for water (especially if there is a yard the landlord wants you to keep up). Tenants usually pay for other services, such as internet, gas, and electricity.

CAUTION

Make sure you're not paying anyone else's utility bills. Some older buildings and some duplexes and triplexes do not have separate gas and electric meters for each unit. In other situations, your meter might also measure gas or electricity for uses outside of your unit—to light the common area or run the laundry room water heater, for example. Whenever you'll be required to pay for utilities that are not 100% under your control, your landlord should disclose this in your lease or rental agreement. (This type of disclosure is required by law in some states.) To avoid hassles later on with neighbors who are wasteful of energy, your best approach is to ask the landlord to install a separate meter for all areas served outside your unit—but be forewarned, it's expensive, and the landlord is likely to say no. Alternatively, you and the landlord should try to come up with a system that fairly measures the common-area usage, which the landlord should pay for.

Assignment and Subletting

Most leases and rental agreements will prohibit you from subletting—renting the unit to another person who's not on the lease or rental agreement— without the prior written consent of your landlord. Also common is a prohibition against "assignments," a legal term that describes what happens when you transfer your entire tenancy to someone else. Landlords include these clauses to prevent you from bringing in tenants whom they haven't approved, and to preserve their occupancy policies.

Even if your lease or rental agreement prohibits sublets and assignments without consent, however, state law usually prohibits your landlord from arbitrarily withholding consent to your request to sublet or assign your lease to someone else.

If your lease or rental agreement doesn't specifically prohibit sublets or assignments, in most states you can do so without your landlord's consent. Nevertheless, it's always wise to get the landlord's permission first, because most landlords will want to know whom they're renting to.

CAUTION

What about using Airbnb? Before you list your apartment on Airbnb or a similar service, be sure to check your lease or rental agreement (see "Tenant Rights to Use Airbnb and Similar Vacation Rental Services" in Chapter 7, for more on this).

Condition of the Rental Unit and Landlord's Responsibilities

Many leases and rental agreements include a clause in which you agree that the premises are in habitable (livable) condition. Before you sign off on a clause like this, inspect the rental unit and note any problems, using the Landlord-Tenant Checklist in Chapter 6. Doing so will help you identify problems that need fixing before you move in, and help you avoid losing your security deposit over a problem that was present when you moved in. It's best to insist that this Checklist be made a part of your lease or rental agreement. You can add a clause like this:

> Tenant has examined the premises, including appliances, fixtures, carpets, drapes, and paint, and has found them to be in good, safe, and clean condition and repair, except as noted in the attached Landlord-Tenant Checklist.

If the landlord won't do this, at least include the landlord's specific promises in the lease or rental agreement. If the landlord promises to fix the oven or install security bars on the ground floor windows, for example, write this into the lease or rental agreement, and set a deadline for work to be completed (ideally, before you move in). (Chapter 6 includes sample agreements regarding repairs.)

You could also use a letter of understanding, as explained earlier in this chapter.

Some states require landlords to notify tenants in writing of procedures for making complaints and repair requests and to alert landlords to defective or dangerous conditions. Good leases and rental agreements include this information, even if it's not required.

> ⓘ CAUTION
>
> **Know your rights to live in a habitable rental unit—and don't give them up.** As a general rule, landlords are legally required to offer livable premises when a tenant originally rents a rental unit and to maintain the premises throughout the rental term. Your lease or rental agreement will probably provide very few details on the landlord's

exact repair and maintenance responsibilities. And you'll probably never see a clause that describes your options, such as withholding rent, if the landlord fails to provide habitable premises. To protect your rights, it is crucial you know the laws on these issues. (See Chapter 8 for details.)

Also, in most states, language a landlord sticks in a lease or rental agreement saying a tenant gives up the right to habitable housing won't be effective. By law, the landlord has to come through with habitable housing, no matter what the agreement says. And even if your state law allows such clauses, as is true in a couple of states, in limited situations, you'll want to avoid any landlord who operates this way.

Landlord's Responsibility for Repairs Caused by Natural Disasters

Many leases and rental agreements outline the landlord's responsibilities if the rental property is damaged or destroyed by a natural disaster, such as an earthquake or flood. For example, the landlord might have the right to declare the lease terminated if the premises are totally destroyed, or the option to simply suspend the lease and begin repairs reasonably quickly. If your lease has no provision regarding destruction, it's likely that state law has something to say on the subject. See Chapter 8.

Tenant's Repair and Maintenance Responsibilities

Most leases and rental agreements state that you are responsible for keeping the rental premises clean, sanitary, and in good condition; and that you must reimburse the landlord for the cost of repairing damage caused by your abuse or neglect. Some clauses go beyond a general statement and actually detail tenants' responsibility for problems like broken windows, clogged drains, or snow removal. And a few landlords go so far as to delegate some of their own repair and maintenance responsibilities to tenants. This is most common, and most practical, for single-family houses or duplexes, because owners of these

How to Choose Renters' Insurance

When considering renters' insurance, follow these steps:

Take a property inventory. In order to choose a policy limit, you'll need to know the value of the items that you'll insure. (The smallest amount of coverage is usually $20,000 to $30,000.) You will be surprised at how fast the totals will mount up, given our ever-expanding inventory of modern necessities—computers, phones, bicycles, cameras, clothing, even pets. Also, taking an inventory will make it easier to make a claim, should you need to do so. The nonprofit organization United Policyholders has useful home inventory worksheets on its website (www.uphelp.org—search for "How to Create a Home Inventory"), as well as information on apps for taking a home inventory. Make a copy of your inventory and keep it in a safe place *away* from home.

Shop around. Find an agent or company representative you trust—possibly your automobile insurance agent, or one recommended by friends or relatives. Keep your inventory handy so that you can compare premiums.

Check what's covered. Ask about things not covered by the policy or where dollar limits are low. Cash is usually not covered, and jewelry, computer, and table silver coverage is typically limited, but you might be able to buy additional coverage (called a "floater" policy). Bicycles are usually covered (but not cars, vans, boats, or trucks). If you run a home business, you probably need to purchase additional coverage for office equipment.

Determine whether the policy is for replacement value. If you suffer a loss, your renters' policy can cover your belongings in one of two ways. It can reimburse you for the actual cash value (what your three-year-old computer would sell for today on the open market) or pay replacement value (what you would have to spend today to get a comparable computer). Obviously, a replacement value policy is preferable but is likely to cost more.

TIP

If you aren't worried about your property, get a high deductible. If your landlord requires renters' insurance to cover any damage you cause to the property, but you really aren't worried about the theft or loss of your own goods (maybe they aren't worth much, or you live in an extremely safe area), you can save a bundle by getting the highest deductible the insurance company offers.

Add your lease guarantor. If the landlord has required a cosigner or guarantor, be sure to add this person as an additional insured to your policy. Although a cosigner's primary role is to provide a source of money if you can't pay the rent, the cosigner could also be sued, along with you, by someone who claims that your negligence caused an injury. Do not expose your generous cosigner to this risk—adding a cosigner to your policy will cost only a few dollars.

Read your policy. Don't assume that the fine print exactly mirrors what you and the insurance agent discussed. Unless you check the important points (and complain, if there are any discrepancies), you'll be stuck.

RESOURCE

More information on renters' insurance. United Policyholders, a highly regarded consumer advocacy group, has helpful articles on renters' insurance on its website at www.uphelp.org. Also, check out the Insurance Information Institute's website (III.org). Many of the apartment-listing websites referred to in Chapter 1 have links to companies that sell renters' insurance.

properties seldom have on-site managers or maintenance people. See "Making Tenants Responsible for Repairs" in Chapter 8 for more on this issue.

Your lease or rental agreement will probably also tell what you what you *can't* do in the way of repairs. Typically, it will prohibit you from making alterations or repairs, such as pounding nails in the walls, painting, or fixing the broken heater, without your landlord's consent. In addition, your lease or rental agreement might specify that if you add any "fixtures"—a legal term that means any addition that is attached to the structure, such as a bolted-on bookcase or built-in dishwasher—they will become the landlord's property and cannot be removed without permission. And because your landlord has the legal right to enter your unit in an emergency, there might be a clause specifically forbidding you from adding or rekeying locks or installing a burglar alarm system without your landlord's consent.

Regardless of what the lease or rental agreement says, tenants have certain limited rights to alter or repair the premises. For example:

- In most states, tenants have the right to repair defects or damage that makes the premises uninhabitable.
- Texas law specifically allows tenants to install security devices without the landlord's prior consent when the landlord has failed to provide or rekey required locks. (Texas Security Devices Act, Tex. Prop. Code §§ 92.151–170.)
- In California, a tenant may install statutorily required door and window locks if the landlord has refused to do so. (Cal. Civ. Code § 1941.3(c).)
- Tenants with a legally recognized disability have certain rights to modify rental living space under the Federal Fair Housing Act. (42 U.S.C. §§ 3601–3619.)
- Federal law gives tenants limited rights to install wireless antennas and small satellite dishes. See "Satellite Dishes and Other Antennas," in Chapter 10, for details.

Who's Responsible for Appliance Repair?

Most state laws do not require landlords to provide major appliances such as refrigerators or stoves, although many landlords do. So, if you see a refrigerator or stove in a rental unit, you would naturally expect it comes with the deal, and that if an appliance breaks through no fault of your own, it's the landlord's job to repair it. Think again. Some landlords, trying to save a buck, include a clause in the lease or rental agreement stating that the appliances are there for the tenant's use but are not part of the rent. The clause goes on to say that if you use the appliances, you are responsible for their repair and maintenance.

This kind of clause is a clear sign that you're dealing with a cheap landlord who's almost certain to do a poor job in the repairs and maintenance department. If the apartment is otherwise terrific and the appliances in pretty good shape, you might decide to put up with this nonsense, but it probably makes more sense not to rent from someone who pinches pennies this hard. (Chapter 9 gives advice on how to pry appliance repairs out of a reluctant landlord.)

Renters' Insurance

Your lease or rental agreement might include a clause alerting you to the fact that your landlord's property insurance will not cover any losses to your personal property that result from an accident on the premises. For example, if a fire that's the fault of the landlord destroys part of your unit and damages your possessions, the landlord's policy will not cover you—it will compensate only the landlord for the cost of repairing the structure. You could demand compensation from the landlord and sue if necessary, but the source of any recovery will be the landlord, personally, not an insurance company.

Similarly, the landlord's liability policy won't cover you if your carelessness causes damage or injury. This means that you might be personally responsible if your actions cause:

- damage to the rental unit or other tenants' property

- loss of or damage to your belongings, or
- injuries to yourself or others.

Because of these realities, you might see a clause requiring you to obtain renters' insurance, which will cover losses to your belongings as a result of fire or theft and also provides coverage if your negligence causes property damage or injury to other people. Landlords with exclusive properties are especially likely to require renters' insurance. Similarly, the landlord's liability policy won't cover you if your carelessness causes damage or injury. This means that you might be personally responsible if your actions cause:

Is It Legal for Landlords to Require Renters' Insurance?

Whether it's legal to require tenants to purchase renters' insurance is a topic of hot debate among lawyers. Judges in some states, including Oklahoma, have held that, by implication, tenants are coinsured under their landlords' own property policy, because their rent helps pay the landlords' premiums. On the other hand, some states have enacted laws specifying the circumstances under which landlords can require renters' insurance. (For example, Virginia (Va. Code § 55.1-1206) and Oregon (Or. Rev. Stat. § 90.222).)

The real reason landlords insist on renters' insurance has little to do with concern for your personal property. Rather, they want it in place so that if you damage the rental property, or if someone is hurt due to your carelessness, your insurance company, not the landlord's, will foot the bill. If you let your renters' policy lapse and refuse to reinstate it, landlords have little recourse other than to terminate your tenancy (assuming their lease or rental agreement provides for that consequence). If you're an otherwise good tenant, landlords will not want to take this ultimate step.

However, the insurance industry handed landlords a way to keep your insurance alive and pressure you to pay the premiums. Landlords can buy a type of insurance called "Apartment Owners Limited Building Policy" that will, if needed, provide you with liability insurance—but not property insurance—if your renters' insurance policy has lapsed. The land-lord sets the rent to include both the rent and a "rent credit" equal to the monthly cost of such a policy, plus a little to cover the landlord's administrative costs. If your insurance policy remains in effect, you get a rent credit every month and pay just the regular rent. But if you can't prove that you have a current policy, the landlord will buy the coverage for you and you'll pay rent plus the "credit." A scheme like this will have a hard time surviving a legal challenge in areas with rent control, unless the rent plus the rent credit is within the rent allowed by law.

What Does Renters' Insurance Cover?

Even if your landlord does not require renters' insurance, buying it can be a good idea if you can afford it. The cost depends on the location and size of the rental unit and the value of your possessions. Renters' insurance typically costs a few hundred dollars a year for a $50,000 policy. Some insurance companies offer discounts if you already have another type of insurance with the company, or if you have risk-reduction measures in place such as a security system.

Renters' insurance usually covers the following:

- loss due to theft, including some losses that occur away from home
- negligent destruction of your or the landlord's property (for example, you start a fire that destroys your kitchen)
- liability for injuries or losses to others (a guest slips and breaks her leg on your freshly washed kitchen floor, or you leave the water on, ruining the downstairs tenant's computer), and
- natural disasters or damage to your property caused by other people (the creek rises, flooding the building, or your neighbor starts a fire that damages your unit).

CAUTION
Renters' insurance will not cover intentional damage. It also will not pay back rent, nor will it cover any sums you might owe the landlord in excess of your security deposit. And, it probably won't cover damages from an Airbnb "guest."

Buying Renters' Insurance With Cotenants

If you rent a place with other people (your cotenants), you might want to explore purchasing one policy that will cover all of you. You shouldn't have a problem getting a joint renters' insurance policy. Under a joint policy, if someone's personal property is stolen or damaged, the insurance company will write just one check for the value of the property. It will be up to you and your cotenants to give the money to the cotenant who suffered the loss. Or, if a fire damages a jointly owned sofa, you'll get one check and you and your roommates will have to apportion the money fairly. The advantage of having one joint policy is that you'll have to satisfy only one deductible. For example, if a burglar steals your bike, one roommate's climbing rack, and another roommate's computer, you'd make one claim for all three items and face only one deductible.

You and your cotenants can also purchase individual policies that cover your individual property, as well as your share of jointly owned property. For instance, if you and your roommate buy a sofa together and each pay half, your individual policy would cover you for up to half the sofa's value. If a fire were to damage the sofa, you could submit a claim for half its value, but you'd probably have to document the fact that you paid for half of it. (You can document your ownership share by signing an agreement with your roommate at the time of sale, or by showing that you wrote a check or incurred a credit card charge for half the price.)

In sum, having just one policy that all cotenants share is cheaper because there's only one premium and one deductible, but having two might be less hassle when it comes to dividing up the proceeds.

Whether you get a joint policy, or each buy an individual policy, it's important to keep clear records of who owns what.

Watch Out for Hold-Harmless and Exculpatory Clauses

Many form leases include illegal provisions that attempt to absolve the landlord in advance from responsibility for all damages, injuries, or losses, including those caused by the landlord's misdeeds. These clauses come in two varieties:

- Exculpatory: "If there's a problem, you won't hold me responsible."
- Hold-harmless: "If there's a problem traceable to me, you're responsible."

For example, the lease generated by one popular legal software package contains an exculpatory provision so broad that it states that your landlord is not responsible, period, for injuries to tenants and guests. If enforced, this would mean that if you fall down broken stairs and break your leg, the landlord isn't responsible (even, apparently, if the landlord knew about the broken stairs for weeks).

Such pro-landlord language is blatantly illegal. If your landlord assaults you, or you're injured because of a dangerous or defective condition the landlord knew about (or should have known about) but failed to fix for several months, no boilerplate lease provision will protect your landlord from civil and possibly even criminal charges. To this end, most states have laws that declare that exculpatory clauses in residential leases and rental agreements are void. This means that a judge will not enforce them.

Violating Laws and Causing Disturbances

Most leases and rental agreements contain a clause forbidding you from using the premises or adjacent areas, such as the sidewalk in front of the building, in such a way as to:

- violate any law or ordinance, including laws prohibiting the use, possession, or sale of illegal drugs

- seriously damage the property (sometimes called "committing waste" in legalese), or

- create a nuisance by annoying or disturbing other tenants or nearby residents.

You might also see a reference to tenants' right to "quiet enjoyment" of the premises. This bit of legal jargon amounts to a promise that your landlord will not act (or fail to act) in a way that seriously interferes with your ability to use the rented premises—for example, by allowing garbage to pile up, tolerating a major rodent infestation, or failing to control (or evict) a neighboring tenant whose constant loud music makes it impossible for tenants to sleep. Fortunately, you have the right to quiet enjoyment even if your lease or rental agreement doesn't mention it.

Many landlords also include specific rules—for example, no loud music played after midnight—in a separate set of rules and regulations. As discussed below, as long as these rules are fairly reasonable—and sometimes even if they are not—your landlord can enforce them.

Pets

In most situations, your landlord has the right to prohibit all pets, or restrict the types allowed—for example, no dogs or cats, but birds are okay, or dogs are okay, but none of a particular breed. However, a landlord may not prohibit trained service animals used by people who have physical or mental disabilities, or emotional support animals, as provided by the federal Fair Housing Amendments Act, discussed in Chapter 5.

Many landlords spell out pet rules—for example, that the tenants will keep the yard free of all animal waste, or that dogs will always be on leash—in a separate set of rules and regulations.

Some landlords allow pets but require tenants to pay a separate deposit to cover any damage that the pet might cause. The laws of a few states specifically allow separate, nonrefundable pet deposits. In others, charging a designated pet deposit is legal only if the total amount your landlord charges for all deposits does not exceed the state maximum for

all deposits. Also, it is illegal to charge an extra pet deposit for people with trained guide dogs, signal dogs, or service animals.

Opening Landlords' Doors to Pets

Several humane societies across the country offer pet-owning tenants helpful materials on how to negotiate with a landlord who doesn't normally allow pets. Check these examples out:

- The Hawaiian Humane Society (www.hawaiian humane.org) includes a special section (search for "Pets In Housing") that offers lots of useful resources for tenants, including a pet addendum to a rental agreement; the site also includes information on state laws in Hawaii, such as regards pet deposits.

- The Humane Society of the U.S. (www. humane society.org) includes useful tips for tenants (search for "information for renters with pets").

Landlord's Right of Access

Some leases and rental agreements spell out rules covering the landlord's right to enter your rental unit, including circumstances allowing access and the minimum amount of notice the landlord must provide. Others are silent on the subject. Even if the lease tries to restrict your right to privacy, however, most states with laws guaranteeing a tenant's privacy prohibit a landlord from enforcing unreasonably strict rules.

Nearly every state clearly recognizes the right of a landlord to enter rented premises under certain narrow circumstances, such as to deal with a genuine emergency (for example, a fire or broken pipe) and when the tenant gives permission. Many states have access laws specifying the other circumstances under which landlords may legally enter—for example, to make repairs and inspect the property and to show property to prospective tenants or buyers. State access laws often require the landlord to give the tenant at least 24 hours' notice for nonemergency entries. A few states simply require the landlord to provide "reasonable" notice, often presumed to be 24 hours. Many states have no statutes covering landlord's access.

To protect your privacy, particularly if your state doesn't set specific rules on landlords' entry, be sure your lease or rental agreement covers the subject. Here's an example of the kind of lease clause you should get your landlord to write into your lease or rental agreement:

"Landlord or Landlord's agent will not enter tenant's home except to deal with an emergency; to make necessary or agreed repairs; to supply necessary or agreed services; or to show the unit to potential purchasers, tenants, or repairpersons. Unless there is an emergency, or it is impractical to do so, Landlord will give tenant at least 24 hours' written notice of the date, time, and purpose of the intended entry."

Extended Absences by Tenant

Some leases and rental agreements require you to notify the landlord in advance if you will be away from the premises for a certain number of consecutive days (often seven or more). Such clauses might give the landlord the right to enter the rental unit during your absence to maintain the property as necessary and to inspect for damage and needed repairs. You'll most often see this type of clause if you live in a place where, in cold weather, pipes in rental units need to be maintained to make sure they don't burst. By state law in Alaska, a rental agreement or lease must say that you need to inform the landlord of any planned absences over seven days (Alaska Stat. § 34.03.150).

Possession of the Premises

Your lease or rental agreement might include a clause explaining what happens if you choose not to move in after signing. Generally, you will still be required to pay rent and satisfy other conditions of the agreement. This does not mean, however,

that the landlord can sit back and expect to collect rent for the entire lease or rental agreement term. Instead, as we explain in Chapter 15, landlords in most states must take reasonably prompt steps to rerent the premises, and must credit the rent they collect against your rent obligation.

Most leases and rental agreements also cover situations when the landlord is unable to turn over possession of the unit to the tenant on time after signing. This clause is included in case fire destroys the building, contracted repairs aren't done on time, or a prior tenant fails to move out. In the absence of a clause like this, the law would usually consider the landlord's failure to allow you to move in on time to mean that the lease was breached, justifying your walking away and looking for another place. But landlords hate to lose a new tenant for reasons beyond their control, so they typically insert a clause that states that the lease will be considered breached only if *the landlord* says it is. Usually, they give themselves 10 to 30 days to make up their minds. In the meantime, you are obligated to honor the lease—even though you can't move in! You might be able to sue the landlord for reasonable costs of temporary housing, although some particularly nasty leases attempt to eliminate that remedy, too.

Another common approach to the "not ready" apartment is to allow the new tenant to walk away—in other words, to acknowledge that the lease has been breached—but to try to limit the landlord's liability for the breach. This is done with a clause that limits the tenant's remedy to the return of any prepaid rent and security deposits ("sums previously paid" is the language common in this type of clause).

If you have a limiting clause like this in your lease, you won't be able to sue the landlord for temporary housing while you wait for repairs or for the prior tenant to move out. You could, however, file a small claims court case and sue the hold-over tenant or the person who caused the delay for your inconvenience and expenses, although your chances of winning are slight.

Tenant Rules and Regulations

Many landlords don't worry about detailed rules and regulations, especially when they rent single-family homes or duplexes. However, in large multitenant buildings, landlords usually set out rules to control the use of common areas and equipment and to protect the rental property from damage. Rules and regulations also help avoid confusion and misunderstandings about day-to-day issues such as garbage, recycling, and use of recreation areas.

Marijuana Smoking

Many states have decriminalized the recreational use of marijuana, often defined as personal possession of a specified, small amount. You surely know whether your state is among them. And you might be wondering whether your landlord can legally prevent your lighting up in your rental. The answer is yes.

Even if recreational marijuana use is legal in your state, your landlord can legally prevent your lighting up in your rental. Smoking marijuana, just like smoking tobacco, creates odors and smoke that can damage the user's rental and travel to other units. Because landlords can legally designate their properties as smoke-free (common areas and individual units), they can consider marijuana smoke a violation of that policy.

Now, what about medical marijuana? The states that provide for legal use do not require landlords to allow such users to smoke on otherwise smoke-free properties. These laws simply protect the users from prosecution by the state; they do not interfere with a landlord's ability to maintain a smoke-free property. The wise practice of a medical marijuana user is to consume the substance in food or liquid, which will not impinge on other tenants' rights to a smokeless property.

Many landlords spell out their rules and regulations right in their lease or rental agreement. However, if the rules and regulations are lengthy, a clause in the agreement usually refers to them as a separate document (lawyers call this "incorporating by reference").

What's Covered in Tenant Rules and Regulations

Tenant rules and regulations typically cover issues such as:

- elevator safety and use
- pool rules
- garbage disposal and recycling
- vehicle and parking regulations—for example, restrictions on the types of vehicles (such as no RVs), or where guests can park
- lock-out and lost-key charges
- pet rules
- security system use
- smoking—prohibiting it altogether or in common areas in multiunit buildings (including the hallways, lobby, garage, or walkways)
- quiet hours (for example, no playing loud music after 10 p.m.)
- dangerous materials—nothing flammable or explosive should be on the premises
- storage of bikes, baby strollers, and other equipment in halls, stairways, and other common areas
- specific landlord and tenant maintenance responsibilities (such as pest control and lawn and yard maintenance)
- use of the grounds
- aesthetic controls—for instance, no drying clothes on balconies
- display of signs in windows
- laundry room rules, and
- rules for using other amenities, such as a pool or workout room.

Unlike the terms and conditions contained in the rental agreement or lease, rules and regulations can be changed by the landlord without waiting until the end of the rental term (for leases) or without giving proper notice (for rental agreements). The landlord has this freedom, however, only if the change is minor and not apt to significantly affect the tenant's use or enjoyment of the rental. For example, shortening the pool hours by a few hours in the winter is rather inconsequential; on the other hand, announcing that the pool will be permanently closed is major—and a tenant would have a good argument that this change constitutes a breach of the rental agreement or lease, even if the landlord characterizes the change as a mere rule change.

Chapter 15 covers your options when important amenities or services are withdrawn.

Tenant rules and regulations can have a significant impact on your daily life and enjoyment of the rental premises. Be sure to read them carefully. Look for a typical landlord ruse: Placing a significant rule or amenity in the rules and regulations, rather than in the lease, to enable the landlord to change the rule without notice (as illustrated in the pool example above).

Attorneys' Fees in a Lawsuit

When people who sign contracts end up in court, each side usually pays its own attorneys' fees and court costs, unless a judge orders the losing side to pay the winner's expenses. This happens rarely, and only when the law that the winner relied upon authorizes attorneys' fees, or when the conduct of the loser was particularly outrageous—for example, filing a totally frivolous lawsuit. If your lease or rental agreement has no "attorneys' fees" clause in it, then you'll be playing by these general rules if you end up in a court spat with your landlord.

But parties to a contract can decide in advance that they would like the rules to be otherwise. Many leases and rental agreements specify who will pay the costs of a lawsuit, by including one of two types of attorneys' fee clauses:

- **The "Loser Pays" Attorneys' Fees Clause.** A common and evenhanded attorneys' fees clause requires the losing side in a landlord-tenant dispute to pay attorneys' fees and court costs (filing fees, service of process charges, deposition costs, and so on) to the winning ("prevailing") party in a lawsuit. With an attorneys' fees clause of this type, if you hire a lawyer to sue your landlord and win, the judge will order your landlord

to pay your costs and attorneys' fees. A "loser pays" clause is attractive if you're confident that you will be a law-abiding and conscientious tenant—in other words, if you expect to be in the right.

On the other hand, if you qualify for legal aid or just feel confident about representing yourself in most situations, you might prefer not to have an attorneys' fees clause, reasoning that a landlord who can't recover attorneys' fees in court might be more willing to compromise any dispute.

- **"Losing Tenant" Pays.** Some landlords aren't content to make the loser (possibly themselves) pay for lawyers' fees. Instead, they write a clause that obligates the tenant to pay the landlord's fees and costs if the landlord wins. But if the landlord loses, the clause says the landlord isn't obligated to pay the tenant's expenses.

This is a pretty shifty arrangement, and it hasn't gone down well. By law in many states, any attorneys' fees clause in a lease or a rental agreement must work both ways, even if it's not written that way. That is, even if the lease states that only your landlord is entitled to attorneys' fees for winning a lawsuit, you will be entitled to collect your attorneys' fees from your landlord if you prevail. Your landlord would be ordered to pay whatever amount the judge decides is reasonable.

Assuming you have a choice in the matter (you often won't), is it a good idea to include an attorneys' fees clause in your lease? It depends. The presence of an attorneys' fees clause will make it far easier for you to find a willing lawyer to take a case that does not have the potential for a hefty money judgment. For example, if you successfully defend against an eviction, you're likely to get the right to stay at the rental, but you probably won't be entitled to any money from the landlord. If your lease has a clause providing that the winner pays the loser, your attorney will get paid by the landlord. Knowing this, a lawyer will be more likely to take your case.

Similarly, if your case has the potential for only a small monetary award but will involve a lot of work, a lawyer will be more willing to take it knowing that the fees will come from the landlord and not from your modest winnings.

Be Careful—Attorneys' Fees Often Go Only to the Winner, Not the Compromiser

In some states, a one-sided attorneys' fees clause (a winning landlord gets attorneys' fees but a winning tenant doesn't) will be read as a two-way, or loser pays, clause only if you *win* the lawsuit. In other words, your state law might regard a settlement or dismissal of the case as having no "winner," in which case a one-sided attorneys' fees clause will operate as written. Say, for example, you have a one-way attorneys' fees clause in your lease, and your landlord files an eviction lawsuit against you for nonpayment of rent. Then the landlord dismisses the case before trial when you come up with good evidence that the unit is uninhabitable. You might think that you won the case (after all, you were not evicted). Unfortunately, in this situation, the law doesn't see you as a "prevailing party." This means you won't be entitled to attorneys' fees from your landlord unless you can get the landlord to sign a statement as part of the landlord's dismissal of the eviction lawsuit that names you as the prevailing party. If you're in this situation, ask your lawyer, or follow the legal research tips in Chapter 20 to find out your state's law.

 CAUTION

Attorneys' fee clauses don't cover all legal disputes. The attorneys' fee clause in your lease or rental agreement covers fees only for lawsuits that concern the meaning or implementation of that document—for example, a dispute about rent, security deposits, or the landlord's right to access (assuming that the rental document includes these subjects). The clause would not apply in a personal injury or discrimination lawsuit.

 RELATED TOPIC

Chapter 20 discusses how to find and work with a lawyer.

Disclosures

Federal, state, or local laws might require your landlord to make certain disclosures before you sign a lease or rental agreement or move in. Examples of common required disclosures include:

- the name of the owner and the person authorized to receive legal papers, such as a property manager
- any known lead-based paint hazards in the rental premises (discussed in Chapter 13)
- hidden (not obvious) defects of the rental property that could cause injury or substantially interfere with your safe enjoyment and use of the dwelling—for example, a warning that the building walls contain asbestos insulation, which could become dangerous if disturbed
- the name and address of the bank where security deposits are held, and the rate of interest and its payment to the tenant (see Chapter 4)
- planned condominium conversions (discussed in Chapter 15), and
- the presence of a methamphetamine lab at the rental in a prior tenant's occupancy.

 RELATED TOPIC

State disclosures. See "Required Landlord Disclosures" in Appendix A for a list of the disclosures required in your state. Your city might impose additional disclosures —call your city attorney or city manager's office for details.

 RENT CONTROL

Rent control laws typically include additional disclosures, such as the name and address of the government agency or elected board that administers the law and special rules governing sublets and assignments.

Authority to Receive Legal Papers

Leases and rental agreements typically include the name and address of the landlord or whoever is authorized to receive notices and legal papers on the landlord's behalf, such as a property manager. Even if your state doesn't require landlords to disclose this information, it's good to have it. You might have to use it if, for example, you need to send a notice that you are ending the tenancy, or if you need to sue the landlord. (If your landlord hasn't given you this information, state law might say that the person or entity to whom you pay rent is the default recipient.)

Grounds for Termination of Tenancy

You'll often find a clause in your lease or rental agreement stating that any violation of its terms by you or your guests is grounds for terminating the tenancy, according to the procedures established by state or local laws.

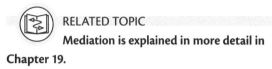

RELATED TOPIC
Chapters 17 and 18 discuss grounds and procedures for terminating tenancies.

Mediation

Often, involving lawyers in disputes between landlords and tenants is not the best approach. Many landlords have learned that these conflicts are best resolved with the help of a skilled, professional mediator.

As a result, you might see a clause obligating you to go through mediation "in good faith" if a dispute arises over the meaning or implementation of your lease or rental agreement. All this means is that you agree not to sue until you have met with the landlord and a mediator in a genuine effort to work out a solution to your dispute.

A mediation requirement is a good thing: It gives you a way to force your landlord into a low-cost, low-stakes discussion about your grievance.

Mediation is not binding—if you don't come to an agreement, you can assert your rights in court.

A mediation clause requires the parties to mediate only disputes that arise from the lease or rental agreement itself. For example, if you intend to sue your landlord for discriminating against you in violation of federal or state fair housing laws, you need not mediate first, because that behavior is not connected with the meaning or implementation of the lease or rental agreement.

RELATED TOPIC
Mediation is explained in more detail in Chapter 19.

Additional Provisions

Some form lease and rental agreements include a blank space for any other agreement you and your landlord wish to make. For example, your landlord might want to add a provision that prohibits smoking or spells out lost key charges.

Write down any agreement that's important to you, such as a landlord's promise to paint the unit before you move in. If you don't, and the promised improvement is put off or not done as promised, you'll be left with little more than your word against the landlord's.

If the form doesn't have a blank to add your own clause, you can modify the lease as shown below in "Changing a Lease or Rental Agreement."

CAUTION
If you don't get everything added to the agreement you sign, be sure to send your landlord a letter of understanding. See the discussion in "Oral Leases and Rental Agreements" and the sample Letter of Understanding, above.

In Chapter 6, "Using Email or Text Messages for Notice or a Letter of Understanding" explains why it's best to send this kind of letter by mail or delivery service, rather than email or text messages.

Validity of Each Part

Leases and rental agreements commonly include what lawyers call a "savings" clause, which means that, if one of the clauses is found to be invalid by a court, the remainder of the agreement will remain in force. Given the number of blatantly illegal clauses that lots of landlords stick in their agreements, it's not hard to see why they need this one.

Entire Agreement

Somewhere in the fine print, usually at the end, most leases have a provision that says that the agreement, and any attachments such as rules and regulations, is the entire agreement of the parties. That means that if the landlord (or you) made any promises that weren't in or attached to the lease or rental agreement, then they don't count and can't be enforced. Note, however, that you both can amend the lease after it's signed, by a formal amendment or a letter, as shown below.

Does this clause mean that your landlord's oral promises ("Of *course* I'll fix the ice maker before you move in!") will never be enforced? Probably not, but convincing a judge that your landlord made the promise will be a lot more difficult without evidence other than your word. For this reason, we counsel you (again) to get all promises from the landlord in writing and part of or attached to the lease.

Miscellaneous Clauses

If the landlord's lease has been prepared by a lawyer or trade organization, there's a good chance that you'll see these additional clauses at the end.

- **Successors.** Many leases state that the lease will be binding on the "successors, heirs, assigns, administrators, and executors" of the parties. This simply means that if the owner dies and the property passes to someone else, if the bank forecloses, or if the owner sells the building or assigns the right to receive rent to someone else, all of these persons will be bound by the agreement. The same goes for you—if you assign the lease (turn it over to a new tenant), you understand that the new tenant will be bound by the lease. (Assignment is explained in Chapter 15.)
- **Applicable law.** Your lease might state that it will be construed according to the laws of a particular state. Most of the time, this will be the state where the property is located. If another state is listed, beware. That state might be where the landlord's business is located, and the landlord might simply want to play by the laws that are familiar (and perhaps less tenant-friendly). In a business-to-business context, this type of choice is often allowed, but it's doubtful that a court would permit a residential landlord to choose another state's law to govern the rental relationship. Any attempt to do so is not a good sign; you'll want to consider whether to negotiate this one away.

Negotiating With the Landlord

Your lease or rental agreement is probably loaded with clauses written to maximize the landlord's rights and minimize yours. That's because these rental documents are typically written by lawyers hired by landlords or their trade associations.

Don't assume, however, that every clause is written in stone. Armed with a little legal knowledge, you'll be able to figure out whether the terms and conditions in your lease or rental agreement are legal or illegal, subject to negotiation or not. Here's how to do it.

We must add, however, that if you're dealing with a large corporation that owns dozens (even thousands) of rentals, you'll have a hard time changing anything other than perhaps the amount of rent. These outfits depend on their leases being uniform, so that leasing agents are asked to be familiar with only one lease per state or city.

TIP

Knowing *when* to negotiate is as important as knowing *how*. Don't start bargaining the minute you see a promising rental. Take some time to establish a rapport with the landlord. Give the landlord reason to want to choose you over other applicants. The landlord might flex on even seemingly mandatory rules (especially no-pets policies) if you appear to be a responsible and trustworthy tenant.

Four Types of Lease Clauses

Every rental clause falls into one of four categories, depending on whether any federal, state, or local laws apply to the subject covered by the clause. How (or whether) you should try to negotiate with your landlord over a rental clause depends on which category the issue fits into.

Category 1: A Restatement of Your Guaranteed Legal Rights

Many states have passed tenant-friendly laws covering topics such as landlords' access to rental property, the amount and use of security deposits, and the right to a livable home. In addition, federal law (particularly in the area of discrimination) and local law (especially if your community has rent control) might grant additional legal rights. *Your landlord cannot legally diminish these rights and cannot ask you to waive them.* You'll learn about the specifics of these non-waivable rights throughout this book.

You don't have to bargain for legal rights that are guaranteed under local, state, or federal law. Even though your landlord is obliged to comply with these tenant rights, including them in your lease or rental agreement is not usually required. If your landlord spells out guaranteed tenant rights in your rental document, that's great—but know that you've got them regardless.

Category 2: A Variation of a Negotiable State or Local Law

Not all tenant-protection laws are off-limits to landlord tinkering, as are the ones in Category 1, above. For example, in some states if *both* the landlord and tenant agree, they can shorten the statutory notice periods for changing or ending a tenancy. If the rental document doesn't mention the issue, however, state law prevails.

If you see a clause that restricts rights you have under a state or local statute, you'll obviously need to know whether this restriction is allowed—in other words, whether the subject instead fits within Category 1, above.

So long as your state or local law allows some wiggle room on a tenant-friendly procedure, the landlord is allowed to take advantage of that liberty. You can ask the landlord to follow the more tenant-friendly procedure—be prepared to offer reasons why restricting the right is either not necessary or not fair. You might be able to work out a compromise or offer a concession of your own in exchange for your full rights under the law. Ultimately, however, if a landlord won't budge and you feel very strongly about the issue, you'll have to look elsewhere.

Category 3: Illegal Clauses

Landlords cannot diminish certain tenant-protections, such as your rights to a habitable rental unit and to be free from illegal discrimination. These are the rights that fit within Category 1, above.

Even so, many landlords attempt to circumvent tenant protection laws by rewriting them in a lease or rental agreement. The best example of this is when landlords try to limit their responsibility to provide habitable housing, despite the laws that prohibit such tactics. Incredibly, some landlords insert clauses in leases and rental agreements declaring that the premises are not warranted as fit, safe, secure, or in good repair. Most states will not uphold these clauses.

This means that even when you sign a lease or rental agreement that contains a clause absolving the landlord of the duty to offer and maintain fit housing, you can still compel the landlord to perform the duty (or use a tenant remedy such as repair and deduct, explained in Chapter 8). If you were to sue over the matter, the court would not hold you to your "waiver."

An attempt to take away a guaranteed tenant right isn't the only kind of illegal clause you might encounter. Some clauses are illegal because they violate an important public policy. For example, many landlords use a lease clause that states that the tenant will not hold the landlord responsible for injuries the tenant might suffer as a result of the landlord's negligence or carelessness. Most courts will not enforce these clauses because our society expects that, for the most part, people should be held accountable for their screw-ups.

Remember that we are dealing here with tenant rights that can't be waived or diminished—in other words, they are *nonnegotiable*. A landlord who attempts to have you sign away your right to enforce your rights is either unaware of or deliberately violating the law. How you respond to a landlord's attempts to avoid legal responsibilities will depend on your assessment of the landlord's intent.

- **The landlord doesn't know the law.** If you think the landlord has made an honest mistake, and especially when the pool of rental options is limited, you might decide that it's worth pointing out that the clause is invalid. Doing so lets the landlord know that you're well informed and won't be taken advantage of. Hopefully, this will prompt the landlord to be more careful in the future. There is a risk, however: You might discover that the landlord will do everything possible to get rid of you, preferring to rent to people who don't know their rights.

- **The landlord is deliberately violating the law.** If every sign suggests that the landlord has deliberately circumvented the law, the wise course is clear: Move on. If you don't, you can count on problems ahead.

Category 4: A Policy or Rule Not Covered by State or Local Law

Finally, you'll see lots of lease clauses that are not regulated by local or state laws or court decisions.

Examples include provisions for parking spaces, amount of rent (rent control excepted), rent due date, move-in date, rules regarding common area use, and procedures for registering complaints and repair requests. Some of these issues are written as clauses in the lease or rental agreement itself, but many are covered in "house rules," which landlords attach to leases.

Minor, day-to-day issues aren't the only ones that might be unregulated, though: In some states, extremely important issues, such as security deposit limits or rules governing landlords' access to rental property, are not governed by law.

For example, Texas does not limit the amount of money a landlord may demand as a security deposit. Clearly, before sounding off with a haughty demand to reform an "illegal" clause, you'll need to know whether your state law does, in fact, regulate the issue.

Issues that aren't governed by law are the truly negotiable ones. Here you are both free to bargain, restrained only by the strength of your position. If it's a renters' market and the landlord's property is littered with "Vacancy" signs, you can expect more cooperation than if there are 17 professional couples lined up waiting to take the unit with no demands. Rather than push now for a better deal, it sometimes makes sense to get the rental and then, after you have established yourself as a stable, desirable tenant, ask the landlord to revisit the issue and possibly change that lease clause (changing rental agreements and leases is covered in Chapter 15).

Concluding Your Negotiations

Negotiation with your landlord should always end with a written version of what the two of you agreed to. Never, ever walk away from a negotiation session without reducing your deal to writing, either by changing the rental document or adding to it. Follow our instructions for changing a lease or rental agreement, below.

Changing a Lease or Rental Agreement

If you and your landlord agree to make changes to your lease or rental agreement, the process is simple.

Deleting Language

When you're able to convince your landlord that a particular clause need not be in your lease, don't rely on the landlord's oral promise to not enforce that part of the lease. Even if the landlord's promise is sincere at the time, an oral promise will not protect you if the landlord decides to renege on the promise or is no longer in the picture because they sold the building. To protect yourself, cross out the unwanted portion of the lease or rental agreement, write in desired changes (if any), and have everyone who is going to sign the document initial and date the changes. Alternatively, have the landlord edit the document and print out a clean copy for everyone to sign.

Adding Language

As explained above, you or your landlord can write or type in minor changes to the lease or rental agreement. If the proposed changes are fairly lengthy, however, your landlord will need to either prepare a new agreement or prepare an amendment (lawyers use the word "addendum") to the original document.

FORM

The Nolo website includes a downloadable Amendment to Lease or Rental Agreement form that you can print out, copy, and use to make changes or insert additions before you sign a lease or rental agreement. A sample is shown in Chapter 15. See Appendix B for the link to the forms in this book.

To use Nolo's Amendment form, follow these steps:

Step 1: On the original document, at the end of the rental provisions and before your signature, add the sentence "See Amendment A for additional provisions." That way, if the attachment gets lost (or the landlord removes it), the fact that it ought to be there will be recorded on the lease, and the landlord cannot claim that it never existed.

Step 2: Fill out the Amendment form included on the Nolo website. If it is the first addition, label it "A" in the space provided in the title and set out the additional lease provision in the space below. (If you later add more provisions, label them "B," "C," and so on, and refer to them on your copy at least of the original lease or rental agreement.) See the sample in Chapter 15.

Step 3: Consider what you want to happen if the landlord fails to follow through. If the amendment is absolutely essential to you—for example, you simply must have a parking space within three months—and you want to be able to legally move out if the landlord doesn't follow through, add this sentence: "Failure of the Landlord to comply with the terms and conditions of this Amendment constitutes a material breach of the Lease/Rental Agreement." This means that the landlord's breach excuses your obligations to stay and pay rent. On the other hand, if noncompliance would not be so devastating to your ability to stay and enjoy your home, specify another consequence, such as that your rent will be reduced a certain amount per day or week until the landlord fulfills the promise.

Step 4: Sign and date the amendment. Because it's part of your lease or rental agreement, store it carefully with the other important documents relating to your tenancy, as suggested in Chapter 6.

Signing a Lease or Rental Agreement

The end of the lease or rental agreement has space to include your landlord's signature, street address, and phone number; or that of the person or entity authorized to receive legal papers, such as a property manager. There's also space for your and other tenants' signatures and phone numbers, as well as any cosigner's signature. (Cosigners are discussed below.)

If your landlord has altered a preprinted form by writing or typing in changes, you and the landlord should initial and date the changes when you sign the document.

Make sure you sign the lease or rental agreement at the same time as the landlord and that you get a copy then and there. If no copy machine is available when you sign, take a picture of the signed document. This assures both sides that no changes can be made after only one party has signed.

Cosigners

A cosigner is someone who agrees to make good on your financial responsibilities under a lease or rental agreement should you fail to do so. If you fail to pay the rent, to replenish your security deposit after the landlord has used it to fix something you've damaged, or to pay for damage whose cost exceeds the limit of the security deposit, the landlord can demand payment from your cosigner. If the cosigner doesn't pay up, the landlord can terminate your tenancy.

Tenants who are students and supported in whole or in part by their parents often ask landlords to accept their parents (or others) as cosigners, hoping that the parents' or friend's solid financial position will make up for the student's meager income.

Landlords who accept cosigners typically have the cosigners fill out a separate rental application and agree to a credit check. Cosigners might bristle at this intrusion, but from the landlord's point of view, an insolvent cosigner is no good at all.

Tenants and their cosigners should also look for a common clause in the cosigner's agreement, one that designates the tenant as the "agent for service of process" should the landlord need to add the cosigner to a lawsuit (over unpaid rent or damage, for example). This clause means that the landlord need only "serve" the tenant with court papers, not the cosigner (the tenant will be expected to relay the unpleasant news to the cosigner, who will be considered "served"). The landlord need not hire a process server to find the cosigner, who is often out of state. If the cosigner ignores the lawsuit, the landlord will win by default, exposing that far-off cosigner to collection efforts. The lesson: Do not count on distance to protect a cosigner from unpleasant legal entanglements and consequences.

With one exception (explained below), landlords do not have to accept cosigners. Many feel that it just isn't worth the hassle of trying to reach someone who might live out of state to pay a tenant's late rent. But the reality of the marketplace usually dictates the practice—for example, landlords in college towns often accept cosigners because so many renters are students.

An important exception applies to the landlord's ability to say no to all cosigners. If an applicant with a disability does not meet the landlord's income threshold but is otherwise qualified, a landlord must at least consider the applicant's proffered cosigner. If that cosigner is financially solvent and stable, the landlord must accommodate the applicant by accepting the cosigner. (*Griebeler v. M & B Associates*, 343 F.3d 1143 (9th Cir. 2003).)

Basic Rent Rules

This chapter addresses important rules about paying rent that every tenant should know, including the following:

- How much rent can my landlord charge?
- Am I allowed a grace period to pay rent?
- What happens if I can't pay on time?
- Are there any limits on late fees?
- How much notice must my landlord give before increasing my rent?
- What are my options if I think the rent increase is unfair?

The general answer to these questions is that you'll need to look at your lease or rental agreement, refer to your state's law (you'll find handy charts in Appendix A), and consider your landlord's unwritten business practices. But figuring out what this means in your specific situation isn't always easy—and that's where this chapter can help.

RELATED TOPIC
Also covered in this book:

- Lease and rental agreement provisions on rent, late fees, and grace periods: Chapter 2.
- Paying first and last month's rent: Chapter 4.
- Negotiating a late rent payment and eviction for nonpayment of rent: Chapter 17.

How Much Can Your Landlord Charge?

Unless the rental is subject to rent control laws, landlords are free to charge as much rent as they like. (In Connecticut, however, tenants in many towns and cities may challenge a rent that they believe is excessive. Conn. Gen. Stat. §§ 7-148b and following. And most states prohibit rent gouging following a declared disaster.)

Most landlords monitor the rental market and price their rental units accordingly. To make sure

you're not overpaying, you should do the same thing: Check rentals on Craigslist and other sites and visit a few similar-sounding places to make sure your rent isn't out of line. Real estate offices are also good sources of information on area rents. (See Chapter 1 for a discussion of how to find an apartment or house.) In addition, local tenants' associations can be a terrific resource. See the "Tenants Working Together" section in Chapter 19 for advice on finding a local tenants' group.

"Section 8"

Many tenants with low incomes qualify for federally subsidized housing assistance. The most common is the Section 8 program of the federal Department of Housing and Urban Development (HUD). ("Section 8" refers to Section 8 of the United States Housing Act of 1937, 42 U.S.C. § 1437f.) That program determines a "market rent" for each rental property and then pays a percentage of the rent directly to the landlord, with the tenant paying the rest. The local housing authority, the landlord, and the tenant enter into a one-year agreement, using a written lease supplied by the county housing authority.

Section 8 housing can often be a good deal, because "market rent" for a unit is often set at a fairly low rate and, of course, part of this amount is subsidized. In addition, Section 8 tenants cannot be evicted except for nonpayment of rent or other serious breaches of the lease. Under federal law, landlords are not required to participate in Section 8, but at least 16 states—California, Colorado, Connecticut, Illinois, Maryland, Massachusetts, New Jersey, New York, North Dakota, Oklahoma, Oregon, Rhode Island, Utah, Vermont, Virginia, and Washington—and the District of Columbia require landlords to do so.

If you think you might be eligible for Section 8 assistance, contact your local HUD office. (Find yours at HUD.gov.)

TIP

If the rent seems low, find out why. When you're apartment-hunting, keep in mind that a lower rent does not always reflect less value. Many wise landlords charge a little less than the going rate as part of a policy designed to find and keep excellent tenants. On the other hand, if you find an attractive unit at an unbelievably low rent, beware. Many scammers list fake rentals at prices that are too good to be true in order to collect a quick holding deposit—never to be seen again. If the listing is legitimate, though, you'll still want to inquire further about a lower-than-market rent: Ask the landlord when the rent last went up. If it's been more than 18 months, you can bet an increase will happen soon. For reassurance, you might want to ask the landlord for a lease of a year or more at the existing rent.

Rent Control

California, Oregon, New York, and Washington, D.C., as well as some cities and counties in Maryland and New Jersey have laws that limit the amount of rent landlords may charge. These rent control laws are sometimes also referred to as "rent stabilization" or "maximum rent regulation" laws.

The Rent Control Board

In most places with rent control, the administration of the program rests in the hands of a rent control board of 5 to 10 people. Board members often decide important issues, such as the maximum amount a landlord can charge for rental units. (In many areas, the law itself limits how and when the rent can be raised.) Depending on the law, rent control board members are elected by voters or appointed by the mayor or city council. Because rent control boards interpret the provisions of the law, they usually have significant power over landlords and tenants.

Where to Get Information About Rent Control

If you are protected by a rent control ordinance, use these resources to get straight information:

- **In Oregon:** Community Alliance of Tenants (www.oregoncat.org).
- **In California:** Tenants Together (Tenants Together.org). Nolo maintains a comprehensive chart of the dozens of ordinances in California: Go to Nolo.com and search for "Updates on California Rent Control and Rent Stabilization Laws." The resulting article includes a link to a detailed Rent Control Chart for California.
- **In Washington, D.C.:** The Department of Housing and Community Development (https://dhcd.dc.gov/rentcontrol).
- **In New York:** New York State Homes and Community Renewal (https://hcr.ny.gov/rent-control).
- **Your city rent control board.** It can supply you with a copy of the current local ordinance, and possibly also with a brochure explaining the main features of the ordinance.
- **Your local tenants' organization.** Virtually every city with a rent control ordinance has an active and vocal tenants' group. (In many cases, the pressure from these groups is why the city has rent control in the first place.) These organizations typically are vigorous watchdogs of the rent board and monitor court decisions and any political goings-on that affect the ordinance (such as proposed ballot amendments). Most important, tenant organizations usually provide a written explanation of the ordinance and how it works, and many have volunteer staff available to explain ambiguous or complex facets of the ordinance.
- **Local attorneys who specialize in landlord-tenant law.** Chapter 20 discusses how to find and work with a lawyer.

RESOURCE

Learn whether your state allows rent control or has just cause eviction laws. If your state doesn't allow rent control, you can skip this section (but note that some states that don't allow rent control might still have just cause eviction laws). We've outlined the status of rent control and just cause evictions for each state in the "State Rent Control Laws" in Appendix A.

RESOURCE

New York and California rent control. Rent control laws for New York are extremely complicated. If you are a New York tenant, consult your local tenants' organization (check out Tenants & Neighbors, www.tandn. org). If you live in California, be sure to check out the Nolo book *California Tenants' Rights*, by J. Scott Weaver.

Rent control laws vary widely. Some, like the ones in New York, have real teeth, while others are practically useless. And rent control is unpopular politically in many areas: State law often restricts local rent control rules or bans them altogether; over 30 states have laws prohibiting local rent control ordinances.

Rent control laws commonly regulate much more than rent—for example, they might limit the circumstances under which landlords may evict tenants. Because these laws are complicated, vary widely, and change often, this book cannot provide fine details on every program, but this general description of what rent control ordinances typically cover will help you understand what to look for.

Property Subject to Rent Control

Not all rental housing within a rent-controlled area is subject to rent control. Commonly, ordinances exempt:

- new buildings
- owner-occupied buildings with no more than three or four units, and

- single-family houses and luxury units that rent for more than a certain amount.

Limits on Rent

Rent control comes in two basic styles: one that protects only the present tenant, and one that regulates rent over the long term, regardless of turnover. In rent control jargon, these varieties are known as "vacancy decontrol" (protects only the current tenant) and "vacancy control" statutes. Here's how they work.

Vacancy Decontrol Statutes: Protecting Current Tenants

In most rent control areas, landlords may raise rent as much as they want when one tenant moves out and a new one moves in (but only when the departing tenant left voluntarily or was evicted "for cause"). This feature, called "vacancy decontrol" or "vacancy rent ceiling adjustment," means that rent control applies to a particular rental unit only as long as a particular tenant (or tenants) stays there. If a tenant voluntarily leaves or, in some places, is evicted for a legal or "just" cause (discussed below), the rental unit is not subject to rent control again until the unit is rerented at a new (and presumably higher) rate.

Some laws automatically allow a specific percentage rent increase each year for existing tenants. The increase might be a fixed percentage of the rent or a percentage tied to a local or national consumer price index.

In addition to built-in annual increases, some rent control laws allow landlords to petition for a rent hike based on an increase in costs, such as taxes or capital improvements.

> **EXAMPLE:** Marla has lived in Edward's apartment building for seven years. During that time, Edward has been allowed to raise the rent only by the modest amount authorized by the local rent board each year. Meanwhile, the market value of the apartment has gone up significantly.

When Marla finally decides to move out, Edward is free to charge the next tenant the market rate. But once set, that tenant's rent will also be subject to the rent control rules, and Edward will again be limited to small annual increases as approved by the rent control board.

Vacancy Control Statutes: Protecting Future Tenants

The type of rent control known as vacancy control sets a base rent for each rental unit. (The brute forces of the market have no place here.) The base rent usually takes into account several factors, including the rent that was charged before rent control took effect, the landlord's operating and maintenance expenses, inflation, and housing supply and demand. The base rent may be raised during the tenancy under certain circumstances, such as an increase in inflation. When the tenant moves out, even voluntarily or after a "for cause" eviction, a landlord cannot raise the rent to market level. Rent stays controlled, subject to the formula of the rent control ordinance.

EXAMPLE: Sergei has been a tenant in Rudolph's apartment complex for two years. Every year on January 1, Rudolph raises the rent according to the rate set by the rent control board. When Sergei moves out on June 1 and Sasha moves in, Rudolph must charge her the same rent as Sergei paid during that year. He cannot raise her rent until the following January 1.

TIP
Slumlords can't raise the rent. When your landlord hasn't adequately repaired and maintained the rental property, your rent control law might prohibit a raise in rent that the landlord might otherwise be entitled to. Read your law carefully to see if you have the right to protest a rent increase based on a pattern of substandard conditions in your building or unit. If your landlord doesn't keep the premises habitable, you probably have other remedies—for example, you might be able to withhold rent—independent of the rent control ordinance. (Chapter 8 discusses your options.)

Evictions in Rent Control Areas

For rent control to work—especially when the law allows rents to rise when a tenant leaves—it must place some restrictions on tenancy terminations. Otherwise, landlords have an incentive to create a vacancy by throwing out existing tenants, either for trivial reasons or by simply refusing to renew a lease. Recognizing this, many laws require landlords to have a "just cause"—that is, a good reason—to terminate and, if necessary, evict. Unless the landlord can point to a "just cause" for tossing you out, you are also entitled to renew under the same terms and conditions, including the length of the rental term. Landlords often refer to this aspect of a rent control ordinance as "the endless lease."

Rent control laws specify a limited number of reasons that justify eviction, including:

- You violate a significant term of the lease or rental agreement—for example, by failing to pay rent, causing substantial damage to the premises, or allowing unauthorized people to live in the rental unit. However, in many situations, state law requires that a landlord must first give you a chance to correct the problem. (See Chapter 17.)
- The landlord wants to move into the rental unit or give it to an immediate family member.

TIP
"Relative move-ins" are often bogus. Unscrupulous landlords often cite the need to have a relative (or themselves) move in as the reason for evicting a tenant. Then, after a ridiculously short tenancy (or none at all), the relative or landlord moves out. In areas with vacancy decontrol, this enables the landlord to raise the rent to market rate for the next tenant.

If you suspect an illegitimate relative move-in, investigate further. See if you can find out whether the landlord or a real relative actually moved in and, if so, for how long. If the tenancy is patently short or the "relation" isn't one at all, consider seeing a lawyer or suing in small claims court to recoup your moving costs and higher new rent. Some rent control laws presume that the move-in is fraudulent if the landlord or relative stays less than a prescribed amount of time.

Additional "just cause" reasons include:

- The landlord wants to remodel the property in a manner that requires you to move out. Under some ordinances, a landlord who rents a number of units (for example, in a good-sized apartment building) must make another similar unit available to you or give you first chance to move back in after the remodeling. In some cases, the landlord may raise the rent based on the improvements.
- You create a serious nuisance—for example, by repeatedly disturbing other tenants or engaging in illegal activity, such as drug-dealing or prostitution, on the premises.

Interest Payments on Security Deposits

Local rent control ordinances sometimes impose rules regarding security deposits that supplement those set out by state law. For example, San Francisco landlords are required to put security deposits in interest-bearing bank accounts, something not required under California law. Check your ordinance to see whether similar protections apply to you. (Chapter 4 discusses interest payments on security deposits.)

Special Notice Requirements

State laws typically require landlords to give a specified amount of notice when it comes to raising the rent or terminating the tenancy. (Notice requirements are explained in Chapter 15.) In rent control situations, however, the notice requirements are often tighter in two respects:

- **Raising the rent.** State law typically requires a 30-day notice for a rent increase. A local rent control law might also require the notice to tell the tenant that the rent control board can verify that the new rental amount is legal under the ordinance.

- **Terminating the tenancy.** Most rent control ordinances forbid the landlord from terminating (or refusing to renew) a tenancy without a "just cause," as explained above. And even where the landlord does have a just cause, the termination or nonrenewal period is longer than that required under general state law.

Your Landlord's Right to Go Out of Business

It's not uncommon for landlords in rent-controlled cities to decide to get out of the residential rental business entirely. To do so, however, they must evict tenants, who will protest that the eviction violates the rent control ordinance.

A rent control ordinance cannot force an unwilling landlord to stay in business, though an ordinance might attempt to restrict the number of condominium conversions (the number-one reason most landlords withdraw from the rental market). However, landlords who withdraw rental units from the market must usually have plenty of evidence that their true motive is not to evade the rent control ordinance: Rent control boards do not want landlords to use going out of business as a ruse for evicting long-term tenants, only to start up again with a fresh batch of tenants whose rents will be substantially higher.

If your landlord files an eviction lawsuit because of going out of business, check your law carefully. It might require the landlord to offer you relocation assistance, and might impose a minimum time period during which the landlord cannot resume business. A landlord who owns multiple units might be prohibited from withdrawing more than a portion of the units; and if the premises are torn down and new units constructed, the law might insist that the landlord offer former tenants a right of first refusal. State laws not related to rent control might also address these issues. Contact your local tenants' group or rent control board for details.

When Is Your Rent Due?

Most leases and rental agreements call for rent to be paid monthly, in advance, on the first day of the month. However, landlords are normally legally free to establish a different monthly payment date—or even to require that rent be paid weekly or biweekly. Some landlords make the rent payable each month on the date the tenant first moved in. Most find it easier, however, to prorate rent for a short first month and thereafter collect rent on the first of the month.

A twice-a-month schedule is the most common variation on the standard monthly payment arrangement. This is often imposed by landlords on tenants who have relatively low-paying jobs and get paid twice a month. Some landlords assume that a tenant can't be trusted to save the needed portion of the midmonth check until the first of the month. Can your landlord require bimonthly checks from you, yet let a wealthier tenant pay once a month? Under certain circumstances, yes; in others, this would be an act of illegal discrimination. (Chapter 5 discusses discrimination in detail.)

 TIP

Special provisions for public assistance recipients. If you receive public assistance in Hawaii, for example, you may choose to establish a due date for your rent that is on or before the third day after the day you usually receive your public assistance check. (For more information, check your state's rent rules. Citations are listed in "State Rent Rules" in Appendix A.)

When Rent Is Due Under an Oral Lease

Oral leases, though never a good idea, are enforceable for tenancies of up to one year. If you have an oral lease and you and your landlord have not discussed when the rent is due, how do you know when to pay?

The safest route is to raise the issue immediately with the landlord. (And, in the process, get a written lease!) Failing that, consider the due date to be the same as it would be if you did, in fact, have a written lease that was silent on the issue (see "When Is Your Rent Due?" above). For example, a tenant with an oral lease in Oregon (and the majority of states) would have to pay at the beginning of the term, but a tenant in California would consider rent to be due at the end. But if you live in a state where rent is due at the end of the rental period, unless otherwise arranged, heed this word of advice: Your landlord probably doesn't know the law, and probably expects rent at the start of the term.

If you live in a state that has no law on the subject, we suggest paying at the start of the term.

When the Due Date Falls on a Weekend or Holiday

Most lease and rental agreements state that when the rent due date falls on a weekend day or legal holiday, the tenant must pay rent by the next business day. This sensible practice is legally required in some states and is the general practice in most. If your landlord insists on receiving the rent check by the first of the month (or other due date), even if mail is not delivered on that day, you might want to check your written agreement. If you get no help there, take a look at the law in your state; you might find that your landlord is violating it. If not, you might have to bite the bullet and get your rent in early.

Grace Periods for Late Rent

Lots of tenants are absolutely convinced that if rent is due on the first, they actually have until the fifth (or sometimes the seventh or even the tenth) of the month to pay, because they are within a legal grace period. Sorry, but this is not true. Rent is legally due on the date specified in your agreement or on the next business day, if your state's law contains that rule. The only wiggle room you might get concerns late fees (some states don't let landlords impose them until the rent is a specified few days late) and (in some states) a few days' protection from a termination notice.

Where and How Rent Is Due

Your lease or rental agreement probably specifies where and how you should pay the rent. In most states, landlords are required to provide tenants with this information.

Where Rent Must Be Paid

Many, if not most, leases and rental agreements specify where you are to pay the rent, such as:

By mail to the landlord's business address. This is the most common method of rent payment. If you mail your rent check, make sure that it arrives on or before the date the rent is due—it is not sufficient to post your check on that date. Given the sluggishness of the U.S. mail, you should allow at least three days for a local delivery. If your rent check will be in the mail on a Sunday or holiday, give yourself an extra day. If the due date is a Sunday or holiday, usually the following business day will suffice—but check your lease or rental agreement and your landlord's policy on this.

At your home. Your landlord might send someone to each unit every month to pick up the rent. This old-fashioned way of collecting the rent isn't used often, but it is a tried-and-true method to pressure a tenant who is chronically late with the rent.

At your landlord's—or manager's—office. This option is practical only for those owners with on-site offices. Often, the office has a drop box or mail slot—but if the office is open when you come by with the rent, spend a few minutes talking with your landlord or manager. It's a perfect time to raise any concerns, suggest improvements, or thank the landlord for attention to previous requests. A conscientious landlord will appreciate the feedback and the opportunity to discuss little problems before they become big ones. Of course, don't make every visit a gripe session, or your landlord will come to dread your visits.

Form of Rent Payment

Most leases and rental agreements also specify how rent must be paid. Cash, check, and money order are still popular ways of paying rent, especially to smaller-scale landlords. But if you're renting from a corporate landlord, chances are you'll be asked to pay your rent through an online portal. Tenants often feel that the form of payment should be up to them, but, just like restaurants and shops, landlords are usually legally free to insist on a particular form of payment (exceptions involve government-subsidized rent payments). California landlords may not require cash rent unless a tenant has bounced a check, and then only for three months; nor may they insist on electronic funds transfers only. (Cal. Civ. Code § 1947.3.)

Pros and Cons of "Easy" Ways to Pay the Rent

Landlords are always looking for ways to ensure that rent payments are quick and reliable. Here are pros and cons of some of the most popular rent collection methods.

Credit card. Some landlords offer tenants the option of using credit cards. Some might even insist on an automatic billing to your credit account at the same time every month, which means you don't have to call or show up at the rental office with your card. This is an extremely convenient arrangement, assuming your credit card can support it. It's obviously not a good idea if you are regularly over your credit limit or if you consistently pay interest on your balance.

Automatic debit. At the time you move in, your landlord might ask your permission—or even require you—to have rent payments debited automatically each month from your bank account. This is convenient but, like the automatic use of your credit card, should not be used by tenants whose checking accounts are thin or often overdrawn. (If you don't have enough money in your account when the debit goes through, the consequences to you are just like having written a bad check.)

Property management software. Many landlords are turning to free or low-cost online property management services to handle rent collection. These programs typically require tenants to create an account, then pay via an online portal. Most programs allow tenants to use either a credit card or automatic debit to pay. Read the fine print carefully: Most of these programs don't charge tenants to pay rent directly from their checking account, but do charge a fee (up to 3% of every payment) for payments made by credit card.

For many landlords, personal checks are the norm—but your landlord doesn't have to accept your personal checks. If you don't have a checking account (or if you have bounced a few checks), your landlord may legally require a certified check or money order. (Below, we explain landlords' rights to change the method of rent payment.)

No law requires a landlord to accept postdated checks, and most won't, because there's absolutely no assurance that necessary funds will ever be deposited in the account. If you are short on funds, far better to handle it in a straightforward manner. See "Negotiating Partial or Delayed Rent Payments," below, for advice on paying late rent.

> **CAUTION**
>
> **Don't pay rent in cash unless you have no choice.** These days, few landlords will accept rent in cash—they are justifiably wary of the risks of keeping large amounts of cash on hand. Your safety, too, will be imperiled if the word gets out that you regularly make a trip to the manager's office carrying a lot of cash. If you must pay in cash, be sure to get a written, dated receipt stating your name and the amount paid (many states require receipts when tenants pay in cash). It's your only proof that you did, indeed, pay the rent.

The Landlord's Right to Change Where and How Rent Is Due

If you've bounced a check or two, chronically pay rent late, or have lost your job, can your landlord suddenly refuse personal checks and accept only certified checks, cash, or money orders? Or, if you've been paying by mail as specified in your lease or rental agreement, can your landlord now require you to bring your rent to the manager's office?

Legally the answer is usually no. Your landlord may not unilaterally change terms in the lease or rental agreement. This means that if you have a year's lease, the payment arrangement is in force for a year; and if you rent month to month, most states require your landlord to give at least 30 days' written notice before changing a rental agreement clause.

How Landlords Can Change Lease or Rental Agreement Terms

To change the terms and conditions of your lease or rental agreement—such as how and where you pay the rent, pet policies, or late rent policies—your landlord must give you proper notice. Here are the basics, which are explained in detail in Chapter 15.

Type of tenancy	Amount of notice
Rental Agreement	Typically 30 days, although some states require as much as 45 or 60 days
Lease	Lease provisions cannot be changed until the lease runs out and a new tenancy begins

If your lease or rental agreement doesn't say where and how rent is to be paid, your landlord's past practice is more likely to legally control how rent is paid. For example, a landlord who has always asked for your rent check on the first of the month has established a due date that you must honor until the landlord formally changes the system with proper notice.

Don't be too quick to assert your rights. Under some circumstances, it might be a mistake to point out to your landlord that the rent payment clause cannot be changed without proper notice, or at all if you have a lease.

If the landlord has a legal ground for eviction (or might be considering giving you a 30-day notice to end a month-to-month tenancy), it's probably far better to go along with the rent payment change than to stand on your rights and give the landlord more reason to move forward with ending your tenancy. Similarly, if your landlord demands payment by certified check or money order after you've bounced several checks, it makes sense to comply for a few months. After you've paid on time for several months and things have calmed down, your landlord might be willing to accept your personal checks again.

If, however, the proposed change is both inconvenient to you and not motivated by your actions (but perhaps instead by the landlord's fear that you might not be able to pay rent in the future), you are within your rights to just say no. As long as you have a lease, the landlord can't evict you, because you've done nothing wrong. But if you have a month-to-month agreement, you probably should go along with the new system—your landlord can change it easily, anyway, by giving you proper notice.

A landlord who has been allowing you to pay rent in a different way than is required by the lease or rental agreement can probably start enforcing the written policy at any time. For example, suppose your lease or rental agreement specifies that rent be paid by certified check, but your landlord regularly and happily accepts your personal checks. Can the landlord suddenly decide to enforce the clause, even if your checks have not bounced? There is no clear answer. If such a dispute ended up in court, it would depend on whether the judge concluded that regular acceptance of your personal checks constituted a valid oral amendment of the written lease or rental agreement. Because your ability to prevail in court is unpredictable, unless you are very seriously inconvenienced by the change it's probably best to accept your landlord's insistence that the written agreement be followed.

Late Charges and Discounts for Early Payments

Rare is the tenant who's never had a problem paying rent on time. If you are a conscientious and honest tenant who is temporarily short on funds, most landlords won't evict you for paying rent a little late one month. However, landlords are wary of sending a message that late payments are okay, and often impose a late fee when rent is even a few days late. But the size of the late fee is subject to legal limits, and in some situations it's not legal to impose one at all.

Are Late Fees Legal?

If your lease or rental agreement says nothing about late fees, your landlord may not impose one, no matter how reasonable it is. For example, if you hand your rent check to the landlord two days late and he tells you he will accept it only if you pay an additional $10, you can refuse unless your lease or rental agreement includes a late fee clause.

However, reconsider asserting your rights if you live in a state that allows landlords to refuse late rent and begin eviction proceedings as soon as the rent is even one day late. (Chapter 17 explains your landlord's legal options when you are late with the rent.)

Limits on Late Fees

Some states put dollar limits on late fees. (See "State Rent Rules" in Appendix A.) In states that don't impose limits, general legal principles still prohibit unreasonably high fees. Courts in a number of states have ruled that contracts that provide for unreasonably high late charges are not enforceable. In other words, if you refuse to pay an outlandish late fee and your landlord attempts to evict you because of it, you should survive the eviction.

 RENT CONTROL
Some rent control laws limit late fees. If you live in an area with rent control, check the law to see if it imposes a limit on late fees.

How do you know if the late fee is "unreasonable"? To make that determination, many courts use these guidelines:

- **The fee shouldn't begin immediately.** Normally, a late fee should not apply until at least three days after the rent due date.
- **The fee should not exceed a certain percentage of your rent.** Late fees that exceed 5% of the rent are likely unreasonable. That's $50 on a $1,000-per-month rental. A few states set lower limits. Even in the majority of states with no statutory limits, a higher late charge, such as

10%, might not be upheld in court, unless the rent was extremely late—at least 10 days.
- **The fee should not increase without limit.** Late charges that increase quickly and without limits are likely to be considered unreasonable. Courts are more likely to uphold late fees that increase each day the rent is late only when the increase is moderate and the total charge has an upper limit. For example, $5 per day for the first four days the rent is late, and $10 for each subsequent day up to a $50 limit on a rent of $1,000 would amount to a maximum fee of 5% and would probably be accepted by a court.

If you believe your late fee is too high under these guidelines, communicate your conclusion—and your rationale—in writing to your landlord.

If you decide not to pay it, be prepared to be asked to move at the first legal opportunity—with proper notice if you rent with a rental agreement, or by the landlord refusing to renew your lease when it expires. A sufficiently annoyed landlord might even initiate eviction proceedings against a tenant with substantial time remaining on the lease. To avoid the risk of eviction, it might make more sense to pay the fee and challenge it in small claims court, where the worst-case scenario is losing your time, the court filing fee, and the offer of a renewal when the lease is up.

Late Fees Disguised as Early Payment Discounts

Some landlords try to disguise excessive late charges by giving a so-called "discount" for on-time rent payment. Here's how this dodge is often structured: A landlord who can't get away with charging a $100 late charge on an $850 monthly rent payment will set the rent at $900 and offer a $50 discount if the rent is no more than three days late. Fortunately, this bit of landlord subterfuge is unlikely to stand up in court unless the discount for on-time payment is modest. Giving a discount of more than 4% to 5% is in effect the same as charging an excessive late fee, and a judge is likely to see it as such.

Of course, if you are always prompt with the rent, a "discount" for prompt payment might not be a problem—after all, if you argue the point with the landlord when you sign the lease or rental agreement, you could end up with a reasonable late fee but a higher rent. And you can still complain about paying an overly high fee if, unfortunately, you are late with the rent a time or two. Most courts will still invalidate an unreasonable late fee although you might have in a sense benefited from its prompt payment "discount" by paying rent on time, or even if you have paid the late fee once or twice before complaining.

Avoiding Late Fees

If you can't pay your rent on time, don't automatically assume that you'll have to pay the late fee. Negotiation is often the tenant's best friend.

You should handle the late fee in the same manner that you handle the late rent payment itself: If you know that you will not be able to make the rent due date, notify your landlord in advance, explain the situation, suggest a payment schedule, and get it in writing. (We explain this process in detail below.) As part of your negotiations, ask for a waiver or reduction of any late penalty—many landlords will appreciate your advance notice and let it go at least once. (The sample letter below shows how to ask.)

Returned Check Charges

Your landlord has the legal right to charge an extra fee if your rent check bounces, but only if you knew in advance (in the lease or rental agreement, orally, or by means of an obvious sign in the rental office where you bring your monthly check) that the landlord would impose the fee.

Like late charges, bounced check charges must be reasonable. Some states regulate the amount landlords can charge; in the absence of such regulation, your landlord should charge no more than the amount the bank charges for a returned

check, probably $25 to $50 per returned item, plus a few dollars for the landlord's trouble. (Visit www.vericheck.com/state-allowed-nsf-fees for information on your state's bounced check limits.)

If your check has bounced, you might get a little breathing room if your landlord follows a policy of letting the bank present the check again to your bank. But don't count on it—experienced landlords instruct their banks to return bad checks after the first rejection, so they can confront the tenant and demand that the check be made good immediately.

Laws in some states allow landlords to charge interest on a bounced check, whether or not your lease or rental agreement says anything about late check charges. For example, California landlords may charge 10% per year interest on a bounced check—so, for example, on a $1,000 rent check that isn't made good for a month, the landlord can demand an additional $8.34. (Cal. Civ. Code § 3289(b).) Your state's consumer protection office should be able to tell you whether your state has a similar law. For a list of state consumer protection agencies, go to www.usa.gov/state-consumer.

Negotiating Partial or Delayed Rent Payments

If you suffer a temporary financial setback that makes it impossible to pay the rent on time or in full, don't immediately assume that you will be evicted or even subjected to a late charge. A landlord who considers you a good tenant won't want to lose you, because it's often difficult and expensive to find and move in good tenants. This means you can probably get the landlord to accept a portion of the rent now—maybe even a small portion—and the rest later. Here are five sensible approaches to take:

1. **Give your landlord written notice (as much as possible) that you will not be able to pay on time.** By taking this responsible and courteous step, you seize the psychological high road. And even more important, you raise the issue *before* your landlord has a chance to work up

a righteous head of steam. This early warning approach could backfire—your landlord could simply give you a legal demand to pay the rent or move out. But you don't have much to lose—most landlords who receive no rent or a bounced check will promptly do exactly the same thing.

2. **Explain your difficulties and emphasize that they are only temporary.** If your landlord is approachable and likely to empathize with your predicament, consider sharing at least some of the reasons behind your request. Emphasize your good, long-term relationship and—if true—that your predicament will be short-lived and not likely to recur. Your goal is merely to put a human face on your situation: It's up to you to decide where your desire for privacy ends and your need to defer your rent begins.

3. **Offer to pay at least some of the rent on time.** Even if you have to borrow money, try to pay at least a portion of the rent on time. By paying even a small amount of money, you offer tangible evidence of your intent to follow through with the rest of your obligation. Your landlord knows that a tenant who has paid a portion of the rent is less likely to skip out than one who has had a totally free ride.

4. **Give your landlord written assurance of your plan to pay.** Most landlords, even the most accommodating, will want a written agreement of your promise to pay the full rent by a certain date, such as the 15th of the month. Your landlord will probably ask for a date that is tied to a verifiable outside event, such as your payday or after your taxes are due. And a written agreement will protect you if, despite an oral agreement, your landlord suddenly decides to evict you for nonpayment of rent. (If, however, you've already received an overdue rent notice and make a partial rent payment, your landlord may still give you a termination notice for the balance.) A sample letter asking the landlord to accept late rent is shown above. If

---

Sample Letter Asking Landlord to Accept Late Rent

123 Shady Lane
Madison, Wisconsin 00000
(608) 555-1234

January 25, 20xx

Mr. Max Mason
100 North Main Street
Madison, Wisconsin 00000

Dear Mr. Mason,

As you know, I have been your tenant at 123 Shady Lane for the past ten months, and I have always met the terms and conditions of my lease. Not only have I paid my rent fully and on time, but I have treated your property with care and respect. I enjoy living at Shady Lane and hope to stay here.

The reason for this letter is to ask you whether I may pay part of next month's rent, due on February 1st, late. I would like to pay half the rent on the 1st, and the balance on the 15th. Unfortunately and with practically no notice, I have been laid off from my job as a computer programmer as a result of downsizing at ABC Software. This layoff happened just after I had spent most of my savings on computer equipment I need for the freelance programming work I do on the side. I have been diligently looking for a new job and already have three interviews scheduled next week. I have also applied for unemployment benefits, and I expect to start receiving checks in a few weeks. After February, I should have no problem paying the rent on time.

I would greatly appreciate it if you could accommodate my request. And since my finances are already stretched, I would also appreciate it if you would waive the late fee. I will be happy to sign an agreement laying out these terms.

Please call me (555-1234) so we can discuss this further. If I don't hear from you within a few days, I'll phone you at your office. Thank you very much for your consideration.

Yours truly,

Tom Tenant

Tom Tenant

the landlord agrees to your request to pay rent late, you should follow up with a written note confirming your exact agreement. Send your letter "return receipt requested," so that you can prove, if need be, that the landlord received it. Some landlords might want to draw up a more formal document.

5. **Keep your promise.** If you run into further difficulties and need to ask for an additional small extension, be sure that you have at least paid an additional portion of the overdue amount first. Obviously, your ability to renegotiate is limited by the landlord's desire to keep you as a tenant, which will probably decline the more your payments are delayed.

Rent Increases

Rent increases are an inevitable part of any tenant's life. But landlords cannot raise the rent on a whim. The timing of a rent increase, and the way your landlord communicates it, are governed by statute in most states; a few states regulate the amount of the increase itself.

When Your Landlord Can Raise the Rent

Except in areas with rent control, your landlord's legal right to raise the rent depends primarily on whether you have a lease or a month-to-month rental agreement.

Leases

Your landlord can't raise the rent until the end of the lease period, unless the lease itself provides for an increase or you agree to an increase. When the lease expires, the landlord can present you with a new lease that has a higher rent or other changed terms.

Rental Agreements

If you rent under a month-to-month rental agreement, the landlord can raise the rent by giving you proper written notice, which is 30 days in most states. (If you pay rent every 15 days, you might be entitled to only 15 days' notice.) In a few states, however, landlords must provide 45 or 60 days' notice to raise the rent for a month-to-month tenancy. (See "State Rules on Notice Required to Change or Terminate a Month-to-Month Tenancy" in Appendix A.)

Improper Notice

Landlords typically violate their notice obligations in one of two ways. Either they don't give enough notice before the increase is set to take effect, or they fail to provide written notice (or don't provide enough details) at all. Your response should depend on which error is involved.

The notice period is too short. If your landlord writes you on June 20 that your rent, due on July 1, has gone up, you haven't been given enough notice. You absolutely do not have to pay the increased rent on July 1, but, of course, you must still make your existing rent payment. However, if your landlord has complied with other notice requirements (discussed below), you *will* be expected to pay the extra rent as of 30 days from the date you got the notice. In other words, your landlord's notice is effective as soon as the legal notice period has elapsed. This might mean you have to pay the next month's rent at the old rate; but, at some point during that month (when the notice period expires), you'll need to pay a prorated share of the rent at the new rate.

> **EXAMPLE:** Simon, a month-to-month tenant, paid his rent for the coming month on the first of the month. State law requires 30 days' notice before a rent increase can take effect. Simon's landlord gave him written notice of an increase on the 20th of June. On July 1, Simon paid full rent at the old rate. On July 20, Simon owed his landlord an additional sum: the rent per day at the new rate minus the rent per day at the old rate, times 11. On August 1, he paid the full increased rent.

Also, check your state's laws for any restriction on how many times in a certain time period a landlord can increase your rent. For example, landlords in Colorado can't raise the rent for the same tenant more than once in a 12-month period. (Colo. Rev. Stat. § 38-12-702.)

Sample Letter Formalizing a Rent Increase

> 789 Walnut Street
> Concord, CA 00000
> (510) 555-4567
>
> June 1, 20xx
>
> Mr. Mike Moskowitz
> 788 Walnut Street
> Pleasanton, CA 00000
>
> Dear Mr. Moskowitz,
>
> In a conversation today you informed me that my rent, currently $850 per month, will go up $50, to $900, as of the first of July. Please sign and date this letter confirming this understanding and return it to me at the above address.
>
> Yours truly,
>
> *William Ames*
> William Ames
>
> _____   _____
> s/Mike Moskowitz   Date

The notice is oral or not properly delivered. State laws all require rent increase notices to be delivered to a tenant in writing; some states require certified mail. Oral notices are ineffective and, unless you specifically agree to the rent increase, you are not obligated to pay more money. But if you ignore a polite oral notice from a landlord, be prepared for an angry confrontation followed by a speedily drafted written notice and a chill in your long-term relationship.

If you receive an oral notice and don't consider it worthwhile, in the long run, to fight your landlord on this issue, be sure to put details on the rent increase (and any other changes in your rental agreement) in writing. One way to do this

is to ask the landlord to prepare a new rental agreement. (Chapter 15 shows how.) Another approach is to write a letter to the landlord confirming the new terms. Ask the landlord to sign and date it and return it to you. (Letters of understanding are explained in Chapter 2.) Getting the increase in writing will protect you against any misunderstanding as to the amount. The sample letter above shows you how to lock in an oral rent raise. You would be wise to send it return receipt requested, and to keep the receipt in a safe place with your other rental papers.

RENT CONTROL
Rent control laws also affect rent increase notices. If you live in an area covered by rent control and get a rent increase notice, be sure the notice (as well as the amount of the increase) complies with the laws of your city. Check the law or contact the rent board.

How High Can the Rent Go?

In areas without rent control, there is no limit on the amount your landlord can increase the rent (except in Connecticut, where most tenants can challenge increases they feel are excessive). The only exception to this rule is if a rent increase is discriminatory or is in retaliation for a tenant's exercising a legal right.

Recognizing that most tenants want to know when and by how much the rent is likely to rise, some landlords announce their rent increase policy in advance. For example, your landlord might say the rent will go up every January, based on a formula tied to the Consumer Price Index. Can you rely on this and successfully resist any other type of rent increase? It depends. If the policy is part of your written lease or rental agreement, the landlord is bound by it. But if it is an oral policy, or one that is part of another tenant's rental agreement but not yours, you'll have a very hard time convincing a judge to hold the landlord to it. If your landlord's policy is not in your lease or rental agreement, ask for a written lease or rental agreement to include it. (See Chapter 15 for advice on how to amend these documents.)

CAUTION

Rent increases often trigger security deposit increases. Many states limit the amount a landlord can charge for a security deposit. Typically, deposits are capped as a multiple of the monthly rent—for example, a maximum of twice the monthly rent. But this means that if the rent has gone up legally, the security deposit may also be legally increased. For example, if the deposit is twice the monthly rent, and your $2,000 rent has gone up $100, the deposit limit rises from $4,000 to $4,200. See Chapter 4 for more on security deposit increases.

Rent Increases as Retaliation or Discrimination

No landlord may raise the rent in a discriminatory manner—for example, only for members of a certain race or religion or for families with children. (Discrimination is explained in detail in Chapter 5.) And in most states, your landlord can't use a rent increase (or evict you or decrease services) in retaliation for your exercise of a legal right—for example, in response to your legitimate complaint to a public agency about defective conditions. (Chapters 8 and 17 discuss your rights to demand fit and habitable housing, free from the threat of eviction.)

How will you know whether a rent increase is in response to your exercise of a legal right? In some states, if you get a rent increase soon—typically, within three to six months—after you've exercised a right, the landlord is presumed to have been acting in retaliation. (See "State Laws Prohibiting Landlord Retaliation" in Appendix A.) This presumption means that if you end up in court (you refuse to pay the increase and the landlord files for eviction), the landlord must convince the judge that the increase was *not* a result of your exercise of a legal right.

But if the increase follows a general policy that your landlord has announced before your use of a legal remedy, and if the landlord has applied the increase to all tenants, it will be hard to show that your recent exercise of a legal right had anything to do with the landlord's action.

For example, many landlords raise rent once a year in an amount that more or less reflects the increase in the Consumer Price Index. Other landlords use a more complicated formula that takes into account other rents in the area, as well as factors such as increased costs of maintenance or rehabilitation. They make sure to inform their tenants about the rent increase in advance and apply the increase uniformly to all their tenants. Consistent increases such as these protect the landlord against any claim of a retaliatory rent increase by a tenant who has coincidentally made a legitimate complaint about the condition of the premises or withheld rent.

If you think a rent hike is motivated by your assertion of a legal right, you can refuse to pay the increase. If the landlord tries to evict you for nonpayment of rent, you can assert in court that the increase was done to retaliate against you. But before you refuse to pay, ask yourself the following questions:

1. **Does state law presume landlord retaliation in some circumstances?** In some states, if rent is increased within a certain time following a tenant's legitimate complaint to a public agency, use of a remedy such as rent withholding, or exercise of a legal right such as organizing a tenants' group, the law presumes that the landlord acted improperly. This brand of antiretaliation statute gives you an important tactical advantage in the courtroom: It is up to the landlord to convince the judge that the increase was not based on retaliation. If the landlord can't convince the judge, you should win without even opening your mouth.

2. **How soon after your action did the rent increase come?** Obviously, the shorter the interval between your exercise of a legal right and the date of the increase, the more suspicious it becomes.

3. **How large was the increase?** Judges are more likely to view a large rent increase (rather than a small one) as the landlord's way to punish or drive away a troublesome tenant.

4. **Does the rent increase affect you alone, or does it apply to many others?** Your chances of proving a retaliatory motive will be greatly increased if you can show that you alone, or you and other activist tenants, but not tenants in similar units, received a rent increase.

5. **Is your landlord known for repeatedly and seriously trampling on tenants' rights?** Your landlord's reputation is certainly a relevant factor if you contemplate challenging a rent increase. You can learn whether the landlord is a frequent visitor to landlord-tenant or small claims court by asking the local tenants' organization or even your fellow tenants. Technically, you aren't supposed to argue in court that the landlord's past illegal rent raises prove guilt now, too; most judges will try to confine you to the facts of your case alone. But it's fairly easy to make sure the judge knows your landlord is a scofflaw—share your information succinctly and quickly, then listen politely while the judge gives you a little lecture on the rules of evidence.

($) RENT CONTROL

Check past rent control records. Your landlord's reputation before the rent control board is just as important as a track record in court. To find out whether your landlord has been repeatedly challenged before the board, check with the local tenants' union.

6. **How disruptive or expensive, from the landlord's point of view, was your exercise of a legal right?** It's easier to win these cases when you can convince a judge that the landlord has a strong motive to get even. Did you cause the landlord considerable time, expense, aggravation, or embarrassment? For example, if you complained to the local health department that your housing is uninhabitable because the roof leaked, and the department ordered your landlord to put on a new roof, that's an expensive job that your landlord might resent highly. You could claim that this resentment prompted a retaliatory rent hike. Similarly, a charge of discrimination (which the landlord might even ultimately defeat) could easily generate strong feelings of bitterness. On the other hand, your isolated request for a necessary and inexpensive repair is far less likely in the eyes of a judge to engender serious landlord revenge. Of course, this theory is based on the assumption that retaliation is always linked to important matters—and we know that some landlords are inclined toward pettiness.

EXAMPLE: Ira rents a two-bedroom unit in a large apartment complex. Within the past year, he has asked his landlord for new carpets and drapes, which were grudgingly provided; and he has organized the rest of the tenants so that they can collectively press for improvements in the property. Ira received a steep rent hike, which he refused to pay. When the landlord tried to evict him for nonpayment of the increased portion, Ira argued that the raise was in retaliation for his requests and political activities. Noting that none of the other two-bedroom tenants received similar hikes, the judge ruled in Ira's favor.

Talking the Landlord Out of a Rent Increase

From a legal standpoint, there is nothing you can do about a legal rent hike that doesn't violate a rent control law and is not discriminatory or retaliatory. The landlord can charge as much as the market will bear. (Connecticut tenants might have some recourse, however, as noted above.) From a practical standpoint, though, you can still try to appeal to your landlord's business sense and heart.

No increase is good business. Smart landlords realize that high rents are not the only route to high profits. Solvent, long-term tenants are the key to a strong business, because they are low maintenance—they don't have to be evicted, sued, coddled, cleaned up after, scolded for breaking the rules, or interviewed and investigated as part of the time- and money-consuming new-tenant application process. If you are a good, long-term tenant and you can convince your landlord that the rent hike will make you move, your landlord might think twice, or at least moderate the increase.

Your leverage with the landlord will increase if you can show that many other stable, long-term tenants are also upset and considering moving. If the rent hike affects others in your building, work together to present your collective plea. (See Chapter 19 for suggestions on working with other tenants.) Remember, even in a tight rental market, lots of long-term tenants are hard to find.

The increase is overreaching. If you think your land-lord will respond to an appeal based on kindness and fairness, give it a try. Calculate the percentage increase of the proposed rent. If it's greater than the current inflation rate or the average yearly rental increase in your area, point this out. Note your surprise at such a steep increase, and explain how it might strain your carefully planned budgeting. Design your appeal on the assumption that the land-lord is a decent person who wants to be a fair and honest landlord (hopefully, this won't be too much of a stretch). You could even accept the inevitable rent increase and propose a more reasonable one. If you have a strong argument, the landlord might think twice about jacking up the rate so much.

Below is a sample letter in response to a rent increase. Obviously, your letter will have to be closely tailored to your own situation. Note how the writers have documented the various ways in which they have been model tenants (the appeal to the landlord's business motives), and have acknowledged how decent the landlord has been (the appeal to the heart). In addition, they have told the landlord, who lives in the same building, that there is a very real chance of losing quiet neighbors. Are these tenants more valuable than an extra $300 a month? Hopefully, yes.

Sample Letter in Response to a Rent Increase

787, 788, & 789 Cherry Street
St. Louis, MO 00000
(314) 555-4567

June 15, 20xx

Mr. Joe Jacks, Owner
790 Cherry Street
St. Louis, MO 00000

Dear Mr. Jacks,

We were dismayed to receive your notice of an intended rent increase of $100 per month. While we realize that you are within your legal rights to raise the rent, we would like to ask you to reconsider this decision.

As you know, the three families who have signed this letter have been your tenants and neighbors in your fourplex for the last four, five, and seven years. None of us have ever been late with the rent; we all have always responded promptly to your requests to inspect and repair various aspects of the building, and have never intentionally damaged your property. During the time that we have lived here, no one has protested the two rent increases (the last being nine months ago). We have been careful to promptly notify you of any problems, and have not insisted on unnecessary, cosmetic improvements.

Having lived in many rentals over the years, we have appreciated your prompt attention to all the large and small details involved in running your business, and we have especially appreciated your kindness and understanding when things went a little bit awry. The increased rent, however, will make it extremely difficult for all of us to continue living here.

We hope that you will take a few moments to consider our request that the increase be rescinded or, at the least, lessened significantly. We have enjoyed living here and hope to continue doing so.

Yours truly,

Alex Corinthos
Benny Spenser
Cathy Webber

Security Deposits

Almost all landlords require their tenants to pay a deposit before moving in, typically at the time they sign a lease or rental agreement.

Landlords charge security deposits to assure that you'll pay rent when due and keep the rental unit in good condition. If you damage the property, fail to pay rent while you're still living there, or leave owing rent, your landlord can use your deposit to cover what you owe.

Security deposits constitute a big investment on your part, and they are a major source of friction between landlords and tenants. Fortunately, most states impose fairly strict rules on how landlords can collect and use deposits and how and when they must return them. Many states and cities even require landlords to put deposits in a separate account and pay interest on them. Landlords who violate security deposit laws are often subject to substantial financial penalties.

 RELATED TOPIC
Also covered in this book:

- Credit-check fees, holding deposits, and other fees landlords may charge: Chapter 1.
- Lease and rental agreement provisions on security deposits: Chapter 2.
- State rules on how and when deposits must be returned, and deductions allowed for cleaning, damage, and unpaid rent: Chapter 16.
- How to handle legal disputes involving deposits when you move out: Chapter 16.

Dollar Limits on Deposits

Many states limit the amount a landlord can collect as a deposit to an amount equal to one or two months of rent. (Sometimes larger deposits are allowed for furnished rentals.) In some states, the rent a landlord collects in advance for the last month is not considered part of the security deposit limit, while in others it is. (Later in this chapter we cover last month's rent.)

Rent that a landlord collects in advance for the first month is never counted towards the security deposit limit. However, a landlord's demand for several months' rent in advance would almost always run afoul of state security deposit limits. In highly competitive rental areas, tenants applying for desirable rental units occasionally offer to prepay several months' rent in order to convince landlords to choose them over other applicants. But is a landlord who collects this money (usually in excess of the state's security deposit limit) in violation of the law? Probably not, as long as it's the tenant's idea and the landlord has not made the extra rent payment a condition of getting the unit. In short, a tenant who wants to waive this protection of the state's deposit limit can do so; but the landlord cannot do it unilaterally.

How much a landlord in your state can charge you for a security deposit might depend on factors such as:

- your age (senior citizens sometimes have a lower deposit ceiling)
- whether the rental unit is furnished
- whether you have a month-to-month rental agreement or a long-term lease
- whether you have a pet or waterbed, and
- the number of rental properties the landlord owns (smaller landlords might be exempt from security deposit limits).

For details, see "State Security Deposit Rules" in Appendix A.

EXAMPLE: Jane, Reuben, and Sandy, who live in different states, each pay $1,900 rent per month for an unfurnished apartment. The maximum security deposit their landlords can collect ranges from $1,900 to $5,700, depending on the state's law:

- Reuben, who lives in Hawaii, pays $1,900—one month's rent
- Jane, who lives in California, pays $3,800 —two months' rent, and
- Sandy, who lives in Nevada, pays $3,800 in cash along with a surety bond for $1,900— a total of three months' rent that can be split between cash and a security bond.

Don't pay an excessive deposit. If your landlord is requesting a deposit that exceeds your state's limit, show the landlord a copy of your state's security deposit statute and ask for a lower deposit that's within the legal limit. If your landlord refuses, contact your city or district attorney's office, tenants' rights group, or state consumer protection agency for advice.

If you have a hard time coming up with the deposit, see if the landlord will reduce the deposit or allow you to pay it in installments. Here are a few tips for approaching your landlord. These strategies are more likely to work if you have a good credit history, strong references, and live in an area with lots of rentals. And, wait until the landlord has offered you the rental unit before you start asking for special considerations.

- **Ask to pay in installments.** Offer to pay half the deposit up front with the rest on an affordable installment plan. Some landlords will say yes only if you can come up with the whole deposit in 30 to 60 days, but others will let you increase the amount a little each month until it's paid off in six months or more.
- **Suggest a cosigner.** A landlord might be reassured if a financially responsible friend or relative agrees to pay the deposit if you can't. (Chapter 2 discusses cosigners.)
- **Offer to buy renters' insurance.** A landlord who's worried about damage might be willing to reduce the deposit if you provide this extra measure of protection to cover any damage accidentally done to the rental property. (Chapter 2 explains renters' insurance.) However, a landlord who is worried about unpaid rent and intentional damage won't be mollified by your purchase of renters' insurance, because your policy won't cover you in these situations.
- **Offer to pay slightly more rent (assuming there are no rent control limits).** Some landlords might agree to a substantially lower deposit in exchange for a higher rent.

True, unlike the security deposit, the extra rent is not refundable. But if it allows you to rent a place you otherwise wouldn't qualify for, paying the extra money over time might be worth it.

Paying Recurring Fees in Place of a Deposit

In at least two states, including Texas and Florida, landlords can offer tenants the option of avoiding a traditional security deposit by paying a monthly fee, which is not refundable and whose amount is not regulated. (Fla. Stat. § 83.491; Tex. Prop. Code § 92.111.) The idea is that the landlord will use the fee to purchase insurance against unpaid rent and damage. Landlords see these arrangements as "win-win," because it allows a tenant who otherwise can't come up with a large deposit to secure the rental.

But many such tenants will not "win" in the end. You might think that the accumulated fee would need to be used for unpaid rent and damage, but that's not so. Paying the fee only allows the tenant to secure the rental without having to pay a deposit (landlords must tell tenants in writing that "…the fee is only for securing occupancy without paying a required security deposit" (Fla. Stat. § 83.491(g)). At any time during the tenancy, tenants can opt out of the fee program and pay a traditional deposit.

When tenants move out leaving damage beyond ordinary wear and tear or unpaid rent, landlords may demand that they pay for it. If the landlord's insurance pays, the insurance company can look to the tenant for reimbursement.

If you are offered such a deal, think carefully.

- You're essentially paying more rent, and will be on the hook for any damage or unpaid rent claimed by the landlord. You'll pay for it, either directly or after being dunned by the insurance company.
- Security deposit replacement is marketed to tenants as "deposit insurance," but it is anything but. When you have actual insurance, your insurance company doesn't pay out and then turn around and sue you for the payments—they cannot seek reimbursement from their own insureds.

- When landlords collect a deposit, many states require pre-move-out inspections, which give tenants a chance to perform needed cleaning and repairs and avoid deposit deductions. But when there's no deposit, that protection will not apply.
- Landlords will benefit when a fee-paying tenant leaves without damage or unpaid rent; all of those fees stay in the landlord's bank account. Landlords also stand to make money when the monthly amount of the fee exceeds the premiums on any insured rental unit.

> **CAUTION**
> **Your landlord's security deposit policy cannot discriminate illegally.** A landlord who charges some tenants the maximum deposit, and others less, should have a good explanation. This means if your landlord is charging the tenant next door a lower deposit because she's purchased renters' insurance, you should be in good legal shape to ask for the same deal. If the landlord refuses, without good reason, to give you an equivalent deal, you might have a discrimination claim in the offing. See Chapter 5 for information on illegal discrimination.

Where to Get More Information on Security Deposits

For more information about security deposit rules in your state, get a current copy of your state's security deposit law (statute). Start by referring to "State Security Deposit Rules" in Appendix A. This table highlights key rules, such as the deposit limit, deadline for landlord to return the deposit, and exemptions to state security deposit laws. Then read the statute online. (See Chapter 20 for information on accessing state statutes online.)

In addition, be sure to check local ordinances. Cities (particularly those with rent control) might add their own rules on security deposits, such as a limit on the amount landlords can charge or a requirement that landlords pay interest on deposits.

How Landlords May Increase Deposits

Tenants often ask whether it's legal for a landlord to raise their security deposit after they move in. The answer is that it depends on the situation.

Leases. If you have a fixed-term lease, your landlord may not raise the security deposit during the term of your lease, unless the lease allows it (most don't). When the lease is renewed or becomes a month-to-month tenancy, however, your landlord may increase the security deposit (subject, of course, to any limits imposed by law).

Written rental agreements. If you have a month-to-month tenancy, your landlord can increase the security deposit in the same manner as rent, typically by giving you a written notice 30 days in advance of the change (see Chapter 3). Again, the deposit can't exceed the maximum amount allowed by your state's security deposit law. (See above.)

> **EXAMPLE:** Jules rents an apartment for $1750 a month in a state that limits security deposits to one month's rent. If his landlord raises the rent to $2,000, the maximum deposit his landlord may collect goes up to $2,000. But the deposit doesn't go up automatically. To raise the deposit amount, his landlord must give Jules the required 30 days' notice (which can be combined with the notice raising the rent).

> **RENT CONTROL**
> **Rent control laws typically limit deposits as well as rents.** (See Chapter 3 for more on rent control.)

Last Month's Rent

A landlord might want you to pay a sum of money called "last month's rent" before you move in, as a hedge against your leaving early without having paid all the rent due under your lease. Problems can arise when:

- the landlord tries to use last month's rent to cover repairs or cleaning, or

- the rent has gone up during the tenancy—and the landlord wants you to top off the last month's rent.

We'll look at these situations below.

Applying Last Month's Rent to Damage or Cleaning

If you have paid your landlord a sum labeled last month's rent and your tenancy is ending (voluntarily or involuntarily), chances are that you will not write a rent check for your last month. After all, you've already paid for that last month, right? Surprisingly, many tenants do pay for the last month anyway, often forgetting that they have prepaid. What happens to that last month's rent?

Ideally, you'll leave the place clean and in good repair, enabling the landlord to refund the entire last month's rent and all or most of your security deposit. But if you leave the place a mess, most states allow your landlord to treat "last month's rent" as part of the security deposit and use all or part of it for cleaning or to repair or replace damaged items.

A few states, such as Massachusetts, restrict the use of money labeled as "last month's rent" to its stated purpose: the rent for the last month of your occupancy. In these states, landlords who use any of a last month's rent deposit to repair or clean a rental are violating the law.

EXAMPLE: Mike's landlord collected a security deposit of one month's rent, plus last month's rent. Mike's state required that landlords use money collected for the last month as last month's rent only, not for cleaning or repairs. When Mike moved out, he didn't owe any rent but he left his apartment a mess. Mike's landlord had to refund his last month's rent and, when the remaining security deposit proved too little to cover the damage Mike had caused, the landlord had to sue Mike in small claims court for the excess.

Last month's rent restrictions are often developed in court cases, not statutes. For this reason, we can't give you a neat list of states that restrict your landlord's use of your last month's rent. If you want to find out how courts in your state have ruled on the use of last month's rent, see our advice on doing legal research in Chapter 20.

Sometimes, landlords want to use money labeled last month's rent before the end of a tenancy. As explained below, the landlord may use your security deposit during your tenancy to pay for repairs that your actions have necessitated. In most states, landlords who also hold last month's rent can use that amount during your tenancy, too, if your security deposit is insufficient.

When Your Rent Goes Up

If you've paid the last month's rent in advance, and the rent at the end of your tenancy is the same as when you began, you're paid up. However, if the rent has increased, but you have not been asked to top off the last month's rent held by the landlord, questions arise. Do you owe the landlord for the difference? If so, can the landlord take money from your security deposit to make it up?

Unfortunately, there are no clear answers. But because landlords in every state are allowed to ask you to top off the last month's rent at the time they increase the rent, judges would probably allow them to go after it at the end of the tenancy, too. Whether they get the difference from your security deposit or sue you in small claims court is somewhat academic.

EXAMPLE: When Rose moved in, the rent was $1,800 a month, and she paid this much in advance as last month's rent, plus an additional $1,800 security deposit. Over the years the landlord, Artie, has raised the rent to $2,000. Rose does not pay any rent during the last month of her tenancy, figuring that the $1,800 she paid up front will cover it. Artie, however, thinks that Rose should pay the $200 difference. Artie and Rose might end up in small claims court fighting over who owes what. They could have avoided the problem had Artie increased the last month's rent amount at the time he increased the rent.

To avoid these disputes, we suggest that you get issues involving last month's rent straight with your landlord at the outset.

Nonrefundable Deposits and Fees

A few states specifically prohibit landlords from charging any fee or deposit that is not refundable. On the other hand, some states specifically allow landlords to collect a fee that is not refundable—such as for pets or cleaning. (See "State Security Deposit Rules," in Appendix A.) A few of these states require that the lease or rental agreement explain how the landlord can use the fee, but most don't, so learn your landlord's policy when you move in. A further complication is that non-refundable fees are sometimes called "deposits"—a contradiction in terms.

If your landlord is charging a nonrefundable fee or deposit, make sure it is legal. This is not always easy, because most state security deposit statutes are silent on the subject of nonrefundable fees. Contact your city or district attorney's office, state or local consumer protection agency, or tenants' rights organization for advice.

> ⓘ **CAUTION**
>
> **In states with deposit limits, creative land-lords have come up with ways to evade the law.** At the beginning of the tenancy, they collect the maximum deposit and also impose nonrefundable fees for processing the tenancy (called "tenant initiation expense fees" or "introductory fees"). Tenants have challenged these as a ruse to avoid the strictures of the deposit law.

Interest on Deposits and Separate Accounts

Unfair as it might seem, less than half of the states require landlords to pay interest on deposits or put the money in a separate bank account. In other words, your landlord can simply put your deposit in a bank account and keep any interest it earns. A number of years ago, when deposits were small, this might not have been such a big deal. But now, when deposits are higher and even in spite of low interest rates, it's extremely unfair.

Separate Accounts

Several states require landlords to put security deposits in a separate account, sometimes called a "trust" account, rather than mixing the funds with their personal or business accounts.

Some states require landlords to give tenants information on the location of this separate trust account at the start of the tenancy, usually as part of the lease or rental agreement. The idea is that by isolating these funds from the landlord's other accounts and telling the tenant where they are kept, the deposit can be traced easily, and it will become immediately evident if the money is improperly used—for example, spent by the landlord for personal purposes, or "misplaced" by a new owner. Landlords are not usually required to set up separate accounts for every tenant, although they should maintain careful records of each tenant's contribution.

Interest

Ideally, your landlord should put your deposit into some kind of interest-bearing account and pay you the interest when you move out, After all, it's your money, not the landlord's.

Unfortunately, only a third of the states require landlords to pay interest on security deposits.

Of course, excellent landlords are willing to pay interest on your deposit as an honest business practice, even if no law requires it. If your landlord doesn't volunteer to do this, there's no harm in asking.

Among the states that require interest, a few, such as Illinois, don't require small landlords (less than 25 rental units) to pay interest on deposits. Others, such as Iowa, allow the landlord to keep the interest earned during the first five years of your tenancy.

State laws typically establish detailed requirements, including:

- **The interest rate.** Usually, it's a little lower than the bank actually pays because the landlord is allowed to keep a small portion for administrative expenses.
- **When interest payments must be made.** Most laws require payments to be made either annually or when you leave.
- **Notification.** Landlords must tell tenants where and how the security deposit is being held and the rate of interest. This should go in the lease or rental agreement.

Several cities (typically those with rent control) require landlords to pay or credit tenants with interest on security deposits even when state law doesn't. A few cities require that the funds be kept in separate interest-bearing accounts.

How Landlords May Use the Deposit

Most states give landlords a set amount of time (usually from 14 to 30 days) to either return your entire deposit or provide an itemized written statement of deductions and refund the rest, if there's anything left.

Although state laws vary on the details, your landlord can almost always withhold all or part of the deposit to pay for:

- unpaid rent
- repairs to fix damage that you or a guest caused (except for "ordinary wear and tear")

- cleaning necessary to restore the rental unit to its level of cleanliness at the beginning of the tenancy (taking into consideration ordinary wear and tear), and
- replacements of rental unit property you've taken.

TIP

Read your lease or rental agreement to be sure deposit refund procedures are spelled out. To protect yourself and avoid misunderstandings with your landlord, make sure your lease or rental agreement is clear on the holding, use, and return of security deposits. If it's not, follow our advice in "Avoiding Fights Over Deposits," in Chapter 16, and write a letter of understanding to your landlord.

Landlords don't necessarily need to wait until you move out to tap into your security deposit. Your landlord may use some of your security deposit during your tenancy—for example, because you broke something and didn't fix it or pay for it. In this case, the landlord will probably require you to replenish the security deposit.

> **EXAMPLE:** Millie pays her landlord Maury a $1,000 security deposit when she moves in. Six months later, Millie goes on vacation, leaving the water running. By the time Maury is notified, the overflow has damaged the paint on the ceiling below. Maury repairs the ceiling at a cost of $250, taking the money out of Millie's security deposit. Maury is entitled to ask Millie to replace that money so that her deposit remains $1,000.

RELATED TOPIC

Chapter 16 provides details on rules landlords must follow when returning deposits. It covers what kinds of deductions landlords can legally make, and how to resolve disputes, including how to sue your landlord in small claims court.

When Your Landlord Sells the Property

In most states, the law requires landlords who sell rental property to do one of two things: return the deposit to the tenant or transfer it to the new owner.

It's been known to happen, however, that a landlord does neither and simply walks off with the money. The tenant might not even be notified that the building has been sold until after the fact. Fortunately, the new owner—even one who never gets the deposit money—cannot require the tenant to replace any security deposit kept by the old landlord. And even better, in most states, whoever happens to be the landlord at the time a tenancy ends is legally responsible for complying with state laws requiring return of security deposits.

If Your Landlord Goes Bankrupt

If your landlord files for bankruptcy, your security deposit is beyond the reach of creditors. That's because, technically speaking, it's not your landlord's money—it's yours, and must be returned to you, unless you fail to pay the rent or damage the property. Chapter 15 explains what happens to your lease or rental agreement if the landlord goes bankrupt.

Discrimination

Not so long ago, a landlord could refuse to rent to you, or could evict you, for almost any reason—because of your skin color or religion, or because you had children or were elderly or disabled. Some landlords discriminated against single women, believing that they would be incapable of paying the rent or would have too many overnight guests.

Recognizing that all Americans who could afford to pay the rent should have the right to live where they chose, Congress and state legislatures passed laws prohibiting housing discrimination. Most notable of these are the federal Fair Housing Act of 1968 and the federal Fair Housing Amendments Act of 1988, which outlaw discrimination based on race or color, national origin, religion, sex, familial status, or disability. (Throughout this chapter, we refer to this federal legislation as the federal Fair Housing Acts or the federal Acts.)

The federal Acts aren't the only laws against housing discrimination: Many states and cities have laws making it illegal to discriminate based on additional factors, such as marital status or source of income. Today, it is safe to say that unless a landlord has a legitimate business reason to reject a prospective tenant (for example, a poor credit history or an application from a more solvent candidate), the landlord risks a potentially costly legal challenge.

It is unusual to encounter a landlord who blatantly discriminates—for example, by stating a preference for all-white tenants or those with-out children. But it is still far too common to encounter more subtle—yet equally illegal—discrimination. For example, some landlords use overly restrictive occupancy standards to hide discrimination against families with children, or design advertisements that send powerful messages that applicants of a certain race are preferred. Or they might simply come up with superficially plausible—but bogus—reasons not to rent to people of a certain race or religion.

In most situations with tenants, landlords have the upper hand. When it comes to discrimination,

however, the balance of power shifts to tenants. By using these strong antidiscrimination laws, a determined tenant or applicant for rental housing who has been wronged can often tie a landlord in legal knots. As discussed below, tenants can complain to the U.S. Department of Housing and Urban Development (HUD), the federal agency that enforces the Fair Housing Acts, or to a state or local fair housing agency. Tenants can also file a lawsuit in federal or state court.

One of the reasons tenants have more of an advantage in the housing discrimination area is that it's not always necessary to show that the landlord or manager intended to discriminate. As long as the tenant can show that the landlord's conduct has a discriminatory effect or impact on members of a legally protected group, the tenant has a strong case. And knowing that cases involving egregious landlord behavior can result in large jury verdicts, insurance companies are often quick to offer settlements outside of court.

If you think that you have been a victim of housing discrimination and you want to do something about it, you face an important choice. You can take your story to the federal or state agency in charge of enforcing fair housing laws, and hope that an agency investigator will pursue your case (you usually won't need your own lawyer). Or, you can talk to an attorney about suing in state or federal court. If your case is successful, you might win an order (or leverage a settlement from the landlord's insurance company) forcing the landlord to rent to you or cease the discriminatory practice. A court might also order the landlord to pay you for your actual losses (having to rent another unit at a higher price, for example) or compensation for the humiliation you have endured.

 RELATED TOPIC
Also covered in this book:
- Legitimate reasons for turning down prospective tenants: Chapter 1.
- Discriminatory rent increases: Chapter 3.
- Discriminatory evictions: Chapter 18.

Federal Law vs. State Law

Federal, state, and local laws all forbid various kinds of discrimination against tenants. The most common kinds of discrimination—race and disability, for example—are prohibited by federal law, which must be followed by landlords in every state. (The key federal laws are the Fair Housing Acts, 42 U.S.C. §§ 3601–3619, 3631.)

Most state laws also make these forms of discrimination illegal, and some states even prohibit additional forms of discrimination. For example, some outlaw housing discrimination based on source of income, which is not illegal under federal law.

If you think you have been illegally discriminated against, it becomes important to know which law covers your situation, because you need to know:

- **Where to make a complaint.** If federal law has been violated, you can complain to a federal agency or sue in federal court; if only state law covers your situation, you are limited to state agencies and courts. If your situation is addressed by both federal and state law, you have a choice between going to a federal agency or court or a state agency or court.
- **Whether your rental is exempt from the law.** Federal antidiscrimination laws (and many state laws) do not apply to every rental. As discussed below, some properties are exempt. Even if both federal and state law prohibit the type of discrimination you experienced, you'll need to know whether an exemption would force you to use one law or the other.

Once you know which law or laws cover your situation, you can begin to evaluate your best avenue for pursuing your case.

Kinds of Discrimination Prohibited by Federal Law

Because federal law applies nationwide, it makes sense to see if your situation is covered by it before delving into state law.

The federal Acts prohibit discrimination on the following grounds (called "protected categories"):

- race
- color
- religion
- national origin
- familial status or age—includes families with children under the age of 18 and pregnant women and elderly persons
- disability or handicap (physical or mental), including recovering alcoholics and past drug addiction, and
- sex, including gender identity and sexual orientation.

The federal Acts apply to all aspects of the landlord-tenant relationship. A landlord may not:

- advertise or make any statement that indicates a limitation or preference based on any protected category
- falsely tell a member of a protected class that no rentals are available
- apply more restrictive screening criteria to applicants in protected categories
- refuse to rent to people in protected groups
- set different terms, conditions, or privileges for rental of a dwelling unit for members of a protected class at any point before or during the tenancy (for example, landlords can't adopt different policies for responding to late payments depending on the tenant's inclusion in a protected class)
- during the tenancy, provide different or diminished housing services or facilities to tenants based on their status as a member (or not a member) of a protected class, or
- terminate a tenancy for a discriminatory reason.

Unfortunately, not every rental is covered by the federal Acts. The following types of property are exempt:

- owner-occupied buildings with four or fewer rental units
- single-family housing rented without the use of discriminatory advertising or without

a real estate broker, as long as the owner doesn't own more than three such houses at any one time

- certain types of housing operated by religious organizations and private clubs that limit occupancy to their own members, and

- with respect to age discrimination only, housing reserved exclusively for senior citizens. There are two kinds of senior citizen housing exempted: communities where every tenant is 62 years of age or older, or communities with individual units that have at least one person 55 years of age or older. To qualify as "55 and older housing," at least 80% of the occupied units in the housing facility must be occupied by at least one person 55 years or older.

TIP

State and local laws might offer additional antidiscrimination protections. If the property you rent is exempt under federal law, similar state or local anti–housing-discrimination laws might nevertheless protect you. For example, owner-occupied buildings with four or fewer rental units are exempt under federal law but not under California law.

More Information From HUD and State Agencies

For more information about the Fair Housing Acts, and technical assistance on accessibility requirements, contact one of HUD's many local offices. You'll find a list of state and local offices on the HUD website at HUD.gov. Look under "Resources" and click on "State Information." You can also call the agency's Housing Discrimination Hotline at 800-669-9777 (or 800-927-9275 TTY).

Your state consumer protection agency can provide more general information and referrals to state law. Many also publish free brochures on landlord-tenant law. For a list of state consumer protection agencies, go to www.usa.gov/state-consumer.

Race or Color

Discrimination based on race or color isn't always obvious, and unintended discriminatory messages are just as illegal as overt ones.

EXAMPLE: The metropolitan area where you live contains large numbers of both Spanish-speaking and Cantonese-speaking people. Several apartment complexes advertise in Spanish only and offer nothing but Spanish-language leases. As an Asian-American who speaks Cantonese (or an Anglo who speaks only English), you naturally conclude that these complexes welcome Hispanics but not you. It is always legal to advertise in English only.

Antidiscrimination laws apply both in the tenant selection process as well as after tenants move in. For example, tenant rules, signs, newsletters, and other communication cannot legally convey any attempt to benefit, support, or discriminate against a racial group or people of a certain color.

EXAMPLE: In an effort to accommodate Spanish-speaking tenants, management translates the move-in letter and house rules into Spanish. Regarding the use of alcohol in the common areas, the Spanish version—but not the English one —begins, "Unlike Mexico, where drinking is practiced in public places, alcoholic beverages may not be consumed in common areas…." Because this phrase isn't included in the English version, it implies an ethnic generalization.

It's important to note that, although discrimination based on color and discrimination based on race often occur together, a tenant could experience discrimination based on race but not color—and vice versa.

Color discrimination is discrimination based solely on the visible color of a person's skin.

EXAMPLE: A landlord who rents to light-skinned African Americans, but refuses to rent to dark-skinned African Americans, is illegally discriminating on the basis of color. This is likely not an example of discrimination on the basis of race, because the landlord will rent to certain members of the African American race.

Race discrimination includes discrimination based on physical characteristics commonly associated with a race (such as facial features, skin color, and hair texture) as well as cultural traditions, practices, and characteristics.

EXAMPLE: An applicant with a last name commonly associated with people of Jewish heritage applies for an apartment. The property manager is part of an anti-Semitic group, and rejects the applicant solely on the basis of the person's last name.

A perpetrator of race- or color-based housing discrimination does not have to be of a different race or color from the victim—the law does not take into account the attributes of someone accused of housing discrimination.

Religion

When a person's beliefs are out of the mainstream or unpopular with other groups, it might seem somewhat reasonable not to rent to that person. For example, a Jewish landlord might be offended by someone's anti-Semitic convictions, but nevertheless could not legally refuse to rent to that person for that reason.

EXAMPLE: Several tenants in Creekside Apartments reserved the common room for a meeting. Creekside management learned that the tenants were members of a white supremacist group claiming to be a religion.

The group encourages its members to suppress nonwhites and non-Christians by whatever means it deems necessary—including violence.

Creekside management was appalled at the thought of these ideas being discussed on its premises, and denied the group the use of the common room. The tenants who were members of this group filed a discrimination complaint with HUD on the basis of freedom of religion. HUD rejected the group's complaint, finding that the management's refusal to let the group use the common room was not illegal discrimination based on religion, because the group was a hate group, not a bona-fide religion.

Subtle messages that might not be intended to discriminate, but demonstrate a preference for people who adhere to a certain faith mindset can also run afoul of antidiscrimination laws. For example, an apartment ad that says "safe Christian community" or "Sunday quiet times enforced" violates federal law, because applicants might reasonably conclude that Christians are preferred as tenants.

National Origin

Discrimination based on national origin is illegal, whether it's practiced deliberately or unintentionally. For example, a landlord who required all residents to be U.S. citizens, or who advertised "Special discounts for members of the Irish-American Club," would likely face a charge of discrimination based on national origin.

Even if your landlord is motivated by what seems like a valid business concern, but rejects tenants in a way that singles out people of a particular nationality, it's still illegal. For example, people in the U.S. without permission can be picked up and held in custody pending deportation at any time. If that were to happen, these tenants might stop paying rent. Does this mean that landlords are entitled to ask every "foreign looking" applicant (but not others) for immigration papers or proof of citizenship? The answer is no, and the reason, of course, is because of the impact this practice is almost sure to have on applicants who look the same but are citizens or in the United States legally. If you're one of them, you're likely to reach the conclusion that you are not welcome because management assumes that everyone like you is living in the United States illegally. A fair housing agency or court would surely agree that this sort of selective "let me see your papers" policy is illegal discrimination.

On the other hand, a landlord who requires *all* prospective tenants to supply satisfactory proof of identity and eligibility to work is on solid ground. Why? Because every applicant, and not just members of one group, is subjected to an inquiry that is reasonably related to the landlord's right to choose tenants who are likely to pay rent over the tenancy term. Note that in California, Colorado, and New York City, though, it's illegal to ask *any* applicant or tenant about their immigration or citizenship status.

TIP

For information on how your landlord may legally verify your citizenship or immigration status, contact the U.S. Citizenship and Immigration Services or USCIS, a bureau of the U.S. Department of Homeland Security, at 800-375-5283, or check their website at USCIS.gov.

Familial Status or Age

A landlord may not legally turn away an applicant because the applicant has children or is pregnant. Similarly, a landlord cannot evict a tenant for having children or being pregnant. In addition, a landlord cannot exclude families by unreasonably limiting the maximum number of people permitted to occupy a rental unit, thereby indirectly preventing families with children from occupying smaller units. Finally, a landlord may not make tenancy decisions based on an applicant's age.

Discrimination Against Families

Discrimination based on family make up can take unexpected forms. Even good intentions do not excuse a landlord's policy or rule that discriminates against families with children or younger people. Consider these examples of familial status discrimination:

- You and your 15-year-old daughter have applied to rent an apartment in an area of town that has experienced several muggings and rapes. Afraid that your daughter, when she returns from school alone each day, will be an easy mark, the manager refuses to accept your application.
- You, your spouse, and your teenage son and daughter have applied for a two-bedroom apartment. The occupancy policy is two-per-bedroom, but the landlord decides that it is inappropriate for teenagers of different sexes to share a room.

The ban against familial status discrimination protects adults without children and singles, too. A landlord may not establish policies that adversely affect childless tenants. This means it is illegal to rent *only* to families, or even to segregate (or restrict) some tenants to certain floors or parts of a building. For example, a policy that requires tenants with children to rent ground floor units indirectly funnels childless tenants to the upper stories. A childless tenant who wanted a ground floor unit would have a valid claim of familial discrimination. Similarly, hosting "families only" social events in the common area excludes childless renters, who could raise a claim of discrimination.

Occupancy Limits: How Many People Can Live in the Rental Unit?

Landlords might try to avoid renting to families with children by setting occupancy policies that appear neutral but have the effect of discriminating. For example, a policy of no more than two people for a two-bedroom apartment would exclude a family with one or two children or a single parent with three children. To counter this subtle discrimination, laws limit landlords' occupancy policies.

Illegal discrimination against families also occurs when an occupancy policy differentiates between adults and children. For example, consider the results of a landlord's policy allowing only one person per bedroom, with a couple counting as one person. Under this rule, the landlord would rent a two-bedroom unit to a husband and wife and their one child, but would not rent the same unit to a mother with two children. The mother and her two children would have a valid discrimination claim.

Familial status discrimination also appears when a landlord applies an occupancy policy in an inconsistent manner. If the way your landlord carries out the occupancy policy has the effect of distinguishing between adults and children, you might be able to challenge those actions as a hidden form of familial discrimination. It doesn't matter if the landlord believes the policy (and its application) is sensible and nondiscriminatory.

EXAMPLE: Jackson owned and managed two identical one-bedroom units, one of which he rented out to three flight attendants who were rarely there at the same time. When the other unit became vacant, Jackson advertised it as a one-bedroom, two-person apartment. Harry and Sue Jones and their teenage daughter were turned away because they exceeded Jackson's occupancy limit of two people. The Jones family learned that the companion unit was rented to three people, and decided to file a complaint with HUD, whose investigator helped negotiate a settlement. Jackson saw that he was legally in the wrong. He agreed to rent to the Jones family and to compensate them for the humiliation they had suffered as a result of being refused.

So what is a reasonable occupancy limit? State and local health and safety codes typically base occupancy limits on the size of the unit and the number of bedrooms and bathrooms.

But the law also addresses the other end of the how-many-occupants issue by setting policies that require a landlord to rent to *at least* a certain number of tenants per unit. The Department of Housing and Urban Development generally considers a limit of two persons per bedroom a reasonable occupancy standard. Because the number of bedrooms is not the only factor—the size of the bedrooms, age of the children, and configuration of the rental unit are also considered—the federal test has become known as the "two per bedroom plus" standard, and helps prevent discrimination against families with children.

States and localities can set their own occupancy standards, and many have. This is where things get tricky: Ordinarily, when the federal government legislates on a particular subject, states and localities are free to pass laws on the subject too, as long as they're equally (or more) protective of the targeted group (in this case, tenants). But the federal government's guidance (a mere memo to regional HUD directors) emphatically stated that Congress didn't intend to develop "a national occupancy code." ("Fair Housing Enforcement—Occupancy Standards Notice of Statement of Policy," Code of Federal Regulations (C.F.R.) Vol. 63, No. 243, Dec. 18, 1998.) The memo practically invited states and localities to set their own occupancy standards, and didn't make it clear whether those standards had to be at least as generous (to tenants) as the federal guidance. As a result, some states developed occupancy standards that were less generous than the federal guidance, while others, such as California, developed standards that were more generous.

If you are renting in a state that has its own occupancy standards (and your city might have its own, too), you'll want to check to see what they are. Landlords are on shaky ground if they follow any standard other than the most generous. To learn about state or local occupancy standards, check with your state's consumer protection agency. You'll find a state-by-state list at www.usa.gov/state-consumer.

Keep in mind that landlords can, however, set an occupancy standard that is lower than the applicable federal, state or local figure if legitimate business reasons will justify it. This is hard to do—while the inability of the infrastructure to support more tenants (perhaps the septic system or plumbing has a limited capacity) might validate a lower occupancy policy, a landlord's desire to ensure a quiet, uncrowded environment for upscale older tenants will not. If your landlord's occupancy policy limits the number of tenants for any reason other than health, safety, and legitimate business needs, it might be illegally discriminating against families.

> CAUTION
>
> **Exceeding the maximum allowable number of tenants is not always a bargain.** Some tenants are delighted to find a landlord who will allow them to live with more than the maximum number of residents allowable under the local health and safety laws. Your rent share will be lower and, in tight rental markets, it might mean the difference between living in a good area and a really bad one, or not even having a home at all. But unless you are desperate, beware! The fact that a landlord is willing to skirt occupancy laws likely reflects how seriously the landlord takes other legal responsibilities (like repairs and maintenance). And by agreeing to live in an overcrowded rental, you hamper your ability to assert your rights—you will naturally hesitate to do anything (like complain to a housing authority about substandard conditions or utilize a repair and deduct remedy) that will bring the illegal rental to the attention of courts or building inspectors.

Age Discrimination

The federal Fair Housing Acts do not expressly ban discrimination based on age. Nevertheless, it is definitely forbidden under the broader concept of prohibiting discrimination on the basis of familial status.

A landlord cannot refuse to rent to an older person or impose special terms and conditions on the tenancy unless these same standards are applied to everyone else. If you have excellent references and credit history, a landlord has no legal basis for refusing you, even if you are 85 and rely to some degree on the regular assistance of a nearby adult child or friend. (Of course, the landlord could legally give the rental to someone else with equal or better references or financial stability.) However, if your current landlord reveals that you suffer from advanced senility to the point that you often wander into the wrong apartment, frequently forget to pay the rent, or are unable to undertake basic housekeeping chores, the prospective landlord can refuse to rent to you based on this age-neutral evidence that you are not likely to be a stable, reliable tenant.

> **EXAMPLE:** Ethel, who is 80 years old, wants to find a smaller place closer to her daughter, Nora. She sells her home and applies for a one-bedroom apartment at Coral Shores. Ethel presents impeccable references from neighbors and employers and an outstanding credit history. Nonetheless, Lucy, the manager of Coral Shores, is fearful that Ethel, at her age, might forget to turn off the stove, fall on the front steps, or do any number of other dangerous things, and decides not to rent to her. Ethel files a fair housing complaint with HUD, which she quickly wins on the basis of Coral Shores' policy of age discrimination.

The issue of age discrimination might also arise during a well-established tenancy. Suppose you have lived alone for years and now, with advanced age, must face the question of whether you are still able to live safely by yourself. Your landlord is honestly concerned that your physical incapacity or mental inattention might result in damage to the premises and injury to you or other tenants. Can your landlord, on the basis of these fears alone, decide not to renew your lease? Absolutely not—there must be real, serious, and probably repeated violations of the criteria that apply to all tenants before nonrenewal of a lease, or eviction, would be legal.

> **TIP**
> **Elderly tenants might also qualify as tenants with a disability, who are entitled to accommodation under the law.** An elderly tenant who cannot meet one of the landlord's policies might be entitled to special treatment as a person with a disability. (See the discussion of discrimination on the basis of disability, below.) For example, an elderly tenant who is chronically late with the rent because of sporadic disorientation might justifiably ask for a grace period, or a friendly reminder when the rent is due; a tenant without a disability who is chronically late with the rent would not be entitled to such special treatment. And if an elderly tenant can't negotiate the stairs, the legal solution is a ramp or a move to a single-level rental, not an eviction notice.

Additional Eviction Protections for Elderly Tenants

Some states and localities, including Connecticut and New York City, protect elderly tenants in the event that their building is sold or converted to condominiums, or if the owner of their rent-controlled unit attempts to evict them in order to move in themselves (or a member of their family). For information on eviction protections for elderly tenants, check your state's fair housing agency.

The prohibition against age discrimination also applies to "emancipated" minors who have the same status as an adult and must be treated like any other adult applicant or tenant. (An emancipated minor is a 17-year-old—or possibly even a 16-year-old in some states—who is legally married, has a court order of emancipation, or is in the military.) On the other hand, a landlord can reject an under-age applicant who is not emancipated, because these minors lack the legal capacity to enter into a binding rental agreement.

Disability

Federal law prohibits discrimination against people who:

- have a physical or mental disability that substantially limits one or more major life activities—including, but not limited to, hearing, mobility, and visual impairments; chronic alcoholism (but only if it is being addressed through a recovery program); mental illness; HIV-positive status, AIDS, and AIDS-Related Complex; and intellectual disability
- have a history or record of such a disability, or
- are regarded by others as though they have such a disability.

Mental or Emotional Impairments

If you had, have, or appear to have mental or emotional impairments, you must be evaluated and treated by the landlord on the basis of your financial stability and history as a tenant, not on the basis of your mental health.

A landlord may consider your mental health as a reason to reject you only if there are specific instances of past behavior that indicate you might be dangerous to others (such as information from a previous landlord that you repeatedly threatened or assaulted other residents). And, if you cannot meet the good-tenant criteria that the landlord applies to all applicants (such as a good credit report), you may be rejected on *that* basis.

Discriminatory Questions and Actions

Landlords are not allowed to ask you whether you have a disability or illness, or ask to see medical records. Even if it is obvious that you have a disability—for example, you use a wheelchair or wear a hearing aid—it is nevertheless illegal to inquire about the severity of your disability. In short, your landlord's actions and questions cannot be designed to treat you differently than other tenants. The policy behind this rule is simple: No matter how well-intentioned, landlords cannot make decisions about where and how tenants will live that they would not make for tenants who don't have a disability. For example, if there are two units for rent—one on the ground floor and one three stories up—the landlord must show both units to a wheelchair-using applicant, however reasonable the landlord thinks it would be for the person to consider only the ground floor unit.

The Rights of Tenants With Disabilities to Live in an Accessible Place

Federal law protects disabled tenants *after* they have moved into a rental unit as well as during the application process. Landlords must:

- accommodate the needs of tenants with disabilities, at the landlord's own expense (42 U.S.C. § 3604(f)(3)(B)), and
- allow tenants with disabilities to make reasonable modifications to their living unit at their expense, if needed for the person to comfortably and safely live in the unit. (42 U.S.C. § 3604(f)(3)(A)).

Let's look briefly at each of these requirements. (You can find more information at HUD.gov (search for "accessibility requirements").)

Accommodations

As a tenant with a disability, you are entitled to expect your landlord to reasonably adjust rules, procedures, or services in order to give you an equal opportunity to use and enjoy your dwelling unit or a common space. Common accommodations address topics such as:

- **Parking.** If the landlord provides parking in the first place, providing a close-in, spacious parking space for a tenant who uses a wheelchair.
- **Service animals.** Allowing a dog or other animal that is individually trained to do work or perform tasks for the benefit of someone with a disability.
- **Payment of rent.** Allowing a special rent payment plan for a tenant whose finances are managed by someone else or by a government agency.
- **Vision problems.** Arranging to read all communications from management to a tenant with vision impairment.
- **Phobias.** For example, providing a washtub and clothesline for a tenant whose anxiety about machines makes her unable to use the facility's washer and dryer.

Does your landlord's duty to accommodate tenants with disabilities mean that you can expect every rule and procedure to be changed at your request? No. Although landlords are expected to accommodate "reasonable" requests, they need not undertake changes that would seriously impair their ability to run their business. For example, if an applicant in a wheelchair prefers the third-story apartment in a walk-up building constructed in 1926 to the one on the ground floor, the landlord does not have to rip the building apart to install an elevator. HUD would consider the expense to be unreasonable.

Modifications

Fortunately, even when the needs of a tenant with disabilities goes beyond what the landlord is expected to reasonably accommodate, the landlord might still have the obligation to allow the tenant to modify the living space. A tenant with a disability has the right to modify the living space to the extent necessary to make the space safe and comfortable, as long as the modifications will not make the unit unacceptable to the next tenant. If a modification would be unacceptable to the next tenant, the current tenant and landlord can agree that the tenant will undo the modification at the end of the tenancy. Examples of modifications undertaken by a tenant with a disability include:

- lowering countertops for a tenant who uses a wheelchair
- installing special faucets or door handles for persons with limited hand use
- modifying kitchen appliances to accommodate a tenant with vision impairment, and
- installing a ramp to allow a tenant who uses a wheelchair to negotiate two steps up to a raised living room.

These modifications must be reasonable and made with prior approval. A landlord is entitled to ask for a description of the proposed modifications, proof that they will be done in an adequate manner, and evidence that any necessary building permits have been secured. In addition, if the proposed modification will require restoration when the tenant leaves (such as the repositioning of lowered kitchen counters), the landlord may require the tenant to pay into an interest-bearing escrow account the amount estimated for the restoration. (The interest belongs to the tenant.)

Unless the property is in Massachusetts or is federally financed, tenants pay for the modification. But if the building opened for occupancy on or after March 13, 1991, and the modification is needed because the building doesn't comply with HUD's accessibility requirements, the landlord must pay.

Service Animals and Comfort or Emotional Support Animals

A lot of uncertainty surrounds the public's understanding of the meaning of a "service animal" and a "comfort" or "emotional support" animal. The confusion is understandable, because different rules apply to housing and public places such as shops, restaurants, and theaters—and public transit (particularly airplanes). In the housing context, a service animal is not limited to a dog, as it is in other public contexts. A tenant with a disability who has a trained animal other than a dog (such as a monkey), that performs work or tasks to help that person live safely and comfortably at home, can ask the landlord to accommodate the animal. But in a public place like a shop, the shopkeeper need not allow the monkey into the shop with his or her owner.

A comfort animal (one that supplies emotional support, well-being, comfort, or companionship, but does no work or tasks) is not part of the definition of a service animal when that animal is in a public place, such as a restaurant. For example, a dog whose presence calms its owner but who is not trained to do work would not qualify as a service animal, and a restaurant or shop would not be expected to accommodate its presence. But for purposes of rental housing, it seems that landlords are required to accommodate the presence of such a comfort animal if they can reasonably do so.

The practical result of two sets of rules is apparent: What is the tenant with a disability who has a trained pig expected to do when shopping or eating at a restaurant?

Keep in mind that before any of these questions can be raised, let alone answered, a tenant must be able to establish a legal disability. No landlord must accommodate any service or comfort animal unless the accommodation is requested by someone with a disability, as that term is defined by law.

Sample Letter
Attesting to the Appropriateness of an Accommodation or Modification

Marcus Welby, M.D.
400 Professional Way, Suite 100
Anytown, Colorado 00000
(719) 555-9999

September 19, 20xx

Hilda Hanson, Manager
Royal Crest Apartments
Anytown, Colorado 00000

Dear Ms. Hanson:

John Anderson, who resides at Royal Crest Apartments, is a patient under my care. He has informed me that he will soon be asking you to modify certain aspects of his apartment. He will also ask you to make some accommodations regarding management policies at Royal Crest.

Modifications

1. Disconnect the electric doorbell and install a hand-knocker on the front door.
2. Allow Mr. Anderson to install curtain rods in the bedroom that will support heavy, light-blocking drapes.
3. Allow Mr. Anderson to put wall-to-wall carpet in the bedroom, which is currently bare hardwood.

Accommodations

1. Communicate any management requests in writing, left in Mr. Anderson's mailbox, rather than by phone.
2. Open the laundry room at 7 a.m., one hour earlier than the current schedule.
3. When management at Royal Crest calls a tenants' meeting to discuss and vote on issues of concern to tenants and management, allow Mr. Anderson to send a proxy who may speak and vote in his place.

In my professional opinion, these requests are necessary and appropriate to enable Mr. Anderson to live at Royal Crest in a safe and enjoyable manner.

Yours truly,

Marcus Welby, M.D.

Marcus Welby, M.D.

cc: Mr. John Anderson

Verification of Disabled Status

Landlords are also entitled to ask for proof that the accommodation or modification you have requested will address your needs. For years, landlords asked for a doctor's letter. Now, according to a HUD and Department of Justice guidance memo, they must be willing to listen to less formal sources. (*Reasonable Accommodations Under the Fair Housing Act*, Joint Statement of the Department of Housing and Urban Development and the Department of Justice, May 17, 2004.) Sources of reliable information include:

- **The individual.** Individuals can prove that they meet the requirements for having a disability (and that a modification or accommodation addresses that disability) by giving the landlord a "credible statement." Unfortunately, the guidance does not define this term.

- **Documents.** A person who is under 65 years of age and receives Supplemental Security Income or Social Security Disability Insurance Benefits is legally disabled. Someone could establish disability by showing a landlord relevant identification cards. Likewise, license plates showing the universal accessibility logo, or a driver's license reflecting the existence of a disability, are sufficient proof.

- **Doctors or other medical professionals, peer support groups, nonmedical service agencies.** Information from these sources might come through letters, phone calls, or personal visits.

- **Reliable third parties.** This wide-open source of information could include friends, associates, and roommates.

If you choose to ask a doctor or therapist to write a letter, ask for a letter attesting that what you are asking for will meet your needs. To protect your privacy, carefully explain that the physician or other writer does not need to explain the disability; rather, the writer needs only to certify that the changes you would like are appropriate to your situation. A sample letter, in which the physician describes the tenant's requests but not the disability, is presented above.

In 2020, HUD issued a guidance memo for housing providers that specifically addressed how to assess a request to have an animal as a reasonable accommodation (*Assessing a Person's Request to Have an Animal as a Reasonable Accommodation Under the Fair Housing Act*, FHEO Notice 2020-01, January 28, 2020).

In particular, the memo sets more restrictive standards than had been in place for what might serve as sources of reliable information for supporting a request to accommodate an animal. For example, the person making the request cannot serve as a source, and a third party who is confirming the disability must be a health care professional such as a physician or a nurse.

HUD's memo also dismisses so-called "certificates" of disability and animal training that anyone can obtain on the internet, simply by answering some questions and paying a fee. By themselves, these phony licenses, certificates, and registrations establish nothing.

To read the full memo, search online for "HUD memo January 28, 2020."

Limited Protection for People in Recovery From Alcohol or Drug Addiction

Federal fair housing law extends limited protection to two carefully defined groups:

- **People who are recovering from alcohol addiction.** Alcoholics who are in recovery may not be denied housing on the basis of their status. Unfortunately, there is no clear definition of what "recovery" means, nor when it begins; but someone who actively and regularly participates in a medically based treatment or AA program probably qualifies.
- **People who were formerly addicted to drugs.** People who were previously addicted to illegal drugs cannot be denied housing on that basis alone. It is also illegal for a landlord to discriminate based on a conviction for illegal drug use. This protection does not extend to

current addiction, nor does it protect someone who has a conviction for drug dealing or manufacture.

It's important to note that other aspects of someone's past might legally serve as the basis for a denial of housing. For example, if the person recovering from alcohol abuse also has bad credit, a spotty employment history, or negative references from previous landlords, a landlord may reject the applicant for these reasons just as readily as any other applicant with these flaws. What a landlord *can't* do is reject the applicant because they used to abuse alcohol or were formerly addicted to drugs.

New Buildings and Accessibility

The Fair Housing Amendments Act (42 U.S.C. §§ 3604 (f)(3)(C) and 3604(f)(7)) imposes requirements on new buildings of four or more units that were first occupied after March 1991. All ground-floor units and every unit in an elevator building must be designed or constructed so that:

- the main building is accessible and on an accessible route
- the public and common areas are "readily accessible to and usable by" the people with disabilities, including parking areas (a good rule of thumb is to reserve 2% of the spaces)
- any stair landing shared by more than one rental unit is handicapped-accessible. (*U.S. v. Edward Rose & Sons,* 384 F.3d 258 (6th Cir. 2004).)
- entryway doorways have 36" of free space *plus* shoulder and elbow room; and interior doorways are at least 32" wide
- interior living spaces have wheelchair-accessible routes throughout, with changes in floor height of no more than ¼"
- light switches, outlets, thermostats, and other environmental controls are within the legal "reach range" (15" to 48" from the ground)
- bathroom walls are sufficiently reinforced to allow the safe installation of "grab bars," and
- kitchens and bathrooms are large enough to allow a wheelchair to maneuver within the room (40" turning radius minimum) and have sinks and appliances positioned to allow side or front use.

EXAMPLE: Patsy applied for an apartment one morning and spoke with Carol, the manager. Patsy said she would have to return that afternoon to complete the application form because she was due at an Alcoholics Anonymous meeting. Carol decided on the spot that she did not want Patsy for a tenant, and she told Patsy that the unit "had just been rented," which was a lie. (Patsy continued to see the newspaper ad for the unit.)

Patsy filed a complaint with HUD, alleging that she had been discriminated against because she was recovering from alcohol abuse. Because Carol could not point to any reason for turning Patsy away other than her assumption that Patsy, because of her former addiction, would be a bad tenant, the judge awarded Patsy several thousand dollars in damages.

Sex and Sexual Harassment

You cannot be denied a place to live (or have special rules imposed on you) solely because you're female or male. Even well-intentioned policies are off-limits—for example, fearful that single women are more likely to be burglarized and assaulted than male tenants, a landlord cannot require single females to live in upper-story apartments, even if, in fact, those units are less prone to break-ins.

A landlord's policy that favors one sex over another might justify a claim of discrimination by either sex. In the example above, the landlord is discriminating against female applicants who want ground-floor apartments, and against male applicants who want an upper-story apartment that is reserved for single women.

Sexual harassment is another form of sexual discrimination. For example, it's illegal for a landlord to reject an applicant because the applicant rejected the landlord's sexual advances or to make life difficult for a tenant who has resisted such advances. In the rental housing context, courts have defined sexual harassment as:

- a pattern of persistent, unwanted attention of a sexual nature, including the making of sexual remarks and physical advances, or a single instance of highly egregious behavior. A manager's persistent requests for social contact, or constant remarks concerning a tenant's appearance or behavior, could constitute sexual harassment, as could a single extraordinarily offensive remark.
- a situation in which a tenant's rights are conditioned upon the acceptance of the owner's or manager's attentions. For example, a manager who refuses to fix the plumbing until the tenant agrees to a date is guilty of sexual harassment. One incident alone can be sufficient to establish this type of harassment.

EXAMPLE: Oscar, the resident manager of Northside Apartments, repeatedly asked Martha, a Northside tenant, for dates. Martha always turned Oscar down and, after his fourth proposition, asked that he leave her alone. Oscar didn't back off, and began hanging around the pool whenever Martha used it, watching her intently and making suggestive remarks about her to the other tenants.

Martha stopped using the pool and filed a sexual harassment complaint with HUD, claiming that Oscar's unwanted attentions made it impossible for her to use and enjoy the pool and even to comfortably live at Northside. Oscar refused to consider a settlement when the HUD investigator spoke to him and Martha about his actions. As a result, HUD pursued the case in court, where a federal judge ordered Oscar to leave Martha alone and awarded her several thousand dollars.

Deciding how to respond to an act of sexual harassment involves considerations that go beyond the usual housing discrimination case, because sexual harassment involves proving certain facts that aren't involved in other sex discrimination lawsuits. In "How to Fight Back," below, we suggest ways to evaluate the strength of your case and include suggestions as to how best to respond to sexual harassment.

Sexual Orientation and Gender Identity

Until relatively recently, housing discrimination based on sexual orientation and gender identity was prohibited by law in only less than half the states. But in February 2021, HUD made such discrimination a type of sex discrimination, which is prohibited by the federal Fair Housing Act. This policy announcement applies in every state to landlords covered by the federal Fair Housing Act, and to local and state governments that receive federal assistance.

Kinds of Discrimination Prohibited by State and Local Law

Most state and local laws prohibiting housing discrimination echo federal antidiscrimination law in that they outlaw discrimination based on race or color, national origin, religion, familial status, disability, and sex. But state and local laws often go into more detail and many also forbid some kinds of discrimination—such as discrimination based on marital status—that aren't covered by federal law. For example, in states that prohibit discrimination based on marital status, it would

be illegal to refuse to rent to divorced people, something that is illegal under federal law.

Here we explain some of the common antidiscrimination laws that states and localities have adopted. For more information on state and local housing discrimination laws, contact your state fair housing agency. See "More Information From HUD and State Agencies" earlier in this chapter for contact information.

Marital Status

About 20 states ban discrimination on the basis of marital status. Most of these states' laws extend protection to married couples only (meaning that landlords can't treat them differently from single tenants). What about the reverse—preferring married couples over single roommates or a single tenant? Does a single person's status as "not married" entitle that person to protection on the basis of "marital status"? A few states have ruled against the disappointed single tenant: Courts in Maryland, Minnesota, New York, and Wisconsin have ruled that the term "marital status" protects only *married* people from being treated differently from single people, not vice versa. In other words, you'll enjoy marital status protection only if you are married.

What about unmarried couples? In most states, landlords may legally refuse to rent to unmarried couples. This means that landlords in these states can ask if two applicants of the same or different sex are lovers or just friendly roommates. In Alaska, California, Massachusetts, Michigan, and New Jersey, though, courts have ruled that the term "marital status" extends to *unmarried* couples.

Zoning Ordinances and Living Together

Some communities have adopted zoning ordinances that prohibit groups of unrelated people from living together (the U.S. Supreme Court has upheld these laws). Most of these ordinances are aimed at barring groups, foster families, shelters, or boarding houses. Very few prohibit two unrelated adults from living together. If you are an unmarried couple, straight or gay, find out whether the neighborhood you're interested in has been zoned only for people related by "blood, marriage, or adoption." If such an ordinance does apply, a landlord could use it to justify refusing to rent to you, though the landlord would be on shaky ground if the law exempts two adults.

Arbitrary Discrimination Is Illegal in California

Federal and state laws clearly prohibit discrimination based on race, religion, sex, and so on. But what about tenant-selection criteria that don't fit into these categories? Can a landlord exclude bearded men and lawyers?

In California, at least, the answer is probably no. Courts have ruled that although California's Unruh Civil Rights Act (Cal. Civ. Code §§ 51–53, 54.1–54.8) contains only the phrases "sex, race, color, religion, ancestry, national origin, disability, medical condition, genetic information, marital status, sexual orientation, citizenship, primary language, or immigration status" to describe types of illegal discrimination, these categories are just examples. The courts have construed the Unruh Act to forbid discrimination on the basis of a "personal characteristic or trait"—also known as "arbitrary discrimination." Other common examples of arbitrary discrimination include obesity, occupation, or style of dress.

Source of Income

In several states, applicants who receive public assistance may not be turned away or otherwise discriminated against because of this fact. (Many cities also extend protection.) Some of these laws require that the assistance be paid directly to the landlord. (Note that some of these states do allow landlords to refuse Section 8 housing vouchers.) This doesn't mean, however, that being on public assistance entitles you to be considered for every rental. A landlord may refuse to rent to you if your available income (regardless of its source) falls below an established level, as long as that standard is applied to every applicant. (See "How Landlords Reject Tenants," in Chapter 1, for information on how landlords may legally use income as a selection criterion.)

For a complete listing of state and local laws on this subject, see the website of the Poverty & Race Research Action Council, at www.prrac.org (search for "Appendix B: State, Local, and Federal Laws Barring Source-of-Income Discrimination").

How to Fight Back

If you believe that a landlord has unlawfully discriminated against you, you don't just have to take it or move on. You can try to work things out with the landlord, or you can take advantage of the powerful antidiscrimination laws discussed earlier.

Your options (discussed in detail below) include:
- trying to negotiate an acceptable settlement with the landlord, possibly with the help of a neutral mediator
- filing a complaint with a federal, state, or local government fair housing agency, or
- filing a lawsuit in federal or state court.

Any of these strategies might force the landlord to do one or more of the following:
- Rent you a particular unit.

- Pay you "actual" or "compensatory" damages. This amount covers your trouble in finding another rental, plus any rent you had to pay to live elsewhere. In addition, you might be entitled to money for any humiliation or emotional distress—if the landlord's conduct was truly awful, this amount can be substantial.
- Pay you punitive damages—extra money as punishment for especially outrageous, intentional discrimination. It is not uncommon for juries to make large awards—$25,000 and up—if a landlord has persistently and obnoxiously violated fair housing laws.
- Pay your attorneys' fees (if you hired an attorney to file a lawsuit).
- Pay a penalty to the federal government. As of 2023, the maximum penalty under the federal Fair Housing Acts is $24,793 for a first violation. Landlords who violate the Acts a second time within five years could be fined $61,982, and landlords who have violated the Acts two or more times in the previous seven years could be fined up to $123,965. Many states have comparable penalties.

Picking the Strategy That Suits Your Goals

Before you can make an intelligent decision about what strategy to pursue, you need to sit down and ask yourself what you're trying to achieve.

If you simply want the offensive or unfair behavior to stop, and aren't interested in seeking compensation for humiliation, inconvenience, or added expense, you won't want to file a complaint or lawsuit right away. For example, if you're an established tenant, you might want a quick resolution of the issue, and be less interested in money damages. A frank discussion with the landlord, perhaps in the company of a mediator or other neutral third party, might work better than a full legal assault. Many a landlord will

listen up quite quickly if you explain, for example, how an occupancy policy discriminates against families. With luck (and the specter of a lawsuit), the landlord might make amends. And if informal techniques don't work, you can still sue or complain to a government agency.

If, on the other hand, you see the landlord's behavior as part of a bigger issue that ought to be settled for the sake of others to come, you might take a different approach: If you reach an informal resolution of your personal discrimination claim, you could be left with the disquieting thought that the next, unwitting applicant or tenant will experience the same treatment. Sexual harassment, in particular, is not likely to end as the result of one person's courageous confrontation.

Lawsuits and agency complaints, however, are adversarial and drawn-out procedures. As anyone who has been involved in a court case will tell you, it is no picnic—even if you win. If you have a strong case and can get a quick court order from a judge, your experience will be mercifully short. Or, if your facts are compelling and your lawyer good, you might be able to settle for a sizable amount of money without going to trial.

Not every case, however, proceeds so easily. If the landlord or the landlord's insurance company fights your claim, the case might drag on for months or even years. In the meantime, the lawsuit could seriously interfere with your personal or business schedule. For example, you will need to be available for depositions (long, drawn-out sessions with the other side's lawyers in which you are questioned under oath) and court dates that are set without regard for your other commitments. As the court or hearing day approaches, your stomach will be in knots and your mind consumed by the battle to come. Many litigants, including the successful ones, come out of the experience vowing never again to go near a lawyer or a courthouse if they can possibly avoid it.

Another important downside of filing a fair housing complaint or lawsuit is that it might hurt your chances of renting later. Future background checks done by prospective landlords will probably reveal the fact that you filed a discrimination complaint. In spite of the existence of some legal protections against direct landlord retaliation (see Chapter 15), the reality is that you have no idea how this information will be used. It would be an unusual landlord indeed who would consider a lawsuit against a former landlord as a mark in your favor, even if your suit was totally justified.

Before making a final decision as to which path to take, ask for the opinion of a trusted and reasonable friend. Discrimination can be a highly emotional subject, and it's always a good idea to seek the counsel of someone who is not involved.

Special Issues in Sexual Harassment Cases

Sexual harassment cases are handled the same way as are other fair housing claims. But because of their special psychological and legal aspects, these cases involve several additional considerations.

As with other kinds of housing discrimination cases, you can directly confront the harasser or seek help from HUD (or a state fair housing agency) or a lawyer. Generally, annoying but not outrageous behavior merits an informal response, but serious, unbearable harassment needs the resources of professionals and courts. Is the behavior threatening? Or does it amount to the social ineptitude of one person? It's usually helpful to share your experience with a wise friend and ask for a candid evaluation of your perceptions.

If you conclude that the behavior warrants a confrontation, demand that it stop. Do so in writing or, at least, follow up your conversation with a written demand. Surprisingly often—some experts say up to 90% of the time—this works, especially in cases where the behavior is fairly low level, such as comments about your appearance, tacky photos on the apartment manager's bulletin board, or off-color jokes. Repeat your demands if necessary.

If the offensive behavior continues in spite of your oral and written requests that it stop, you'll need to consider your next step. In general, you have three options:

Stay put and hope for the best. It's not a good idea to choose this option unless you simply cannot move or file a complaint. Many hardcore harassers escalate their behavior over time.

Break the lease and move out. The landlord has a legal responsibility to make sure you have the undisturbed, quiet enjoyment of your leased home. If a court decides that a landlord has not met this responsibility, the tenant is excused from the lease.

What this amounts to in the context of sexual harassment is that, if the landlord, manager, or employee is harassing you and interfering with your ability to enjoy your tenancy, you might be able to point to this as a justification for breaking the lease. But the harassment must be serious and persistent in order for this strategy to work, and if your landlord challenges your decision to move without giving proper notice, you must be prepared to produce convincing evidence—for example, copies of your written demands that the behavior stop and, if possible, testimony from other tenants who have experienced similar mistreatment.

File a fair housing claim or lawsuit. In general, consider this option only if you can show clearly that the advances were unwanted, rebuffed, repeated, and fairly serious; that you lost no time in confronting the harasser and, when repeated requests were unheeded, you promptly filed a complaint. Filing a sexual harassment complaint is almost sure to be a painful experience, especially if you alone have endured the mistreatment. The other side will probably base much of its defense on trying to discredit you.

To prove a claim of sexual harassment, you must usually show that the behavior was *unwanted*. This can be hard to do, since it's usually a matter of your word against the harasser's. To help your lawyer or HUD investigator establish your case, you should:

- **Collect evidence.** Keep any offensive cards, emails, notices, or photographs; photograph evidence (such as off-color jokes or cartoons posted on bulletin boards) that you cannot seize.

- **Keep a detailed journal.** Keep a detailed journal of every offensive incident. Include the names of everyone involved, dates, times, and locations. If your case goes to court, the contents of your journal might be admitted to substantiate your testimony; in any event, it will be an invaluable aid to the lawyer or investigator preparing your case.
- **Talk with other tenants.** If your story is echoed by other tenants, it's harder for the harasser to claim that you are lying or unreasonably interpreting his ardent but innocent interest. Talk to other tenants and find out whether others are in the same boat. (Chapter 19 discusses ways for tenants to act together effectively.)
- **Talk with friends.** Promptly sharing your experience with trusted friends serves two purposes: First, it helps you sort out your emotions and relieves the burden of keeping an upsetting secret. Second, it creates potentially valuable witnesses who can testify that you were angry or upset. It will also preclude a harasser's inevitable argument that, had you been truly offended, you would have turned to a friend for solace and advice.

Negotiating With the Landlord

If the landlord's insurance company or lawyer realizes you have complained (or are about to do so) to a fair housing agency or are poised to file a lawsuit, they might offer to settle. Be wary of dealing with these professional types without the presence of a neutral third party—a mediator, for example. Chapter 19 explains the mediation process in detail, and gives you information on locating and working with a mediator.

During negotiations, you might be offered a sum of money to settle a sexual harassment or race-based discrimination claim. If you think the offered amount is too low, you might be tempted to go shopping for a lawyer in hopes of getting more

money. Fine, but remember, once the lawyer's fee and pretrial expenses are figured in, you'll have to get quite a bit more in order to come out ahead.

EXAMPLE: Your landlord offers you $5,000 to settle your discrimination claim. Thinking that you can get more, you hire a lawyer, agreeing to an attorney's fee of one-third of your settlement or jury verdict plus court costs. Assuming costs amount to $1,500, this means you'll have to recover almost $10,000 in order to actually receive $5,000—what you were offered in the first place. If you end up getting only a couple of thousand dollars more with a lawyer than without, you'll recover less than you were originally offered.

How Strong Is Your Case?

If you've thought it through and decided you do want to file a complaint with a fair housing agency or sue the landlord, you need to evaluate the strength of your case and the chances of your success. How serious was the discrimination, and how convincing is your proof?

Severity of the Illegal Act

The more serious the harm you suffered, the more likely you are to win. For example, if you are a family of four and encounter a landlord who clearly uses occupancy standards to discriminate against families with children, an investigator at the local HUD office might be quite interested in your case. The key issue—being able to rent as a family—is extremely important. Less serious acts of discrimination might be better addressed in a meeting with the landlord.

Be realistic in your assessment of the harm. Remember, your fate will depend on how a judge, jury, or insurance adjuster reacts to the landlord's behavior. For example, when a manager screams racial epithets at minority tenants, it's a big case in anyone's book; if the manager puts all families with kids in the back of the building, it's less so.

Also try to determine whether the act was part of a pattern. Landlords who repeatedly discriminate against applicants and tenants are of far greater interest to enforcement agencies than those who commit an isolated wrong. Judges and juries, too, are more prone to punish inveterate bigots than first-timers.

How Landlords Get Caught

Landlords who turn away prospective tenants on the basis of race, ethnic background, or other group characteristics don't usually come out and admit what they're doing. But especially if they own many rental units, their illegal practices often become known to private fair housing advocacy groups (sometimes known as "fair housing councils") or HUD investigators, who hear repeated complaints.

HUD and fair housing organizations are adept at uncovering discriminatory housing practices by attempting to test the practices of housing providers who have been accused of illegal discrimination. For example, in response to an applicant's complaint of racial discrimination, one of these groups will have a white "tester" apply for housing offered by the same landlord, listing credit and income information that is similar—or sometimes not even as good—as that given by the minority applicant. A landlord who offers to rent to a white tester, after having rejected the minority applicant with the same or better qualifications, is very likely to become the subject of a fair housing complaint or lawsuit.

Landlords are also sometimes caught by amateur testers. For example, if you are Black and think that you have been treated differently only because of your skin color, there is nothing to stop you from asking friends who aren't Black to apply for the same vacancy. Be sure that your "testers" have background and credit histories that are similar to yours. If they are offered the apartment, it's strong evidence that you were rejected because of your skin color.

Intentional vs. Unintentional Discrimination

Housing discrimination comes in two forms:
- intentional, such as a statement that the owner doesn't rent to non-Christians, and
- unintentional, such as a policy that lets only two people occupy a two-bedroom flat. This indirectly discriminates against families, even if the landlord's genuine reason is to limit noise and congestion.

Even though the law bans both kinds of discrimination, landlords who practice intentional discrimination are, in general, far more vulnerable to a fair housing charge. Indirect discrimination cases often must be proved by argument and statistics—you must show that the landlord's behavior or policy tends to hurt a protected group more than tenants in general. Also, intentional discrimination carries with it the possibility of punitive damages, which makes the case more attractive to a private attorney and often pressures landlords into settling.

Coming Up With Proof

However right you might be, to win in an administrative hearing or in court you'll have to prove it. If you're lucky, you can use the landlord's own words—like a printed ad that asks for "mature adults only"—as proof. But it's just as likely that there will be no hard proof of discrimination, and that your case will come down to your word against the landlord's.

For example, consider the landlord who tells you during the application process, when no one else is present, that he doesn't rent to single women because he is afraid of his liability if a woman is assaulted on his property. He can be expected to deny having made that statement. In this situation, your case would be greatly strengthened if you could find other single women with decent credit and employment records who had also been turned down by this landlord.

Complaining to a Fair Housing Agency

You may file a discrimination complaint with HUD (if you believe a federal law has been violated) by phone (800-669-9777), mail, or on the HUD website (www.hud.gov/fairhousing/fileacomplaint). You can also file a complaint with a state antidiscrimination agency (if your state's antidiscrimination law has been violated), and in some places also with a local fair housing agency. State and local fair housing agencies are listed on the HUD website at HUD.gov (check the "Resources" menu tab and visit the "State Information" section). You can also get information by calling HUD's Housing Discrimination hotline at 800-669-9777. You can get more details about the complaint-filing procedure by contacting either the state or regional federal agency office.

How It Works

A federal HUD complaint must be filed within one year of the alleged violation; state statutes and local ordinances might set shorter deadlines. The complaint form for HUD is short, simple, and easily completed online without the help of a lawyer. If the complaint is filed with HUD, the agency should (but doesn't always) conduct an investigation within 180 days. The response time of state housing agencies varies.

After HUD investigates (and this is true of most state agencies as well), it will decide whether to dismiss your complaint or take it further. If the agency proceeds with your complaint, they'll attempt to have you reach a conciliation agreement (compromise) with the landlord. For example, you might agree to drop your complaint in exchange for a sum of money and the landlord's written promise to rent you an apartment or, if you're a current tenant, to stop discriminatory policies.

If conciliation is unsuccessful, the fair housing agency will hold an administrative hearing, which is like a trial without a jury, to determine whether discrimination has occurred. If the administrative law judge decides there was a fair housing violation, the agency will order the landlord to pay you money damages, rent you the unit you were denied, or take other appropriate action.

State or Federal Fair Housing Agency: Which Is Better?

If the fair housing violation you've encountered involves both federal and state law, you'll have a choice as to which enforcement agency to approach. Some points to consider are:

- **Your time frame.** HUD cases are typically long, drawn-out affairs—some have dragged on for years. If you want a court order that a landlord offer you a particular rental, you probably won't get quick action from HUD, but you could receive money damages later. Some states handle their cases more quickly. Call your state's fair housing agency and ask how long it takes to resolve a typical case.

- **What you must prove.** It might be tougher to prove your case under one law than another. For example, the federal Fair Housing Acts don't require you to prove that the landlord acted intentionally, but some state laws (California's Unruh Act, for one) do. It would be wise to talk to a fair housing group or lawyer to compare the available laws.

- **What you could win.** Some state statutes put a cap on money damages, both compensatory and punitive; federal law does not. If your case is serious, you might give up a substantial amount of money by pursuing a state law claim instead of a federal claim.

- **Your state's reputation for protection of tenant rights.** A state fair housing agency will mirror the general attitude of the state toward tenants' rights. If you live in California, Massachusetts, or New York, for example, you can expect more protection than if you live in a hands-off state such as Alabama. If you aren't familiar with your state's approach to housing discrimination law, you'll have to do a bit of homework, such as going to the public library and asking the reference librarian to guide you to helpful articles or resources. A librarian at a local law library could be especially helpful. (See Chapter 20 for information on doing legal research.)

Filing a Lawsuit in Federal or State Court

If you have experienced clear and outrageous discrimination, going directly to court might be quicker and more rewarding than going to a government agency. You'll need the help of an experienced lawyer if you choose this route. Assistance from a lawyer will significantly increase your chances of forcing the landlord to rent you the premises and to pay you money damages.

You can sue in federal court or state court even if you have filed a complaint with a fair housing agency (deciding whether to do both is one of the reasons you'll need to hire a good lawyer). The exceptions to this rule are if you have signed a conciliation agreement, or if a formal HUD administrative hearing has already begun. If you file in federal court, you must do so within two years of the alleged violation.

How It Works

Your attorney might decide to file papers asking the court for an expedited hearing (often within a few days), with the hope that a judge will find that the landlord's actions or policies are discriminatory and order the landlord to cease them immediately. These orders are called "temporary restraining orders" (TROs) or sometimes "preliminary injunctions." They are granted only if you convince the judge that:

- You have a good chance of winning the case (that is, the landlord really did illegally discriminate).
- You will suffer irreparable harm if immediate relief isn't granted.

In theory, the TRO remains in place until a more formal hearing is held. In practice, when discrimination is clear enough for a judge to issue a TRO, normally the parties settle out of court. A typical settlement might involve the tenant getting the rental unit, attorneys' fees, and money damages—which, depending on the severity of the discrimination, might be $2,000 to $20,000 or more.

Hiring a Lawyer

Finding a lawyer to represent you in a federal or state lawsuit of this kind might be tough. In the past, legal aid attorneys, hired by government-financed law clinics, often handled discrimination cases for people with low incomes, but federal cutbacks have greatly reduced the availability of legal aid services. As a result, you will probably need to work with a private attorney. (Chapter 20 offers tips on how to find and work with a lawyer.)

If you have a strong case, an attorney might take it "on contingency." This means you pay nothing up front but agree to give the attorney a percentage, usually 20% to 40%, of whatever you win or agree to in a settlement. Depending on your arrangement with the lawyer, you might be responsible for paying the costs of filing the lawsuit and other expenses, such as those for depositions, investigators, and expert witnesses out of pocket. However, many attorneys who handle these cases will cover these expenses, and then deduct them from any award (your take-home amount of the award would be calculated after the expenses—which can be considerable—are deducted).

An attorney who is not confident your case is a winner might require an up-front retainer of at least several thousand dollars, to cover the costs of preparing the legal papers and filing the suit. When the case is over, the lawyer will return to you any amount that was not needed for costs and fees. If you have won, the whole award is divided according to your contingency fee agreement (since you've already paid for expenses). If the case settles or ends in your favor, you might also be awarded court costs, attorneys' fees, and damages, but you can't count on it.

As explained above, if you've gotten a reasonable settlement offer from a landlord, your lawyer needs to win considerably more for you in order for you to come out ahead. To ensure that a lawyer doesn't end up actually costing you money, one strategy is to insist on paying a percentage of only the portion of any award or settlement that exceeds the amount you were already offered. Read between the lines: A lawyer who balks at this suggestion probably believes that the case isn't worth much more than your original offer. On the other hand, a lawyer who thinks that the case is really worth a lot more (for example, $25,000 to $50,000) will be pleased to base the fee on a percentage of any recovery over the low initial settlement offer you received.

> **CAUTION**
>
> **If your lease or rental agreement has an "attorneys' fees" clause, it might not apply to a discrimination lawsuit.** Typically, these clauses, which require the loser to pay the winner's attorneys' fees in a lawsuit between the landlord and tenant, apply only when the lawsuit is over a lease clause. For example, if you don't pay the rent and your landlord evicts you, the clause will apply, because paying rent is part of the lease. But if your landlord's discriminatory behavior does not involve a lease term—you sue for sexual harassment, for example—the fees clause won't apply.

Who Gets Sued or Targeted in a Complaint

Landlords and their employees aren't the only targets of fair housing enforcement. Newspapers that publish discriminatory ads are also covered by the federal fair housing rules, and many have been sued or named by fair housing enforcement agencies for ads like "quiet and mature neighborhood" and "Tenant wanted: Christian handyman." Publishers are especially attractive targets, since they usually have hefty insurance policies that can pay a settlement or court judgment. Online publishers are also covered by fair housing laws, and can be sued for posting discriminatory ads.

Management companies hired by landlords to oversee their rental properties can also be sued. Frequently, it's the company's manager who commits the discriminatory act—for example, by improperly screening tenants or setting discriminatory policies. Usually the company is every bit as liable as if the owner had done the deed; sometimes, an administrative judge or jury decides that both owner and management company are responsible. Large management companies that handle hundreds of rentals are often more solvent (have "deeper pockets") than the small-fry landlords they represent.

Inspecting the Rental Unit and Moving In

Disputes over the return of security deposits are common, and often arise when a landlord keeps all or part of a security deposit, claiming the tenant left the place filthy or damaged. Not surprisingly, the tenant often disagrees, arguing that:

- the problems existed at move-in
- the property damaged was so old that it wasn't worth anything in the first place or was impossible to clean, or
- the landlord is substantially exaggerating the cost of cleaning up or fixing damage that did occur.

This chapter shows how you can avoid such disputes by inspecting and photographing or videoing the rental unit *before* you move in. (Chapter 16 covers the subject of moving out and getting your security deposit returned in detail.) This chapter also discusses the value of keeping organized records and why it's best to send important notices and requests to the landlord in writing (rather than relying only on email or text communications).

How to Inspect the Rental Unit

When you first visited your new place, you got a general impression of the rental unit's condition. To avert all sorts of future arguments with your land-lord, now that you've signed a lease, you need to go deeper. It is absolutely essential that you check the place over for damage, dirt, mildew, and obvious wear and tear before moving in.

Filling Out a Landlord-Tenant Checklist

Creating a written inventory of the condition of the rental property at the beginning (and end) of the tenancy is an excellent way to protect yourself when it comes time to getting your security deposit returned. Completing a written checklist is also the law in some states, as you'll see in "State Security Deposit Rules" and "Required Landlord Disclosures" in Appendix A.

 FORM

A sample Landlord-Tenant Checklist is shown below, and the Nolo website includes a downloadable copy. See Appendix B for the link to the forms in this book.

You and your landlord or manager should fill out the checklist together. If that's impossible, complete the form on your own. It's a good idea to take along a friend as a potential witness, who could testify about the unit's condition in court (or provide you with a signed declaration) if you have a dispute over security deposit deductions when you move out.

The checklist is in two parts. The first side covers the general condition of each room; the second covers furnishings.

You will be filling out the first column—*Move-In Condition*—before you move in. The second column—*Move-Out Condition*—is for when you move out and (ideally) the two of you inspect the unit again. At that time the checklist will document any damage to the rental unit during your tenancy, which the landlord might attempt to recoup by withholding all or part of your security deposit.

Some states give tenants the option of requesting a pre-move-out inspection, which gives them notice of needed cleaning or repairs. If your state requires landlords to offer this step, use the second column and draw a line down the center, for pre-move-out notes and actual move-out notes. (Chapter 16 further discusses how to complete the Landlord-Tenant Checklist when you move out.)

General Condition of Rental Unit and Premises

In the *Move-In Condition* column, you should note both serious problems, such as a broken heater or leaking roof, and minor flaws such as stained kitchen counters. Be sure to note areas or items (especially in the kitchen or bathroom) that are dirty, including mildew, pest, or rodent problems.

Mark "OK" next to items that are in satisfactory condition—basically, clean, safe, sanitary, and in good working order.

Landlord-Tenant Checklist

Property Address: _____ 572 Fourth St., Apt. 11, Washington, D.C. _____

General Condition of Rental Unit and Premises

	Move-In Condition Date of Walk-Through: May 1, 20xx	Move-Out Condition Date of Walk-Through:
Living Room		
Flooring	OK	
Walls & ceilings	OK	
Light fixtures	OK	
Window treatments	Miniblinds discolored	
Windows & screens	Window facing street rattles	
Doors & handles/locks	OK	
Fireplace	OK	
Smoke detector & CO detector	OK	
Other	N/A	
Kitchen		
Flooring	Cigarette burn hole in linoleum near fridge	
Walls & ceilings	OK	
Light fixtures	OK	
Window treatments	OK	
Windows & screens	OK	
Doors & handles/locks	OK	
Cabinets	Paint chipped in lots of areas	
Counters	Stained but clean	
Stove/oven/range	Burners are filthy (covered in grease)	
Refrigerator	OK, but ice maker doesn't work	
Dishwasher	N/A	
Garbage disposal	OK	
Microwave	N/A	
Stove hood	Clean on top but greasy on underside	
Sink & plumbing	OK	
Other appliances	N/A	
Smoke detector & CO detector	OK	
Other	Insides of drawers are filled with crumbs and lining is peeling	

General Condition of Rental Unit and Premises (continued)

	Move-In Condition Date of Walk-Through: May 1, 20xx	Move-Out Condition Date of Walk-Through:
Dining Room		
Flooring	OK	
Walls & ceilings	Crack in ceiling	
Light fixtures	OK	
Window treatments	OK	
Windows & screens	OK	
Doors & handles/locks	OK	
Smoke detector & CO detector	N/A	
Other		
Bathroom		
Flooring	OK	
Walls & ceilings	Wallpaper peeling	
Light fixtures	OK	
Window treatments	N/A	
Windows & screens	No screen	
Doors & handles/locks	OK	
Bathtub/shower (incl. attached door)	Tub is chipped and stained	
Sink, counters, & plumbing	OK	
Cabinets & storage	OK	
Mirror(s)	OK	
Toilet	Base of toilet very dirty	
Ceiling fan/ventilation	No ceiling fan	
Other	N/A	
Bedroom		
Flooring	Bedroom #1 (master): OK Bedroom #2: OK	
Walls & ceilings	#1: OK #2: OK	
Lighting fixtures	#1: ceiling light dented #2: OK	
Window treatments	#1: dusty #2: none	
Windows & screens	#1: OK #2: OK	

General Condition of Rental Unit and Premises (continued)

	Move-In Condition Date of Walk-Through: May 1, 20xx	Move-Out Condition Date of Walk-Through:
Doors & handles/locks	#1: Lock on door OK #2: No lock on door	
Closet	#1: Water stains in closet #2: OK	
Smoke detector & CO detector	#1: OK #2: OK	
Other	N/A	
Other Areas		
Heating, A/C (mechanical room)	OK	
Lawn/garden	N/A	
Stairs and landings	OK	
Patio, terrace, deck, etc.	N/A	
Basement	OK	
Garage	N/A	
Attic	N/A	
Entryway	scuffed walls and baseboards	
Laundry room	N/A	
Other		

[X] Tenants acknowledge that all smoke detectors were tested in their presence and found to be in working order, and that the testing procedure was explained to them. Tenants agree to promptly notify Landlord in writing should any smoke detector appear to be malfunctioning or inoperable. Tenants will not refuse Landlord access for the purpose of inspecting, maintaining, repairing, or installing legally-required smoke detectors.

[X] Tenants acknowledge that all carbon monoxide detectors were tested in their presence and found to be in working order, and that the testing procedure was explained to them. Tenants agree to promptly notify Landlord in writing should any carbon monoxide detector appear to be malfunctioning or inoperable. Tenants will not refuse Landlord access for the purpose of inspecting, maintaining, repairing, or installing legally-required carbon monoxide detectors.

Checklist for Furnished Property

	Move-In Condition Date of Walk-Through: May 1, 20xx	Move-Out Condition Date of Walk-Through:
Living Room		
Coffee table	Two scratches on top	
End tables	OK	
Lamps	OK	
Chairs	OK	
Sofa	OK	
Decorative items (unattached mirrors, rugs, pictures, vases, etc.)	2 framed pictures on wall, look OK	
Electronics	N/A	
Other	N/A	
Kitchen		
Countertop appliances	N/A	
Dishes, silverware, & cookware	N/A	
Linens	N/A	
Chairs & stools	N/A	
Table	N/A	
Decorative items (unattached mirrors, rugs, pictures, vases, etc.)	N/A	
Other	N/A	
Dining Room		
Chairs	OK	
Stools	N/A	
Table	Leg bent slightly	
Lamps	N/A	
Decorative items (unattached mirrors, rugs, pictures, vases, etc.)	N/A	
Electronics	N/A	
Other	N/A	
Bathroom		
Shelves & storage (unattached)	N/A	
Shower curtain & rod	Shower curtain torn	
Hamper	N/A	
Linens	N/A	
Decorative items (unattached mirrors, rugs, pictures, vases, etc.)	N/A	
Other	N/A	

Checklist for Furnished Property (continued)

	Move-In Condition Date of Walk-Through: May 1, 20xx	Move-Out Condition Date of Walk-Through:
Bedroom		
Bed(s)	#1: OK #2: OK	
Chairs	#1: OK #2: OK	
Bureau	#1: OK #2: OK	
Chests	N/A	
Dressing table	N/A	
Bedside tables	#1: OK #2: OK	
Lamps	#1: OK #2: N/A	
Linens	N/A	
Decorative items (unattached mirrors, rugs, pictures, vases, etc.)	N/A	
Electronics	N/A	
Other	N/A	
Other Areas		
Desks	N/A	
Shelves	N/A	
Books, games, media	N/A	
Decorative items (unattached mirrors, rugs, pictures, vases, etc.)	Hallway picture frame chipped	
Electronics	N/A	
Tools (yard and workshop)	N/A	
Trash & recycling bins	N/A	
Outdoor furniture	N/A	
Recreational equipment	N/A	
Other	N/A	

Use this space to provide any additional explanation:

_____

_____

_____

_____

_____

_____

Landlord-Tenant Checklist completed on moving in on _____ May 1, 20xx _____ and approved by:

Bernard Cohen _____ and _Maria Crouse_ _____
Landlord/Manager   Tenant

                                          Sandra Martino _____
                                          Tenant

                                          _____
                                          Tenant

Landlord-Tenant Checklist completed on moving out on _____ and approved by:

_____ and _____
Landlord/Manager   Tenant

                                          _____
                                          Tenant

                                          _____
                                          Tenant

Make a note—as specific as possible—describing items that are broken, stained, worn, grime-covered, scratched, leaking, smelly, dented, chipped, or simply not in the best condition. For example, instead of writing "stove dirty," state that the burners are covered with grease. Don't simply note that the refrigerator "needs fixing" if an ice maker doesn't work. It's just as easy to write "ice maker broken, should not be used." This way, the landlord can't claim you broke the ice maker and should pay for its repair or replacement.

Furnishings

The second part of the checklist covers furnishings, such as lamps or shower curtains. Obviously, you can simply mark "Not Applicable" or "N/A" in most of these boxes if your unit is not furnished.

If your rental property has rooms or furnishings not listed on the checklist, note them in "Other Areas" or cross out something that you don't have and write in the changes. If you are renting a large house or apartment or providing many furnishings, you might want to attach a separate sheet. Just make a separate list for additional items and staple it to the checklist.

What to Look For

Structure
- holes or cracks in floors, walls, or ceiling
- dark round spots on the ceiling or dark streaks on the walls, indicating water leaks or mold

Plumbing
- toilet takes too long to flush or leaks on the floor
- tap water is discolored
- low water pressure (evidenced by scalding hot water in the shower when you flush the toilet)
- water drains slowly in sinks, tubs, and showers
- mold stains on walls, ceilings

Heating
- no heat or inadequate or dangerous heating facilities
- old air filters (ask when they were last replaced)

Light and Ventilation
- poor ventilation in bathrooms (no outside window or fan)
- inadequate natural light through windows
- poor lighting in hallways, stairs, entranceways, or parking areas

Wiring and Electricity
- loose or exposed wiring
- insufficient outlets or light fixtures

Insects, Vermin, and Rodents
- rodent trails or excrement
- evidence of cockroaches in cupboards, in closets, or behind appliances
- bed bugs (under carpets, within light fixtures)

Security
- flimsy or inadequate locks on doors and windows
- windows don't open and close easily (painted or nailed shut)

Fire Safety
- smoke detectors absent or not working
- fire extinguishers absent or not working
- exits leading to street or hallway unsafe or full of litter
- combustible materials in storage rooms, garages, or basements

Trash and Garbage Receptacles
- inadequate garbage and recycling storage and removal

Test Smoke Detectors, Carbon Monoxide Detectors, and Fire Extinguishers

State and local laws often require landlords to provide fire extinguishers, carbon monoxide detectors, and smoke detectors in rental units.

As part of your move-in procedures, make sure the landlord tests all smoke detectors and carbon monoxide (CO) detectors in your presence and shows them to be in good working order. Be sure you understand how to:

- test the fire and CO detectors
- recognize the signs of failing detectors—for example, a beeping noise, and
- replace the batteries, if applicable.

Make sure the pressure needles on fire extinguishers are well within the green zone, and that the tool is not dented or rusty. Check the maintenance record (some require maintenance every 5 years). The headcap locking pin (what you pull to use the extinguisher) should be in place and the security seal unbroken.

Do not disable a smoke or carbon monoxide detector. Not only is it foolish—it could expose you to liability if a fire or the presence of carbon monoxide causes damage that could have been prevented had there been a working detector.

The boxes at the bottom of the General Condition of Rental Unit and Premises section of the checklist acknowledge that you tested the smoke detector and carbon monoxide detector in the landlord's presence and found them to be in working order.

Signing the Checklist

After you and your landlord agree on all of the particulars on the rental unit, you each should sign and date every page of the checklist, including any attachments. The landlord will probably keep the original and give you a copy. If you filled out the checklist on your own, do your best to have the landlord review your comments, note any

disagreement, and return a copy to you promptly. You should ask the landlord to make the checklist part of your lease or rental agreement, as explained in Chapter 2.

A savvy landlord will update the checklist after making repairs or replacing, adding, or removing items after you move in. You should both initial and date any changes.

Photographing or Filming the Rental Unit

Taking photos and video of the unit before you move in is another excellent way to avoid disputes over your responsibility for damage and dirt. In addition to the checklist, you'll be able to compare "before" and "after" images when you leave. This should help refresh your landlord's memory, and if you end up in small claims court fighting over the security deposit, documenting your point of view with photos or videos will be invaluable.

Whether you take a photo with your phone or use a separate camera, save the photos as soon as possible. Email a copy of one set to your landlord or, if your landlord uses an online management portal, see if there's a shared folder to which you can upload the images for safekeeping. If you make a video, clearly state the time and date when the video was made and send the landlord a copy.

You should repeat this process when you leave. Chapter 16 discusses moving out.

How to Handle Problems

If you discover any problems, try to get your new landlord to fix them before you move in.

Serious Problems

The landlord must fix certain defects—such as a broken heater or leaking roof—under state and local housing codes. (Chapter 8 discusses landlords' repair and maintenance responsibilities.) A landlord who does not immediately agree to fix serious problems probably isn't taking the obligation to repair very seriously. You're probably better off refusing to rent the place and walking away.

If the landlord promises to make repairs or alterations after you move in, be careful. First, ask other tenants how good the landlord is at keeping promises. Second, get the promises in writing and signed, ideally as part of the lease or rental agreement (see Chapter 2). Your written agreement should specify the:

- exact repair or alteration—for example, installation of a deadbolt lock
- deadline by which repairs will be made, and
- consequence for the landlord's failure to complete repairs by the promised date—for example, a certain reduction in your rent or even your ability to move out without liability for future rent.

Some samples are shown below.

Sample Agreements Regarding Repairs

Serious Problem:

> Landlord will clear the drains and fix the leaking toilet by February 28, the day before the Tenant's rental agreement begins. If Landlord fails to fix these plumbing problems by March 1, Tenant may withhold rent until Landlord fixes the problem.

Nonessential Repair or Improvement:

> Landlord will supply up to $250 worth of "Color Pro" paint and painting supplies. Tenant will paint the living room, hall, and two bedrooms, using off-white latex paint on the walls and ceiling and enamel paint on all wood surfaces (doors and trim). Paint and supplies will be picked up by Tenant from ABC Hardware and billed to Landlord.

Nonessential Repairs or Improvements

If repairs are not essential—such as a new coat of paint or more electrical outlets in the study—try to work something out.

Many landlords are open to making reasonable improvements and alterations, especially in higher-rent areas that have lots of places for rent and not too many people looking, or if you've impressed the landlord as a good, responsible tenant.

You might offer to pay part of the expense of nonessential repairs or improvements, such as adding additional electrical outlets to accommodate your electronic equipment, or fixing the backyard fence so that your dog can't get out. If you want the apartment painted, offer to do the work if the landlord buys the paint. Chapter 10 provides advice on how to convince the landlord to improve or alter the premises, and how to keep your monetary outlay to a minimum.

If the landlord seems completely unreasonable, or really put out simply by your request, beware. This doesn't sound like a good way to start the tenancy.

 TIP
If you have a disability and are seeking a reasonable modification of your living space to meet your needs, your landlord will not be able to legally stand in your way. Under the federal Fair Housing Amendments Act of 1988, you are entitled to make reasonable modifications to your rental to make it safe and enjoyable. Chapter 5 explains how to go about obtaining permission to perform necessary modifications.

Clarifying Important Terms of the Tenancy

A good lease or rental agreement should cover the basic issues of your tenancy, including rent, deposits, rent increases, and sublets. (Chapter 2 discusses leases and rental agreements.)

If your landlord does little more than sign a tersely worded lease or rental agreement and hand you a key, make sure you have all necessary information before you move in. For example, be sure you know:

- the landlord or manager's phone numbers (day and night) and emails
- how to report maintenance and repair problems
- any rules for the use of grounds, garage, and storage space
- location of garbage cans, details on recycling programs and trash pickup days, and
- other issues that affect the rental, such as pool hours or use of a laundry room.

Organizing Your Rental Records

Establishing a simple system to record all correspondence with your landlord, such as repair requests, will provide a valuable paper trail should disputes later develop—for example, regarding your landlord's failure to make necessary repairs. Without good records, the outcome of a dispute might come down to your word against your landlord's, always a precarious situation.

If your landlord uses a quality online rental management portal, your job will be easy: A record of all correspondence should be available just by logging in. Don't leave the safe storage of your records to luck, though—all it takes is one system update gone bad for the program to inadvertently lose everything. Download your data monthly, if possible, or just keep a backup file of your correspondence the old-fashioned way.

To get started right, set up a file folder for the following documents:

- a copy of your rental application, references, and credit report
- your copy of the signed lease or rental agreement
- any building rules and regulations or move-in letter from the landlord

- deposit information, including the amount and (if known) the location and interest rate terms of your deposit (Chapter 4 discusses basic security deposit rules), and
- Landlord-Tenant Checklist and photos or video taken at move-in.

After you move in, add these documents to your file:

- your landlord's written requests for entry (Chapter 11 discusses tenant privacy rights)
- rent increase notices
- records of your repair requests, including how and when they were handled (Chapters 8, 9, and 10 discuss repairs, maintenance, improvements, and alterations), and
- any other correspondence with your landlord, including copies of emails.

Using Email or Text Messages for Notice or a Letter of Understanding

You and your landlord are probably a lot more likely to send each other messages by email or text rather than by post—for example, if you're trying to schedule a time for the landlord to fix your heater. But will those electronic communications serve you as well as a mailed letter, if you need evidence that the message was received at the other end?

Suppose, for example, that you want to give notice of your intention to end your month-to-month tenancy, and do so by sending an email that's 30 days in advance of your planned departure. Or, say you need to send your landlord a request for repairs (this is the first, necessary step before you can use a remedy like repair-and-deduct, if the landlord fails to take action). If you end up in a legal dispute and your landlord challenges you in court, and claims ignorance about your decision to leave or the repair problem, you'll need confirmation that the emails or text messages were received.

! CAUTION

Read the statute (or the lease) for notice instructions! Now and then, a statute will tell you exactly how to deliver notices and demands to the other party. As email and text communications become more and more common, lawmakers are incorporating specifications for electronic communication in their laws. And lawyers are drafting leases with notice clauses that take electronic communications into account. It's still common however, to see the generic requirement that demands and notices be delivered "in writing," which doesn't help very much.

E-signatures are legal everywhere under the ESIGN (Electronic Signatures in Global and National Commerce) Act, a federal law. In addition, all states have passed either the "UETA" (the Uniform Electronic Transactions Act) or their own laws, to cover situations where federal law doesn't apply.

It's also very common for landlords to use e-signature programs or property management programs that allow all parties to sign electronically and download fully executed versions for their records. Print your documents and save them to your physical file folder.

! CAUTION

Do not use text messages for important decisions, like a landlord's agreement to do a repair or especially an agreement to lease. Texts are hard to track, and evidence of receipt isn't available short of complex searches through users' accounts. Rarely would a landlord-tenant dispute support the expense of such a search. If you're worried about being able to prove the receipt of a text, you'd be best served to also print it and mail it return receipt requested … the old-fashioned way. Consider doing the same for your emails.

Why It's Difficult to Prove That Your Landlord Received Your Email

You might think that you'll be able to produce evidence of the landlord's receipt of your emails, by using your computer's stored files or receipt requests. Think again. Here are some common myths about how to prove that email messages were delivered.

The email didn't return to you. Emails that cannot be delivered to an account often come back with an error message. If you don't receive an error message, you might feel confident that the email was delivered. But how can you prove it? The best you can do is to print the email and hope that it shows that there was no response like "Re: Undelivered email" or something similar. This approach has a problem, however. Because of the large volume of spam, many email servers will send undeliverable email to one big account, rather than generating individual "cannot deliver" replies. So the absence of a "cannot deliver" email might not prove the opposite—that the message was delivered to your landlord. In short, archived email shows what you sent (though you can easily alter the text after you've sent it), but no legal proof that the original email was received by the other side.

Printed email. Printing your sent message provides no proof that the other side got it. Printed emails can easily be challenged for authenticity (the text can be altered after the message was sent). For this reason, it won't be admitted in court.

A delivery confirmation request. This method asks the recipient to send back a message (just a click) that they got the email. But here, too, problems abound: The recipient can simply decide not to send the message, and many large email servers (like Yahoo and Hotmail) don't support these features.

Request a read receipt. This is a feature on most email systems, and it simply asks the user who receives the message to send you a receipt. Again, it's dependent on the user agreeing to send the receipt. A landlord who doesn't want to give you proof of the date of your repair request is not likely to send a receipt.

Hidden scripts. These bits of software are embedded in your email, and secretly trigger a notification when the message is read. But most current email programs will detect the presence of the script, and warn you that the message you're about to open contains possibly unsafe content. Most email users will not open those emails.

Roommates, Guests, and Airbnb

Whatever your reasons for having roommates, one thing is likely: The makeup of your living group will change over time as jobs, schooling, friendships, love, and even illness or death play their part in rearranging the names on your mailbox. Unfortunately, most landlords are not as flexible as you might wish when it comes to adding new roommates or letting one out of a lease.

This chapter discusses crucial issues about sharing rental housing, such as:

- your legal obligations and responsibilities with respect to your roommate
- moving in a roommate and what to do if your landlord objects
- what to do if relations with your roommates deteriorate, particularly when roommates won't pay their share of the rent
- your rights to bring in paying "guests" through Airbnb and similar services, and
- whether you can rent space to a roomer.

RELATED TOPIC
Also covered in this book:

- How to find a compatible and responsible roommate: Chapter 1.
- Lease or rental agreement limits on number of occupants and restrictions on overnight guests, sublets, and assignments: Chapter 2.
- Your right to sublet your apartment for a while, and what happens if your landlord objects: Chapter 15.
- Whether you can get someone else to take over the rest of your lease and, if you do, whether you are off the financial hook: Chapter 15.
- What happens if you break your lease and move out early: Chapter 15.
- Getting your security deposit back if you leave but your roommates stay: Chapter 16.

Renting a Place With Others

When two or more people all sign the same rental agreement or lease—or enter into the same oral rental agreement—they are cotenants and share the same legal rights and responsibilities. Most of the time, cotenants sign the rental document at the beginning of the tenancy. A person can become a cotenant later, too, by moving in when an original cotenant leaves, and either signing the existing lease or rental agreement or being accepted and treated as a full-fledged cotenant by the landlord.

Common Terms

Original tenant. The initial tenant (or tenants) who signed the lease or rental agreement. This is a shortcut term with no precise legal meaning.

Tenant. Someone who has signed a lease or a rental agreement, or whose residency has been accepted by the landlord, typically evidenced by the landlord's acceptance of their or rent payment.

Cotenants. Two or more tenants who rent the same property under the same lease or rental agreement. Each is 100% responsible for carrying out the agreement (lawyers call this "joint and several liability"), including paying all the rent.

Roommates. Two or more people, usually unrelated, living under the same roof and sharing rent and expenses. Roommates are usually cotenants, but a roommate might be a subtenant of the original tenant. In other situations, a roommate might have the legal status of a long-term guest, with no formal legal relationship with the tenant or the landlord.

Joint and several liability. This refers to the sharing of legal obligations by two or more people. When cotenants are "jointly and severally liable" for rent, it means the landlord can seek the entire rent from any one of the cotenants, and a court can hold any one of them responsible for paying the entire rent. You and your cotenants are jointly and severally liable for rent and other obligations—*even if your lease or rental agreement does not include this clause*. It applies to oral leases, too.

Roomer. A person who rents space in your home. If you are a tenant, the roomer is your subtenant, and you are the roomer's landlord.

Guest. Someone who lives in the rental but who does not pay rent, either to the tenant or the landlord. "Rent" can include more than money, such as services rendered in exchange for a place to live. Removing a guest is not covered in states' landlord-tenant statutes.

Understanding the legal consequences of being a cotenant is important: One cotenant's negative behavior—not paying the rent, for example—can affect everyone's tenancy. The sections below explain how this works.

When One Roommate Doesn't Pay Rent

Cotenants can decide to split the rent equally or unequally, depending on their own personal wishes. However, such agreements don't have any impact on the landlord. Each cotenant is independently liable to the landlord for all of the rent. Landlords often remind cotenants of this obligation by inserting into the lease a chunk of legalese that says that the tenants are "jointly and severally" liable for paying rent and adhering to terms of the agreement. (See "Common Terms," above.) If one tenant can't pay a share of the rent in a particular month, or simply moves out, the other tenant(s) must still pay the full rent or risk termination and eviction.

> **EXAMPLE:** James and Helen sign a month-to-month rental agreement for an apartment rented by Blue Oak Properties, for $1,800 per month. James and Helen agree between themselves to each pay half of the rent. After three months, James moves out without notifying Helen or Blue Oak. Helen is legally obligated to pay Blue Oak all the rent until she legally ends the tenancy. (In their state, that's 30 days' written notice.) If Helen can't pay the rent, Blue Oak may terminate the rental and, if she doesn't move, evict her.
>
> In the meantime, if she can prove the existence of her agreement with James, Helen could try to recover James's share of the rent by suing him in small claims court.
>
> If, instead of leaving, she gets a new roommate whom the landlord approves of and who pays half the rent, Helen can recover from James only the extra rent she had to pay before the new person moved in.

Landlords often insist on receiving one rent check for the entire rent—they don't want to be bothered with multiple checks from cotenants, even if each cotenant pays on time and the checks add up to the full rent. As long as you have been advised of this policy in the rental agreement or lease, it's legal for your landlord to impose it.

When One Roommate Violates the Lease or Rental Agreement

Although it is painful for an innocent tenant to hear, the landlord can legally hold all cotenants responsible for the negative actions of just one, and terminate everyone's tenancy with the appropriate notice. For example, both cotenants can be evicted if just one of them seriously damages the property, moves in an extra roommate on the sly, keeps a dog in violation of a no-pets rule, or otherwise violates the lease or rental agreement.

> **EXAMPLE:** Dan and Mike were cotenants whose lease prohibited pets. Dan's friend Kate implored him to take Spot, her cat, when she joined the Peace Corps. Mike didn't like the idea, but Dan won him over by promising that both he and Spot would move if the landlord found out. To Mike's dismay, when the landlord discovered Spot, he sent both Mike and Dan termination notices.

In practice, however, landlords sometimes ignore the legal rule that all tenants are equally liable for lease violations, and don't penalize a blameless one. If the nonoffending roommates pay the rent on time, don't damage the landlord's property, and can plausibly argue that the misbehavior will not recur, the landlord might want to keep them.

A landlord who is willing to keep just the non-offending tenants must, technically, go through a two-step process. The landlord will have to terminate the original rental agreement or lease as to everyone, then offer the remaining tenants the chance to sign a new agreement. This two-step is necessary because unless the lease says otherwise, landlords don't have the right to selectively terminate a multi-tenant lease—either all of you get the boot, or none of you. (This rule has been changed in a number of states when domestic violence is the cause for the termination: The laws allow landlords to selectively terminate only the perpetrator, leaving the lease of the victim intact. For more information on domestic violence, see below.)

If you want to convince your landlord to let you remain in your rental after a cotenant gets the boot, it helps to understand the landlord's principal concerns—to have good, stable tenants who pay the rent on time. A gentle reminder that throwing everyone out and starting over doesn't best serve those goals might persuade the landlord to not evict you. Of course, you will have to absorb the departed tenant's share of the rent for the time it takes to find an acceptable new cotenant. And, your landlord will need to approve any new cotenant. ("Adding a New Roommate," below, shows the best way to find a roommate who passes your landlord's muster.)

Unfortunately, if you can't handle the increased rent until you find a new tenant, or the landlord feels you can't be trusted to find a trustworthy one, the landlord is likely to evict all of you at the same time. It's far simpler and quicker than first evicting the troublemaker for the lease violation and then later ousting the rest of you when you fail to come up with the entire rent.

Agreements—and Disagreements— Among Roommates

Roommates make lots of informal agreements about splitting rent, occupying bedrooms, and sharing chores. Your landlord isn't bound by these agreements, and has no power to enforce them. For all sorts of reasons, roommate arrangements regularly go awry. If the situation gets bad enough, you'll likely end up arguing with your roommates about who should leave.

Only Landlords Can Evict Tenants

As a general rule, you can't terminate your roommate's tenancy by filing an eviction action. (The situation is different if you rent to a subtenant; see "Taking in a Roomer," below.)

This rule has one rather rare exception: A few rent control statutes (such as the one in San Francisco) allow a landlord to designate a "master tenant"— usually a long-term tenant who was there first—to perform many of the functions of a landlord. Master tenants have the right to choose— as well as to evict—tenants who share their rental. If your rental is subject to rent control, find out whether the law includes a provision for a master tenant.

The more you can anticipate possible problems from the start, the better prepared you'll be to handle disputes. First, try to choose responsible and compatible housemates. (Follow our advice in Chapter 1.)

Then, before you move in, sit down with your roommates and create your own agreement covering major issues, such as:

1. **Rent.** What is everyone's share? Who will write the rent check if the landlord requires only one check?
2. **Space.** Who will occupy which bedrooms? How will you divvy up other spaces, such as bathrooms, closets, and parking spots?
3. **Household chores.** Who's responsible for cleaning, and on what schedule?
4. **Food sharing.** Will you be sharing food, shopping, and cooking responsibilities? How will you split the costs and work?
5. **Noise.** When should music be turned off or down low?
6. **Overnight guests.** Is it okay for friends or significant others to stay over? With what frequency?
7. **Moving out.** If one of you decides to move, how much notice must be given? Must the departing tenant find an acceptable substitute?

Sample Roommate Agreement

Alex Andrews, Brian Bates, and Charles Chew are cotenants at Apartment 2, 360 Capitol Avenue, Oakdale, Kentucky, under a year-long lease that expires on February 1, 20xx. They have all signed a lease with the landlord, Reuben Shaw, and have each paid $500 toward the security deposit of $1,500. Alex, Brian, and Charles all agree as follows:

1. **Rent.** The rent of $1,500 per month will be shared equally, at $500 per person. Alex will write a check for the total month's rent and take it to the manager's office on the first of each month (or the next day if the 1st falls on a holiday). Brian and Charles will pay their share to Alex on or before the due date.

2. **Bedrooms.** Alex and Brian will share the large bedroom with the adjacent deck; Charles will have the small bedroom.

3. **Food.** Each cotenant is responsible for his own food purchases.

4. **Cleaning.** Charles will clean his own room and Alex and Brian will clean theirs. The household chores for the rest of the apartment—living room, dining room, kitchen, and bathroom—will rotate, with each cotenant responsible for vacuuming, dusting, mopping, and bathroom maintenance on a weekly basis.

   Each cotenant will promptly clean up after himself in the kitchen. No one will leave dishes in the sink for more than 24 hours, and everyone will promptly clean up when asked.

5. **Utilities.** Everyone will pay an equal share of the electricity, gas, internet, and cable bills. Alex will arrange for these services and will pay the bills. Within three days of receiving the bills, Charles and Brian will each pay Alex one-third of the total.

6. **Guests.** Because of the apartment's small size, each tenant agrees to have no more than one overnight guest at a time and to inform the others in advance, if possible. Each cotenant agrees to no more than four guests overnight in a month.

7. **Exam Periods.** During midterm and final exam periods, no cotenant will have overnight guests or parties.

8. **Violations of the Agreement.** The cotenants agree that repeated and serious violations of one or more of these understandings will be grounds for any two cotenants to ask the other to leave. If a cotenant is asked to leave, he will do so within two weeks, and will forfeit any outstanding prepaid rent.

9. **Leaving Before the Lease Ends.** If a cotenant wants to leave before the lease expires on February 1, 20xx, he will give as much notice as possible (and not less than one month) and diligently try to find a replacement tenant who is acceptable to the remaining cotenants and the landlord.

Sample Roommate Agreement (continued)

10. **Security Deposits.** The cotenant who leaves early (voluntarily or involuntarily) will get his share of the security deposit returned, minus costs of repairs, replacement, and cleaning attributable to the departing tenant, when and if an acceptable cotenant signs the lease and contributes his share to the security deposit. If an acceptable cotenant cannot be found, the departing tenant will not receive any portion of his share of the security deposit.

11. **Dispute Resolution.** If a dispute arises concerning this agreement or any aspect of the shared living situation, the cotenants will ask our town's Mediation Service for assistance before they terminate the cotenancy or initiate a lawsuit. This will involve all three tenants sitting down with a mediator in good faith to try to resolve the problems.

Alex Andrews	_February 1, 20xx_
Alex Andrews	Date
Brian Bates	_Feb. 1, 20xx_
Brian Bates	Date
Charles Chew	_Feb. 1, 20xx_
Charles Chew	Date

It's best to put your understandings in writing. (See the sample roommate agreement, above.) Oral agreements are too easily forgotten or misinterpreted after the fact.

Be as specific as possible, especially on issues that are important to you. If dirty dishes in the sink drive you up the wall, write it down. If occasional guests are no problem, but you can't stand the thought of your roommate's (nonrent-paying) friend hogging the bathroom for two week stretches, make sure your agreement is clear on guests.

Some parts of this kind of agreement are not legally binding—that is, a judge won't order a tenant to clean the bathroom. Judges will, however, enforce financial agreements, such as how rent is to be shared.

EXAMPLE: Roommates Janet and Jacob orally agree that Jacob will get the larger bedroom and pay 60% of the rent, and Janet will pay 40%. Right after they move in, Jacob loses his job and is unable to pay his share. Janet pays the whole amount for two months, until finally she talks Jacob into moving. Six months later, after landing a good job, Jacob still hasn't paid Janet, who sues him in small claims court. Jacob admits in court that he owes Janet his share of two months' rent, but says there was never a deal to split it 60-40. The judge, faced with two different stories and nothing in writing, decides to split the rental obligation 50-50.

If Janet and Jacob had shared the rental for some time and given separate rent checks to the landlord every month (Jacob paying 60% and Janet 40%), Janet would probably have been able to convince the judge of the 60-40 agreement by producing her string of canceled checks. Of course, a written and signed Roommate Agreement that reflected the 60-40 split would have won the case for Janet.

By far the greatest value of committing your understanding of cotenant rights and responsibilities to writing is that it forces you and your housemates to take your cotenancy responsibilities seriously. To underline this commitment, it's always wise to include a clause requiring cotenants to participate in mediation before one of you breaks the agreement by moving out or running off to court. Our sample roommate agreement, above, includes such a clause. Chapter 19 discusses how mediation works.

It is usually best not to involve your landlord in disputes among roommates. The reasons—both practical and legal—include the following:

- The landlord can't enforce any decisions among tenants. For example, short of continual—and, of course, illegal—monitoring of your living situation, how could a landlord make tenants share housecleaning?

- Any complaint you make about a cotenant is likely to be reciprocated, with the result that your landlord is likely to receive a negative picture of all of you. Especially if you have a month-to-month tenancy, your landlord might get tired of your constant complaining and decide to get rid of the whole bunch of you. (Terminating a month-to-month rental agreement in this situation would not be illegal, because landlords are legally free to oust tenants whose demands and behavior are unreasonable and too time-consuming.)

CAUTION
Don't change the locks. If a roommate dispute gets serious—especially if your cotenant hasn't paid the rent—you might be tempted to change the locks or ask the landlord to do so. Don't. A landlord cannot legally bar entry to a tenant without a court order. Similarly, if you unilaterally bar your roommate from the rental, you, too, risk legal liability if the locked-out roommate is forced to find shelter elsewhere and sues you for the cost of alternate housing. Finally, changing the locks without your landlord's permission is almost always prohibited in the lease, and gives your landlord a legal justification to evict all of you.

Domestic Violence Situations

Most states extend special protections to victims of domestic violence. (See "State Laws in Domestic Violence Situations," in Appendix A.) If you are dealing with domestic violence, take steps to protect your personal safety, and consider contacting local law enforcement or a battered women's shelter for help. Your state might have laws that protect you, such as the following:

- **Antidiscrimination status and eviction protection.** Many states prohibit landlords from refusing to rent to applicants who have restraining orders, whether it's refusing to renew leases or terminating on the basis of domestic violence status alone. (Increasingly, however, states are allowing termination when the situation poses a threat to other tenants.)
- **Early termination rights.** Many states allow victims of domestic violence to terminate a lease and move without responsibility for the balance of the rent. Tenants usually must present evidence of domestic violence status, such as a police report (each state specifies the types of admissible evidence).
- **A requirement of confidentiality.** Some states prohibit landlords from disclosing to prospective landlords a former tenant's status as a victim of domestic violence.
- **The power to evict the aggressor.** Some states allow a landlord to evict only the wrongdoer, leaving the lease intact for the victim.
- **Lock change requirements.** Most states require landlords to change the locks once an abuser has left or a restraining order has been issued by a judge.

In the absence of a state law giving victims of domestic violence early termination rights or other protections, don't assume your landlord will say "No" to an early termination or other related request. First, because a blanket policy will usually affect female, not male, tenants, it can be attacked in court as indirectly discriminating on the basis

of sex (several lawsuits brought in states without statutory protections have succeeded on this theory). Aside from the landlord's vulnerability to being sued, emphasize that it might be essential to your safety to allow you to move quickly. Finally, point out that the landlord's bottom line might benefit from allowing the tenancy to end immediately—what the landlord stands to lose in rent might pale in comparison with repair costs if the property is damaged, not to speak of the fallout from negative publicity if the situation escalates.

Although your state might give some special protections to domestic violence victims, these accommodations do not prohibit the landlord from terminating, if necessary, for nonpayment of rent. Unfortunately, all too often the abuser will leave the property but the remaining victim struggles to pay the rent. Landlords may legally terminate the tenancy of a domestic violence victim who falls behind in the rent, just as they can for any tenant who hasn't paid.

When You Fear Violence

If you fear for your immediate physical safety (or that of one of your cotenants), or when serious law-breaking such as drug dealing is involved, call the police. Short of that, if you have a sound factual basis to believe that one of your roommates intends to harm you, communicate these fears to your landlord, who might begin proceedings to evict the aggressor. You might need to mention that a land-lord who fails to sensibly intervene where violence is clearly threatened might be successfully sued by the victim if the aggressor in fact carries through with the threat. (See a related discussion of assaults by one tenant against another tenant in Chapter 14.)

In the meantime, if you fear violence from a cotenant, consider taking the following precautions:

- **Get out of harm's way.** This might mean spending a few days at a motel, shelter, or friend's place, but if you feel seriously threatened, the incon-venience and possible expense of removing yourself from danger will be well worth it. If continuing your cotenancy turns out to be impossible, taking a breather might give you a chance to plan your exit.

- **Contact the local police department, the court clerk's office, or a battered women's shelter for information on obtaining a temporary restraining order.** In most areas, it's fairly quick and easy to bring this type of problem before a judge, without needing to pay a lawyer. And if the judge decides that the situation merits it, the judge will issue an order forbidding the aggressor from coming near you. Temporary restraining orders (TROs)—and how to use them—are explained in Chapter 14.

Safety and Privacy Considerations for Victims

Be sure to consider the privacy of your computer, smartphone, or tablet when seeking help online or over the phone. Some victims might use the same device, network, or phone plan as the abuser, allowing the abuser to see the victim's search or call history or otherwise track their activity.

Many smart devices contain cameras or GPS tracking that can be used to locate and monitor your whereabouts. An abuser can even slip a small tracking device in your car, bag, pocket, or other belongings without your knowledge.

If you're concerned about your privacy while searching online, contact one of several organizations that provide assistance and resources, including the National Domestic Violence Hotline (it can provide you with links to state coalitions against domestic violence) and RAINN (National Sexual Assault Hotline). Another useful resource is WomensLaw.org, which includes extensive information on state laws relevant to domestic violence, sexual assault, and stalking. You can also check out Nolo's Resources for Victims of Crime at Nolo.com (choose Articles on the home page and type the name of the article as it appears above).

If you and other blameless cotenants want to stay, follow our suggestions for bringing in a substitute tenant as explained below in "Adding a New Roommate."

EXAMPLE: Andy and his roommate Bill turned out to be completely incompatible. Before long, arguments about housekeeping, regular guests, and late rent payments by Andy escalated to the point where Bill felt physically threatened. Bill asked their landlord, Anita, to evict Andy. Andy responded by telling Anita that he had never threatened Bill, and that Bill's complaints were a clear illustration of how paranoid and hard to live with he was.

After listening to Andy's and Bill's complaints, Anita referred them to a local mediation service. Both agreed to participate. The mediator's influence worked for a while, but Andy and Bill were soon back to loud, unpleasant shouting matches. After satisfying herself that Andy really had made a series of physical threats, Anita terminated the tenancy as to both of them, on the grounds that their tenancy posed a real danger that one of them would be hurt. The termination made Andy even madder, and Bill sensibly moved in with his girlfriend for a week, until Andy moved out.

Because Bill wanted to live in the rental and could pay the full rent for a while, Anita offered him a month-to-month rental agreement, specifying the full rent. Bill posted a "roommate wanted" notice on a bulletin board at work and eventually found Charlie, who had a solid employment and rental history. After confirming Charlie's qualifications, Anita terminated the brief rental agreement with Bill and wrote a new one, naming Bill and Charlie as cotenants.

Although Bill had ended up paying some of Andy's share of the rent, he decided that his peace of mind and safety were worth more than the money, and did not sue Andy for the debt.

If your living situation has deteriorated to the point that the police have paid you a visit, or you think that they will soon, you might find yourself being asked by police whether they can come in and look around. When the police have a search or arrest warrant, you must let them in (they'll force their way in if you refuse); and they can enter without a warrant if they are in "hot pursuit" of a fleeing criminal, or need to preserve evidence of a serious crime. But if they have no warrant, and no other justification for warrantless entry, and your roommate is present and objects to a proposed search of your home or apartment, your roommate's objection will probably stop the entry (the cops will have to return with a warrant). If your roommate is absent, however, you have the power to consent to the search. (*Georgia v. Randolph*, 547 U.S. 103 (2006).)

When a Roommate Leaves

A cotenant who wants to leave in the middle of a tenancy is legally responsible, if the resident is a month-to-month tenant, for giving the landlord proper written notice and paying rent through the end of the notice period. If there's a lease, the tenant must either get permission from the landlord to leave early or, if this is impossible, find a new tenant (acceptable to the landlord) to take over. If a cotenant simply leaves, the fallout can be serious. Chapter 15 explains in detail the likely consequences to the departing tenant. Here we discuss the predicament of the remaining cotenants.

What to Do If You Want to Stay

The unauthorized departure of a cotenant gives the landlord the option of evicting the rest of you, even if you can pay the full rent. The landlord has this option because breaking the lease or rental agreement is a violation of a key lease term (the length of stay), for which all tenants are liable. (See "Renting a Place With Others," above.)

In practice, however, your landlord will probably let you stay if it will keep a steady stream of rent money coming in and keep the place occupied by stable, nondestructive tenants. So if you pay the rent after a cotenant has broken the lease and left, the landlord will probably not evict you and other tenants unless:

- You are a troublesome tenant, and this is a golden opportunity to be rid of you.
- Your income doesn't appear sufficient to cover the rent in the future. In this case, if you can assure the landlord that you can promptly bring in a good, law-and-lease-abiding new cotenant, you might be able to salvage your tenancy. In the meantime, you might need to ask permission to pay the rent late or in installments. Or, ask the landlord to use the departed tenant's share of the security deposit to help pay the rent until you find an acceptable replacement. See Chapter 3 for ideas on how to approach your landlord.

CAUTION

Always get your landlord's approval before moving in a new roommate. If a cotenant takes off and leaves you facing the entire rent, you might be tempted to simply move in another roommate, bypassing the landlord's application process. Don't! Your lease or rental agreement probably prohibits unauthorized sublets. If it does, bringing in a new tenant—even a great one—without your landlord's okay violates your agreement and gives your landlord a watertight reason to evict you. Instead, keep your relationship on an honest footing and get your landlord's approval for a replacement tenant. "Adding a New Roommate," below, shows how.

How to Deal With a Departing Roommate

Remaining roommates need to cover their legal flanks with respect to the departed tenant as well as the landlord. If your housemate has left during the middle of a lease or without proper notice in a month-to-month tenancy, leaving you responsible for all the rent, your personal relations will be rocky at best. Probably the last thing you want is to have your errant roommate reappear, expecting to move back in.

To avoid such surprises, try to get your former roommate to sign an agreement, making it clear that the departing tenant will do all of the following:

- **Pay a stated amount of rent and utilities.** If you rent under a written rental agreement, this will normally be rent and utilities for 30 days from the date the departing tenant gave written notice (or left without notice) unless a new roommate comes in earlier and covers these costs. If you rent under a lease, the amount owed will depend on when a new cotenant, acceptable to the landlord, is ready to take over. If, despite your best efforts, you cannot find an acceptable replacement, the departing tenant will be liable for the rent for the balance of the lease.
- **Pay for any damage the individual personally caused to the rental unit.** (See the Chapter 16 discussion of how landlords charge for damage. You can apply the same strategy.)
- **Pay for rent and damage no later than a stated date.**
- **Move out for good and give up any claim of being a tenant.**

Chapter 16 discusses what happens to the departing cotenant's security deposit.

But what if you and the departing cotenant can't work things out, and the departed cotenant shows no signs of paying? If your roommate is long gone or out of state, it might be best to grit your teeth, pay the rent owed, and forget it—trying to find, sue, and collect from the former roommate is likely to be more trouble than it's worth.

On the other hand, if your ex-roommate is still in town and has a source of income, consider taking the time to sue in small claims court for unpaid rent, damage to the rental unit, unpaid utilities, and your costs to find a replacement cotenant, such as advertising. Then, if your ex-roommate still doesn't pay up, you can collect what you won in court from the person's bank account or wages. (Landlords often use these methods; see Chapter 16.)

What to Do If You Want to Move Out, Too

If your cotenant skips out, leaving you in the lurch, you might decide that it's not worth the hassle of trying to stay and rustle up another roommate.

To ease your departure and losing your security deposit to make up for unpaid rent, or to avoid having the landlord report you as a deadbeat to the credit bureau, follow these steps:

- If you are a month-to-month tenant, give the required amount of written notice (usually 30 days) immediately. Don't wait until you can't pay the next month's rent and receive a termination notice. (Chapter 15 shows how to give proper notice.)
- If you have a lease, let the landlord know in writing that you plan to move because you cannot afford the rent without your cotenant. Before you move, be extra accommodating when it comes to showing the unit to prospective renters. Facilitating a quick rerental is not just a courtesy to your landlord, but is to your advantage as well, because the sooner a new tenant takes over, the sooner your liability for the balance of the rent due under the lease ends. In addition, do your best to find an acceptable replacement tenant yourself. (See Chapter 15 for an explanation of the landlord's responsibility to look for a new tenant, and "Adding a New Roommate," below, for advice on finding and presenting a replacement.)

Adding a New Roommate

Suppose now that love, poverty, or the desire for some friendly conversation convinces you to add a roommate—or you just need to replace a departing one. Most landlords will insist that the new roommate become a cotenant, having the same rights and responsibilities that you do. This is normally best for you, too, but in a few situations, you might want the newcomer to be a subtenant, who rents from you and has no direct relationship with the landlord. For example, if you want to have the power to evict your new roommate, you'll need to set up a subtenancy. Either way, though, you'll need the consent of the landlord. Here, we explain how to bring the roommate in as a cotenant. "Taking in a Roomer," below, discusses how to sublet to a roomer.

Getting the Landlord's Approval

Obviously, you want to be sure that your new roommate is financially stable and compatible with you.

But even if you satisfy yourself as to your intended cotenant's stellar qualifications, it doesn't mean the landlord will take your word for it. Landlords have their own good-tenant criteria. To increase your chances of getting an official okay, consider these questions before approaching the landlord:

- **Will adding a roommate exceed the occupancy limit?** Landlords are entitled to set reasonable limits on the number of occupants per rental unit. (See Chapter 5.)
- **Will the new roommate meet your landlord's good-tenant criteria?** Many landlords subject prospective tenants to a thorough screening process, checking credit, employment, rental history, and references. Put yourself in your landlord's shoes and find out as much as you can about the person's financial status and rental history. It not only will help assure the landlord's approval, but will also protect you from getting saddled with a deadbeat roommate. Ask your prospective roommate

to request a personal credit report. (See Chapter 1.) If the credit report is good, you'll want to hand it to the landlord with your proposed new tenant's application. Because the landlord will almost surely want to pull the prospect's credit report, doing it first gives you the opportunity to develop a plausible explanation for any negative information— for example, a prior eviction or bankruptcy.

Sample Letter Requesting Permission to Add a Roommate

---

250 Main Street #3A
St. Paul, Minnesota 00000

January 5, 20xx

Barrie Newsome
247 Oakleaf Road
St. Paul, Minnesota 00000

Dear Ms. Newsome,

As you know, I rent a spacious one-bedroom apartment, #3A, at 250 Main Street, St. Paul, Minnesota. I would like to add my friend Mary Mason to my lease, as a cotenant. Mary has just learned that her lease will not be renewed at the end of February because the owners of her flat, where she has lived for five years, have decided to move in themselves.

Mary and I have been friends for years. She works with me in the fulfillment department of Better Graphics, Ltd., and has been there for ten years. Her supervisor, Jim Barton, will be happy to answer any questions you might have, and Mary will be glad to provide a recent copy of her credit report. You can also contact her current and former landlords for references.

I would like to drop by the rental office this week and pick up a rental application for Mary.

Thank you very much for your consideration of my request.

Yours truly,

Tanya Tenant
Tanya Tenant

Unless you are on fairly close personal terms with your landlord, it's usually a good idea to write your landlord a note about your desire to add a roommate. This gives the landlord an unpressured opportunity to think about it. It is also your chance to sell your proposal by pointing out that your rental is big enough for another tenant and, assuming you already have someone lined up, that your new roommate will be a great tenant. A sample letter is shown above.

Adding a Roommate to the Lease or Rental Agreement

If your intended roommate passes the landlord's credit and background checks, the landlord will probably ask both of you to sign a new lease or written month-to-month agreement. From your landlord's point of view, this is far more than a formality, since it makes the new arrival a cotenant who is 100% liable to pay rent and make good on any damage. It's also desirable from your perspective, because it makes it completely clear that your new roommate shares the same legal rights and responsibilities that you do.

More Roommates, More Rent

A landlord who agrees to an additional cotenant might ask for a rent increase, on the theory that more residents means more wear and tear. By signing a new lease or rental agreement, you are in effect starting a new tenancy, so the landlord can increase rent immediately, rather than give you the usual 30 days' notice (for a month-to-month rental agreement) or wait until the lease ends.

Unless your rental unit is covered by rent control—or if the landlord is using a big rent increase as a not-so-subtle way to discriminate against you for an illegal reason (see Chapter 5)—your landlord can ask for as much extra money as the market will bear.

TIP

Negotiate the rent increase. Just because your landlord asks for a big rent increase doesn't mean you have to say yes. One good approach is to counteroffer a lower amount. Let the landlord know that you might rethink adding a roommate, or even move out yourself, if you can't reach an acceptable compromise.

Security Deposit Increases

The landlord also has the legal right to change other conditions of your tenancy when you add a roommate and sign a new agreement. One change that is particularly likely is an increase in the security deposit. However, this is one area where the sky is not the limit, because many states limit the amount of security deposits. Usually the limit is a multiple of the monthly rent. (See "State Security Deposit Rules" in Appendix A.) Keep in mind that if the deposit is already at the maximum, but the landlord raises the rent for the new occupant, the maximum security deposit goes up, too.

Guests

You should always be clear with your roommates regarding how you feel about overnight guests, whether you have a written roommate agreement (as we recommend early in this chapter) or you just discuss the subject before you move in. You might not be happy about your roommate's friend staying over every night and hogging up the shower in the morning; and you certainly might not want your roommate renting out your place on Airbnb during winter break (issues regarding Airbnb are discussed in the following section).

Tenant Rights to Use Airbnb and Similar Vacation Rental Services

You might be tempted to earn some extra cash by renting out your apartment on a short-term basis though websites such as Airbnb, Vrbo, or FlipKey. Doing so, however, might result in the landlord filing an eviction lawsuit against you. Here are some things you should do before engaging in short-term hosting.

Read Your Lease or Rental Agreement

As discussed in Chapter 2, your lease likely prohibits sublets without your landlord's prior written consent (and might even specifically forbid your use of short-term rental services). If you violate a no-sublets provision, or a lease clause limiting guest stays, your landlord may terminate your rental and, if you refuse to move, evict you.

Work Something Out With Your Landlord

Most renters who do short-term hosting on sites such as Airbnb never tell their landlords about it (especially if their landlord lives out of town and rarely stops by the rental). But if the neighbors complain or the landlord otherwise discovers what you're doing, you could be in trouble. Instead of taking this chance, consider asking your landlord's permission before you list your apartment on Airbnb or another short-term hosting site. Offering to split with your landlord part of the money you earn, or pay more rent, might seal the deal.

There are other things you can do to make your landlord more amenable to your short-term hosting, such as:

- promise to have paying guests only on an occasional basis, rather than all the time
- carefully screen your guests, and
- rent out only a portion of your apartment, rather than the entire unit, and agree to be present to deal with the guests (and limit problems with neighbors).

If you do get your landlord's permission to short-term host, be sure to summarize your agreement in writing.

If you don't have it already, you should also obtain renters' insurance (discussed in Chapter 2) with plenty of liability coverage. That said, having renters' insurance might not, in the end, cover you if a paying "guest" causes damage. The insurance company might claim that its coverage extends only to damage caused by you and your true guests, not damage caused by a paying occupant. And be forewarned: If you approach your insurance company proactively, asking whether they will cover you for your short-term rentals, the insurance company might respond by canceling your policy outright, adding an expensive rider, or telling you that you need a separate policy.

If your landlord won't agree to permit you to short-term host, don't do it. The extra money you might earn likely won't make up for getting evicted.

Research Your Local Zoning or Land Use Laws

Many cities restrict or prohibit short-term rental hosting (by setting maximum days per year for short-term rentals, requiring the host to be present, restricting such activities to specified neighborhoods, and so on). If short-term rentals are regulated where you live, unless you can comply with the restrictions, forget about it—even if it's okay with your landlord.

Taking in a Roomer

You might be reluctant to completely share your home with a roommate, but want someone to share costs of your rental. The solution might be to take in a roomer as a "subtenant," making it clear that this person is not a full-fledged cotenant.

When you take in a subtenant, you're that person's landlord. We suggest that you sign a month-to-month rental agreement, specifying rent and any restrictions on the roomer's use of your home. And although your roomer doesn't sign the rental document you have with your landlord, the roomer must comply with its rules as well as yours. Think of the arrangement as a set of nesting dolls: You live within your landlord's rules and regulations, and your subtenant lives within yours. So if your landlord prohibits using the pool after 10 p.m., you can't promise your roomer the joy of midnight swims.

The main advantage of making your roomer a subtenant instead of a cotenant is that it gives you the legal right to terminate the roomer's tenancy if things don't work out as planned. By contrast, you can't end the tenancy of a roommate who is a full-fledged cotenant—only the landlord can do this.

Don't get too enthusiastic about bringing someone in as a roomer without first talking with your landlord. You'll need your landlord's approval to create a subtenancy—and many landlords would rather not. Even if your landlord gives approval, you might have problems getting a roomer out.

You'll probably have to follow the same procedures all landlords use to terminate a tenancy.

For more on the pros and cons of subtenancies, see the discussion of subletting in Chapter 15.

 CAUTION

The New York Roommate Law is special.
Tenants in New York enjoy the benefits of its Roommate Law (N.Y. Real Prop. Law § 235(f)), which gives tenants the right to bring in specified roommates, subject only to local laws on overcrowding.

Major Repairs and Maintenance

In every state, you are legally entitled to rental property that is in good repair and that meets basic structural, health, and safety standards. When your rental doesn't meet these basic requirements, you might have the legal right to:

- withhold rent
- pay for repairs yourself and deduct the cost from the rent
- sue the landlord, or
- move out without notice.

This chapter describes your right to a safe and livable home that provides you with basic necessities. It also provides practical advice on how to get a reluctant landlord to perform needed repairs. Less important maintenance and repair issues—such as unclogging kitchen drains or mowing the front lawn—are covered in the next chapter.

 RELATED TOPIC
Also covered in this book:

- How to be sure your lease or rental agreement has clear provisions on repair and maintenance: Chapter 2.
- How to use a Landlord-Tenant Checklist to keep track of the condition of the premises before and after you move in: Chapter 6.
- Landlord's responsibility for minor repairs such as small plumbing jobs: Chapter 9.
- How to make improvements or alterations to your rental unit without violating your lease or rental agreement or donating improvements to the landlord: Chapter 10.
- Landlord's liability for injuries caused by defective housing conditions: Chapter 12.
- Landlord's liability for cleaning up environmental hazards, such as asbestos and lead: Chapter 13.
- Landlord's responsibility to provide safe, reasonably crime-free rental housing: Chapter 14.

Your Basic Right to Livable Premises

Landlords are legally required to offer livable premises when they originally rent a unit and throughout the tenancy. In legal terminology, this duty has the lofty-sounding name "the implied warranty of habitability."

The vast majority of tenants have the right to a decent place to live even if their rental didn't meet habitability standards at move-in, and even if the lease states that the landlord doesn't have to provide a habitable unit. In a rare showing of unanimity, almost all courts have rejected landlords' attempts to enforce sleazy tenant "waivers" and landlord "disclaimers." Except for a handful of states in very limited circumstances (including Florida, Maine, and Texas), neither a tenant waiver (at the beginning of the tenancy or during its life) nor a disclaimer in the lease will relieve the landlord of the responsibility to provide housing that begins—and remains—fit and habitable.

The landlord's responsibility to provide habitable housing includes:

- keeping structural elements of the building, including floors, stairs, walls, and roofs, safe and intact
- maintaining all common areas, such as hallways and stairways
- keeping electrical, plumbing, sanitary, heating, ventilating, and air-conditioning systems and elevators operating safely
- supplying cold and hot water and heat in reasonable amounts at reasonable times
- providing trash receptacles and arranging for their removal, and
- exterminating infestations of rodents and other vermin.

In some states, building codes alone define what it means for housing to be habitable, while in others, court decisions define the concept. And in still other states, both apply. It can be important for you to know which source (building codes, court decisions, or both) is the basis for the implied warranty of habitability in your state: The source of the warranty might define the landlord's responsibilities and determine your options when the landlord does not comply.

State Laws and Local Housing Codes

Your landlord must comply with state and local building and housing laws. This section explains what these laws typically require of a landlord; if yours runs afoul of them, see the discussions below, for what to do.

Local Ordinances

City or county building or housing codes regulate structural aspects of buildings and usually set space and occupancy standards, such as the minimum size of sleeping rooms. They also establish minimum requirements for light and ventilation, sanitation and sewage disposal, heating, water supply (such as how hot the water must be), fire protection, and wiring (such as the number of electrical outlets per room). In addition, housing codes typically make property owners responsible for keeping hallways, lobbies, elevators, and the other parts of the premises the owner controls clean, sanitary, and safe.

Your local building or housing authority, and health or fire department, might have an informational booklet that describes the exact requirements your landlord must meet. In most urban areas, these local codes are more thorough than the state's general housing law—for example, many cities require landlords to install smoke detectors and some security items, such as dead bolt locks and peepholes, in exterior doors. However, local laws usually don't explain what you can do—withhold rent, for example—if your landlord fails to comply. To find out, you'll need to consult your state's general housing law.

Most local housing codes also have a catch-all provision that prohibits something called "nuisances." A nuisance is a situation that is dangerous to human life, detrimental to health, or morally offensive and obnoxious—for example, overcrowding a room with occupants, providing insufficient ventilation or illumination, inadequate sewage or plumbing facilities, permitting illegal activities, or allowing excessive noise or commotion, making it impossible to use or enjoy one's property. Drug use and dealing on the premises is also a legal nuisance.

Exemptions for Older Buildings

When a new housing code is adopted, or an old one changed, it doesn't necessarily mean that all existing buildings are illegal because they are not "up to code." Especially when it comes to items that would involve major structural changes, lawmakers will often exempt older buildings by writing a "grandfather clause" into the code, exempting all buildings constructed before a certain date. Typically, however, a landlord who later undertakes major renovations or remodeling must comply with the new rules. If you suspect that major work is being planned or done without bringing the building up to code, contact your local housing department. If you fear landlord retaliation, do so anonymously, if possible. (Tenants' protections against retaliatory conduct are discussed in Chapter 15.) Other new code requirements that are easy and inexpensive to make—for example, installing locks, peepholes, or smoke detectors—must be made regardless of the age of the building.

State Housing Laws

If you live in an urban area covered by a detailed building or housing code, statewide housing code won't be as relevant—on topics where state and local law overlap, your landlord will need to follow the stricter local codes. However, if you live in a small town or rural area not covered by a detailed building code, your state's housing law will dictate what your landlord must do to keep your rental habitable. Some states have detailed laws—for example, requiring certain kinds of locks.

To find out whether your state has statutes that pertain to the maintenance of your rental, follow these steps:

- Refer to "State Landlord-Tenant Statutes" in Appendix A. (See Chapter 20 for information on how to access your state and local statutes online.)
- Check out the laws that apply to you in more detail by looking in the index to your state's statutes for subentries under "Landlord-Tenant" such as "Landlord Obligations to Maintain Premises," "Repairs," and "Duty to Maintain."
- Contact your state consumer protection agency to see if it publishes pamphlets or brochures that describe landlords' repair and maintenance responsibilities in less legalistic terms. (For a list of state consumer protection agencies, see www.usa.gov/state-consumer.)

Court-Imposed Rules

In many states, your right to habitable housing doesn't depend on only a state or local housing code. In these states, housing must be up to code *and* "fit for human occupation" or "fit and habitable." While a serious housing code violation will almost always qualify as a breach of the warranty of habitability, other shortfalls will constitute a violation of the warranty, too. This means that if your locality has nonexistent or poorly written housing codes, a judge could still find that your landlord breached the warranty because, in the judge's opinion, the premises are not fit for human habitation. And even if local housing or building codes apply, a court might require stricter standards than the codes.

In evaluating whether a landlord is providing habitable housing, courts can consider unique characteristics of the rental property, such as the weather conditions it experiences, the terrain, and its general location and neighborhood. Features or services that might be considered nonessential extras in some parts of the country are absolutely necessary

components of habitable housing in others. For example, in climates with severe winters, storm windows might be considered basic features.

Finally, keep in mind that how courts interpret "habitable housing" fluctuates based on changes in living conditions and technology. For example, courts consider the prevalence of crime in urban areas when determining what constitutes habitable housing. Good locks, security personnel, exterior lighting, and secure common areas are now considered, in some cities, to be as important to tenants as are water and heat. (Chapter 14 discusses your rights to adequate security measures.)

Your Repair and Maintenance Responsibilities

Your landlord isn't the only one responsible for keeping the rental clean and safe. State and local housing laws generally require you as a tenant to:

Dispose of garbage, rubbish, and other waste in a clean and safe manner. For instance, if mice or ants invaded your kitchen because you forgot to take out the garbage before you left on a two-week vacation, you would be responsible for paying any necessary extermination costs.

Keep plumbing fixtures as clean as their condition permits. For example, bathtub caulking that has sprouted mold and mildew might render the tub unusable. Because it could have been prevented by proper cleaning, you are responsible for cleanup and repairs necessary to get the tub back in working condition. On the other hand, if the bathroom has no fan and the window has been painted shut, the bathroom will be hard to air out; resulting mildew might be your landlord's responsibility.

Use electrical, plumbing, sanitary, heating, ventilating, air-conditioning, and other facilities and other systems, including elevators, properly. Examples of abuse by tenants include overloading electrical outlets and flushing large objects down the toilet.

Fix things you break or damage. If you cause a serious habitability problem in your unit—for example, you carelessly break the heater—you are responsible.

You can't avoid responsibility by just deciding to live without heat for a while to save money. If you drag your feet, the landlord can use your security deposit to pay for it, and if that isn't enough, sue you for the remaining uncovered expenses. Your landlord can't, however, charge you for problems caused by normal wear and tear—for example, to replace a carpet that has worn out from use. (Chapter 16 discusses the difference between normal wear and tear and damage.)

Making Tenants Responsible for Repairs

Your landlord may legally delegate some repair and maintenance responsibilities to you, typically in exchange for less rent. Landlords cannot, however, force tenants to give up their rights to habitable housing.

Landlords rarely give tenants responsibility for major repair and maintenance duties (such as roof repairs and other structural work), because most tenants don't have the time, skill, or interest to devote to extensive construction. (Taking on responsibility for minor repairs and maintenance is discussed in Chapter 9.) In addition, many states have rules regarding the types of repairs that landlords can delegate to tenants and unlicensed contractors.

The picture is often different, however, when you rent a single-family residence. In several states, the landlord and tenant may agree in writing that the tenant will perform some of the landlord's legal duties—for example, arranging for garbage disposal, plumbing, heating, or other specified repairs. (In other states, agreements like this are void.) States allowing this arrangement typically require that each side completely understands their rights and responsibilities and that neither pressures the other (otherwise, a court won't enforce the agreement).

Damage Caused by Criminals

If a burglar breaks into your home, smashing the cupboards and generally making a mess, who pays? Usually, the landlord, as long as your carelessness (failing to lock a window, for example) didn't facilitate the intruder's entry. If you were careless, are you 100% liable for the damage? Theoretically, no, because the criminal also contributed to the damage. But it's very unlikely that a jury would be asked to apportion responsibility between the two of you. More likely, your landlord will demand payment and, if you have renters' insurance, you could try to get it to cover at least some of the cost. If you don't have renters' insurance, expect the landlord to use your security deposit and demand that you swiftly replenish that.

Carelessness is not the only way you might be liable for a criminal's acts. For example, if you and your landlord agree that you will maintain the doors and windows in your single-family rental and you fail to do so, you might be held partially liable for the burglar's damage. And if the criminal happens to be someone whom you have let into the building, a jury will almost surely hold you at least partly responsible if they conclude that you knew or should have known that a criminal incident was likely.

How to Get Your Landlord to Act

Knowing that you have a legal right to habitable housing doesn't guarantee you'll get it. Here are some tips to maximize your chances of getting your landlord to respond promptly to your repair requests.

Read Your Lease or Rental Agreement

Read your lease or rental agreement to find out if it lays out a required method for making repair requests—and follow it. For example, many institutional landlords require tenants to make repair requests through an online portal. Or, your landlord might require you to text about repairs that need immediate attention. Follow the instructions in the lease or rental agreement, but also keep a separate written record of when (and how) you made the request. It also doesn't hurt to send an additional request in writing—and you absolutely should follow up in writing if your landlord ignores your request.

Put Repair Requests in Writing

If your lease or rental agreement is silent on how you must request repairs, the best approach is to put every repair and maintenance request in writing, keeping a copy for your files. You might want to call first, but be sure to follow up with a written request. (Send your letter certified, "return receipt requested," to confirm delivery.)

Written communications to your landlord are important because they:

- are far more likely to be taken seriously than face-to-face conversations or phone calls, because it's clear to the landlord you're keeping a record of your requests
- are less likely to be forgotten or misunderstood
- satisfy the legal requirement that you give your landlord a reasonable opportunity to fix a problem before you withhold rent or exercise other legal rights (see below), and
- serve as potential evidence in case you ever need to prove that the serious problems with your unit were the subject of repeated repair requests.

In Chapter 6, the section "Using Email or Text Messages for Notice or a Letter of Understanding" explains why it's best to send important communications, such as repair requests, by mail or delivery service, rather than by email or text message.

In your repair request, be as specific as possible regarding the problem, how it's affecting your ability to live in your rental, what you want done and when. For example, if the thermostat on your heater is always finicky and often doesn't function at all, explain that you have been without heat during the last two days during which the nighttime low was below freezing—don't simply say "the heater needs to be fixed." If the problem poses a health or safety threat, such as a broken front door lock or loose step, say so and ask for it to be fixed immediately. Competent landlords will respond extra quickly to genuinely dangerous (as opposed to merely inconvenient) situations. Finally, be sure to note the date of the request and how many requests, if any, have preceded this one. For more tips on writing a persuasive repair request, see Chapter 9.

Sample Request for Repair or Maintenance

TO: Kay Sera, Landlord
        Stately View Apartments

FROM: Will Tripp
        376 Seventh Avenue
        Apartment No. 45
        Brighton, New Jersey 00000

RE: Roof leak

DATE: March 10, 20xx

As I mentioned to you on the phone yesterday, on March 9, 20xx, I noticed dark stains on the ceilings of the upstairs bedroom and bath. These stains are moist and appear to be the result of the recent heavy rains. I would very much appreciate it if you would promptly look into the apparent roof leak. If the leak continues, my property might be damaged and two rooms might become unusable. Please email or call me so that I'll know when to expect you or a repairperson. You can reach me at work during the day (555-1234) or at home at night (555-4546). My email is wtrip@tripp.com.

Thank you very much for your attention to this problem. I expect to hear from you within the next few days, and expect that the situation will be corrected within a couple of weeks.

Yours truly,

Will Tripp

Will Tripp

If your landlord provides a repair request form, use it. If not, create your own. (See the sample shown above.) Always make a copy of your request and keep it in a safe place in your files.

CAUTION

In dangerous situations, you must take precautions, too. Once you're aware of a dangerous situation, you must take reasonable steps to avoid injury. For example, don't continue to use the outlet when you see sparks fly from the wall; don't park in the garage at night if the lights are burned out and there is a safer alternative. If you don't take reasonable care and are injured and sue the landlord, you can expect a judge or jury to hold the landlord only partially responsible. (See Chapter 12.)

Deliver Your Repair Request to the Landlord

If your landlord has an on-site office or a resident manager, deliver your repair request personally. If you mail it, consider sending it certified (return receipt requested), or use a delivery service that will give you a receipt establishing delivery. If you email your request, ask for a call (or a return email) acknowledging receipt (but understand that if the landlord doesn't comply, you'll have no proof of receipt).

- It will get the landlord's attention and highlight the fact that you are serious about your request.
- The signed receipt is evidence that the landlord did, in fact, receive the letter. You might need this in the event that the landlord fails to make the repair and you decide to do it yourself or withhold rent. If a dispute arises as to your right to use a self-help measure, you'll be able to prove in court that you satisfied the legal requirement of notifying the landlord first.

If your first request doesn't produce results—or at least a call or note from the landlord telling you when repairs will be made—send another. Mention that this is the second (or third) time you have brought the matter to the landlord's attention. If the problem is getting worse, emphasize this fact. And, of course, be sure to keep a record of all repair requests.

Keep Notes on All Conversations and Copies of All Emails

Besides keeping a copy of every written repair request, don't neglect to keep a record of oral communications, too. If the landlord calls you in response to your repair request, make notes during the conversation or immediately afterward; write down the date and time that the conversation occurred and when you made your notes. These notes might come in handy to refresh your memory and help you reconstruct the history of your case. In most states, if a dispute ends up in court, and you are unable to remember the details of the conversation, your notes can be introduced in court to fill the gap.

You can keep track of other kinds of communications, too. For example, if your dealings with your landlord are accomplished online, simply print out each message. But keep in mind that email does not provide the type of legal proof that you'd get with a written communication sent certified mail or return receipt requested. See "Using Email or Text Messages for Notice or a Letter of Understanding" in Chapter 6 for details.

CAUTION

Think twice before taping telephone conversations. Many tenants are tempted to tape phone conversations with their landlords or managers, figuring that this is one sure-fire way to preserve evidence of a promise to repair. Under federal law (18 U.S.C. § 2511), some phone conversations can be taped with the consent of one party (that would be you), but laws in many states require the consent of all parties before a conversation can be recorded. Penalties include fines and, in some instances, jail time. While it is unlikely that a one-time offender will be prosecuted, it is likely that this illegal conduct will weaken your case should you wind up in court defending your use of a tenant repair option.

Sample Letter of Understanding Regarding Repairs

1234 Appian Way, #3
Bloom City, Indiana 00000

September 3, 20xx

Ms. Iona Lott, Landlord
100 Civic Center Drive
Bloom City, Indiana 00000

Dear Ms. Lott,

Thank you for calling me yesterday, September 2, 20xx, regarding my request for repairs, dated August 27, 20xx. In that request, I told you that the hot water in my unit is very hot (123° F. on my thermometer), even though the temperature gauge on the water heater is turned down as far as it can go. I am concerned that my young daughter might be injured by this scalding water, and am anxious that the temperature be lowered as soon as possible.

As I understand it, you agreed to have Ralph, your handyman, come check the problem on Saturday morning, September 6, between 9 and 10 a.m. Ralph will bring along a new thermostat should he need to replace the old one.

Please let me know if your recollection of our conversation and plans differs from mine.

Yours truly,

Howard Hillman

Howard Hillman

Put the Landlord's Promises in Writing

If you and your landlord agree on a plan of action, it's wise to write down your understanding of this agreement. Send a copy to the landlord, inviting a reply if the landlord thinks that you have missed or misstated anything.

If you don't get a response, the law presumes that the landlord agreed with your version of the conversation. See the sample Letter of Understanding Regarding Repairs, above.

What to Do If the Landlord Won't Make Repairs

If your persistent and businesslike requests for repairs are ignored, you can take stronger measures. Your options will probably include one or more of what we call the "big sticks" in a tenant's self-help arsenal. (See "State Laws on Rent Withholding and Repair and Deduct Remedies," in Appendix A.) These remedies include:

- calling state or local building or health inspectors
- withholding the rent (if allowed by your state law)
- repairing the problem (or having it repaired by a professional) and deducting the cost from your rent (if allowed by your state law)
- moving out, or
- paying the rent and then suing the landlord for the difference between the rent you paid and the value of the defective premises.

If the landlord hasn't fixed a serious problem that makes your rental unit truly uninhabitable—rats in the kitchen, for example—you will want to take fast action. But not every case is so clear-cut. Before you withhold rent, move out, or adopt another extreme remedy, make sure every one of these conditions is met:

- **The problem is serious, not just annoying, and imperils your health or safety.** Not every building code violation or annoying defect in your rental home (like your water heater's ability to reach only 107° F, short of the code-specified 110°) justifies use of a "big stick" against the landlord.

- **You (or a guest) did not cause the problem, either deliberately or through carelessness or neglect.** If so, you can't pursue the self-help options.
- **You told the landlord about the problem and provided a reasonable opportunity to get it fixed, or provided the minimum amount of notice required by state law.** You can't use big-stick options without first informing the landlord of the problem and providing a chance to fix the problem. You'll need to check your state's law for the exact requirements for the option you are pursuing.
- **You are willing to risk termination of your tenancy by an annoyed landlord.** Exercising any of the rights discussed here will not endear you to your landlord. Many states forbid your landlord from retaliating against you by raising the rent or terminating your tenancy, but, unfortunately, some states don't. If your lease is about to run out (or you're a month-to-month tenant) and your state does not protect you from retaliatory rent increases or evictions, a complaint to health inspectors or use of a self-help big stick could end up causing you to lose your rental. (Chapter 15 discusses retaliation and gives information on state laws.)
- **You are willing to risk eviction if a judge decides that you shouldn't have used the big stick, and your credit report can bear this negative mark.** Even if you're sure that you were justified in using a big stick, a judge might decide otherwise. For example, if you withhold rent, the landlord could sue to evict you based on nonpayment of rent. In most states and in most situations, you'll have a second chance to pay the balance before being sued for eviction, but not always. (See Chapter 17.) For some tenants, additional negative marks on their credit records will cause extremely serious problems for future rentals, loans, and employment.

- **If you move out, either voluntarily or because the building is closed due to code violations you have reported, you can find a comparable or better unit.** In some states, landlords whose buildings are closed due to code violations must help their tenants with relocation expenses.

TIP

Before doing repairs yourself, withholding rent, or using another "big stick," make sure you have proof of how bad the problem was. One good approach is to take pictures or a video of the problem; another is to have witnesses. Also consider asking an experienced and impartial contractor or repairperson to examine the situation and give you a written description of the problem and estimate for repair. Be sure the description is signed and dated.

Reporting Code Violations to Housing Inspectors

Local building, health, or fire department inspectors discover code violations, such as hazardous electrical wiring or a leaking roof, in various ways. A tenant complaint could trigger an inspection, as could a change in property ownership or financing—for example, if the owner takes out a new loan. Code violations can also be discovered through routine inspections (discussed in Chapter 11).

After discovering a code violation, the housing inspector will give the owner an order to correct the problem. Fines and penalties usually follow if the owner fails to comply within a certain amount of time (often 5 to 30 business days). After that, the city or county might sue the landlord. In many cities, a landlord's failure to promptly fix cited violations of local housing laws is a misdemeanor (minor crime) punishable by hefty fines or even imprisonment. In rare cases, especially if tenants' health is imperiled, local officials might even require that the building be vacated.

If You Must Move Because of Building Code Violations

If a judge decides that a building's condition substantially endangers the health and safety of its tenants, and repairs are so extensive they can't be made while tenants inhabit the building, the judge might order all residents to move out. You usually won't have a chance to come to the court hearing to object to this dire consequence—you'll simply be told to get out, sometimes within hours.

In some states, the landlord must pay your rent in comparable temporary housing nearby. Some statutes also make the landlord cover moving expenses and utility connection charges and give you the first chance to move back in when the repairs are completed. In other states, however, you might be on your own, which explains why tenants are often reluctant to call the inspectors.

If you're tempted to call the inspectors for major habitability problems, it might be wise to find out whether you can get relocation assistance if the building is closed. There's nothing to prevent you from calling the housing department for your city or state and simply asking, without registering a complaint. Or, you can check your state statutes (listed in "State Landlord-Tenant Statutes" in Appendix A). Look in the index to your state's codes, under "Landlord-Tenant," for subheadings such as "Relocation Assistance" or "Padlock Orders." (See Chapter 20 for general advice on doing legal research.)

In many areas, reporting a landlord to a building inspector is a very big deal—an inspector who finds lots of problems can force the landlord to clear them up immediately. But the effectiveness of building inspectors varies widely. Some cities have woefully few inspectors compared to the number of tenant complaints, and courts are largely unable to follow up on the properties that are cited.

Withholding the Rent

If you conclude that your landlord has not met the responsibility of keeping your unit livable, state law might allow you to stop paying any rent to the landlord until the repairs are made. This is called rent withholding. Many states allow rent withholding under statutory law or a past court decision. See "State Laws on Rent Withholding and Repair and Deduct Remedies" in Appendix A.

The term "withholding" is actually a bit misleading, because in most states and cities you can't simply keep the rent money until your landlord fixes the problem. Instead, you have to deposit the withheld rent with the court or a neutral third party or escrow account set up by a local court or housing agency until the repairs are accomplished. (Even if your statute doesn't require it, it's a good idea to escrow the rent yourself, as explained below.)

Before you can properly withhold the rent, three requirements must be met:

- The lack of maintenance or repair has made your dwelling unlivable.
- The problems were not caused by you or your guest, either deliberately or through neglect.
- You told the landlord about the problem and provided a reasonable time to fix it, or the minimum amount required by state law.

In addition, under most rent withholding laws, you cannot withhold rent if you are behind in the rent or in violation of an important lease clause. In short, you need to be squeaky clean.

The Consequences of Withholding Rent

When your rent check fails to arrive, your landlord's response probably will be to terminate your tenancy for nonpayment of rent and file for eviction if you don't move voluntarily.

If you have met the requirements explained above and have carefully followed the procedures set out in your rent withholding statute, you'll have a good defense to the eviction lawsuit.

You might feel confident enough to head into court without a lawyer, or you might want to consult with an attorney first. If you have improperly used the remedy (for a minor repair, for example), you'll be evicted. Because of the possibility of this dire consequence, it's crucial to understand your rent withholding law and use it appropriately.

How to Withhold Rent

Here are the steps to follow when considering whether to withhold rent.

Step 1: Research the law.

If rent withholding is allowed in your state, the statute will be listed in Appendix A. Also, check if any local laws apply. In a few localities subject to rent control, the remedy might be part of your local ordinance. In either case, read the law to find out:

- what circumstances justify rent withholding
- whether you must give the landlord a certain amount of time to fix the defect (10 to 30 days' notice is typical), or whether the notice and response time must simply be "reasonable" under the circumstances, and
- whether you must place the unpaid rent in a separate bank account or deposit it with a court or local housing agency, and how this is done.

We explain how to find and look up your state's law in Chapter 20.

Illegal Lease Clauses: Your Landlord Can't Limit Your Right to Withhold the Rent Under State Law

Some leases and rental agreements attempt to prohibit a tenant from withholding the rent, even when a property is uninhabitable. In many states, the rent withholding law itself makes such a clause illegal. But even where a state statute or court decision doesn't specifically prohibit these clauses, courts often don't uphold them. Why? Because a judge will approve your supposed waiver of your right to withhold rent only if your "waiver" has been the subject of real negotiations between you and the landlord—not something the landlord insisted upon without your input. Considering that most leases are preprinted forms that landlords present to tenants in a take-it-or-leave-it situation, a judge is likely to decide that the so-called "waiver" was not negotiated and is invalid.

Step 2: Notify your landlord.

Give your landlord written notice of the problem and your intent to withhold rent. A sample letter is shown below. Refer to the state or local law that allows withholding and include a copy of it. We recommend including a proposal that if for any reason your landlord disagrees that repairs are needed, you quickly mediate the dispute. (Chapter 19 discusses mediation services.) Send the letter "return receipt requested."

Step 3: Collect evidence.

As soon as you decide to withhold rent, prepare to defend yourself against an eviction lawsuit. You'll need to prove to the judge that the problem is serious and that you complied with the notice requirements of the rent withholding law. Keep copies of all correspondence with the landlord, plus photographs or video of the problem. Consider other ways (besides your own testimony) you can prove that the problem was real and serious. For example, if you're dealing with a broken furnace in winter, print out the local weather report for each day you didn't have heat. Get an estimate from a heating repairperson that corroborates the fact that the heater doesn't work. And because evictions are usually handled in a regular trial court, which has stricter rules of evidence than small claims court, you cannot simply present a repairperson's written description of the problem. The repairperson would have to appear in court and testify about the condition of the repair job. Introducing evidence is covered in detail in "Rules of Evidence in Formal Court" in Chapter 18.

Step 4: Repeat your request for repairs.

If the landlord hasn't responded satisfactorily to your first letter, give the landlord one last deadline—say, 48 hours or whatever period you feel is reasonable under the circumstances.

Step 5: File any court papers.

Under some state laws, you must ask a local court for permission to withhold rent, provide compelling reasons why your rental is not livable, and follow procedures. This process usually isn't difficult and doesn't require the use of a lawyer. You can get the necessary information and forms from the court or local housing department.

Step 6: Deposit your rent in escrow.

In some states, you will have to deposit your rent with the specified local court or housing agency or in a separate bank account. Some states do not require a separate escrow account.

Sample Letter Telling the Landlord You Intend to Withhold Rent

58 Coral Shores, #37
Sandy Bay, FL 00000
407-555-5632

August 5, 20xx

Mr. Roy Hernandez
3200 Harbor Drive
Sandy Bay, FL 00000

Dear Mr. Hernandez:

My family and I are your tenants at the above address. As you know, I called you on August 3 to report that the front porch has collapsed from dry rot at the top of the stairs, making it impossible to enter the flat except by the back door. You assured me that you would send a contractor the next day. No one came on August 4.

Under Florida Statutes Section 83.51(b), you are responsible for keeping the porch in good repair. Florida law gives tenants the right to withhold rent if you fail to do so and the condition is serious (Florida Stat. § 83.201). Tenants may begin withholding rent if the landlord, after receiving 20 days' notice, fails to fix the problem.

By hand-delivering this notice to you today, August 5, I am giving you the notice as required by law. If the porch is not repaired by August 25, I will withhold rent until it is.

Yours truly,

Alicia Sanchez

Alicia Sanchez

Enclosure: Florida Statutes Sections 83.51 & 83.201

Even if your statute doesn't require that you deposit the withheld rent into an escrow account held by a neutral third party, do so anyway. This will dispel any suggestion that you are withholding rent simply in order to avoid paying it.

If a court or housing department isn't set up to handle withheld rent, try asking a mediation service if it will establish an account for this purpose. Any attorney you might hire will also have a "trust account" in which the money can be held. Alternatively, you can set up a separate bank account of your own and use it only for withheld rent.

If you must pay for any of these services, you can ask the court to order the landlord to reimburse you if the landlord brings an eviction action.

What Happens to the Withheld Rent

If the rent money is being held by a court or housing authority, landlords can sometimes ask for release of some of the withheld rent to pay for repairs. While repairs are being made, you might continue to pay the entire rent to the court or housing authority, or you might be directed to pay some rent to the landlord and the balance to the court or housing authority.

When the dwelling is certified as fit by the local housing authorities or the court, any money in the account is returned to the landlord, minus court costs and inspection fees.

If your withholding law doesn't require you to escrow the rent and a court hasn't been involved, you and the landlord will make your own arrangements as to the distribution of the money. Your landlord will probably expect full payment of the withheld rent once the repairs are complete. If you don't pay up, you can expect your landlord to file an eviction lawsuit for nonpayment of rent.

Depending on your state's law, whether a court is involved, the severity of the repair problem, and your landlord's willingness to negotiate, you could seek compensation for the time you have spent living in a substandard home. One option is to ask for a retroactive reduction in rent, starting from the time that the premises became uninhabitable. (Some states will limit you to a reduction starting from the time you notified the landlord of the problem.) Reducing the rent is known in legalese as rent "abatement."

A court might order a retroactive rent abatement, or you might be able to negotiate one with your landlord. The following section describes how a judge will determine how much the landlord should compensate you for the inconvenience of having lived in a substandard rental unit. If a court is not involved, you and the landlord can use one of these methods.

Determining the Value of a Defective Rental Unit

Judges typically use one of two following ways to determine the difference between the withheld rent and what a defective, unlivable unit was really worth:

Figuring the market value. Under this approach, all you owe the landlord is the fair market value of the premises in its defective condition. For example, if an apartment with a broken heater normally rented for $1,200 per month but was worth only $600 without operable heating, the landlord would be entitled to only $600 per month from the escrowed funds. Of course, the difficulty with this approach—as with many things in law—is that it is staggeringly unrealistic. An apartment with no heat in winter has *no* market value, because no one would rent it. This approach works better when the defect doesn't render the unit unmarketable. For example, when one of two bathrooms becomes unusable, the rental's market value becomes equal to that of a one-, not two-bathroom rental.

By percentage reduction. Another approach is to identify what part of the unit is affected by the defect, and then calculate the percentage of the rent attributable to that part. For example, if the roof leaked into the living room of your apartment, rendering the room unusable, you could reduce the rent by the percentage of the rent attributable to the living room.

Although you could calculate the proportion of rent based off of square footage, if the living room was the main living space and the other rooms were too small to live in comfortably, the percentage of loss would be much greater than it would be in more spacious apartments. Obviously, this approach is far from an exact science, too.

We recommend you use both methods to calculate the unit's reduced, real value. Sometimes, the calculations will be simple—for example, using the fair market value approach, if a broken air conditioner turns your flat into an oven, its rental value can be determined by consulting ads for non–air-conditioned flats in your area. The percentage reduction method might, in some situations, yield a lower rental value. After you've used both methods, ask the judge to adopt the lower figure and to rule that the landlord is entitled only to that amount of rent per month, times the number of months that you endured the substandard conditions. The difference between the full rent and the realistic rent should go to you.

> **EXAMPLE:** When Henry and Sue moved into their apartment, it was neat and well-maintained. Soon after, the building was sold to an out-of-state owner, who hired an off-site manager to handle repairs and maintenance. Gradually, the premises began to deteriorate. At the beginning of May, 15 months into their 2-year lease, Henry and Sue could count several violations of the building code, including the landlord's failure to maintain the common areas, remove the garbage promptly, and fix a broken water heater.
>
> Henry and Sue sent numerous requests for repairs to their landlord over a two-month period, during which they gritted their teeth and put up with the situation. Finally they had enough and checked out their state's rent withholding law. They learned a tenant could pay rent into an escrow account set up by their local court. Henry and Sue went ahead and deposited their rent into this account.

In response, Henry and Sue's landlord filed an eviction lawsuit. In their defense, Henry and Sue pointed to the numerous code and habitability violations. The court agreed with the couple, did not allow the eviction, and ordered the following:

- During the time that they lived in these uninhabitable conditions, Henry and Sue were not required to pay full rent. Using the "market value" approach, the court decided that their defective rental was worth half its stated rent. Accordingly, since the landlord owed them a refund for portions of their rent for May and June, Henry and Sue would be paid this amount from the escrow account.

- The balance of the rent in the account would be released to the landlord (minus the costs of the escrow and the tenants' attorneys' fees), but only when the building inspector certified to the court that the building was up to code and fit for human habitation.

- Henry and Sue could continue to pay 50% of the rent until needed repairs were made and certified by the building inspector.

Making Repairs and Deducting the Cost—"Repair and Deduct"

Another powerful legal remedy, called "repair and deduct," is available to tenants in most states and some large cities. (See "State Laws on Rent Withholding and Repair and Deduct Remedies" in Appendix A.) If your state doesn't allow repair and deduct, check your local housing ordinances to determine whether your city allows it. If your state or city doesn't have a repair and deduct statute, this procedure is not available to you.

It works like this: If you have tried and failed to get the landlord to fix a serious defect, you can hire a repairperson to fix it and subtract the cost from the following month's rent. In most states, the amount you can spend and deduct is limited to a

specific figure or a percentage of the month's rent. Most states also limit the frequency with which you can use the procedure, and require that you notify the landlord in writing and provide the legally required or a reasonable amount of time to repair the problem. Be sure to read your state statute for details on the repair and deduct option.

State laws vary greatly as to the amount of rent you can withhold and the frequency you can use this remedy for repairs. For example, in Massachusetts, you can spend up to four months' rent (for health code violations certified by an inspector only). (Mass. Gen. Laws ch. 111, § 127L.) In California, you can spend only one month's rent, and only use this option twice a year. (Cal. Civ. Code §§ 1941 to 1942.5.) And in Louisiana, there is practically no guidance at all: You are simply allowed to repair and deduct a "reasonable" amount for "necessary" repairs that are the landlord's responsibility. (La. Civ. Code art. 2694.)

Reducing the Rent on Your Own

If your state doesn't have a rent withholding statute, you might be tempted to reduce the rent on your own. For example, if the water heater is broken and the landlord won't fix it despite your repeated requests, you might believe that your cold-water flat is worth only a fraction of the rent you're responsible for under the lease.

It's very risky to give your landlord a short rent check. You can expect a speedily delivered termination notice, followed by an eviction lawsuit, for nonpayment of rent. Your theory—that the landlord was entitled to less rent because your unit wasn't livable—is not likely to be well-received in a state that hasn't taken the issue seriously enough to establish rent-withholding procedures to ensure that landlords live up to their duty to provide habitable housing. If the court doesn't approve of your approach, you'll lose your rented home.

If your state doesn't give you the option of rent withholding, use one of the other remedies mentioned here, including repair and deduct (if available), moving out, or filing a lawsuit in small claims court asking for a retroactive rent reduction for substandard conditions.

Sample Letter Telling the Landlord You Intend to Repair and Deduct

8976 Maple Avenue
Carson, WA 00000
360-555-6543

January 14, 20xx

Hattie Connifer
200 Capitol Expressway, Suite 300
Carson, WA 12345

Dear Ms. Connifer:

On January 10, I called your office and spoke to you about a major problem: I have no hot water. As I explained on the phone, on the evening of January 9 the water heater for my flat sprang a leak. Luckily, I was home and was able to divert the water to the outside with a hose, turn off the intake valve, and shut off the pilot.

At the end of our conversation on January 10, you assured me that you would send a repairperson to the flat the next day, January 11. As of today, no one has showed up, and I am enduring my fourth day of no hot water.

Under Washington law, I am entitled to remedy the problem and deduct the cost from my rent if you do not attend to the problem within 24 hours (Washington Rev. Code § 59.18.100). I intend to do this if the heater is not replaced within 24 hours after you receive this letter, which I am personally delivering to your office. As required by law, I have enclosed an estimate of the replacement cost: A-1 Appliance Repair has estimated the cost and installation of a new, comparable heater at $1,100.

Yours truly,

Wanda Wright

Wanda Wright

Enclosure: Estimate of A-1 Appliance Repair

These restrictions make the repair and deduct remedy a poor choice for tenants when it comes to big-ticket projects such as a major roof repair. Obviously, if you're limited to a twice-a-year expenditure of half your monthly rent, you are not going to be able to pay for a $20,000 roof retrofit. Sometimes, however, a number of tenants might pool their dollar limits to accomplish a costly repair. (Tenants working together is covered in Chapter 19.)

 CAUTION

Most repair and deduct statutes require you to spend only a reasonable amount of money on repairs. In some states, you might have to hire the (qualified) contractor who presents the lowest bid. If your landlord challenges the amount you spent on the repair, you'll need to be able to prove that the cost was the going rate for the job. Get bids from several reputable contractors or licensed repairpersons, and choose wisely. In most states, the best choice is not necessarily to go with the lowest bid, but the best value for a decent job.

Moving Out

If your dwelling isn't habitable and hasn't been made so despite your complaints and repair requests, you also have the right to move out—either temporarily or permanently. This drastic measure is justified only when the problems are truly serious, such as the lack of essential services or the total or partial destruction of the premises. You might hear the term "constructive eviction," which simply means that the landlord's failure to provide fit housing has, for all intents and purposes, forced you out. (Chapter 13 explains your right to move out because of environmental toxins.)

Under your state's statute, you might have to take certain steps before moving out. For example, the statute might describe the type of notice you must provide, and require you to give your landlord anywhere from 5 to 21 days to fix the problem. Check your state law for details.

Temporary moves. In many states, if the landlord fails to provide heat or other essential services, you can procure reasonable substitute housing during the period of the landlord's noncompliance. You typically can recover the costs of substitute housing up to an amount equal to your rent. If you can demonstrate to a judge that you were unable to find reasonable, substantially similar temporary accommodations at a price equal to or lower than your existing rent, you might be awarded a greater amount.

Permanent moves. If you move out permanently because of habitability problems, you might also be entitled to money from the landlord to compensate you for out-of-pocket losses. For example, you might be able to recover moving expenses and the cost of a hotel for a few days until you find a new place.

Also, if the conditions were substandard during prior months when you did pay the full rent, you could sue to be reimbursed for the difference between the value of the defective dwelling and the rent paid. In addition, if you are unable to find comparable housing for the same rent (often the case in areas with rent control or a tight rental market), and end up paying more rent than you would have under the old lease, you might be able to recover the difference.

Damage to the Premises

If your home is totally damaged by natural disaster or any other reason beyond your control, it only makes sense that you have the legal right to consider the lease at an end and to move out.

Partial destruction, however, is another matter.

If you must find another place to live because of damage to or significant destruction of the premises—no matter the cause—you must decide whether to terminate the lease or rental agreement or just suspend it while repairs are made.

CAUTION

Check your lease or rental agreement for a clause covering what happens if the premises are partially damaged or destroyed. Your lease or rental agreement might give the landlord—and only the landlord—the right to decide whether to terminate your rental or merely suspend it. If you disagree with the landlord's call, you'll need to try some negotiation.

Terminating the lease or rental agreement. You'll want to terminate the lease if you can find new housing of comparable quality and cost. You won't have to live with the uncertainty of when you'll move back to the original dwelling, and it will save you the time and aggravation of an extra household move. And if your new housing comes with a lease, you might *have* to terminate the old one, because the new lease won't allow you to move when you want.

If you decide to terminate the original lease or rental agreement, finalize the decision in writing. Have the landlord write "Terminated" on each page of your lease or rental agreement. Both of you should sign and date each page. Your landlord should refund your security deposit according to your state's procedures. (See Chapter 16.)

Leaving temporarily without terminating the lease. If your rental is a particularly great deal, the local market is very tight, or the repairs can be accomplished within a reasonable time, you'll want to hang on to your unit. If you are protected by rent control and you have lived in your rental for a significant period of time, you'll probably be loath to move. Find a month-to-month rental while the original unit is repaired.

You and the landlord should add a page to the lease entitled "Suspension," which states that the landlord's and tenant's responsibilities have been suspended from a certain date until the day you move back in. Be sure to include the landlord's promise to notify you promptly as soon as the rental is ready. If relocation costs are being covered by the landlord, note them. Both of you should sign and date this document.

In some circumstances, and regardless of whether you decide to terminate or just suspend the original lease, you might have the legal right to financial assistance from the landlord to pay for temporary substitute housing. It depends on how your rental unit was destroyed. If a natural disaster struck, the landlord is less likely to be obligated than if your home was destroyed by fire caused by the landlord botching an electrical repair job. And if your home burns down because of your own carelessness, don't expect financial help—in fact, the landlord might be able to sue *you*.

Natural or third-party disasters. If your unit is destroyed by earthquake, tornado, flood, or arson, your duty to pay rent is at an end. State laws vary on the extent of the landlord's responsibility to aid you with relocation or temporary housing costs. If you have renters' insurance, your best bet is to file a claim for help in resettlement and coverage for your lost or destroyed possessions. (Renters' insurance is covered in Chapter 2.)

If you have a month-to-month tenancy, the landlord might be required by law to pay for your substitute housing for 30 days. If you have a lease, the landlord is probably obligated to pay for substitute housing for a longer period—often until you find a comparable replacement or, if you drag your feet, until a court thinks you should have been able to.

Destruction that is traceable to the landlord. If the landlord or the landlord's employees were even partially responsible for the damage, your legal right to assistance almost surely increases. Even if your tenancy is just month to month, the landlord is likely to be obligated by state law to pay for a reasonable period of temporary housing. If the permanent substitute housing you find is more expensive, the landlord might be obliged to pay the difference between your old rent and the new rent for one or two months. If you have a lease, the landlord's responsibility to pay the difference might extend to the end of your lease term.

If the landlord doesn't offer you a fair settlement, you can bring a lawsuit to recover the cost of temporary and substitute housing and the value of your lost possessions. Often, cases like these settle before trial, because your claims are likely to be covered by the landlord's insurance policy. (Business policies generally include coverage for the landlord's negligent acts, but they exclude coverage for natural disasters.)

Suing the Landlord

A consumer who purchases a product—be it a car, a hair dryer, or a steak dinner—is justified in expecting a minimum level of quality, and is entitled to compensation if the product is seriously flawed. The same goes for tenants. If your rental is not habitable, you can sue the landlord—whether or not you move out. You can use small claims court, which allows claims of up to several thousand dollars. (For your state's ceiling, see the table in Chapter 19.) You won't need to hire a lawyer.

Suing the landlord makes sense only if you can safely continue to live in your rental. For example, if the roof leaks only into the second bedroom, and you can move the kids into the living room for a while, you might want to stay and sue in order to avoid the hassle of moving, arranging for the repair yourself (repair and deduct), or figuring out the complications of rent withholding. But you wouldn't want to stay and sue if you are without heat in the winter or in danger of electrocution every time you use the kitchen stove.

What are the pros and cons of suing your landlord instead of using repair and deduct or rent withholding? On the positive side, if you lose your lawsuit you'll have lost some time and money, but you won't be evicted, as can happen with the unsuccessful use of repair and deduct or rent withholding. But suing isn't entirely risk-free, especially if you're a month-to-month tenant or nearing the end of a lease you would like to renew. Your annoyed landlord might simply decide to terminate or not renew. Tenants who are protected by state antiretaliation laws will have some protection, but to assert your rights you'll have to bring a lawsuit, a dreary prospect. (Landlord retaliation is covered in Chapter 15.)

In your lawsuit, you ask the judge to rule that your unrepaired rental was not worth what you've paid for it. You want to be paid the difference between the monthly rent and the real value of the unit, times the number of months that you've lived with the substandard conditions. In short, you'll ask for a retroactive rent decrease. In addition, you can sue your landlord for:

- lost or damaged property—for example, furniture ruined by water leaking through the roof
- compensation for personal injuries—including pain and suffering—caused by the defect (see Chapter 12), and
- your attorneys' fees and court costs if you had to hire a lawyer to sue the landlord (Chapter 2 discusses attorneys' fees).

In some states, you can ask the court for an order directing the landlord to repair the defects, with rent reduced until they are fixed. In others, small claims courts can only order the landlord to pay you for your losses, but usually the money judgment prompts the landlord to make the repairs.

Minor Repairs and Maintenance

Ask a group of tenants which rental problem is most annoying, and chances are you'd hear "Repairs!" And most wouldn't be referring to major problems that make a unit unlivable. Far more common are the day-to-day but nonetheless important problems: leaky faucets, malfunctioning appliances, and dozens of other frustrating breakdowns.

Unfortunately, if your landlord refuses to attend to minor repairs, you cannot use the "big stick" legal weapons—such as withholding rent and moving out—discussed in Chapter 8. You're not out of luck, though—this chapter discusses several proven strategies for getting your landlord to keep up with basic repairs and maintenance.

 RELATED TOPIC
Also covered in this book:

- How to clarify repair and maintenance responsibilities at the start of your tenancy: Chapter 2.
- How to use a Landlord-Tenant Checklist to note problems with the rental unit when you move in: Chapter 6.
- Dealing with serious problems that make housing uninhabitable: Chapter 8.
- Your responsibility to keep your rental unit clean, safe, and in good condition: Chapter 8.
- Making improvements or alterations to your rental on your own: Chapter 10.
- Your landlord's liability for injuries caused by defective premises: Chapter 12.

Minor Repairs: What Are They?

When your landlord won't make a repair, your first step is to decide whether the problem is major (affecting the habitability of your rental unit) or minor. You have different legal options depending on your conclusion.

Common minor repairs and maintenance issues include:

- small plumbing problems (as long as they are not creating major leaks or floods), like replacing washers and cleaning drains

- system upkeep, like changing heating filters and cleaning exhaust fans
- item upkeep, such as replacing excessively worn flooring or patching small holes in walls
- routine maintenance, like replacing the grout around bathtub tile, and
- maintenance of and monitoring common areas, such as pools, spas, and laundry rooms.

Don't assume that inexpensive repairs are always minor repairs—or vice versa. Sometimes an extremely important repair costs very little. For example, if the only thing between you and a heated apartment is the replacement of a $45 furnace part, the repair is "major" because an unheated dwelling is uninhabitable, even though the repair cost is insignificant. Because lack of heating is a habitability problem, if the landlord didn't replace the furnace part promptly, you would probably be entitled to withhold rent or use one of the other "big stick" strategies discussed in Chapter 8. By contrast, replacing the living room carpet, which is worn but not a hazard, will be very expensive, but will be considered a minor repair because the consequence of not replacing it is not an unfit dwelling.

Most minor repairs are the landlord's responsibility. But landlords aren't required to keep the premises looking like new, and ordinary wear and tear doesn't have to be repaired during your tenancy. (And, when you move out, your landlord cannot use your security deposit to cover the cost of dealing with ordinary wear and tear. See Chapter 16.)

Sources of the Landlord's Responsibilities

Your landlord is not legally responsible for every minor repair. For example, if you or one of your guests caused damage, carelessly or intentionally, you are responsible for repairing it. If your lease or rental agreement prohibits you from making repairs, then you are responsible for the landlord's repair costs. Typically, landlords deduct repair costs from your security deposit, as discussed in Chapter 16.

Common Misconceptions About Routine Maintenance

Many tenants (and landlords) are under the mistaken impression that every time a rental unit turns over, or a certain number of years have passed, the landlord must supply a new paint job, clean drapes and carpets, or otherwise refresh the unit. Unfortunately for tenants, the law almost never mandates cosmetic changes—even badly needed ones.

Here are some of the common misconceptions regarding rental sprucing-up:

Paint. No state's law requires landlords to repaint the interior every so often. (Very rarely, local ordinances such as those in New York City might impose minimal repainting obligations.) Unless the paint creates a habitability problem—for example, it's so thick around a window that the window can't be opened, or flaking lead-based paint poses obvious health risks—the landlord probably isn't required by law to repaint. (Lead-based paint creates so many potential problems that we discuss it separately in Chapter 13.)

Drapes and Carpets. So long as drapes and carpets are not so damp or mildewy as to amount to a health hazard, and so long as carpets don't have dangerous holes that could cause someone to trip and fall, your landlord isn't legally required to replace them.

Windows. You're responsible for fixing (or paying to fix) a broken window that you or your guest intentionally or carelessly break. If a burglar, vandal, or neighborhood child breaks a window, however, the landlord is usually legally responsible for the repair. (Broken windows can sometimes be a habitability problem; see Chapter 8.)

Keys and Locks. Unfortunately, in many areas of the country, landlords are not legally required to change the locks for new tenants or even to provide serious, heavy-duty door and window locks. However, if you tell a landlord in writing that you are worried about renting a unit secured by locks for which previous tenants (and perhaps their friends) have keys, most landlords rekey the locks. (If the landlord knows of your concern but does not respond, and you are attacked or your place is burglarized by someone using an old key, the chances of the landlord being held liable in a lawsuit go way up. See Chapter 14.)

On the other hand, if you had nothing to do with the repair problem and it's not merely cosmetic, your landlord is probably responsible, for one of the following reasons:

- A state or local building code requires the landlord to keep the damaged item in good repair.
- A state or local law assigns responsibility for the specific repair to the landlord.
- A lease or rental agreement provision or advertisement describes or lists particular items, such as hot tubs, trash compactors, and air conditioners; by implication, this makes the landlord responsible for maintaining or repairing them.
- The landlord made explicit promises to repair or replace items when showing you the unit.
- The landlord's past maintenance of a particular feature, such as a whirlpool bathtub, has created an implied promise to continue its maintenance.

Each of these grounds for holding your landlord responsible for repairs is discussed in detail below.

Building Codes

States (and sometimes cities) enact building codes that create standards for structural components such as roofs, flooring, and windows, as well as essential services, such as hot water and heat. If the repair problem in your rental violates the building code, you might be facing a habitability problem, as discussed in Chapter 8.

Building codes often cover minor, less essential details as well as major, habitability-related ones. For example, codes might specify a minimum number of electrical outlets per room. If, for example, a broken circuit breaker at your rental results in your having fewer working outlets than the code requires, the consequence is probably not an unfit dwelling, but the landlord is still legally required to fix the problem.

Landlord-Tenant Laws

Some state laws place responsibility for specific minor repairs and maintenance on the landlord. A common example is the requirement that landlords provide renters with garbage receptacles and arrange for garbage pickup. Many states have their own rules, so be sure to check your state's statutes regarding landlords' responsibility to maintain the premises.

In many states, renters of single-family residences can agree to take on responsibilities that would otherwise belong to the landlord, such as disposing of garbage. For details, check your state's landlord-tenant codes under "State Landlord-Tenant Statutes," which are listed in Appendix A.

Your Lease or Rental Agreement

When it comes to legal responsibility for repairs, your own lease or rental agreement is often just as important (or more so) than building codes or state laws. If your written agreement describes or lists specific items such as drapes, washing machines, swimming pools, saunas, parking places, or dishwashers, your landlord must provide them in decent repair. The promise to provide them carries with it the implied promise to maintain them throughout the entirety of the tenancy, unless you and your landlord agreed otherwise.

Advertisements and Marketing

Advertisements and marketing materials that describe or list included features, such as high-speed internet or an onsite gym, constitute promises to provide these amenities should you decide to rent at the advertised rate. When a landlord offers included amenities, and this offer affects your decision to move in, you have the right to hold the landlord to these promises.

Even if your written lease or rental agreement says nothing about appliances, if the landlord's ad listed a dishwasher, clothes washer and dryer, and microwave oven, you have a right to expect that all of them will be maintained and repaired by the landlord if they break through no fault of yours.

> **EXAMPLE:** Tina sees Joel's ad for an apartment, which says "heated swimming pool." After Tina moves in, Joel stops heating the pool regularly because his utility costs have risen. Joel has violated his promise to keep the pool heated.

The promise doesn't have to be in words.

> **EXAMPLE:** The onsite leasing officer at a large apartment complex showed Tom a glossy color photo of an available apartment. The photo featured a smiling resident using an intercom to welcome a guest. The apartment Tom rented did not have a working intercom, and he complained to the management, arguing that the advertisement implied that all units were so equipped. The property's management realized that they would have to fix the intercom.

Promises Made Before You Rented the Unit

Almost every landlord engages in a bit of puffing when showing a rental to a prospective tenant. You might even hear rosy plans for amenities or services that haven't yet materialized ("We plan to redo this kitchen—you'll love the new trash compactor!"). Whenever you hear promises like these, it's wise to get them in writing, as part of (or attached to) your lease or rental agreement or, at the very least, in a prompt letter of understanding that cannot be repudiated later.

If you've already moved in and you don't have the landlord's promise in writing, don't give up hope. An oral promise is valid and enforceable—it's just a little harder to prove that it was made. If the promised trash compactor never appears, it's your word against the landlord's unless you have witnesses to the conversation. You'll be in a stronger position, proof-wise, if the promised feature is present in your unit but just doesn't work or breaks down after you move in, as explained just below.

EXAMPLE: When the rental agent shows Tom around the building, she goes out of her way to show off the laundry room, saying, "Here's the laundry room—we have two machines now, but will be adding two more soon." Tom rents the apartment. Two months go by and management still hasn't added the new machines. The landlord has violated the promise to equip the laundry room with four machines.

Implied Promises

Suppose your rental agreement doesn't mention a garbage disposal, and neither does any ad you saw before moving in. And, in fairness, you don't remember your landlord even mentioning one when showing you the unit. But the unit has a garbage disposal, and it worked when you moved in. Now the garbage disposal is broken and, despite repeated requests, your landlord hasn't fixed it. You have the legal right to demand that your landlord make this repair: Many courts will hold a landlord legally responsible for maintaining all significant aspects of your rental unit. And, if a feature is in working order when you move in, many judges reason that the landlord has made an implied contract to keep them in workable order throughout your tenancy.

The flip side of this principle is that if you pay for a hamburger, the waiter doesn't have to deliver a steak. In other words, if your rental was shabby when you moved in, and the landlord never gave you reason to believe that it would be spruced up, you have no legal right to demand improvements—unless, of course, you can show health hazards or code violations. It's just like buying secondhand goods "as is" for a low price—legally, you're stuck with the deal you made. (But "Getting the Landlord to Make Minor Repairs," below, suggests some strategies that might convince a reluctant landlord to take better care of the rental.)

Another factor that is evidence of an implied contract is the landlord's past conduct. By consistently fixing or maintaining a particular feature of your rental, your landlord has made an implied obligation to continue doing so.

EXAMPLE: Tina's apartment has a built-in dishwasher. When she rented the apartment, neither the lease nor the landlord said anything about the dishwasher or who was responsible for repairing it. The dishwasher has broken down a few times and whenever Tina asked Joel to fix it, he did. By doing so, Joel has established a practice that he—not the tenant—is responsible for repairing the dishwasher.

TIP

Check your lease. Landlords who want to avoid responsibility for appliance repairs often insert clauses in their leases or rental agreements warning that the appliances are not maintained by the landlord. (See "Typical Provisions in Leases and Rental Agreements" in Chapter 2.)

TIP

Using the Landlord-Tenant Checklist at the start of your tenancy will give you a record of appliances and features—and their condition. If something needs repairs, you'll be able to use the Checklist as proof of its original condition.

Tenant Responsibilities

Leases and rental agreements usually include a general statement that you are responsible for keeping your rental unit clean, safe, and in good condition; and for reimbursing your landlord for the cost of repairing damage you cause. Your lease or rental agreement will probably also say that you can't make alterations or repairs, such as painting the walls, installing bookcases, or fixing electrical problems, without your landlord's permission. (See Chapter 2.)

Landlords who are tired of maintenance and repair jobs sometimes use the lease, rental agreement, or separate contract to give these responsibilities to a tenant. This is especially true for rentals of single-family homes and duplexes—landlords often ask tenants to agree to mow the lawn, trim the bushes, and do minor plumbing jobs and painting.

Many state laws regulate the kind of repairs and maintenance that landlords can hand off to tenants. In general, if the landlord is not required to provide an item in the first place (a sauna, for example), the lease or rental agreement can delegate responsibility for repairing it to the tenant. Landlords cannot, however, make tenants responsible for repairing or maintaining essential features required by law. (See Chapter 8.) Also, laws in some states limit duties that landlords can delegate to tenants in multiunit buildings, but allow tenants in single-family dwellings and duplexes to assume more responsibilities.

Landlords often offer a rent reduction in exchange for a tenant's agreement to take on certain maintenance and repairs. Alternatively, landlords might offer other perks (a parking space, for example), or a bonus amenity if the tenant will perform the maintenance—for example, a hot tub in exchange for your promise to clean it.

Although usually legal, these arrangements often lead to dissatisfaction—typically, the landlord feels that the tenant has neglected certain tasks, or the tenant feels that too much work is involved. If the dispute boils over, the landlord tries to evict the tenant.

Here's how to protect yourself and avoid disputes:

- **Sign an employment agreement separate from your rental agreement or lease.** This is especially important if you plan to do considerable work for your landlord on a continuing basis, such as keeping common areas clean or maintaining the landscaping. Tenants who are also building managers are in this position. Ask your landlord to pay you for your work, rather than give you a rent reduction. That way, if the landlord claims that the job is not done right, the worst that can happen is that you will be fired; your tenancy should not be affected. But if your maintenance duties are tied to a rent reduction and things go wrong, you and the landlord will have to amend the lease or rental agreement in order to remove your duties and reestablish the original rent. And if the maintenance jobs are spelled out in a lease clause, the landlord also has the option of terminating the lease, on the grounds that your poor performance constitutes a breach of the lease.

- **As an employee, you are subject to your state's and federal employment laws, as is your landlord.** Workers' compensation requirements, as well as tax reporting duties, will apply. If your landlord ignores this aspect of your job, it's a bad sign.

- **Clearly write out your responsibilities and the landlord's expectations.** List your tasks and the frequency with which your landlord expects them to be done. Weekly tasks might include, for example, cleaning the laundry room, sweeping and wet mopping the lobby, and mowing the grass. Be sure to also include details about who will provide tools for completing the tasks. Otherwise, you might get hit with the unexpected (and possibly significant) expense of having to buy, for example, a lawnmower or cleaning supplies.

- **Make sure the agreement is fair.** Ideally, your landlord will pay you a fair hourly rate. If your only choice is a rent reduction, make sure the trade-off is equitable. If you're getting only a $50 rent reduction for work that would cost the landlord $200 to hire a cleaning service, you're being ripped off.

- **Discuss problems with the landlord and try to work out a mutually satisfactory agreement.** If the landlord has complained about your performance under the arrangement, try to work it out. Perhaps your landlord has underestimated what's involved in cleaning the hallways and grounds. Your landlord might be willing to pay you more for better results or shorten your list of jobs. If not, cancel the arrangement. In extreme cases, you might need to move out.

Watch Out for Illegal Retaliation

Delegating some maintenance tasks does not relieve your landlord of all repair and maintenance responsibilities. For example, if your landlord believes that the gardening work you agreed to do in exchange for a rent reduction isn't up to par, your landlord cannot react by shutting off your water.

CAUTION

Don't perform repairs involving hazardous materials. Any repair involving old paint or insulation (opening up a ceiling or wall cavity, for example) can expose you or others to dangerous levels of toxic materials. For example, sanding a surface for a seemingly innocuous paint job might actually create lead-based paint dust; the quick installation of a smoke alarm could involve disturbing an asbestos-filled ceiling. See Chapter 13 for more information on environmental hazards.

Getting the Landlord to Make Minor Repairs

Once you've determined that your landlord is legally responsible for fixing the particular minor problem that is bedeviling you, your next job is to get the landlord to act.

Appealing to Your Landlord

If your informal requests for repairs haven't worked, it's time to write a formal demand letter— or, if you have already sent one, a second one.

Before you start writing, take a minute to think about your landlord's overriding business concerns:

to make money, avoid hassles with tenants, and stay out of legal hot water. A request that zeroes in on these issues will likely get the job done.

How to Write a Persuasive Repair Request

Whether this is your first or second formal demand letter, frame your repair request along one or more of the following lines, if possible:

- **It's a small problem now, but has the potential to be a very big deal.** A bathtub faucet that drips badly might simply be annoying now, but devastating later if it fails completely while you're not home, flooding the tub and ruining the floor and downstairs neighbor's ceiling. When you ask that the faucet be repaired, point out the possible consequences of ignoring the problem.
- **There is a potential for injury.** Landlords hate to be sued. If you point out the problem's potential to cause injury, it's likely that your landlord's fear of lawsuits will serve as an impetus for repairs.
- **There is a security problem that imperils your safety.** Landlords are increasingly aware that they can be sued for criminal assaults against tenants if the premises aren't reasonably secure. (Chapter 14 discusses this topic in detail.) Emphasizing the security risks of not fixing a problem—for example, a burned-out lightbulb in the garage or a door that doesn't always latch properly—might motivate the landlord to act promptly.
- **The problem affects other tenants.** Explaining that the issue could result in disaster for more than one tenant will greatly increase your chances of some action. For example, accumulated oil puddles in the garage threaten the safety of all tenants and guests, not just you. Faced with the possibility of a small army of potential plaintiffs, each accompanied by an eager attorney, even the most slothful landlord might spring into action. See Chapter 19 for tips on working with other tenants to accomplish common goals.

See the sample letter below for more ideas on writing a persuasive repair request.

A written demand for repair or maintenance lets your landlord know that you are serious about the issue and will not just let it go. In addition, if your dispute ends up in small claims court, the demand letter can usually be introduced as evidence. Like this sample letter, your demand letter should:

- be neatly typed
- use businesslike language
- state the important facts accurately and concisely (keeping in mind that a judge might later use your letter to become familiar with the situation)
- be polite and civil. Accusations and personal attacks on your landlord will only hurt you. You want to appeal to the landlord's business interests, and encourage a response that is thoughtful and rational—not emotional and defensive.
- state exactly what you want—a new paint job, for example.

> **CAUTION**
>
> **Think twice about emailing or texting your requests.** In Chapter 6, "Using Email or Text Messages for Notice or a Letter of Understanding" explains why it's best to send important communications, such as repair requests, by mail (certified or return receipt requested) or delivery service, rather than email or text messages.

Always keep a copy of the letter for your files, and hand-deliver the letter or send it "return-receipt requested."

Proposing Mediation

If your demand letter does not produce results, consider involving the help of a local mediation center. Most community services handle lots of landlord and tenant problems, for free or at a very low cost. If they can coax the landlord to talk with you (and they're very good at doing that), you have a decent chance of ending up with an agreement. See Chapter 19 for more information on mediation.

Sample Letter Asking for Minor Repairs

90 Willow Run, Apartment 3A
Morgantown, Arizona 00000

February 28, 20xx

Mr. Lee Sloan
37 Main Street, Suite 100
Morgantown, Arizona 00000

Dear Mr. Sloan:

I would appreciate it if you could schedule an appointment with me to look at three problems in my apartment that have come up recently.

First, the kitchen sink is dripping, and it's getting worse. I'm concerned that a plate or dish towel might stop up the drain, leading to an overflow. At any rate, I'm sure that you don't want to pay for wasted water.

I've also been having trouble opening the sliding doors on the bedroom closet. The track appears to be coming away from the wall, and the doors wobble and look like they might fall into the room when I open and close the closet.

Thanks very much for thinking about my requests. I hope to hear from you soon.

Yours truly,

Chris Jensen
Chris Jensen

Reporting Code Violations

If appealing to your landlord's business sensibilities doesn't work, other strategies are available to pry minor repairs out of your landlord.

If the problem you want fixed constitutes a code violation, such as inadequate electrical outlets or low water pressure, you should find an ally in the building or housing agency in charge of enforcing the code. (Chapter 8 covers how to find and what to expect from these local agencies.) Whether you'll get any action out of the agency will depend on the seriousness of the violation, the workload of the agency, and its ability to enforce its compliance orders. When your problem is minor, though, don't be surprised if already overworked code enforcement officials give it low priority.

Suing in Small Claims Court

If you can reasonably argue that you aren't getting what you paid for, you might decide to sue in small claims court. But before you do, write a second demand letter if you haven't already. Like the first letter (see the sample above), your second letter should describe the problems and alert the landlord to the negative consequences that might result if repairs aren't made. In addition, make it clear that you intend to sue if you don't get results.

EXAMPLE: Chris Jensen wrote to her landlord on February 28, requesting repairs as shown in the sample letter above. She got no reply. Ten days later, she sent a second letter that summarized the first and concluded with this paragraph:

"If you are unable to attend to these repairs, I'll need to call in a handyman to repair the faucet and doors, and I will seek reimbursement from you in small claims court if necessary. Of course, I sincerely hope that this will not be necessary."

If the second letter doesn't produce results, it's time to head for small claims court. You won't need a lawyer; just download small claims court forms from the court's website or go to the clerk of court and ask for the forms. In small claims court, you can't get an order from the judge directing your landlord to paint, fix the dishwasher, or repair the intercom. You might, however, be compensated in dollars for living in a rental unit with repair problems. Here's how it works.

When you file your small claims court suit, you'll ask for an amount that reflects the difference between your rent and the value of the unit with repair problems. (To calculate this amount, use

one of the methods described in "What to Do If the Landlord Won't Make Repairs" in Chapter 8.) In court, your argument will be that you are not getting the benefit of what you're paying rent for—for example, a functioning dishwasher, presentable paint, or a working air conditioner.

You're more likely to succeed with this line of argument if you have a lease rather than a month-to-month agreement. If you have a long-term lease, you can argue that you are locked into paying a fixed rent for an extended period, but each time you make a payment you're getting less than what you're entitled to. In contrast, a month-to-month tenant has no long-standing obligation; if you don't like the fact that the shower door now won't close, you can leave after giving relatively short notice, with no legal liability for future rent. A judge is likely to point this out and to tell you that, in effect, you agreed to the increasing shabbiness every month when you failed to send in a termination notice.

Special Concerns for Month-to-Month Tenants

If you have a month-to-month tenancy, your landlord can, in most states, terminate your tenancy with just 30 days' notice. That means you should think twice before trying an adversarial strategy such as reporting or suing your landlord in response to minor problems with your rental.

An antiretaliation law, if one is in force where you live, might protect you from a termination notice. (See "State Laws Prohibiting Landlord Retaliation" in Appendix A for details on your state rules.) But if you have to go to court, you might end up wishing you'd never complained about that cracked tile. Remember, as a month-to-month tenant, you have the option of ending your tenancy with 30 days' notice— so if you're really unhappy with your place, maybe you should look for another.

Ⓘ **CAUTION**

Don't stop paying rent. Although fairness dictates that if your rental unit is full of repair problems you ought to pay less rent, it's a mistake to pay your landlord less than the full monthly rent. Rent withholding, as discussed in Chapter 8, is legally appropriate only for major repairs. If you withhold even a portion of the rent because of a minor repair problem, you risk termination and, if you don't pay up, eviction for nonpayment of rent.

Your goal in small claims court is to convince the judge that these problems really make your rental unit worth less money. Use common sense—it's not worth your time or money to sue over small things. A small claims court judge is not going to adjust your rent because a little grout is missing from your bathroom tile. But if your dishwasher is broken, three faucets leak noisily, and the bathroom door won't close properly, your chances of winning go way up. You'll need to show the judge that:

- there are lots of minor defects, not just an isolated one, and
- you've given the landlord plenty of time and notice to fix the problems.

Bring evidence. Winning in small claims court depends more on what you bring into court to prove your story than on what you say. Examples of key evidence include:

- copies of letters you've written asking for repairs
- your written notes on your landlord's response to your repair requests, including the number of times they were ignored or promised repairs didn't materialize
- witnesses—a family member, for example, who can describe the inoperable air conditioner
- photographs and video—your images of the cracked, flaking plaster, for example
- a copy of the local building or housing code that addresses the issue (if applicable)
- your lease or rental agreement (bring this no matter what, but it will be especially relevant if it lists (as items included in the rental) any of the items that need repair, or if it prohibits you from making repairs yourself)
- a copy of the Landlord-Tenant Checklist, which you hopefully completed when you moved in and that was signed by you and the landlord, showing that the problem did not exist at the start of your tenancy, and
- ads, brochures, or "For Rent" signs describing features of your rental that are missing or malfunctioning.

For more advice on preparing for and filing a small claims court case, see Chapter 16.

EXAMPLE: Judy signed a one-year lease for a studio apartment at $750 a month. When she moved in, the place was in good shape. But six months into her tenancy, the apartment began to deteriorate. A water leak from the roof stained and buckled several areas of the hardwood floors; the kitchen cabinets, which were badly made, warped and would not shut; the dishwasher became so noisy the neighbor banged on the wall when it was in use; the soap dish fell off the bathroom wall; and the white entryway rug started to fall apart. Judy asked her landlord to attend to these problems and followed up with several written demand letters. Two months after her original request, Judy wrote a final demand letter.

When the landlord still did nothing, Judy filed suit in small claims court, asking the judge to award her damages (money) representing the difference between her rent and the value of the deteriorated apartment. After considering Judy's evidence, including copies of her demand letter, photographs of the defects, and the testimony of her neighbor, the judge agreed with Judy. She figured that the deteriorated apartment would have rented for $150 less a month, and ordered the landlord to pay Judy $450 to make up for the three months she had lived with the defects. Judy's landlord was quick to make repairs after learning this expensive lesson in court.

RESOURCE

Everybody's Guide to Small Claims Court, by Cara O'Neill (Nolo), has all the details you need to file a small claims court lawsuit.

Making Minor Repairs Yourself

If you've concluded that a repair job isn't your landlord's responsibility, that means it's your responsibility.

Before you head out to the hardware store, pause for a moment. You need to know, first, whether it makes sense from a practical point of view for you to do the repair or maintenance, and, second, whether it's legal.

Evaluating Your Skills and Time

Before you embark on a job, realistically assess its magnitude and your skills, tools, and time. Seemingly easy repairs often have hidden complexities. A simple job, like replacing the flexible hoses under the sink that connect the pipes to the faucet, might require special wrenches because of the cramped workspace. Do you have this equipment, or are you willing to purchase it? Time is also an issue: Are you willing to commit precious non-work time to a plumbing project? Only an experienced, equipped handyperson (or one willing to consult a good do-it-yourself manual) should consider doing most home repairs.

You must also consider whether you are willing to take the risk of being held liable if one of your repair projects goes awry and results in property damage or, worse, someone's injury. Your landlord's insurance policy will not cover your misdeeds, and unless you have renters' insurance, you stand to lose a lot of money.

EXAMPLE: Colin decided to replace a window that was broken by his daughter's basketball. He removed the shards of glass, fitted a new pane in place and caulked the circumference. Colin mistakenly used the wrong type of caulk, and a year later it had cracked, allowing rainwater to seep onto the windowsill and down the wall. The landlord was furious when he realized that he would have to replace the sill and the drywall, simply because Colin had DIY'ed a job he wasn't qualified to do. The cost of these repairs was taken out of Colin's security deposit.

Getting the Landlord's Permission

First, look at your lease or rental agreement. You might see a clause that forbids you from undertaking any "repairs, alterations, or improvements" without the landlord's consent. (Alterations and improvements are discussed in Chapter 10.) These clauses are legal, and their purpose is to ensure the landlord's control over physical changes to the property (while making sure that tenants pay for any damage they cause).

If your lease has a "no repairs" clause, you'll have to convince the landlord to give you permission to fix something. (See the sample letter below.) And even if you don't have such a clause, check with the landlord first, anyway. You won't need to do this if the repair or replacement is truly insignificant and nontechnical (or if it's unlikely to be noticed by the landlord), like replacing the entryway rug or installing new miniblinds identical to the old ones.

But for jobs that have the potential to get complicated, expensive, or have dire consequences if things go wrong, you'll want to have the official okay before proceeding. Having your landlord's permission might prevent or limit your landlord's ability to hold you responsible if things go awry.

Of course, a potential negative outcome might be the very reason your landlord will say "No way" and call for the bonded repairperson. But many landlords—if they trust you—will be happy to save themselves the time and trouble of lining up a worker, scheduling a time to be in your apartment, getting you to pay the bill, or deducting the expense from your security deposit and then getting you to bring the deposit up to its original level.

To protect yourself, put your repair proposal in writing, phrase it in a way that tells the landlord you'll proceed unless you hear to the contrary within a reasonable amount of time, and keep a copy for your records. That way, you have a record that your work was undertaken with the landlord's consent. A sample letter is shown below. Notice how the tenant has clearly identified the problem, described her experience with similar repairs, and laid out a plan for repairing the item. The tenant's thorough letter outlining a well-thought-out approach to the problem is designed to inspire the landlord's confidence.

Sample Letter Requesting Permission to Do a Minor Repair

890 Market Street, #3
Central City, Texas 00000
214-555-7890

January 4, 20xx

Jackson Montgomery
234 Fourth Street
Central City, Texas 00000

Dear Mr. Montgomery,

Last night, a fork accidentally fell into my garbage disposal, jamming the blades and causing the unit to stop. The disposal will have to be taken out and the blade assembly examined. The shear key, which prevents the engine from seizing, will need to be replaced.

I am familiar with the installation and maintenance of these appliances, having worked on one at my former residence. I have the tools to do the job. I'll proceed with this repair unless I hear from you to the contrary. Please leave me a note or call me before January 10 if you do not wish me to do the job. If I don't hear from you by then, I'll go ahead.

Yours truly,

Janet Green

Janet Green

Making Improvements and Alterations

Your lease or rental agreement probably includes a clause prohibiting you from making any alterations or improvements to your unit without the express, written consent of the landlord. Landlords use these clauses—some of which contain a long list of prohibitions—so that tenants don't change the light fixtures, knock out a wall, install a built-in dishwasher, or even pound in a nail to hang a picture unless the landlord agrees first.

But what if you make one of these alterations or improvements without getting your landlord's permission—for example, you bolt a closet storage system to the wall? In most states, unless you get the landlord's permission to remove the item, such improvements and additions become the landlord's property when you leave.

Discovering too late that you must leave behind what you thought of as a portable improvement can be a real blow. To help you avoid problems, this chapter explains:

- what types of improvements and alterations become the landlord's property
- what you can do, ahead of time, to prevent donating the improvement to your landlord
- how to minimize your losses if your landlord insists that the improvement remain on the property, and
- special rules for cable TV access and satellite dishes.

 RELATED TOPIC
Also covered in this book:
- Typical lease and rental agreement restrictions on tenant improvements and alterations: Chapter 2.
- The rights of tenants with disabilities to modify their living space: Chapter 5.
- Performing minor repairs with the landlord's consent: Chapter 9.

Improvements That Become Part of the Property

Anything you attach to the ground or to a building, fence, or deck belongs to the landlord, absent an agreement saying it's yours. (Lawyers call such items "fixtures.") As a result, when you move out, the landlord is legally entitled to prohibit you from removing the fixture and returning the premises to its original state.

This basic legal principle is spelled out in most leases and rental agreements. In addition, many leases and rental agreements specify what types of improvements belong to the landlord. A typical clause looks something like this: "Any alterations, installations, or improvements, including shelving and attached floor coverings, will become the property of the owner and will remain with and as part of the rental premises at the end of the term."

Sometimes, a landlord and departing tenant disagree over whether an item—such as an appliance, flooring, or shelving—is the tenant's movable property or a fixture that must remain in the rental. When these disputes end up in court, judges use a variety of legal rules to determine the nature of the object or improvement. Here are some of the questions that judges ask:

- **Did you get the landlord's permission?** If you never asked the landlord to install a closet organizer, or you asked and got no for an answer, a judge is likely to rule for your landlord—particularly if your lease or rental agreement prohibits alterations or improvements.
- **Did you make any structural changes that affect the use or appearance of the property?** If so, chances are that the item will be deemed the landlord's, because removing it will often leave an unsightly area or alter the use of part

of the property. For example, if you modify the kitchen counter to accommodate a built-in dishwasher you purchased, and then take the dishwasher with you, the landlord will have to install another dishwasher of the same dimensions or rebuild the space. The law doesn't impose this extra work on landlords, nor does it force them to let you do the return-to-original work yourself.

- **Is the object firmly attached to the property?** In general, additions and improvements that are nailed, screwed, or cemented to the building are likely to be deemed "fixtures." For example, drywall screws that anchor a bookcase might convert an otherwise free-standing unit belonging to the tenant to a fixture belonging to the landlord. Similarly, closet systems bolted to the wall become part of the structure and would usually be counted as fixtures. Even if you have a very good reason for firmly attaching your addition—bolting a bookcase to the wall for earthquake protection, for example—you might still end up having to leave it behind. On the other hand, shelving systems that are secured by isometric pressure (spring-loaded rods that press against the ceiling and floor) involve no actual attachment to the wall and for that reason are not likely to be classified as fixtures.

- **What did you and the landlord intend?** Courts will look at statements made by you and the landlord to determine whether there was any understanding as to your right to remove an improvement. In some circumstances, courts will even infer an agreement from your actions—for instance, if your landlord stopped by and gave permission for you to install what you've described as a portable air conditioner, or helped you lift it into place.

Improvements That Plug or Screw In

The act of plugging in an appliance doesn't make the appliance a part of the premises. The same is true for simple wiring or pipe attachments to join an appliance to an electrical or water source. For example, a refrigerator or free-standing stove remains the property of the tenant. Similarly, portable dishwashers that connect to the kitchen faucet by means of a coupling are not considered fixtures.

By contrast, if you remove the light fixtures in your rental and, without your landlord's knowledge, install a custom-made fixture that could not be used in any other space, it is unlikely that you could convince a judge that you reasonably expected to take it with you at the end of your tenancy.

Improving Your Rental Unit Without Enriching Your Landlord

Your best protection against losing an item you want to take with you when you leave is not to attach it to a wall in your unit. Fortunately, hundreds of items are on the market—bookcases, lighting systems, closet organizers, and even dishwashers—that you can take with you when you leave. Home improvement or organization stores are great places to get ideas, as are websites geared to tenants or small-home living.

If you are determined to attach something to the wall or floor, talk to the landlord before you get out your tools. If you can, get the landlord to agree to pay for the improvement or to let you remove it when you leave.

Before talking with your landlord, determine your ideal outcome for the improvement. For example, if you'd like to install a custom track lighting system that won't work in any other space, find out whether

Agreement Regarding Tenant Improvements to Rental Unit

Mark Henderson _____ ("Tenant")

and _____ Robin Reese _____ ("Landlord")

agree as follows:

Tenant may make the following alterations to the rental unit at: _____ 370 Alpine Way, San Jose, _____
California 00000

Install window unit air conditioner in the master bedroom. _____

_____ .

Tenant will accomplish the improvements by using the following materials and procedures:
Purchasing a Cold Spot window air conditioner unit, Model 34A, and anchoring it to the window frame

using manufacturer's enclosed brackets. _____ .

Landlord and Tenant further agree that *[check either 1 or 2]*

☑ 1. The improvement will become Landlord's property and is not to be removed by Tenant. Landlord will

reimburse Tenant for *[check a or b or both]*:

    ☑ a. the cost of material, and/or

    ☐ b. labor costs at a rate of $_____ per hour, after Tenant provides receipts and the
        Landlord determines that the work has been done in a workmanlike and acceptable manner.

    Landlord will reimburse Tenant *[check c or d]*:

    ☑ c. by lump sum payment, within a reasonable time, or

    ☐ d. by reducing Tenant's rent, according to the following schedule: _____

    _____

☐ 2. The improvement will be considered Tenant's personal property, and as such may be removed by

Tenant at any time up to the end of the tenancy. Tenant promises to return the premises to their

original condition upon removing the improvement. If Tenant fails to do this, Landlord may deduct

the cost of restoring the premises to their original condition from Tenant's security deposit.

_____ *Mark Henderson* _____   *May 10, 20xx* _____
Landlord   Date

_____ *Robin Reese* _____   *May 10, 20xx* _____
Tenant   Date

the landlord will pay for it. On the other hand, if you want to take the fixture with you, impress upon the landlord your intent to carefully restore the property to its original condition. Keep in mind that if your restoration attempts are less than acceptable, the landlord will be justified in deducting from your security deposit the amount of money necessary to do the job right. And if the deposit is insufficient, the landlord can sue you for the excess.

Approach your landlord as one businessperson dealing with another. If the improvement will remain and you seek reimbursement, point out that it will make the property more attractive. It might even justify a higher rent for the next tenant and thus pay for itself over the long run. Remind the landlord that the cost of a durable, expensive item could be amortized, enabling the landlord to take incremental tax deductions for several years. Your landlord might agree to reduce your rent a little each month or simply reimburse you all at once.

If you and the landlord reach an understanding, put it in writing. As shown in the sample agreement above, you should carefully describe the project and materials and state whether you are to be reimbursed or allowed to take the improvement with you.

TIP

Save all receipts for materials and labor. It is important to keep a good record of the amount of money you spend on the project—regardless of your current agreement with your landlord. If your landlord plans to reimburse you, you'll need proof of exactly how much you spent. And, if the landlord doesn't let you remove the improvement at the end of your tenancy, despite a promise to do so, you'll have receipts to back up your small claims lawsuit for the value of the addition.

FORM

The Nolo website includes a downloadable copy of the Agreement Regarding Tenant Improvements to Rental Unit form. See Appendix B for a link to the forms in this book.

Cable TV Access and High-Speed Internet

Many rental properties already have access to cable TV and high-speed internet. But what can you do if your rental doesn't have access, or if the landlord has a contract with a provider other than the one you want to use?

In the event that your rental property does not have cable, the landlord is entitled to say "No" to your request for access. If this is your situation, and if high-speed internet is available in your area, investigate your options for on-demand and live TV streaming services. Aside from the benefit of being able to pick and choose which services to use, you might find that this is a less expensive option than traditional cable.

Alternatively, you could consider mounting a satellite dish. See "Satellite Dishes and Other Antennas," below, for rules governing these devices.

Satellite Dishes and Other Antennas

Until the advent of online streaming, satellite dishes were an attractive alternative to cable TV. These days, if you have high-speed internet, you'll almost always be better served by a streaming service than a pizza-sized dish hanging off your balcony. But, if satellite is your best option, your landlord can't impose restrictions that unreasonably impair your ability to install, maintain, or use an antenna or dish that meets guidance issued by the Federal Communications Commission (FCC). (Search online for the Over-the-Air Reception Devices Rule, 47 C.F.R. § 1.4000, further explained in the FCC's Fact Sheet, "Over-the-Air Reception Devices Rule.")

RESOURCE

For details on permissible restrictions, visit www.fcc.gov/consumers/guides/installing-consumer-owned-antennas-and-satellite-dishes, or call the FCC at 888-225-5322 (toll free).

Your Right to Privacy

There's no place like home—unless, of course, you have a landlord who doesn't respect your right to privacy. Usually, it's a landlord or manager who cannot stop fussing over the property or who presses for an invitation into your home to look around. Even worse are landlords and managers who use a passkey to enter without notice when you're not at home and there is no emergency.

This chapter covers your basic rights to privacy and what to do about a landlord or manager who violates these rights. You can sue your landlord for entering unlawfully—but it's rarely worth the time or trouble. Unfortunately, the law won't solve all problems inherent in dealing with difficult people. In some instances, you might find that you'll either have to bear the actions of an intrusive landlord or move on.

RELATED TOPIC

To avoid problems with obnoxious landlords at your next place, be sure to talk with other tenants before you move in. Chapter 1 provides advice on checking out prospective landlords. Also, see Chapter 2 for typical lease and rental provisions regarding landlord right of access.

State Laws on Landlord's Entry

About half the states have statutes specifying when and how landlords may legally enter rented property. (See "State Laws on Landlord's Access to Rental Property" in Appendix A for details.) In other states, your right to privacy is determined by your state's and the federal Constitution, as interpreted by the courts. If you want to know its precise extent, you'll have to research the law yourself or get help from a lawyer or tenants' rights group. See Chapter 20 for information on legal research.

Entry by the Landlord

Your landlord must have a good reason to enter your apartment and must meet legal notice requirements.

Allowable Reasons

Landlords always can come in when you give permission or any time there is a genuine emergency that threatens life or property. Nearly every state has, by judicial decision or statute, decided that landlords also can enter (after proper notification) to:

- assess the need for repairs or improvements
- make needed repairs or improvements, or
- show property to prospective tenants or purchasers.

In addition, a landlord who believes you have abandoned the property—that is, skipped out without giving notice or returning the key—may legally enter.

The following sections provide details on each of these reasons.

Entry With Your Permission

Obviously, your landlord can enter your rental when you give authorization. But don't let your landlord coerce your permission. A landlord who pressures you, perhaps implying or even threatening eviction if you don't allow immediate or virtually unrestricted access, is clearly violating your privacy rights. See "What to Do About Invasions of Privacy," below, for advice on how to deal with this situation.

Emergencies

In all states, landlords can enter your rental unit without giving notice to respond to a true emergency that threatens injury or property damage. An emergency entry is likely warranted in the following examples:

- Smoke is pouring out of your apartment window. Your landlord calls the fire department and uses a master key—or even breaks in if necessary—to try to deal with the fire.
- Your landlord sees water coming out of the bottom of your back door. It's okay to enter and find the water leak.
- You hear screams coming from the rental unit next door and call the manager. She knocks on the apartment door, but gets no answer. After calling the police, the manager uses her master key to enter and see what's wrong.
- Your family and friends, worried that you haven't been at work or reachable by phone over the long weekend, ask your landlord to enter your apartment to make sure everything's okay. He does so and finds nothing amiss; you show up a day later, having taken a spur-of-the-moment vacation.

On the other hand, a property owner's urge to repair a problem that's important but doesn't threaten life or property—say, a stopped-up drain that is not causing any damage—isn't a true emergency.

A landlord who needs to enter your apartment in an emergency should leave a note or call you explaining the circumstances and the date and time of entry. If you don't get this kind of notification, make it clear in writing that you expect it.

TIP

Your landlord is legally entitled to a key to your rental unit. Check your lease or rental agreement; many forbid tenants from rekeying, adding additional locks, or installing a security system without the landlord's permission. If you get permission to change or add locks, you probably will need to give your landlord a copy of the new keys. Similarly, if you install a security system, you probably will need to give your landlord the name and phone number of the alarm company or instructions on how to disarm the system in an emergency.

Repairs

Many states, either by statute or court decision, allow a landlord or repairperson to enter rental property to assess the need for or cost of repairs, and to make necessary or agreed-upon repairs, alterations, or improvements—for example, to fix a broken oven or replace the carpet.

In these situations, the landlord generally must enter only at reasonable times and must give you at least the required amount of notice, usually 24 hours. (Notice requirements are discussed below.) However, if this is impracticable—for example, a repairperson is available on a few hours' notice—a landlord will probably be on solid ground by explaining the situation to you and giving shorter notice. Of course, if you agree to a shorter notice period, your landlord has no problem.

EXAMPLE: Amy told her landlord Brett that her bathroom sink was stopped up and draining very slowly. Brett called the plumber, who said that he had several large jobs in progress, but would be able to squeeze in Amy's repair at some point within the next few days. The plumber promised to call Brett before he came over. Brett relayed this information to Amy, telling her he would give her at least four hours' notice before the plumber came.

TIP

Avoid hassles with repairpeople. Here's how:

- Be sure your landlord knows and trusts the service and repairpeople allowed to enter your rental unit. If new service providers are used, their references should be checked, and your landlord or manager should be present at all times.
- Try to be home (or ask your landlord to be present) when repairs will be made to avoid possible loss of or damage to your belongings or the rental unit.
- Always get the repairperson's phone number in advance, so you can reschedule if need be.
- Make sure your landlord notifies you if plans change.

• Make your landlord and the repairperson aware of any unique considerations for entering your unit, such as medical concerns (if, for example, you want them to wear a mask or gloves in your unit), loose pets, or people who might be sleeping in another room.

Maintenance While You're Away

Several states with privacy statutes give landlords the legal right to enter rental premises if you are away for an extended period, often defined as seven days or more. Under these laws, the landlord is allowed to maintain the property as necessary and to inspect for damage and needed repairs. For example, if you live in a cold-weather place such as Connecticut, your landlord might want to check the pipes in your house to make sure they haven't burst when you are away in the winter.

While many states do not address this issue, either by way of statute or court decision, your landlord is probably on safe legal ground to enter your rental unit during your extended absence if there is a genuine need to protect the property from damage. But your landlord should enter only if something really needs to be done—that is, something you would do if you were home as part of your obligation to keep the property clean, safe, and in good repair. (See Chapter 8 for a discussion of tenant repair and maintenance responsibilities.) For example, if you leave your windows wide open just before a driving rainstorm, your landlord would probably be justified in entering to close them.

TIP

Check if your lease or rental agreement requires you to report extended absences. It might require you to inform your landlord when you will be gone for an extended time, such as two weeks, and give the landlord the right to enter the premises during these times. For example, in Alaska, where tenants must notify their landlords if they plan to be absent more than seven days, a landlord may enter without notice if the tenant has been gone for more than seven days without notification. (Alaska Stat. §§ 34.03.140, 34.03.150, and 34.03.230(b).)

In general, if you plan to be gone for an extended time, it makes good sense to inform your landlord. Your landlord might be able to take steps that will obviate the need to enter while you're gone (like draining the pipes).

Inspections

Some conscientious landlords schedule regular safety and maintenance inspections of their rental properties once or twice a year, in an effort to find small problems before they become big ones.

If this is your landlord's practice, your lease or rental agreement probably gives your landlord the right to enter your unit—after giving reasonable notice—to make this inspection. Even if it doesn't, your state law probably allows this type of entry. All states with privacy statutes grant landlords the right to inspect rental property. (See "State Laws on Landlord's Access to Rental Property" in Appendix A.)

CAUTION

Don't put up with unnecessary, repeated inspections. No unit should need inspecting more than once or twice a year absent a very specific reason—for example, to track down the source of a water leak, or to check the point of entry of a persistent ant or rodent infestation. If your landlord asks to inspect your unit too frequently, it might constitute illegal harassment. "What to Do About Invasions of Privacy," below, shows how to deal with this situation.

Showing the Property to Prospective Tenants or Purchasers

Most states with access laws allow landlords to enter rented property to show it to prospective tenants. If your landlord doesn't plan to renew your about-to-expire lease, or you have given or received a notice terminating your month-to-month tenancy, your landlord can show prospective new tenants around during the last few weeks (or even months) of your stay.

Also, a landlord can show your rental unit—whether an apartment in a multiple-unit building, single-family house, or condominium unit—to potential buyers, lenders, or mortgage companies.

Your landlord must follow the notice procedures discussed below. Typically, you are entitled to at least 24 hours' notice, and the landlord must enter at reasonable times.

It's no fun to have your last weeks or months in your current place constantly interrupted by prospective new tenants or buyers—after all, you are still paying the rent. Especially if you're not moving out voluntarily, it can seem like an intolerable intrusion to have your landlord or rental agent constantly parading people through.

For Sale or For Rent Signs

Occasionally, friction is caused by landlords who put "For Sale" or "For Rent" signs in front of an apartment building or a rented single-family house. Prospective buyers or renters sometimes interpret these signs as an invitation to ring the doorbell—an annoyance that can rise to the level of invading your privacy.

With online multiple-listing services, many real estate offices can, and commonly do, sell rental houses and buildings without ever placing a For Sale sign on the property, except perhaps when an open house is in progress. If a real estate office puts a sign in front of your building, you should insist that it clearly state a telephone number to call and warn against disturbing you, using words like "Inquire at 555-1357—Do Not Disturb Occupant." If this doesn't do the trick, and informal conversations with the landlord do not result in removal of the sign, write a firm letter explaining why your privacy is being invaded and ask your landlord to remove the sign. If this doesn't work, remove the sign yourself and return it to the landlord. If your landlord simply replaces the sign, you could sue for invasion of privacy, just as if the landlord personally had made repeated illegal entries.

If the landlord constantly wants to show the unit to prospective tenants or buyers on short notice, you have two options:

Notify your landlord in writing to follow the law or you will sue for invasion of privacy. If you are planning to move out anyway, you might have nothing to lose by fully asserting your legal rights. But if you don't have a place lined up and are banking on a good recommendation, it's probably not a good idea to give your landlord a hard time.

Allow the unit to be shown on shorter notice in exchange for a reduction in the rent. This is a fair proposition because, after all, you are giving up some of the value of your rental home by letting strangers waltz though. A smart landlord will probably see the value in agreeing to pay a little something for your cooperation. For example, you might work out a deal with your landlord that two-hour notice is reasonable for up to three rental showings a week when you are home and three when you aren't, in exchange for having your rent reduced by a certain amount. Depending on how much you will be inconvenienced, a 10%–30% rent reduction might be reasonable.

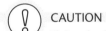 CAUTION

If there's a lockbox on your rental, make sure you know who will have access. A lockbox is a metal box that attaches to the front door. It can be opened with a code, and inside there's a key to the house. If the house is on the Multiple Listing Service, a potential buyer's agent can open the box by using a combination or, if it's electronic, a code. Buyers' agents must request permission to visit the property, and when the seller agrees to the showing, the buyer's agent receives the combination or code. With electronic boxes, the code is usually good for only a designated period of time. But with the older combination models, anyone who has the combination could potentially return at any time to obtain the key again. Although misuse of combinations and codes is very rare, you should be aware of the risks. Discuss with your landlord how access to the lockbox will be given. If you have any concerns based on what you hear, you can request that a lockbox not be used, or that the combination or code be changed frequently.

Notice Requirements

Most state access laws require landlords to give you 24 hours' to two days' notice before entering your rental unit in nonemergency situations. A few states simply require landlords to provide "reasonable" notice. See "State Laws on Landlord's Access to Rental Property," in Appendix A.

In many situations, you might not care about getting the legally required amount of notice—especially when your landlord wants to enter to make long-needed repairs. In other situations, though, like when you're in the middle of dinner or hosting a guest, a landlord's request to enter to fix or inspect something is totally unreasonable. When a landlord's proposed entry is inconvenient or unreasonable, you have a legal right to deny entry and ask that a later appointment be scheduled. If you do so politely and in a cooperative spirit, it shouldn't cause a problem.

Similarly, if your building is for sale and an overeager real estate salesperson shows up on your doorstep with clients in tow, or your landlord calls on 20 minutes' notice and asks to be let in to show the place to a potential tenant, you are entirely within your rights to say politely but firmly, "I'm busy right now—try again in a day or so after we've set a time convenient for all of us."

 TIP

You can provide your landlord with ways other than writing to reach you to give you notice of entry. Even if your state requires your landlord to give you notice of entry in writing, it often makes sense to provide your landlord with at least one other way of reaching you. This is especially true if you don't think you'll see a written notice in time. For example, it's okay to ask your landlord to text or email you for access, if that's what works best for you. Let your landlord know that you're much more likely to respond in a timely manner to your preferred contact method than to a written notice. Save or take notes about texts, emails, and phone calls from your landlord just as you would a written notice.

What's Reasonable Notice?

If your state requires your landlord to give you only "reasonable" notice before entering your rented home, you'll naturally want to know how this translates into hours and days. 24 hours is generally presumed to be reasonable notice. Less notice (say, 10 or 15 hours) might be fine if the situation warrants it—for example, if your landlord finds out Thursday evening that an electrician is available Friday morning to put extra outlets in your apartment. Except for an emergency, less than four hours' notice is not ordinarily considered reasonable.

To find out precisely how your state's courts have interpreted the concept of reasonable notice, you'll need to look up recent court decisions. (Chapter 20 explains how to find statutes and the cases that have dealt with them.)

TIP

Tenants with disabilities might be entitled to special notice. A landlord who knows of a tenant with a disability's unusual needs for privacy will be expected to accommodate the tenant's needs in all but true emergencies. (Chapter 5 discusses the rights of tenants with disabilities.)

Must Notice Be in Writing?

Not all states require that notice be in writing. But it's a good idea to ask your landlord for written notice whenever possible, especially if the landlord has entered without permission previously. Keep copies of these written notices in your rental file, and also make a note of any oral or electronic requests for entry. Most important, if your landlord has entered without your permission or without giving proper notice, make a note of the time, date, and circumstances, listing the names of anyone else who witnessed or knows about the incident. This information will come in handy should you end up in a legal dispute with your landlord over this issue.

Time of Day Landlord May Enter

Most state access laws either don't specify what hours a landlord may enter your rental unit or simply allow entry at reasonable times. Weekdays between 9 a.m. and 6 p.m. would seem to be reasonable times, and perhaps Saturdays between 10 a.m. and 1 p.m. Some statutes are more specific.

Clarifying Access Rules

To make sure you and your landlord are operating on the same wavelength, be sure your lease or rental agreement includes a clause regarding landlord access to the property. If it doesn't, you might want to add a clause, or write a letter of understanding after you and the landlord have discussed the issue and come to an agreement. (Chapter 2 covers how to write a letter of understanding. Chapter 15 explains how to amend a lease or rental agreement.)

Spelling out clear guidelines is especially important if your state doesn't set specific rules regarding your landlord's entry. Ask your landlord to give you at least 24 hours' notice before entering your unit, except when there is a genuine emergency or you invite the landlord to enter. You could point out that this is the standard in many states. See the suggested lease clause in Chapter 2 for a good model.

Cooperating With Requests to Enter

Common sense suggests that if your landlord usually is respectful of your privacy, you're better off accommodating requests for entry, especially if the purpose is to make repairs that will benefit you. By taking a reasonably cooperative approach, you'll go a long way toward avoiding disputes and legal problems. Here's why.

You might be evicted. In every state, your landlord has certain legal rights of access. As long as your landlord complies with your state law as to reasons for entry and notice periods, your refusal to allow access can result in an eviction lawsuit.

Your tenancy might be terminated. Unless you have a long-term lease or live in a rent control area that requires the landlord to state a good reason (just cause) for eviction, you face the threat of losing your rental unit if your landlord concludes you are too difficult to deal with. Even though you might be within your legal or moral rights to deny your landlord access, your landlord could simply give you a 30-day notice and terminate your tenancy (or decline to renew your lease) rather than put up with you.

Your landlord might be less cooperative when you want a favor. If your landlord considers your desire for absolute privacy hard to cope with, don't expect much help when you make other requests. And you might get a negative reference when you eventually move on.

Adopting a reasonable attitude to landlord requests doesn't mean you should surrender your right to privacy and let your landlord enter at all hours of the day or night. There's no doubt about it: You should respond quickly to a landlord (or manager) who is entering without notice or good reason and make it clear that you won't tolerate clear violations of your privacy. But don't be hard-nosed just for the principle involved.

Entry by Others

Your landlord is not the only one who may enter your rental unit. This section describes your rights and responsibilities when other people, such as municipal inspectors, request entry.

Health, Safety, or Building Inspections

Rules regarding entry by state or local health, safety, or building inspectors are different from those that govern your landlord's right of access.

Responding to Neighbors' Complaints

If inspectors have a reasonable suspicion that your unit violates housing codes or local standards—for example, a credible source has complained about noxious smells coming from your home or about your 20 cats—they will usually knock on your door and ask permission to enter. Except in the case of genuine emergency, you have the right to say no.

Inspectors have ways to get around tenant refusals. A logical first step (maybe even before they stop by your rental unit) is to ask your landlord in advance to let them in. Because your landlord can usually enter on 24 hours' notice, this is probably the simplest approach. If inspectors can't reach your landlord or get cooperation, their next step will probably be to get a search warrant based on the information from your neighbors. The inspectors must first convince a judge that the source of their information—the neighbors—is reliable, and that there is a strong likelihood that public health or safety is at risk. Inspectors who believe that you will refuse entry often bring along police officers who have the right to overcome your objections.

Random Inspections

Fire, health, and other municipal inspectors sometimes randomly inspect apartment buildings even when they don't suspect noncompliance. These inspection programs have become increasingly popular, not only because they uncover substandard housing conditions, but because they are a revenue-generating scheme in some cities (landlords pay an inspection fee). These inspections might be allowed under state law or local ordinance. (Most ordinances exempt single-family homes and condominiums.)

The inspectors might contact your landlord first and ask permission to enter. If the landlord says yes and gives you 24 hours' notice (or whatever your state requires), the inspection can proceed. If the landlord refuses entry, the inspector will almost surely have a judge issue a search warrant. Such a warrant would allow inspectors to enter without

your or your landlord's permission to check for fire or safety violations. Again, if inspectors expect that you might resist, a police officer will usually accompany the inspector.

An inspector who arrives when you're not home might ask the landlord to open your door on the spot, disregarding your state's privacy laws. If the inspectors come with a warrant, the landlord can probably give consent, because even you couldn't prevent entry. But if the inspector is there without a warrant, your landlord probably cannot speak for you and say "Come on in." However, the answer will depend on each state's interpretation of its laws regarding warrantless entries. Cautious landlords will ask an inspector without a warrant to enter after the landlord has given you the proper amount of notice under your state's law or the terms of your lease or rental agreement.

Inspection Fees

Many cities impose fees for inspections, on a per unit or building basis or a sliding scale based on the number of a landlord's holdings. Some fees are imposed only if violations are found. If your ordinance imposes fees regardless of violations, your landlord might ultimately pass on the cost of the inspection to you in the form of a fee. It's not illegal for your landlord to do this, as long as your lease or rental agreement provides for it.

If your ordinance imposes a fee only when violations are found, your landlord should not pass the cost on to you if the noncompliance is not your fault. For example, if inspectors find that the landlord has failed to install state-mandated smoke alarms, the landlord should pay for the inspection; but if you have allowed garbage to pile up in violation of city health laws, you can expect to pay for the inspection (and the removal of the garbage).

Law Enforcement

Even the police cannot enter your rental unit unless they can show you or your landlord a recently issued search or arrest warrant, signed by a judge.

The police don't need a search warrant, however, if they need to enter to prevent a catastrophe, such as an assault or fire, if they are in hot pursuit of a fleeing criminal, or if they need to enter to preserve evidence of a serious crime. Also, different rules might apply if law enforcement suspects terrorist activity by a tenant.

Your Landlord's Right to Let Others In

Your landlord has no right to give others permission to enter your home. (The possible exceptions to this rule for municipal inspectors and police are discussed above.)

Occasionally a landlord or resident manager will be faced with a very convincing stranger who will tell a heart-rending story concerning the need to get into the rental right away.

If the landlord contacts you and you authorize entry, there's no problem. But what if the landlord can't contact you to ask whether it's okay to let the desperate individual in? This is one reason why your landlord should always know how to reach you during the day.

If the desperate person is telling your landlord the truth, chances are that if you could be contacted, you would say "Yes, let Uncle Harry in immediately." But even if your landlord could somehow verify the person's story without contacting you, letting anyone enter your home without your permission invades your privacy. The landlord risks being legally responsible should your property be stolen or damaged. If your landlord does let a stranger in without your permission, you can sue for any loss you suffer as a result.

Other Invasions of Privacy

Entering your home without your knowledge or consent isn't the only way a landlord can interfere with your privacy. Here are a few other common intrusions, with advice on how to handle them.

Giving Information About You to Strangers

Strangers, including creditors, banks, and prospective landlords, might ask your landlord to provide credit or other information about you.

Did you pay the rent on time? Did you maintain the rental property? Cause any problems?

Basically, your landlord has a legal right to truthfully respond to legitimate questions about you that are asked for verifiable business reasons. Examples include questions from your bank when you apply for a loan or from a prospective landlord who wants a reference. An extra-cautious landlord will ask for your written permission to release credit and similar information, but as long as the landlord's answer is in response to a legitimate request, a formal release is not legally required. (See the release form at the bottom of the rental application in Chapter 1.)

Landlords are within their rights to give out negative information on you, so long as it is absolutely factual. If your landlord spreads false stories about you—for example, says you filed for bankruptcy if this isn't true—and you suffer a loss as a result (for example, you don't get a job)—you can sue the landlord for defamation (libel or slander).

A landlord (or, more typically, an on-site manager) who spreads negative information about you (whether or not true) risks an invasion of privacy lawsuit. Examples include calling other landlords in your area to bad-mouth you, broadcasting that you haven't paid the rent, or telling others that you drink too much. This sort of gossip has no legitimate purpose and is malicious and damaging. It can rise to the level of an invasion of privacy that gives you valid reason to sue.

Bothering You at Work

In case of emergency, your landlord should have whatever phone number is necessary to reach you when you're at work. For many people, this is their cell phone number. But if you're unable to answer your cell phone during your work day, you should give your landlord your employer's or work number.

However, situations justifying a landlord's calling you at work are fairly rare. If a landlord calls you to complain about late rent payments or other problems, politely say you'll talk when you're at home. If this doesn't work, follow up with a brief note.

If the landlord persists or tries to talk to your boss or others about the problem, your privacy is being invaded. Write a letter asking the landlord to stop immediately. If the conduct continues, consider going to small claims court to sue for damages. If you lose your job or a promotion as the result of the landlord's conduct, see a lawyer. You might have the basis for a successful lawsuit.

Unduly Restricting Guests

Some landlords limit guests' visits—for example, no more than 10 days in any six-month period—to avoid having a guest turn into an unpermitted cotenant or subtenant. (See Chapter 7 for an explanation on how a resident can gain the status of a tenant.) A few landlords, overly concerned about possible rogue occupants, go overboard in keeping tabs on legitimate guests who stay overnight or for a few days. Some leases, rental agreements, or rules and regulations will require you to register any overnight guest. While your landlord has a legitimate concern about visitors becoming permanent unauthorized residents, it is overkill to require you to inform your landlord of a guest whose stay is only for a day or two.

In short, while your landlord does have a right to control who lives in the rental unit, your social life is your own business. Extreme behavior in this area—whether by an owner or a management employee—can be considered an invasion of privacy for which you may sue.

Spying on You

A few landlords have attempted to interrogate visitors, knock on tenants' doors at odd hours to see who answers, monitor your activities by way of a camera, or even peek through windows. Needless to say, this sort of conduct can give you cause to sue a landlord for invasion of privacy—and grounds for contacting the police.

Self-Help Evictions

It is illegal for the landlord to come on the property and perform acts intended to force you to move out. For example, it's illegal for landlords to do such things as remove windows and doors, turn off the utilities, or change the locks. (Chapter 18 discusses illegal "self-help" evictions.)

Sexual Harassment or Assault

If your landlord or manager comes onto your property or into your home and harms you in any way, sexually harasses you (see Chapter 5), threatens you, or damages any of your property, you should report the matter to the police. Some local police departments have taken the excellent step of setting up special landlord-tenant units. The officers and legal experts in these units have been given special training in landlord-tenant law and are often helpful in settling disputes and setting straight a landlord who has taken illegal measures against a tenant.

 RELATED TOPIC
You might have a discrimination claim.
As we explain in Chapter 5, if you are single, female, or a member of a protected class, and you have been harassed by the landlord, the landlord might also be violating fair housing laws.

What to Do About Invasions of Privacy

As you have undoubtedly figured out, it is one thing to have a right, and quite another thing to enforce it. This is especially true for tenants who don't have a long-term lease and don't live in an area where rent control laws require just cause for eviction. In these situations, a softer approach to invasions of privacy might be sensible, as an aggressive assertion of your rights might get you nothing more than a termination notice. Although you should be firm and determined in asserting your rights, being strident might be counterproductive.

By using the following step-by-step approach, you'll gradually increase the heat on a landlord who is violating your right to privacy. Usually, you'll get positive results without having to progress past the second step.

Step 1. Talk to the Landlord or Manager

As a first step, voice your concerns in a friendly but firm way. If you come to an understanding, follow up with a note to confirm it. See the Sample Letter When Landlord Violates Privacy (Friendly Approach), below. As with all important communications with your landlord, send your letter by mail, rather than email, so you'll have proof of what you sent, should you end up asserting your privacy rights in court.

TIP

Management companies often don't know what their managers are doing. If your property is managed by a professional management company, and the manager is invading your privacy, you might have to go over the manager's head to the company itself. It's best to assume the company doesn't know what's going on, and will take action to remedy the situation once you describe the situation. Look at your lease or rental agreement for contact information for the management company. If the lease is silent, you'll probably be able to find the information on the company's website. Call and

ask to speak to a company manager, politely tell them about the problem, and that you expect better. Follow up with a written letter if the problem continues.

Sample Letter When Landlord Violates Privacy (Friendly Approach)

February 5, 20xx

Joan Smith
123 Main St.
Portland, Oregon 00000

Dear Ms. Smith:

Thanks for sending your plumber over yesterday to fix my bathtub leak. I really appreciate your prompt response. As I mentioned, I would have preferred not to be home when the plumber came because I often work at home and need to be able to count on uninterrupted periods of time. As we discussed, next time you'll give me at least 24 hours' notice so I can plan accordingly.

Thanks again.

Sincerely,
Jon Klein
Jon Klein
Green Gables Apartment #4B
526 Grover Road
Portland, Oregon 00000

TIP

Work with other tenants. Chances are that if your landlord has entered your home repeatedly and without good reason or notice, find out whether other tenants in the building or complex have had the same problem. If so, you have a golden opportunity to organize your neighbors and exert concerted pressure by using, together, the steps outlined in this section. For all the obvious reasons, your group complaints will be taken more seriously and given more attention than if you are acting alone. (See Chapter 19 for tips on how to organize fellow tenants.)

Step 2. Write a Tough Letter

If the friendly, informal approach doesn't work, or if your landlord doesn't follow the agreement that you have worked out, it's time for a stronger, more formal letter that sets forth your legal rights and explains what you'll do if they aren't respected. To create a record of your demand, use a mail or delivery service that will provide proof of delivery. Assuming you are willing to risk alienating your landlord— perhaps because you have a lease and don't feel vulnerable or because your relationship is already bad—your letter should threaten a lawsuit if the illegal conduct doesn't stop pronto. This can be an especially effective technique if a group of tenants is working together.

A sample letter (for the get-tough approach) is shown below. Writing a letter like this—and keeping a copy of it and proof of delivery—will greatly improve your chances of winning in court if you decide to sue.

> **TIP**
>
> **Try mediation before filing a lawsuit.** It's always preferable in terms of cost, energy, and outcome. Mediation by a neutral third party is an especially good way to resolve disputes with your landlord when you want to continue living in your current rental unit. See Chapter 19 for details on finding and using a mediation service.

Step 3. Sue Your Landlord

If, despite your second letter, the invasions of your privacy continue, document them and either see a lawyer or take your landlord to small claims court.

Depending on the circumstances, you might be able to sue your landlord for:

- **Trespass:** entering your rental space without consent or proper authority.
- **Invasion of privacy:** interfering with your right to be left alone.

- **Breach of implied covenant of quiet enjoyment:** interfering with your right to undisturbed use of your home. ("Your Basic Right to Livable Premises," in Chapter 8, discusses the implied covenant of quiet enjoyment.)
- **Infliction of emotional distress:** a pattern of illegal acts—or one outrageous instance— by someone (in this case, the landlord or manager) who caused serious emotional consequences to you.

One difficulty with a lawsuit against a landlord for unlawful entry is that often you will have no demonstrable monetary damages. As a result, a judge likely will conclude that your landlord's walking on your rug and opening and closing your door didn't cause much harm—and you won't be awarded much money.

However, if you can show a pattern of illegal entry (and the fact that you asked the landlord to stop it), or even one clear example of outrageous conduct, you might be awarded a substantial recovery. You'll probably want an attorney for this kind of case, especially if you decide to sue in a court other than small claims court.

Here are examples of two court cases based on a landlord's unlawful entry.

EXAMPLE: Debra rented a townhouse from Grace. Grace approached Debra with a suggestion that they go into business together, but Debra declined. Feeling spurned, Grace demanded that Debra's cotenant leave. She called both tenants at home and at work, changed their locks, yelled obscenities, and ripped out their phone jack. Debra moved out, losing her prepaid rent and security deposit and incurring temporary housing costs. Debra sued Grace for trespass and, because the trespass was deliberate and outrageous, for emotional distress as well. The state appellate court directed the trial court, which had initially thrown the case out, to let it go to the jury. (*Johnson v. Marcel*, 465 S.E.2d 815. (Va. 1996).)

Sample Letter When Landlord Violates Privacy (Get-Tough Approach)

789 Porter St., #3
Cleveland, Ohio 00000

September 19, 20xx

Jan Roper Real Estate Co.
11 Peach Street
Cleveland, Ohio 00000

Dear Mr. Roper:

Several times in the last two months your resident manager, Pete Tuttle, has entered my apartment when I was not at home and without notifying me in advance. Following the second such visit, I wrote to you on August 20, demanding that these unannounced entries stop at once.

In spite of my letter, Pete continued to enter when I was not home and without notice. One time when I was home sick from work, he simply walked in without knocking.

In no situation was any emergency involved, and there was no real purpose for these visits. These intrusions have caused me considerable anxiety and stress, to the point that my peaceful enjoyment of my tenancy has been seriously disrupted.

This letter is to formally notify you that I value my privacy highly and insist that my legal rights to that privacy, as guaranteed to me under Ohio Rev. Code Ann. §§ 5321.04 and 5321.05, be respected. Specifically, in nonemergency situations, I am entitled to 24 hours' notice of your (or your employee's) intent to enter my home, and a clearly stated purpose of the entry.

I assume this notice will be sufficient to correct this matter. If you want to talk about this, please call me at home (555-7890) at night before 10 p.m.

Yours truly,

Sally South

Sally South

EXAMPLE: In New York, a landlord entered his tenant's apartment several times without permission. Although the entries did not make the premises unusable, they violated the tenant's reasonable expectation of privacy and New York's law that required the landlord to provide habitable premises. A judge ruled that the tenant was entitled to a retroactive rent abatement of 15%. (*Steltzer v. Spesaison*, 614 N.Y.S.2d 488 (1994).)

 RELATED TOPIC
Chapter 20 shows how to find and work with a lawyer. Chapter 19 discusses small claims court suits and dollar limits in each state.

Step 4. Move Out

A landlord's (extreme or repeated) violation of your right of privacy might give you a legal excuse to break a lease or end a tenancy early, without liability for further rent. If the landlord sues you for the rent after you leave, your defense can be that the extreme or repeated intrusions made it impossible for you to "quietly enjoy" your rented home—a right guaranteed to every tenant. Or you can argue that the landlord's behavior itself amounted to an eviction (lawyers call it "constructive eviction"), justifying your departure.

TIP
Don't take the law into your own hands. You do not have the right to use physical force against a land-lord who invades your privacy unless you can reasonably conclude that self-defense is needed. Do your best to remove yourself from the situation, then call the police.

Injuries on the Premises

If you have been injured on your landlord's property, you might have a legal claim against your landlord. That doesn't mean you'll have to file a lawsuit—most valid claims against landlords are settled without trial. It might be to your advantage to negotiate with the landlord's insurance adjuster or lawyer yourself, rather than to immediately hire a lawyer, who will typically take one-third of your recovery. If the landlord or insurer proves unreasonable, you can always hire a lawyer.

This chapter explains how to evaluate whether your landlord is liable for your injury, and what to do to maximize your chances of an acceptable settlement or lawsuit verdict.

 RELATED TOPIC
Also covered in this book:

- Landlords' repair and maintenance responsibilities: Chapters 8 and 9.
- Landlords' legal responsibility to provide premises that are safe from criminal acts: Chapter 14.
- How to recognize and deal with common environmental hazards: Chapter 13.
- How to sue for a landlord's tolerance of a legal "nuisance": Chapter 14.
- How to research your state's laws on personal injuries: Chapter 20.
- How to choose and work with a lawyer: Chapter 20.

What to Do If You're Injured

What is the best course of action to take if you're injured? If your injury is significant and costly—it has resulted in lost income, doctor's bills, and physical or emotional discomfort—and you think the landlord is at fault, you'll want to consider legal action. First, though, you'll need to decide whether to handle the claim yourself (at least initially) or hire a lawyer right away.

If your injury is severe, it's a good idea to consult a lawyer as soon as possible. The more severe your injury, the more likely it is that you will suffer

long-term effects—and medical bills—as a result. Personal injury lawyers specialize in accounting for and making sure you are compensated for both the short-term and long-term consequences of your injury.

You'll want to hire a lawyer to pursue your claim when you've experienced:

- a long-term or permanently disabling injury, such as the loss of a limb
- an injury that results in medical costs and lost income over $10,000, or
- heavy-duty toxic exposure, such as pesticide poisoning.

This book can't cover all the ins and outs of pursuing a personal injury claim. However, this chapter will discuss the basic steps of documenting, evaluating, and pursuing a claim, and will provide a good start for injured tenants seeking to represent themselves in pursuing their claim.

Get Immediate Medical Attention

The success of an accident claim often depends on what you do in the first hours and days after your injury. Although it can be difficult, attending to these details immediately following the incident will pay off later.

It is essential to get prompt medical attention for your injury, even if you consider it to be of marginal help to your physical recovery. No insurance company, judge, or jury will take your word alone for the extent of your injury, pain, and suffering. Even though it seems obvious that a sprained ankle could cause immobility, swelling, and pain that makes you miss a week's work, you'll need to have the nature and extent of your injury confirmed *and documented* by a physician. You'll need a written professional opinion to convince a skeptical insurance adjuster or jury that you didn't suffer a mere bruise that had minimal impact on your life.

Moreover, if you intend to hold the landlord financially responsible for your injuries, the law expects you to take whatever steps are possible to lessen the extent of your injuries and speed your recovery. The reason for this has little to do with concern for your physical well-being; rather, the law expects you to take reasonable steps to lessen the accident's financial impact on the landlord. In short, you'll need verification that you were a conscientious patient who did not ignore or prolong the effects of your injuries.

> **EXAMPLE:** May-Ling, a new tenant, slipped on a puddle of oil-slicked rainwater that habitually accumulated at the base of the garage stairs. She fell and badly twisted her back. Thinking that time would heal her wounds, she did not seek medical attention, though she did stay home from work for a week.
>
> She then filed a claim with the landlord's insurance company, seeking compensation for her pain and suffering and lost wages. The insurance adjuster questioned the severity of her injury and suggested that, had she consulted a doctor, she might have recovered sooner with the aid of treatment. Unable to verify the extent of her injury and having no way to effectively answer the claim that medical attention might have helped her, May-Ling settled her claim for a disappointing amount.

Write Everything Down

As soon as possible after the accident, jot down everything you can remember about how it happened. Include a complete list of everyone who was present and what they said. For example, if, after you tripped on a loose stair, the manager rushed over and blurted out, "I told Jim [the landlord] we should have replaced that last month!" be sure to write it down and note the names of anyone who heard the manager say it.

Describe the precise nature of your injuries, including pain, anxiety, and loss of sleep. Make notes daily, if you can. Take pictures of any visible wounds. Note every economic loss, such as lost wages, missed classes and events, and transportation and medical costs. If you have a conversation regarding the incident with anyone (the landlord, other tenants, an insurance adjuster, or medical personnel), make a written summary of the conversation.

Preserve Evidence

Claims are often won by the production of a persuasive piece of physical evidence: the worn or broken stair that caused the fall, the unattached throw rug that slipped when stepped on, the electrical outlet faceplate that showed burn marks from a short. Physical evidence that is not preserved within a short time can be lost, modified by time or weather, repaired, or destroyed. For example, the landlord, not wanting more accidents, might quickly replace a loose stair that caused you to fall, and throw the old one away.

If preservation of the evidence would involve dismantling the landlord's property, you might have to settle for the next-best alternative, photographs or videos. Don't wait—you need to make your record before repairs are made. Be sure to upload your photos to a secure place in the cloud, lest they be lost if you lose your phone.

To forestall challenges to the accuracy of your pictures (or a claim they were doctored), have someone else take them. Be prepared to testify in court that the photos are a fair and accurate depiction of the scene.

If you are experiencing pain or any incapacity, keep what's known as a "pain diary." Every day (and more often if appropriate), jot down how you feel, what you can and cannot do, and what medication you're taking to alleviate the injury. This log might come in handy if you are asked to document your condition.

Contact Witnesses

Having an eyewitness can be an immeasurable help. Witnesses can corroborate your version of events and might even have seen important aspects of the situation that you missed. But you must act very quickly to find and preserve the observations and memories of those who could bolster your case—people's memories fade quickly, and strangers can be very hard to track down later.

CAUTION

Don't tell witnesses not to talk to the "other side." Witnesses have no legal obligation to talk to you, although most will if they feel you have been wronged. Similarly, you have no legal right to tell them not to talk to others. Moreover, doing so might invite a suggestion that you had something to hide. If a favorable witness tells an insurance adjuster a different story, you can expose the inconsistencies later in court.

Get the names, addresses, and contact information of anyone who witnessed the incident, and as much information as possible about what they saw. Write up a summary of what they saw, and ask them if they would be willing to review it for accuracy so you have an idea of what to expect if they're interviewed by insurance or testify at a trial.

TIP

Don't overlook the witness who heard or saw another witness. It can often be important to have a witness to what another witness said or did. For example, the manager who blurted out, "I told him we should have fixed that last month" will have every incentive to deny making that statement, because it pins knowledge of the defect on the the manager's boss. If someone else also heard the manager say it, they'll have a tougher time disowning it.

Evaluate Your Case

Before making demands for money from your landlord or an insurance company, you need to know whether you have a legal leg to stand on. That's what most of the rest of this chapter expla `ins.

Get the Insurance Carrier Involved

Check your lease or rental agreement to find out who is the contact person to receive notices regarding your rental. If your lease or rental agreement is silent on who should receive notices, it's safe to assume that you'll need to contact your landlord or the property management company.

Notify the designated party or your landlord or property manager in writing that you have been injured. A sample letter is shown below. If your case is substantial, you can expect that the landlord will contact the insurer right away. On the other hand, a landlord who suspects that the claim is phony or trivial might hold off notifying the insurance company, fearing a rate increase or policy cancellation. At this point, you cannot force the landlord to refer the case or disclose the name of the insurer; all you can do is persevere until your persistence and the threat of a lawsuit become real enough for the landlord to call in the insurance company's help.

If a third party is involved, it won't hurt to notify them, too, if there is some basis for thinking that they might have been at least partially responsible. For example, a contractor or subcontractor might have created or contributed to the dangerous situation, or a repairperson might have done a faulty job, causing your injury.

**Sample Letter to Landlord
Regarding Tenant Injury**

37 Ninth Avenue North
South Fork, RI 00000
401-555-4567

February 28, 20xx

Fernando Diaz
3757 East Seventh Street
South Fork, RI 00000

Dear Mr. Diaz:

On February 25, 20xx, I was injured in a fall on the front steps of the duplex that I rent from you. The middle step splintered and collapsed as I walked down the stairs. Please refer this matter to the carrier of your business liability insurance and have them contact me at the above address.

Thank you for your cooperation.

Yours truly,

Alex Watson

Alex Watson

Negotiate, Mediate, or Sue

If the landlord's insurance carrier is involved, chances are that you'll negotiate a settlement. You can ask to submit the dispute to a mediator (a neutral third party who helps both sides reach a settlement) if you feel that the insurance company is interested in settling the matter and will deal with you fairly. (Mediation isn't binding; if you don't reach a mutually-agreeable settlement, you can always file a lawsuit.)

But if the landlord stonewalls you, refusing to refer your claim to the insurance carrier or a lawyer, you might need to consider a lawsuit. Chapter 19 gives detailed information on negotiating with, mediating with, and suing your landlord if necessary. It also helps you decide whether to take your case to small claims court yourself (saving time and the expense of hiring a lawyer) or whether you are better off in a formal court with a lawyer.

TIP

Don't wait too long before filing suit. You must file your lawsuit within the time specified by your state's "statute of limitations." Most states give you one to four years after your injury. Check the state-specific articles on Nolo.com (on the home page, choose "Articles" and type "personal injury statute of limitations [your state]"). Chapter 20 gives information on how to look up the underlying statute.

RESOURCE

How to Win Your Personal Injury Claim, by Joseph Matthews (Nolo), explains personal injury cases and how to work out a fair settlement without going to court.

Everybody's Guide to Small Claims Court, by Cara O'Neill (Nolo), provides great advice on small claims courts, which, in most states, allow you to sue for amounts up to $5,000 to $25,000.

Represent Yourself in Court: How to Prepare & Try a Winning Case, by Paul Bergman and Sara J. Berman (Nolo), will help you prepare and present your case should you end up in court.

Is the Landlord Liable?

It isn't always easy to determine whether the landlord is legally responsible for an injury. Basically, your landlord might be liable for your injuries if those injuries resulted from the landlord's:

- unreasonably careless conduct
- violation of a health or safety law
- failure to make certain repairs
- failure to keep the premises habitable, or
- reckless or intentional acts.

And in rare instances, the landlord might be liable because courts or the legislature in your state have decided that landlords are automatically liable for certain kinds of injuries, even though they haven't been careless.

Keep in mind that several of these legal theories might apply in your situation, and you (and your lawyer) can use all of them when pressing your claim. Basing your claim on more than one plausible theory of liability will likely yield better results when you negotiate with the landlord's insurance company.

The Landlord Was Unreasonably Careless

Most personal injury claims against landlords charge that the landlord acted negligently—that is, acted carelessly, in a way that wasn't reasonable under the circumstances—and that the injury was caused by that behavior.

Negligence is always determined in light of the facts of each situation. For example, it would be reasonable for a landlord to add lights to a dark, remote stairwell. If your landlord doesn't, and you're hurt because you couldn't see the steps and fell, your landlord's failure to install the lights might be negligence. On the other hand, if the stairwell had adequate lighting but a fuse blew ten minutes before your fall, it would be unreasonable to expect the landlord to have instantly fixed the problem.

To determine whether your landlord was negligent and should be held responsible for your injury, you must answer six questions. The insurance adjuster will use these same questions to evaluate your claim. If your case looks strong, you'll probably be able to wrest a good settlement offer from the company. And if the insurance company isn't forthcoming, you'll be able to head to court confidently, where a judge or jury will use the same questions when deciding your case.

Question 1: Did your landlord control the area where you were hurt or the thing that hurt you? The law will pin responsibility on your landlord only if your landlord had the legal ability to maintain or fix the area or item that injured you. For example, the property owner normally has control over a stairway in a common area, and if its chronic disrepair causes a tenant to fall, the owner will likely be held liable. The owner also has control over the building's utility systems, so if a malfunction causes injury (for example, you burn your hand when a broken water heater causes boiling water to come out of your tap), the owner might be held responsible for your injuries. On the other hand, if you're hurt when your own bookcase falls on you, your landlord—who has zero control over how the bookcase is built, set up, or maintained—will not be held responsible for your injuries.

Landlords can also be held responsible for dangerous conditions on adjacent land that they do not own, but over which they exercise some control (particularly when they know that tenants are using the area). For example, a landlord who knows that tenants are using an adjacent empty lot as a shortcut might have the duty to at least warn of any dangers (such as uneven ground). Or, local law might make owners responsible for repairing property-adjacent sidewalks.

Question 2: How likely was it that an accident would occur? The landlord isn't responsible if the accident wasn't foreseeable. For example, common sense would tell anyone that loose handrails or stairs are likely to lead to accidents. On the other hand, it would be unusual for peeling wallpaper to cause an injury. So, if a freak, unforeseeable accident does happen, chances are your landlord will not be held liable.

Question 3: How difficult or expensive would it have been for the landlord to reduce the risk of injury? A court is more likely to hold your landlord liable for your injuries if your landlord could have prevented the accident by taking reasonably priced measures. In other words, could something as simple as warning signs, a bright light, or caution tape have prevented people from even encountering the hazard? Or would major structural remodeling have been necessary to reduce the likelihood of injury? A court would expect a landlord to take reasonable low-cost steps to prevent even minor foreseeable injuries, but would not expect a landlord to take expensive steps to prevent a freak accident that could cause minor injuries.

When there is a great risk of very serious injury, landlords are expected to spend money to avert it. For example, a high-rise deck with rotten support beams must be repaired, regardless of the cost, because there is a great risk of collapse and dreadful injuries to anyone on the deck. A landlord who knew about the condition of the deck and failed to repair it would surely be held liable if an accident did occur.

Question 4: Was a serious injury likely to result from the problem? The amount of time and money your landlord is expected to spend on making the premises safe will also depend on the seriousness of the probable injury. For example, no one would expect an inoperable poolside umbrella to cause serious injury: If you're sunburned at the pool as a result, it's not likely that a judge would rule that your landlord had the duty of keeping you from getting burned. But if a dangerous situation is likely to result in serious injury—the ladder on the diving board is broken and might cause someone to fall to the ground—the owner is expected to take the situation more seriously and fix it faster.

The answers to these first four questions should tell you (or an insurance adjuster or judge) whether a dangerous condition existed on the property that the landlord had a legal duty to deal with. Lawyers call this having a "duty of due care." If, based on these questions, you think the landlord had a legal duty to deal with a condition on the premises that posed a danger to you, keep going. You have two more questions to answer.

Question 5: Did your landlord fail to take reasonable steps to prevent an accident? The law won't expect your landlord to undertake Herculean measures to shield you from a condition that poses some risk. Instead, the landlord is required to take only reasonable steps. For example, if you've demonstrated that a stair was broken, you also need to show that the landlord's failure to fix it was unreasonable in the circumstances.

Question 6: Did your landlord's failure to take reasonable steps to fix the hazard cause your injury? This last question establishes the crucial link between the landlord's negligence and your injury. Not every dangerous situation results in an accident. You'll have to prove that your injury was the result of the landlord's carelessness, and not some other reason. Sometimes this is self-evident: One minute you're fine, and the next minute you've slipped on a freshly waxed floor and have a broken arm. But it's not always so simple. For example, in the case of the loose stair, the landlord might be able to show that the tenant barely lost his balance because of the loose stair and that he had really injured his ankle during a touch football game he'd just played.

Examples of Injuries From Landlord Negligence

Here are some examples of injuries for which tenants have recovered money damages due to the landlord's negligence:

- Tenant falls down a staircase due to a defective handrail.
- Tenant trips over a hole in the carpet on a common stairway not properly maintained by the landlord.
- Tenant injured and property damaged by fire resulting from an obviously defective heater or wiring.
- Tenant gets sick from pesticide sprayed in common areas and on exterior walls without advance notice.
- Tenant's child is scalded by water from a water heater with a broken thermostat.
- Tenant slips and falls on a puddle of oil-slicked rainwater in the garage.
- Tenant's guest injured when she slips on ultraslick floor wax applied by the landlord's cleaning service.
- Tenant receives electrical burns when attempting to insert the stove's damaged plug into the wall outlet.
- Tenant slips and falls on wet grass cuttings left on a common walkway.

The Landlord Violated a Health or Safety Law

Many state and local governments have enacted health and safety laws requiring smoke detectors, sprinklers, inside-release security bars on windows, childproof fences around swimming pools, and so on. To put real teeth behind these important laws, legislators (and sometimes the courts) have decided that landlords who don't take reasonable steps to comply with certain health or safety statutes, will automatically be deemed legally negligent. And if that negligence results in an injury, the landlord is liable for it. You don't need to prove that an accident was foreseeable or likely to be serious; nor do you have to show that complying with the law would have been relatively inexpensive. The legal term for this rule is "negligence per se."

> **EXAMPLE:** A local housing code specifies that all kitchens must have grounded power plugs. Your kitchen does not have grounded plugs. As a result, you're injured when using an appliance in an otherwise safe manner. In many states, the law would presume negligence on the part of your landlord. If you can show that the ungrounded plug caused your injury, the landlord will be held liable.

Bear in mind that landlords are expected to take only reasonable steps to comply with safety and health laws that fall within the negligence per se realm. For example, most states require landlords to supply smoke detectors. If your landlord has supplied one, but you have disabled it, your landlord won't be held responsible if you are hurt by a fire that could have been stopped had you left the detector alone.

The landlord's violation of a health or safety law might also indirectly cause an injury. For example, if the landlord lets the furnace deteriorate in violation of local law, and you are injured trying to repair it, the landlord will probably be liable unless your repair efforts are extremely careless themselves.

> **EXAMPLE:** The state housing code requires landlords to provide hot water. In the middle of the winter, your hot water heater has been broken for a week, despite your repeated complaints to the landlord. Finally, to give your child a hot bath, you carry pots of steaming water from the stove to the bathtub. Doing this, you spill the hot water and burn yourself seriously.
>
> You sue the landlord for failure to provide hot water as required by state law. If the case goes to court, it will be up to the jury to decide whether the landlord's failure to provide hot water caused your injury. Many juries would think that your response to the lack of hot water was reasonable and foreseeable. Acknowledging this, your landlord's insurance company would probably be willing to offer a fair settlement.

The Landlord Didn't Make Certain Repairs

For perfectly sensible reasons, many landlords do not want tenants to undertake even relatively simple tasks like painting, plastering, or unclogging a drain. Your lease or rental agreement might prohibit you from making any repairs or alterations without the owner's consent, or limit what you can do. (Chapter 10 discusses this.)

But in exchange for a landlord's reserving the right to make all these repairs, the law imposes a responsibility. If, after being told about a problem, the landlord doesn't maintain or repair something you aren't allowed to touch, and you are injured as a result, the landlord is probably liable. The legal reason is that the landlord breached the contract (the lease) by not making the repairs. (The landlord might be negligent as well; remember, you can argue that there are multiple reasons why the landlord should be held liable.)

> **EXAMPLE:** The rules and regulations attached to Lori's lease state that management will inspect and clean the fan above her stove every six months. Jake, an affable but somewhat scatterbrained graduate student in charge of maintenance at the apartment complex, was supposed to do the fan checks. But deep into his studies and social life, Jake scheduled no inspections and, ten months later, Lori was injured when the accumulated grease in the fan filter caught fire.
>
> Lori sued the landlord, alleging that his failure to live up to his contractual promise to clean the fan was the cause of her injuries. The jury agreed and awarded her a large sum.

Some other common examples might include:

- **Environmental hazards.** If your lease forbids repainting without the landlord's consent, the landlord is obligated to maintain the painted surfaces. If the landlord is aware that the paint contains lead, and allows it to crack and deteriorate, the landlord will be liable for the health problems that follow. (Chapter 13 covers environmental health hazards such as lead-based paint.)

- **Security breaches.** Landlords typically forbid tenants from installing locks of their own. That means your landlord might be liable if the failure to provide secure locks contributes to a crime. (See Chapter 14.)

The Landlord Didn't Keep the Premises Habitable

One of a landlord's basic responsibilities is to keep the rental property in a "habitable" condition. A landlord who fails to maintain a habitable dwelling might be liable for injuries caused by the substandard conditions. For example, a tenant who is bitten by a rat in a vermin-infested building could argue that the owner's failure to maintain a rat-free building constituted a breach of duty to keep the place habitable, which in turn led to the injury. The injured tenant must show that the landlord knew of the defect and had a reasonable amount of time to fix it (but didn't).

This theory applies only when the defect is so serious that the rental unit is unfit for human habitation. For example, a window that won't close even partway would probably make a North Dakota rental unfit for habitation in the winter, but a torn screen door in a Florida apartment in the summer would not. The North Dakota tenant who cut herself trying to force the window to close might sue the landlord for negligence and for violating the implied warranty of habitability, while the Florida tenant would be limited to suing the landlord for negligence.

EXAMPLE: Jose notified his landlord about the mice that he had seen several times in his kitchen. Despite Jose's repeated complaints, the landlord did nothing to eliminate the problem. When Jose reached into his cupboard for a box of cereal, he was bitten by a mouse. Jose sued his landlord for the medical treatment he required, including extremely painful rabies shots. He alleged that the landlord's failure to eradicate the rodent problem constituted a breach of the implied warranty of habitability, and that this breach was responsible for his injury.

In the example above, the jury agreed and gave Jose a large monetary award. The injury sustained by Jose could also justify a claim that the injury resulted from the landlord's negligence. And, if Jose's landlord had failed to take reasonable steps to comply with a state or local statute concerning rodent control, the landlord might automatically be considered negligent. Finally, the owner might also be liable if the lease forbade Jose from making repairs, such as repairing improper sewage connections or changing the way garbage was stored. As you can see, sometimes several legal theories fit the facts and support your claim for damages.

The Landlord Acted Recklessly

In the legal sense of the word, "recklessness" usually means extreme carelessness regarding an obvious defect or problem. A landlord who is aware of a long-existing and obviously dangerous defect but neglects to correct it might be guilty of recklessness, not just ordinary carelessness.

If your landlord or the landlord's employee acted recklessly, your monetary recovery could be significant. This is because a jury has the power to award not only actual damages (which include medical bills, loss of earnings, and pain and suffering) but also extra, "punitive" damages. (See "How Much Money You're Entitled To," below.) Punitive damages are almost never given in simple negligence cases, but are appropriate to punish recklessness and to send a sobering message to others who might behave similarly. But don't count your millions before you have them: The line between ordinary negligence and recklessness is wherever the jury thinks it should be. The size of the punitive award is likewise up to the jury, and can often be reduced later by a judge or appellate court.

The unpredictability of punitive damage awards, however, can be to your advantage when negotiating with the landlord. The landlord might settle your claim rather than risk letting an indignant jury award you punitive damages.

EXAMPLE: The handrail along the stairs to the first floor of the apartment house Jack owned had been hanging loose for several months. Jack attempted to fix it two or three times by taping the supports to the wall. The tape did no good, however, and the railing was literally flapping in the breeze. One dark night when Hilda, one of Jack's tenants, reached for the railing, the entire thing came off in her hand, causing her to fall and break her hip.

Hilda sued Jack for her injuries. In her lawsuit, she pointed to the ridiculously ineffective measures that Jack had taken to deal with an obviously dangerous situation, and charged that he had acted with reckless disregard for the safety of his tenants. (Hilda also argued that Jack was negligent because of his unreasonable behavior and because he had violated a local ordinance regarding maintenance of handrails.) The jury agreed with Hilda and awarded her punitive damages.

The Landlord Intentionally Harmed You

Intentional injuries are rare but, unfortunately, they occur more often than you might guess. For example, if a landlord or manager struck and injured you during an argument, the landlord is liable for any injuries that result from this intentional act.

Less obvious, but no less serious, are emotional or psychological injuries which can, in extreme circumstances, also be inflicted intentionally. Intentional infliction of emotional distress often arises in these situations:

- **Sexual harassment.** Repeated, disturbing attentions of a sexual nature can leave the victim fearful, humiliated, and upset; and can form the basis for a claim of intentional harm. (See Chapter 5 for a detailed discussion of possible responses.)

    EXAMPLE: Rita's landlord Brad frequently made suggestive comments about her looks and social life. When she asked him to stop, he replied that he was "just looking out for her," and he stepped up his unwanted attentions. Rita finally had enough, broke the lease and moved out. When Brad sued her for unpaid rent, she turned around and sued him for the emotional distress caused by his harassment. To his surprise, Brad was slapped with a multi-thousand-dollar judgment that included punitive damages.

- **Assault.** Threatening or menacing someone without actually touching them is an assault, which can be enormously frightening and lead to psychological damage.
- **Repeated invasions of privacy.** Deliberately invading a tenant's privacy—by entering the rental without permission, for example—can cause extreme worry and distress. (Chapter 11 covers tenants' privacy rights.)

The Law Makes the Landlord Liable

In a few rare circumstances, even landlords who do their best to create and maintain safe rentals can be held responsible for tenants' injuries. In other words, a landlord who is not negligent might still be responsible for a tenant's injuries. This legal principle is called "strict liability," or liability without fault. It's similar to "no fault" auto insurance payments—the injured party collects without having to prove that the accident was the other person's fault.

Dog Bites and Other Animal Attacks

It's not uncommon for tenants (or their guests) to be injured by other tenants' dogs or other animals. In some situations, the landlord as well as the animal's owner will be legally liable for your injuries.

Dangerous domestic pets. You might be able to hold your landlord responsible for an injury caused by another tenant's dangerous domestic pet, such as a vicious dog, if you can convince a judge or jury that the landlord:

- knew (or, under the circumstances, must have known) of the animal's dangerous propensities, and
- could have prevented the injury—for example, by imposing a leash-only rule or evicting the rule-breaking pet owner.

Dangerous exotic pets. Keeping a wild animal such as a monkey or wolf as a pet is an "ultrahazardous" activity. In the eyes of the law, injured victims don't have to prove that the pet was dangerous—it's presumed dangerous, period. A landlord who knows that a wild animal is on the premises will likely be held liable along with the animal's owner if the animal injures a guest or tenant.

It's always advantageous for an injured tenant or guest to be able to sue the landlord as well as the pet's owner, because the landlord will almost always have an insurance policy to cover the claim. If the animal owner has renters' insurance, that policy might also cover a claim. Animal owners without renters' or homeowners' insurance are not covered for the consequences of their pets' misbehavior, and your ability to collect from them will depend on whether they have enough assets to satisfy a settlement or judgment.

In most states, strict liability is imposed by courts or lawmakers only when a hidden defect poses an unusually dangerous risk of harm to a group of persons unable to detect or avoid the danger. For example, Massachusetts landlords who fail to comply with specific statutory requirements are subject to strict liability if children under age six are poisoned by lead-based paint at the rental. (Mass. Gen. Laws ch. 111, § 199.)

Louisiana is the only state that makes strict liability available for a wide range of tenant injuries, but the quirkiness of the law (you must have been injured by a building's "ruin" caused by neglect or a "vice or defect" in the building's "original construction") mean it's rarely used in practice. (La. Civ. Code Art. 2322.) Most injured Louisiana tenants sue their landlords for negligence.

If You're at Fault, Too

If you sue your landlord for negligence, the landlord might turn right around and accuse you of negligence, too. And if you are partially to blame for your injury, the landlord's liability for your losses will be reduced accordingly.

Your Own Carelessness

If you are also guilty of carelessness—for example, you were drunk and, as a result, didn't (or couldn't) watch your step when you tripped on a loose tread on a poorly maintained stairway—in most states the landlord's liability will be proportionately reduced.

The legal principle is called "comparative negligence." Basically, this means that if you are partially at fault, you can collect only part of the value of your losses. For example, if a judge or jury ruled that you had suffered $10,000 in damages (such as medical costs or lost earnings) but that you were 20% at fault, you would recover only $8,000.

Comparative negligence is applied in different ways in different states. Depending on the law in their state, injured tenants might collect:

- 100% of their damages or losses, no matter how careless they were—even if they were 99% at fault.
- Only if their own carelessness was less than the landlord's. If it's equal to or greater than the landlord's, they get nothing.

- When their negligence was *equal to* or lower than the landlord's. If the jury concludes that the tenant and landlord were equally at fault, the tenant will collect half the damages.
- Nothing. In a few states, the doctrine of comparative negligence doesn't exist. When tenants are even the least bit negligent, they cannot collect anything.

It's not worth your while to learn the rule in your state—it's likely to be a fairly difficult call, anyway, and one that lawyers argue long and hard about. Instead, understand that if you are injured and intend to file a claim or lawsuit against your landlord, you'll need to consider whether your own carelessness played a part. If it did (or if you can expect the landlord to claim that it did), check with a lawyer or do your own legal research to find out what impact, if any, your carelessness might have on your chance of recovering.

Your Risk-Taking

Carelessness on your part is not the only way that your monetary recovery can be reduced. If you deliberately chose to act in a way that caused or worsened your injury, another doctrine might apply. Called "assumption of risk," it refers to the situation where a tenant knows the danger of a certain action but decides to take the chance anyway.

> **EXAMPLE:** In a hurry to get to work, you take a shortcut to the garage by using a walkway that you know has uneven, broken pavement. You disregard the sign posted by your landlord: "Use Front Walkway Only." If you trip and hurt your knee, you'll have a hard time pinning blame on your landlord, because you deliberately chose a known, dangerous route to the garage.

Injuries to Guests

Will your landlord be legally liable if a guest of yours is hurt on the rental property? In most states yes, as long as the guest was there at your invitation and was hurt while involved in an activity that the landlord could reasonably expect a guest to engage in. For example, your dinner guest who trips on a poorly maintained step while on the way to your front door could fairly look to the landlord for compensation, because using the steps is something the landlord would expect your guest to do. But suppose the laundry room is clearly posted, "For tenants' use only," and your guest is hurt there? The injured guest might not prevail.

If you are injured as a result of putting yourself in harm's way, you're in the same boat as those who contributed to their misery (comparative negligence, above), and the same rules of recovery apply.

How Much Money You're Entitled To

If you were injured on your landlord's property and have convinced an insurance adjuster or jury that the landlord is responsible, at least in part, you can ask for monetary compensation, called "compensatory damages." Injured tenants can recover the money they have lost (wages) and spent (doctors' bills), plus compensation for physical pain and suffering, mental anguish, and lost opportunities.

Medical care and related expenses. You can recover for doctors' and physical therapists' bills, including future care. Even if your bills were covered by your own insurance company or medical plan, you can still sue for the amounts—but expect your insurance company to come after you, via a lien claim, if you recover anything in excess of your co-payments or deductibles.

Missed work time. You can sue for lost wages and income while you were unable to work and undergoing treatment for your injuries. You can also recover for expected losses due to continuing care. The fact that you used sick or vacation pay to cover your time off from work is irrelevant. You are entitled to save this pay to use at your discretion at other times. In short, using up vacation or sick pay is considered the same as losing the pay itself.

Pain and other physical suffering. The type of injury you have suffered and its expected duration will affect the amount you can expect for pain and suffering. But insurance adjusters won't take your word for the level of discomfort you're experiencing. If you can show that your doctor has prescribed strong antipain medication, you'll have some objective corroboration of your distress. And the longer your recovery period, the greater your pain and suffering.

Permanent physical disability or disfigurement. If your injury has clear long-lasting or permanent effects—such as scars, back or joint stiffness, or a significant reduction in your mobility—the amount of your damages goes way up.

Loss of family, social, career, and educational experiences or opportunities. If you can demonstrate that the injury prevented you from advancing in your job or landing a better one, you can ask to be compensated for the lost income. Of course, it's hard to prove that missing a job interview resulted in income loss (after all, you didn't yet have the job). But the possibility that you might have moved ahead might be enough to convince the insurance company to sweeten its offer.

Emotional damages resulting from any of the above. Emotional pain, including stress, embarrassment, depression, and strains on family relationships, can be compensated. Like pain and suffering, however, it's hard to prove. If you have consulted a therapist, physician, or counselor, their evaluations of your reported symptoms can serve as corroborating evidence of your problems. Be aware, however, that when you choose to sue for mental or emotional injuries, to bolster your case, you'll usually need to provide the other side with copies of your doctor's notes and files regarding your symptoms and treatment. Claiming mental or emotional injuries might also open the door for the other side to investigate prior mental or emotional issues.

In some cases, injured tenants can collect more than compensatory damages. Punitive damages are awarded if a judge or jury decides that the landlord acted outrageously, either intentionally or with extreme carelessness (recklessness). Punitive damages are punishments for this conduct.

Environmental Hazards

andlords must also take steps to ensure that you and your family aren't sickened by several common hazards, including lead, asbestos, and radon. In many states, landlords are also responsible for addressing hazardous mold and bed bug infestations.

This chapter explains landlords' obligations and offers some suggestions on how to spot problems, work with the landlord (or housing authorities), and take steps to protect yourself.

> **RELATED TOPIC**
>
> **Also covered in this book:**
> - Your right to safe and habitable housing: Chapters 8 and 9.
> - Your legal options if you are injured by defective housing conditions: Chapter 12.

Asbestos

Exposure to asbestos has long been linked to an increased risk of cancer, particularly for asbestos manufacturing workers and construction workers who use asbestos materials. The danger of asbestos in homes has also been recognized.

Homes built before the mid-1970s often contain asbestos insulation around heating systems, in ceilings, in roof tiles, and in other areas. Until 1981, asbestos was also widely used in other building materials, such as vinyl flooring and tiles. Asbestos that is intact (or covered up) generally isn't a problem, and the current wisdom is to leave it in place but monitor it for signs of deterioration. However, asbestos that has begun to break down and enter the air—for example, when it is disturbed during maintenance or renovation work—can become a significant health problem to people who inhale it.

OSHA Regulations

Fortunately for tenants in every state, owners of buildings constructed before 1981 must install

warning labels, train staff, and notify people who work in areas that might contain asbestos. Unless the owner rules out the presence of asbestos by having a licensed inspector test the property, the law presumes that asbestos is present.

These requirements are imposed by the U.S. Occupational Safety and Health Administration (OSHA) to protect workers. In the process of complying with OSHA's requirements to inform and protect employees or outside contractors, your landlord learns whether there is asbestos on the property and (based on its type and quantity) what must be done to protect the workers. These precautions just happen to benefit tenants, too.

The only way landlords escape complying with OSHA's asbestos rules is if they never hire an employee, never use an outside contractor, and never otherwise learn about asbestos on the property. It would be a very rare landlord who never hires an outside contractor to perform services at a rental.

Once a landlord knows about the presence of any dangerous defect on the rental property, including asbestos, the law imposes a duty to take reasonable steps to make sure that tenants aren't harmed. In short, once the asbestos genie is out of the bottle, the landlord must take reasonable steps to protect your health or face the legal consequences.

Deteriorating Asbestos: An Obvious, Dangerous Defect

Problems with asbestos often arise when neither the landlord nor the tenant realizes that the material is embedded in ceilings and floors. Sometimes, however, the situation is not so subtle. Deteriorating asbestos that is open and obvious is a dangerous defect that your landlord must address pronto. It's no different from a broken front step or an inoperable front door lock. As the owner, the landlord is responsible for fixing conditions that could cause significant injury.

OSHA regulations cover two classes of materials: those that definitely contain asbestos (such as certain kinds of flooring and ceilings) and those that the law presumes contain asbestos. The second class is extremely inclusive, describing, among other things, any surfacing material that is "sprayed, troweled on, or otherwise applied." Under this definition, virtually every dwelling built before 1980 must be suspected of containing asbestos. Asbestos or asbestos-containing materials are typically found in or on:

- sprayed-on "popcorn" or "cottage cheese" ceilings
- acoustic tile ceilings
- vinyl flooring, and
- insulation around heating and hot water pipes.

When the Landlord Must Test for Asbestos

Landlords are required to comply with OSHA's asbestos testing and protective rules when they undertake a major remodel or renovation of a building built before 1981. They must also follow OSHA's asbestos rules for less-intensive projects that might in any way disturb asbestos (such as preparing an asbestos-containing ceiling or wall for repainting). Even relatively noninvasive custodial work—such as stripping floor tiles containing asbestos—comes within the long reach of OSHA.

OSHA has concluded that post-1981 buildings are unlikely to contain asbestos, but if your post-1981 building *does* have asbestos (perhaps the builder or remodeler used recycled building materials), OSHA regulations cover it, too.

Protection From Asbestos

OSHA requires very specific training, work techniques, and protective clothing for employees whose work involves disturbing asbestos. But OSHA does not specifically address the measures that landlords must take to protect tenants from exposure. However, the worker protection requirements give very useful clues as to what you can reasonably expect from your landlord in the way of tenant protections.

In short, whenever a landlord must take measures to protect workers from asbestos, the landlord must take steps to warn and protect tenants, too. Landlords who know they must take steps to protect workers but fail to take steps to protect tenants risk being liable for any tenant injuries that result from the asbestos. (See Chapter 12.)

- **Custodial work.** At the low end of the asbestos-disturbing spectrum, workers doing custodial work—for example, stripping the floor tiles in the lobby—must be trained (and supervised by a trained superior) in safe asbestos-handling techniques. Your landlord should warn all tenants that the work is planned, giving you an opportunity to avoid the area if you choose. The landlord should also make sure that tenants, their guests, and children don't come into contact with the debris. Conscientious landlords will use written notices to alert tenants, and place cones and caution tape around the area.
- **Major repairs or renovations.** If renovation or repair work is planned for a pre-1981 building, the landlord must test for asbestos and provide more protection, including air monitoring, protective clothing, and medical surveillance of workers. Tenants are entitled to appropriate warnings, and the landlord should minimize tenants' exposure through fastidious worksite procedures and isolation of dangerous materials.

EXAMPLE: Sally returned home to her apartment to find that workers were planning to remove the ugly, stained ceiling tile in the lobby and hallways. She learned from the contractor that the project would last four days. Sally was concerned that her young sons, returning home from school in the afternoon and curious about the renovations, would hang around the halls and lobby or at least pass through them as they went in and out to play. Either way, Sally's sons would be exposed to the airborne fibers. Sally wrote a note to the landlord, explaining her concerns.

Sally's landlord recognized the reasonableness of her fears and the potential for injury. He spoke with the contractor, one who had been specially trained in asbestos removal, and arranged for the work to be done between the hours of 8 a.m. and 3 p.m. He insisted, and the contractor readily agreed, that the old tiles be removed and any asbestos-containing material covered at the end of each work day. Finally, the landlord hired two adults to monitor foot traffic in and around the renovation site, to ensure that no one lingered near the workers or came into contact with the removed materials.

Alerting and Motivating Your Landlord

Many landlords, unfortunately, have no idea about their duty to deal with the risks posed by asbestos. If you live in an older building and suspect that there is asbestos on the premises that is not being managed properly, alert your landlord and see to it that your health is protected. Here are some strategies.

When the asbestos is obvious but intact. Asbestos that is intact—for example, asbestos insulation that is covered with foil or wrapped with tape—probably does not pose a significant health risk to you, because the covered fibers can't enter the air. It is important, however, that asbestos be monitored for signs of deterioration. For example, if the tape wrapping is tearing or falling away, it is no longer doing its job of containment. If you are worried about asbestos-containing materials in your home, ask your landlord, in writing, to have the material inspected by a trained professional.

CAUTION
Never disturb asbestos-containing materials.
You shouldn't drill holes in walls or ceilings that contain asbestos, or sand asbestos tiles in preparation for a new coat of paint. First, you want to protect your health. Second, intentionally disturbing asbestos will almost certainly reduce, if not defeat, any legal claim you might have if you're injured by asbestos in your rental. The law won't hold your landlord responsible for an injury that you deliberately courted, ignoring a risk you knew about. (See Chapter 12.)

When the asbestos is obvious and airborne. Take immediate action if asbestos in your living space has begun to break down or slough off. Asbestos that has begun to break down is extremely dangerous. If it is present in your living space in any significant amount, it makes your premises legally uninhabitable. (See Chapter 8 for your legal options, which might include withholding rent. Also, below, we discuss the option of moving out.) A sample letter from a tenant concerned about deteriorating asbestos is shown below.

TIP
Keep copies of all correspondence regarding asbestos or other environmental health hazards. If your landlord fails to take the right steps and you want to move out or seek other legal remedies, you'll need to be able to prove that you notified the landlord of the problem and waited a reasonable amount of time for a response.

When custodial or repair work is done improperly. When it comes to asbestos removal, the people who suffer most from a landlord's disregard of workplace safety are the workers themselves. But improper asbestos removal or disturbance is likely to affect you, too. Fortunately, there is something you can do about it. OSHA wants to hear about violations of workplace safety rules. You can reach OSHA by calling the phone number listed below in "Asbestos Resources." Many states have state equivalents of OSHA, and you can also call your state's consumer protection agency for information.

CAUTION
Beware of landlord retaliation. A landlord who learns about your complaint to OSHA won't be pleased. Many (but not all) states have laws that prohibit landlords from taking actions against tenants (such as rent hikes, diminution of services, or ending a tenancy) after tenants have exercised their legal rights by contacting a federal or state agency regarding a violation of law. (See "State Laws Prohibiting Landlord Retaliation" in Appendix A.) If you aren't protected by an antiretaliation statute, proceed carefully and, if possible, anonymously.

Sample Letter Regarding Deteriorating Asbestos

37 Ninth Avenue North
Chicago, Illinois 00000
312-555-4567

February 28, 20xx

Margaret Mears
3757 East Seventh Street
Chicago, Illinois 00000

Dear Ms. Mears:

As you know, the ceilings in my apartment are sprayed-on acoustical plaster. I have begun to notice an excessive amount of fine, white dust in the apartment, and I believe it is the result of the breakdown of the asbestos fibers in the plaster. I am quite concerned about this, because inhaling asbestos can cause serious illness. Please contact me immediately so that you can take a look and arrange for a licensed inspector to examine the ceilings.

Yours truly,

Terry Lu

Terry Lu

Sample Letter Requesting Reimbursement for Temporary Housing

1289 Central Avenue, Apartment 8
Toofar, TX 00000
713-555-7890

June 13, 20xx

Mr. Frank Brown, Owner
Sunshine Properties
75 Main Street
Toofar, TX 00000

Dear Mr. Brown:

I have just received the notice you sent to all tenants on the first floor, alerting us to the fact that you intend to tear out the heating ducts and insulation during the week of July 6. The work will involve removal of heating vents inside our apartment and removal of the asbestos insulation through the openings. You estimate that the work will take two days for each apartment.

I do not think that it would be a good idea for me and my elderly mother to live in the apartment during this process. I am concerned that we will inhale airborne fibers that might cause difficulties in breathing. My mother suffers from chronic bronchitis and cannot risk exposure to anything that might worsen the condition. Dr. Jones, who treats my mother, would be happy to corroborate this fact.

I think that the best solution would be for us to move out while this work is being done. The nearby Best Midwestern Motel has reasonable rates and would be convenient to our jobs and transportation. Please contact me so that we might discuss this before the renovation work begins. You can call me at home at the above number most nights and weekends.

Yours truly,

Sharon Rock

Sharon Rock

cc: Dr. Jones

Moving Out If Necessary

Sometimes it isn't possible to shield yourself from the effects of deteriorating asbestos, or even your landlord's major repairs or renovations involving asbestos. For example, if the acoustic ceilings in your apartment are being removed, it is unlikely (even if you and your landlord are prepared to take every precaution) that you can avoid inhaling some dangerous airborne fibers. In situations like this, the best option might be to move out temporarily until the work is completed. (See Chapter 8 for a discussion of moving out because your rental is uninhabitable.) Because the responsibility to repair and maintain the structure is the landlord's, the cost of temporary shelter should be covered by the landlord as long as you can convincingly establish that remaining on the premises would constitute a significant health risk. See the sample letter below.

If you are able to give valid reasons why you should be absent until the asbestos removal work is done, and if you have a reasonable landlord who appreciates the potentially serious legal consequences of denying your reasonable request, chances are you'll be able to come to an agreement. (Don't ask to stay at the Ritz, however!)

But what if the landlord stubbornly refuses? Obviously, to protect your health, you'll want to move out anyway. And assuming the asbestos problems really are serious, you should stand a good chance of prevailing in a small claims court lawsuit for the cost of your temporary housing. Be sure to keep a copy of the letter you have sent (preferably by certified mail) to the landlord, a record of any refusal to pay for temporary accommodations, and all receipts for your expenses.

TIP
Come to court prepared with asbestos-related information. If you go to small claims court, be prepared to explain the serious dangers of breathing asbestos fibers to the judge and why the landlord's work was so invasive that temporarily moving out was your only sensible alternative. See "Asbestos Resources," below. Also, see Chapter 19 for a discussion of small claims lawsuits.

Instead of suing in small claims court, you might be tempted to utilize what the law calls a "repair and deduct" remedy (discussed in Chapter 8) by simply deducting the cost of replacement housing from your rent. Even though it sounds like a reasonable solution, a judge might not allow it. Seizing upon this uncertainty, your landlord's response will probably be to terminate your tenancy and file for eviction for nonpayment of rent. If you lose, you will not only have to pay for the cost of the temporary housing, but face eviction from your rental as well. (In addition, you might be stuck with the landlord's attorneys' fees if your lease has an "attorneys' fees" clause. See Chapter 2.) Far better to file a straightforward lawsuit asking for reimbursement, where the risk is simply losing the suit, not your home.

If your landlord refuses to cover temporary housing expenses, you might also want to consider moving out permanently. This option is most appropriate when the risk is great and the length of exposure relatively long. But to justify breaking the lease (and to avoid liability for future rent), you will have to be able to show that airborne asbestos really did make the premises uninhabitable. (See Chapter 8 for a full discussion of breaking the lease due to uninhabitability.) If the landlord is ripping out whole ceilings over a month's time, this argument will be strong. However, it will not amount to much if the landlord is drilling two small holes in the ceiling to install a smoke detector.

TIP
Check to see if your state law allows landlords to terminate tenancies for major renovation. Some states allow landlords to terminate tenancies early when they plan to do major renovation, so long as they provide relocation assistance for tenants. "State Landlord-Tenant Statutes" in Appendix A gives citations to your state's landlord-tenant codes, and "State Laws on Unconditional Quit Terminations" gives citations to laws that explain when landlords may terminate your tenancy. In one or another of those sets of laws, you might find that your state requires your landlord to pay for moving expenses if your tenancy is terminated because a major project (such as wide-scale asbestos removal) makes it impossible for you to stay on the premises.

Asbestos Resources

For further information on asbestos rules, inspections, and control, contact the nearest office of the U.S. Occupational Safety and Health Administration (OSHA) (find yours at OSHA.gov or call 800-321-OSHA). For additional information on asbestos, its negative health effects, and what you can do to protect your family, visit the EPA website, at www.epa.gov/asbestos.

Lead

Exposure to lead-based paint and lead water pipes can lead to serious health problems, particularly in children. Brain damage, attention disorders, and hyperactivity have all been associated with lead poisoning. Studies show that the effects of lead poisoning are lifelong, affecting both personality and intelligence. In adults, lead poisoning can cause nerve disorders, high blood pressure, reproductive disorders, and muscle and joint pain.

How Lead Poisoning Occurs

Lead-laden dust caused by the deterioration of exposed lead-based paint is the greatest source of lead poisoning. Falling on windowsills, walls, and floors, this dust makes its way into the human body when it is stirred up, becomes airborne and is inhaled, or when it is transmitted directly from hand to mouth. Exterior lead-based house paint is also a potential problem because it can slough off walls directly into the soil and be tracked into the house.

Lead dust results from simple deterioration, as well as renovations or remodeling—including, unfortunately, those very projects undertaken to rid premises of the lead-based paint. Lead poisoning can also occur from drinking water that contains leached-out lead from lead pipes or from deteriorating lead solder used in copper pipes.

Children between the ages of 18 months and five years are the most likely to be poisoned by lead-based paint. Their poisoning is detected when they become ill or, increasingly, in routine examinations that check for elevated blood levels of lead.

Buildings constructed before 1978 are likely to contain some source of lead: lead-based paint, lead pipes, or lead-based solder used on copper pipes. In 1978, the federal government required the reduction of lead in house paint; lead pipes are generally only found in homes built before 1930, and lead-based solder in home plumbing systems was banned in 1988. Pre-1950 housing in poor and urban neighborhoods that has been allowed to deteriorate is by far the greatest source of lead-based paint poisonings.

Discovering (or being told by the landlord) that there is lead on the premises is not necessarily the end of a healthy and safe tenancy. Below, we offer advice on how to cope with a lead problem.

Federal Protections

Unfortunately, federal law does *not* require landlords to test for lead, nor does it require them to get rid of it even when they know it's present. Still, federal law aimed at reducing lead poisoning does provide some important benefits to tenants. Many states give additional protections.

Disclosure

Most landlords who rent property built before 1978 must inform tenants of any information they possess on lead paint hazard conditions on the property. Federal law requires landlords to provide this information, along with certain disclosures (discussed below), to tenants before the tenants sign or renew a lease or rental agreement.

Landlords must disclose the presence of lead in individual rental units, common areas and garages, tool sheds, other outbuildings, signs, fences, and play areas. If the property has been tested for lead (testing must be done only by state-certified lead inspectors), a copy of the report, or a summary written by the inspector, must be shown to tenants.

With certain exceptions (listed below), every lease and rental agreement must include a disclosure page, even if the landlord has not tested. A copy of the federally approved disclosure form "Disclosure of Information on Lead-Based Paint and/or Lead-Based Paint Hazards" is reproduced below.

Lead Inspections

Federal law does not require landlords to inspect their properties for lead. However, landlords can voluntarily arrange for an inspection in order to certify on the disclosure form that the property is lead free and exempt from federal regulations. (See list of exemptions, below.) When a property owner takes out a loan or buys insurance, the bank or insurance company might require a lead inspection.

Professional lead inspectors don't always inspect every unit in large, multifamily properties. Instead, they inspect a sampling of the units and apply their conclusions to the property as a whole. Giving the landlord the results and conclusions of a building-wide evaluation satisfies the law, even if your particular unit was not tested. If, however, your landlord has specific information regarding your unit that is inconsistent with the building-wide evaluation, your landlord must disclose it to you.

For information on arranging a professional lead inspection or using a home testing kit, see "Recognizing Lead in Your Home," below.

Information

The landlord must give all tenants the lead hazard information booklet *Protect Your Family From Lead in Your Home,* written by the Environmental Protection Agency (EPA). If they choose, landlords can reproduce the booklet in a legal-size, 8½ x 14-inch format, and attach it to the lease. Any copy of the booklet must include the graphics that are in the original. State agencies can develop their own pamphlets, but they cannot be used in place of the EPA version unless the EPA has approved them.

Along with the EPA booklet and any known information about the presence of lead-based paint, your landlord must also provide you with a "Lead Warning Statement." This statement, which confirms that the landlord has complied with all notification requirements, can be included in or attached as a separate document to the lease or rental agreement.

If your landlord has not given you a disclosure form or an EPA booklet, ask for them. If you get no results, notify the EPA. This will probably result in no more than a letter or call from the inspectors, because the EPA will usually not cite landlords unless their noncompliance with the laws is willful and continuing. But a landlord who continues to ignore the law might be subject to the penalties described below.

Enforcement and Penalties

HUD and the EPA enforce renters' rights to know about the presence of lead-based paint by using "testers," as they do when looking for illegal discrimination (see Chapter 5). Posing as applicants, testers who get the rental will document whether landlords disclosed lead paint information before the lease or rental agreement was signed. Individual complaints from tenants who have not received the required booklets can trigger an investigation, too.

Landlords who fail to provide all the required disclosures are subject to one or more of the following penalties:

- a notice of noncompliance (the mildest form of reprimand)

- a civil penalty (which can include fines of up to $21,018 per violation for willful and continuing noncompliance)
- an order to pay an injured tenant up to three times his actual damages, or
- a criminal fine of up to many thousands of dollars per violation.

Rental Properties Exempt From Federal Regulations

- **Housing for which a construction permit was obtained, or on which construction was started, after January 1, 1978.** Older buildings that have been completely renovated since 1978 are not exempt, even if every painted surface was removed or replaced.
- **Housing certified as lead-free by a state-accredited lead inspector.** Lead-free means the absence of any lead paint, even paint that has been completely painted over and encapsulated.
- **Lofts, efficiencies, studios, and other "zero-bedroom" units, including dormitory housing and rentals in sorority and fraternity houses.** University-owned apartments and married student housing are not exempted.
- **Short-term vacation rentals.**
- **A single room rented in a residential home.**
- **Housing designed for persons with disabilities** (as explained in HUD's Fair Housing Accessibility Guidelines, 24 C.F.R., ch. I, Subchapter A, App. II), unless any child less than six years old resides there or is expected to reside there.
- **Retirement communities** (housing designed for seniors, where one or more tenant is at least 62 years old), unless children under the age of six are present or expected to live there.

Government testers are also on the lookout for property owners who falsely claim that they have no knowledge of lead-based paint hazards on their property. Here's how it often comes up: A tenant complains to HUD after becoming ill with lead poisoning despite the landlord's disclosure stating

Disclosure of Information on Lead-Based Paint and/or Lead-Based Paint Hazards

Lead Warning Statement

Housing built before 1978 may contain lead-based paint. Lead from paint, paint chips, and dust can pose health hazards if not managed properly. Lead exposure is especially harmful to young children and pregnant women. Before renting pre-1978 housing, lessors must disclose the presence of known lead-based paint and/or lead-based paint hazards in the dwelling. Lessees must also receive a federally approved pamphlet on lead poisoning prevention.

Lessor's Disclosure

(a) Presence of lead-based paint and/or lead-based paint hazards (check (i) or (ii) below):

   (i) _____ Known lead-based paint and/or lead-based paint hazards are present in the housing (explain).

   _____

   _____

   (ii) _____ Lessor has no knowledge of lead-based paint and/or lead-based paint hazards in the housing.

(b) Records and reports available to the lessor (check (i) or (ii) below):

   (i) _____ Lessor has provided the lessee with all available records and reports pertaining to lead-based paint and/or lead-based paint hazards in the housing (list documents below).

   _____

   _____

   (ii) _____ Lessor has no reports or records pertaining to lead-based paint and/or lead-based paint hazards in the housing.

Lessee's Acknowledgment (initial)

(c) _____ Lessee has received copies of all information listed above.

(d) _____ Lessee has received the pamphlet *Protect Your Family from Lead in Your Home.*

Agent's Acknowledgment (initial)

(e) _____ Agent has informed the lessor of the lessor's obligations under 42 U.S.C. 4852d and is aware of his/her responsibility to ensure compliance.

Certification of Accuracy

The following parties have reviewed the information above and certify, to the best of their knowledge, that the information they have provided is true and accurate.

_____	_____	_____	_____
Lessor	Date	Lessor	Date
_____	_____	_____	_____
Lessee	Date	Lessee	Date
_____	_____	_____	_____
Agent	Date	Agent	Date

that the landlord had no knowledge of lead-based paint hazards on the premises. If HUD decides to investigate whether, in fact, the landlord knew about the hazard and failed to tell the tenant, their investigators get access to the landlord's records. They comb leasing, maintenance, and repair files—virtually the landlord's entire business records. If HUD finds evidence that the landlord knew (or had reason to know) of lead paint hazards, such as a contract from a painting firm that includes costs for lead paint removal, or a loan document indicating the presence of lead paint, the landlord will be hard pressed to explain why the box on the disclosure form stating that there are no reports or records regarding the presence of lead-based paint on the property is checked. The tenant, in turn, will have good evidence to use in court.

RESOURCE

The Residential Lead-Based Paint Hazard Reduction Act was enacted in 1992 to reduce lead levels. It is commonly referred to as Title X [Ten] (42 U.S.C. § 4852d). The Environmental Protection Agency (EPA) has written regulations that explain how landlords should implement lead hazard reduction (24 C.F.R. Part 35 and 40 C.F.R. Part 745). For more information, see "Lead Hazard Resources," below.

Federal Rules Covering Renovations

When occupied rental units or common areas in buildings constructed before 1978 are renovated, EPA regulations require that current tenants receive lead hazard information before the renovation work begins. (40 C.F.R. §§ 745.80–88.) The regulations were developed under the federal Toxic Substances Control Act (15 U.S.C. §§ 2681–2692) and became effective on June 1, 1999.

The obligation to distribute lead information rests with the "renovator." If the landlord hires an outside contractor to perform renovation work, the contractor is the renovator. But if the landlord,

property manager, or superintendent or other employees perform the renovation work, the landlord is the renovator and is obliged to give tenants the required information.

The type of information that the renovator must give to tenants depends on where the renovation is taking place. If an occupied rental unit is being worked on, resident tenants must get a copy of the EPA pamphlet *The Lead-Safe Certified Guide to Renovate Right* (even if you already got one when you moved in). If common areas will be affected, the landlord must distribute a notice to every rental unit in the building.

What Qualifies as a Renovation?

According to EPA regulations, a "renovation" is any change to an occupied rental unit or common area of the building that disturbs painted surfaces. Here are some examples:

- removing or modifying a painted door, wall, baseboard, or ceiling
- scraping or sanding paint, and
- removing a large structure like a wall, partition, or window.

Not every renovation triggers the federal law, though. The law recognizes four big exceptions:

Emergency renovations. If a sudden or unexpected event, such as a fire or flood, requires emergency repairs to a rental unit or to the property's common areas, there's no need to distribute lead hazard information to tenants before work begins.

Minor repairs or maintenance. Minor work that affects *two square feet or less* of a painted surface is also exempt. Minor repairs include routine electrical and plumbing work, so long as no more than two square feet of the wall, ceiling, or other painted surface gets disturbed by the work.

Renovations in lead-free properties. If the rental unit or building in which the renovation takes place has been certified as containing no lead paint, the landlord isn't required to give out the required information.

Common area renovations in buildings with three or fewer units. Tenants in buildings with three or fewer units are not entitled to information about common area renovations.

If your landlord has repainted a rental unit in preparation for your arrival, this won't qualify as a "renovation" unless accompanied by sanding, scraping, or other surface preparation activities that might generate paint dust. Minor "spot" scraping or sanding can qualify for the "minor repairs and maintenance" exception if no more than two square feet of paint is disturbed on any surface to be painted. To learn more, go to the EPA website (EPA.gov) and type Renovation, Repair, and Painting Program in the search box on the home page.

Receiving the EPA Pamphlet When Your Rental Is Renovated

Before starting a renovation to an occupied rental unit, the renovator must give the EPA pamphlet *The Lead-Safe Certified Guide to Renovate Right* to at least one adult occupant of the unit being occupied, preferably the tenant. This requirement applies to all rental properties, including single-family homes and duplexes, unless the property has been certified lead-free by an inspector.

The renovator (whether your landlord or an outside contractor) can mail or hand-deliver the pamphlet to you. Renovators who mail the notice must get a "certificate of mailing" from the post office dated at least seven days before the renovation work begins. If the renovator hand-delivers it, you'll probably be asked to sign and date a receipt acknowledging that you received the pamphlet before renovation work began in the unit. You should get the pamphlet 60 days (or less) before the work begins (delivering the pamphlet more than 60 days in advance won't satisfy the renovator's obligations under the law).

Notice of Common Area Renovation

If the building has four or more units, the renovator must notify tenants of all "affected units" about the renovation and tell them how to obtain a free copy of the EPA pamphlet *The Lead-Safe Certified Guide to Renovate Right*. (C.F.R. § 745.84(b)(2).) In most cases, common area renovations will affect all units in the property, meaning that all tenants must be notified about the renovation. But when renovating a "limited use common area" in a large apartment building, such as the 16th floor hallway but no others, the landlord need only notify those units serviced by, or in close proximity to, the limited use common area. The EPA defines large buildings as those having 50 or more units.

To comply, the renovator must deliver a notice to every affected unit describing the nature and location of the renovation work, its location, and the dates the renovator expects to begin and finish work. Renovators who cannot provide specific dates may use terms like "on or about," "in early June," or "in late July" to describe expected starting and ending dates for the renovation. The notices *must be delivered within 60 days before work begins.* The notices may be slipped under apartment doors or given to any adult occupant of the rental unit. Renovators may *not* mail the notices.

Penalties

Failing to give tenants the required information about renovation lead hazards can result in harsh penalties. Renovators who knowingly violate the regulations can get hit with a penalty of up to $37,500 per day for each violation. (15 U.S.C. § 2615.) Willful violations can also result in additional fines and imprisonment.

State Laws on Lead Affecting Tenants

Many states have also addressed the lead issue by prohibiting the use of lead-based paint in residences and requiring the careful maintenance of existing lead paint and lead-based building materials. Some states require property owners to disclose lead hazards to prospective tenants. If your state has its own lead statute, you're entitled to its protections as well as the federal law.

If your state has its own lead hazard reduction law, you'll see that, like its federal cousin, it does not directly require the landlord to test for lead. Does this mean that the landlord need not conduct inspections? Not necessarily. In New York City, for example, landlords must perform annual visual inspections of rental units where a child under age six resides. Landlords must inspect for "lead-based paint hazards," defined as peeling paint or deteriorated subsurfaces. New York City landlords must also visually inspect any vacant apartments before the unit may be reoccupied. For more information on the New York City Childhood Lead Poisoning Prevention Act of 2003, commonly known as Local Law 1 (Administrative Code of City of N.Y. § 27-2012[h]), see the City's informational booklet, *What Every Tenant Should Know About LOCAL LAW 1* (type this title into your browser to access the booklet).

Recognizing Lead in Your Home

If your landlord has tested for lead and complied with federal disclosure requirements, you can skip this section. However, most landlords have not tested for lead. There are several clues as to whether there is lead in or around your home, and ways that you (or, ideally, your landlord) can find out for sure.

You will need to hire a licensed lead tester to get a precise assessment of the risk of lead in your home. Unfortunately, the cost is high—a few hundred dollars at least. If you (and possibly other tenants) choose to do an assessment, you'll be in a good position to lobby the landlord to do something about containing the risk. But even if you do not get a professional's opinion, but are fairly sure that lead is present in your home, you can still act prudently on your own to reduce the risk. (Below, we explain what you can do yourself and how to get the landlord to act.)

Paint

Your first step should be to determine the age of the building. If the landlord doesn't know or won't say, go to the local building permit office and ask to see the building's construction permit. You might also find the building's age by searching the tax assessor's website, or most online real estate websites (such as Realtor.com and Zillow.com) list the year a residence was built. If these methods don't give you the age, you'll have to estimate.

As noted above, housing that was built before January 1, 1978 is almost certain to have lead-based paint. But buildings constructed later might have it, too, because the 1978 ban did not include a product recall, so lead-based paint remained on the shelves.

You can do your own test for lead. Home testing kits work like this: After you swab a chemical solution over a painted surface, the swab will turn a certain color if lead is present. Kits are widely available at hardware and paint stores and are inexpensive, but unfortunately are unreliable about 30% of the time. For more reliable results, hire a professional tester who will use an X-ray gun to give an instant reading through all the layers of paint. A professional inspection will cost a few hundred dollars; if you can, share the cost with other tenants. (See "Lead Hazard Resources," below, for information on finding a HUD-approved contractor to test for lead.)

Lead Pipes

Pre-1930 construction often contains lead pipes. It's difficult to know for sure whether you have lead pipes until you examine the plumbing. When you look under the sink, you might be able to see the pipe coming out from the wall; if so, look for the tell-tale dark gray color. A plumber can easily identify the pipes.

Lead Solder

Lead solder was used to join sections of pipe as recently as 1988. You won't know whether it was used unless you can look at several soldered junctions; even then, you will probably need a plumber to tell you whether the solder was leaded.

Imported, Nonglossy Vinyl Miniblinds

Miniblinds from China, Taiwan, Indonesia, and Mexico that were manufactured before 1996 are likely to contain lead. As the surface vinyl deteriorates in the sun, lead dust enters the air. Landlords are not required to tell you about leaded miniblinds *unless* they know that the blinds have begun to deteriorate and produce lead dust. Be smart: Ask the landlord to replace the blinds now, before a problem occurs.

Soil

For decades, American cars ran on leaded gasoline—and the effects are still with us. Exhaust from lead-burning cars contains lead, which falls to the ground where it remains, relatively inert, for years. Neighborhoods adjacent to heavily traveled roadways have significant amounts of lead in the soil; the readings drop off dramatically as the distance from the roads increases. If you live near a busy freeway or throughway, assume the worst and take care of yourself. See below for suggestions on self-help.

Dealing With Lead on Your Own

You don't need to automatically reject, or move out of, a rental that contains lead. Remember, only deteriorating lead is the culprit.

If you do discover hazardous lead, an aggressive approach is often best. If you live in older housing where lead is almost surely present and deteriorating, assume a worst-case scenario and adjust your housekeeping and hygiene habits accordingly. (Ideally, you'll want the landlord to eventually take more drastic measures, such as careful repainting,

as discussed below.) Here's what the experts recommend that you do:

- Vacuum thoroughly and regularly, using a "HEPA" ("high energy particle arresting") vacuum that will filter out the fine lead dust. Ask your landlord to provide one.
- Even when a unit has been repainted, the old lead paint layer will eventually be reexposed on some painted surfaces that get a lot of wear, such as door thresholds and windowsills. Wash them with a phosphate-based cleaner or a solution (like "Leadisolve") designed for lead pickup.

CAUTION

Don't disturb lead paint in buildings built before 1978. Do not sand walls, windowsills, doors, or other surfaces—it risks releasing lead into the air (possibly even from paint several layers down), creating the very hazards you are attempting to avoid. Renovations of this type should be handled by painters who have been trained and equipped to capture and remove lead dust and chips. If you intentionally disturb lead and suffer an injury, it will be difficult to place legal responsibility on your landlord.

- If your unit has lead pipes or copper pipe with lead solder, draw water out of the pipes by letting the taps run for 30 seconds before using—even if you plan to boil it for tea. Don't use hot water for cooking. Better yet, use bottled water for drinking and cooking.
- If lead is in the soil outside, provide throw rugs at each entrance and ask guests to remove their shoes before entering.
- Consider covering lead-laced soil with sod or an impermeable material.
- If your household has young children (especially those who are still crawling), use extra care to clean floors, especially the areas under and near windows. Wash children's toys and hands frequently, and clean pacifiers and bottles after they fall on the floor.

- Test your children for lead poisoning. Elevated blood levels in young children can be picked up in a simple blood test. The test is often done as part of routine check-ups. If you live in a building that you suspect places your child at risk for lead poisoning, you need this information to protect your child. The Centers for Disease Control and Prevention recommend giving children a blood level test at age six months to one year. Do follow-up tests as needed.

! **CAUTION**

If a child's blood lead level is very high, move promptly and see a lawyer. Evidence of lead poisoning will almost certainly entitle you to move out on the grounds of uninhabitability. (See "Moving Out If Necessary," below.) In Connecticut, a dwelling with lead is considered unfit by law. You will definitely need expert legal assistance if you sue for damages.

Getting the Landlord to Act

Getting your landlord to hire a professional to test and assess the risk of lead poisoning can be a tall order—after all, no federal or state law requires it. And it might be next to impossible to get your landlord to paint over deteriorating lead paint. But even the most penurious, callous, or short-sighted landlord might respond to an appeal to the bottom line.

Many landlords have learned (sometimes the hard way) that testing for lead and taking measures before tenants get sick is well worth the cost and time. Although landlords aren't liable for lead poisoning unless it can be shown that they knew that lead was present, these days it is increasingly difficult for landlords to plausibly argue that they were ignorant of this well-publicized issue. Lawsuits for lead poisoning can result in astronomical jury awards or settlements if the landlord is held responsible for the lifetime effects of an infant's

brain damage. The cost of testing, risk assessment, and lead management pales in comparison.

If the landlord isn't aware of the potentially enormous liability for lead poisoning, suggest that your landlord Google "lead poisoning tenant jury awards." The resulting articles describe the millions of dollars that juries have awarded poisoned tenants. Many state health agencies publish their own pamphlets that also explain the risks to landowners who ignore the writing (and the paint) on the wall.

Sample Letter Regarding Lead Test Results

45 East Avenue North
Central City, MO 00000
816-555-7890

February 28, 20xx

Lester Levine
3757 East Seventh Street
Central City, MO 00000

Dear Mr. Levine:

We recently hired the environmental engineering firm of Checkit & Howe to test our duplex for the presence of lead-based paint. A report of their findings is enclosed. As you can see, there is indeed old, unstable lead paint on most of the windowsills and in the upstairs hall.

We are concerned about the effect that this deteriorating paint will have on the health of our children, aged three months and three years. At a minimum, we would like to discuss a safe and effective response to this problem. Please contact us as soon as possible so that we can arrange a meeting. We're home in the evenings and on weekends.

Yours truly,

Maynard G. Krebs

Zelda Krebs

Maynard G. and Zelda Krebs

Encl: Report of Checkit & Howe

Notify the Landlord of Problems

If you discover a lead hazard on the property, tell the landlord at once, in writing. A sample letter is shown above.

Although the goal of your efforts is a safe place to live, not a successful lawsuit, don't lose sight of the fact that your landlord might avoid liability for lead injuries unless you can show that your landlord knew (or should have known) of lead hazards and failed to take reasonable steps to reduce them. In short, if you believe there is a lead risk on your property, you want to make it impossible for the landlord to plausibly deny knowing about it. If you use a kit to test your rental unit or its water supply and find the presence of lead, send the results (certified mail) to the landlord. If your child has elevated blood levels, do the same. Keep these receipts and any other evidence of the landlord's knowledge, such as notes of a conversation in which the landlord acknowledged the presence of pre-1978, chipping paint but refused to buy a HEPA vacuum.

Involve State, Local, or Federal Inspectors

Some states with aggressive lead-containment laws (such as Maryland, Connecticut, and California), and even some cities (such as San Francisco), have the power to inspect and order cleanups when a tenant complains to their enforcement agencies or reports a child's elevated blood level. Check whether your state has a lead abatement law; if so, contact the enforcing agency for help.

If your state does not have a lead hazard reduction law or effective enforcing agency, contact the EPA for advice.

Consider a Lawsuit

Some lead-management measures, such as scrupulous housekeeping, are more time-consuming than expensive. However, money enters the picture when there's so much lead dust that containment is the only reasonable response—for example, sealing lead-based paint by covering it with a durable finish. If actual removal of the painted surfaces is necessary (perhaps the underlying structure is so deteriorated that it must be replaced), considerable expense is in the offing.

Forcing the landlord to deal with lead on the property will involve asking a judge to issue an order that directs that the work be accomplished in a certain way within a certain time. Lawsuits like this cannot be filed in small claims court. These lawsuits are typically complicated affairs that require lawyers. They can be very effective when a group of tenants sue together. See Chapter 20 for suggestions on finding and working with a lawyer.

If you spend time and money dealing with lead containment—using special detergents or vacuums, devoting extra time to fastidious housekeeping, putting up with the intrusion of contractors trying to deal with the lead problem—ask your landlord to reduce the rent accordingly. (See Chapter 8 for advice on how to determine the value of a defective rental unit.) After all, these expenses are necessitated by the dilapidation of the property. If your landlord refuses and you have a lease requiring that you live in the unit for months or years, consider going to small claims court for an order reducing your rent, and ask that you be compensated for past labor and expenses, too. See Chapter 8 and *Everybody's Guide to Small Claims Court,* by Cara O'Neill (Nolo), for help.

Moving Out If Necessary

If the risk of lead poisoning is high and cannot be controlled, the smartest move might be to move out. Here are two scenarios that usually justify a move:

The rental is permeated with lead that you cannot effectively control. If lead constitutes a serious danger to your health—perhaps deteriorating paint has caused a serious lead dust problem, or old lead pipes have contaminated the water supply—you would be justified in breaking the lease and moving out on the grounds that your unit is legally uninhabitable. (See Chapter 8 for more on this topic.) To help counter any possible lawsuit by the landlord against you for future unpaid rent, be sure that you have your evidence in hand, such as a report from an EPA inspector or a state agency in charge of enforcing your state's lead law.

Lead Hazard Resources

Information on the evaluation and control of lead-based paint, dust, and other hazards, disclosure forms, copies of the *Protect Your Family From Lead in Your Home* and other pamphlets, and lists of EPA-certified lead paint professionals can be obtained from the National Lead Information Center by calling 800-424-LEAD, or check the EPA website at EPA.gov/lead. The EPA also provides pamphlets, documents, forms, and information on all lead paint hazards and federal laws and regulations on its website, as well as useful advice on topics such as finding a contractor licensed to test for and remove lead.

State housing departments will have information on state laws and regulations. Start by calling your state consumer protection agency (find yours at www.usa.gov/state-consumer).

Renovations will create a lead problem. If the landlord plans repairs or renovations in an effort to contain a serious lead problem, you might be wise to leave the premises. Even meticulous cleanup procedures cannot eliminate the risk of inhaling lead dust created by renovation. Some state statutes require the landlord to cover tenants' temporary housing expenses incurred during lead abatement work.

Even in the absence of such a statute, however, nothing prevents you from suing in small claims court. (Above, we discuss reimbursement for housing during asbestos-removal work.)

Radon

Radon is a naturally occurring radioactive gas that is associated with lung cancer. The U.S. Environmental Protection Agency (EPA)

estimates that millions of American homes have unacceptably high levels of radon. Radon can enter and contaminate a house built on soil and rock containing uranium deposits. It can also enter through water from private wells drilled in uranium-rich soil.

Radon becomes a lethal health threat when it enters from the soil and is trapped in homes that are tightly insulated or poorly ventilated. Radon is a smaller risk when it escapes from building materials that have incorporated uranium-filled rocks and soils (like certain types of composite tiles or bricks) or is released into the air from aerated household water that has passed through underground concentrations of uranium.

Problems occur most frequently in areas where rocky soil is relatively rich in uranium and in climates where occupants keep their windows tightly shut to maintain heat in the winter and air conditioning in the summer. No state is immune, however—according to the EPA, high levels of radon have been detected in every state. If you smoke and your house has high radon levels, your risk of developing lung cancer is especially high.

Fortunately, there are usually simple, inexpensive ways to measure and reduce radon levels in buildings. For example, good ventilation will disperse the gas in most situations. Solutions range from the obvious (open the windows) to the somewhat complex (use fans), but none of them involves tremendous expense.

No laws currently require a private landlord to try to detect or get rid of radon. The radon problem has not become the subject of national laws requiring testing or even disclosure. But if you suspect radon in your rented home, there are still things you can do.

Finding Radon

Radon is invisible and odorless. To test the air in your house, you can buy a do-it-yourself kit (make sure it says "Meets EPA Requirements") or hire a professional (get one who is certified by the

EPA's Proficiency Program). Testing takes at least three days, and sometimes months. Kansas State University's National Radon Program Services (www.sosradon.org/test-kits) is a good source of discounted radon testing kits. Before you pay for a radon test, though, check to see whether your state offers a free test—many (especially those in areas prone to radon problems) do.

RESOURCE

How to find information about radon in your state. The EPA's website is a great resource. You can look up your state's radon zone map to find out if radon is an issue where you live, and you can find the link to your state's radon website. (Your state's radon website will be where you can find out whether your state offers free or deeply discounted radon tests.) Visit www.epa.gov/radon/epa-map-radon-zones-and-supplemental-information.

Testing for radon makes sense if you live in an area that is naturally rich in uranium soil and rock. (In Colorado, for instance, radon is often a problem.) To find out, check out the EPA's zone map for your state (see resource box above for link).

Solving Radon Problems

If radon is present in significant amounts, it needs to be kept out or blown out of the building.

Getting it out. Once radon has entered the house, it needs to be dispelled with fans and open windows. Because of the increased costs of heating and air-conditioning, and the loss of security when windows are left open, these methods should be only temporary. The only good long-term solution is to prevent radon from entering the structure.

Keeping it out. Sealing cracks and other openings in the foundation is a basic radon reduction technique. Another method is soil suction—sucking the radon out of the soil before it enters the foundation or basement, and venting it into the air above the roof through a pipe. Increasing the air pressure within a house can also work, because radon enters houses when the air pressure inside is less than that of the surrounding soil. Equalizing the pressure in the basement or foundation reduces this pull.

The Landlord's Responsibility

Keeping radon from entering your dwelling involves major expenditures and modifications to the building's structure. Obviously, this kind of work is your landlord's responsibility.

If you have grounds for concern—your neighborhood has several buildings that are vented for radon control, or the geology of the area suggests the presence of uranium-rich soils—suggest that your landlord hire a testing firm, and provide your landlord with a copy of the EPA booklet explaining the dangers of radon. (See "Radon Resources," below.) As always, if a group of tenants voices their concern, the landlord is more likely to pay attention than if you act alone. Obviously, if you perform a test, send the landlord a certified letter with a copy of the report.

Keep copies of letters and reports, and write a letter of understanding to the landlord summarizing any oral discussions of the issue. (A sample letter of understanding can be found in Chapter 2.) Meticulous business practices like these impress your landlord with your seriousness and willingness to take legal action if necessary.

Radon Resources

For information on the detection and removal of radon, as well as a database of qualified radon reduction providers, contact the U.S. Environmental Protection Agency Radon Hotline at 800-557-2366 or visit the EPA website (EPA.gov/radon). You can also download a copy of the booklet "A Radon Guide for Tenants" and other publications, including "A Citizen's Guide to Radon."

Moving Out If Necessary

Unacceptably high levels of radon render a home unfit for habitation. If a certified tester has reached that conclusion, you have all that you need to demand that the landlord take prompt steps to remedy the problem. If the landlord fails to address it within a very short time, you can break your lease or month-to-month rental agreement and move out, citing a breach of the implied warranty of habitability (see Chapter 8). However, your suspicion alone that radon is present (perhaps because your neighbor has a radon problem) will probably not protect you if the landlord sues you for unpaid rent. It might be appropriate to move out temporarily if the landlord plans to install pumps or vents, which can take some time to regulate the amount of radon. See the discussion above, which suggests strategies for recouping expenses of temporary housing.

Carbon Monoxide

Carbon monoxide (CO) is a colorless, odorless, lethal gas. Unlike radon, whose deadly effects work over time, CO can build up and kill within a matter of hours. And, unlike any of the environmental hazards discussed so far, CO cannot be covered up or managed.

When CO is inhaled, it enters the bloodstream and replaces oxygen. Dizziness, nausea, confusion, and tiredness can result; high concentrations bring on unconsciousness, brain damage, and death. It is possible to be poisoned from CO while you sleep.

Sources of Carbon Monoxide

Carbon monoxide is a byproduct of fuel combustion; electric appliances cannot produce it. Common home appliances, such as gas dryers, refrigerators, ranges, water heaters or space heaters, oil furnaces, fireplaces, charcoal grills, and wood stoves all produce CO. Automobiles and gas gardening equipment also produce CO.

If appliances or fireplaces are not vented properly, CO can build up within a home and poison the occupants. In tight, "energy-efficient" apartments, indoor accumulations are especially dangerous.

> **TIP**
>
> **If you smell gas, it's not CO.** Carbon monoxide has no smell. Only a CO detector will alert you to its presence. To help identify leaking natural gas, utility companies add a smelly ingredient; when you "smell gas," you are smelling that additive. Because natural gas is so combustible, call the utility company or 911 immediately if you smell it.

Preventing Carbon Monoxide Problems

If your landlord has a regular maintenance program, it should prevent the common malfunctions that cause CO buildup. But even the most careful service program cannot rule out unexpected problems like the blocking of a chimney by a bird's nest or the sudden failure of a machine part.

Fortunately, relatively inexpensive devices, similar to smoke detectors, can monitor CO levels and sound an alarm if they get too high. If you purchase one, make sure it is UL-certified.

> **CAUTION**
>
> **If your CO detector sounds an alarm, leave immediately and do a household head count.** Because one of the effects of CO poisoning is confusion and disorientation, get everyone out immediately—then check for signs of poisoning and call the fire department or 911.

Unlike smoke detectors, which are required by almost all states (or local ordinances), CO detectors are not universally required. But many states have passed laws that require builders, sellers, and landlords to install monitors, particularly in single-family homes. For a list of states that have carbon monoxide detector laws, go to the website of the National Conference of State Legislatures (NCSL.org) and type "carbon monoxide detectors" into the search box on the home page. You'll get a list of state statutes—check the dates for currency.

Even if your state doesn't require your landlord to install a CO monitor, that doesn't mean that you cannot persuade your landlord to install one. Detectors that are connected to the interior wiring of the house and backed up with emergency batteries are best. In a letter, emphasize your concerns and the relative ease with which the landlord could put your mind at rest. A sample letter is set out below.

Sample Letter Asking for CO Detector

34 Maple Avenue North, #3
Badlands, CO 00000
303-555-1234

February 14, 20xx

Cindy Cerene
1818 East Seventh Street
Badlands, CO 00000

Dear Ms. Cerene:

The kitchen in the apartment we rent from you has a gas stove and cooktop, which are about 15 years old, and there is a gas furnace in the hallway. These appliances appear to be working normally, but especially in the winter, when storm windows make the house airtight, I am concerned about the possible buildup of carbon monoxide. I would like to ask you to install a CO detector in the hallway near the bedrooms.

As you know, CO is a deadly gas that can kill within hours. We can't see it or smell it, and it could accumulate and poison us during the night. The only way to protect ourselves (besides your regular maintenance of these appliances) is with a detector. These devices are not very expensive, and can be easily installed. I would do it myself, except that our lease prevents me from undertaking alterations or improvements without your consent.

I hope that you'll give some thought to my request. Thanks very much for your consideration of this matter.

Yours truly,

Brian O'Rourke

Brian O'Rourke

Avoiding Carbon Monoxide Problems

- Check chimneys and appliance vents for blockages.
- Never use portable gas grills or charcoal grills inside your home.
- Never use a gas range, clothes dryer, or oven for heating.
- If you use a nonelectric space heater, have it inspected annually. You can get recommendations from fuel suppliers.
- Never run a car engine or any gas-powered equipment in an attached garage; the fumes can seep into the house.
- Check the pilot lights of gas appliances every few months. They should show a clear blue flame; a yellow or orange flame might indicate a problem.

Responsibility for Carbon Monoxide

Most CO hazards are caused by a malfunctioning appliance or a clogged vent, flue, or chimney. It follows that the responsibility for preventing a CO buildup depends on who is responsible for the upkeep of the appliance.

Appliances. Appliances that are part of the rental, especially built-in units, are typically the responsibility of the landlord, although you are responsible for intentional or unreasonably careless damage. For example, if the pilot light on the gas stove that came with the rental is improperly calibrated and emits high amounts of CO, the landlord is responsible for fixing it. On the other hand, if you bring in a portable oil space heater that malfunctions, that is your responsibility.

Vents. Vents, chimneys, and flues are part of the structure, and their maintenance is typically handled by the landlord. In single-family houses, however, it is not unusual for landlord and tenant to agree to shift maintenance responsibility to the tenant.

If you have or suspect a CO problem that can be traced to the landlord's faulty maintenance, promptly request that the landlord fix it. If you are poisoned because your landlord failed to routinely maintain the appliances or to respond promptly to your repair request, the landlord will have a difficult time avoiding legal responsibility. (See Chapter 12.) To motivate your landlord to fix the CO-spewing gas dryer, it might be sufficient to subtly point out that failure to do so could cause a tragedy—and a lawsuit.

A sample letter bringing a CO problem to the landlord's attention is shown above. If you write such a letter, you would be smart to hand-deliver it to your landlord or manager, because the problem needs immediate attention. And in the meantime, don't use the appliance you suspect of causing the problem.

Carbon Monoxide Resources

The EPA website offers useful instructional material, including downloadable educational pamphlets, at EPA.gov./indoor-air-quality-iaq. Local natural gas utility companies often have consumer information brochures available to their customers. You can also contact the American Gas Association for consumer pamphlets on carbon monoxide. It can be reached by calling 202-824-7000 or visiting the Association's website at AGA.org.

Mold

Mold is one of the more common environmental hazards that cause concern among renters. Across the country, tenants have won multimillion-dollar cases against landlords for significant health problems—such as rashes, chronic fatigue, nausea, cognitive losses, hemorrhaging, and asthma—allegedly caused by exposure to "toxic molds" in their building.

Mold is also among the most controversial of environmental hazards. There is considerable debate within the scientific and medical community about which molds, and in what concentrations and situations, pose serious health risks to people in their homes. Unlike lead poisoning, for example, where lead levels in blood can be accurately measured (and their effects scientifically predicted), demonstrating health effects from mold is difficult. There is no debate, however, among tenants who have suffered the consequences of living amidst (and inhaling) mold spores.

Where Mold Is Found

Mold comes in various colors and shapes. The villains—with names like stachybotrys, penicillium, aspergillus, paecilomyces, and fusarium—are black, white, green, or gray. Some are powdery, others shiny. Some molds look and smell disgusting; others are barely seen—hidden between walls, under floors and ceilings, or in less accessible spots such as basements and attics.

Mold often grows on water-soaked materials, such as wall paneling, paint, fabric, ceiling tiles, newspapers, or cardboard boxes. However, all that's really needed is an organic food source, water, and time. Throw in a little warmth and the organism will grow very quickly, sometimes spreading within 24 hours.

Humidity sets up prime growing conditions for mold. Buildings in the naturally humid climates of Texas, parts of California, and the South have experienced more mold problems than residences in drier climates. But mold can grow irrespective of the natural climate, as long as moisture is present. Here's how:

- Floods, leaking pipes, windows, or roofs can introduce moisture that will lead to mold growth in any structure—in fact, these are the leading causes of mold.
- Tightly sealed buildings (common with new construction) can trap mold-producing moisture inside.
- Overcrowding, poor ventilation, numerous over-watered houseplants, and poor housekeeping can also contribute to the spread of mold.

Unsightly as it might be, most mold is not harmful to your health—for example, the mold that grows on shower tiles is not dangerous. It takes an expert to know whether a particular mold is harmful or just annoying. Your first response to discovering mold shouldn't be to demand that the landlord call in the folks with the white suits and ventilators. Most of the time, proper cleanup and maintenance will remove mold. Better yet, focus on early detection and prevention of mold, as discussed below.

Laws on Mold Affecting Landlords

Unlike other environmental hazards such as lead, landlord responsibilities regarding mold have not been clearly spelled out in building codes, ordinances, statutes, and regulations. The main reason for the lack of standards is that the dangers are hard to quantify. Some states have responded to mold problems in schools, but legislation on residential issues has been slow to come.

To do your own research on state or local ordinances covering mold, see the advice on doing legal research in Chapter 20.

Federal Law

No federal law sets permissible exposure limits or building tolerance standards for mold.

State Law

California is the first state to take steps toward establishing permissible mold standards. The "Toxic Mold Protection Act of 2001" authorizes the state's Department of Health Services (DHS) to adopt, if feasible, permissible exposure levels ("PELs") for indoor mold for sensitive populations, such as children and people with compromised immune systems or respiratory problems. If this is not feasible, the DHS may develop guidelines for determining when the presence of mold is a health threat. In addition, the California DHS will develop identification and remediation standards, which will guide contractors, owners, and landlords in how to inspect for mold and safely remove it. California's law also requires landlords to disclose to current and prospective tenants the presence of any known or suspected mold. (Cal. Health & Safety Code §§ 26100 and following.) (See the DHS website, given below in "Mold Resources.") Several other states have passed similar legislation, aimed specifically at the development of guidelines and regulations for mold in indoor air.

Local Law

A few cities have enacted ordinances related to mold:

- New York City's Department of Health and Mental Hygiene has developed guidelines for indoor air quality, which landlords in New York City should follow. In fact, any landlord would be wise to consult them, but you cannot force your landlord to abide by them. You can read them online at www.nyc.gov/site/doh/health/health-topics/mold.page
- San Francisco has added mold to its list of nuisances, thereby allowing tenants to sue landlords under private and public nuisance laws if they fail to clean up serious outbreaks (San Francisco Health Code § 581).

Landlord Liability for Tenant Exposure to Mold

With little law on the specific subject of mold, you'll have to rely on your landlord's general responsibility to maintain and repair rental property (the subject of Chapter 8) for guidance. The landlord's legal duty to provide and maintain habitable premises naturally extends to fixing leaking pipes, windows, and roofs—the causes of most mold. If the landlord doesn't take care of leaks and mold grows as a result, you might be able to hold the landlord responsible if you can convince a judge or jury that the mold has caused a health problem. Your position, legally, is really no different from what happens when the landlord fails to deal with any health or safety hazard on the property. For example, if the owner knows about (but fails to fix) a loose step, he'll foot the bill if someone is injured as a result of tripping on the step.

Naturally, some landlords have responded to the possibility of tenants' mold-related health claims by writing lease clauses that purport to relieve them from any liability resulting from mold growth.

Some state laws explicitly prohibit these "exculpatory clauses" that absolve a landlord from liability, and many courts have refused to enforce these clauses on the grounds of public policy.

The liability picture changes when mold grows as the result of your own behavior, such as keeping the apartment tightly shut, creating high humidity, and failing to maintain necessary cleanliness. Just as you don't want the landlord to police your lifestyle, you don't want your landlord poking in to examine your housekeeping habits (and in many states, privacy statutes prevent landlords from unannounced inspections, as explained in Chapter 11). When a tenant's own negligence is the sole cause of injury, the landlord is not liable.

Prevention—The Best Way to Avoid Mold Problems

A smart landlord's efforts should be directed squarely at preventing the conditions that lead to the growth of mold—and you should be the landlord's partner in this effort. This approach requires maintaining the structural integrity of the property (the roof, plumbing, and windows), which is the landlord's job. You, in turn, need to follow some practical steps and promptly report problems that need the landlord's attention.

The following steps are especially important if you live in a humid environment or have spotted mold problems in the past:

- **Check over the premises and note any mold problems; ask the landlord to fix them before you move in.** Fill out the Landlord-Tenant Checklist form in Chapter 6 and follow the advice on inspecting rental property at the start of a tenancy.
- **Understand the risks of poor housekeeping practices and recognize the factors that contribute to the growth of mold. In particular, be sure you know how to:**
  - ventilate the rental unit
  - avoid creating areas of standing water— for example, by emptying saucers under houseplants, and
  - clean vulnerable areas, such as bathrooms, with cleaning solutions that will discourage the growth of mold.

The EPA website includes lots of practical tips for discouraging the appearance of mold in residential settings.

- **Immediately report specific signs of mold, or conditions that could lead to mold, such as plumbing leaks and weatherproofing problems.**
- **Ask for all repairs and maintenance needed to clean up or reduce mold—for example:**
  - Request exhaust fans in rooms with high humidity (bathrooms, kitchens, and service porches), especially if window ventilation is poor in these areas.
  - Ask for dehumidifiers in chronically damp climates.
  - Reduce the amount of window condensation by using storm windows, if they're available.

These preventive steps will do more than decrease the chances that mold will begin to grow. If you have asked for them in writing and included the underlying reason for the request, you'll have good evidence to show a judge if a landlord refuses to step forward and your possessions are damaged or you are made ill by the persistence of the problem.

EXAMPLE: The closet in Jay's bedroom begins to sprout mold along the walls and ceiling. Jay asks his landlord, Sam, to address the problem (Jay suspects that the roof is leaking). Sam refuses, and Jay begins to feel sick; his clothes and shoes are also ruined by the mold. When Jay sues Sam for the value of his ruined possessions, he shows the judge the written requests for repairs that Sam ignored. After showing the judge photos and an impressively moldy pair of shoes, Jay wins his case.

How to Clean Up Mold

Although reports of mold sightings are alarming, the fact is that most mold is relatively harmless and easily dealt with. Most of the time, a weak bleach solution (one cup of bleach per gallon of water) will remove mold from nonporous materials. You should follow these commonsense steps to clean up mold if the job is small (if a lot of work is involved, ask the landlord to do the work). Use gloves and avoid exposing eyes and lungs to airborne mold dust (if you disturb mold and cause it to enter the air, use masks). Allow for frequent work breaks in areas with plenty of fresh air.

- Clean or remove all affected areas, such as a bathroom or closet wall. Begin work on a small patch and watch to see if you develop adverse health reactions, such as nausea or headaches. If so, stop and contact the landlord, who will need to call in the professionals.
- Don't try removing mold from fabrics such as towels, linens, drapes, carpets, and clothing—you'll have to dispose of these items.
- Contain the work space by using plastic sheeting and enclosing debris in plastic bags.

For more information, check out the sites noted in "Mold Resources," below.

CAUTION

People with respiratory problems, fragile health, or compromised immune systems should not participate in cleanup activities. If you have health concerns, ask for cleanup assistance. You might want to gently remind your landlord that it's a lot cheaper than responding to a lawsuit.

Mold Resources

For information on the detection, removal, and prevention of mold, see the EPA website at EPA.gov/mold. See their document "A Brief Guide to Mold, Moisture, and Your Home" and "Mold Remediation in Schools and Commercial Buildings Guide" (which includes multifamily properties). Publications written with the homeowner in mind are available from the California Department of Public Health at www.cdph.ca.gov (search "Mold").

Testing for Toxicity

If you discover mold on the property, should you test it to determine the nature of the mold and its harmfulness? Most of the time, no. You and the landlord are much better off directing your efforts to speedy cleanup and replacement of damaged areas. Knowing the type of mold present and whether it produces toxins will not, in most cases, affect the appropriate method of cleanup. Properly testing for mold is also extremely costly.

Unlike detecting lead paint by using a swab kit, you cannot perform a reliable mold test yourself. (Over-the-counter kits, which cost around $50, provide questionable results.) A professional's basic investigation for a single-family home can cost $3,000 or more. And to further complicate matters, there are relatively few competent professionals in this new field—unlike lead and asbestos inspectors who must meet state requirements for training and competence, there are no state or federal certification programs for mold busters.

This said, it will be necessary to call in the testers if you contemplate suing the landlord. If you're suing for significant health impairment, you'll need a lawyer. In that event, the lawyer will have the mold tested as part of the "discovery" phase of the lawsuit—that period of time when each side gets to ask for and examine the other side's facts.

Compensation for Mold Damage

If your belongings have been damaged by mold, your recourse will depend on who is responsible for the mold (you, or the landlord?). Sometimes this is easy to know, as when the roof leaks and the resulting soggy closet has sprouted mold. But, if you are watering a large number of plants and have leaky saucers of standing water in a closed-up apartment, arguably your housekeeping habits have created the conditions ripe for mold. Alas, it's often not so clear-cut. But here, at least, are the guidelines:

- **The landlord is responsible for the conditions that lead to mold growth.** When this is the case, the landlord is legally responsible for foreseeable damages, which include ruined tenant property. A polite, written request for compensation, followed by a suit in small claims court if necessary, is your course of action. Note that the landlord's property insurance policy will not cover this situation, but the landlord's liability policy might. It's your landlord's decision on whether or not to turn the case over to the insurance carrier, however.

- **The tenant is responsible for conditions that resulted in mold.** In this case, you're on your own, unless you have renters' insurance. Even with a policy, however, you may not have coverage for damage due to mold. Check your policy for its definitions of coverage and exclusions.

Bed Bugs

Bed bugs are the latest scourge to plague tenants (and landlords). A single female will lay 500 eggs in her lifetime. You'll find them in sleazy digs with sloppy tenants, as well as upscale apartments with fastidious residents. They're expert hitchhikers who can catch a ride on your suitcase or clothing. No one really knows how to kill them. If they show up at your rental property, you'll probably conclude that mold, asbestos, or lead-based paint would be benign by comparison. If you learn nothing else from reading this section, or want to stop right here, know this: If your landlord proposes aggressive, albeit inconvenient, methods to eradicate the bugs, join in the effort.

Expert Help on Bed Bugs

For detailed information on identifying and dealing with bed bugs, check out www.bed-bugs-handbook. com. The site contains information about preventing and identifying bed bugs, along with a directory of exterminators. Give this information to your landlord if necessary.

What's a Bed Bug—And Where Does It Come From?

Bed bugs are wingless insects that are about one-quarter inch in length, oval but flattened from top to bottom. They're nearly white (after molting) and range from tan or deep brown or burnt orange (after they've sipped some blood, a dark red mass appears within the insect's body). They seek crevices and dark cracks, commonly hiding during the day and finding their hosts at night. Bed bugs nest in mattresses, bed frames, and adjacent furniture, though they can also infest an entire room or apartment. They easily spread from apartment to apartment via cracks in the walls, heating systems, and other openings.

Relatively scarce during the latter part of the 20th century, bed bug populations have resurged recently in Europe, North America, and Australia, possibly a result of the banning of effective but toxic pesticides such as DDT. Bed bugs do not carry disease-causing germs (perhaps their one saving feature). Their bites resemble those of a flea or mosquito. Bed bugs are expert stowaways, crawling into luggage, clothing, pillows, boxes, and furniture as these items are moved from an infested home or hotel to another location. Secondhand furniture is a common source of infestation.

How to Deal With an Infestation

You'll learn that bed bugs have infested your property when you or another resident notices widespread, annoying bites that appear during the night. To minimize the outbreak and attempt to stop the spread of the pests to other rental units, take the following steps immediately. We can't emphasize this enough: Unless you and your landlord move swiftly and aggressively, identifying infested areas and treating them thoroughly, you will be doomed to a never-ending infestation.

Confirm the Infestation

First, make sure that you're in fact dealing with bed bugs and not some other pest, such as fleas. Because several kinds of insects resemble bed bugs, you'll need to capture a critter or two and study them. Go online to the sites mentioned above for more pictures of bed bugs than you ever wanted to see, and compare your samples. If it looks like a bed bug, that's good enough. Your landlord should be able to confirm it by calling a pest control outfit.

Tell the Landlord

Notify your landlord or manager immediately if you suspect a bed bug problem (even if you haven't confirmed it). You probably don't need to make a midnight phone call, but a call on the weekend is definitely in order. The following sections explain what happens when the landlord steps up and addresses the problem; below are some suggestions on what to do if the landlord will not take care of the issue.

Get Ready for an Inspection

In a multiunit building, bed bugs can travel from one unit to another, leading to the nightmare of an entirely infested building. But chances are that one unit is the original source (and it will have the highest concentrations of bed bugs). Landlords who know what they're doing will hire a competent exterminator to measure the concentration of bugs in the complaining tenant's unit, and to also inspect and measure all adjoining units (on both sides and above and below the infested unit). You should get proper notice of the exterminator's inspection and be told what's involved (expect a competent exterminator to look closely into drawers, closets, and shelves). By "boxing" or "mapping" the source, the professional will confirm where the bed bug problem originated and learn whether and how far the problem has spread (this tells the owner whether it needs to treat adjoining units). Mapping the infestation (particularly if the exterminator does it more than once, over a period of time) might also help determine when a particular unit became infested, which the landlord might use to apportion financial responsibility for the extermination (see "Extermination and Relocation costs: Who Pays," below).

> **TIP**
> **Using an experienced exterminator is the *only* way to deal with a bed bug infestation.** A can of Raid is not going to do the job.

Declutter, Move Out, Exterminate, Vacuum—And Do It Again

Bed bugs thrive in clutter, which simply gives them more hiding places. Before you can effectively deal with the bugs, tenants in infested units must first remove clutter and neaten up (what to do with possibly-infested items is covered below). Tenants must remove all items from closets, shelves, and drawers; and wash all bedding and clothing (putting washed items in sealed plastic bags). Then, you need to move out during treatment, and return when the exterminator gives the all clear. Most of the time, you can return the same day.

Upon return, tenants must thoroughly vacuum. Experienced exterminators will recommend a second and even a third treatment, with exhaustive cleaning and clutter-removing in between. You must take these steps. If you don't and the infestation reappears and spreads, you're in for the whole process all over again.

Infested items that can't be treated must be destroyed. Do not remove infested items and simply bring them back. And use extreme care when removing infested belongings and furniture. Bag them in plastic before carting them away—otherwise, you might inadvertently distribute the bugs to the rest of the building.

Exterminations and Relocation Costs: Who Pays?

In keeping with their obligation to provide fit and habitable housing, landlords must pay to exterminate pests that tenants have not introduced. In Florida, this duty is explicit: Since 1973, bed bugs are specified as one of the many vermin that landlords are required to get rid of, in order to maintain a fit and habitable rental. (Fla. Stat. § 83.51.) Eradicating infestations caused by the tenant, however, can rightly be put on the tenant's tab. But determining who introduced the bed bugs is often very difficult.

Bed Bugs in Multifamily Buildings

In a multiunit building, if your landlord has approached a bed bug problem by "boxing" the building as explained above, it might be possible to identify the most infested rental unit. But identifying the source (or most infested) unit is not the same as proving that these tenants caused the problem. For example, suppose the landlord traces the infestation to Unit 2, whose occupant moved into the building a few weeks ago. Serial mapping might show that adjoining Units 1 and 3 became infested after Unit 2 did, thereby suggesting that tenants in Units 1 and 3 were not responsible for their infestations. But the tenant in the source unit (Unit 2) might argue that the *former* occupants introduced the bed bug eggs that conveniently hatched after their departure. How will a landlord disprove this? Maybe it will discover that the new tenant came from a building that was also infested, but lacking this, the landlord will have a hard time laying responsibility on the new resident. Even if management did a thorough inspection of the unit before rerenting, there's no guarantee that it didn't miss some miniscule eggs. In short, because of the practical difficulty of identifying the tenant who introduced the bugs, the landlord will probably end up footing the bill for extermination and relocation costs.

If mapping identifies a source unit that's occupied by a long-term resident, it will be similarly difficult to develop the facts needed to prove that this tenant introduced the bugs. How will management learn about its tenants' habits, purchases, and travels, short of a full-blown lawsuit? And even if the landlord discovers, for example, that tenants bought a secondhand couch recently, how will it prove that the couch contained bed bugs? Or that bugs came home with a tenant following his recent stay in a hotel, or travel abroad? The bottom line is that landlords usually end up footing the bill for cleaning up bed bugs in multiunit buildings.

Bed Bugs in Single-Family Rentals

Renters of single-family rentals might more easily be saddled with the responsibility for an infestation, simply because there won't be any other residents to look to. Especially if you are a long-term tenant, it will be difficult to avoid the conclusion that your activities resulted in the infestation. (Tenants who have just moved in might be able to argue that the former residents introduced the eggs.)

Ruined Belongings: Who Pays?

In extreme cases, bed bugs infest every nook and cranny of a rental and its contents—books, clothes, furniture, appliances. One New York landlord reported getting a phone call from his tenant who discovered bed bugs and moved out with only the clothes on his back, leaving everything— everything—behind. This tenant sued the owner for the replacement cost of his belongings, claiming that the landlord's ineffective eradication methods left him no choice. Who pays?

Should this claim get before a judge, the answer would probably depend on the judge's view of the reasonableness of the landlord's response and the tenant's reaction. The more you can show that you took immediate and effective steps to report the problem, and cooperated with every reasonable request of the landlord and the exterminator, the better you would fare.

Will Your Insurance Step Up for Bed Bugs?

If you're facing a bed bug problem, you'll want to know whether your renters' insurance (or your landlord's policies) will help you with the cost of moving out and replacing any ruined belongings. Here's the scoop:

- **Expenses of moving out temporarily.** The landlord's commercial general liability policy might cover these expenses, which you will have to submit initially to your landlord. However, the trend has been for standard landlords' policies not to cover bed bug damage—instead, the landlord must purchase a rider (additional coverage).
- **Claims for lost or damaged belongings, and medical expenses.** Again, your landlord's policy might step up.

Now, suppose *you* are the source of the infestation? Your landlord might attempt to place the eradication cost on you. Unfortunately, most renters' insurance policies don't cover bed bug infestations. If you're the source of the infestation, the costs of eradication will likely come out of your security deposit or your pocket.

Your Right to Know About a Bed Bug Problem—And What to Do If Your Landlord Doesn't Tell the Truth

As the public learns about bed bugs, many applicants worry about the building's history. Knowing that full eradication is rare unless the landlord acts swiftly and thoroughly, many tenants simply won't consider renting in a property that ever had a problem, period. Knowing this, some landlords believe that disclosing a rental's bed bug past will make it unrentable. State and local legislators are increasingly addressing the issue of whether landlords should be required to disclose a property's bed bug history, as well as tenant and landlord duties when an infestation appears.

The majority of tenants, however, will not have the benefit of explicit disclosure laws. But that doesn't mean that you can't try to find out, and by asking, set the stage for some powerful responses on your part if the landlord is untruthful. First, if you question the landlord directly about a bed bug problem, especially if you make it clear that this issue is of critical importance to you, the landlord must answer truthfully or risk the consequences:

- **Breaking the lease.** A tenant who learns after the fact that the landlord hasn't answered truthfully will have legal grounds for breaking the lease and leaving without responsibility for future rent. Your theory is fraud, which will undo a contract and leave you free to walk away.

- **Increased chances of damages.** In the event that the bug problem reappears and you sue over lost or damaged possessions, costs of moving and increased rent, and the psychological consequences of having lived with the bugs, your chances of recovering will be enhanced by the owner's lack of candor. A competent lawyer will argue that the landlord's failure to disclose a potentially dangerous situation set you up for misery that could have been avoided.

Electromagnetic Fields

Electromagnetic fields (EMFs) are another one of the household "environmental hazards" that concern tenants.

Power lines, electrical wiring, and appliances emit low-level electric and magnetic fields. The intensity of both fields are thousands of times lower than the natural fields generated by the electrical activity of the human heart, brain, and muscles. The farther away you are from the source of these fields, the weaker their force.

The controversy surrounding EMFs concerns whether exposure to them increases a person's chances of getting certain cancers—specifically, childhood leukemia. Although some early research raised the possibility of a link, recent scientific studies have discounted it. Interestingly, the scientific inquiry on the effects of EMFs has now shifted to the effects of cell phone reception and use. You probably have nothing to worry about regarding EMF exposure even if your rental sits under or near a set of power lines.

Since the landlord cannot insist that the power companies move their transmitters or block the emissions, the landlord is not responsible for EMFs or their effect—if any—on you. If you're worried, your only practical option is to move. If you have a month-to-month rental agreement or the lease is up, you can easily move on without legal repercussions. But what if you decide midlease that the EMFs are intolerable? Legally, you would be justified in breaking a lease or rental agreement only if the property presents a significant threat to your health or safety. (Breaking a lease when the property is unfit is explained at length in Chapter 8.) Given the professional debate regarding the danger from EMFs, it is unclear whether that a court would decide that their presence makes the property unlivable.

 RELATED TOPIC
Electromagnetic field resources. The National Institute of Environmental Health Sciences has useful resources on EMFs. To find these, simply do a search on their website at www.niehs.nih.gov.

- **Using repair and deduct or rent withholding remedies.** If your state allows you to use these remedies for serious fixes that the landlord has failed to do, you might want to consider them now (see "State Laws on Rent Withholding and Repair and Deduct Remedies" in Appendix A, and "What to Do if the Landlord Won't Make Repairs" in Chapter 8). But because an infestation, particularly in a multitenant building, will be costly to address, these remedies might not practically do you much good. In a single-family rental, you might have more success.

- **Call the health inspectors.** Health inspectors are aware of the seriousness of bed bug infestations. Your local department might be prepared to deal with the landlord on your behalf.

Now, suppose you don't question a landlord about a rental's bed bug history, the landlord remains silent, and a problem reappears. Will you have a strong case for breaking the lease without responsibility for future rent, or using the landlord's silence as a way to increase your chances of collecting damages? It's impossible to answer this in the abstract—like many legal questions, the answer will depend on the facts, such as how aggressively and thoroughly the owner attempted to rid the property of bugs.

Crime on the Premises

Landlords in most states have some degree of legal responsibility to provide secure housing. This means they must take reasonable steps to:

- protect tenants from foreseeable assailants, thieves, and other criminals
- protect tenants from the criminal acts of fellow tenants
- warn tenants about dangerous situations they are aware of but cannot eliminate, and
- protect the neighborhood from their tenants' known illegal and noxious activities, such as drug dealing.

Landlords who don't take these steps might be liable for any injuries or losses that occur as a result.

This chapter explores the security measures that you can legally expect while renting, and how to enforce your right to a safe rental.

 RELATED TOPIC

Also covered in this book:

- Prohibition of illegal activities and disturbances in leases and rental agreements: Chapter 2.
- Landlords' responsibilities for repair and maintenance: Chapters 8 and 9.
- Tenants' rights to privacy: Chapter 11.
- Landlords' liability for injuries from defective housing conditions: Chapter 12.

The Landlord's Basic Duty to Keep You Safe

In every state, landlords are expected to take reasonable precautions to protect tenants from foreseeable harm. You can't expect your landlord to build a moat around the rental property and provide round-the-clock armed security. On the other hand, your landlord's duty to provide safe housing extends beyond handing you a set of keys to the front door.

State and Local Laws

Many state and local building and housing codes are loaded with rules designed to protect tenants. For example, some laws require rentals to have front-door peepholes and specific types of locks.

In contrast, some state and local laws offer little specific guidance. For example, they might require "clean and safe" or "secure" housing, without defining these terms. Courts in several states have ruled that these requirements apply only to the condition of the physical structure. In other words, a landlord in these areas might be expected to do nothing more than make sure that the rental structure won't collapse or otherwise cause injury.

But as the following example shows, some courts have taken a broader view of the term "safe."

EXAMPLE: The housing code in the city where Andrew owned rental property set minimum standards for apartment houses, including a requirement that all areas of rental property be kept clean and safe. The garage in Andrew's apartment building was poorly lit and accessible from the street because the automatic door worked excruciatingly slowly. The tenants met to discuss the situation and decided to send a group letter to Andrew, setting out their concerns. They had done a little legal research first, and were able to explain to Andrew that if a tenant (or guest) were hurt by an assailant who had entered through the unsecured entrance, Andrew might be liable.

Andrew showed the letter to his lawyer, who explained that the apartment building's dark and easy-to-enter parking garage violated the "clean and safe" requirement of the housing code, and that the tenants were right regarding his potential liability. Andrew fixed the door and added lights in the garage.

If your state and local laws are vague, you might want to see how local agencies or the courts have interpreted the meaning of broad terms such as "clean" and "safe."

Tenants can report landlords who don't comply with requirements to the agency in charge of enforcing the codes, often a local building or housing authority. (See below.) And, if you're injured as a result of your landlord's violating a safety law—for example, an intruder enters your apartment building by way of a lock that's been broken for weeks—the landlord might be liable for your injuries.

> **TIP**
>
> **To get a copy of your local housing code or ordinance, call your city manager's or mayor's office or look it up online.** Many cities link to their housing codes from their main website. In addition, you might be able to get information from a state or local housing agency or local tenants' association.

The Landlord's General Responsibility

In addition to complying with local and state laws that require basic security measures, landlords have a general common law duty to act reasonably under the circumstances—or, expressed in legal jargon, to "act with due care." For example, common areas must be maintained so that they do not create a risk of accidents. When it comes to security, too, courts in most states have ruled that landlords must take reasonable precautions to protect tenants from foreseeable criminal assaults and property crimes.

What precautions are reasonable depends on the situation. If you have been the victim of a crime on the premises—or are afraid you will be, sooner or later—ask yourself six questions to help you determine your landlord's responsibility:

1. Did your landlord control the area where the crime occurred?

Your landlord isn't expected to police the entire world. For example, a lobby, hallway, or other common area is an area of high landlord control. However, the landlord exerts much less control over the sidewalk outside the front door.

2. How likely is it that a crime would occur?

Landlords are duty-bound to respond to the foreseeable, not the improbable. Have there been prior criminal incidents at the particular spot you are worried about? Elsewhere in the neighborhood? A landlord who knows that an offense is likely (because of a rash of break-ins or prior crime on the property) has a heightened legal responsibility in most states to guard against future crime.

3. How difficult or expensive would it have been for the landlord to reduce the risk of crime?

If relatively cheap or simple measures could significantly lower the risk of crime, it is likely that a court would find that your landlord had a duty to undertake them, especially in an area where criminal activity is high. For instance, a court might expect your landlord to install reasonably priced new locks and better lighting if these measures were likely to discourage thieves. However, it is doubtful that a court would require your landlord to implement a very costly solution, such as structural remodeling or hiring a full-time doorman, unless the danger is very great.

4. How serious an injury was likely to result from the crime?

Almost any criminal incident has the potential to result in horrific consequences.

If, based on these first four questions, you think the landlord had a legal duty to deal with a condition on the premises that exposed you to the risk of crime, keep going. You have two more questions to answer.

5. Did your landlord fail to take reasonable steps to prevent a crime?

As ever, "reasonableness" is evaluated within the context of each situation. The greater the danger, the more a landlord must do. Past criminal activity on the premises increases your landlord's duty to keep tenants safe. "Reasonable precautions" in a crime-free neighborhood are not the same as those called for when three apartments in the landlord's building have been burglarized within the past month.

Many courts have ruled that prior criminal activity in the neighborhood increases a landlord's duty to tenants only if the prior crimes were similar to the current one. For example, a string of car break-ins in the neighborhood will probably not obligate a landlord to provide extra security measures to prevent apartment break-ins.

Landlords cannot eliminate all danger to tenants. In some situations, a warning might be enough. Just as caution tape and construction cones alert tenants to a freshly washed floor, landlords can warn tenants about possible criminal problems by using:

- newsletters that remind tenants to be on the alert and use good sense
- letters that communicate specific information, such as a physical description of an assailant who has struck nearby, and
- signs that remind tenants to use the building's safety features, such as a notice posted in the lobby asking tenants to securely lock the front door behind them.

6. Did your landlord's failure to take reasonable steps to keep you safe contribute to the crime?

You must be able to connect the landlord's failure to provide reasonable security with the criminal incident. It is often very difficult for tenants to convince a jury that the landlord's breach caused (or contributed to) the assault or burglary.

Think of it this way: If you fall because the rotten front step collapsed, you can trace the collapse directly to the landlord's failure to maintain the property. But when an intruder enters through an unsecured front door, the burglar's independent decision to commit the crime must be taken into account when determining liability. The landlord is not responsible for the criminal's decision to break the law, and many juries will hesitate to place responsibility on the landlord, even if, for example, failure to install a lock made the entry possible.

To convince a jury otherwise, you must emphasize that a crime of this nature was highly foreseeable and would probably have been prevented had the landlord taken appropriate measures. If a jury decides that the landlord didn't meet the duty to keep you safe, and that this failure facilitated the crime, it will typically split the responsibility for the crime between the landlord and the criminal. For example, jurors might decide that the landlord was 60% at fault and the criminal 40%. The landlord must compensate you accordingly. Not surprisingly, the criminal's share is usually never collected.

How Much Money You're Entitled To

To get financial compensation, you must show that you were harmed by the criminal incident. Tragically, this is often quite obvious, and the only issue that lawyers argue about is the worth, in dollars, of dreadful injuries. Compensation might also be awarded for the continuing psychological impact and mental anguish resulting from the encounter.

The Landlord's Promises

A landlord who promises specific security features—such as a doorman, security patrols, interior cameras, or an alarm system—must either provide them or risk being liable (at least partially) for any criminal act that they would have prevented. Remember, your lease is a contract, and if it includes a "24-hour security" promise or a commitment to have a doorman on duty at night, your landlord is required to uphold these promises. Even oral descriptions of security bind the landlord if they were a factor that led you to rent the unit. You can often also rely on statements about security in advertisements.

Your landlord won't be liable for failing to provide what was promised, however, unless this failure caused or contributed to the crime. Burned-out lightbulbs in the parking lot won't mean anything if the burglar got in by breaking the lock on the trapdoor on the roof.

EXAMPLE 1: The manager of Jeff's apartment building gave him a thorough tour of the "highly secure" building before Jeff decided to move in. Jeff was particularly impressed with the security locks on the gates of the high fences at the front and rear of the property. Confident that the interior of the property was accessible only to tenants and their guests, Jeff didn't hesitate to take his kitchen garbage to the dumpsters at the rear of the building late one evening. There he was accosted by an intruder who got in through a rear gate which had a broken lock. Jeff's landlord was held liable because the landlord had failed to maintain the sophisticated, effective locks that had been promised.

EXAMPLE 2: The information packet given to Maria when she moved into her apartment stressed the need to keep careful track of door keys: "If you lose your keys, call the management and the lock will be changed immediately." When Maria lost her purse containing her keys, she immediately called the management company but couldn't reach them because it was after 5 p.m. and there was no after-hours emergency procedure. That evening, Maria was assaulted by someone who got into her apartment by using her lost key.

Maria sued the owner and management company on the grounds that they had completely disregarded their own standard (to change the locks promptly) and so were partially responsible (along with the criminal) for the assailant's entry. The jury agreed and awarded Maria a large sum.

Problems With Other Tenants

Sometimes danger lurks within as well as beyond the gate. Your landlord has a duty to take reasonable steps to protect you if another resident on the property (including a roommate) threatens to harm you or your property.

Your landlord's responsibility to deal with a troublesome tenant is similar to the responsibility to respond to a loose stair or broken front-door lock. A landlord who knows about a problem (or should know about it) is expected to take reasonable steps to prevent foreseeable harm to tenants. If the landlord fails to do that, and you are injured or robbed by another tenant, you can sue and recover damages.

If your roommate's the problem, be sure to read the related discussion of violent roommates in Chapter 7.

When the Landlord Must Act

The landlord won't be held partially responsible for a tenant's illegal acts unless the problem tenant had done or threatened similar criminal conduct in the recent past, and the landlord knew about it. In short, you'll need to convince an insurance adjuster, judge, or jury that:

- it was reasonable to expect the landlord to know or discover the details of a tenant's past, and
- once known, the landlord could have taken steps to control or evict the troublemaker.

Unless there's a clear history of serious problems with the offending tenant, landlords usually win these cases.

EXAMPLE 1: Evelyn decided to rent an apartment to David, although she knew that he had been convicted of spousal abuse many years earlier. For two years David appeared to be a model tenant, until he hit another tenant, Chuck, in the laundry room over a disagreement as to who was next in line for the dryer. Chuck was unable to convince the jury that Evelyn should bear some responsibility for his injuries, because he could not show that the incident was foreseeable.

EXAMPLE 2: Mary rented an apartment to Carl, who appeared to be a nice young man with adequate references. Carl stated that he had no criminal convictions when he answered this standard question on the rental application. Several months later, Carl was arrested for the burglary and assault of another tenant in the building. At trial, it came out that Carl had recently been released from state prison for burglary and rape. Because Mary had no knowledge of Carl's criminal past, she was not held liable for his actions.

What the Landlord Must Do

A landlord who knows about the potential for danger from another tenant must do something about the problem tenant, such as warn other tenants or evict the troublemaker.

For example, suppose your neighbor bangs on the walls every time you practice the violin during the afternoon—and the pounding is getting louder. If you've tried to talk things out and been greeted with a raised fist, it's time to alert the landlord. You can reasonably expect the landlord to intervene

Getting a Restraining Order

If you are seriously threatened by another tenant who will not leave you alone, and your landlord either won't evict the aggressor or the eviction is taking some time, consider seeking a restraining order.

To obtain a restraining order, you will demonstrate to a court that you are in imminent danger of being harmed if the order is not issued. For example, repeated verbal threats of harm to you or your family would be sufficient to obtain a restraining order. The order directs the threatening individual to stay away from you. Its principal value is that when you have a restraining order and call emergency services for assistance, the police will react faster and more firmly than they might otherwise.

The exact procedure for obtaining restraining orders depends on the rules where you live—call your local courthouse or law enforcement station to obtain more information (many courts and law enforcement offices also post the procedures and necessary forms on their websites).

If you obtain a restraining order, make a copy and give it to your landlord and to the manager. Ask them to alert other on-site personnel, such as security guards and maintenance personnel, of the existence and meaning of the order.

You can provide a picture of the aggressor with the copy of the order if you think it would be helpful.

A wise landlord will usually consider a restraining order as ample grounds for terminating the tenancy of the aggressor (and evicting, if necessary). If, after being evicted, the aggressor returns to the rental property, request that the landlord call the police and order the aggressor to leave the property.

If you get no cooperation from your landlord and are still fearful, move. Your safety is worth far more than your right to live in a particular rental space.

Your landlord might take the position that you have broken the lease and try to keep your security deposit to cover unpaid rent for the balance of the lease or rental agreement. Should this happen, and you decide to sue your landlord to get your deposit back, your chances of winning are good. (Chapter 16 discusses small claims suits over security deposits.) You can argue that by failing to evict the troublemaker, the landlord breached the covenant of quiet enjoyment and made your rental unfit and uninhabitable, which justified your moving out. (See Chapter 8.)

In addition to the protection provided by a restraining order, if your situation involves domestic violence, your state law might grant you specific rights (see Chapter 7, section "Domestic Violence Situations," and "State Laws in Domestic Violence Situations" in Appendix A).

and attempt to broker a solution—perhaps an adjustment of your practice schedule or some heavy-duty earplugs for the neighbor. If the circumstances are more threatening—for example, your neighbor brandishes a gun—you can reasonably expect your landlord to call the police, terminate the aggressor's tenancy immediately (and follow with an eviction lawsuit if necessary), and warn other tenants pending the departure of the dangerous tenant.

Many states have laws that make it relatively simple for landlords to evict trouble- makers, particularly when domestic violence is involved. These laws allow landlords to terminate the tenancies of dangerous tenants on short notice, and do not require landlords to give these tenants the opportunity to remedy their behavior. (See Chapter 17 for details on expedited evictions.)

EXAMPLE: Bill received several complaints from his tenants about Carol, a tenant who had pushed another resident out of the elevator, slapped a child for making too much noise, and verbally abused a tenant's guest for parking in Carol's space. Despite these warning signs, Bill didn't terminate Carol's tenancy or even speak with her about her behavior. When Carol picked a fight with a resident whom she accused of reading her newspaper and badly beat her up, Bill was held partly liable on the grounds that he knew of a potentially dangerous situation and failed to take appropriate steps to safeguard his tenants.

TIP

If you fear violence from another tenant, let your landlord know in writing. Not only does this underscore the seriousness of the situation, but it will be irrefutable proof that the landlord was on notice that problems were brewing. When more than one resident complains, the landlord will face more pressure to take action. And if there is an altercation later, the landlord cannot plausibly claim ignorance.

CAUTION

Get your facts straight before making accusations. If you believe that certain individuals are breaking the law—or just causing trouble—be certain that you have the facts straight before telling others about them. Otherwise, you might find yourself on the wrong end of a libel or slander lawsuit.

Intervention and eviction of the troublemaker are the usual ways that landlords meet their duty to take care that residents don't harm other residents. But the law doesn't require your landlord to have a crystal ball.

EXAMPLE: Abbot and his mother rented a duplex from Xavier, who knew that Abbot had a behavior disability and took regular medication to control it. Unknown to his mother or Xavier, Abbot began skipping his medication and eventually attacked Larry, another tenant, with a baseball bat. Xavier was not held liable, because it would have been illegal to refuse to rent to Abbot, a person with a legally recognized disability, under the Federal Fair Housing Amendments Act. Xavier did not know that Abbot had discontinued his medication, nor would it have been reasonable to expect Xavier to monitor Abbot's dosages. If Xavier had known that Abbot was off his medication and acting out, however, he would have been duty-bound to speak to Abbot and his mother and possibly to warn the other resident. (Note, however, that if Abbot had a history of violent behavior toward other tenants or damaging rental property that the landlord, Xavier, was aware of when Abbot and his mother applied for the tenancy, Xavier would probably have been on solid legal ground to deny the application.)

Illegal Activity on the Property and Nearby

Illegal activities on the premises create problems for law-abiding tenants and enormous financial risks and penalties for landlords. In addition to losing law-abiding tenants, landlords might be hit with:

- lawsuits by tenants who are hurt or annoyed by drug dealers or other criminals
- fines issued by local, state, or federal authorities for tolerating a legal nuisance
- criminal charges for tolerating illegal behavior, and
- in extreme cases, court-ordered seizure of their rental property.

Understanding your landlord's legal duties (and liabilities) when it comes to illegal activity at your rental is the first step you can take to avoid trouble. The balance of this chapter gives suggestions on what you can do to convince the landlord to take action against drug dealing and other activities and, at the same time, take steps to protect yourself.

Government Lawsuits Against the Landlord

The legal meaning of "nuisance" bears only a little resemblance to its meaning in everyday life. A legal nuisance is a pervasive, continuing, and serious condition—like a pile of stinking garbage or a group of drug dealers—that threatens public health, safety, or morals. In some states, it also includes activity that is simply offensive, like excessive noise or open sexual conduct.

Every state has some type of nuisance abatement law, which allows the government, and sometimes the neighbors, to sue to stop these sorts of problems. Using public nuisance abatement laws against crime-tolerant landlords is increasingly common in large cities with pervasive drug problems. Landlords themselves face civil fines or criminal punishment for tolerating the behavior.

Public nuisance laws come in two forms: civil and criminal. The table below explains the differences between the two types.

Civil and Criminal Nuisance Laws		
	Civil Nuisance Laws	**Criminal Nuisance Laws**
Activities the laws target	Unhealthy, immoral, or obnoxious behavior that might be, but is not necessarily, a violation of the criminal law as well	Criminal behavior
Examples of targeted activities	Excessive noise, piles of garbage and trash, and inordinate amounts of foot or car traffic	Drug dealing, prostitution, gambling, and gang activities
Who can sue	Public agencies such as city health departments, law enforcement agencies, and, in many states, affected neighbors, who can band together and sue for large sums in small claims court (see below)	Law enforcement agencies only
Possible consequences to the landlord	A court ordering the offending tenant, and sometimes the landlord, to compensate other tenants. If a health, fire, or other enforcement agency brings the nuisance action based on many violations, the court might order the closing of the entire building.	Liability for money damages plus fines and imprisonment

Nice Properties Are Not Immune

Drug-related crime isn't limited to seedy neighborhoods—illegal drug use is spread widely throughout American society. In fact, smaller apartment complexes with some measure of security are often preferred by drug dealers over large, unprotected housing units. The reason for this preference might surprise you: A drug dealer, like a law-abiding tenant, is interested in a safe, controlled environment. But drug dealers who are smart enough to choose nice properties aren't always smart enough to keep their illegal activity from affecting other tenants.

Seizure of the Landlord's Property

It's rare, but the government sometimes seizes property because of the illegal activities of one or more tenants. The landlord loses not only the property, but also all the rent money that the landlord received from the drug-dealing tenants.

If you're a tenant, forfeiture won't improve your lot. Few tenants want to live in government-run housing that starts off as a drug den. But a landlord who hears the word "forfeiture" will probably be highly motivated to get rid of the offending tenants.

EXAMPLE: Sterling Properties hired a management firm to run several apartment buildings in a high-crime area. At one of the buildings, there were repeated drug arrests and complaints from neighbors regarding incessant comings and goings of people at all hours. The federal government initiated forfeiture proceedings. Sterling Properties argued that because it had not been informed by its management company of the situation, it had no knowledge of the illegal activities of the tenants. The court ruled that the neighborhood was a virtual "anthill" of illegality that any reasonable person would know about, and that the knowledge of the management company could be imputed to the owners. The building was forfeited and became the property of the U.S. government.

Other landlords in the area, shocked at this result, began meeting to work out strategies to rid their neighborhood of residents suspected of drug dealing.

Small Claims Lawsuits Filed by Neighbors

Overworked and understaffed police and health departments are often unable to make a real dent in problem-plagued neighborhoods. Determined tenants and neighbors have stepped in to fill the enforcement gap, bringing their own small claims court lawsuits in an attempt to eliminate the offensive behavior. Tenants and neighbors may sue a landlord for failing to take steps to clean up the property, and seek:

- **Monetary compensation.** Each neighbor generally sues for the maximum allowed in state small claims court ($5,000 to $10,000 in most states), and the landlord often pays the maximum to *each one*. (See the discussion of small claims courts in Chapter 19.)
- **Direction from the court.** The tenants and neighbors can ask the court for an order directing the landlord to evict the trouble-makers, install security, and repair the premises. Such orders are not available in all states.

Small claims court might be "small," but it can be mighty. In one case in Berkeley, California, after failing to get the police and city council to close down a crack house, neighbors sought damages stemming from the noxious activities. Each of the 18 plaintiffs collected the maximum amount allowed in small claims court ($3,500 at the time), avoided the expense of hiring counsel, and sent the landlord a very clear and expensive message. The problem was solved within a few weeks.

Getting Results From the Landlord

Here are some suggestions on how to encourage your landlord to fulfill the responsibility to provide a safe place to live.

Evaluate the Situation

Before approaching your landlord with requests for improved security, collect hard evidence concerning the building's vulnerability to crime. The best way to evaluate the safety of your rented home is to conduct a security inspection of the rental property. Your goal is to answer two questions:

- If I (or a family member, roommate, or guest) were here alone at night, would I feel safe?
- If I were an assailant or a thief, how difficult would it be to get into the building or individual rental unit?

Analyze the Building

Start by circulating a letter to other residents, explaining your concerns and suggestions for improved security on the property, and solicit their comments. Call a meeting to discuss the results and plan your next moves.

You'll learn the most about your building's vulnerability if several tenants walk or drive around the rental property at different times of the day and night—you might see something at 11 p.m. that you wouldn't notice at 11 a.m. A reasonably safe and secure single-family home, duplex, or multiunit rental will have strong locks on windows and doors, good interior and exterior lighting, and other features that will hinder trespassers. To see how your rental unit, building, and grounds measure up, use the checklist of Important Security Features, below.

You might also want to get a security evaluation and advice from your renters' insurance agent—even more important, encourage your landlord to do the same and learn about equipment and safety systems that can prevent break-ins and assaults. Your local law enforcement agency might offer free on-site evaluations and recommendations.

Important Security Features

- **Exterior lighting.** Exterior lights are most effective near entranceways and walkways. The lighting should be activated by motion or a timer, not dependent on the memory of managers or tenants to turn it on. Many security experts consider the absence or failure of exterior lights as the single most common failing that facilitates break-ins and crime.
- **Interior lighting.** Bright interior lights in hallways, stairwells, doorways, parking garages, and common areas should illuminate potential hiding places.
- **Secure doors.** Look for sturdy dead bolt door locks on individual rental units and solid window and patio door locks, as well as peepholes at the front door of each unit (with a wide-angle lens for viewing). Lobby doors should have dead bolt locks. Solid metal window bars or grills over ground floor windows are often a good idea in higher-crime neighborhoods, but landlords might be subject to restrictions of local fire codes. All grills or bars should have an interior release mechanism.
- **Intercom and buzzer systems.** The best ones allow you to identify the person at the door (either by voice or by video) and control the opening of the front door from the safety of your unit.
- **Neat and compact landscaping.** It should not obscure entryways or afford easy hiding places adjacent to doorways or windows.
- **Live doorkeeper or concierge.** In some areas, a 24-hour doorman is essential and can do more to reduce crime outside the building than anything else.
- **Secure parking.** Driveways, garages, and underground parking must be well lit and secure from unauthorized entries. Fences and automatic gates might be a necessity in some areas.
- **Secure elevators.** Elevators that require a passkey for entry are ideal. You might even want to request that the landlord install closed-circuit monitoring. Having someone watch the monitor is expensive, but it's worth suggesting if your building has fairly high rents or is in a particularly crime-prone area.

Consider the Neighborhood

The extent of your vulnerability depends on not only the security systems in your building, but also on the surrounding neighborhood. If there has been little or no crime in your area, you have less to worry about and less legal reason to expect your landlord to equip the property with extensive security devices. On the other hand, if crime is a problem, gather information about local illegal activity from people in the neighborhood and the police department. Then use this information to suggest appropriate measures both your landlord and other tenants can take to keep the rental property safe.

Request Improvements

After you've read this chapter and done your homework on local crime statistics, it's quite likely that you know more about the security needs of the rental units and building (and landlords' legal responsibilities) than the owner, especially if the owner is an absentee landlord. To further support your position, you might first have to educate your landlord about:

- **Statutory security requirements.** If local or state ordinances or laws require specific security devices, such as dead bolts, peepholes, or window locks, start by asking your landlord to comply with the law. Put your request in writing. (Of course, keep copies of all correspondence.) Attach a copy of the ordinance or statute to your request. If you get no response, submit a second request. Then, if there is still no compliance, consider your options. (See "Protecting Yourself," below.)
- **Promised security measures that are missing or malfunctioning.** If the landlord promised security beyond the basics dictated by law—such as an advertisement promising garage parking or security personnel—you have a legal right to expect that the landlord deliver; see "The Landlord's Basic Duty to Keep You

Safe," above. Send a written reminder to the landlord and attach a copy of the advertisement or lease provision that backs up your request.

Involve Other Tenants

If you are a renter in a multiunit building, chances are that you aren't the only one concerned with safety. Working with other tenants on this issue (or others) has definite advantages:

- **Landlords respond to armies more readily than to individuals.** Once you get other tenants involved, your chances of getting the landlord to implement anticrime measures greatly increase. The consequences of rent withholding, complaints to the police, or small claims actions are much greater if done by a group than by a sole tenant. (These tactics are discussed below.)
- **Involving others reduces the chances of retaliation.** Tenants in most states are protected against landlord retaliation (such as terminations, rent hikes, and withdrawal of services) for exercising their rights to voice their opinions to the landlord, complain to enforcement agencies, and organize collectively. (See Chapter 15 for a thorough explanation of antiretaliation laws.) But if your state doesn't protect you against retaliation, acting as a group might make it harder for your landlord to retaliate—few landlords want instantly empty buildings or, worse, buildings full of angry residents.
- **You'll learn more about security problems.** For example, maybe the upstairs neighbor, who is home during the day, can tell you that the 24-hour security guard really lounges in the manager's office all afternoon, watching YouTube videos.
- **Involving others increases your safety.** Once you and your neighbors realize that you are all in the same boat, it is more likely that you will look out for each other.

See Chapter 19 for tips on working with other tenants.

- **Security necessitated by the surroundings and circumstances.** Your own assessment of the property and the neighborhood may lead you to conclude that the landlord is shirking their duty to protect tenants. But if you don't have a clear-cut ordinance or statute to point to, motivating the landlord will take some extra work. Use the information you've gathered to convince the landlord that, given the area's crime problems, more effective security measures are required—and that if security isn't improved, the landlord could be legally liable for injuries that result.

Oral requests sometimes get results, but more often they are ignored. Putting security requests in writing and having them signed by as many tenants as possible is a far better way to get results. Even the most dim-witted landlord understands that if tenants have a written record of their complaints about personal safety issues—especially when the landlord has not kept promises to provide security systems—and nothing is done, the chances of a successful lawsuit go way up.

So write a letter even if you think it's hopeless, even if your landlord is notoriously stingy or impossibly stubborn. By creating a paper trail, you have increased the landlord's incentive to take action. Your letter should:

- point out that the landlord alone has control over what measures can be put in place
- set out the foreseeable consequence (an assault) of not dealing with the property's obvious lack of security
- propose that the solution is relatively easy, and
- suggest that the consequences—a burglary or assault—are serious.

A sample letter alerting the landlord to dangerous conditions is shown below.

Sample Letter Alerting the Landlord to Dangerous Conditions

789 Westmoreland Avenue, #5
Central City, WA 00000
555-123-4567

January 3, 20xx

Mr. Wesley Smith, Landlord
123 East Street
Central City, WA 00000

Dear Mr. Smith:

As tenants of the Westmoreland Avenue building, we are concerned that there is a dangerous condition on the property that deserves your prompt attention.

As you know, the large sliding windows on the bottom floor (in the lobby) are secured by turn locks that can be easily forced open. On occasion we have seen a dowel placed in the track to prevent the windows from being opened, but lately the dowels have often been missing. Several times, the windows have even been left open all night.

We are worried that an intruder can easily get into the building. There have been several burglaries in the neighborhood within the past two months. The situation would be greatly helped if you could send a glass repairperson to replace the locks with much stronger ones. Needless to say, a burglary or assault is a worrisome prospect.

Thank you for your prompt consideration of this matter.

[signed by as many tenants as possible]

_____

_____

_____

TIP
Contact the landlord's insurance company.
If you can find out who insures the landlord (a tenant who has filed any type of previous claim might know) and the landlord persists in not taking reasonable safety precautions, send copies of all your correspondence to the company. Because the insurer might have to pay a substantial claim or jury award if a tenant is assaulted, it has an obvious interest in getting the landlord to act. Pressure from the insurance company (and the worry that it might cancel the policy or increase rates) might have an immediate effect on a lazy or stubborn landlord.

Meet With the Landlord

If your written requests don't produce results, invite your landlord to meet with you (and other tenants, if possible) to discuss your concerns. You might want to involve a local mediation service, which has the advantage of giving you a skillful and neutral moderator. You'll be especially glad for the presence of the mediator if your landlord arrives with an attorney. If you or other tenants end up in court over your landlord's failure to keep the premises safe, the refusal to discuss the situation with you will hardly help the landlord's case. (Chapter 19 gives suggestions on finding and working with a mediator.)

Get Help From the Government

If gentle (or even concerted) persuasion fails to get desired security improvements, call in the reinforcements. Depending on what the exact problem is and where you live, contact either building or health inspectors or local law enforcement agencies, who have the power to order the landlord to comply with the law. For example, if a local ordinance requires dead bolts on all exterior doors, it probably names the agency (such as the health department or the building inspectors) responsible for enforcing the code. Often, all you need to do is to contact that agency and begin the complaint procedure. Send copies of your complaint (signed by as many tenants as possible) to the landlord. This alone might result in the landlord taking the desired actions.

The effectiveness of turning to building or health inspectors varies hugely. In some areas, inspectors are so overwhelmed with complaints that they are rarely able to respond promptly. On the other hand, some enforcement agencies are quite effective, and you might get a quick and satisfying response. Because they respond fastest to situations that pose serious and immediate threats to health or safety, emphasize the seriousness of the problem.

> **EXAMPLE:** When Lucy moved into her apartment two years ago, the neighborhood was reasonably safe and untroubled. In the last two months, however, Lucy's street had become the site of rival gang activity. After two muggings nearby and a burglary next door, Lucy was worried about her safety and decided to do something about it.
>
> Lucy looked at her city ordinances online, which included a requirement that multiunit rental property be equipped with dead bolts and locks on lower-level windows. Along with several other tenants, she also evaluated the property and concluded that the shrubbery needed trimming, the exterior lights were inadequate, and the parking garage was unsafe. They talked with the other tenants, and decided to present their concerns to the landlord as a group.
>
> When a meeting failed to produce significant change, they contacted the building inspector, who cited the landlord for code-related violations of the dead bolt lock law. At that point, another tenant had an idea that proved to be a small stroke of genius: She complained to the fire department about the condition of the bushes, which resulted in a scheduled inspection. Even though the size of the bushes might not have resulted in a citation, notification of the inspection was enough to motivate the landlord to immediately cut them back.

Finally, realizing that the tenants were determined to make changes—and to avoid being hassled in the future—the landlord hired a regular landscaper, installed floodlights, and added a locking gate to the garage.

Withhold Rent

A truly dangerous rental might be considered legally uninhabitable. Most states recognize the failure to provide adequate security as a failure to provide an essential service. If that's the situation where you live, you might be justified in withholding rent. (Chapter 8 explains this option.)

Here are some guidelines that must be met by any claim that a unit is uninhabitable because of high crime danger.

- **The problem is truly serious now, not merely annoying or a potential problem.** For example, having to walk past dope dealers on your way through the front hall is unavoidable, frightening, and loaded with potential for violence. On the other hand, unverified stories regarding prostitution in your neighborhood or even in your building are less compelling.

- **You've given the landlord notice of the problem and time to respond.** In general, as discussed in Chapter 8, you must tell the landlord about it and provide sufficient time for the landlord to fix the problem or approach legal authorities (police or city attorney) who are better equipped to deal with it. For example, if drug dealers have moved in next door, you must alert the landlord and allow ample time for termination and eviction procedures; if gangs have invaded your neighborhood, you must complain to the landlord and give the police time to act.

CAUTION
Withholding rent, even if it's totally justified, might prompt the landlord to terminate your tenancy if you're a month-to-month renter. Although many states have laws that are supposed to protect you from such retaliation, you might still have to fight it out in court if your landlord sues to evict you. (See Chapter 8.)

Break the Lease

If your rented home is uninhabitable due to inadequate security, you might be justified in moving out, for the same reasons you might be able to withhold rent.

You might also be justified in breaking the lease and moving out if *promised* security was an important factor in your decision to rent your place, and the landlord failed to follow through on that promise (see "The Landlord's Basic Duty to Keep You Safe," above). This remedy is explained in Chapter 8 in connection with repairs or maintenance that have been promised but not delivered.

EXAMPLE: Wendy, a nurse who worked many night shifts, rented her apartment in Safe Harbor after reading its advertisement in the local newspaper that promised "Security personnel on duty at all times." When she was shown around the property, Wendy told the manager that she often came home late at night. She was assured that there was a 24-hour guard service. However, after coming home several nights in the early morning hours and discovering that there were no security guards on duty, Wendy confronted the management and was told that financial constraints had made it necessary to cut back on the guards' hours. Wendy wrote the landlord a letter asking that the guard service be restored. When it wasn't, she promptly moved out.

Safe Harbor kept Wendy's entire security deposit claiming that her departure violated the lease and that management had been unable to find a replacement tenant for four weeks. Wendy sued Safe Harbor for the return of her entire deposit, arguing that in fact it was Safe Harbor who had broken the lease by failing to provide security as promised. The judge decided that the promise of 24-hour security was an important part of Safe Harbor's obligations and that its failure to deliver constituted a breach of the lease, which excused Wendy from her obligation to stay and pay rent. And the judge ordered Safe Harbor to refund Wendy a portion of the rent she had already paid, on the grounds that she had paid for an apartment with a guard but had not received it.

You might be able to break a lease and move with little or no financial consequence. In most states, your landlord will have a duty to make reasonable efforts to rerent your unit and apply the new rent to what you owe on the balance of your lease. (This duty is discussed in detail in Chapter 15.) If the rental market is tight and your rental is reasonably attractive and competitively priced, your landlord will have little excuse for not rerenting quickly. Of course, if the dangerous conditions that prompted your early departure are noticed by prospective tenants (who reject the rental for that reason), the landlord might have a hard time rerenting. Fortunately for you, the harder it is for the landlord to rerent, the stronger your case that the rental was unacceptably unsafe, justifying your breaking the lease. In short, you win either way.

Sue in Small Claims Court

Small claims court can be an appropriate tool to deal both with simple problems like the installation of a dead bolt and complex ones like ridding the building of drug-dealing tenants.

If you're lucky, the difference between a secure apartment and an unsecured one might be the simple addition of a code-mandated door or window lock, trimming some bushes, or replacing burned-out lightbulbs in the garage or hall. If your repeated requests for action have fallen on closed ears, and local inspectors can't or won't come to your aid, what should you do?

If you can, perform the work yourself (preferably with other tenants) and then sue the landlord for the cost. This route does, however, put you at risk, especially if your lease or rental agreement says "no improvements or alterations without the landlord's consent." Your risk of eviction for violating that lease clause will probably be less if the job you do is required by local law, such as a code-required dead bolt, rather than a modification like trimming the bushes that *you* have concluded is required for your safety.

> ⓘ **CAUTION**
> **Notify your landlord if you install an alarm or permanent locks.** Laws in most states require tenants to give the landlord access (keys and codes).

Protecting Yourself

Faced with an unsafe living situation, your only option might be to pursue self-help remedies such as installing your own security protections or moving out, as explained above. But short of that, consider the following.

Use Good Judgment

If you live in a dangerous building or high-crime neighborhood, your first thought must be to watch out for yourself. Just as defensive driving techniques can do more to keep you safe than confronting dangerous drivers or equipping your car with every imaginable safety device, you'll want to rely primarily on your own good judgment and willingness to change your habits.

If you have identified vulnerable aspects of your building or rental unit, chances are that others have, too. If you were a burglar or mugger, how would you strike? Avoid dangerous situations—for example:

- Don't use an isolated parking lot late at night.
- Consider curtailing your evening activities. No late-night movie is worth the risk of an assault.
- Use a fan for air circulation instead of opening easily accessible windows at night.

Install Your Own Security Protections

In some situations, you might be able to take matters into your own hands, at least as regards your own rented space. Even if your lease prohibits you from making alterations or repairs without the landlord's permission (see Chapter 10), lots of effective security devices do not require permanent installation. For example, sliding windows often can be secured with removable interior blocks, and sliding doors can be tightly locked with specially designed rods. In addition, local or state law might expressly permit tenants to install certain devices when the landlord has failed to do so. (For suggestions on supplying code-required equipment and

not footing the bill, see "Getting Results From the Landlord," above.)

Remember, your landlord has the right to enter in an emergency, so you must provide keys and codes. (Chapter 11 discusses your landlord's right of entry.)

Consider Moving

Sad to say, often your most effective response to a dangerous rental situation is to move. Many tenants on a tight budget believe they can't afford any better alternatives. While understandable, this view is often wrong. Look around your area for places where low rents don't mean high crime. Although sometimes well-kept secrets, these neighborhoods often exist. Or consider the possibility of getting a roommate or sharing a house so you can afford to live in a better part of town.

If you have a month-to-month rental agreement, you can usually move out with 30 days' notice. Breaking a lease might be a little more difficult, unless you're moving out because your rental is uninhabitable or your landlord failed to follow through with promised security measures, as discussed above. (Chapter 15 discusses notice requirements for ending a tenancy.)

How Tenancies End or Change

Whether you move often or tend to stay put for years, you should understand the important legal issues that arise at the end of a tenancy, including:

- the type of notice a landlord or tenant must provide to end a month-to-month tenancy
- legal restrictions on your landlord's ability to end a month-to-month tenancy, including the ban on "retaliatory evictions"
- what happens if you leave without giving required notice
- the landlord's legal options if you don't leave after receiving (or giving) a termination notice or after the lease has expired
- your options if you want to get out of a lease early or sublet your home temporarily, and
- what happens if your landlord goes out of business or declares bankruptcy.

This chapter starts with a brief discussion of a related topic: When and how either you or your landlord can change your lease or rental agreement during your tenancy.

RELATED TOPIC

Also covered in this book:

- Lease and rental agreement provisions on notice required to end a tenancy: Chapter 2.
- Notice required for rent increases: Chapter 3.
- Getting your security deposit back after you leave: Chapter 16.
- When the landlord can terminate your tenancy because you violated the lease or rental agreement: Chapter 17.
- Overview of eviction lawsuits: Chapter 18.

Changing Terms During Your Tenancy

Once you sign a lease or rental agreement, it's a legal contract between you and your landlord. All changes should be in writing and signed by each of you.

SKIP AHEAD

If you have a lease, your landlord cannot unilaterally change its terms until the lease period ends. After all, the whole point of a lease is to fix the terms of the tenancy—including rent—for the length of the lease. If you have a lease, skip ahead to "How Fixed-Term Leases End."

Amending a Month-to-Month Rental Agreement

A landlord who wants to change something in a month-to-month rental agreement doesn't need your consent. Legally, the only step your landlord needs to take is to send you a notice of the change. The most common reason landlords amend a rental agreement is to increase the rent. Chapter 3 provides a detailed discussion of this issue (including constraints resulting from rent control or eviction protection).

To change a month-to-month tenancy, most states require 30 days' notice, subject to any rent control laws. (See "State Rules on Notice Required to Change or Terminate a Month-to-Month Tenancy" in Appendix A for a list of each state's notice requirements.) In most states, the landlord can deliver the notice by first-class mail.

A landlord doesn't legally have to redo the entire rental agreement in order to make a change or two. It's just as legal and effective to attach a copy of the notice making the change to the rental agreement. However, many landlords will want the change to appear on the written rental agreement itself.

If the change is small and simply alters part of an existing clause—such as increasing the rent or making the rent payable every 14 days instead of every 30 days—your landlord can cross out the old language in the rental agreement, write in the new and sign in the margin next to the new words. The landlord will probably also want you to sign and date the change.

Amendment to Lease or Rental Agreement

This is an Amendment to the lease or rental agreement dated _____March 1, 20xx_____ ("the Agreement")

between _____Olivia Matthew_____ ("Landlord")

and _____Steve Phillips_____ ("Tenant")

regarding property located at _____1578 Maple St., Seattle, WA_____ ("the Premises").

Landlord and Tenant agree to the following changes and/or additions to the Agreement:

1. Beginning on June 1, 20xx, Tenant shall rent a one-car garage, adjacent to the main premises, from
    Landlord for the sum of $75 per month.

2. Tenant may keep one German shepherd dog on the premises. The dog shall be kept in the backyard
    and not in the side yard. Tenant shall clean up all animal waste from the yard on a daily basis. Tenant
    agrees to repair any damages to the yard or premises caused by his dog, at Tenant's expense.

_____

_____

_____

_____

_____

_____

_____

_____

_____

_____

_____

_____

_____

Olivia Matthew	*May 20, 20xx*
Landlord/Manager	Date
Steve Phillips	*May 20, 20xx*
Tenant	Date
Tenant	Date
Tenant	Date

If the changes are lengthy, your landlord might either add an amendment page to the original document or prepare a new rental agreement, as discussed below. If an amendment is used, it should clearly refer to the agreement it's changing and be signed by the same people who signed the original agreement. See the sample amendment above.

 FORM
The Nolo website includes a downloadable copy of the Amendment to Lease or Rental Agreement form. See Appendix B for the link to the forms in this book.

Preparing a New Rental Agreement

A landlord who is adding a new clause or making several changes to your rental agreement will probably find it easiest to substitute a whole new agreement for the old one. For example, your landlord will probably want a new agreement if you're adding or replacing a roommate or if a "no pets" clause is being added. If your landlord prepares an entire new agreement, it's best that you both write "Canceled by mutual consent, effective [_date_]" on the old one, and sign it. All tenants (and any cosigner or guarantors) should sign the new agreement. (Chapter 7 discusses having a roommate sign a new agreement.) The new agreement should take effect on the date the old one is canceled.

How Month-to-Month Tenancies End

This section discusses how you or the landlord can end a month-to-month tenancy.

 RELATED TOPIC
Ending a rental agreement involuntarily. If your landlord terminates your tenancy on the grounds that you have violated a rental clause—for example, by not paying rent or by disturbing your neighbors—turn to Chapter 17.

How Landlords Can End a Tenancy

It's easy for a landlord to end a month-to-month tenancy. In most places (and absent any eviction protection laws), landlords do not have to have a reason. A landlord can simply give you a written notice to move, allowing you the minimum number of days required by state law and specifying the date on which your tenancy will end. (See "State Rules on Notice Required to Change or Terminate a Month-to-Month Tenancy" in Appendix A.) After that date, you no longer have the legal right to occupy the premises.

$ **RENT CONTROL**
Protections of rent control. Most rent control laws do not allow a landlord to terminate a month-to-month tenancy except for just cause (legally recognized reason). Chapter 3 discusses rent control.

If you want more security, your only real alternative is to sign a fixed-term lease. But if you want to stay after getting a 30-day notice telling you to leave, either for a short time (until you find another place) or indefinitely, there is nothing to stop you from negotiating with the landlord. ("How to Stay When Your Landlord Wants You Out," below, gives some practical advice on how to approach this.)

Each state, and even some cities, has its own very detailed rules and procedures for how landlords must prepare and serve termination notices. For example, some states require that the notice be printed in a certain size or font. If your landlord doesn't follow these procedures, the termination notice might be invalid. But once you point out the mistake, either informally or as a defense to an eviction lawsuit, your landlord will be able to try again—and will probably do it right the second time. If you want information on your state's exact requirements, consult your state statutes. (See "State Landlord-Tenant Statutes" in Appendix A.) Your state consumer protection agency or local tenants' rights organization might also have useful advice.

If you stay on despite receiving a properly written and served termination notice, your landlord will be able to file an eviction lawsuit.

TIP
The 30-day period might start on the day the notice is mailed, not received. Say your landlord mailed a 30-day notice on June 1, asking you to be out by July 1. If you don't get the notice until June 4, you might believe you are legally entitled to stay until July 4, even though the notice gives a July 1 termination date. Not necessarily. In some states, putting the notice in the mail is enough to start the 30-day notice period running. If you need every day possible to move out and can't arrange a compromise date with your landlord, check this point in your state's statutes. (Chapter 20 discusses how to look up a statute.)

How You Can End a Month-to-Month Tenancy

The landlord isn't the only one who can end a month-to-month tenancy easily and quickly; you can, too. In fact, the overwhelming number of rental relationships are ended when the tenant voluntarily decides to move on.

How and When to Give Notice

In most states, and for most rentals, you must provide the same amount of notice as (sometimes less than) a landlord—typically, 30 days.

For details on your state's rules, see "State Rules on Notice Required to Change or Terminate a Month-to-Month Tenancy" in Appendix A. You'll see that in some states, if you pay rent more frequently than once a month, you can give notice to terminate that matches your rent payment interval. For example, if you pay rent every two weeks, you need give only 14 days' notice.

If your state allows you to mail your termination notice, use certified mail, and mail it a few days early. You'll get a receipt that shows exactly when the landlord received it. Depending on the state, it might be legal to mail your 30-day notice exactly 30 days before you wish to end your tenancy, even though the landlord gets it a few days later. But

in other states, a landlord is entitled to receive the notice at least 30 days before you plan to leave. If you intend to leave on July 1 and mail your notice on June 1, your landlord might not get it until June 4. If the notice period is 30 days, your tenancy won't end until July 4. Your landlord might try to withhold four days' worth of "unpaid rent" from your security deposit if you move out as planned on July 1.

To protect yourself, mail a notice in plenty of time to give the landlord 30 days' notice. To be on the safe side, don't count the last day if it falls on a Sunday or holiday. Or, if time is tight, deliver it in person, and request a receipt.

It's not a good idea to give your notice orally. Even if you know the landlord well and feel that your word is enough, the law usually requires written notice. Use our form, Tenant's Notice of Intent to Move Out. A filled-out sample is shown below.

FORM
The Nolo website includes a downloadable copy of the Tenant's Notice of Intent to Move Out form. See Appendix B for the link to the forms in this book. Copy this form, fill it out, and give it to your landlord.

In most states, you can give notice at any time. In other words, you don't have to give notice so that your tenancy will end on the last day of the month or the last day of your rental cycle. If your tenancy ends midmonth, you'll be paying rent until that date. For example, if you pay rent on the first of the month but give notice on the tenth, you will be obliged to pay for 10 days' rent for the next month, even if you move out earlier. To calculate the amount, prorate the monthly rent.

The exception to this general rule comes if your rental agreement states that notice may be given only on a certain date, typically the date the rent is due. This means that if you decide on the tenth that you need to move, you'll have to wait until the first to give notice and will be obliged to pay for the entire next month, even if you leave earlier. An argument could be made that requiring tenants to give notice on a specified day of the month has the effect of

Tenant's Notice of Intent to Move Out

April 3, 20xx
_____
Date

Anne Sakamoto
_____
Landlord

888 Mill Avenue
_____
Street Address

Nashville, Tennessee 00000
_____
City and State

Dear _____Ms. Sakamoto_____ ,
                        Landlord

This is to notify you that the undersigned tenants, _____Patti and Joe Ellis_____

_____ , will be moving from

____999 Brook Lane, Apartment Number 11, Nashville, Tenn._____ ,

on ____May 3, 20xx_____ , ____30 days_____ from today.

This provides at least _____30 days'_____ written notice as required in our rental agreement.

Sincerely,

Patti Ellis
_____
Tenant

Joe Ellis
_____
Tenant

_____
Tenant

lengthening the state-mandated notice period, which landlords may not do explicitly. Whether such an argument would work for you depends on local and state practice; better to plan ahead if you can and give notice on the required date.

You are legally free to give your landlord more notice than is required by law. But giving extra notice does not give you an initial period of time in which to change your mind. For example, if you give 45 days' notice in a state that legally requires 30, you have no legal right to change your mind during the first 15 days.

If You Change Your Mind

For all sorts of reasons, you might change your mind after giving your landlord formal notice of your intent to move. But if you can't convince the landlord to reinstate your tenancy, or the unit has already been rented again, it's too late. You'll have to move.

If you want to stay after giving notice, promptly call the landlord and explain why your plans have changed—for example, you were moving because you thought you had just bought a house, but the deal collapsed in escrow. You are more likely to influence the landlord to reinstate your tenancy if you can show that you now plan to stay for an extended period of time, not just a few weeks.

If the landlord agrees to reinstate your tenancy informally—perhaps over the phone—fine, but be sure to follow up with a confirming letter. If your landlord doesn't immediately write back disagreeing with your understanding, this is probably enough to legally reinstate the old rental agreement. But, to be safe, offer to sign a new rental agreement. A sample letter to a landlord is shown below. Note how the tenant has built in a favorable outcome: The letter states that if she doesn't hear from her landlord within a reasonable time, the old rental agreement will be back in force. (Locking the landlord into your position is the essence of this kind of letter, which is explained in detail in "Oral Leases and Rental Agreements" in Chapter 2.)

If you are having trouble communicating with your landlord, see if a local mediation program can help. (See Chapter 19 for more on mediating landlord-tenant disputes.)

Paying Rent After You've Given or Received Notice

If your landlord accepts rent (excluding past-due rent) after your notice period has ended, it cancels the termination notice and creates a new month-to-month tenancy. This means you (or your landlord) must give another 30-day notice to start the termination process again.

Sample Letter Requesting Reinstatement of Tenancy

945 Willow Road, #8
Marysville, RI 00000

June 10, 20xx

Mr. Paul Johnston
123 Capitol Mall
Capital City, RI 00000

Dear Mr. Johnston,

On June 1, I gave you written notice of my intent to move on the first of July, in order to accept a transfer to my company's headquarters in New York.

After I gave notice, however, my job transfer was canceled, and I would like to continue living here. I hope that you have not rented my apartment already, and will cancel my 30-day notice and continue to rent to me as you have done for the past two years. My hope is to continue to live here for the foreseeable future.

Thank you very much for considering my request. Assuming I can stay on, I would be happy to sign another rental agreement or, if you prefer, we can resume using the old agreement. If I don't hear from you within a few days, I'll assume that we'll be operating under the old rental agreement. I have enclosed a copy of my supervisor's recent memo canceling my job transfer.

Yours truly,

Sally Blum

Sally Blum

Extending Your Tenancy a Few Days

Suppose that, after giving notice, you need a little more time to move. Assuming no new tenant is set to move in right away or the landlord has not scheduled maintenance or refurbishing work, your landlord might be willing to let you pay prorated rent for a specified number of extra days. If so, you should sign an agreement setting out what you have agreed to.

If your landlord refuses your request to stay a few days and you simply don't move at the end of the notice period, you'll probably receive a termination notice from the landlord right away. The landlord will probably also promptly file papers to evict you or, if it's allowed in your state, go directly to court.

Leaving on Short Notice

Even the most conscientious tenant might not be able to give the landlord the required amount of notice. Perhaps a family medical emergency or a new job requires you to move out immediately. If you leave without giving enough notice, you lose your right to occupy the premises, but are still obligated to pay rent through the end of the required notice period. (In some states, there's an exception for victims of domestic violence, who have early termination rights. See "Renting a Place With Others" in Chapter 7 for more information.)

> **EXAMPLE:** Edna moves out after giving her landlord 15 days' written notice of her intent to move. Because Edna lives in a state that requires 30 days' notice, she owes rent for an additional 15 days. Of course, Edna's landlord might let her leave early without paying the additional rent, especially if another tenant is ready to move in very soon. But a landlord who can't rent the apartment within 15 days can deduct any unpaid rent from Edna's security or last month's rent deposit.

Special Rules for Tenants Who Enter Military Service

Tenants who enter military service after signing a lease or rental agreement have a federally legislated right to get out of their rental obligations. (War and National Defense Servicemembers' Civil Relief Act, 50 App. U.S. Code. §§ 501 and following.) You must mail written notice of your intent to terminate your tenancy for military reasons to the landlord or manager.

Rental agreements. Once you have mailed or delivered the notice, the tenancy will terminate 30 days after the day that rent is next due. For example, if rent is due on the first of June and you mail a notice on May 28, the tenancy will terminate on July 1. This rule takes precedence over any longer notice periods that might be specified in your rental agreement or by state law. If state law or your agreement provides for shorter notice periods, however, the shorter notice will control. Recently, many states have passed laws that offer the same or greater protections to members of the state militia or National Guard.

Leases. A tenant who enters military service after signing a lease may terminate the lease by following the procedure for rental agreements, above. For example, suppose you sign a one-year lease in April, agreeing to pay rent on the first of the month. You enlist October 10 and mail a termination notice to the landlord on October 11. In this case, your tenancy will terminate on December 1, 30 days after the first time that rent is due (November 1) following the mailing of your notice. You will have no continuing obligation for rent past December 1, even though this is several months before the lease expires.

The Act also restricts the landlord's ability to evict covered active-duty personnel and their dependents for nonpayment of rent.

TIP

Most landlords must try to minimize their losses when tenants leave early. In most states, your landlord has a legal duty to try to limit ("mitigate," in legalese) the amount lost because you leave early. To do that, the landlord must try to rerent the property promptly. (This responsibility is discussed in detail in "Getting Out of a Lease," below.) But few courts expect a landlord to accomplish this in less than a month. So if you leave without giving enough notice, expect to pay rent for at least the next month.

How Fixed-Term Leases End

A lease lasts for a fixed term, typically one year. As a general rule, neither you nor your landlord may unilaterally end the tenancy, unless you have violated the terms of the lease or the landlord has failed to meet a responsibility, such as to provide a habitable place to live.

If you and your landlord both live up to your promises, however, the lease simply ends of its own accord at the end of the lease term. At this point, you must either:

- move
- sign a new lease (with the same or different terms), or
- stay on as a month-to-month tenant with your landlord's approval.

If you do none of these things and your landlord wants you to move on, you are considered a "holdover" tenant and will probably be evicted.

RENT CONTROL

Your landlord might be required to give you the option to renew your lease in a rent control area. If your tenancy is covered by rent control, your landlord might be required to renew your lease unless there is a legally approved reason (just cause) not to. (See Chapter 3 for more on rent control.) Reasons such as your failure to pay rent or your landlord's desire to move in a close relative commonly justify nonrenewal. If your landlord does not renew your lease, but the reason given doesn't legally qualify as just cause, you will probably become a month-to-month tenant. Your landlord will still need a good reason to get you out. Check your city's or state's rent control law carefully.

What to Do Before the Lease Expires

A lease clearly states when it will expire, and you are responsible for knowing this date. Some states or cities (especially those with rent control), however, require landlords to remind tenants in writing of the impending expiration date, and give the tenant the option to renew or let them know the lease isn't being renewed.

If you want to renew your lease or stay on as a month-to-month tenant, talk to your landlord well before your lease expires. This is also the time to suggest changes you want—for example, if you want to add a roommate or bring in a pet.

If you plan to leave at the end of the lease, it's courteous to give your landlord notice of your intent.

Staying and Paying Rent Without a New Lease

It's fairly common for landlords and tenants not to care, or not even to notice, that a lease has expired. The tenant keeps paying the rent, and the landlord keeps accepting it. Is everything just the same as it was before the lease expired? The answer depends on where you live.

Creating a month-to-month tenancy. In most states, you will have created a new, oral month-to-month tenancy on the same terms as those in the old lease. Now your landlord can treat you as a month-to-month tenant—for example, the rent can be raised with proper notice.

> **EXAMPLE:** Shawn's lease ended on July 1, but neither he nor his landlord Helen realized that the lease was up. Shawn paid the regular month's rent on July 1. On July 20, Helen realized that the lease had expired, and decided that she wanted Shawn to stay—but at a higher rent. She decided not to offer Shawn another lease, because rents were going up in her area. She sent him a note telling him that he would have to pay $100 more on August 1.
>
> When Shawn got Helen's note, he realized that he was no longer renting under his old lease. But he understood that, by accepting

rent on July 1, Helen had created a month-to-month tenancy. This meant that Helen could not change any terms unless she gave Shawn the proper amount of notice—30 days in their state. Because Helen gave notice on July 20, Shawn's rent could not go up until August 20.

Of course, your landlord can belatedly present you with a new lease. If you decide not to sign it, you can stay on as a month-to-month tenant, under the terms of the old lease, until the landlord gives you proper written notice to move on.

Automatically renewing the lease. In a few states the rule is quite different. If your lease expires and your landlord continues to accept rent, the two of you have created a new lease for the same length (such as one year) and terms (such as the amount of rent) as in the old lease. In other words, you have automatically renewed the lease. The effects are dramatic: You and the landlord are now legally obligated for a new lease with the same term as the old one.

To avoid inadvertently signing up for an entire new term, never pay rent past the date the lease expires without discussing it first with your landlord.

When a Lease Ends and Your Landlord Wants You Out

Once the lease expires, your landlord doesn't have to keep you on as a tenant. If you stay on after the lease ends and offer rent that your landlord *does not* accept, you're a "holdover" tenant. In some states, the landlord must still give you notice, telling you to leave within a few days; if you don't leave at the end of this period, you can be evicted. A few states allow the landlord to file for eviction immediately, as soon as the lease expires.

Unless you have a reasonably good chance of proving that your landlord's refusal to renew the lease is illegal (see "Retaliation and Other Illegal Tenancy Terminations," below), or you believe you can work out a compromise with your landlord (see "How to Stay When Your Landlord Wants You Out," below), it's probably time to pack up and move. There's no reason to head into an eviction lawsuit that's a pretty sure loser.

First, if your intent is to buy time, you'll get relatively little of it by staying on and going to court. That's because holdover eviction lawsuits where the tenant has no good defense are given speedy treatment in most states. And while the exact time will vary depending on state law and how fast the landlord jumps through required procedural hoops, it can often be accomplished in two to three weeks. (See the overview of evictions in Chapter 18.)

Second, take a good look at your lease or rental agreement. Chances are it has an "attorneys' fees and costs" clause in it. (See "Typical Provisions in Leases and Rental Agreements" in Chapter 2.) This means that if you lose (or even if you capitulate on the courthouse steps before the actual hearing), you'll probably be on the hook for your landlord's attorneys' fees and costs. Those can add up to a few thousand dollars for even the most perfunctory eviction lawsuit. These costs will come out of your security deposit. If that doesn't cover them, the landlord can sue you in small claims court and come after your wages or bank account if you don't pay the judgment.

In short, holding on to your apartment for no legally defensible reason in an effort to avoid moving for a few weeks is very rarely worth the negative consequences.

CAUTION
Watch out for lease and rental agreement clauses that make holdover tenants pay a higher rent. Your landlord might attempt to discourage you from staying past the end of your tenancy by making you agree, in advance, to pay as much as three times the rent if you do. Clauses like this might not be enforceable—they are a form of "liquidated damages" (damages that are set in advance, without regard to the actual harm suffered by the landlord), which are illegal in residential rentals in many states, including California. The clause would probably not hold up in a rent control area; nor would it survive a challenge if the clause describes the rent hike as a "penalty."

Retaliation and Other Illegal Tenancy Terminations

Landlords can terminate a tenancy for a variety of reasons, such as nonpayment of rent, serious violations of the lease, and illegal activity such as drug-dealing on the rental property. And unless state or local laws require a reason, a landlord can, with proper notice, terminate a month-to-month rental agreement or decline to renew a lease without giving any reason at all. But they can't terminate a tenancy for the *wrong* reason— in retaliation against you for exercising your legal rights or in a way that discriminates illegally.

Illegal Discrimination

Just as landlords can't engage in illegal discrimination when they rent a unit and manage it during your tenancy, they can't unlawfully discriminate when it comes to terminating a month-to-month tenancy or deciding not to renew a lease—for example, by deciding not to continue to rent to persons of a certain ethnicity. Chapter 5 covers the topic of discrimination, and also explains what you can do if you think you have been illegally discriminated against. All of the options discussed there—such as complaining to the federal Department of Housing and Urban Development and filing a lawsuit—are available to you if your lease or rental agreement is not renewed for discriminatory reasons.

Retaliation

The second major landlord "no-no" when it comes to tenancy nonrenewals is retaliation. In most states, landlords may not end a tenancy in retaliation for your legally protected activities, such as complaining to a building inspector that a rental unit is uninhabitable. If they do, and you stay on despite the landlord's wishes, you can defend yourself against a lawsuit to evict you by proving retaliation.

Prohibitions against retaliatory evictions were the natural outgrowth of tenant protection laws that began to appear in the 1970s. Lawmakers reasoned, quite rightly, that it made no sense to arm tenants with the legal right to insist on fit and habitable housing (see discussion in Chapter 8) if the landlord could simply evict a tenant who exercised this right. Only five states—Louisiana, Missouri, North Dakota, Oklahoma, and Wyoming—do not have statutes or court decisions protecting tenants against retaliation. The rest protect you if you have:

- complained to government agencies, such as housing authorities, health departments, or fire departments
- exercised your First Amendment rights to assemble and present your views collectively, as in joining or organizing a tenant union, and
- availed yourself of strategies allowed by your state's law, such as deducting money from the rent and using it to fix defects in the rental unit, or even withholding the rent entirely for an uninhabitable unit (see Chapter 8).

See "State Laws Prohibiting Landlord Retaliation" in Appendix A for the specifics of these state laws.

How do you prove your landlord is trying to retaliate against you? In the real world, landlords are rarely so foolish as to say directly, "I'm terminating your tenancy because you complained to the health department!" Instead, they're likely to terminate a tenancy for a trumped-up reason, hoping to mask the fact that the real motive is to get rid of a tenant whom they regard as a troublemaker. Common examples of cover-ups that are really retaliations are:

- a termination that follows hard on the heels of a long-term tenant's legitimate decision to withhold the rent
- an unexplained refusal to renew a lease following a tenant's complaint to the health department, and
- a termination notice alleging misuse of common facilities after a tenant has used the common room to bring tenants together to fight a proposed rent increase.

Fortunately, however, many states give tenants an edge when it comes to unmasking illegal reasons to end a tenancy. In many states, the landlord is presumed to be retaliating against you if a tenancy is ended (or services decreased) within a certain amount of time, typically six months but sometimes 90 days or one year, following your exercise of a legal right.

How to Stay When Your Landlord Wants You Out

Even if you don't have a winning objection to your landlord's tenancy termination notice—for example, you can't convincingly claim that your landlord is retaliating for your exercise of a legal right, or you can't characterize it as an instance of illegal discrimination—all is not necessarily lost. In fact, your best chance of staying comes not from legal arguments but from honest negotiations. Even if your landlord has been behaving in a highly unreasonable way, it is still in your interest to try to arrive at an acceptable compromise. The following steps might help get your lease or rental agreement renewed.

Promptly Ask for a Meeting

Set up an appointment with the landlord or manager. Don't wait—the more time that passes, the less likely that the landlord will come around. If possible, save the specifics of what you want to talk about until you meet face to face. It's harder to say no across a table than it is on the phone.

Prepare Your Case in Advance

If the termination or nonrenewal is apparently not based on something the landlord thinks you did wrong (these situations are covered in Chapter 17), try to figure out the reason behind the landlord's decision before you meet.

Common reasons for a landlord to end a tenancy include:

- **A misunderstanding.** For example, maybe your landlord's been told—incorrectly—that you'll be moving in a couple of months, and wants to rent the unit now, when a renter is lined up.
- **A matter of personal taste.** Your landlord is annoyed with the family parties you hold around the outdoor grill every Saturday night or has been influenced by the manager, who doesn't like you, your teenage son, or any one of a dozen other things.
- **Irrational whim.** Your landlord likes to periodically rotate tenants, even stable ones, on the theory that—contrary to accepted landlord lore—regular turnover makes it easier to push through rent increases.

Negotiate With Your Landlord

When you meet with your landlord, explain why you want to stay, and prepare convincing arguments to counter the landlord's concerns. Chapter 19 discusses how to negotiate with your landlord.

TIP

Look for hidden, illegal reasons behind your landlord's termination. It's possible that, in the process of negotiation, you'll discover that the true motivation is, indeed, illegal—such as your proper exercise of a repair and deduct statute or the addition of a baby to your apartment. In that event, you might want to stay and fight. Chapter 18 gives you some tips on how to defend an eviction lawsuit.

If You're Successful, Sign a New Lease or Rental Agreement

Don't leave the negotiation table without a written version of the conclusions reached. Ask to sign a new lease or rental agreement or, at the very least, write a summary of your understandings, date it, and ask the landlord to sign it. If that can't be accomplished, immediately write a letter of understanding detailing the promises made by each of you, including the reinstatement of your tenancy. Letters of understanding are explained in Chapter 2.

Getting Out of a Lease

Ideally, you'll sign a lease for just the amount of time you need the rental—a year to attend school, for instance. But despite your best efforts to match your lease term with your plans, you might need to move, temporarily or permanently, before the lease is up.

If you have no intention of returning, one option is to simply move out without sweating the legalities. Leaving before a fixed-term lease expires without paying the remainder of the rent due under the lease is called breaking the lease.

Breaking the lease might not cost you much. If the landlord rerents the property quickly, all you'll be responsible for paying is the rent for the brief time the unit was vacant.

But if you want to leave early, you can do better than just moving out and hoping your landlord gets a new tenant quickly. You should try to minimize your financial responsibility for rent left on the lease, and ensure a good reference from the landlord when you're looking for your next place to live.

This section discusses all your options:

1. **Get the landlord to cancel the lease.** By far the most painless method.

2. **Find a new tenant to sign a new lease with the landlord.** A little more trouble, but usually worth it if the landlord won't just let you off the hook.

3. **Assign your lease.** Turn over your lease to someone else—not a bad choice, but the lease must allow it, and it keeps you on the legal hook to some extent.

4. **Sublet, leave temporarily, and return later.** Subletting makes sense only if you truly want go back to your rental later and you are certain that your subletter will move as planned (and again, your lease might prohibit it).

When Breaking a Lease Is Justified

Some important exceptions apply to the blanket rule that a tenant who breaks a lease owes the rent for the entire lease term. You might be able to legally move out without providing the proper notice in the following situations:

- **The rental unit is unsafe or otherwise uninhabitable.** If your landlord does not provide habitable housing—for example, if the unit violates health or safety codes—a court would probably conclude that you have been "constructively evicted." That releases you from further obligations under the lease. (See Chapter 8.)

- **State or federal law allows you to leave early under the circumstances.** A few states' laws list reasons that allow a tenant to break a lease. For example, in many states, victims of domestic violence have early termination rights (see "Renting a Place With Others" in Chapter 7). Some states allow members of the military to break a lease because of a change in orders. In all states, tenants who enter active duty after signing a lease must be released after delivering proper notice (see "Special Rules for Tenants Who Enter Military Service," above). If you have a good reason for a sudden move, check your state's law. Check the "Being Evicted or Breaking a Lease" section in the tenants' area of Nolo.com for details.

- **The rental unit is damaged or destroyed.** If your home is significantly damaged—either by natural disaster or any other reason beyond your control—you have the right to consider the lease terminated and to move out. (See Chapter 8.)

- **Your landlord harasses you or violates your privacy rights.** (See Chapter 11.)

Getting the Landlord to Cancel the Lease

Lots of tenants assume that their landlord will never agree to end their lease early. This is a mistake. And anyway, it can't hurt to ask. Depending on the circumstances, your landlord might actually be delighted to see you go.

Reasons why your landlord might cheerfully tear up your lease include:

- **It's a chance to raise the rent.** Especially if you are a long-term tenant and your rent is below the current going rate, your departure gives your landlord the chance to offer the unit at a higher rate.

 RENT CONTROL

Most rent control laws let landlords raise rent to the market rate when a tenant moves out. This gives landlords a huge financial incentive to get rid of old tenants. In the few rent control areas that limit rent increases even when a tenant voluntarily moves out, the landlord's profit motive to end your tenancy will be weaker. (Chapter 3 discusses rent control.)

- **The landlord will be able to make major repairs or renovations.** Laws in many states require the landlord to pay for relocation and temporary housing costs if a tenant must move because of renovations or repairs. Or the landlord might have to reduce the rent if part of an apartment becomes unusable. (See Chapter 8.) So landlords usually put these jobs off until the unit is vacant; your departure might be just what your landlord was waiting for.
- **The landlord doesn't like you.** Here is one situation where a less-than-perfect tenant might have an edge. If, in your landlord's eyes, you are a pain in the neck (but your actions have not justified eviction), your request to leave early might be met with a sigh of relief.
- **Your landlord is a decent sort.** If you have been honest and considerate with the landlord, and you have a good reason for leaving—for example, to nurse a sick parent or find a new job after getting laid off—your landlord might be willing to extend you the favor of letting you go. In fact, your landlord might be legally required to allow you to leave early because of

a job change or health problem. (see "When Breaking a Lease is Justified," above.)

When you ask to get out of your lease, be prepared to sweeten the deal by offering to pay a little bit extra. In the business world, this is known as a "buyout." For example, if you want to leave three months early, you might offer to pay half a month's extra rent and promise to be extra accommodating when the landlord wants to show the unit to prospective tenants. A sample Buyout Agreement is shown below.

If your landlord agrees to let you out of your lease early—even if your parting is friendly—it's vital to get the agreement in writing. (See the sample Landlord-Tenant Agreement to Terminate Lease, below.) It protects you in the event that the landlord (or a new owner) tries to hold you responsible for future rent or damages done by the next tenant.

Help With Moving Costs From Your Employer

If you need to move because of a new job or transfer, check to see if your company will cover the cost of getting out of a lease. Many will, recognizing that relocation expenses aren't limited to hiring movers and storing furniture. Especially if your transfer is involuntary or you have been aggressively courted by a new company, use your leverage as a valued employee to ask the company to buy out at least a month or two of your lease. In most areas, that should give the landlord plenty of time to find a new tenant.

FORM

The Nolo website includes a downloadable copy of the Landlord-Tenant Agreement to Terminate Lease form. See Appendix B for the link to the forms in this book.

Sample Buyout Agreement Between Landlord and Tenant

This Agreement is entered into on January 3, 20xx, between Colin Crest, Tenant, who leases the premises at 123 Shady Lane, Capitol City, California, and Marie Peterson, Landlord.

1. Under the attached lease, Tenant agreed to pay Landlord monthly rent of $2,200. Tenant has paid rent for the month of January, 20xx.

2. Tenant's lease expires on June 30, 20xx, but Tenant needs to break the lease and move out on January 15, 20xx.

3. Landlord agrees to release Tenant on January 15, 20xx, from any further obligation to pay rent in exchange for Tenant's promise to pay one-and-one-half month's rent ($3,300) by January 15, 20xx.

4. Tenant agrees to allow Landlord to show the apartment to prospective new tenants on two hours' notice, seven days a week. If Tenant cannot be reached after Landlord has made a good-faith effort to do so, Landlord may enter and show the apartment.

5. If Tenant does not fulfill his promises as described in paragraphs 3 and 4 above, the attached lease, entered into on January 3, 20xx, will remain in effect.

Colin Crest
Colin Crest, Tenant
1/3/xx
Date

Marie Peterson
Marie Peterson, Landlord
1/3/xx
Date

Terminating the Lease and Providing a New Tenant

If your landlord is not willing to end your lease early, another approach might let you break your lease at little or no cost. Simply present your landlord with an acceptable substitute tenant, who will take over right away and continue the flow of rent uninterrupted. Another benefit of this strategy is that it prevents the landlord from passing along to you the costs of finding a new tenant.

To come up with an acceptable new tenant, you'll need to advertise the unit and screen applicants. Doing this is similar to finding someone to be a cotenant. (See Chapter 7.) If you find a good person whom the landlord accepts, be sure the landlord signs a termination of lease form, shown below.

In most states, your landlord must try to find a replacement tenant when you break the lease. Along those lines, if you present a suitable tenant whom the landlord rejects, and the landlord later tries to collect from you, that unreasonable rejection should bar the recovery. (See the discussion below.) But what if your landlord simply refuses to talk to the perfectly acceptable people you find, and demands that you pay rent for the rest of the lease? You'll need to preserve the evidence that you presented one or more good, new tenants, and that the landlord unreasonably refused to consider them or unreasonably rejected them. Without good evidence, you may lose your deposit, be liable for unpaid future rent, and suffer other negative consequences of breaking a lease.

TIP

Keep good records of suitable new tenants. Your files should include their employment and rental history and letters of reference. Better yet, have candidates fill out the rental application in Chapter 1 and give you a copy of their credit report. If your prospective sub's background and credit history is as good as or better than your own, the landlord is going to have a tough time explaining a rejection to a judge if the dispute goes to court.

Landlord-Tenant Agreement to Terminate Lease

_____Robert Chin_____ ("Landlord")

and _____Carl Mosk_____ ("Tenant")

agree that the lease they entered into on _____November 1, 20xx_____ , for premises at

___56 Alpine Terrace, Hamilton, Tennessee_____ ,

will terminate on ____January 5, 20xx_____ .

_Robert Chin_____   _December 28, 20xx_____
Landlord/Manager   Date

_Carl Mosk_____   _December 28, 20xx_____
Tenant   Date

Assigning Your Lease

If you intend to leave permanently, but your landlord will not cancel the lease, consider the third option: assignment. Even though you might have to spend time finding a new tenant, a landlord who is reluctant to simply release you from the lease might be willing to work with this arrangement, as explained below. But because you face some potential legal liability with assignments, this option is always less attractive than the previous two. And keep in mind that most leases prohibit assignment "without consent," so you'll need your landlord's cooperation.

How Assignments Work

Assigning a lease means you turn over the entire rest of your lease to another person, called an "assignee." (You're the "assignor.") You move out, and the new person takes over the lease and moves in. If a dispute erupts over the lease—for example, the assignee fails to pay the rent or the landlord fails to maintain the property—the new tenant can sue or be sued by the landlord.

But making an assignment doesn't completely sever your legal relationship with the landlord. _Unless you agree otherwise, you remain responsible for the rent if the assignee fails to pay._ You are not, however, liable for damage to the premises caused by the assignee. The bottom line: It's much better to get your lease officially terminated and have the new tenant sign a new lease. Then you're totally off the hook.

Generally, the landlord and new tenant are bound by all the terms of the lease you, the original tenant, signed. For example, a lease provision in which the landlord agreed to supply a specified parking spot is still in effect, but it now benefits the new tenant. Only in very unusual situations, where a lease provision is personal, does the obligation not transfer. For example, under the law of most states, a promise by a tenant to do a landlord's housekeeping in exchange for a rent reduction would not automatically pass to an assignee.

Some landlords will agree to an assignment when they might not agree to terminate your tenancy and simply rent to a new tenant. That's because with an assignment, the landlord has two people who are legally responsible to pay the rent: you and the assignee. In a sense, you've become a rent guarantor. Of course, if you are moving out of state and will be beyond the power of a local court, the landlord is unlikely to be able to collect from you.

Finding an Assignee

Finding someone to take over your lease is similar to finding an acceptable new tenant. The advice in Chapter 7 will help you locate and present someone whom your landlord is likely to accept.

There is one important added consideration, however. Because an assignment means that you remain on the hook financially if the new tenant falls behind on the rent, you will want to be absolutely sure that the assignee is solvent and responsible. For that reason, you might want to be even fussier than your landlord. Once you move, you never want to hear about your old rental unit again.

If You Take Over Someone's Lease

If you move in as an assignee of an old tenant's lease, your legal position is very good. You can stay until the lease runs out and enjoy all the rights of a regular tenant—for example, you can sue your landlord for failure to fix a hole in the roof, insist on the use of a parking space as promised in the lease, or use your state's repair and deduct statute for appropriate repairs. Be aware that if you don't pay the rent, the landlord can still evict you; but if it turns out that the original tenant is easier to locate or collect from, the landlord might pursue that person, not you.

Be aware that if you take over a lease that has only a few more months to run, you might face a rent increase if you want to stay when the lease expires. To avoid any surprises, you might consider asking the landlord if you can sign a new, year-long lease and lock in a favorable rent.

How to Assign a Lease

Accomplishing an assignment isn't difficult. One simple, legal approach is to print "Assigned to John Doe" on your current lease at each place your name appears. This will usually be the first clause that identifies the "parties" of the lease and the signature line at the end of the lease. The new tenant, you, and the landlord should then sign your names next to the words "Assigned to John Doe," each place these words are inserted on the lease.

A less messy approach involves giving your landlord a formal "Consent to Assignment of Lease" form, like the sample shown below. Using this form protects you in two important respects:

- It makes it clear that the newcomer (the assignee) is responsible for every term and condition of the lease.
- It gives you an opportunity to have the landlord agree that, contrary to the default rule explained above, you are off the hook even if the new tenant fails to pay the rent.

In this assignment document, the landlord specifically gives up the right to collect any further rent from you. The landlord might balk and demand that this provision be removed. But then again, lots of landlords, not that worried about this aspect of assignments (or unaware that it even exists), might just go ahead and sign.

 FORM
The Nolo website includes a downloadable copy of the Consent to Assignment of Lease form. See Appendix B for the link to the forms in this book.

Subletting Your Home Temporarily

If you have a fairly long lease and a particularly wonderful rental, you might want to move out for a while but then move back in. If you really want to keep your place, you can try to sublet it—that is, rent it to a short-term tenant who will leave when you wish to return.

Consent to Assignment of Lease

Carolyn Friedman _____ ("Landlord") and

Joel Oliver _____ ("Tenant")

and Sam Parker _____ ("Assignee")

agree as follows:

1. Tenant has leased the premises at _____ 5 Fulton, Indianapolis, Indiana _____

   _____

   from Landlord.

2. The lease was signed on _____ April 1, 20xx _____ and will expire on

   _____ March 31, 20xx _____.

3. Tenant is assigning the balance of Tenant's lease to Assignee, beginning on _____ November 1, 20xx _____,

   (the "Effective Date"), and ending on _____ March 31, 20xx _____.

4. Tenant's financial responsibilities under the terms of the lease end as of the Effective Date.

5. As of the Effective Date of the assignment, Tenant permanently gives up the right to occupy the premises.

6. Assignee is bound by every term and condition in the lease that is the subject of this assignment.

Carolyn Friedman _____ _October 1, 20xx_ _____
Landlord/Manager   Date

Joel Oliver _____ _October 1, 20xx_ _____
Tenant   Date

Sam Parker _____ _October 1, 20xx_ _____
Assignee   Date

Subletting might sound like a good option, but think long and hard before you dive in. Subletting has some serious potential drawbacks, explained below. As a general rule, sublease only if all four of these conditions are met:

- You really want your old rental unit back.
- You are completely confident of the integrity, financial stability, and housekeeping habits of your intended subtenant.
- Your landlord has approved the person you have presented.
- You are sure you will return and you're sure the subletter will leave as planned.

EXAMPLE: Denis has lived in his apartment in a university town for 20 years. His landlord, Sally, happily renews the lease every year, appreciating the fact that Denis pays the rent on time and takes good care of the property. When Denis began planning a four-month trip to Europe, he asked Sally if he could sublet to his cousin Ralph, who would be a visiting professor during that time.

Sally was hesitant, having heard from other landlords that sublets were loaded with legal problems. But Denis gave Sally a copy of Ralph's excellent résumé and explained that he just couldn't afford to leave the unit empty for four months; he might have to move out permanently if Sally didn't let Ralph take over. After checking Ralph's references and credit report, Sally agreed to the sublet. The subtenancy proceeded without a hitch and Denis returned to a well-kept home.

Downsides of Subletting

Here are some important issues to consider before you go hunting for a subtenant.

You're still on the hook, financially. If the new tenant (the subtenant) fails to pay the rent or damages the premises, you will be 100% legally responsible.

It's hard to find good subtenants. The pool of reliable short-term tenants is fairly small: visiting students or professors, people waiting for escrow to close on a home they've purchased, and so on. And it's important to find a very, very reliable subtenant; if you don't, you might end up getting sued by the landlord for losses caused by the subtenant. (See Chapter 7 for advice on choosing a replacement tenant.)

	Comparing Subleases and Assignments	
	Sublease	**Assignment**
Rent	New tenant (subtenant) is liable to the original tenant, not to the landlord. Original tenant is liable to landlord.	New tenant (assignee) is liable to the landlord. Absent an agreement to the contrary, old tenant is liable if new tenant doesn't pay.
Damage to premises	Original tenant is liable for damage caused by new tenant.	Absent an agreement to the contrary, original tenant is not liable for damage caused by new tenant.
Violations of lease	Landlord can't sue new tenant for money losses caused by violating lease, because new tenant never signed lease. New tenant can't sue landlord for lease violations, either.	New tenant and landlord are bound by all terms in lease except those that were purely personal to the landlord and old tenant.
Eviction	Landlord can sue to evict new tenant for any reason old tenant could have been evicted. But to evict subtenant, landlord must also evict old tenant.	Landlord can evict new tenant for any reason old tenant could have been evicted.

Your landlord can refuse. Most leases require the landlord's permission before you can sublet. (See Chapter 2.) This is because most landlords don't like sublets—they prefer to end the tenancy and rent to a new tenant, let the tenant assign the rest of the lease to a new tenant, or insist that the new occupant become a full-fledged cotenant.

The big reason landlords don't like sublets is that if the subtenant screws up, the landlord might not be able to sue the subtenant directly. For example, in some states, if a subtenant ruins the premises and the security deposit doesn't cover the loss, the landlord can sue only you—not the subtenant who caused the damage. If you are far away and suddenly decide not to return, the landlord has a big problem. Or if the subtenant's behavior is grounds for eviction—for example, the subtenant is dealing drugs on the rental property or disturbing the neighbors—the landlord might need to evict you in order to get rid of the subtenant.

The subtenant might refuse to leave when you return. This puts you—and your landlord—in an awkward legal situation. The only way the landlord might be able to evict the subtenant is to evict you, too. And, even if you are able to evict the subtenant yourself, no landlord wants to become embroiled in a lawsuit between you and the subtenant.

A subtenant can turn into a tenant. If you and the landlord treat a subtenant like a tenant, that subtenant might gain legal status as the landlord's tenant. For example, a subtenant who repeatedly pays rent directly to the landlord and not to you might be able to claim the status of a tenant (technically, a cotenant). And once that happens, the new tenant has all the rights and responsibilities of a cotenant, which can have important legal consequences for you. (See the Chapter 7 discussion of cotenants and the joint and several liability rule.) To avoid this, make sure that the subtenant pays you the rent, no matter what it says in a written subtenancy

agreement. Deposit the subtenant's check in your account and write your own check to the landlord (or use whatever payment method you and the landlord follow).

Housesitters as Subtenants

Many tenants have a housesitter stay in their home when they will be gone for an extended period of time, especially if they have a pet that needs care. It might surprise you to learn that unless your housesitter will be there for just a few days (or, if your lease or rental agreement has a guest clause, no longer than the number of days guests are allowed to stay) that housesitter is poised to become a subtenant. Or, if your landlord doesn't accept your housesitter as a subtenant, the sitter might be deemed an unauthorized occupant. The question is, should you take the time and trouble to alert the landlord and create a sublease, as the rest of this section explains?

The answer depends entirely on your relationship with the landlord, the circumstances of the rental, and how comfortable you are with taking a chance that your tenancy will be imperiled unless you operate "by the book." Don't take a chance if you have a touchy relationship with the landlord, who is itching to find a reason to boot you, and who is likely to find out about the arrangement. Long-term tenants with rent control have a lot to lose, in particular. On the other hand, if the landlord will probably not find out, and neighboring tenants in the building have been alerted and have no issues, you might do just fine going under the radar.

If you decide to approach the landlord, emphasize the value of having someone on-site during your absence, and assure the landlord that the sitter has every intention to depart. Still, follow the suggestions in this section for choosing your sitter wisely and documenting the arrangement with a sublease, signed also by the landlord.

CAUTION
Choose your in-home service providers carefully. Tenants often give keys to service providers such as dogwalkers, housekeepers, and even in-home delivery services. Because these people will not be living in your home, legally speaking they are guests to whom you've given a key or electronic access. Unless their presence creates a nuisance, the landlord should have no legal basis for objecting to their comings and goings. But obviously, choose these service providers with care: The entire contents of your home—as well as any beloved pets—will be at the service provider's fingertips. Look for providers that are bonded or have professional liability insurance (ask to see proof; they should be able to show you a certificate of insurance). Do your due diligence to make sure that they have established, good reputations.

Creating a Sublease

If you have decided to sublease—and have gotten your landlord's okay—you have just donned a new legal hat: You are your subtenant's landlord. As a landlord, you should take steps to protect your interests and, above all, ensure that your tenant will not do anything that will jeopardize your own tenancy.

You'll need a clear written agreement, signed by you and the subtenant, that lays out the details about rent, the length of the subtenancy, the security deposit, and so on. For example, you'll need to state whether the subtenant has a month-to-month subtenancy or a sublease for a certain period. One way is to simply use the same form you signed with your landlord, changing the title from "Lease" to "Sublease" and making yourself the sublessor and the other person the subtenant. Attach a copy to your original lease, the terms and conditions of which the sublessee agrees to follow as well.

CAUTION
Don't discriminate illegally. As a sublessor, you must abide by fair housing laws. (See Chapter 5.) Be especially careful in your advertisements. An index card tacked to a grocery store bulletin board advertising "Room to rent, single Christian woman preferred" might be a violation of your state's law. On the other hand, if you spread word of your search by informal word-of-mouth only, you'll probably be okay.

> ### Now That You're a Landlord
>
> Once you take on a subtenant, you must meet your responsibilities as a landlord. Follow these steps to make sure you cover the basics:
>
> - Screen and choose your subtenant carefully.
> - Get a security deposit equal to the maximum allowed by law—or, if there's no applicable law, at the minimum equal to the amount you paid for your security deposit.
> - Do your best to provide the subtenant a safe place to live. As you would do for your own safety, alert the subtenant about any hazards and clean up any dangerous situation you've created within your rental unit.
> - Use the Landlord-Tenant Checklist to note the condition of the premises when the subtenant moves in.
> - Use the Landlord-Tenant Checklist again when the subtenant moves out and promptly refund the security deposit, less any legitimate deductions for unpaid rent, cleaning, or damage. If you make deductions, immediately give the subtenant a written explanation.

Ending a Subtenancy

If your subtenant rents month to month and you'd like to end the arrangement, you'll need to give the amount of notice required by your state to terminate a month-to-month tenant. Typically, this is 30 days. (Appendix A lists every state's rule.) If your subtenant has a lease that you would prefer not to renew, send a reminder in advance that the end is approaching and that you do not intend to renew the lease or start a month-to-month relationship.

If the subtenant doesn't leave, do not accept any more rent. You'll probably need to follow regular eviction procedures, like any other landlord.

You also might find it necessary to evict if the subtenant hasn't paid you the rent, or has broken the house rules or a lease clause. You'll probably need to follow your state's procedures for eviction "for cause." (Chapter 17 discusses termination notices for tenant wrongdoing. Read Chapter 18 for an overview of evictions.)

 RENT CONTROL

Rent control might limit your options. Check any applicable rent control laws to see if they apply to subtenants. If it's unclear, ask the local rent control board or a tenants' group.

Breaking the Lease

When you sign a lease, you are legally bound to pay rent for the full lease term, whether or not you continue to occupy the dwelling. Simply moving out, even if you notify the landlord in advance, does not get you off the hook as far as paying rent is concerned.

There's good news, though: You might not have to pay much, if any, additional rent. In most states, you must pay only the amount your landlord loses because you moved out early. If the rental market is tight, the landlord will probably get a new tenant quickly, at the same rent you paid (or even more). Once there's a new rent-paying tenant, your obligation to pay rent ends.

Your Landlord's Duty to Find a New Tenant

Most states require landlords to take reasonable steps to keep their losses to a minimum—in legalese, to "mitigate damages." (Each state's rule is listed in "Landlord's Duty to Rerent" in Appendix A.) So if you break your lease and move out without legal justification, your landlord usually cannot just sit back and wait until the end

of the lease, and then sue you for the total amount of lost rent. In most states, your landlord must try to rerent the property reasonably quickly and subtract the rent received from new tenants from the amount you owe. The landlord can, however, add legitimate expenses to your bill—for example, the cost of advertising the property or using credit reporting agencies to investigate potential renters.

 TIP

Negotiate over the landlord's normal tenant-finding expenses. Why should you pay for the landlord's costs of advertising, showing the apartment, and screening applicants? After all, these are expenses that your landlord would have incurred anyway if you had stayed and left at the end of your term.

Especially if you left only a month or so early, tell the landlord that you are willing to pay lost rent, but shouldn't have to underwrite regular business expenses. If the landlord doesn't buy it and withholds a sizable portion of your security deposit for this purpose, consider suing in small claims court. Many judges will conclude that your landlord should bear at least a portion of the cost of finding a new tenant. (Chapter 16 explains the use of small claims court to dispute security deposit deductions.)

Your landlord is required to make reasonable efforts to rerent the property to a good tenant at a reasonable rent. The landlord does not need to relax standards for acceptable tenants—for example, to accept applicants with poor credit or shady rental histories. Also, the landlord is not required to rent the premises for below fair market value or to immediately turn all attention to renting your unit, disregarding other business.

EXAMPLE: Susan rented an apartment from Stephen in January for a term of one year, at the monthly rent of $1,000. At the end of August, Susan paid her September rent and gave notice of her intent to move at the end of September to be closer to her invalid mother. Susan is legally liable to Stephen for $3,000—the rent for October, November, and December.

However, Stephen posts an ad, checks out prospective tenants, and rents the apartment again on October 15. The new tenant pays $500 for the last half of October and $1,000 in November and December. Stephen must subtract this $2,500 from Susan's $3,000 debt. This leaves her liable for only $500, plus Stephen's advertising costs and credit check fees.

If the Landlord Sues You

If you move out and break your lease, your landlord can, and probably will, charge you for the time and cost of advertising for a new tenant, particularly if the rental market is slow.

Your landlord will probably first use your security deposit to cover these amounts. (See Chapter 16.) But if your deposit doesn't cover what you owe, your landlord might sue you. The landlord can go to court as soon as the property is rented again. Once a new tenant is in place, the landlord's losses—such as advertising expenses and the rent differential, if any—are known. In many states, the landlord has up to four, or even five, years to sue.

If you are sued, you will receive legal documents setting out the landlord's claim. Read them carefully, to see if the amount the landlord asks for is fair. As explained above, if you took the proper steps to protect yourself by finding an acceptable replacement tenant whom your landlord unreasonably rejected, your landlord's suit might be bogus, and you will definitely want to defend yourself.

Chances are you'll be sued in small claims court, assuming the amount the landlord claims isn't above the court's upper limit—about $3,000 to $15,000 in most states. But if it is, and if your lease contains a clause allowing your landlord to recover attorneys' fees, the landlord can file in regular court, where you stand to lose much more.

EXAMPLE: Cree has a year's lease at $800 per month. She moves out with six months ($4,800 of rent) left on the lease. Cree's landlord, Robin, cannot find a new tenant for six weeks, and when she finally does, the new tenant will pay only $600 per month.

Unless Cree can show Robin acted unreasonably, Cree would be liable for the $200 per month difference between what she paid and what the new tenant pays, multiplied by the number of months left in the lease at the time she moved out. Cree would also be responsible for $1,200 for the time the unit was vacant, plus Robin's costs to find a new tenant. Cree would thus owe Robin $2,400 plus advertising and applicant screening costs. If Robin sues Cree for this money and uses a lawyer, if there is an "attorneys' fees and costs" in her lease Cree will also owe Robin these costs, which can be upwards of a few thousand dollars.

If you are sued in small claims court for an amount that seems excessive, simply tell the judge your side of the case. Bring with you any witnesses and documentation that would help tell your story —for example, any evidence that the landlord did not advertise the rental unit, failed to consider prospective tenants you suggested, or overpriced the unit, making it harder to find new tenants.

In some states, in order to win *you* might be required to prove that the landlord took no steps to find a new tenant. In other states, courts require landlords to prove that they did in fact take reasonable steps.

To be on the safe side, assume that the burden of proof will be on you, and be prepared to make your case in court if your landlord sits back and makes no attempt to rerent.

Chapter 16 discusses how to defend yourself in small claims court. If you are sued in regular court and want legal advice, see Chapter 20, which covers how to find and work with a lawyer.

Termination Fees

If your lease contains a termination fee clause—a provision requiring you to pay the landlord a certain amount of money if you break the lease—the landlord may sue you for that amount. In some states, liquidated damages clauses like this in residential leases are flatly illegal. (A few other states, however, allow them under certain circumstances). This means that the landlord would not be able to automatically collect this amount. The court would probably, however, allow the landlord to prove any actual losses, which you'd have to pay if the landlord demonstrates that reasonable cost-free efforts to rerent didn't produce a suitable tenant, and that spending a certain amount of money to find one was justified.

Even in states that allow liquidated damages, the termination fee must not be excessive. If the amount you are supposed to pay greatly exceeds what the landlord actually lost—or would have spent by actively looking for another tenant—a court might consider it an invalid "penalty" and order you to compensate the landlord only for actual losses. But even if you ultimately don't have to pay the whole amount, you'll expend considerable time and energy fighting your landlord in court.

RESOURCE

Everybody's Guide to Small Claims Court, by Cara O'Neill (Nolo), explains how to defend yourself against a landlord who sues you in small claims court.

For more information on the mechanics of a civil lawsuit and how to conduct yourself in court, see *Represent Yourself in Court: How to Prepare & Try a Winning Case*, by Paul Bergman and Sara J. Berman (Nolo).

Condominium Conversions

Landlords can sometimes make a lot of money by converting their rental properties into condominiums, which will often mean the end of your tenancy. Condo conversions can be especially attractive to landlords in areas with rent control, because rent control restricts the profit landlords can make by renting, but doesn't regulate the selling price of condominiums.

Many states regulate the conversion of rental property into condominiums—that is, they limit the number of conversions and give existing tenants considerable rights, as explained below. Here are some of the basic issues that your state's condo conversion law might address:

Government approval. An owner who intends to convert rental property to condos must usually get a plan approval (often called a "subdivision map approval") from a local planning agency. If the property is subject to rent control, additional requirements probably apply.

Public input. In most situations, the public—including current tenants—can speak out at planning agency hearings regarding the proposed condominium conversion and its impact on the rental housing market. Owners are usually required to give tenants notice of the time and place of these hearings.

Tenants' right of first refusal. Most condominium conversion laws demand that the owner offer the units for sale first to the existing tenants, at prices that are the same as or lower than the intended public offering. Often, to keep tenant opposition to a minimum, landlords voluntarily offer existing tenants a chance to buy at a significantly lower price.

Tenancy terminations. Month-to-month tenants who don't buy their units will receive a notice to move at some point during the sales process. Tenants with leases usually have a right to remain through the end of the lease. The entire condo conversion approval process typically takes many months—time enough for current leases to expire before the final okay has been given.

Renting after the conversion has been approved. If you sign a lease or rental agreement *after* the condo conversion has been approved, many states require the owner to give you plenty of clear written warnings (in large, boldface type) that your unit might be sold and your tenancy terminated on short notice. Knowing this, landlords who continue to rent units after they've gotten their subdivision approval usually do so on a month-to-month basis, so the short notice really won't be any different from what any month-to-month tenant would receive.

Relocation assistance and special protections. Some statutes require owners to pay current tenants a flat fee to help with relocation. Some also require owners to provide more notice or additional relocation assistance for elderly tenants or those with small children. There is nothing to stop you from bargaining with the owner for additional compensation—in exchange for your agreement to vacate earlier, for example.

What can you do if your landlord fails to comply with your state or city's conversion laws? Generally, you might be able to delay the conversion and possibly obtain money damages (if you sue your landlord), but you won't be able to stop the process.

 RELATED TOPIC
Legal research on condo conversions. For advice on researching your state's statutes and court cases on condominium conversions, see the discussion of legal research in Chapter 20.

When the Landlord Sells or Goes Out of Business

What happens to your lease if your landlord goes out of the business of renting residential property before the end of the lease term? If a new owner buys the property, in most cases the new owner must honor the existing leases.

If a landlord no longer wants to be a landlord (suppose the landlord wants to take the property out of circulation in order to fix it up for sale), you can't just be tossed out. The regular rules discussed just above apply. If you don't have a lease, the landlord can give you a 30-day notice.

If you do have a lease, it must be honored. But when your lease is up, the landlord has no obligation to continue renting to you or anyone else. A landlord who really wants leaseholding tenants out early will offer to buy them out.

 RENT CONTROL
Phony going-out-of-business ploys. Some landlords in areas with rent control claim to go out of business, oust all their tenants, but then relist the vacancies a few months later. The landlords do this in order to charge a market-rate rent to a new batch of tenants—which of course will be higher than the current, controlled rent. To prevent this, many rent control laws require withdrawn property to remain off the market for a lengthy amount of time, and impose penalties if the landlord rerents too soon. The laws might also specify that former tenants be given the right of first refusal when the property is returned to the rental market.

When the Landlord Declares Bankruptcy

If your landlord files for bankruptcy, your tenancy will not automatically end. To explain what will happen, we need to give you a little background information.

First, if the landlord has filed a Chapter 7 bankruptcy, the landlord's assets will be used to pay off as many debts as possible (the rest are wiped out). The bankruptcy court will appoint someone called a bankruptcy trustee to oversee the case and manage (and then sell) the landlord's property for the benefit of the creditors. If the landlord has filed a Chapter 11 bankruptcy, where the landlord comes up with a plan to pay off debts while still running the business, the landlord stays in the picture as the trustee and is known as the "debtor in possession." (11 U.S.C. § 1101.) Both types of trustees have broad power over the landlord's assets—and income-producing rental property is considered an asset. Your security deposit, however, is not an asset of the bankruptcy estate, because it's your money, not the landlord's. (11 U.S.C. § 365(h).)

Both trustees have the ability to "assume" or "reject" the landlord's leases. Very little will change for you if the trustee assumes the lease— you might even continue to pay rent to the landlord, and the landlord might remain your contact person for requesting repairs. If the trustee rejects the lease, you will have a choice. You can:

- treat the lease as terminated and move out, or
- stay put and retain all your rights under the lease.

As you can see, the term "rejects" is a bit misleading, because it does not mean that your tenancy will end. However, your ability to use your state-given tenant remedies, such as rent withholding and repair and deduct, will be replaced by the remedy provided by the bankruptcy code. If, for example, your landlord fails to provide heat, you'll have to apply to the bankruptcy court for an "off-set" against rent—in effect, a rent abatement based on the diminished value of your rental. (11 U.S.C. § 365(h)(1)(B).)

In practical terms, your landlord's bankruptcy might not greatly affect the quality of your tenancy. In a Chapter 7 bankruptcy, the property will probably be sold eventually, in which case you'll be dealing with a new owner who will have to honor your lease (the same situation you'd face if the landlord sold the property voluntarily). In a Chapter 11 bankruptcy, if there is enough value in the property to justify its continued operation, you might notice little change. There is always the chance, however, that the trustee will decide to sell the property, in which case you will find yourself with a new owner and landlord—but again, one who will have to honor the terms of your lease.

When the Rental Property Is Foreclosed

If the landlord falls behind on mortgage payments on the rental property, the bank (or mortgage holder) can foreclose, and then sell the property to satisfy the landlord's debt out of the proceeds of the sale. At such sales, the mortgage holder usually ends up owning the property, though sometimes a third party outbids the mortgage holder and becomes the owner.

Eviction Protection After a Foreclosure

The federal Protecting Tenants at Foreclosure Act (PTFA) enables tenants whose rental is in foreclosure to remain in their homes for at least 90 days or until the end of their lease, whichever is greater. (12 U.S.C. § 5220.) The PTFA applies to rentals in all states, but states and cities might have additional protections for tenants whose home is in foreclosure.

If you are caught in the middle between a defaulting landlord and a foreclosing bank, and you want to preserve your rental, consider consulting a local real estate or foreclosure lawyer, who should know the details of the PTFA as well as any applicable state or local laws. The website of the National Housing Law Project, NHLP. org, is also a useful resource on state and local protections for tenants in foreclosure situations (go to "Tenants and Foreclosure" under the "Initiatives" tab in the menu).

State and Local Foreclosure Protections for Tenants

Many states (and some cities) give tenants additional protection from eviction in default and foreclosure situations. For example, some state and local laws require a foreclosing bank to give tenants notice about an impending foreclosure, require a new owner to give tenants a certain number of days' notice to vacate before starting an eviction after a foreclosure, or require a new owner to honor existing leases under specific circumstances.

"Cash for Keys"

To encourage tenants to leave quickly, banks sometimes offer tenants a cash payout in exchange for their rapid departure. Thinking that they have little choice, many tenants—even Section 8 and other protected tenants—take the deal.

Rules in Areas With Just Cause Eviction Protection

Tenants who live in areas with "just cause" eviction protection are also protected from terminations at the hands of an acquiring bank or new owner. These tenants can rely on their rent control law's list of allowable reasons for termination. Because a change of ownership, without more, does not justify a termination, the fact that the change occurred through foreclosure will not justify a termination. However, a new owner who wants to do an "owner move-in" eviction may do so, as long as the owner complies with the ordinance's procedures.

Paying Rent—Before or After Foreclosure

The issue of whom you pay rent to pending or after a foreclosure can be confusing. Here's a summary of the key issues.

Paying Rent Before the Foreclosure

Tenants who learn that their landlords are in default on the mortgage (they've fallen behind on their payments) or already in foreclosure (the lender has announced their intent to foreclose) are often confused about who is entitled to the rent money. You are likely to hear demands from many quarters—the desperate owner, a management company, or a bank. It's important to know who is—and who isn't—entitled to the rent check. First, a little background.

Lending banks (the mortgage holders) typically attach a rider, or special agreement, to the mortgage or deed of trust documents when a buyer intends to use the building as a rental. This rider, called a 1-4 Family Rider (Assignment of Rents) is used by lenders in most states for properties that have one to four rental units. Its main purpose is to give the lender the right to receive the rent when the buyer has defaulted on the mortgage.

Foreclosures in Multifamily Properties

The 1-4 Family Rider is a standard form that's used for small properties (four or fewer rental units). Banks and buyers use a standard form because they assume that the relatively small size of the deal doesn't merit lengthy negotiations between the parties.

Larger properties almost always have the same sort of arrangement—if the owner falls behind on the mortgage payments, the lender gets the right to receive the rent. Usually, these arrangements are negotiated by the banks and the buyers' lawyers and might include unique provisions that are hammered out by the parties. But as far as the tenants are concerned, the bottom line is the same: With proper notice, you will be expected to pay the rent to the bank.

To understand how the rider works, think like a banker for a minute. The property is generating income and the buyer is falling behind on mortgage payments. In order to cut its losses as quickly and as thoroughly as possible, the lender wants to get its hands on the rent.

In most states, once the lender gives the owner a written notice of default, the lender has the right to receive the rent directly from the tenants. Lenders have to give written notice to the tenants, and they typically do so by letter, posted notice on the property, or in person.

Paying Rent After the Foreclosure

After the foreclosure has happened, the new owner, whether a bank or an investor, can insist that the tenant comply with the lease or rental agreement that the tenant entered into with the old owner. This means that on the first rent due date after the property changes hands, you must pay the same rent to the new owner. If you don't pay, the new owner can give you a notice to pay rent or quit, and if you do neither, begin eviction proceedings.

If you receive notice that the property in which you live has been foreclosed (that is, a "trustee's sale" has been held), you should stop paying rent to the now-former owner and pay it to the new owner. If you don't know who that is, set aside your rent payment each month (to be extra careful, set up an escrow account and deposit it there), so that you can pay it to the new owner once you find out who that is. If you receive a three-day notice to pay rent or quit from the new owner, you might want to confirm with your county's Recorder's Office—usually located at the county seat—that the person or entity giving you the notice is truly the new owner.

Repairs and Maintenance Preforeclosure

Even though the bank is receiving the rent payments, all other rights and responsibilities that the owner/landlord has with respect to the tenants remain in place. Until the bank actually forecloses, the owner is still the owner. This leads to problems if you need maintenance or repairs.

Owners whose properties are in preforeclosure are often unwilling to make repairs.

Without a source of income from the rental property, most owners will be unable (or unwilling) to maintain it. For you, however, the owner's disillusionment is beside the point when it comes to safe and secure rental housing, because landlords must maintain fit and habitable rental housing. How does a tenant enforce this right against a demoralized (and possibly broke) owner?

The lender is not obligated to help. According to the Family Rider, the lender must apply the rent money to property management costs, including maintenance, before it applies the money to the unpaid mortgage. But the Rider explicitly does not obligate the lender to assume the maintenance duties of the owner. Unless there's a specific local or state law to the contrary, the lender's right to receive rent money doesn't turn that lender into the landlord for purposes of maintaining the property. (A few states are beginning to make banks legally responsible for maintenance. For example, in California, banks have specified maintenance duties.) If conditions seriously deteriorate to the point where the home is not fit to live in, you might find yourself stuck between an owner who has no ability to take care of business, and a lender who has no obligation to do so.

Self-help remedies are tricky. You might need to avail yourself of a tenant's "self-help" remedy, such as rent withholding and repair-and-deduct (not all states give these remedies to tenants). In many cities, housing and health departments are charged with responding to unsafe and unsanitary conditions in rental housing. They typically have powers that range from ordering the owners to take care of business (under threat of contempt of court), to taking over the property altogether and running it until they've fixed the problems (and charging the owner for the privilege).

Although these government agencies can, and should, still do their jobs, their intervention might be ineffective. The agencies will be dealing with an owner who has no resources to contribute (and who might even be impossible to locate), and a bank that has no legal duty to step up. Results will differ when the government takes over because the efficiency of local and state agencies varies tremendously.

Moving Out and Getting Your Security Deposit Back

Fights over security deposits make up a large percentage of the landlord-tenant disputes that wind up in court. Tenants are normally the plaintiffs (the ones who file the lawsuit), alleging improper use of the deposit money or a refusal to return the deposit at all.

This chapter discusses some simple steps you can take to protect your security deposit and minimize the chances of ending up in court with your landlord. It also includes advice and information on:

- when and how landlords must return deposits and what deductions are allowed under the law
- how to make sure you meet your landlord's expectations for the condition in which the unit should be left
- how to protect yourself by documenting the condition of the rental unit when you move out
- how to write demand letters for the return of your deposit
- how to negotiate with your landlord and use a mediation service, if appropriate, and, should it be necessary,
- how to file and prepare a winning lawsuit against your landlord.

As always, you'll want to put your communications with your landlord in writing. You can use the tried-and-true sample forms and letters provided in this chapter to create your paper trail. As with all important communications, use a mail or delivery service that will provide proof of delivery (you might need this should you end up in court fighting about your deposit). In Chapter 6, "Using Email or Text Messages for Notice or a Letter of Understanding" explains why it's best to send important communications by mail (certified or return receipt requested) or delivery service, rather than email or text.

 RELATED TOPIC
Also covered in this book:

- State laws on how and how much your landlord can collect for deposits, as well as what happens to your deposit if the landlord sells the property: Chapter 4.
- How to use a Landlord-Tenant Checklist to document the condition of the rental unit when you move in: Chapter 6.
- Landlord and tenant repair and maintenance responsibilities: Chapters 8, 9, and 10.
- What happens to your deposit if the landlord files for bankruptcy or the property is foreclosed: Chapter 15.

Basic Rules for Returning Deposits

Most states hold landlords to a strict set of rules regarding security deposits. Landlords are expected to account for tenants' money promptly or face penalties. For example, in many states a landlord who deliberately violates the security deposit statute might have to return all of the tenant's deposit plus two or three times the amount wrongfully withheld, plus attorneys' fees and costs.

Advance Notice of Deductions

In many states, landlords must give tenants a heads-up before they deduct any amounts from a security deposit. Most of the time, landlords provide this advance notice during a pre-move-out inspection (the second inspection is done when the tenant leaves). This practice gives tenants an opportunity to avoid deposit deductions by cleaning and making repairs before they move out.

Although these pre–move-out inspections can be very helpful for tenants, they do not eliminate the landlord's ability to make deductions at move out. For example, landlords can still deduct for damage or uncleanliness that appeared after the first inspection, or for problems they couldn't see because of the presence of the tenant's belongings. For specifics on your state's law, see "State Security Deposit Rules" in Appendix A.

Deadlines

Depending on the state, landlords have between 14 and 30 days after you leave—whether voluntarily or by eviction—to return your deposit.

The landlord must mail the following to your last known address (or forwarding address, if known):

- your entire deposit, with interest if required (Chapter 4 provides more information about interest on security deposits), or
- a written, itemized statement as to how the deposit has been applied (toward back rent, cleaning costs, and damage repair), together with whatever is left of the deposit, including any interest that is required. In most states, landlords send the itemization along with any deposit balance. A few states add an additional step that gives tenants time to respond to proposed deductions before they are actually made.

For specifics on your state's law, see "State Security Deposit Rules" in Appendix A.

Unfortunately, landlords in some states are not subject to deadlines or rules governing the return of deposits. If you live in one of these states, ask your landlord when you move out when you can expect to get your deposit back. A reasonable landlord should return your deposit within one month. If more than a month has passed or you suspect you might never see your deposit again, follow the steps in "How to Handle Deposit Disputes," below.

> **CAUTION**
> **Leave a forwarding address.** A few states excuse landlords from complying with some of the return rules if the tenant has not left a forwarding address. Don't take a chance.

Itemized Statements

In most states, you are entitled to a statement that explains the purpose of each deduction and states the dollar amount withheld. Your landlord should never send a statement that simply says, "$200 deduction for cleaning and repairs." If you get this kind of vague statement, you have the legal right to ask for more details.

If cleaning and repair work have already been done, your landlord should provide details on labor and supplies, including receipts, in the final itemization. For example:

- "Carpet cleaning by ABC Carpet Cleaners, $160, required because of several large grease stains and candle wax imbedded in living room rug."
- "Dry wall repair of several holes in bedroom wall and painting of new drywall. $400."
- "$250 to replace living room drapes that were damaged by cigarette smoke and holes."

See the sample Security Deposit Itemization below.

If your landlord can't complete the necessary repairs or cleaning within the time required to return the security deposit, the statement should contain a reasonable estimate of the cost. If you end up disputing the security deposit deductions in court, your landlord will need to produce receipts for the final, actual amounts deducted.

When a tenant breaks or substantially shortens the useful life of an item, it can be a little tougher to put a dollar amount on damages. In fairness, the landlord ought to take into account how old the item was, how long it might have lasted otherwise, and its original cost.

> **EXAMPLE:** Lee's dog ruined an eight-year-old rug that had a life expectancy of ten years. If the rug cost $1,000, Lee's landlord should charge $200 for the two years of life that would have remained in the rug had Lee's dog not ruined it.

Security Deposit Itemization
(Deductions for Repairs, Cleaning, and Unpaid Rent)

Date: November 8, 20xx

From: Rachel Tolan

123 Larchmont Lane

St. Louis, Missouri

To: Lena Coleman

456 Penny Lane, #101

St. Louis, Missouri

Property address: 789 Cora Court, St. Louis, Missouri

Rental period: January 1, 20xx to October 31, 20xx

1. Security deposit received: $ 1,500

2. Interest on deposit (if required by lease or law): $ N/A

3. Total credit (sum of lines 1 and 2): $ 1,500

4. Itemized repairs and related losses:

   Repainting of living room walls, required by crayon

   and chalk marks $ 260

5. Necessary cleaning:

   Sum paid to resident manager for 4 hours cleaning at

   $30/hour: debris-filled garage, dirty stove, and refrigerator $ 120

6. Defaults in rent not covered by any court judgment
   (list dates and rates): _____

7. Amount of court judgment for rent, costs, attorneys' fees: N/A

8. Other deductions (specify): $ N/A

9. Total amount owed landlord (sum of lines 4 through 8): $ 380

10. Final balance (line 3 minus line 9)

    ☑ Tenant Owes Landlord: $ _____

    ☐ Landlord Owes Tenant: $ 1,120

Comments: A check for $1,120 is enclosed.

The approach illustrated in the example above amortizes the cost of the damaged item over its useful life. The tenant ends up paying for the value of the item at the time the damage occurred. We think this approach is fair because it takes into account the fact that items wear out through normal use and landlords must shoulder the cost of replacing them. When you shorten the useful life of an item, your landlord will have to make a capital expenditure earlier than planned, so it's fitting that you should compensate the landlord accordingly.

This is not the only method that landlords use, however. Some will charge you for the item's original cost, regardless of its age; and some will charge you for the full replacement cost. Both of these methods result in the tenant essentially underwriting the landlord's cost of doing business. Look back at the example—why should Lee pay the landlord $1,000 (the rug's original cost) when, in two years, the landlord would have had to spend that amount to replace an item that had lost its usefulness? Even worse, if the rug would now cost more, why should Lee take on the additional burden of paying the inflated cost?

Unfortunately, we aren't aware of any statutes that directly address the question of how landlords should figure the cost of an item when it's ruined by a tenant. But you can arrive at a sensible amount by following the depreciation rules that landlords follow when they want to amortize the cost of a durable item and deduct its cost as a business expense over several years. Here's how "straight-line" depreciation works: Suppose your dog left several indelible stains on an area rug that cost $2,000. The landlord wants to charge you for replacing it. Start by deducting the rug's salvage value from its cost—in this case, maybe the landlord could get $50 for it at a garage sale. Then divide the result by the number of years one could expect the rug to last (its useful life)—say, six. The result ($2,000 minus $50 = $1,950 divided by 6 = $325) is the amount by which the value decreases every

year. If the rug was 2 years old, it was worth $1,950 minus 2 × $325, or $1,300, and it would be reasonable for your landlord to deduct that amount from your deposit.

If you believe your landlord is overcharging you, it's time to consider challenging the deductions. In the next few sections, we cover what your landlord can legally charge you for, steps to take to avoid going to court, and what to do if you're left with no alternative but to go to court.

Sample Life Expectancies from HUD

Landlords who provide affordable housing through a HUD-sponsored program can ask HUD for reimbursement for damages that are not covered by a tenant's security deposit. HUD's "Sample Life Expectancy Chart" is not legally binding but would be taken seriously by a judge.

Item	Expected life expectancy	Rental unit or type of occupancy
Hot Water Heaters	10 years	All units
Plush Carpeting	5 years	Family
	7 years	Elderly
Air-Conditioning Units	10 years	All units
Ranges	20 years	All units
Refrigerators	10 years	All units
Interior Painting— Enamel	5 years	Family
	7 years	Elderly
Interior Painting—Flat	3 years	Family
	5 years	Elderly
Tiles/Linoleum	5 years	Family
	7 years	Elderly
Window shades, screens, blinds	3 years	Family, Elderly

Source: Special Claims Processing Guide, June 2006, Appendix 5D.

Deductions for Cleaning and Damage

Legally, a landlord may charge for any cleaning or repairs necessary to restore the rental unit to its condition at the beginning of the tenancy. The landlord may not use your security deposit for the cost of remedying ordinary wear and tear.

Unfortunately, it's not always easy to decide what constitutes ordinary wear and tear, or what must be done to leave a rental unit clean.

Reasonable Deductions

In general, landlords may charge only for cleaning and repairs that are really necessary, such as replacing stained or ripped carpets or drapes (particularly smoke-contaminated ones), fixing damaged furniture, and cleaning dirty stoves, refrigerators, and kitchen and bathroom fixtures. Landlords might also need to take care of such things as flea infestations left behind by a dog or mildew in the bathroom caused by a failure to clean properly.

Your landlord can't set unreasonable standards for cleaning. For example, if the place was less than immaculate when you moved in, your landlord has no legal right to require a perfect cleaning job now. And no judge would uphold a requirement that you clean the floor with a toothbrush.

What Can Your Landlord Charge For?	
Ordinary Wear and Tear: **Your Landlord's Responsibility**	**Damage or Excessive Filth:** **Your Responsibility**
Curtains faded by the sun	Cigarette burns in curtains or carpets
Curling linoleum in bathroom	Broken tiles in bathroom
Minor marks on or nicks in wall	Large marks on or holes in wall
Dents in the wall where a door handle bumped it	Door off its hinges
Moderate dirt or spotting on carpet	Rips in carpet or urine stains from pets
A few small tack or nail holes in wall	Lots of picture holes or gouges in walls that require patching and repainting
A rug worn thin by normal use	Stains in rug caused by your leaking fish tank
Worn gaskets on refrigerator doors	Broken refrigerator shelf
Faded paint on bedroom wall	Water damage on wall from hanging plants
Dark patches of ingrained soil on hardwood floors that have lost their finish and have been worn down to bare wood	Water stains on wood floors and windowsills caused by windows being left open during rainstorms
Warped cabinet doors that won't close	Sticky cabinets and interiors
Stains on old porcelain fixtures that have lost their protective coating	Grime-coated bathtub and toilet
Moderately dirty miniblinds	Missing miniblinds
Bathroom mirror beginning to "de-silver" (black spots)	Mirrors caked with lipstick and makeup
Clothes dryer that delivers cold air because the thermostat has given out	Dryer that won't turn at all because it's been overloaded
Toilet flushes inadequately because mineral deposits have clogged the jets	Toilet won't flush properly because it's stopped up with a diaper

That said, every move-out is different in its details, and no hard and fast rules dictate how to determine what is wear and tear and what is your responsibility. But here are some basic guidelines:

- You should not be charged for filth or damage that was present when you moved in.
- You should not be charged for replacing an item when a repair would be sufficient. For example, if you damaged the kitchen counter by placing a hot pan on it, you shouldn't be required to replace the entire counter if an expertly done patch will do the job. Of course, you have to evaluate the overall condition of the unit—if it is a luxury property that looks like an ad in *Architectural Digest*, don't expect your landlord to make do with a patch.
- The longer you've lived in a place, the more wear and tear can be expected on things like carpets, floors, and walls.
- Landlords in some states are allowed to charge a cleaning fee, which is separate from the security deposit and is specifically labeled as nonrefundable. (See Chapter 4.) You should not be charged at move-out for cleaning if you've already paid a nonrefundable cleaning fee.
- You should be charged a fair price for repairs and replacements. You should not be asked to foot the bill for a high-priced handyman or unreasonably expensive replacement items. Legally, your landlord is obligated to spend only what is needed to accomplish the job in a reasonably professional manner.

> **TIP**
>
> **Check prices yourself.** If you believe you are being price-gouged, it might be worth it to get a few quotes from repairpersons and compare them with the landlord's bill, or to shop around for the item that the landlord replaced. Say, for example, your landlord charges you $900 to replace a stove you damaged. First, argue that you should be liable only for the value of the (used) stove you ruined. But as a backup, agree for the purposes of argument only that you'll pay for a replacement. If you find the same stove on sale at a nearby discount warehouse for $600 (and you can't convince the judge to adopt your first theory), you have the makings of a winning small claims case if, after learning of the discrepancy, the landlord doesn't reduce your bill by $300.

See "What Can Your Landlord Charge For?" above, for some examples of what a court will consider to be ordinary wear and tear, and what crosses the line and is commonly considered to be a condition for which you must pay for cleaning, replacement, or repair.

> **RENT CONTROL**
>
> **Your rent control law might provide guidance on what is "normal wear and tear" and what is "damage."** Most rent control laws allow the landlord to raise the rent for specific capital expenses. Typically, maintenance expenses spent in response to normal wear and tear are not considered capital expenses. But if the landlord must replace an item, it might qualify as a capital expense, which justifies a rent increase. Protenant rent boards have reacted against this rent-increase justification by classifying the replacement of appliances, carpets, repainting, and so on as mere "maintenance" necessitated by normal wear and tear. Your argument: If it's maintenance to the rent board, it ought to be maintenance with respect to your security deposit, too, and your deposit shouldn't be used for it.

Common Disagreements

Common areas of disagreement between landlords and tenants concern repainting, carpets, and fixtures.

Painting

Although state and local laws (with the exception of some cities, including New York City) provide no firm guidelines as to who is responsible for repainting when a rental unit needs it, courts usually rule that if you have lived in your unit for several years, painting should be done at your landlord's expense, not yours. On the other hand, if you have lived in a unit for less than a year, and the walls were freshly painted when you moved in but are now a mess, your landlord is probably entitled to charge you for all costs of cleaning the walls. If repainting badly smudged walls is cheaper and more effective than cleaning, the landlord can probably charge for repainting.

Rugs and Carpets

If the living room rug was already threadbare when you moved in and looks even worse now, it's pretty obvious that your footsteps have simply contributed to the inevitable, and that this wear and tear is not your responsibility. On the other hand, a brand-new good quality rug that becomes stained and full of bare spots within months has probably been subjected to the type of abuse you will have to pay for. In between, it's anyone's guess. But, clearly, the longer you have lived in a unit, and the cheaper or older the carpet was when you moved in, the less likely you are to be held responsible for its deterioration.

Fixtures

The law considers pieces of furniture or equipment that are physically attached to the rental property, such as bolted-in bookshelves, to be your landlord's property, even if you paid for or installed them. This means that if you leave behind a row of bookshelves, your landlord can legally remove them, subtract the cost of removal from your security deposit, *and* keep the bookshelves. (Chapter 10 discusses how to avoid disputes over fixtures when you move out.)

 TIP

Report damage immediately to your landlord. If your landlord doesn't take action and the problem gets worse, a written notice of the damage will create a record of your attempts to nip it in the bud. You shouldn't have to pay, at move-out time, for any issues that were exacerbated by the landlord's inaction.

Deductions for Unpaid Rent

If you move out owing rent, your landlord can deduct any unpaid rent from your security deposit, including any unpaid utility charges or other financial obligations required under your lease or rental agreement. Even if your debt far exceeds the amount of the security deposit, most laws still require your landlord to itemize and notify you of how the security deposit was applied to your debt.

Chapter 15 discusses how month-to-month tenancies and fixed-term leases end, including notice requirements and what happens if you leave early or stay late.

Month-to-Month Tenancies

Ideally, as a month-to-month renter, you'll give the right amount of notice and pay for your last month's rent. Usually, the notice period is the same as your rental period, 30 days. Then, when you leave as planned, the only issue with respect to your security deposit is whether you've caused any damage or left the place dirty. But, in the real world, the following hiccups occur frequently, and they all result in deductions from your security deposit for unpaid rent:

- You leave as announced, but owe rent.
- You leave later than planned, and haven't paid for your extra days.
- You leave as announced, but you haven't given the right amount of notice.

Let's look at each situation.

Owing Rent When You Leave

If you've managed to convince a good-hearted (or lazy) landlord to let unpaid rent slide, the landlord is entitled to deduct what you owe from the security deposit—either during the tenancy or when you leave. There's a limit, however: The landlord is bound by the laws that require people to bring a claim for unpaid rent within a certain number of years (called the "statute of limitations"). When the unpaid rent extends beyond this period, your landlord cannot claim it. In the unusual event that your landlord has failed to collect rent for a long time, you might need the protection of these limits.

Staying After Your Announced Departure Date

If you fail to leave when planned (or when requested, if the landlord has terminated the rental agreement), you obviously aren't entitled to stay on rent-free. When you eventually leave, your landlord will calculate the exact amount you owe by prorating the monthly rent for the number of days you have failed to pay.

> **EXAMPLE:** Erin gives notice on March 1 of her intent to move out. She pays her landlord Ann the rent of $1,800 for March. But because she can't get into her new place on time, Erin stays until April 5 without paying anything more. Ann is entitled to deduct 5/30 (one-sixth) of the total month's rent, or $300, from Erin's security deposit.

Giving Inadequate Notice

When you terminate a month-to-month tenancy, you must give your landlord the legally required amount of notice before leaving; in most states, that's 30 days. You must pay rent for that entire period. If you gave less than the legally required amount of notice and moved out, you are responsible for paying rent for the balance of the notice period unless the place is rerented within the 30 days. (Chapter 15 covers notice requirements for terminating a tenancy.)

> **EXAMPLE:** Tom pays his rent on the first of every month. State law requires 30 days' notice to terminate a tenancy. On June 20, Tom gives notice that he will leave on July 1. The rental market is soft and Jim, his landlord, is unable to rerent for two months. Because Tom gave only 10 days' notice, Jim is entitled to deduct two-thirds of a months' rent (representing the 20 days of unpaid rent) from Tom's deposit.

**Letter #1:
Tenant's Cleaning Plans**

1492 Fraser Avenue, #363
Chicago, Illinois, 00000

May 15, 20xx

Brett Steiner
5 Hilton Ave.
Chicago, Illinois 00000

Dear Ms. Steiner:

As you know, I gave notice on April 30, 20xx that the last day of my tenancy will be May 30, 20xx.

I intend to leave the apartment clean and undamaged. Specifically, I plan to:

1. Vacuum all floors and carpets and wash kitchen and bathroom floors.
2. Wash bathroom tile and all painted surfaces.
3. Clean all bathroom and kitchen appliances with cleaning products designed for these areas; clean oven and clean refrigerator.
4. Cold-water wash the curtains in the kitchen and bathroom.
5. Wash the interior surfaces of the windows.
6. Remove all rubbish and personal items.

I believe that thoroughly accomplishing these tasks will satisfy my obligations under Illinois law to leave my rental unit clean. And because my apartment has not been damaged (beyond ordinary wear and tear), I expect a full and prompt refund of my $1,750 security deposit. Please let me know within five days if my cleaning plan is not acceptable to you. If I don't hear from you, I'll assume that you are in agreement with it.

Yours truly,

Stephan Pierce

Stephan Pierce

Fixed-Term Leases

If you leave before a fixed-term lease expires, your landlord is entitled to the balance of the rent due under the lease. That rule is softened considerably by the fact that in most states your landlord is required to try to rerent the property, and once a new tenant starts paying rent, your obligation ends.

If you leave less than a month before your lease is scheduled to end, you can be sure that, if the case goes to court, a judge will conclude you owe rent for the entire lease term. It would be unreasonable to expect a landlord to immediately find a new tenant to take over the few days left of your lease. But if you leave more than 30 days before the end of a lease, your landlord's duty to look for a new tenant will be given more weight by the courts. (See Chapter 15 for more on your landlord's duty to try to rerent the property promptly.)

> **EXAMPLE:** On January 1, Anthony rents a house from Will for $2,200 a month and signs a one-year lease. He moves out on June 30, even though six months remain on the lease, making him responsible for a total rent of $13,200. Will rerents the property on July 10, this time for $2,250 a month (the new tenants pay $1,500 for the last 20 days in July), which means that he'll receive a total rent of $12,750 through December 31. That's $450 less than the $13,200 he would have received from Anthony had he lived up to the lease, so Will may deduct $450 from Anthony's deposit. In addition, if Will spent a reasonable amount of money to find a new tenant (for ads, rental agency commissions, and credit checks), he may also deduct this sum from the deposit.

After an Eviction

If you lose an eviction lawsuit, the landlord can legally expect payment for rent until you actually leave.

> **EXAMPLE:** When Allen fails to pay May's rent of $1,500, Marilyn sues to evict him. On June 10, she gets an eviction judgment from the court, ordering Allen to pay rent through that date. He doesn't actually leave until June 17. Marilyn can deduct the following items from the deposit:
> - costs of necessary cleaning and repairs, as allowed by state law
> - the amount of the judgment (for rent through June 10), and
> - rent for the week between June 10 and June 17 at $50 per day, or $350.

If the security deposit is not large enough to cover everything you owe, and the landlord has obtained a court judgment, the landlord can collect the balance in all sorts of ways—for example, by going after your wages or bank account.

Avoiding Fights Over Deposits

Most security deposit hassles between landlords and tenants concern cleaning, not repairs or replacement costs. That's because replacement and repair costs are objective and can be verified, but cleanliness is subjective. You need to figure out what your landlord expects, and adopt those standards if they're reasonable—at least until you've moved out.

Your Cleaning Plans

Some landlords are wise enough to establish fair cleaning and damage guidelines right in the lease or rental agreement, a move-out letter, or set of rules and regulations. But what if your lease says nothing beyond obligating you to leave the unit in "clean and acceptable condition"? If you've lived in your place long enough, you might have a good idea of your landlord's standards.

But if you have any doubt, you should seize the initiative by giving your landlord written notice of your cleaning plans—for example, washing the kitchen floor, laundering the cotton bedroom curtains, thoroughly cleaning all appliances and bathroom fixtures, and so on. Your letter should also ask your landlord to respond within a few days with any comments or disagreements with your cleaning plans. See the sample letter #1 above.

Is it really necessary to take the time and trouble to give your landlord a preview of your cleaning plans? Yes.

First, giving the landlord the chance to respond in advance to your cleaning plans puts you in the driver's seat. This type of letter of understanding legally obligates your landlord to tell you if your cleaning plans aren't sufficient. If you don't receive a response, you can assume that your landlord accepts your plan of action. If, later, the landlord deducts because you didn't shampoo the carpets, when you stated that you intended to do a thorough vacuuming, you have solid evidence that the deduction is unreasonable.

But keep in mind that you must do a thorough job on the tasks you set yourself, and that it is always possible for you and the landlord to argue about whether you vacuumed well enough.

Telling your landlord in advance how you intend to clean might save you some trouble, too: Your landlord might tell you to cross some items off your list if, for example, your landlord intends to replace the bedroom drapes that you plan to dry clean, repaint the walls you intend to clean, or replace the old stove you plan to scrub.

A letter of understanding might also save you money. For example, when you suggest washing the walls with a strong cleaner, your landlord might react in horror, saying that it could strip the paint of its glossy finish. If you don't know about these risks and your cleaning makes things worse, you can be sure that your landlord will tap into your deposit.

Legally speaking, you are required only to return your rental in the same condition in which you found it, minus ordinary wear and tear. If your rental was on the grubby end of the cleanliness spectrum when you moved in, you'll hardly be in the mood to return it any cleaner. But leaving a dirty apartment, even for good reason, all but guarantees that your landlord will dip into your deposit for cleaning charges. Knowing this, you

Letter #2: Tenant's Cleaning Plans

1492 Fraser Avenue, #363
Chicago, Illinois, 00000

May 15, 20xx

Brett Steiner
5 Hilton Ave.
Chicago, Illinois 00000

Dear Ms. Steiner:

As you know, on April 30, 20xx I gave notice to terminate my tenancy effective May 30, 20xx.

When I moved in on October 1, 20xx, the previous tenant had just left a day earlier. There were full garbage bags in the kitchen and entry hall; the kitchen, hallway and bathroom floors had been swept but not washed; the kitchen cabinets had peeling, sticky shelf paper; the windows had not been washed; the refrigerator still had containers of food; the oven had not been cleaned and the burners on the stove were encrusted with charred spills. After we toured the apartment and noted all of these problems on the Landlord-Tenant Checklist (copy attached), you promised to have a cleaning service come the next day.

Despite my written reminder to you the next day (copy attached), the cleaning crew never materialized. I was forced to spend six hours dealing with the mess. In case you don't remember just how bad it was, I have a set of date-stamped photos showing all the disgusting details, which I'd be happy to show you. I also have receipts for my cleaning materials.

Under state law, I am required to return the rental unit to you in substantially the same condition as I found it, minus ordinary wear and tear. I intend to live up to my legal duty. In fact, the condition of the apartment is far better than it was when I moved in. I will be here to go over the apartment with you on my last day as we arranged, and will have with me our original Checklist, my camera, and my friend Ray, who helped me clean when I moved in.

Yours truly,

Stephan Pierce

Stephan Pierce

must be willing and equipped to assert your rights in a lawsuit in small claims court if you wish to get the entire deposit back. To win, you'll need to have a good deal of evidence of the rental unit's filthy or damaged condition at move-in (such as a signed Landlord-Tenant Checklist, photos, and witnesses).

The sample letter #2 above shows you how to set up a less-than-perfect cleaning job for an apartment that was presented in less-than-perfect shape. Note how the tenant, Stephan, lets his landlord know that he has plenty of hard evidence concerning the miserable condition of the unit when he moved in.

Of course, there is the possibility that your landlord will use your letter as a point of departure, adding extra tasks from replacing degraded tile grout to painting the ceiling. If so, politely refuse, explaining that such requests are excessive.

Cleaning Thoroughly

You can't expect to get your deposit back if you've left the place a mess. So clean the place thoroughly, including all the items you promised in the letter (if any) you sent to your landlord. This doesn't normally mean you have to dry-clean the drapes or wash the ceiling. A good thorough cleaning, including all appliances, fixtures, floors, and window coverings, should be adequate. Be sure to apply some extra elbow grease when cleaning the kitchen and bathrooms.

Remove all your belongings before you leave. That includes bags of garbage, clothes, food, newspapers, furniture, appliances, dishes, plants, cleaning supplies, and other items. Leaving them causes extra work for your landlord, which you'll end up paying for from your deposit. If you leave items of value behind, your landlord can, in some states, dispose of them or keep them. Below we explain how landlords handle abandoned property.

Documenting the Condition of the Unit

In Chapter 6, we recommend that you fill out a Landlord-Tenant Checklist when you move in, documenting the condition of the rental unit. We also suggest you photograph and videotape the unit. You should do the same when you move out. Pictures will provide great visual proof of your claim if you later have to sue the landlord to get your deposit returned. (See Chapter 6 for suggestions on taking photos that you can rely on later.)

Be sure to keep all your receipts for cleaning and repair materials and expenses as evidence that you did clean, in case you later have to sue in small claims court in order to get your deposit back.

Finally, be sure to have a friend or neighbor witness the final result. A person who helped clean often makes a very convincing witness. Make sure it's someone who will be willing to give you a signed declaration as to the condition of the unit pre- and post-cleaning; or better, someone who will testify in court on your behalf, if necessary, should you end up in court.

Arranging a Final Inspection

After you've moved your belongings out and cleaned up, and just before you return the key, ask your landlord to inspect the unit in your presence to determine whether any deductions from your security deposit are warranted.

Try to avoid having your landlord do the final inspection alone. A landlord is less likely to claim dirty or damaged conditions when a tenant is present. A few states, including Arizona and California, actually give the tenants the legal right to be present when landlords conduct the final inspection. But wherever you live, you'll want to insist on being there. Write the landlord a brief note such as the one below.

Request to Clean Further

75 Bolton Road

Evanston, Illinois, 00000

May 28, 20xx

Brett Steiner

5 Hilton Ave.

Chicago, Illinois 00000

Dear Ms. Steiner:

Thank you for meeting me today to go over the condition of my old apartment on Fraser Avenue (#363). My tenancy expires on May 30, although I have already moved my belongings and have moved out. I had hoped that you would approve completely of my cleaning job.

It is my understanding that you approved of the condition of the apartment except for the bathroom walls and tiles. I used a conventional household cleaner, not wanting to risk marring the surface of the tiles with anything stronger. As a result, I could not remove every bit of discoloration and mildew in the grout. You expressed disappointment at this and stated that you would have to hire a cleaning crew to do the job over, and would deduct two hours of their time (at $40 an hour) from my security deposit.

I asked you at the time, and I repeat the request now, to have the opportunity to do the work myself. I am sure that I can remove the offending stains with a stronger cleanser just as well as a cleaning company could. I know that this will mean that you will need to inspect again, but since you visit the property daily, it seems to me that this would not be an undue imposition. And because I am no longer occupying the unit, you would need to look at this one room only, since the rest of the apartment is acceptable. I can arrange to meet you at any time.

Please extend me the favor of another 10-minute inspection of the bathroom walls. Getting my entire security deposit ($1,750) back is very important to me, since I am facing a hefty security deposit obligation in my new duplex.

Yours truly,

Stephan Pierce

Stephan Pierce

Request to Be Present at Inspection

1492 Fraser Avenue, Apt. #363

Chicago, Illinois 00000

May 24, 20xx

Brett Steiner

5 Hilton Ave.

Chicago, Illinois 00000

Dear Ms. Steiner:

As you know, on April 30, 20xx I gave notice to terminate my tenancy effective May 30, 20xx. On May 15, I wrote to you explaining my plans for cleaning the apartment. Since I didn't hear back from you, I went ahead and cleaned as planned.

I would like to arrange to meet you and conduct a final inspection of my apartment this week. Saturday morning is best for me, but I can be somewhat flexible. I have a copy of the Checklist we completed when I moved in two years ago. I'm sure that you will be pleased with the condition of the apartment.

Please call me at 123-4567 so that we can arrange for a convenient time to meet.

Yours truly,

Stephan Pierce

Stephan Pierce

When you tour the apartment together, give your landlord a copy of the Landlord-Tenant Checklist you completed when you moved in and any other before-and-after proof you have that the unit is in essentially the same condition, excluding normal wear and tear. Any item that your landlord claims needs cleaning, repair, or replacement should be noted in the Move-Out Condition column. When possible, also note the estimated cost of repair or replacement. An excerpt of the Checklist is shown below. See Chapter 6 for a complete Checklist.

Be ready to calmly and pleasantly assert your point of view, backed up, if possible, with photos showing the condition of the unit when you moved in. Try to work out any disagreements on the spot. If your landlord points to a damaged or dirty item that would be inexpensive to clean or replace, be willing to compromise. It is usually better to give up a few dollars than go to all the trouble of suing later. (You would sue for the portion improperly withheld.) If you come to an agreement, ask the landlord to return your security deposit before you leave.

If your landlord claims that your unit needs more cleaning or repairs, ask for a second chance to do it. By law, at least one state (Montana) requires landlords to offer tenants a second chance at cleaning (if it's done within 24 hours) before deducting cleaning charges from the security deposit.

As long as you are still technically a tenant (your 30-day notice period hasn't run out), you should have no problem. But if your time to move out is up and your landlord needs to get the apartment ready quickly for another tenant, the answer probably will be no, especially if repairs are required in addition to cleaning.

If your request to reclean is denied, put it in writing. (A sample letter is shown above.) A written request that is also turned down might serve you well if you decide later to sue over deposit money withheld for cleaning. Especially if the case is close,

a judge is likely to look askance at a landlord who refused your repeated offers to do a better job.

Requesting Your Deposit in Writing

It's always a good idea to ask for the return of your deposit in a letter to your landlord. In some states, you *must* make a written "demand" for its return, and provide a mailing address— if you don't, you risk losing it altogether. Even if your state does not require it, promptly writing to your landlord when your tenancy is up is important for several reasons:

- **Your letter gives the landlord your forwarding address.** This simple, essential information is often overlooked by tenants in a hurry to pack up and move. In some states, landlords may keep the deposit if they can't locate you within a specified amount of time.

- **Writing a demand letter is another opportunity to build your case if you decide to sue for the return of your security deposit.** Writing down what you think your landlord owes invites one of two responses: paying up or disputing your version. If your landlord doesn't pay and doesn't take the time or trouble to discuss the matter with you, you're in a good position to argue in court

Landlord-Tenant Checklist

Property Address: _____ 572 Fourth St., Apt. 11, Washington, D.C. _____

General Condition of Rental Unit and Premises

	Move-In Condition Date of Walk-Through: May 1, 20xx	Move-Out Condition Date of Walk-Through:
Living Room		
Flooring	OK	
Walls & Ceilings	OK	
Light Fixtures	OK	
Window Treatments	miniblinds discolored	
...ows & screens	Window facing street rattles	
...les/locks	OK	

Demand for Return of Security Deposit

May 25, 20xx

Ms. Samuel

100 East Tenth Street

Mayflower, ME 00000

Dear _____ Ms. Samuel _____ :

On _____ April 1, 20xx _____ , we vacated the apartment at _____ 7 Bonny Court _____

and gave you our new address and phone number. As of today, we haven't received our $ 1,000

security deposit, nor any accounting from you for that money. We were entitled to receive our deposit by

_____ May 1, 20xx _____ . You are now _____ 25 days _____ late.

We left our apartment clean and undamaged, paid all of our rent, and gave you proper notice of our intention

to move. In these circumstances, it's difficult to understand your oversight in not promptly returning our

money.

Perhaps your check is in the mail. If not, please put it there promptly. Should we fail to hear from you by

_____ June 5, 20xx _____ , we'll take this matter to court. And please understand that if we are

compelled to do this, we will also sue you for any additional punitive damages allowed by state law.

Please mail our deposit immediately to the address below. If you have any questions, please contact us at the

number below.

Very truly yours,

Michael Burns

Michael Burns

Theresa Burns

Theresa Burns

2520 Homestead Lane

Mayflower, ME 00000

555-123-4567

Home phone

555-456-7890

Work phone

that your landlord lost the opportunity to work things out and should now pay up.

- **Your letter makes it more likely that you'll get penalty damages if the landlord fails to follow the law.** Laws in many states penalize landlords who intentionally break security deposit laws. If you have written a clear letter that tells the landlord exactly what to do and you still don't get your deposit, the landlord certainly can't claim ignorance of the law or of your whereabouts.

If you're asking for your entire deposit back, use our form, "Demand for Return of Security Deposit" (a sample is shown above). Fill in the date and the landlord's (or manager's or management company's) address at the top. Consult your state law to calculate when, by law, your landlord should have returned the deposit. Give the landlord at least ten days before you resort to stronger measures (court).

You'll want to do your own letter, tailored to fit your circumstances, if you and the landlord have reached an understanding as to specific deductions, as illustrated in the "Demand for Partial Return of Security Deposit," below. Either send the letter certified mail (return receipt requested), or use a delivery service that will give you a receipt establishing delivery. Keep a copy of your letter and the delivery receipt—you'll need them if you end up in court.

FORM

The Nolo website includes a downloadable copy of the Demand for Return of Security Deposit form. See Appendix B for the link to the forms in this book.

If Stephan doesn't hear from Brett within a month, he'll want to send a stronger letter. An example is shown in "How to Handle Deposit Disputes," below.

Using the Deposit as Last Month's Rent

If you have not paid the rent for your last month of residence, the landlord can always apply your security deposit to this unpaid sum. It's just another way of saying that the deposit can be used to cover

unpaid rent. In fact, this is exactly what you might want the landlord to do. It saves you from writing a check for the last month's rent and having to wait until after you move out to get your deposit refund.

(If your landlord collected a separate sum labeled "last month's rent," see Chapter 4.)

Demand for Partial Return of Security Deposit

75 Bolton Road
Evanston, Illinois, 00000

June 2, 20xx

Brett Steiner
5 Hilton Ave.
Chicago, Illinois 00000

Dear Ms. Steiner:

As you doubtless remember, I was your tenant in Apartment #363 at 1492 Fraser Avenue in Chicago. I paid you a deposit of $1,750. My tenancy ended on May 30.

Thanks for giving me the opportunity to redo the bathroom tiles and clean them to your satisfaction. We agreed yesterday that the entire apartment was clean and in good condition but for two cracked tiles on the counter. We agreed that you would deduct $175 for this damage. Since I have no unpaid rent to account for, I expect that my security deposit will be refunded in the amount of $1,575 to the address above.

Yours truly,

Stephan Pierce

Stephan Pierce

If you want your landlord to apply your deposit for the last month's rent, get approval in writing. Why should your landlord object? Because the landlord can't know in advance what the property will look like when you leave. If you leave the property a mess, but the whole security deposit (or a good part of it) has gone to pay the last month's rent, nothing (or not enough) will be left to use to repair or clean the property. The landlord will have to absorb the loss or sue you.

If you're a fastidious tenant who is almost sure to leave the unit in tip-top shape, your landlord might decide to take a chance that the deposit won't be needed for repairs or cleaning. Offer to let the landlord make a quick inspection first, to see that the property is clean and undamaged. Be forewarned, however, that many landlords will refuse to do a preinspection, arguing that the presence of all of your belongings will make it difficult to get an accurate picture of the condition of the entire unit, and that damage might be caused during your move-out.

Even if your landlord objects to your decision not to write a final rent check, the chances that you will be evicted for nonpayment of rent are slim, because you'll be out of there in a month anyway. (But don't expect a recommendation from this landlord when your next one calls for a reference.)

CAUTION

If the landlord doesn't agree to your request, be sure you know your state's law before deciding not to write your last month's rent check. In a few states, expecting the landlord to apply the deposit to the last month's rent can be disastrous. For example, in Kansas, if you attempt to use the security deposit for the last month's rent, you lose the entire deposit and can be sued for the last month's rent besides. Minnesota and Texas also impose statutory penalties when tenants try this maneuver. Check your state's statutes and the cases that have interpreted them before you act. (Citations to the security deposit statutes of each state mentioned above are in "State Security Deposit Rules" in Appendix A.)

Security Deposits From Cotenants

A common dispute among roommates is what happens to the security deposit when one leaves and the others stay. If you're the one leaving, you would most certainly like your share of the deposit back when you move out. Unfortunately, you might have to wait a while.

When cotenants all sign a lease or rental agreement together, your landlord has no legal duty to return or account for any portion of the deposit until all of the cotenants leave. Practically speaking, this means cotenants must work out among themselves what to do when one roommate leaves.

It's common for a new tenant to pay a deposit directly to the departing tenant, to reimburse the departing tenant's original deposit payment. From the new tenant's point of view, however, this is wise only if the unit is being maintained properly, because the new tenant won't want to end up paying for preexisting damage. If no one is replacing you, see if the other cotenants will chip in and pay you your share—but be prepared to accept less if damage is attributable to you that the landlord will eventually deduct for.

Some landlords, however, will refund your share of the deposit when you leave even though it's not legally required. However, as part of doing so, the landlord will probably want to inspect the property. That's good for the new tenant, too, who gets to start with a clean slate, knowing that all damage has been noted and paid for from the former tenant's portion of the security deposit.

> **EXAMPLE:** Bill and Mark were cotenants who had each contributed $1,000 toward the $2,000 security deposit. Bill needed to move before the lease was up, and asked Len, their landlord, if he would accept Tom as a new cotenant. Len agreed.
>
> Bill wanted his $1,000 back, and although Tom was willing to contribute his share of the deposit, he did not want to end up paying for damage that had been caused before he moved in. To take care of this, Len agreed to inspect if Tom would first give him a check for $1,000. When he got the check, Len inspected and found $200 worth of damage. Bill disagreed, and they compromised on $150. Len deducted this amount from Bill's share of the deposit and wrote Bill a check for $850. Len left it up to Bill and Mark to fairly apportion the responsibility for the damage.

Second Demand for Return of Security Deposit

75 Bolton Road
Evanston, Illinois, 00000

July 15, 20xx

Brett Steiner
5 Hilton Ave.
Chicago, Illinois 00000

Dear Ms. Steiner:

As you know, until May 30, 20xx, I rented apartment #363 at 1492 Fraser Avenue in Chicago. When I moved out, the apartment was thoroughly cleaned. I recleaned the bathroom and you inspected it May 28, pronouncing the bathroom (and the rest of the unit) acceptable. Actually, I left the place in far better shape than it was when I moved in. In addition, the apartment was not damaged other than for two chipped tiles, which we agreed would cost me $175. I left owing no rent.

On June 2, 20xx, I sent you a letter asking that my deposit be refunded in the amount of $1,575 and gave you my new address. I called you on June 20 to remind you about returning my deposit and again gave you my new address. You assured me that you'd "Get right on it in a day or two."

As of today, I have received neither my $1,575 security deposit nor any accounting from you for that money. Under Illinois law (765 Ill. Comp. Stat. § 710), I was entitled to receive my deposit, including an itemization of any deductions, 30 days after my tenancy ended—that is, by June 30, 20xx. You are now over two weeks late.

If I do not receive my money by July 25, I will regard your retention of my deposit as showing bad faith and will sue you in small claims court for $3,150, which is double the amount of the deposit due as allowed under Illinois law.

Please mail my deposit immediately to the above address.

Very truly yours,

Stephan Pierce

Stephan Pierce

If the landlord refuses your request to inspect and return a portion of the security deposit to the departing tenant, get together with your roommates and realistically appraise the situation. The new cotenant should be asked to pay the departing tenant a full share of the deposit if there is no damage, or a portion if there is damage attributable to the departing tenant.

How to Handle Deposit Disputes

Let's assume that several weeks have passed since you moved out and wrote to your landlord asking for your deposit to be returned. However, you haven't gotten either a check or an explanation of why the landlord is keeping your money. Or maybe you have received an itemization from the landlord—and you're convinced that the deductions are unjustified. Or maybe your landlord has violated another law, such as a requirement that you receive interest on your deposit.

It's time to take action. Start with a simple phone call to your landlord, follow up with a letter, and, if all else fails, go to court.

Call the Landlord

Start by phoning the landlord to discuss the problem. We don't recommend texting, because this invites a conversation via text, which can lead to a dragged-out exchange that's hard to track and show to a judge if you need to. Especially if your deposit is only a few days late, there might be a reasonable explanation for your landlord's tardiness—maybe the landlord is waiting for some repair work and doesn't yet know its exact cost. Make a note of the date and time of your phone call, and write down as many specifics of the conversation as you can remember. If you leave a voice message, note the day and time you left it, as well as what you said. If you go to court, you might need to show these notes to the judge.

Make a Second Written Demand

If you didn't get a good answer and a firm promise that you'll get the deposit or itemization right away, it's time for stronger action. Write another demand letter like the one shown above. (If this if your first letter, you might want to soften the tone a bit.)

If you're tempted to skip this step because you're sure it's a waste of time, don't. Your demand letter might serve as a catalyst to get your landlord to agree to a fair settlement. Even if the landlord never reads it, setting out your case in a formal letter gives you an excellent opportunity to prepare your case for small claims court. And remember: Some state security deposit statutes require you to make a written request; and in some states, small claims court rules require you to write a demand letter before you can sue.

Your letter should lay out the reasons your landlord owes you deposit money and make it clear that if you don't get it, you plan to go to court. Now, instead of being just another cranky voice on the telephone, you and your dispute become a sobering reality to your landlord. Your landlord will realize that you won't simply go away, and that you plan to have your day in court.

Here are some tips on writing a demand letter:

1. Summarize the main facts. If you end up in small claims court, your letter will be read by a judge. It should explain what happened.

2. Be polite. Don't personally attack your landlord —even if you think it's deserved. The more annoying you are, the more you invite your landlord to respond similarly. Your goal is to get your landlord to make a businesslike analysis of the dispute and ask:

- What are my risks of losing?
- How much time will a defense take?
- Do I want the dispute to be decided in public?
- Even if I think the tenant is partly at fault, isn't it more cost-effective to return the deposit or offer a settlement?

3. Ask for exactly what you want. For example, if you want your full deposit returned, ask for it.

4. Explain your legal rights. Cite state security deposit law, using the summaries in this book and the "State Security Deposit Rules" chart in Appendix A.

If your state allows extra, punitive damages when a landlord intentionally withholds a deposit, point out that you are entitled to them now.

5. Conclude by stating you will sue if necessary. If you will be suing for extra (punitive) damages allowed under your state law, make this point, too. (Check your state security deposit statute for details on punitive damages.) It will be hard for your landlord to try to avoid punitive damages by claiming blissful ignorance of the law or simple inadvertence when you show the judge the letters you've written.

Keep a copy of all correspondence and your notes. You'll need these records if you go to court.

Consider Compromising

When you've written your landlord a demand letter and haven't received a satisfactory response, in most states you can file suit immediately. (Some states require that you try mediation first; check your state's statute.) But before you do, try to meet the landlord halfway. You don't need to go overboard trying to reach a compromise, especially if you believe your landlord's original assessment of the cost of repairs and cleaning was grossly unfair and you believe you can prove your position in court.

Just the same, it usually doesn't make sense for you to prepare a small claims case and spend time in court to argue over $50 or even $100. This is especially true because, fair or not, some judges are prone to split the difference between the landlord's and the tenant's claims.

If you and the landlord reach a compromise, it's wise to sign an agreement right away. Writing things down gives you a chance to make sure you and your landlord really agree. And if the landlord fails to honor the agreement, you can enforce the agreement in small claims court. You won't have to argue over any of the underlying facts (concerning your clean or not-so-clean apartment, for example); the agreement will clearly show that the landlord promised you a certain amount of money. A sample agreement is shown below.

Sample Agreement Regarding Return of Security Deposit

Brett Steiner, Landlord, and Stephan Pierce, Tenant, agree as follows:

1. Tenant's tenancy at 1492 Fraser Avenue, Apartment #363, Chicago, terminated on May 30, 20xx. Landlord holds a $1,750 security deposit.

2. Tenant left owing no unpaid rent. Landlord and Tenant have agreed that Tenant had caused $175 worth of damage to the bathroom counter tiles.

3. Tenant requested the return of $1,575 but has not yet received any of it.

4. Landlord will deduct an additional $25 from the deposit for recleaning of the bathroom tiles and will return $1,550 to Tenant by mailing a check no later than three days after the date of this Agreement.

5. In exchange for receiving the $1,550 as required by this Agreement, Tenant will not sue Landlord for failing to return the deposit within the time required by state law.

6. This Agreement is a final and complete resolution of the dispute over use and retention of Tenant's security deposit.

Brett Steiner	8/20/xx
Brett Steiner, Landlord	Date
Stephan Pierce	8/20/xx
Stephan Pierce, Tenant	Date

If you and your landlord can't arrive at a reasonable compromise, you might wish to try mediation. That's a procedure in which you meet with a neutral third person who helps you arrive at your own solution. Many cities, counties, and nonprofit organizations offer mediation services designed to help tenants and landlords. In fact, mediation might be a prerequisite to filing a lawsuit in small claims court. Check your state's small claims court procedures, and read the discussion on how to negotiate with landlords on various issues in Chapter 19. It also covers mediation.

Suing Your Landlord in Small Claims Court

If the formal demand doesn't work and there is no reasonable prospect of compromise, consider suing your landlord in small claims court. It's inexpensive, usually $20 to $300, to file a case (in many courts, the higher your claim is, the higher the filing fee will be).

You don't need a lawyer, and disputes typically go before a judge (there are no juries) within 30 to 60 days. The trial itself, which consists of both sides explaining what happened from their point of view and presenting any evidence or witnesses, seldom takes more than 15 or 20 minutes. The judge either announces a decision right there in the courtroom or releases it (sometimes online) within a few days.

You can sue your landlord for your security deposit and for any required interest. As a general rule, you have to request a precise amount when you file your suit. In many states, you might be eligible to receive punitive damages if the landlord intentionally failed to return your deposit on time. (See "Basic Rules for Returning Deposits," above.) Whether the landlord's conduct was bad enough to entitle you to punitive damages is up to the judge. In practice, your chances of collecting significant punitive damages will be good only if the landlord has delayed a considerable time without a plausible explanation for the delay.

If you win, the judge will often have the discretion to add these punitive damages and possibly court costs, such as filing fees, onto the final award.

By Any Other Name

We use the term small claims court here, but the exact name depends upon the state. These courts are called "Justice of the Peace," "Conciliation," "District," "Justice," "City," or "County" in different places.

The maximum amount for which you can sue in small claims court varies among the states, from $2,500 to $25,000. (Appendix A lists each state's limit.) If you believe your landlord owes you more than the amount you can seek in small claims court, you must either file your lawsuit in the local trial court or reduce your demand to an amount at or below the small court limit. Most of the time, it's worth reducing your demand in order to take advantage of the simpler procedures and lower costs associated with small claims courts.

TIP

Don't wait to file your case. Each state limits the time within which lawsuits can be filed. In a dispute over a written rental agreement or lease, you probably have up to four or five years to sue. Just the same, it's foolish to wait very long, because the memories of witnesses fade (or the witnesses themselves might be impossible to find), and your landlord might even go out of business. Also, judges are not very sympathetic to old disputes.

RESOURCE

The Small Claims Court & Lawsuits section of Nolo.com includes useful articles on each state's small claims court rules, as well as general articles, such as how to prepare evidence for a small claims suit. Also, *Everybody's Guide to Small Claims Court,* by Cara O'Neill (Nolo), explains small claims court strategy and procedure, including how and where to serve court papers, how to collect your money, and details on appeals.

Preparation: The Key to Winning

Winning your small claims court case can be easy or difficult, depending on the facts of the situation and how much homework you do before appearing in court.

First, get a copy of your state's security deposit law and any local ordinances that apply. Many courts also publish small claims court guides. Read these thoroughly before you go to court. You can get copies online. (See Chapter 20 for advice on legal research.)

Second, gather tangible evidence. If you simply testify that your apartment was clean and in good shape, and your landlord says just the opposite, the judge is stuck making a decision that is little more than a guess. Most judges will split the difference. If your landlord comes to court with a witness who reads off a long list of damaged and dirty conditions you allegedly left behind, you might even lose.

To win, you must have enough evidence to convince the judge you are right. Ideally, preparation should start when you move into the rental unit and make a record of its condition. When you moved out, you should have made another similar written record and taken photos. (See above.)

But even if you weren't so thorough, you might still convince the judge that you left the rental in good shape if you can provide the following types of evidence:

- A clear statement of how much money your landlord owes you, the interest (if any) owed, penalties you seek, and an accounting of your expenses such as cleaning supplies.
- A copy of your signed lease or rental agreement and any written guidelines your landlord provided on cleaning, damage repair, and security deposits.
- Photos or a video of the premises taken before you moved in that show how dirty or damaged the place was.
- Photos or a video taken after you left that show no additional mess or damage.
- One, or preferably two, witnesses who were familiar with the property, saw it just after you left and will testify that the place was clean or that certain items were not damaged.
- If it's difficult for a witness to come to court, a signed letter or a statement (declaration) signed "under penalty of perjury" can be used in most states. Make sure the statement includes the date of the event, exactly what the witness saw, any credentials that make the person qualified to testify on the subject, and any other facts that are relevant to the dispute. (No need to have the witness sign in front of a notary.)

- Details on the amount of time you spent cleaning the unit.
- Copies of receipts for cleaning supplies you used in the final cleanup or for professional cleaning (for carpets and drapes) or repair.
- A copy of the Landlord-Tenant Checklist that you filled out with the landlord when you moved in and when you moved out, signed by both you and your landlord. This is particularly important if the landlord admitted, on the Checklist, to damaged or dirty conditions when you moved in.
- Copies of all correspondence: a letter outlining your cleaning plans (if any), the demand letters, and written notes of your conversations about the deposit.
- If the landlord is overcharging for cleaning or repairs, a written estimate from another cleaning or repair service showing it would have done the job for less. For example, if your landlord claims to have paid $400 for cleaning, you could submit a statement from ABC cleaning that they charge $30 per hour and can clean a one-bedroom apartment in six hours, for a total bill of $180.
- If the landlord is charging you the full replacement cost or original cost of a ruined item, bring an estimate of the item's age, its expected useful lifetime, and its original cost. Amortize the cost over the item's life, and agree to pay the remaining value only (see the explanation of straight-line depreciation, above). Check with appliance stores or do some research online to get original cost figures for rugs or appliances and their expected (or proven) lifetime. This process is a bit inexact but worth it if you're being hit with a hefty replacement bill for something that was on its last legs already.
- If you dispute your landlord's claim that you broke or damaged an item such as an appliance, the opinion of a repairperson or other expert as to why the appliance failed.

If you take the trouble to understand your state's law and to gather good evidence, you should have no trouble convincing a judge to rule in your favor.

> **EXAMPLE:** Shawna's landlord claims that Shawna is responsible for the broken refrigerator ice maker, claiming that she must have caused the problem by blocking the air circulation when she stuffed too much food in the freezer. Shawna, who rarely has more than a half-gallon of ice cream in her freezer, is not about to stand by and give up the $400 the landlord claims it will cost to fix the ice maker, which she is convinced was on its last legs when she moved in.
>
> To fight back, Shawna talks to a local refrigerator repairperson. He scoffs at the idea that the problem could be caused by over-filling the freezer and tells Shawna that this particular model is notorious for ice maker failures. Shawna asks him to write a letter to the court saying this, and then follows up by looking in *Consumer Reports* magazine, which lists this brand of ice maker as a problem. Shawna brings the letter and article to court, shows them to the judge, testifies that she never misused the freezer, and wins the case.

How to Present Your Case in Court

Small claims courts are informal places, intended to be used by regular folks presenting their own cases. If you do not have experience with a court, consider watching a few cases a day or two before your case. You will see that it is a very simple procedure. Many small claims courts also provide helpful pamphlets, videos, and even video tutorials on how small claims courts work. Some courts offer free legal adviser programs to help you prepare your case properly.

A few days before your case will be heard, practice your presentation in front of a tough-minded friend acting as the judge. Present your case from start to finish, introducing witnesses and explaining evidence. Chances are that your presentation will be awkward, and you might even forget key points. Fine, keep practicing until you can make your presentation in an efficient and convincing way. Keep in mind that the judge will give you only a few minutes to make your case.

Stick to the important facts.

On the day your case will be heard, get to the court a little early and check for your courtroom (in some places referred to as a "department").

Tell the clerk or bailiff that you are present, and sit down and wait until your case is called. When your turn comes, stand at the large table at the front of the room to speak. Remember, judges hear many cases every day and will not be particularly excited by yours. If you are long-winded, your judge might stop listening and start thinking about lunch.

Start your presentation with the problem; for example, "Brett Steiner hasn't returned my security deposit to me, and it's been almost two months since I moved out of her apartment at 1492 Fraser Avenue. State law says she is supposed to return it within 30 days." Then present the directly relevant facts that explain why you should win; for example, "The apartment was clean, my rent was paid in full, and we had agreed that my deposit of $1,750 would be returned but for $275 in damage costs." Again, be brief and to the point; don't ramble. You can show pictures and documents to the judge. When you are done with your oral presentation, tell the judge whether you have witnesses who want to testify.

The landlord, of course, will also have a chance to speak. In most states, the landlord has the responsibility of proving that he's entitled to keep all or part of a deposit. If the landlord exaggerates the extent of any damage or dirt, stay cool. You should get another chance to speak—and your evidence should back up your version. If you don't have a lot of tangible evidence or witnesses, simply state the facts as you see them. For example, you

might say, "Your Honor, when I moved in three years ago, the walls had not been freshly painted. And because the previous tenant lived in the unit for two years, I'm pretty sure it's been at least five years since the unit was painted. The fact that they need freshening up now is due to ordinary wear and tear, and it should be the landlord's responsibility."

> ### If Your Landlord Doesn't Show Up
>
> In the unlikely event your landlord doesn't show up, you'll probably win. In most states, the judge will ask you to briefly state the basic facts of your case and to provide some evidence, such as a set of photos showing the condition of the rental unit when you moved in and out. The judge might also check to see that your landlord was properly served with the court papers and might ask you a question or two to make sure your case has no obvious flaws. Of course, you'll still have to collect the judgment.

TIP

When to see a lawyer. Although generally it's not cost-effective to hire a lawyer when you head to small claims court, one possible exception to this rule applies only when your state allows you to have an attorney represent you in court. If your lease or rental agreement requires you to pay the landlord's attorneys' fees if the landlord wins a lawsuit, then in most states, you, too, are entitled to attorneys' fees if you win a lawsuit. In short, if there's a fair sum of money involved (which might be the case if there's a possibility for punitive damages) and you're confident of winning, you might look for a lawyer experienced in representing tenants to handle the matter for you. (If your state doesn't allow lawyers to represent litigants in court, the lawyer can at least advise you. If you win, it won't hurt to ask for attorneys' fees—you should be able to collect for the cost of that lawyer's advice.) Be sure you thoroughly discuss fee arrangements ahead of time. (See Chapter 20 for advice on finding and working with an attorney.)

If Your Deposit Doesn't Cover What You Owe

Tenants aren't the only ones who can use small claims court. If the security deposit doesn't cover what you owe for back rent, cleaning, or repairs, your landlord can file a small claims suit against you.

If you are sued, you should show up in court even if you think the landlord is in the right or you know you can't pay what you owe. Even if your landlord has a good case, it gives you a chance to present any facts that might reduce the amount of the judgment. Also, in some states, you can ask the judge to allow you to make payments in installments.

If you don't show up, the landlord will probably win by default and can collect the judgment by garnishing your wages or going after other assets, like a bank account. The judgment can be collected against you for many years and will be a negative mark on your credit file.

If you have good evidence of a valid defense, you definitely want to argue your side of things. For example, if you feel that the landlord charged too much for the cleaning job, get estimates from at least two reputable cleaning firms as to how much they would have charged. Calmly and clearly present your side of the dispute. If you have no proof about the dispute itself, you'll need to demonstrate that the landlord's case is flawed in some procedural respect—for example, the landlord failed to send an itemized list of proposed deductions, as required by your state's law.

Your Abandoned Property

If you've handled your move-out in a way that maximizes your chances of getting your security deposit back, it's unlikely that you'll be leaving anything behind, least of all items of value. Even the most organized tenant, however, can inadvertently miss something—for example, you might neglect a closet or forget the storage area in the garage; or walk out thinking that your partner had picked up everything ("What? I thought *you* had the laptop!"). And, let's face it—when the U-Haul is packed and

the engine is running, the temptation to leave a bag full of junk for the landlord to deal with might be just too great to resist. Far too often, however, you realize later that the bag contained something you really wanted to keep.

Tenants who leave involuntarily face a higher risk of leaving something behind. If your tenancy is terminated on short notice and you decide to leave rather than fight, you might not have the time to double-check for missed belongings. Tenants who have lost an eviction lawsuit and wait until the sheriff or constable arrives to take their belongings off the property for them face the greatest danger of not being able to account for all of their possessions when the dust settles.

Regardless of the reason why your things are still on the landlord's property, you'll want to know how, if at all, you can get them back. First, understand that if the items are obvious trash, the landlord can dispose of them immediately. This means that if a reasonable person would conclude that an item had no value, the landlord is justified in tossing it—even if, to you, it has enormous sentimental value or is even a valuable antique or collectible. Landlords aren't expected to be sensitive to your sentiments, nor need they be professional appraisers.

But for things that are clearly of some value—such as a bicycle, a new TV, clothes, or furniture—it's another story. In some states, landlords face serious liability for disposing of your personal property (other than obvious trash) unless they follow specific state rules. Typically, the more valuable the property left behind by a tenant, the more formalities the landlord must comply with when disposing of it.

Not surprisingly, states that heavily regulate other aspects of landlords' dealings with tenants also impose complicated requirements on how they must handle abandoned property. States with fewer laws governing the landlord-tenant relationship tend to pay scant attention to this subject.

This section provides an overview of how to go about reclaiming your abandoned property. Because state laws vary so much, we cannot give you detailed state-by-state information on what to do and expect from your landlord. For this reason, it is critical that you read your own state statute for details on issues such as how your landlord must notify you and how much time you'll have before the landlord may dispose of or sell your things. Your local tenants' association or state consumer protection agency might be helpful. In some states, courts have modified the procedures in the statutes, often imposing additional requirements—and unfortunately, legislatures don't always revisit their statutes to bring them into line with court-ordered changes. The "State Laws on Handling Abandoned Property" chart in Appendix A gives you citations to your state's statutes and includes some case citations.

Why Did You Move Out?

In many states, the landlord's options when dealing with your property will differ depending on the circumstances of your departure. To understand the issue, let's look at the reasons tenants leave. Here are typical scenarios:

- You decide to move at the end of a lease or after giving a termination notice. In this situation, many states give the landlord maximum flexibility to dispose of leftover belongings.
- You decide to move after receiving a termination notice (even one for cause, such as nonpayment of rent). Many states give the landlord maximum flexibility to dispose of leftover belongings in this situation.
- You are physically evicted along with your personal belongings, which might be dumped on the street or sidewalk by the sheriff. Some states require landlords to take more pains with the property of a tenant who has been evicted—though some require less effort.
- You simply move out without notice. In a few states, property belonging to tenants who move out unexpectedly must be treated differently from property that's left after a clearly deliberate move.

When you read your state's law, be on the lookout for different rules based on the reason for your departure.

Planned Moves

If you have left voluntarily, in most states the landlord will have considerable latitude when it comes to dealing with abandoned property. The reasoning here is that tenants who decide upon and plan their own departure—even the ones who leave after receiving a three-day notice—have time to pack or dispose of their belongings themselves. Tenants who fail to take care of business are in no position to demand that the landlord handle their property with kid gloves—and many state laws don't require that landlords do so.

Evicted Tenants

Law enforcement officials who physically evict tenants will also remove property from the rental unit. In these situations, tenants arguably have less opportunity to arrange for proper packing, storing, or moving than they would if they were moving voluntarily (even though most states give tenants a few days' warning of the sheriff's impending visit). For this reason, landlords in some states must make more of an effort to preserve the property, locate the tenant, and wait before selling or disposing of items left behind. Typically, law enforcement officials are permitted to place the tenant's possessions on the sidewalk or street; then the landlord might be required to step in and store the possessions.

Paradoxically, some states take the opposite approach, reasoning that a tenant who has lost an eviction lawsuit isn't entitled to special treatment when it comes to reclaiming items left behind.

Unannounced Departures

Odd as it seems, it's not unusual for tenants to simply disappear with no notice, leaving considerable belongings behind. Sometimes, the tenant is behind on the rent and figures that abandoning possessions and disappearing will be cheaper, in the long run, than paying the rent. Here again, your state might impose special procedures that require the landlord to store the property for a significant time or make extra efforts to locate the tenant.

Although landlords chafe at the notion that they must take special care of the belongings of someone who has left without notice, there is a very good reason behind the rule. It protects tenants who have *not* abandoned the tenancy or their possessions, but have gone on an extended trip or vacation and simply didn't tell the landlord. By making the landlord take special pains to determine that the tenant is gone for good, it's likely that the landlord will learn that you plan to return. In the meantime, your goods will be safe.

When You're Behind in the Rent

If you have moved voluntarily, been evicted, or simply disappeared but also owe back rent or money for damages, you might expect that your landlord would take or sell whatever property of value that's left behind. As tempting as this course appears, it's a risky one in many states—even when the landlord has a court judgment for money damages.

Some states do allow the landlord to keep or sell abandoned property if the tenant owes money, even in the absence of a court judgment directing the tenant to pay. In legal parlance, the landlord has an "automatic lien" on your belongings. This differs from the normal lien process, which involves formally recording the creditor's claim (the landlord's lien) against the tenant's property, then "getting in line" in case others have filed ahead of the landlord.

If your state statute gives your landlord a lien on a tenant's property, you might not see your belongings again, although some statutes require landlords to publicize their intent to keep an item before it definitively becomes theirs. Many states that give landlords an automatic lien will exempt certain items from the landlord's grasp, such as season-appropriate clothing, blankets, tools, and items needed for a minor child's education.

If the landlord takes an item on which you still owe money (furniture purchased with an installment plan, for example), the landlord might end up in a fight with the merchant, but that spat doesn't concern (or benefit) you.

Distress and Distraint

A few states still have statutes on the books that provide for "distress" or "distraint." These were medieval procedures that allowed landlords who were owed money, after or even during the tenancy, to simply grab tenants' possessions. In the words of one judge, it "allowed a man to be his own avenger." In America, the practice of requiring security deposits was developed in states that did not allow landlords to use distress and distraint.

This crude, quick, and drastic remedy was the ultimate in self-help. It won't surprise you to learn that in states that still have laws providing for distress or distraint, courts have stepped in and ruled them unconstitutional, or have added so many safeguards (notice, a hearing, and so on) that the original process is unrecognizable. If you encounter a distress or distraint statute when reading your state's laws, don't assume that your landlord will swoop in and grab your stuff. Chances are your state's courts have imposed so many restrictions that the process is too complicated to be worth it.

Legal Notice Requirements

Many states require landlords to provide tenants written notice that they are holding abandoned property. A few states even provide a form, which you'll see printed right in the statute. Typically, the notice must give the tenant a set amount of time to reclaim the property, after which the landlord can act. Some state rules require specific information in the notice, such as:

- **A detailed description of the property left behind.** This inventory of the abandoned property should be specific but need not involve snooping. Landlords shouldn't open locked trunks or suitcases; photographs or videos are often used.
- **The estimated value of the abandoned property.** This is basically the landlord's estimate of how much the item would fetch at a flea market or garage sale.
- **Where the property can be claimed.** Many states require landlords to provide the address of the rental premises or an outside storage place.
- **The deadline for the tenant to reclaim property, such as 7 or 10 days.**
- **What will happen if property is not reclaimed.**

What Will Happen to Your Property

Getting property back begins with some very commonsense steps: Contact the landlord and give a definite day and time when you'll be back to pick it up. If the landlord has stored your property, you will have to pay a reasonable storage fee. If you've received a notice from the landlord that the property is being held, follow the instructions on the notice for reclaiming your goods.

In some states, landlords are pretty much free to do what they want if the tenant does not respond within the specified amount of time, such as 30 days—that is, they can throw the property out, sell it, or donate it to a nonprofit organization. In some states, as explained above, landlords can use the property to satisfy unpaid rent or damages, or might even be allowed to keep it when there's no debt. Other states require them to give the property to the state. Depending on how thoroughly your state has legislated in this area, the law might address:

- **Procedures based on the value of the property.** Several states allow landlords to keep or dispose of property only if the expense of storing or selling it exceeds a specified figure (such as a few hundred dollars) or the property's value.
- **Sale of abandoned property.** Some states require landlords to inventory, store, and sell tenants' property. A few require landlords to sell the property at a public sale (supervised by a licensed and bonded public auctioneer), after first publishing a notice in the newspaper.
- **Disposition of the proceeds from selling the property.** States that require landlords to store and sell the property on behalf of the tenant also allow them to use any money they make from the sale to cover the costs of advertising and holding the sale and storing the property. For example, you might be charged for the prorated daily rental value for keeping the property on the landlord's premises or any out-of-pocket costs the landlord incurs for renting storage space (including moving the property to the storage space). As explained above, some states allow landlords to use the proceeds to pay for any money owed by the tenant—for example, for unpaid rent or damage to the premises. In many states, the excess proceeds of selling the tenant's property belongs to the tenant, or the landlord might be required to pay the balance to a government agency, such as the state treasurer.

Landlord Liability for Damage to or Loss of Your Property

Although lots of states legislate how landlords should handle abandoned property, the laws provide no guarantee that landlords will comply. The landlord might decide to dispose of it, keep it, sell it, or return it damaged. Your options depend on how extensively your state has protected you in this situation (you must read and understand your state's law). In general, here's what you can expect.

<table>
<tr><td>

Exceptions to State Rules on Abandoned Property

Your state's rules on abandoned property don't apply to obvious garbage—nor do they apply in the following situations:

Fixtures. If a tenant attaches something more or less permanently to the wall, such as built-in bookshelves, it is called a "fixture." As described in Chapter 10, absent a specific written agreement such as a lease provision, fixtures installed by the tenant become a part of the premises. Fixtures belong to the landlord and do not have to be returned to the tenant. On the other hand, a left-behind fixture that the landlord never approved might be something that the landlord wants to remove. The cost of doing so and returning the property to its original condition will be your responsibility.

Motor vehicles. Occasionally, a departing tenant will leave an inoperable or "junker" automobile in the parking lot or garage. Motor vehicles are often a special category of personal property to which state rules on abandoned property don't apply. If you leave a car or other vehicle behind, the local police will probably arrange to have it towed after tagging it and determining that it is abandoned.

</td></tr>
</table>

Property Returned But Damaged

A landlord will not generally be held liable for damage to property unless the damage is caused by the landlord's negligence. Whether the landlord has been negligent will depend on the circumstances. For example, storing your laptop outside, exposed to the sun and weather, would be considered negligent by most judges. Placing your photo albums in a garage where they were gnawed on by mice might not be.

If you decide to seek legal redress for damage to your property, begin by writing a letter explaining the problem and the amount you want. If this produces no results, write another letter and mention that you'll sue if the matter isn't resolved. Then, sue if necessary. Unless the amount exceeds your state's small claims limit, you'll want to use that in court. Follow the advice in Chapter 19 for presenting a case in small claims court.

Property the Landlord Has Kept or Sold

As explained above, some states allow landlords to sell or keep property to satisfy outstanding tenant debts for damage or back rent. After checking your state's law and rechecking your own records, you might conclude that the landlord had no basis to keep or sell the property. If so, follow the advice just above by writing a letter and suing if necessary. Your legal theory will be that the landlord has "converted" the property, without your permission.

When the Landlord Hasn't Followed the Rules Exactly

After checking your state's law, you might discover that the landlord followed the procedure, but not exactly—and now you don't have your goods. For example, the landlord might have given you notice and time to respond, but the time to collect might have been shorter than provided by the statute. You might feel that, had you been given the proper amount of time to get your things, you would have done so. But now they're gone. What to do?

Unfortunately, you won't necessarily have a rock-solid case against the landlord for the value of your belongings. State statutes vary tremendously in how they'll punish landlords who haven't followed the rules. Keep in mind that many judges simply won't penalize a landlord who attempted to comply with the law—especially in view of your carelessness in leaving the items behind.

Termination Notices Based on Nonpayment of Rent and Other Acts

When tenants violate their leases or engage in unacceptable behavior—by paying the rent late, keeping a dog in violation of a no-pets clause in the lease, throwing loud parties that disturb neighbors—landlords can terminate their tenancies.

Termination is the first step toward an eventual eviction. The landlord sends you a notice announcing that your tenancy is over and that if you don't leave within a few days, you'll be sued for eviction. Alternatively, the notice might give you a few days to clean up your act (pay the rent, find a new home for the dog). If you leave or reform as directed, no one goes to court. In a few situations, landlords can terminate tenancies effective immediately, giving tenants no chance to save their tenancies.

Eviction itself—that is, physically throwing you and your possessions out of the property—can't be done until the landlord has gone to court and proved that you've done something that justifies eviction. And even when landlords win an eviction lawsuit, they can't just move you and your things out onto the sidewalk. In most states, landlords must hire the sheriff or marshal to perform that unpleasant task.

This chapter explains when and how a landlord can terminate your tenancy. It also explains some strategies to consider if you are the unhappy recipient of a termination notice.

 RELATED TOPIC
Also covered in this book:
- Terminations when you haven't done anything wrong: Chapter 15.
- Overview of the eviction process, including illegal "self-help" evictions: Chapter 18.
- State laws that require your landlord to give you proper notice before beginning an eviction: Appendix A.

Termination Notices

Before filing an eviction lawsuit (sometimes called an unlawful detainer, or UD lawsuit), the landlord must give you a properly written notice describing a valid reason why the landlord wants you to leave.

Most states' laws require termination notices to be written and delivered ("served") according to very picky rules that dictate the information contained and dates mentioned. Some states even specify the type size of the notice and method of delivery. Check your state's statutes to determine whether the notice you received complies with the law. If it doesn't, you might be able to defeat the landlord's eviction lawsuit on this basis:

Most courts will dismiss the lawsuit when the landlord hasn't followed proper procedures. But a determined landlord will be simply delayed, not deterred. If you prove that the landlord's notice was faulty, you'll probably receive a correct one very soon after.

When a landlord wants you to leave because of some wrongdoing on your part, you'll receive one of three different types of termination notices.

Although terminology varies somewhat from state to state, the substance of the three types of notices is essentially the same.

- **Pay rent or quit** notices are used when the tenant has not paid the rent. Tenants are given a few days (three to five in most states) to pay or move out ("quit"). If they don't, the landlord can file for eviction. But not every state requires a landlord to give tenants this chance to pay the rent; in a few states, when tenants fail to pay rent on time, the landlord can simply demand that they leave (see "Unconditional quit," below).

- **Cure or quit** notices are typically given after a violation of a term or condition of the lease or rental agreement, such as a no-pets clause or the promise to refrain from making excessive noise. Typically, tenants are given a set amount of time in which to correct, or "cure," the violation; if they fail to do so, they must move in order to avoid an eviction lawsuit.

- **Unconditional quit** notices are the harshest of all. They order tenants to vacate the premises with no chance to pay the rent or correct the violation of the lease or rental agreement. In most states, unconditional quit notices are allowed only when tenants have:

- repeatedly violated a lease or rental agreement clause
- been late with the rent more than once within a specified period of time
- seriously damaged the premises, or
- engaged in illegal activity.

Most states' statutes require that landlords use one of these three types of notices, depending on the situation. However, some states, such as Texas and Louisiana, don't require landlords to give tenants a second chance by using pay or quit or cure or quit notices—their laws provide only for unconditional quit notices. Landlords in these states do have the option to voluntarily give tenants a chance to pay the rent or adjust their behavior, but are not required to do so.

The tables in Appendix A ("State Laws on Termination for Nonpayment of Rent," "State Laws on Termination for Violation of Lease," and "State Laws on Unconditional Quit Terminations") give the details and citations to your state's statutes.

Not surprisingly, the number one reason for getting kicked out of a rental is not paying the rent on time. In most states, when tenants pay rent late, landlords can send a termination notice immediately.

Fortunately, in most states the termination notice must give tenants a few days—usually three to five—in which to pay up. The exact number of days varies from state to state. (For details, see "State Laws on Termination for Nonpayment of Rent" in Appendix A.)

EXAMPLE: Willy's $1,900 rent was due on the first of the month. When he had not paid by the third, his landlord sent him a five-day pay rent or quit notice. Willy understood that he had to pay his rent by the end of the eighth day of the month (or move out) in order to avoid being sued for eviction. On the seventh, Willy paid the entire rent of $1,900, avoiding a lawsuit that would have surely led to his eviction.

Unfortunately, if your state doesn't require the landlord to give you a few days to scrape the rent together, your landlord may immediately terminate your tenancy for not paying the rent. Usually, you have a few days before the landlord can file for eviction. Of course, even in the harshest states, some landlords will allow you to stay on if you pay reasonably quickly and convincingly argue that you'll pay your rent on time in the future.

Required Grace Periods

A handful of states don't let landlords send a termination notice (either a pay rent or quit notice or an unconditional quit notice) until the rent is a certain number of days late. In these states, tenants enjoy a statutory "grace period." (Details are in "State Laws on Termination for Nonpayment of Rent" in Appendix A.) If you live in one of these states, haven't paid the rent, and receive a pay rent or quit notice, you have a pretty good cushion before your landlord can file for eviction: the grace period plus the time specified in the pay rent or quit notice.

EXAMPLE: Lara, a Maine tenant, couldn't pay her rent on time. State law required the landlord to wait until the rent was seven days late before he could send a termination notice. He did so on the eighth, giving Lara notice that she must pay or move within seven days. In all, Lara had 14 days in which to pay the rent (or move out) before her landlord could file for eviction.

TIP
Late rent fees are unaffected by pay rent or quit notice periods or statutory grace periods. If you are subject to late rent fees, they'll kick in as soon as your lease or rental agreement (or in some states, state law) says they can. The number of days specified in your pay rent or quit notice will not affect when these fees are due, nor will a legally required grace period. (Chapter 3 discusses late fees.)

Paying Rent After You Get a Termination Notice

If you are late with the rent and get a termination notice—whether or not it gives you a few days to pay the rent—call the landlord immediately and try to work something out. "Negotiating With the Landlord," below, offers some pointers on dealing with the landlord. Here are the legal rules.

Paying the Whole Rent

If the landlord has sent you a termination notice but then accepts rent for the entire rental term, you are entitled to stay for that period. In most states, it's as if you paid on time in the first place.

> **EXAMPLE:** Zoe's rent was due on the first of the month. She didn't pay on time, and her landlord sent her a three-day pay rent or quit notice. Zoe borrowed money from her parents and paid on the third day, saving her tenancy and avoiding an eviction lawsuit.

In some states, however, your late payment can come back to haunt you if you are late again, as explained below.

If You're Chronically Late

In several states, landlords don't have to give you a second chance to pay the rent if you are habitually late. Typically, they are legally required to give you a chance to pay and stay only once or twice within a certain timeframe. For example, the law might state that landlords can send an unconditional quit notice when a tenant has paid rent late three times within the past year.

Some states insist that the landlord must have given you a written pay rent or quit notice for the first late payment, so that there is proof that you were late. Other statutes allow landlords to use an unconditional quit notice for "repeated lateness," meaning that landlords need not have used a notice to pay rent or quit the first time rent was late.

 CAUTION
Don't wear your landlord's patience thin. Even if your landlord accepts late rent without giving you a pay rent or quit notice ("writing you up," landlords call it), don't count on endless forbearance. Remember, unless you have a lease, in most states the landlord can terminate your tenancy with a 30-day notice. Even if you live in a rent control area that requires landlords to have good reason to evict you, repeatedly paying late is ample legal reason to evict. ("Negotiating With the Landlord," below, explains how to protect yourself when negotiating late rent payments.)

If you receive a pay rent or quit notice, don't assume that you have to pack up and move immediately—even if you're not immediately able to pay rent in full. "Negotiating With the Landlord," below, explores your options.

Making a Partial Rent Payment

When you pay (and your landlord accepts) a partial rent payment after receiving a termination notice, the most that you've bought is a little time. If the landlord accepts an amount of rent that covers only part of what you owe (for past months or even just the current month), that will, in most states, cancel the effect of the notice. But your landlord can pocket your offering with one hand and simultaneously serve you with a fresh termination notice with the other, demanding that you pay the new balance or leave.

> **EXAMPLE:** Danny's rent of $1,600 was due on the first of the month. Danny didn't pay January's rent and didn't have enough for February, either. On February 2, his landlord sent him a three-day notice to pay $3,200 or leave. Danny paid $1,600 on February 3 and thought that he'd saved his tenancy. He was amazed when, later that day, his landlord handed him a new three-day notice to pay $1,600 or leave. The landlord filed for eviction on February 7 when Danny failed to pay.

Other Violations of the Lease or Rental Agreement

In addition to nonpayment of rent, landlords may terminate a tenancy when the tenant violates other terms of the lease or rental agreement. Violations that commonly prompt termination notices include:

- keeping a pet in violation of a no-pets rule
- bringing in an unauthorized roommate
- subleasing or assigning without permission, and
- repeatedly violating "house rules" that are part of the lease or rental agreement, such as common area, noise, and guest rules.

The laws in most states insist that landlords give tenants an opportunity to correct, or "cure," violations before the tenancy can end. Landlords must use a "cure or quit" notice, giving the offending tenants about 5 to 30 days to mend their ways. However, state laws often recognize two important "but ifs," good reasons for landlords to skip the cure or quit notice and go straight to an unconditional quit notice:

Repeated violations. Tenants who violate the same lease clause two or more times within a certain period of time, will probably lose the right to a second chance.

The violation cannot be corrected. Some lease violations cannot be corrected because the effect of the violation is permanent. If a lease violation cannot be cured, the landlord may serve the tenant with an unconditional quit notice. For instance, suppose your lease contains the common prohibition against making alterations or improvements without the landlord's consent. For example, suppose you dismantle and discard the built-in dining room buffet, which you think is cheap and ugly but your landlord considers a valuable antique. Your landlord can send you an unconditional quit notice because it is simply too late to save the buffet.

If you get a notice telling you to cease a curable violation of your lease or rental agreement, your response will depend on the legitimacy of the landlord's claim. See "Negotiating With the Landlord," below, for suggestions.

"Waste" and "Nuisance"

Termination notices for bad behavior often contain two archaic legal terms that need a bit of explaining:

Waste. A tenant who either intentionally or through extreme carelessness damages the landlord's property is said to have committed waste. Waste does not include normal wear and tear or accidents that are the result of simple carelessness. For example, a carpet that needs to be replaced because your fish tank inexplicably sprung a leak would probably not constitute waste; but if you turn the dining room into a motorcycle repair shop, ruining the carpet, subfloor, and walls in the process, you can expect a termination notice based on waste.

Nuisance. Public nuisances are activities that result in a substantial danger to the health or safety of occupants or neighbors, such as drug dealing. Private nuisances are activities, not necessarily illegal, that seriously limit the neighbors' ability to use and enjoy their homes, such as playing music so loudly that no one can sleep or using the backyard for midnight volleyball tournaments every Friday and Saturday night. Many state statutes allow a landlord to terminate a tenancy based on either form of nuisance. (Chapter 14 explains how to use public nuisance laws to pressure a landlord to evict troublemaking tenants.)

Violations of Your Legal Responsibilities as a Tenant

Virtually every state allows landlords to terminate the tenancy of someone who violates basic responsibilities imposed by law. These responsibilities include the duty to maintain at least minimally acceptable housekeeping standards and to refrain from highly disruptive activities. For example, a tenant who commits any of the following acts is a likely candidate for a termination notice:

- grossly deficient housekeeping practices that cause an unhealthy situation, such as allowing garbage to pile up

- seriously misusing appliances, like damaging the oven while attempting to clean it with steel wool
- repeatedly interfering with other tenants' ability to peacefully enjoy their homes, such as hosting late parties, playing incessant loud music, or running a noisy small business (repairing cars in the driveway of a rental duplex, for example)
- substantially damaging the property—for instance, knocking holes in the walls or doors, and
- allowing or participating in illegal activities on or near the premises, such as drug dealing or gambling.

Many landlords specifically include these obligations in their leases or rental agreements. But even when these documents do not mention these obligations, tenants are still legally bound to observe them.

If you or your guests substantially damage the premises, expect an unconditional quit notice. The law doesn't require landlords to give tenants accused of serious misbehavior a second chance. You'll probably get only 5 to 10 days to move out. The details are in "State Laws on Unconditional Quit Terminations" in Appendix A.

Illegal Activity on the Premises

In recent years, many states have responded aggressively to widespread drug dealing in residential neighborhoods by making it easier for landlords to evict based on these activities. Indeed, in some states a landlord must evict known drug dealers or users or risk having authorities close down or even confiscate the entire property. (This process, known as "forfeiture," is explained in Chapter 14). To say the least, the threat of losing their rental property has motivated many landlords to quickly evict tenants they suspect are engaging in illegal acts.

The landlord doesn't always have to wait until the tenant is convicted of a crime or even arrested. In some states, landlords may evict as long as they have a "reasonable suspicion" that illegal activity is afoot and the tenant or the tenant's guests are involved. By contrast, in other states an eviction for illegal drug activity may not begin unless there's been a criminal conviction for criminal acts on the rented premises.

Evictions based on criminal activity are often called "expedited evictions" because courts push them through and send law enforcement out to finish the job quicker than for a normal eviction. Expedited evictions are preceded by an unconditional quit notice that tells the tenant to move out (and do so quickly). If the tenant stays, the landlord can go to court and file for eviction. The court hearing on the eviction is typically held within a few days, and, if the landlord wins, the tenant is given little time to move. Details are set out in "State Laws on Unconditional Quit Terminations" in Appendix A.

Negotiating With the Landlord

If you receive a termination notice, you might experience at least a momentary surge of panic, despair, or anger. It's understandable: Someone is attempting to remove you from your home.

As difficult as it might be, don't let emotions dictate your response. How to best respond to a termination notice depends on whether and how long you would like to stay and whether you have a good defense to the landlord's stated reason for giving you the termination notice. You'll also want to consider the big picture: the time and trouble it will take you to fight an eviction, and the possible effect a lawsuit might have on your ability to secure future rentals, even if you win.

If you don't want to move, negotiation should be your first response—regardless of the merits of your defense. For example, if there is some validity behind your landlord's termination notice—if you are, in fact, late with the rent, or your last two parties truly were a bit raucous—your best bet is to meet with your landlord and agree to change your behavior. Don't be shy about negotiating. After all, from your landlord's point of view, striking a deal can make far more sense than going to court to evict you. Remember, lawsuits are time-consuming, expensive, and filled with technicalities; they are certainly a lot less attractive, businesswise, than negotiating a firm settlement that the landlord believes you will abide by.

It goes without saying that a landlord who perceives you as an inveterate troublemaker is unlikely to want to bargain. And, of course, some landlords are so unapproachable or irrational that meeting on a one-to-one basis is sure to be fruitless. If so, you'll have to consider the other options covered in the two sections below.

Suggestions on how to negotiate with the landlord are also covered in Chapter 15. All of the considerations explained there apply in the situations discussed in this chapter. In an eviction situation, though, you'll want to consider the following strategies, as well.

When You're at Fault

When the landlord has a valid reason for terminating your tenancy, you'll find that negotiation is most likely to work under two conditions:
- you have generally been a stable, law-abiding tenant, and
- the alleged violation is relatively minor and can be completely remedied.

For example, if you've kept your son's dog for a couple of weeks in violation of the no-pets rule, and the animal has not caused substantial damage or annoyance, your landlord might give you a few extra days (beyond the time specified in the cure or quit notice) to find a home for the pooch. Similarly,

if the landlord is mad because you've had an overnight guest a few too many times in violation of the lease clause, let your landlord know that things have changed, because your pal has:
- moved on (show the landlord your friend's new lease)
- agreed not to stay over on a regular basis in the future, or
- wants to become a tenant (your roommate) for a reasonable increase in your rent.

When you're late with the rent, an offer to pay part now and the rest on your next payday might mollify the landlord. (It's even better to tell the landlord if you anticipate a payment problem and set up a partial payment agreement in advance; see Chapter 3.)

Other strategies include offering to make payments in person for the next three months or, if checks have been bouncing, paying with a money order rather than a check. To assure the landlord that rent will be paid, offer to add a very solvent parent or friend as a cosigner on the lease or rental agreement.

As you negotiate, keep these points in mind:
- Emphasize your track record as a desirable tenant.
- Explain that the problem can be resolved easily, will leave no lasting ill effects, and won't happen again.
- If possible, offer to compensate the landlord in place of moving out—for example, if the landlord is furious at your "remodeling" work in the kitchen, offer to pay for further work that will remedy the situation.
- As subtly as possible, point out to the landlord that compromising with you is far less expensive and time-consuming than going to court to evict you.
- Remember that it might be to your advantage, too, to live with a less-than-perfect solution rather than take the time to respond to—and possibly lose—an eviction lawsuit.

> **TIP**
> **If the manager is unreasonable,** try to meet and deal with the manager's boss (if they work for a professional management company) or the owner.

When You've Done Nothing Wrong

When a termination notice accuses you of something you didn't do—or, at least, didn't intend to do—you're in a difficult position. True, if the case goes to court, the landlord will have to prove your misdeeds. But if you attempt to negotiate, you'll have to convince the landlord that you're not guilty. And, of course, it's never easy—and sometimes impossible—to get some people to contemplate the possibility that they have exaggerated the situation or are just plain mistaken. Here are some approaches to consider in situations where you believe there's been a misunderstanding.

- **When the landlord has made a mistake.** The landlord thinks you were the one responsible for the mess left in the common room, or were the host of the destructive wild party. Unlike TV lawyers, you might not be able to produce the culprit, but you might be able to bring evidence—for example, statements from neighbors—that will establish your blamelessness. Here you need not only evidence, but a good deal of tact. Don't rub your landlord's face in the error. Not only might this poison your future relations, it's also likely to cause your landlord to terminate your month-to-month tenancy or refuse to renew your lease when it runs out.
- **When you made a good-faith error.** You violated a lease or rental agreement term, but really didn't intend to do so. For example, perhaps you made the common mistake of assuming that all tenants enjoy a legal grace period when it comes to paying rent late before a termination notice can be sent. Arriving with your entire month's rent and honestly explaining your confusion to the landlord might get results.

Getting Help From a Mediator

In many areas, community mediation programs—or sometimes even mediation programs limited to landlord-tenant disputes—are available to help feuding landlords and tenants. They can be a huge help when direct negotiation with your landlord fails, but they are a realistic alternative for you only if you think your landlord might budge. A landlord who is dead-set on getting you out has no reason to agree to mediation.

One big advantage to initiating mediation is that often you won't even have to contact the landlord yourself. Instead, case workers at the mediation program will contact the landlord for you and set up the session. At the mediation session, a skilled person—the mediator—will attempt to help you both craft an acceptable compromise.

Remarkably, most mediation programs report a better-than-50% success rate working with people who believed no compromise was possible.

Chapter 19 gives details on using mediation to resolve landlord-tenant disputes.

To find out if a mediation program exists near you, call your city government (manager or mayor), county offices, or court clerk.

Refusing to Move Out

When the deadline in your termination notice passes, you will not be automatically evicted. In almost every state, the landlord must file and win an eviction lawsuit before the sheriff or marshal can physically evict you. It follows that if you and the landlord haven't arrived at a solution, you face a choice:

- abide by the demands of the termination notice, or
- force the landlord to start eviction proceedings.

Refusing to obey a termination notice makes sense in three situations: when the landlord's reasons for terminating your tenancy are wrong, when they are illegal, or (possibly) when you need to buy time to find another place.

Depending on the state, your case will be heard in a general trial court, a small claims court, or a designated landlord-tenant court. If you're headed for a general trial court, you might want to hire a lawyer. Chapter 18 gives an overview of eviction lawsuits.

When You're in the Right

The most obvious reason to ignore a termination notice and fight an eviction lawsuit is when you're right and you're prepared to take the time and the risk of going to court to prove it. For example, suppose, despite your repeated requests over a reasonable period of time, your landlord failed to replace your broken heater, with the result that you eventually called a heater service and had it fixed yourself. After deducting the cost of the repair from the next month's rent, you received a pay rent or quit notice. If you carefully read Chapter 8 and followed your state's law allowing you to make the repair, and have documented your communications with the landlord, you will probably be in no mood to move or compromise.

As any lawyer or citizen who has been through a lawsuit will tell you, however, being in the right is no guarantee that you will prevail in court. You must have the law and the facts on your side—and sometimes a fair amount of luck besides.

If you're headed for court, no matter what the reason, check these points:

Did the landlord comply with the notice requirements to end your tenancy? Carefully read your state's statutes and entries on the three tables in Appendix A ("State Laws on Termination for Nonpayment of Rent," "State Laws on Termination for Violation of Lease," and "State Laws on Unconditional Quit Terminations") and compare them with the notice that you have received. Here are some common landlord mistakes you'll want to check for:

- **Did the landlord give you the correct notice?** For example, if you received an unconditional quit notice when you were entitled to a cure or quit notice, this is a serious error. Failure to use the right notice is probably the most common

landlord mistake, and often results in a judge refusing to grant an eviction. A landlord can then start over with the proper notice.

- **Did the landlord deliver the notice to you in the way required by your state law?** For example, did the person who served the notice attempt to do so personally?

- **Did the termination notice contain the legally required wording?** For example, many states require the landlord to explain, in plain English, exactly what you've done (or not done) that justifies the notice. In these states, a notice is legally insufficient if it simply says that you have five days to cease violation of the lease or leave. The landlord must explain, for example, that you owe a specified amount of rent, or that the lease violation consists of your repeated use of the pool at night, which is prohibited in your lease. In areas covered by rent control, landlords often must add specified warnings and advisements to termination notices.

- **Did a lawyer who regularly collects rent debts send your notice?** Under the Federal Debt Collection Practices Act ("FDCPA"), written pay or quit demands signed by attorneys who regularly collect rent debts violate federal law unless they afford you 30 days' notice (rather than the minimum required under state law) (FDCPA, 15 U.S. Code §§ 1692 et seq.; *Romea v. Heiberger & Associates*, 988 F.Supp. 712 (S.D.N.Y. 1997) aff'd 163 F.3d 111 (2d Cir. 1998)). If you received a rent demand notice from a lawyer that gives you less than 30 days to pay the rent or move out, you might be able to seek damages against the lawyer under the FDCPA. However, this violation won't nullify the effect of the notice: A notice issued by a lawyer that provides less than 30 days' notice is nevertheless valid. If you do not pay the rent demanded or move out within the time provided, the landlord can still commence an eviction proceeding against you based on the rent demand.

TIP

Consider doing some legal research. You might want to go to your local law library or online to read the termination notice laws and the cases that have interpreted them before concluding whether the notice was properly chosen, drafted, and given. See Chapter 20 for advice.

- **Do you have documentary evidence?** Obviously, it's helpful in court to back up your claims with as much hard-copy evidence as possible. For example, if the basis of the termination is that you have violated a rental rule (by using the pool at midnight), yet no rule prohibiting night swimming appears in the lease or house rules, be sure that you have a copy of the lease and rules.

- **Do you have visual evidence?** The chances for winning will increase if you can give a judge or jury a real picture of the situation. If you withheld rent because of a leaking roof, take a picture of the sodden wall and your bucket of water.

- **Do you have live testimony?** A neutral witness who supports your side of the story is invaluable. For instance, if you withheld rent because the landlord refused to repair your stove, ask a repairperson to examine the stove and testify as to its condition. Or, if the landlord claims that you've made excessive noise, ask a neighbor to testify that, in fact, there was really no problem.

When the Landlord Is Retaliating

In most states, landlords are not allowed to terminate your tenancy as punishment for exercising a legal right, such as complaining to a health inspector, organizing a tenants' group, or properly withholding rent or using repair and deduct. (Landlord retaliation is discussed in detail in Chapter 15.) But suppose you have spoken to a housing inspector but you are *also* late with the rent—will it do you any good to prove that the landlord's real motive is retaliation? Or, put another way, does your conduct have to be "squeaky clean" in order to get a judge to stop an eviction lawsuit based on your landlord's retaliatory conduct?

It stands to reason that you'll always be in a better position if you can present yourself as a completely blameless tenant. But even if you are less than perfect, all might not be lost. Some states address this issue in their written law; others leave it to the courts to decide. If you plan to mount a retaliatory eviction defense but you know that there is a skeleton or two hiding in your closet, be sure to read your state's retaliation statutes and look for court decisions interpreting them. (Chapter 20 gives advice on how to do basic legal research.)

Buying Time (at a Price)

If you don't have a good legal reason for ignoring a termination notice, you might still choose to force the landlord to proceed to an eviction lawsuit if you have no place to move. The process (other than expedited evictions) normally takes from two to six weeks, time you might need in order to find another rental or finish a job or school year. And depending on the law and practice in your state, you might be able to obtain additional delays for hardship circumstances (see Chapter 18).

Understand that buying time often comes at a price: When an eviction lawsuit is filed against you—even if it's dismissed because you voluntarily move—if your lease or rental agreement allows your landlord to recover for attorneys' fees, you'll be charged for these. Courts in some states can order you to pay these fees even in the absence of such a clause, if the judge decides that your conduct has been extreme and outrageous. These fees can total hundreds or thousands of dollars, depending on the complexity of the case. (Chapter 2 explains attorneys' fees.)

Cutting Your Losses and Moving

Even if you believe you are in the legal right, finding another place to live might be your best option after getting a termination notice. There are many times in life when it is not worth your time and money to fight. Consider moving to a more congenial situation if:

- You can find comparable or better housing without major inconvenience.
- The landlord has always been difficult to deal with and you can expect future hassles.
- You cannot afford the time off from work, school, or your personal life to get involved in a lawsuit, nor can you afford to hire a lawyer.
- You are not absolutely sure you will win and your lease or rental agreement contains an

attorneys' "fees and costs" clause, meaning that if you lose you'll pay the landlord's costs as well as your own.

Moving in response to a termination notice, or even an eviction, does not mean that you forfeit your security deposit. Of course, if you have failed to pay the rent or have damaged the rental unit beyond normal wear and tear, the landlord can subtract what you owe from the deposit. (Chapter 16 discusses basic rules on returning security deposits.)

What about any future rent you owe under a lease the landlord terminates early? Chances are that even if the landlord has a good reason to end your lease early, a court hearing the eviction will not hold you liable for rent for any period after you leave (that's because until the landlord rerents, the landlord's damages—lost rents—are unknown).

Evictions

This chapter is for readers who have received a termination notice but are unwilling or unable to move out before the deadline given in the notice. For more details about termination notices (unconditional quit notices, notices to pay rent or quit, and notices to cure or quit), see Chapter 17. Read this chapter to get an idea of what you'll face if the landlord goes ahead and files a lawsuit to evict you.

We can't tell you exactly how to fight back—laws vary too much from state to state, and every situation is unique. But we can give you a good overview of the eviction procedure that follows a termination notice and tell you what your landlord can—and cannot—do under the law. To win an eviction lawsuit, you'll need to hire a lawyer or learn the particulars of your state's laws and procedures on your own. (Chapter 20 tells you how to get started by looking up your state's eviction statutes.)

TIP

Consider hiring a lawyer if your lease or rental agreement has an attorneys' fees clause. If you will be entitled to attorneys' fees if you win, and you are confident that you have a strong case, you might want to hire an attorney. Some lawyers even take eviction defense cases on a contingency—that is, you owe nothing if you lose, and they collect their fees from the landlord if you win. (Chapter 20 discusses contingency fees.)

RESOURCE

Find your state's eviction rules and procedures. California tenants should consult *California Tenants' Rights*, by J. Scott Weaver (Nolo); this book contains California-specific eviction defense information and tear-out court forms. Tenants in other states should check the Tenants section of Nolo.com for useful state-specific articles on topics such as tenant defenses to evictions. Appendix A of this book also contains information about state-specific rules and statutes.

When to Fight—And When to Move

Unless you have the law and provable facts on your side, fighting a termination notice is usually short-sighted. If you lose an eviction lawsuit, you might end up hundreds (even thousands) of dollars in debt and face a negative credit rating.

So, when does it make sense to fight an eviction? Here is a bare-bones list of the main legal reasons (grounds) for contesting an eviction:

- Your landlord gave you the wrong notice—for example, an unconditional notice to quit when you were entitled, under state law, to a pay rent or quit notice. However, fighting an eviction on this ground does nothing more than buy you a bit of time. See Chapter 17.
- Your landlord canceled the termination notice—for example, your landlord accepted rent after giving you a pay rent or quit notice—but filed for eviction anyway. See Chapter 17.
- You received a pay rent or quit notice and you offered rent within the specified time, but the landlord wouldn't accept it. See Chapter 17.
- The premises are legally uninhabitable, which excuses you from paying rent. See Chapter 8.
- You didn't pay all the rent because you properly used a tenant remedy allowed in your state, such as rent withholding or the state's repair and deduct procedures. See Chapter 8.
- An agreement with your landlord justified your paying less rent—for example, because you had taken on responsibility for maintenance. See Chapter 9.
- You're being evicted in retaliation for exercising a legal right, such as complaining to a housing inspector about your unit. See Chapter 15.
- Your landlord has an illegal discriminatory motive for eviction—for example, your race, sex, age, family status, or disability. See Chapter 5.

Illegal "Self-Help" Evictions

In years past, nothing stopped a landlord from changing the locks, removing the front door, cutting off the utilities, or even moving furniture onto the street if the tenant failed to pay rent, violated a lease clause, or damaged the property. Fortunately, today every state has forbidden these "self-help" evictions. Instead, landlords must get a court order directing tenants to leave, and if they don't, authorizing a local sheriff or marshal to physically remove the tenants.

Many states that have outlawed self-help evictions have put some teeth behind the ban. Tenants who have been locked out, frozen out by having the heat cut off, or denied electricity or water by their landlord can sue not only for their actual money losses (such as the need for temporary housing, the value of food that spoiled when the refrigerator stopped running, or the cost of an electric heater when the gas was shut off), but also for penalties as well. In some states, tenants can collect a money judgment and still remain in the premises; in others, illegally evicted tenants are entitled to monetary compensation only. (See the chart "Consequences of Self-Help Evictions," in Appendix A.)

If you decide to sue your landlord for an illegal eviction, research your state's statutes and consider consulting an experienced tenants' lawyer. (See Chapter 20 for advice on legal research and using an attorney as a coach.)

TIP

Watch out for the landlord who removes your property under the guise of handling "abandoned" property. A few states allow landlords to freely dispose of a tenant's property when the tenant has permanently moved out. So when a landlord has locked up, taken, or moved a tenant's property, it's not surprising to hear the landlord claim that the tenant had abandoned the property—even when abandonment is not obvious. If a tenant who in fact didn't intend to abandon sues over the property, the landlord must prove by clear and decisive evidence that the tenant intended to leave permanently and turn the place (and its contents) over to the landlord. "Your Abandoned Property" in Chapter 16 explains how landlords handle abandoned property.

How Eviction Lawsuits Work

Here's a guide to the basic elements of an eviction lawsuit.

CAUTION

"Expedited evictions" are fast and do not follow the typical path. If you are being evicted for serious illegal activity, such as drug dealing or use, your landlord might be able to take advantage of a speedy eviction procedure that will give you little, if any, time to prepare a defense.

What Court Hears Evictions?

Your landlord will file an eviction lawsuit in a formal trial court (called "municipal," "county," or "justice"), a specially-designated "landlord-tenant court," or in small claims court. Some states give landlords the choice; others confine eviction lawsuits to one or the other. If your landlord has a choice, the decision of which court to use will depend on:

- **Amount of unpaid rent.** If the landlord is also suing for unpaid rent that is higher than the small claims court's jurisdictional amount, the landlord must use a higher court. (States' small claims court jurisdictional limits are listed in Chapter 19.) Alternatively, the landlord can stay in small claims court by trimming the demand for damages to at or below the jurisdictional limit.

- **Attorneys' fees clause.** If your lease or rental agreement contains an attorneys' fees clause and the case against you is strong, your landlord is likely to hire an attorney and go to formal court, figuring that the fee will come from your pocket. On the other hand, if your landlord realizes that you have little or no funds—making chances of collection low—your landlord might choose small claims instead. Big landlords (who usually include attorneys' fees clauses in their rental contracts) are especially likely to choose formal court, regardless of the strength of their case, because they intend to hire attorneys and do not have the time to go to court themselves.

Regular trial court and small claims (or landlord-tenant) court have significant differences in how they operate:

- In small claims court, the regular rules of evidence are greatly relaxed, and you can show or tell the court your side of the story without adhering to the "foundation" requirements that apply in higher courts. ("Laying a foundation" is explained in "Rules of Evidence in Formal Court," below.)

- In regular court, you and the landlord will likely engage in a pretrial process called "discovery," in which you ask each other about the evidence that supports your positions. Discovery includes depositions (where witnesses are questioned under oath) and interrogatories (discussed in "Pretrial Discovery," below). This process is normally not available in small claims or landlord-tenant courts.

- In regular court, you and the landlord can each attempt to wash the case out of court quickly by filing pretrial requests to the court to dismiss or limit the case (discussed below). In small claims and landlord-tenant court, the idea is to decide the entire case after one efficient court hearing, and pretrial requests and motions usually are not used.

RESOURCE

Everybody's Guide to Small Claims Court, by Cara O'Neill (Nolo), describes the workings of your state's small claims court in detail.

Represent Yourself in Court: How to Prepare & Try a Winning Case, by Paul Bergman and Sara J. Berman (Nolo), explains how to present evidence and arguments in formal court.

First Steps: The Complaint and Summons

An eviction lawsuit begins when the landlord files a legal document called a "Complaint" or similar term. The Complaint, which is usually loaded with legal jargon, lists the facts that the landlord thinks justify your eviction. It also asks the court to order you to leave and to pay back rent, damages directly caused by your unlawfully remaining on the property, court costs, and (sometimes) attorneys' fees.

Normally, your landlord cannot sue you for anything but back rent and the damages associated with your failure to pay. Because an eviction procedure is so quick, most states do not allow a landlord to add other legal beefs to an eviction Complaint. For example, if your landlord claims that you have damaged the sofa and your security deposit won't cover the cost of replacement, the landlord must sue you in a separate lawsuit. In some states, landlords cannot add unpaid late fees. Similarly, if you would like to bring up an unrelated bit of landlord misbehavior, such as your landlord's repeated violations of your privacy, you will have to do so in a separate legal action.

When the landlord files a Complaint, the clerk will assign a date for the court to hear the case. That date is entered on the Summons, a piece of paper that says that you've been sued and must answer the landlord's charges and appear in court within a specified number of days or lose the lawsuit. The landlord must then give you the Complaint and the Summons, which officially inform you of your right to appear before a judge. In legal jargon, this is called "service of process."

State laws are quite detailed as to the proper way to give you, or "serve," court papers. Typically, the preferred method is "personal" service, which means that a law enforcement officer or professional process server personally hands you the papers. (Don't think that you can slam the door in the process server's face to avoid service—the process server can leave them on the doorstep to complete service.) In most states, any adult not involved in the lawsuit can serve papers.

If, despite repeated attempts, the process server cannot locate you, most states allow something called "substituted service." This means the process server leaves a copy of the papers with a competent adult at your home, or mails the papers first-class and also leaves a copy in a place where you'll likely see it, such as posted on your front door.

Failure to properly serve the tenant is one of the most common errors landlords make. For example, when landlords try to serve the papers themselves, they violate a rule that is found in almost all service laws: Parties to a lawsuit must have a third party serve papers. Another common mistake is not making enough attempts at personal service before resorting to substituted service. The most common violation of the service rules is that the process server simply lies about having personally contacted the party. This happens especially in rough areas of town, where process servers are afraid to go.

If your landlord did not follow state statutes correctly, you can usually ask the judge to dismiss the lawsuit before trial. However, in some states the fact that you did, in fact, receive the papers will defeat your claim. And even if you win, your landlord might be prepared with a new Summons, which will be handed to you right in court.

CAUTION

Don't ignore a Summons. If you have already ignored a notice telling you to move out, you might be tempted to also ignore a Summons and Complaint, too, figuring that you'll move out just before the case goes to court or the sheriff arrives to escort you out. This plan is a mistake. Far better to immediately call the landlord

and negotiate a move-out date. If you owe back rent and attorneys' fees and costs that amount to more than the security deposit, the landlord might agree to not sue you for the excess in exchange for your speedy departure. But don't expect more than a few days at this point.

If you don't respond to the Summons and Complaint, the landlord will automatically win the eviction lawsuit. The court will grant what's called a "default judgment" against you, ordering you to pay unpaid rent and, if your lease or rental agreement has an attorneys' fees and costs clause, those expenses as well. The default will show up on your credit report.

Knocking the Lawsuit Out of Court Before Trial

Failure to properly serve you isn't the only procedural objection you can raise to the landlord's lawsuit (and even then, as noted above, it's a short-lived victory). Other landlord mistakes can also justify dismissal of the case before trial. To get the case dismissed, you might need to file brief documents called a "motion to dismiss" the landlord's case, or to "strike" (eliminate) a key part of it. You must also serve a copy of your motion on the landlord, in the manner required by law in your state. Here are the main arguments tenants can use to argue for dismissal of the eviction case:

The landlord used the wrong notice. In many states, landlords must give tenants a certain amount of time—often three to five days—to pay the rent or cure the lease violation before filing an eviction lawsuit. (See Chapter 17.) However, very serious misbehavior (such as damage to the property), illegal activities, or repeated late rent or lease violations might enable the landlord to serve an unconditional quit notice, which does not give the tenant a chance to cure the problem. If you are being evicted for behavior that triggers a pay rent or quit or cure or quit notice, but the landlord gave you an unconditional quit notice instead, you can challenge it in court. If you win, the landlord will be told to start over and use the right termination notice. Once you're served with the right notice, you will have the opportunity to comply ("cure" the problem) and save your tenancy.

The landlord filed the lawsuit too soon. If you've been given a termination notice that does give you time to pay or cure, the landlord cannot file for eviction until that time has run out. For example, if you have five days to pay the rent or move and you don't pay, the lawsuit cannot be filed until the sixth day.

Your Answer to the Complaint

The next step in a typical eviction lawsuit involves your response to the landlord's claim that something you've done (or not done) justifies your eviction. At this point, you've gone beyond the technicalities of the way your landlord filed the lawsuit, and are addressing the reasons for the eviction head-on.

You must file a document called an Answer on or before the date printed on the Summons. Fortunately, your answer need not take the shape of a lengthy legal brief. In many states, you can even use a preprinted answer form prepared by the court that allows you to simply check appropriate boxes, depending on what you intend to argue. If you're in one of the few states that still follow the old-fashioned rule of requiring that documents be prepared on numbered legal paper, you can find free templates online (type "numbered legal paper" in your browser's search box).

In general, your Answer can contain two kinds of responses:

- **Denials.** By responding with a denial, you are asserting that what the landlord has said is untrue. For example, if you paid your rent to the manager but the landlord claims it was never received, you will simply deny that the rent is unpaid. Or, if the landlord is evicting you because you have a dog but the animal was on the property for only an hour when its owner visited you, you'll also simply check the "deny" box. Or, if your state does not offer a form, you would type something like this: "Defendant denies the allegations in Paragraph X of Plaintiff's Complaint." (The landlord is the plaintiff in the lawsuit; you're the defendant.)

- **Affirmative Defenses.** The Answer is also the place to state what the law calls "affirmative defenses"—good legal reasons that legitimize what would otherwise be grounds for eviction. For example, if you're being evicted for not paying the rent, you could explain that you used some of the rent money to pay for repairing a serious problem your landlord knew about but ignored, as is allowed under your state's repair and deduct law. Some preprinted answer forms actually list the common defenses that we described at the beginning of this chapter. Normally, you'll need to provide a one-paragraph statement of the facts that justify your use of the affirmative defense you have selected.

EXAMPLE: Wilson, a gay man, was sure that his termination and eviction were motivated by the landlord's discovery of his sexual orientation. The answer form provided by the court clerk listed "Discrimination" as an affirmative defense. Wilson checked the box next to it, and wrote in the space next to the checkbox, "Plaintiff served me with a 30-day notice because he doesn't want gay people living in his building."

Not every state, however, gives you the convenience of a list of preprinted affirmative defenses. But don't worry: You won't have to write your Answer entirely from scratch. You can probably find a fill-in-the-blanks form online at the court's website. If you come up empty-handed, you might need to go to a physical law library and consult one of the form books that lawyers use (these are not typically available for free online). Form books are designed to cover every typical situation, so you're sure to find a "canned" form that will fit your situation. (See Chapter 20 for information on legal research.)

Answer Raising Affirmative Defense

First Affirmative Defense

1. Defendant admits that she did not pay the amount of rent due as stated in the Complaint. She argues, however, that the entire rent was not due because she was legally entitled to pay less than the stated rent because of her valid use of the repair and deduct statute of the state of California, Civil Code Section 1942.

2. Plaintiff is required by law to provide hot water of at least 110 degrees Fahrenheit, as specified by title 25 of the California Code of Regulations, section 32. However, the water temperature in defendant's apartment did not rise above 50 degrees as of January 4, 20xx.

3. Plaintiff had actual knowledge of the inability of defendant's water heater to deliver legally sufficient hot water, since defendant wrote him two letters (dated January 5 and 10, 20xx), asking that the situation be corrected, but he failed to do so.

4. The defective condition was not caused by any willful or negligent act of the defendant or any person acting under her authority.

5. As a direct and proximate result of plaintiff's failure to correct the violation of law within a reasonable time, defendant hired a plumber on January 25, 20xx, to inspect and repair the water heater. The heater was fixed by installing a new valve, at a reasonable cost of $125.

6. Defendant deducted $125 from her rent check on February 1, 20xx.

7. Defendant has not used this state's repair and deduct statute more than the number of times allowed by law, nor is the amount deducted more than one month's rent.

THEREFORE, DEFENDANT ASKS THAT:

1. Plaintiff take nothing by his action;

2. Costs of this action be awarded to defendant; and

3. Defendant be awarded such further relief as the Court considers proper.

February 9, 20xx   _Sally Strong_
Date   Sally Strong, in Pro Per

When you sign your Answer, be sure to note under or after your typed name that you are appearing "Pro per" or "Pro se," which means that you are representing yourself and have not hired a lawyer. A sample is shown above.

Pretrial Discovery

Sometimes, the facts of a case are not straightforward, and the tenant or the landlord might wish to find out more about the other's arguments and legal position before the trial. Called "discovery," this process is not available in small claims court. During the discovery period, each party is entitled to serve the other with one or all of the following.

- Deposition notices, requiring the recipient (a witness, expert, or party to the lawsuit) to attend a meeting (the deposition) to answer questions under oath, which creates a record (the transcript of the meeting) that can be used in court.

- Requests to produce documents in the recipient's possession, such as the landlord's repair request form or a landlord's letter to all tenants.

- Sets of preprinted questions, called "interrogatories," that cover information normally involved in a landlord-tenant dispute. For example, the landlord might be asked to "State the names and addresses of all owners of record of the property."

- Specific statements of fact (called "requests for admissions") that the recipient must, under oath, admit or deny. For example, a tenant might ask the landlord to admit or deny the statement, "Landlord does not maintain an on-site office at [your apartment complex]."

Many states also require parties to produce this type of information even when the other side does not serve official requests. Typically, the information gathered during discovery can be used at trial.

Rules of Evidence in Formal Court

Depending on the state, evictions are heard in a formal trial court, small claims court, or an informal landlord-tenant court. In small claims court, you can usually present any evidence you want to the judge. But if you are in a formal court, the judge will not examine documentary evidence until you have established that it is likely to be trustworthy and relevant to the issues in the case. Presenting the legal background of evidence is called "laying a foundation." Here are a few hints on how to prepare evidence for formal court:

- **Photographs.** If your landlord's termination notice is based on your knocking a hole in the kitchen wall, you'll want to show the judge a photograph of the place where, in fact, there is a mere scuff mark. But before the picture can be admitted into evidence, someone will have to testify that the picture is a fair and accurate depiction of the way the wall looked. It's best to ask a neutral witness to come to your apartment, look at the wall, and come to court prepared to testify that, yes, the photo is an accurate portrayal. Your witness need not take the photo.

- **Letters.** You might have received a termination notice stating (incorrectly) that you improperly used the repair and deduct remedy by failing to notify your landlord of the problem in the first place. In court, this means you'll need to introduce into evidence your copy of the letter you sent your landlord requesting repairs as proof that you complied with this requirement. To do this, you can simply testify that the letter is a true copy, that the signature is your own, and that you mailed or handed it to your landlord.

- **Petitions.** Perhaps your defense to your termination and eviction is that the landlord is retaliating against you because you circulated a petition asking for cleaner common areas or because you protested a rent increase. To introduce the petition, you can testify that you circulated it or, even better, have someone who signed it testify that it is genuine.

- **Government documents.** If you've withheld rent because of what you claim are uninhabitable conditions (an inoperable, sole toilet, for example), your landlord might attempt to evict you for nonpayment of rent. If you made a complaint to a local health department and they issued a report critical of your landlord, you'll want to have the report considered by the court (admitted into evidence). You'll have to have someone from the health department (preferably the individual who actually wrote the report or performed the inspection) testify that the report was written as part of the department's normal duties when investigating possible health violations. To get the inspector or representative to court, you'll need to use an order, called a "subpoena," that you can serve on the department or its representative.

The Trial

The way your trial will look and sound will depend primarily on whether it's in a formal court or a small claims or landlord-tenant court. In formal court, you'll have to abide by your state's rules of evidence. But in an informal court, you might be able to introduce letters and secondhand testimony ("I heard her say that …"). Also, you can introduce evidence without elaborate "foundations." (See "Rules of Evidence in Formal Court," above.) See Chapter 19 for an explanation of the kinds of evidence you'll need to win.

The Judgment

If you win, the landlord cannot evict you, and you'll likely get a judgment for your court costs and fees. You might also be awarded money damages if the landlord acted illegally, as in the case of discrimination. If the landlord wins, you must move out. The landlord might also be awarded unpaid rent, damages, court costs, and attorneys' fees.

If you win by asserting a habitability defense, the court might hold onto your case even after the trial is over. That's because the court doesn't want to simply return you to an unfit dwelling. In some states, a judge can order the landlord to make repairs while the rent is paid into a court account; when an inspector certifies that the dwelling is habitable, the judge will release the funds.

If You Lose: Stopping or Postponing an Eviction

If you lose the eviction lawsuit, you can expect your landlord to move quickly to physically remove you from the property. In rare instances, you might be able to get the trial judge to stop the eviction, but only if you can convince the court of two things:

- Eviction would cause a severe hardship for you or your family. For example, you might be able to persuade the judge that alternate housing is unavailable and your job will be in jeopardy if you are forced to move.
- You are willing and able to pay any back rent owed (and the landlord's costs to bring the lawsuit) and future rent, as well.

It's very unusual for a judge to stop an eviction, for the simple reason that if your sympathetic predicament (and sufficient monetary reserves) weren't persuasive enough to win the case for you in the first place, it's unlikely that these arguments can prevail after the trial.

It might, however, be more realistic to ask for a postponement of the eviction. Typically, evictions are postponed in three situations:

- **Pending your appeal.** If you file an appeal, you can ask the trial judge to postpone ("stay") the eviction until the appellate court decides the case. If you've been evicted in small claims court, in a few states you might have an automatic postponement during the appeal. Of course, this is one reason why smart landlords never use small claims court in these states.
- **Until your circumstances improve.** You might be able to persuade a judge to give you a little more time to find a new home.

- **Until the weather improves.** Contrary to popular belief, judges in many cold-climate states are not required to postpone an eviction on frigid days. The District of Columbia is an exception: a landlord cannot evict on a day when the National Weather Service predicts at 8 a.m. that the temperature at the National Airport will fall below freezing within the next 24 hours or when precipitation is falling at the rental. (D.C. Code § 42-3505.01(k).) But you can always just ask the judge, anyway.

Eviction

In most states, a landlord cannot move your belongings out on the street, even after winning an eviction lawsuit. (See "Illegal 'Self-Help' Evictions," above.) Typically, the landlord must give the judgment to a local law enforcement officer, along with a fee that you've been charged as part of the landlord's costs. The sheriff or constable gives you a notice telling you that law enforcement will be back, sometimes within just a few days, to physically remove you if you aren't gone. At this point, it's time to move. No one, even the most unfairly wronged tenant, wants the experience of being tossed out.

Stopping Eviction by Filing for Bankruptcy

Tenants with significant financial burdens might decide to declare bankruptcy. There are several kinds of bankruptcy; the most common are "Chapter 7," in which most debts are wiped out after as many creditors as possible have been paid; or "Chapter 13," in which qualifying debts get wiped out after paying into a court-approved plan for three to five years.

What Happens to Your Lease

Filing for a Chapter 7 bankruptcy affects your tenancy even if you are not behind in the rent or otherwise in violation of your lease. After you file, the Chapter 7 "bankruptcy trustee" (a person appointed by the bankruptcy court to oversee the case) must decide whether to assume your lease or rental agreement (take it over) or reject it.

A trustee who assumes your residential contract will step into your shoes. The trustee gets no more than what you contracted for and must pay whatever you owe, including the monthly payment and any past due amount. Doing so can be expensive, so it will happen only if you pay below-market rent, and when subletting your place (assigning your agreement to someone else) will net your creditors a profit. If you're paying the current market rate, or your contract forbids subletting, there won't be any profit to be made and the trustee will let you keep the lease.

It works a bit differently in a Chapter 13 bankruptcy. As long as you're current on your payments, you won't have to worry about losing your residential rental, because the Chapter 13 trustee doesn't sell or liquidate your property.

However, if you're behind in the rent, you must pay unpaid rent regardless of the chapter that you file. (11 U.S.C. §§ 365(b)(1)(A), (B), & (C).)

If you have filed for either Chapter 7 or Chapter 13 bankruptcy and are behind in the rent, or become unable to pay the rent, or if you violate another term of your tenancy (such as having a dog in spite of a no-pets clause), the landlord cannot deliver a termination notice or proceed with an eviction. This prohibition is known as the "automatic stay," and it means that the landlord must go to the federal bankruptcy court and ask the judge to "lift," or remove the stay. (11 U.S.C. § 365(e).)

In most cases, the judge will lift the stay within a matter of days and the landlord can proceed with the termination and eviction. (The landlord won't have to go to court if the tenant is using illegal drugs or endangering the property, as explained below in "Bankrupt Tenants, Drugs, and Damage.")

The automatic stay does not apply, however if the landlord completed the eviction proceeding and got a judgment for possession before the tenant filed for bankruptcy. In this scenario, landlords can proceed with the eviction without having to go to court and ask for the stay to be lifted.

In very narrow circumstances, and only for evictions based on rent nonpayment, a tenant can stop the eviction even when the landlord got a judgment before the tenant filed for bankruptcy. A tenant has only 30 days after filing for bankruptcy to try this. Here are the specifics:

- You must go to court and file a paper certifying that state law allows you to avoid eviction by paying the unpaid rent, even after the landlord has won a judgment for possession. Very few states extend this option to tenants. The certification must be served on the landlord.

- You must deposit with the clerk of the bankruptcy court any rent that would be due 30 days from the date the petition was filed, and

- You must certify to the bankruptcy court (and serve the landlord with this certification) that you have paid the back rent.

At any point during these 30 days, the landlord can file an objection to the tenant's certification. The judge will schedule a hearing in the bankruptcy court within ten days. If the landlord convinces the judge that the tenant's certifications are not true, the court will lift the stay and the landlord can proceed to recover possession of the property.

Bankrupt Tenants, Drugs, and Damage

In most states, landlords can evict tenants who are using illegal drugs or endangering the property. If the tenant files for bankruptcy before the landlord wins a judgment for possession, the landlord will be able to proceed with the eviction without asking the bankruptcy judge to lift the stay. How these eviction cases proceed depends on the timing:

- **When the landlord has begun an eviction case but doesn't have a judgment.** The landlord will file a certification, or sworn statement, that there is an active unlawful detainer case based on the tenant's endangerment of the property or use of illegal drugs (or such use by the tenant's guests).
- **When the landlord hasn't yet filed an eviction lawsuit.** The landlord will file a certification, or sworn statement, that the activity described above has happened within the past 30 days.

In either situation, the landlord will serve the tenant as they would serve any legal notice.

If the tenant does not file an objection within 15 days of being served, the landlord can proceed with the eviction without asking the court for relief from the stay.

A tenant who wishes to object must file with the court, and serve on the landlord, a certification challenging the truth of the landlord's certification.

The bankruptcy court will hold a hearing within ten days, at which the tenant must convince the court that the situation the landlord describes did not exist or has been remedied. If the court rules for the landlord, the eviction can proceed without the landlord having to ask that the stay be lifted; but if the tenant wins, the eviction cannot proceed.

Resolving Problems Without a Lawyer

Legal disputes between tenants and landlords come in all shapes and sizes. Here are some examples of the more common ones:

- **Rent.** You disagree about the validity, timing, or method of a rent increase.

- **Habitability.** You've complained several times about the leaky roof that has made the living room unusable. After getting no response from your landlord, you don't pay the next month's rent. Your landlord is threatening eviction.

- **Privacy.** You don't want the landlord to keep entering your apartment on very short notice and at inconvenient times. Your landlord thinks you're being unreasonable.

- **Security deposits.** At the end of your tenancy, you claim that you left the rental unit reasonably clean and undamaged. The landlord says it didn't pass the white glove test.

- **Lease or rental agreement violation.** Your landlord complains that you are violating your lease by having noisy parties and frequent overnight guests. You feel your private life is your business, and that your landlord is jealous of your social life.

How you handle problems with your landlord can have a profound effect on your ability to enjoy your rental home. In some cases, such as when a landlord persistently refuses to attend to major repairs, enters unannounced, and generally makes your life miserable on a number of fronts, your best bet might be to end the tenancy and move to a more congenial place. Or, if you are the victim of serious discrimination or other illegal acts, your best bet might be to move out and go straight to a lawyer.

Often, however, you can take steps that will improve matters—or at least resolve the dispute in your favor. Hiring a lawyer should be your first choice in only rare circumstances. Before you go the (expensive) route of hiring counsel, try:

- negotiation
- mediation, or
- small claims court.

Most landlord-tenant disputes involve only the occupants of a single unit and the landlord. But if you're in a situation where other tenants share your concerns, you'll find it effective to approach your landlord as a group.

In this chapter, we'll show you how to attempt to resolve solo disputes as well as group disputes without a lawyer.

RESOURCE

Nolo has compiled a comprehensive list of websites and articles for renters looking for help related to landlord-tenant issues and evictions. The page includes a list of sites for finding low- or no-cost legal assistance, answers to tenant FAQs, and much more. You can find "Legal Resources for Tenants" by typing the title into the search box on Nolo's home page.

How to Negotiate a Settlement

No matter how serious the problem, you're almost always better off trying to resolve disputes directly with your landlord. This is especially true if your concerns don't warrant the use of a heavy-duty legal strategy in the first place. So put aside the possibility of suing—except possibly in small claims court (see below)—and instead direct your efforts toward negotiating a settlement.

You'll be most successful if you focus on what exactly you want the landlord to do, rather than fighting for the principle involved. Berating your landlord for insensitivity or ignorance might give you a sense of righteous vindication, but not necessarily better results.

Here are some helpful pointers for negotiating with landlords:

- **Set up an appointment to discuss the problem.** Don't drop in unannounced—making an appointment will emphasize how important you consider the matter to be, and reduces your landlord's ability to brush you off. Try to arrange sufficient time, without distractions such as children, so you can both express your concerns and work out an agreement.

- **Solicit the landlord's point of view.** Once the landlord starts talking, listen closely and don't interrupt, even if some points are not true or some opinions are inflammatory.

- **State that you understand and respect the landlord's key points.** Even if you strongly disagree with your landlord's position, it's often a good idea to accurately restate the concerns as you're hearing them. This should help focus the conversation and keep your landlord from endlessly repeating the same point.

- **Avoid personal attacks.** Even if true, suggesting that your landlord is a slumlord or is profiteering at the expense of tenants will only raise the level of hostility and make settlement more difficult. Equally important, it's usually best to stay calm and not to react impulsively or emotionally to your landlord's misstatements.

- **Be courteous, not weak.** If the law is on your side or you have the firm backing of other tenants, let the landlord know that you're coming from a position of strength. Make it clear that you prefer negotiating an agreement but that, if necessary, you have the resources and evidence to fight and win.

- **Emphasize problem solving.** Try to structure the negotiation as a mutual attempt to solve a problem. For instance, if you're complaining about a landlord's policy of entering tenants' apartments unannounced to make repairs, seek solutions that recognize the interests of both parties—for example, an understanding that repairs are necessary and even desirable but most can be prearranged.

- **Put yourself in the landlord's shoes.** How would you want to work with unhappy tenants if roles were reversed? Your answer might be something like, "I'd want to feel that I've won." As it turns out, this is a great insight—the best settlements are often those in which both sides feel they've won, at least to some extent.

- **If you reach an understanding with your landlord, promptly write it down and sign it.** You should volunteer to prepare the first draft. If you agree to pay the landlord some money as part of the settlement, make it clear that the payment fully satisfies the landlord's claim: "Tenant's $200 payment of August 1, 20xx, fully satisfies any claim Landlord has against Tenant regarding damaged patio furniture."

RESOURCE

Getting to Yes: Negotiating Agreement Without Giving In, by Roger Fisher, William Ury, and Bruce Patton (Penguin Books). This classic book offers a strategy for coming to mutually acceptable agreements in all kinds of situations, including landlord-tenant disputes.

Using a Mediator

If you're unsuccessful negotiating a settlement with your landlord, or relations are so strained that no meeting seems possible, don't give up on the idea of negotiation. Instead, your best approach is often to enlist the help of a neutral third-party mediator. Even if your landlord won't speak to you, a skilled and experienced mediator might be able to bring everyone to the table.

Many people confuse mediation with arbitration, which is seldom, if ever, used in residential landlord-tenant disputes. While both are nonjudicial ways to resolve disputes, there's a huge difference: Arbitration, like lawsuits, results in a binding decision. Mediators, by contrast, have no power to impose a decision. Their job is simply to help the parties work out a mutually acceptable solution to their dispute. Put another way, if you and your landlord don't agree on a solution, there is no forced solution.

Mediation makes good sense if:

- your landlord doesn't realize what a poor job the resident manager or management company has been doing, and you want the opportunity to bring this up

- you are dealing with a good or at least halfway decent landlord, and you think there's hope for resolution, or
- you think the landlord is savvy enough to want to avoid a protracted court battle.

TIP
Mediation can also help resolve roommate disputes. If you and your roommate disagree about noise, overnight guests, or some other issue, consider trying mediation.

Does mediation really work? Surprisingly, yes. One big reason is the cooperative spirit that emerges. By agreeing to mediate a dispute in the first place, you and the landlord implicitly agree to solve your own problems. Also, the fact that no judge or arbitrator has the power to impose what might be an unacceptable solution reduces fear and defensiveness on both sides. This, in turn, often means both landlord and tenant take less extreme—and more conciliatory—positions.

Sometimes mediation is not the best approach. For example, if your landlord has discriminated against you based on your race, sex, or some other illegal reason, you should probably file a fair housing complaint or a lawsuit, as explained in Chapter 5.

How to Find a Mediation Service

Many cities and counties offer free or low-cost community mediation programs that handle landlord-tenant disputes. For information, call your mayor's or city manager's office and ask for the staff member who handles landlord-tenant mediation matters or housing disputes. That person should refer you to the public office or community group that attempts to informally—and at little or no cost—resolve landlord-tenant disputes before they reach the court stage. You can also get referrals for fee-based mediation services from the American Arbitration Association (visit their website at www.adr.org) or a neighborhood dispute resolution center.

TIP
If there's a charge for the mediation service, offer to split it with your landlord. That way, you'll both feel equally vested in the outcome.

How Mediation Works

Mediation in landlord-tenant disputes is fairly informal. More likely than not, the mediator will have you and your landlord sit down together. Each side is usually asked to discuss all issues they consider important—even emotional ones. This process of airing the entire dispute often cools people off considerably and can lay the foundation for a fairly quick compromise.

If the dispute is not resolved easily, the mediator might suggest ways to resolve the problem, or might keep everyone talking long enough to realize that the real problem goes deeper than the one being mediated. Typically this is helped along through a caucus process, where each side is asked to occupy a separate room, with the mediator shuttling back and forth with offers and counteroffers. When settlement appears near, everyone gets back together, and the mediator helps guide the parties to an agreement everyone approves.

For example, assume you and your landlord are mediating because you have threatened to withhold rent due to a serious defect in the premises, such as a broken heater. In a court hearing, this issue would be the only one considered. In contrast, a mediator can use the looser mediation process to discover that a major part of your grievance is that the manager has been slow to make all types of repairs, and the heat problem is simply the final straw.

You're not the only one who will have a chance to discuss other issues. You might discover that your landlord is angry at you for letting your kids run wild and ruin the garden, or is sick and tired of getting calls from the police responding to noise complaints filed by your neighbors. Once all of this is on the table, a compromise solution might fall easily into place: For example, you could agree to provide better supervision of your kids and cut out overly loud parties in exchange for the manager getting the heat fixed and doing other repairs quickly.

And to keep future conflicts from developing, both sides might agree to meet monthly so that misunderstandings can be resolved before they grow into major battles.

Suing in Small Claims Court

If your attempts at settling a dispute with your landlord fail, you might end up in a lawsuit. Fortunately, there are many situations when you can competently and efficiently represent yourself in court. This is almost always true when your case is worth a few thousand dollars and you choose to use small claims court.

You can use a small claims court lawsuit to pursue many rental-related goals, including:

- forcing a landlord to perform needed major repairs (see Chapter 8)
- pressuring a landlord to do minor repairs (see Chapter 9)
- dealing with a landlord who repeatedly and seriously intrudes upon your privacy (see Chapter 11)
- winning a money judgment against a landlord who has failed to get rid of drug-dealing tenants (see Chapter 14), and
- obtaining an order that your landlord must return your security deposit (see Chapter 16).

Most people who go to small claims court handle their own cases. In fact, in some states, lawyers aren't allowed to represent clients in small claims court. (Some states allow attorneys in certain situations, such as with permission of the court or only when both sides have counsel.) There's no rule against conferring with a lawyer before court, to help you prepare your case.

In any event, representing yourself is almost always the best choice—after all, the main reason to use the small claims court is because the size of the case doesn't justify the cost of hiring a lawyer.

Learning the Rules

Small claims court procedures are relatively simple and easy to master. Basically, you pay a small fee, file your lawsuit with the court clerk, see to it that the papers are served on your landlord (this can often be done by mail), show up on the appointed day, tell the judge your story, and present any witnesses and other evidence.

Evidence that backs up your story is usually the key to winning in small claims court. For example, if you are suing your landlord to get your security deposit returned, all you need to win is a photograph of a clean and undamaged apartment and the convincing testimony of someone who helped you clean up. (Chapter 16 explains how to gather and present evidence in small claims court disputes about security deposits.)

Court rules that cover such things as where you file your lawsuit, how legal papers must be delivered to your opponent ("service of process"), and how promptly you must sue are usually available on the court's website or from the small claims clerk. In addition, clerks in small claims court are expected to explain procedures to you. In some states, they can even help you fill out the required forms. If necessary, be persistent. If you ask enough questions, you'll get the answers you need to handle your own case comfortably. Also, in some states such as California, you can consult a free small claims court adviser.

How Much Can You Sue For?

Exactly how much can you sue for in small claims court? The maximum varies from state to state. In most, it is $3,000 to $15,000. (See "State Small Claims Court Limits" in Appendix A, or ask your court clerk for the most current limit.)

Don't assume that your case can't be brought in small claims court if it's slightly over the limit. Rather than hiring a lawyer or trying to go it alone in formal court, your most cost-effective option might be to sue for the small claims maximum and forget the rest.

RESOURCE

Everybody's Guide to Small Claims Court, by Cara O'Neill (Nolo), provides detailed advice on bringing or defending a small claims court case, preparing evidence and witnesses for court, and collecting your money judgment when you win. Especially if you have never been to small claims court, you'll want to closely study the material on how to present your testimony and witnesses in court. *Everybody's Guide to Small Claims Court* will also be useful in defending yourself against a landlord who sues you in small claims court—for example, claiming that you owe money for damage to the premises.

Tenants Working Together

When it comes to confronting a recalcitrant land-lord, one strategy is potentially more productive than all others: Work together with other tenants. A landlord who has the resources and determination to outwait, outspend, or outmaneuver one tenant will often be much more willing to compromise when a number of tenants all threaten to act together. For example, you and other tenants could file a complaint with a government agency, sue, threaten a rent strike, or move out.

Keep in mind, however, that a group of tenants will be effective only if they speak with a clear, consistent voice. For a variety of reasons, it can be hard or even impossible to form a tenants' group—for example, if tenant turnover is high or many tenants fear or dislike one another. But even if it's only a handful of tenants, you might find that there's power in numbers.

What Tenants' Groups Can Do

A tenant organization can be an informal group that comes together on one major issue, such as getting the landlord to make repairs or fighting a rent increase. Or a group can be more formally organized with regular meetings and address a wide variety of issues, such as getting the landlord to stop arbitrary mistreatment of tenants or making the building safer.

The tenant organization could use negotiation or mediation to convince the landlord to work more cooperatively with tenants. If push comes to shove, however, the tenants' group could even sue the landlord in small claims court. Faced with a multitenant lawsuit, many landlords suddenly become more willing to sign a formal agreement giving the tenants all or some of what they request. A cohesive tenant organization should be able to convince the landlord to deal with it on a continuing basis.

Tenants' organizations can also help work out problems among tenants. As any tenant in a multiunit building knows, a neighbor with a loud stereo (or child, dog, or spouse) can cause more day-to-day misery than the most obnoxious landlord. To deal with ongoing problems, an effective tenants' group can set up a voluntary mediation procedure to help members settle problems before they fester. And when it comes to drugs, prostitution, and gang activity, a tenants' organization can be very effective in pressuring the landlord to evict the troublemaker.

CAUTION

Beware of retaliation against tenant groups. Laws in most states protect tenants from landlord retaliation when the tenant exercises a legal right such as withholding rent when conditions justify it. Unfortunately, some states don't extend this legal protection to activist tenants, which means that a hostile landlord might try to get rid of those who organize or participate in tenant groups. Of course, the stronger and more unified the group, the harder this will be to do. See "State Laws Prohibiting Landlord Retaliation" in Appendix A and the discussion of retaliation in Chapter 15. Proceed at your own risk if tenants' organizing activities are not protected by your state's antiretaliation laws.

Getting Tenants Together

Two or three concerned tenants can start an effective tenants' group. Start by holding a meeting so people can get to know each other and speak about problems they have had with the building or the landlord.

You'll need a small group to get things started. If you live in a large apartment complex or more than one building is involved, make sure you have the active involvement of someone from each building.

To get other tenants interested, identify one or more problems most tenants face. A big rent increase, fear of crime, safety of children, and parking problems are common. Focus on problems that should concern most tenants, not just your personal beef with your landlord.

Set a convenient meeting time and place to discuss these issues, and contact tenants individually to ask them to come. If you and the other organizers can afford the time, do this in person, door-to-door. Post or distribute notices only as a last resort or as a supplement to personal contact. Don't be too confrontational. You don't want to present yourselves to moderate tenants as a bunch of hotheads, and, of course, you don't want to alienate the landlord, whom you hope to persuade to work with your group.

The first meeting should begin informally. People should be given a chance to get to know each other and see that they really do have common problems that can be tackled by a group.

Try to anticipate and deal with tenants' fears about participating in the group. Some people might worry about being evicted if they ask for better treatment, while others might be concerned that the tenants' group is controlled by unreasonable or self-centered people. Even if not expressed, these fears are likely to be present. If they are not brought into the light and dealt with, they might cause tenants to drop out later, when the action starts.

At the close of your first meeting, assuming you have clearly identified one or more key problems that badly need to be addressed, you'll want to assign a little legal homework. For example, if your landlord has refused to repair the front door lock, someone needs to see if state or local laws require specified security equipment. Fortunately, the research you need to do shouldn't be difficult. If this book doesn't answer your questions, Chapter 20 goes into considerable detail about how you can learn more.

TIP

Bring a copy of laws that back up your position. Wavering tenants are often convinced to support a tenants' group when they see that the law is on their side. If you have a copy of your state's antiretaliation statute or repair and deduct statute, for example, it will reassure other tenants.

How to Structure Your Group

At some point, your group will need to decide how to structure itself. Do you want a formal organization, with officers, committees, chairpersons, and regular meetings? Or are you content with a looser, as-needed organization that requires less work and commitment? If you are lucky enough to have a relatively small, committed group of long-term tenants, you might be able to create a cohesive, structured organization. But in most places, the tenant population is ever-changing, and tenants are not particularly connected to each other. Most tenant organizations look less like a labor union and more like a group of neighbors responding to a particular problem.

Petition to the Landlord

Harbor View Apartments
3700 Marina Way
Shady Bay, OR 00000

September 1, 20xx

PETITION TO RENEE ECKER, LANDLORD

We are all tenants at Harbor View Apartments. We direct your attention to the following problems, and ask that prompt action be taken to correct them.

1. **Closed laundry facility.** Because advertisements for Harbor View state that there are two on-site laundry facilities, and the apartment tour includes a visit to one of the two laundry rooms, we are entitled to the use of both rooms. Since June 15, 20xx, the laundry room in the West building has been closed, forcing all tenants to use the one remaining room. There are not enough washing machines in that room to reasonably accommodate the needs of the tenants.

2. **Inadequate security.** We request that the security of Harbor View be improved. At present, there are no deadbolt locks on residents' doors, no peepholes in front doors, and no lighting (other than a softly lit decorative sign) in the front of the building. This situation is intolerable given the fact that there have recently been three burglaries at a neighboring apartment building, Sea Breeze. In addition, Officer Friday, who covers this beat on a regular basis, has informed us that there has been an increase in the number of robberies, car thefts, and incidents of vandalism in this neighborhood.

   We ask that you immediately install deadbolt locks, peepholes, and better lighting. We also ask that you consult a security specialist to develop an overall plan for improved building security.

3. **Dirty common areas.** We request that the cleanliness and maintenance of our building be improved. As the landlord, you have the responsibility under state law to keep these common areas neat and clean by maintaining them on a regular basis. The lobby, hallways, and stairways are not being cleaned on a regular basis. Specifically, the lobby has large dustballs, piles of discarded junk mail, and unwashed windows. The stairways and halls are not regularly swept and washed, and the exterior breezeways have not been thoroughly cleaned since last spring.

We would like to meet with you to discuss these issues. Please contact Andy Ableson, in Apartment 3C, within the next five days to arrange for a mutually convenient time and place. A weekday evening in the Clubhouse common room might work best. We look forward to talking with you and working out a solution to these concerns.

Signed,

[Signed by as many tenants as possible] _____

_____

_____

TIP
Contact groups that are concerned with tenants' rights. Many communities, especially those with rent control, have active tenant associations that can furnish technical and legal advice as well as publicity and moral support. Examples of tenants' rights groups in California include the San Francisco Tenants Union (SFTU.org) and Tenants Together (TenantsTogether.org); a useful resource for tenants in New York is Tenants & Neighbors (www.tandn.org). To find local tenant advocacy groups, check out the Tenant Rights section of the U.S. Department of Housing and Urban Development (HUD) website (www.hud.gov/topics/rental_assistance/tenantrights). HUD provides a wide variety of local resources, including links to tenant unions and legal aid organizations for each state; even if you don't qualify for legal aid services, you will find useful information on tenant rights on many legal aid websites. Also, be sure to see the links to tenant rights' guides by state in the Tenants section of Nolo.com.

RENT CONTROL
If you live in a city or state covered by rent control, be sure to study the law and its regulations. You might be able to bring your group's grievance before the rent board—in fact, you might be required to do so before going to court.

Petitioning the Landlord and Taking Action

Especially if you face a serious problem, your group's second meeting should be devoted to developing a strategy to deal with the landlord. First, report on what you've found out about the legal options available to you. For example, if you all are fed up with the building's lack of hot water and have determined that its temperature often falls below the minimum mandated by your state's building codes, you might have learned that it's legal to withhold rent until the situation is corrected. (See Chapter 8.) But you also might have learned that you cannot legally do this until you have notified the landlord in writing and provided a reasonable amount of time to attend to the problem. (This is a good idea, regardless of whether it's legally required or not.)

Draw up a list of your complaints and concerns, present them to the landlord, and ask for a meeting. Your letter or petition should:

- be worded politely but firmly
- clearly set out your requests, and
- ask for a response within a specific time (such as seven days).

Unless the situation is extremely serious (for example, drug dealers are shooting at each other in the parking lot, or the building's sewage systems are backing up daily), your first letter should not threaten specific repercussions if the landlord is not cooperative. Better to have your letter carry the clear implication that your group takes its requests seriously and that it will act in some as-yet-unspecified way if a favorable response is not forthcoming. To reinforce this point, it is usually best if all the tenants in the group sign the petition. See the sample Petition to the Landlord, above.

Meet With the Landlord

Follow our suggestions for negotiating, above. But be careful not to overwhelm the landlord with sheer numbers. Consider nominating one or two people to speak on behalf of the group.

If that doesn't work, follow through with mediation and then, as a final resort, sue in small claims court or take other appropriate court action.

Lawyers and Legal Research

Throughout this book, we point out instances when an attorney's advice or services might be useful. Usually, attorneys should be involved in disputes that involve lots of money, are very complicated, or whose consequences to you could be very important (like losing your home). For example, if you become involved in a lawsuit over housing discrimination, withhold rent because your rental unit is uninhabitable, or claim that your landlord's wrongful acts resulted in your being seriously injured, you'll likely benefit from a lawyer's help. Or, if you're the target of an eviction and can't abide the thought of losing, you might want to lawyer up to increase your chances of winning. This chapter explains how to work with a lawyer efficiently, ensuring that you get the most for your money.

Aside from the situations above, if you attempt to buy much legal information at the rates lawyers charge—$150 to $350 an hour—you'll quickly go broke. Fortunately, you don't need a lawyer to acquire a good working knowledge of the basic legal principles that apply to most problems with landlords. You've probably learned a lot already by reading this book. When more questions come up, turn to this chapter for advice on how to research the law for yourself.

How a Lawyer Can Help You

Here are some important ways lawyers can help tenants, besides representing them in eviction cases:

Make a quick phone call or write a letter to the landlord. For example, say your landlord persists in entering your apartment to perform nonemergency repairs upon 20-minutes' notice and ignores your complaints about these intrusions. In this case, a letter from your lawyer explaining your state's interpretation of "reasonable notice" requirements might do the trick, especially if it outlines repercussions of your landlord's continued violation of the law.

Evaluate a complicated case. If you're considering filing a lawsuit, you could ask a lawyer to evaluate its merits. This could ultimately save you a lot of money if the lawyer opines that your claim is unlikely to succeed.

Handle big lawsuits for a contingency fee. If you have a legal problem that might result in a big recovery, such as a personal injury lawsuit or discrimination charge, a lawyer might be willing to work on contingency, which means the lawyer gets paid only if you win. Some lawyers who work on contingency will require you to pay up front the costs of the lawsuit, such as filing fees, the costs of mailing and photocopying, and service fees, though.

Represent you in disputes over terms of your lease or rental agreement. If the lease or agreement has an "attorneys' fees" clause and you win the lawsuit, your landlord will end up paying your attorney bills. Lawyers are more willing to take on tenant causes when there's an attorneys' fee clause, because landlords often have deeper pockets (and possibly insurance policies) to cover litigation costs than tenants do.

Review a long-term lease before you sign it. Most people don't need to involve a lawyer when they sign a lease. But if you plan to lease a place for several years, and especially if you're adding custom provisions such as an option to purchase, the advice of a knowledgeable lawyer will be worth the expense.

Finding a Good Lawyer

Most lawyers in general practice have limited experience in landlord-tenant legal issues. (In fact, by now you might know more than many lawyers.) So if you just pick a name from an online directory, or go with the attorney who prepared your will, you're unlikely to get someone who's qualified to deal with your problem.

Unfortunately for tenants, lawyers who are thoroughly familiar with landlord-tenant law often represent property owners. Because of possible conflicts and the desire to not appear disloyal, these lawyers might be unwilling to take on tenant cases—or charge so much that tenants can't afford them anyway.

But the good news is that in every metropolitan area you can find competent tenants' lawyers who charge fairly for their services. Not only do these attorneys already know the law (you don't pay for them to research it), they understand how the landlord-tenant business works and can often suggest effective strategies that general practitioners don't even know about.

RESOURCE

Looking for a lawyer? Consider looking at one or both of these Nolo resources:

Lawyers.com. At Lawyers.com you'll find a user-friendly tool that allows you to search for attorneys in your area, who have certain areas of expertise, and who speak Spanish. You can also search for attorneys by name. Attorney profiles prominently display contact information, list topics of expertise, and show ratings—by both clients and other legal professionals.

Avvo.com. Avvo.com allows you to search by practice area and location. Whether you look for lawyers by name or expertise, you'll find listings with detailed background information, peer and client ratings, and even profile visibility.

Keep in mind that the lawyers listed on online directories have paid to have their names show up prominently on the relevant pages. That's not necessarily a bad thing—lawyers who have taken the time to build out a profile usually specify the types of cases they specialize in, which will save you the time of having to sort out who will and will not take on landlord-tenant matters. Also, most of these sites allow any client—not just happy ones—to post reviews, and attorneys usually cannot edit or remove unfavorable reviews. So if you find an attorney with overwhelmingly good reviews, it's a good sign that you might want to add that attorney to your contact list.

Compile a List of Prospects

The best way to find a suitable attorney is through one or more of these sources:

A trustworthy person or organization with experience in the landlord-tenant field. A local tenants' organization is often a good place to get a referral.

Organizations that focus on a particular area of the law, or special interest groups. Fair housing groups can give referrals for discrimination cases. Women's organizations, such as the National Women's Law Center (NWLC.org), might recommend attorneys who handle sexual harassment cases; groups representing the rights of disabled people, such as the Disability Rights Legal Center (www.thedrlc. org), might recommend attorneys who specialize in disability rights litigation.

An experienced local lawyer who practices in another area. Ask for a referral to someone who regularly represents tenants. For example, if you or a friend has been pleased with the services of a local family law practitioner, chances are that this attorney will steer you to an equally good tenants' lawyer.

Local legal aid (legal services) office. Legal aid usually has lawyers experienced in representing tenants. If you have a limited income, you might be eligible for their services. Even if you are not eligible, ask for a reference—the legal aid office might know local lawyers who are experienced, honest, and skillful.

Attorneys who write articles about landlord-tenant law in trade magazines and newspapers. Even if these lawyers live in other parts of the country, it can make sense to track them down. Experts in this increasingly complex field share information at national conferences or online, and might be able to provide top-notch referrals in your area.

Your state's continuing legal education program— usually run by a bar association, a law school, or both. These programs offer seminars and publications for attorneys and can often identify lawyers with expertise in landlord-tenant law.

Help From Nonlawyers

In some large metropolitan areas where the practice is allowed, look to tenants' organizations for help if you're sued for eviction. Some tenants' groups provide free one-on-one eviction defense help, and others offer classes or seminars on particular issues, such as eviction defense or rent withholding.

Legal typing or document preparation services, on the other hand, are private businesses that help consumers do their own legal paperwork, for fees that are usually much lower than lawyers. They normally specialize in typing your eviction papers (such as your Answer to the landlord's Complaint) so they'll be accepted by the court, arranging for filing, and then serving court papers on the landlord. Typically, they charge by the page or by the document.

Typing services can't give legal advice about your case and can't represent you in court at the eviction trial. You must decide what steps to take in your case and provide the information to complete the needed forms.

To find a nonlawyer typing service, search online or in your phone book for "Eviction Services" or "Paralegals" in your area. Ask how many years they have been in business, and also ask for and check references.

TIP

Don't forget your renters' insurance. If you followed our advice in Chapter 2 and purchased renters' insurance, you have bought legal representation if you are sued by your landlord, a guest, or other tenant for specified acts. (Your policy does not entitle you to a lawyer in an eviction or if you are the one who intends to file a lawsuit.) Contact your insurance company immediately if you are served with legal papers (usually called a Complaint and Summons).

RENT CONTROL

Where there's rent control, there are lawyers. Because many rent control laws are complicated or poorly written, attorneys are almost always on the scene. Ask the rent control board, if applicable, or visit a meeting or hearing and see who shows up on behalf of the tenants.

Shop Around

After several reliable organizations or individuals give you the names of prospective lawyers, your job has just begun. First, take a look at your list of names. If several people recommend the same attorney, start with that one.

The best way to evaluate a prospective lawyer is to arrange a brief meeting to evaluate your case. If your case has the potential for a significant monetary award (as do discrimination or personal injury cases), many lawyers will be glad to speak to you for a half hour or so at no charge, or at a reduced rate.

When you meet, briefly explain your legal problem and how much work you plan to do yourself. Try to get a feeling for the lawyer's experience and accessibility.

Does the lawyer frankly answer your questions about fees, the lawyer's experience in landlord-tenant matters, and your specific legal issue? Stay away from lawyers who make you feel uncomfortable asking questions. And be sure you understand how the lawyer charges for services. (We discuss various fee arrangements below.)

Will the lawyer provide the kind of legal help you want? If you plan to be actively involved in dealing with your legal problem, look for a lawyer who doesn't resent your participation. If it will make the lawyer uncomfortable, you have the wrong lawyer.

Does the lawyer clearly lay out all your options? A good lawyer should almost always discuss the possibility of trying to resolve your dispute through negotiation or mediation instead of immediately going to court.

Will the lawyer be accessible? This is a huge issue—probably the most common complaint against lawyers is that they don't return phone calls or email and are not available to their clients in times of need. If every time you have a question there's a delay of several days before you can talk to your lawyer, you'll lose precious time, not to mention sleep. So be sure to discuss with any lawyer how fast you can expect to have phone calls returned and how you can contact the lawyer in an emergency.

Is the lawyer experienced in your particular legal problem? If your property is in a rent-controlled city or state, be sure the lawyer knows its rent control laws and practices.

Does the lawyer represent landlords, too? Chances are that a lawyer who represents both landlords and tenants has the knowledge to do a good job for you.

TIP

Talk with other tenant clients. It's a good idea to ask for references from some of the lawyer's other tenant clients, particularly those with similar legal problems. Find out how satisfied other tenants were with the lawyer's work.

Fee Arrangements With Lawyers

How you pay your lawyer depends on the type of legal service you need and the amount of legal work involved. Once you choose a lawyer, ask for a written fee agreement explaining how fees and costs will be billed and paid. In some states, a written agreement is required by law; even if it isn't, it's always a good idea. Be sure to include an overall cap on what you can be billed for without being asked first.

If your case involves a significant amount of attorney time, and your lawyer will be delegating some of the work to a less experienced associate, paralegal, or secretary, the delegated work should be billed at a lower hourly rate. Be sure this information is recorded in your written fee agreement.

RESOURCE

Do you have a legal right to counsel in an eviction or landlord-tenant lawsuit? Almost everyone is familiar with the fact that criminal defendants have the right to an attorney even when they cannot afford one. Traditionally, this right to counsel has been limited to criminal matters. However, a growing movement guarantees legal representation to defendants in eviction lawsuits and other noncriminal (civil) matters. While the right to counsel for indigent tenants in eviction lawsuits is provided statewide in only four states (Connecticut, Maryland, Minnesota, and Washington), a growing number of cities are passing their own laws. Check the National Coalition for a Civil Right to Counsel's Status Map (www.civilrighttocounsel.org/map) to learn the status of civil right to counsel where you live.

Lawyers' Billing Practices

Lawyers charge for their services in four basic ways.

Hourly fees. In most areas, you can get competent representation for $125 to $300 an hour. Most lawyers bill in 6-, 10-, or 15-minute increments. If you're doing much of the legal legwork yourself, and just want specific questions answered, you'll probably be billed this way. Comparison shopping among lawyers can help you avoid overpaying, but only if you are comparing lawyers with similar expertise. A highly experienced tenants' attorney might be cheaper in the long run than a general practitioner, even at a higher hourly rate. The fact that the tenants' attorney is further along the learning curve means it should take less time to come up with good answers and advice.

How Legal Costs Can Mount Up

In addition to the fees they charge for their time, lawyers bill for a variety of items as well—and if you're not wary, these costs can add up quickly. Costs can include charges for:

- photocopying
- faxes
- overnight mail
- messenger service
- expert witness fees
- court filing fees
- long distance phone calls
- process servers
- work by investigators
- work by legal assistants or paralegals
- deposition transcripts
- online legal research, and
- travel.

Many lawyers absorb the cost of photocopying, faxes, local phone calls, and the like as normal office overhead—part of the cost of doing business—but that's not always the case. So in working out the fee arrangements, ask for a list of costs you'll be expected to pay. If a lawyer seems intent on nickel-and-diming you to death, look elsewhere. For example, if you learn the law office charges $3 or more for each page it copies, red flags should go up. On the other hand, it is reasonable for a lawyer to pass along expenses like court costs, process server fees, and work by investigators.

Flat fees. Sometimes a lawyer will quote you a flat fee for a specific job—for example, to defend you in an eviction lawsuit. In a flat fee agreement, you pay the same amount regardless of how much time the lawyer spends on the job. If a lawyer is highly recommended by others as trustworthy and the flat fee is moderate, this can be a great arrangement for you. You should expect to pay 50% to 100% of the fee up front.

Contingency fees. This is a percentage—commonly, one-third—of the amount the lawyer obtains for you in a negotiated settlement or through a trial. If the lawyer recovers nothing for you, you pay only for the costs of filing suit and other expenses (for example, expert fees and depositions). Contingency fees are common in personal injury and discrimination cases, but relatively unusual for eviction defense. (For more details on contingency fees, see Chapter 5.)

The landlord pays. If your lease or written rental agreement has a two-way ("loser pays") attorneys' fees provision (discussed in Chapter 2), you are entitled to recover your attorneys' fees if you win a lawsuit that concerns the meaning or implementation of that agreement. The clause does not cover fees if the dispute arose independently of the lease or rental contract, such as a discrimination claim, personal injury lawsuit, or sexual harassment case. If you have a strong case that's backed up with a loser-pays clause, many lawyers will take your case for little or nothing, in the expectation that they will get paid by the losing landlord.

Saving on Legal Fees

Here are some key ways to hold down the cost of legal services:

Do your own research. Read any consumer-oriented legal materials in your state or city, such as informational booklets prepared by your state's attorney general's office or consumer protection agency. If your state or locality has rent control, go to the administration website, which will probably be full of information. The HUD website (HUD. gov) includes many useful links for each state. Search "[name of your state] tenant rights" to get started. Also, see the suggestions in "Doing Your Own Legal Research," below, as to how you can easily find relevant statutes, ordinances, and court decisions that affect your problem.

Be organized. Especially when you are paying by the hour, it's important to gather important documents, write a short chronology of events, and concisely explain a problem to your lawyer. Gather and copy important documents, such as your lease or rental agreement, move-in letter from your landlord, correspondence with the landlord, repair requests, and other records. Keep the originals for your records, and have the copies ready to give to your lawyer.

Be prepared before you meet your lawyer. Whenever possible, put your questions in writing and email them to your lawyer before all meetings or phone conversations. That way your lawyer can be prepared to answer your questions and won't have to schedule another conference or phone conversation. Early preparation also helps focus the meeting so there is less chance of digressing (at your expense) into unrelated topics.

Carefully review lawyer bills. Like everyone else, lawyers make mistakes. For example, a ".1" of an hour (six minutes) might be transposed into a "1." (one hour) when the data are entered into the billing system. That's $200 instead of $20 if your lawyer charges $200 per hour. Don't hesitate to politely question your bill. You have the right to a clear explanation of costs.

Resolving Problems With Your Lawyer

If you see a problem emerging with your lawyer, don't just sit back and fume; call, email, or write to your lawyer. Whatever it is that rankles—a shockingly high bill or a missed deadline—have an honest discussion about your feelings.

Your Rights as a Client

As a client, you have the right to expect the following:

- courteous treatment by your lawyer and staff members
- an itemized statement of services rendered and a full advance explanation of billing practices
- charges for agreed-upon fees only
- prompt responses to phone calls, emails, and letters
- confidential legal conferences, free from unwarranted interruptions
- up-to-date information on the status of your case
- diligent and competent legal representation, and
- clear answers to all questions.

If you can't frankly discuss these sometimes sensitive matters with your lawyer, change lawyers. If you don't, you'll surely waste money on unnecessary legal fees and risk having matters turn out badly.

If you decide to change lawyers, be sure to fire your old lawyer—in writing—before you hire a new one. If you don't, you could find yourself being billed by two lawyers at the same time. Get all important legal documents back from the first lawyer, as well as any remaining retainer money you might have paid. Tell your new lawyer what your old one has done to date and pass on the file.

Here are some tips on resolving specific problems:

- If you have a dispute over fees, the local bar association might be able to mediate it for you, although the extent to which they are willing to go after one of their own varies greatly.
- If a lawyer has violated legal ethics—for example, had an undisclosed conflict of interest, overbilled you, or didn't represent you zealously—the state agency that licenses lawyers might discipline or even disbar the lawyer. Although lawyer oversight groups are typically biased in favor of the legal profession, they will often take action if your lawyer has done something seriously wrong.
- When a major mistake has been made— for example, a lawyer missed the deadline for filing your papers in response to an eviction lawsuit—you can sue for malpractice. Many lawyers carry malpractice insurance; insurance companies typically offer settlements out of court.

Doing Your Own Legal Research

When faced with a serious, complex, or expensive problem with your landlord, you'll probably need more information. For example, if you were assaulted in the hall of your building by an intruder, and want to know to what extent you might be able to hold your landlord responsible, you'll almost surely want to look up your state court decisions involving similar incidents.

Using this book is a good way to educate yourself about the law that affects your rights as a tenant. But because landlord-tenant issues involve the laws and court decisions of all the states, plus the ordinances of many thousands of municipalities, no one book can do the whole job.

Lawyers aren't the only source for legal help. You can do a lot on your own. You can get the text of key federal and state statutes free on many states' websites (check both the state's official website as well as the state legislature's website). Rules put out by federal and state regulatory agencies are usually available online as well. Rent control ordinances are all online.

Most of the time, your research needs can be met by searching online (more on that below). In a few instances, however, the materials you need will not be available, or will not be free. For example:

- **Practice guides for lawyers.** These are the lawyers' best friends, replete with summaries, sample letters, and forms. Lawyers pay hefty fees for online access. Print books are usually available in public or private (law school) libraries.
- **Form books.** Like practice guides, these include forms designed for many situations. Access is subscription-based, though they might also be in a local physical library.
- **Law reviews and journals.** If you want to get "the big picture," or learn about cutting-edge issues and arguments, you'll need to consult these scholarly works. They are generally not available for free—but some might be in your local library.

If you want access to one of the resources mentioned above, your first step is to find a law library that's open to the public. You might find such a library in your county courthouse or at your state capitol. Publicly funded law schools generally permit the public to use their libraries, and some private law schools grant access to their libraries— sometimes for a modest fee.

Don't overlook the reference department of the public library if you're in a large city. Many large public libraries have a fairly decent legal research collection. Your library might even provide access to the legal research collection online to patrons with a library account. Also, ask about using the law library in your own lawyer's office. Some lawyers, on request, will share their books with their clients.

RESOURCE

Recommended reading on legal research. We don't have space here to show you how to do your own legal research in anything approaching a comprehensive fashion. To get started, go to Nolo's website at Nolo.com/ legal-research. Here you'll find information on legal research, advice on finding local ordinances and court cases, and more. To go further, we recommend *Legal Research: How to Find & Understand the Law,* by the Editors of Nolo (Nolo). This nontechnical book gives easy-to-use, step-by-step instructions on how find legal information.

Statutes and Ordinances

Every tenant and every landlord is governed by a mix of state, local, and federal law, with state law almost always being the most important. In some areas, such as discrimination, federal, state, and local laws overlap. When this happens, the laws that give tenants the most protection usually prevail.

When you're beginning the search for an answer to a legal question, it's usually best to start by looking for a state, federal, or local law that covers your issue.

State Statutes

State law regulates, among other things, rent rules, deposits, your right to privacy, housing standards, maintenance responsibilities, and eviction procedures. Your state consumer protection agency or attorney general might provide helpful publications or phone advice summarizing and explaining these laws. (Find yours at www.usa.gov/state-consumer.)

A good place to begin is by using the legal references (citations) to your state's key landlord-tenant laws contained in this book. Armed with the citation, go online to your state's official website (www.[state abbreviation].gov). Every state has posted its statutes online, although each has presented them in a unique way, so we can't give you precise directions for locating a law in your state. But in general, you'll find links to state legislation or state laws, and once in that section of the site, you should be able to plug in your citation and get to the law you want to read.

The website maintained by the Cornell Legal Information Institute (www.law.cornell.edu) also provides access to federal and state statutes, cases, and informative articles.

Finding out how courts have interpreted the law you're dealing with is significantly more involved than finding statutes. You might have to go to a physical law library and read the law in an "annotated code" collection (annotated code sets aren't available for free online). These are books that include not only the statutes, but cases that have involved them. You might find similar cases to yours, which could be very helpful. Annotated codes have comprehensive indexes by topic, and are kept up to date with paperback supplements ("pocket parts") stuck inside the back cover of each volume.

Some case research tools are available online for free, such as:

- Google Scholar (scholar.google.com)
- Justia (justia.com)
- CourtListener (courtlistener.com), and
- FindLaw (https://caselaw.findlaw.com).

Many of these options allow you to search for case law by state and keyword (such as "eviction"), and a list of cases will pop up. However, figuring out which cases are relevant and still good law is not an easy task. Another option might be to sign up for a free trial of a subscription-based online legal research program, such as FastCase

(fastcase.com). Beware, though: Most paid research programs are quite expensive if you forget to cancel your free trial, and learning how to use them can be challenging.

> **CAUTION**
> **Never rely on old law.** Many laws change every year. Make sure you are up to date by referring to the insert you'll almost always find inside the back cover of code books. (If there isn't an insert, it's because the hardbound book was published that year and is completely current.) These pocket parts, which are organized by code number, should contain all law changes through the end of your state's last legislative session.

Local Ordinances

Local ordinances, such as rent control rules, noise regulations, health and safety standards, requirements for interest on tenants' security deposits, and antidiscrimination rules will also affect your tenancy. Many municipalities have local ordinances online—just search for the name of a particular city. Sometimes this presence is nothing more than a not-so-slick public relations page, but sometimes it includes a large body of information, including local ordinances available for searching and downloading. Be sure to check out State and Local Government on the Net (www.statelocalgov.net), and the municode library (https://library.municode.com).

Finally, your local public library or office of the city attorney, mayor, or city manager can provide information on local ordinances that affect tenants. If you rent in a city with rent control, be sure to get a copy of the ordinance, as well as all rules issued by the rent board covering rent increases and hearings.

Federal Statutes and Regulations

Congress has enacted laws, and federal agencies such as the U.S. Department of Housing and Urban Development (HUD) have adopted regulations, that cover important aspects of landlord-tenant law.

Common Abbreviations in Case Citations		
Abbreviation	**Title**	**Courts Covered**
A., A.2d, and A.3d	Atlantic Reporter (first, second, and third series)	Connecticut, Delaware, the District of Columbia, Maine, Maryland, New Hampshire, New Jersey, Pennsylvania, Rhode Island, and Vermont
N.E., N.E.2d, and N.E.3d	North Eastern Reporter (first, second, and third series)	Illinois, Indiana, Massachusetts, New York (except for appellate court decisions), and Ohio
N.Y.S. and N.Y.S.2d	New York Supplement (first and second series)	New York appellate court
N.W. and N.W.2d	North Western Reporter (first and second series)	Iowa, Michigan, Minnesota, Nebraska, North Dakota, South Dakota, and Wisconsin
P., P.2d, and P.3d	Pacific Reporter (first, second, and third series)	Alaska, Arizona, California (except for appellate court decisions), Colorado, Hawaii, Idaho, Kansas, Montana, Nevada, New Mexico, Oklahoma, Oregon, Utah, Washington, and Wyoming
Cal. Rptr., Cal. Rptr.2d, and Cal.Rptr.3d	California Reporter (first, second, and third series)	California appellate court
S.E. and S.E.2d	South Eastern Reporter (first and second series)	Georgia, North Carolina, South Carolina, Virginia, and West Virginia
So., So.2d, and So.3d	Southern Reporter (first, second, and third series)	Alabama, Florida, Louisiana, and Mississippi
S.W., S.W.2d, and S.W.3d	South Western Reporter (first, second, and third series)	Arkansas, Kentucky, Missouri, Tennessee, and Texas
U.S.	United States Reports	U.S. Supreme Court
S.Ct.	Supreme Court Reporter	U.S. Supreme Court
F., F.2d, and F.3d	Federal Reporter (first, second, and third series)	Federal appellate courts
F. Supp., F.Supp.2d, and F.Supp.3d	Federal Supplement (first, second, and third series)	Federal trial courts

Examples include antidiscrimination laws, wage and hour rules that affect the employment of tenant-managers, and statutes requiring the disclosure of environmental health hazards.

Federal laws affecting tenants are contained in a multivolume series of books called the U.S. Code. It consists of 53 separate numbered titles. Each title covers a specific subject matter. For example, the federal Fair Housing Acts are contained in title 42 and begin with Section 3601.

Federal regulations that explain the law in detail are published in the Code of Federal Regulations (C.F.R.), organized by subject into 50 separate titles. For example, regulations issued by the Environmental Protection Agency interpreting the federal lead paint legislation ("Title Ten") can be found in Title 24, Part 35, and Title 40, Part 745.

To access the U.S. Code online, visit the Office of the Law Revision Counsel's website at https://uscode.house.gov, or see the Cornell Legal Information Institute at www.law.cornell.edu.

Court Decisions

Sometimes the answer to a legal question cannot be found in a statute. This happens when:

- court cases and opinions have greatly expanded or explained the statute, taking it beyond its obvious or literal meaning, or
- the law that applies to your question has been made by judges, not legislators.

Court Decisions That Explain Statutes

Statutes and ordinances rarely explain themselves. For example, a state law might guarantee you the right to housing that is weatherproofed, but that statute might not specify if that means your landlord must provide storm windows. However, other tenants might have asked the same question and ended up in court. If a judge interpreted the statute and wrote an opinion on the matter, that written opinion, once published, will become the law as much as the statute itself. If a higher court (an appellate court) has also examined the question, then its opinion becomes the law statewide.

To find out whether written court decisions interpret a particular statute or ordinance you're interested in, a good place to start is an annotated code (discussed above). If a case that seems to answer your question or relate to your problem is listed in the code, your first step is to find and read it.

Next, if you find a court decision that's useful to your case, make sure the decision is still good law—that a more recent opinion from a higher court has not reached a different conclusion. To do this, use a set of books known as *Shepard's*. Explaining how to do this takes more space than is available here, but a friendly law librarian can guide you. *Legal Research: How to Find & Understand the Law*, by the Editors of Nolo (Nolo), has a good, easy-to-follow explanation of how to use the *Shepard's* system to expand and update your research (*Shepard's* is not available online).

Court Decisions That Make Law

Some laws that govern your rights will not have a starting point in a statute or ordinance. These laws, which are entirely court-made, are known as common law. An example of common law in many states is the landlord's responsibility to provide tenants with habitable housing, discussed in Chapter 8 (over the years, legislatures caught up with the courts and wrote statutes that mirrored, or "codified," the court decisions).

Researching common law is more difficult than researching statutory law, because you do not have the launching pad of a statute or ordinance. But with a little perseverance, you can find your way to the court cases that have developed and explained the legal concept you wish to understand. For example, if you're interested in a landlord's liability for burglary committed after the landlord installed a faulty lock, try using a search engine to see if you get results that include cases (or reports of cases). This is an area where you'll be hampered if you are relying solely on free online resources.

At the physical law library, you will have access to materials that will help you get to the relevant cases. A good beginning is to ask the librarian for any lawyer's practice guides in the field of landlord-tenant law (these are not available for free online). These outlines of the law, which are written to provide basic information to lawyers, are usually up to date. Because lawyers' practice guides are so popular, they are usually kept behind the reference counter and cannot be taken out of the library.

How to Read a Case Citation

If you find a citation to a case that looks important, you might want to read the opinion. You'll need the title of the case and its citation, which is like an address for the set of books, volume, and page where the case can be found. Ask the law librarian for help.

Although it might look about as decipherable as hieroglyphics, once understood, a case citation gives lots of useful information in a small space. It tells you the names of the people or companies involved, the volume of the reporter (series of books) in which the case is published, the page number on which it begins, and the year in which the case was decided.

> **EXAMPLE:** *Smith v. Jones Int'l,* 123 N.Y.S.2d 456 (1994). Smith and Jones are the names of the parties having the legal dispute. The case is reported in volume 123 of the New York Supplement, Second Series, beginning on page 456; the court issued the decision in 1994.

Law Review Articles

Law schools and other state and local bar associations publish periodicals that might contain timely articles on legal issues that affect tenants. But academic journals rarely contain useful, practical information. Local bar association journals and other publications aimed at practicing lawyers are likely to be much more helpful.

Most states publish their own official state reports. All published state court decisions are also included in seven regional reporters. There are also special reports for U.S. Supreme Court and other federal court decisions. (See "Common Abbreviations in Case Citations," above.)

LexisNexis and Westlaw: Helpful but Costly

Two companies, West Publishing and Lexis, offer full-scale legal research services that make it relatively easy to search a huge database of statutes, court decisions, regulations, and legal articles. The cost is very high.

If you are not connected with a large law office or law school, you will likely find it difficult to get access to either Westlaw or Lexis for free. A small but growing number of law libraries or public libraries, however, offer these services.

Keep in mind that it takes time and training to learn how to navigate these legal research systems efficiently. However, if you are already savvy on how to use computerized information retrieval services, you might want to give it a try.

State Landlord-Tenant Law Charts

How to Use the State Landlord-Tenant Law Charts

The State Landlord-Tenant Law Charts are comprehensive, 50-state charts that give you
two kinds of information:

- citations for key statutes and cases, which you can use if you want to read the
  law yourself or look for more information (see the legal research discussion in
  Chapter 20), and
- the state rules themselves, such as notice periods and deposit limits—in other words,
  what the statutes and cases say.

When you're looking for information for your state, simply find your state along the
left-hand list on the chart, and read to the right—you'll see the statute or case, and the rule.

State Landlord-Tenant Statutes

Here are some of the key statutes pertaining to landlord-tenant law in each state. In some states, important legal principles are contained in court opinions, not codes or statutes. Court-made law is not reflected in this chart. Note that because some states exempt certain occupancies, such as rentals of mobile homes and short-term rentals, from their general landlord-tenant statutes, it's a good idea to confirm that these statutes apply to your rental situation. You'll find the details about each state's exemption statutes, if any, in the following chart titled "State Landlord-Tenant Law Exemption Statutes."

State	Statute	State	Statute
Alabama	Ala. Code §§ 35-9-1 to 35-9-100; 35-9A-101 to 35-9A-603	Louisiana	La. Rev. Stat. §§ 9:3251 to 9:3261.2; La. Civ. Code art. 2002; 2668 to 2729
Alaska	Alaska Stat. §§ 34.03.010 to 34.03.380	Maine	Me. Rev. Stat. tit. 14, §§ 6000 to 6046; tit. 22, § 1331; tit. 35-A, § 10117
Arizona	Ariz. Rev. Stat. §§ 12-1171 to 12-1183; 33-301 to 33-381; 33-1301 to 33-1381; 36-1637	Maryland	Md. Code Real Prop., §§ 8-101 to 8-604; 8-901 to 8-911; 14-126; 14-801 to 14-806
Arkansas	Ark. Code §§ 18-16-101 to 18-16-306; 18-16-501 to 18-16-509; 18-17-101 to 18-17-913	Massachusetts	Mass. Gen. Laws ch. 111, §§ 127F, 127L; ch. 186, §§ 1A to 31; ch. 186a, §§ 1 to 6; ch. 239, §§ 1 to 15
California	Cal. Civ. Code §§ 789.3; 790 to 793; 827; 1925 to 1934; 1940 to 1954.05; 1954.50 to 1954.605; 1961 to 1995.340; 2079.10a; Cal. Civ. Proc. Code §§ 1159 to 1161, 1161.2 to 1161.5, 1161b to 1179a; Cal. Health & Safety Code §§ 25400.28; 26147 to 26148; Cal. Bus. & Prof. Code § 8538; Cal. Gov't Code §§ 8589.45, 53165.1	Michigan	Mich. Comp. Laws §§ 125.530; 554.131 to 554.201; 554.601 to 554.641; 600.2918
		Minnesota	Minn. Stat. §§ 504B.001 to 504B.471
		Mississippi	Miss. Code §§ 89-7-1 to 89-7-125; 89-8-1 to 89-8-45
		Missouri	Mo. Rev. Stat. §§ 441.005 to 441.920; 442.055; 535.010 to 535.300
Colorado	Colo. Rev. Stat. §§ 13-40-101 to 13-40-123; 13-40.1-101 to 13-40.1-102; 38-12-101 to 38-12-106; 38-12-301 to 38-12-1007; 38-12-1201 to 38-12-1205	Montana	Mont. Code §§ 7-1-111; 70-24-101 to 70-26-110; 70-27-101 to 70-27-212; 75-10-1305
Connecticut	Conn. Gen. Stat. §§ 19a-37, 47a-1 to 47a-75; 2023 Conn. Legis. Serv. P.A. 23-207 (S.B. 998)	Nebraska	Neb. Rev. Stat. §§ 69-2301 to 69-2314; 76-1401 to 76-1449
Delaware	Del. Code tit. 4, § 1308; tit. 25, §§ 5101 to 5907	Nevada	Nev. Rev. Stat. §§ 40.215 to 40.425; 118A.010 to 118A.530, 2023 Nevada Laws Ch. 118 (S.B. 223)
Dist. of Columbia	D.C. Code §§ 42-3201 to 42-3651.08; D.C. Mun. Regs., tit. 14, §§ 300 to 399	New Hampshire	N.H. Rev. Stat. §§ 477:4-g; 540:1 to 540:30; 540-A:1 to 540-A:8; 540-B:1 to 540-B:10
Florida	Fla. Stat. §§ 83.40 to 83.683; 125.0103; 404.056; 715.10 to 715.111	New Jersey	N.J. Stat. §§ 2A:18-51 to 2A:18-61.67; 2A:18-72 to 2A:18-84; 2A:42-1 to 2A:42-96; 2A:42-144 to 2A:42-148; 46:8-1 to 46:8-64; 55:13A-1 to 55:13A-31; N.J.A.C. §§ 5:10-1.1 to 5:10-29.1
Georgia	Ga. Code §§ 44-1-16; 44-7-1 to 44-7-81		
Hawaii	Haw. Rev. Stat. §§ 368-1 to 368-4; 521-1 to 521-83		
Idaho	Idaho Code §§ 6-301 to 6-324; 55-208 to 55-308; 55-314	New Mexico	N.M. Stat. §§ 47-8-1 to 47-8-51; N.M. Admin. Code § 20.4.5.13
Illinois	420 Ill. Comp. Stat. §§ 46/25, 46/30; 425 Ill. Comp. Stat. § 60/3; 430 Ill. Comp. Stat. § 135/10; 735 Ill. Comp. Stat. §§ 5/9-201 to 5/9-321; 765 Ill. Comp. Stat. §§ 705/0.01 to 742/30; 750/1 to 750/35; 755/1 to 755/999; 1085/35	New York	N.Y. Real Prop. Law §§ 220 to 238-a; Real Prop. Acts §§ 701 to 853; Mult. Dwell. Law (all); Mult. Res. Law (all); Gen. Oblig. Law §§ 7-101 to 7-109; N.Y. Envtl. Conserv. Law § 27-2405; N.Y. Exec. Law §§ 170-d, 296; N.Y. Penal Law §§ 241.00 to 241.05; N.Y. Unconsol. Law §§ 8581 to 8597 (Emergency Housing Rent Control Law); 8601 to 8617 (Local Emergency Housing Rent Control Act); 8621 to 8634 (Emergency Tenant Protection Act); 9 NYCRR § 466.15; N.Y. Pub. Serv. § 104
Indiana	Ind. Code §§ 8-1-2-1.2; 32-31-1-1 to 32-31-11-5; 36-1-24.2-1 to 36-1-24.2-4		
Iowa	Iowa Code §§ 562A.1 to 562A.37		
Kansas	Kan. Stat. §§ 58-2501 to 58-2573; 58-25,127; 58-25,137	North Carolina	N.C. Gen. Stat. §§ 42-1 to 42-14.2; 42-14.4 to 42-14.6; 42-25.6 to 42-76; 62-110
Kentucky	Ky. Rev. Stat. §§ 224.1-410; 383.010 to 383.715; 902 Ky. Admin. Regs. 47:200	North Dakota	N.D. Cent. Code §§ 23-13-15; 47-06-04; 47-16-01 to 47-16-41; 47-17-01 to 47-17-05

State Landlord-Tenant Statutes (continued)

Ohio	Ohio Rev. Code §§ 1923.01 to 1923.15, 5321.01 to 5321.20	**Texas**	Tex. Prop. Code §§ 91.001 to 92.355
Oklahoma	Okla. Stat. tit. 41, §§ 101 to 201; tit. 74, § 324.11a	**Utah**	Utah Code §§ 57-17-1 to 57-17-5; 57-20-1; 57-22-1 to 57-22-7; 57-27-201; 78B-6-801 to 78B-6-816
Oregon	Or. Rev. Stat. §§ 90.100 to 90.228; 90.243 to 90.265; 90.295 to 90.493; 105.005 to 105.168; 105.190; 479.270 to 479.280; 479.290; 479.300; 479.305; Or. Rev. Stat. Ch. 13, § 55; Or. Rev. Stat. Ch. 82, § 2	**Vermont**	Vt. Stat. tit. 9, §§ 4451 to 4475
		Virginia	Va. Code §§ 54.1-2108.1; 55.1-1200 to 55.1-1262
		Washington	Wash. Rev. Code §§ 43.31.605; 59.04.010 to 59.18.912; 59.24.010 to 59.24.060
Pennsylvania	68 Pa. Cons. Stat. §§ 250.101 to 399.19		
Rhode Island	R.I. Gen. Laws §§ 34-18-1 to 34-18-60; 42-128.1-14	**West Virginia**	W. Va. Code §§ 37-6-1 to 37-6-30; 37-6A-1 to 37-6A-6; 37-7-1 to 37-7-5; W. Va. Code St. R. § 64-92-7
South Carolina	S.C. Code §§ 5-25-1330; 27-40-10 to 27-40-940		
		Wisconsin	Wis. Stat. §§ 704.01 to 704.95; Wis. Admin. Code ATCP §§ 134.01 to 134.10
South Dakota	S.D. Codified Laws §§ 43-32-1 to 43-32-36		
Tennessee	Tenn. Code §§ 66-7-101 to 66-7-102; 66-7-104; 66-7-106 to 66-7-107; 66-7-109 to 66-7-112; 66-28-101 to 66-28-522	**Wyoming**	Wyo. Stat. §§ 1-21-1001 to 1-21-1017; 1-21-1201 to 1-21-1211; 1-21-1301 to 1-21-1304; 34-2-128 to 34-2-129

State Landlord-Tenant Exemption Statutes

Your state's general landlord-tenant statutes (listed in the "State Landlord-Tenant Statutes" chart above) might not apply to all types of rentals and landlord-tenant relationships: Most states define what a rental is for purposes of the statutes. Other states might not define what a rental is, but instead exempt certain types of occupancies from the general landlord-tenant statutes. Some states do both. To check whether your state's general landlord-tenant statutes apply to your situation, review the statutes listed in the "State Landlord-Tenant Statutes" chart for any definition of what your state considers a rental. Next, you'll need to find out whether your situation falls within any exemptions from the general landlord-tenant statutes. This chart provides information about the exemptions that are most relevant to readers of this book. If your state does not have an exemption statute, you'll see "No statute" written in the Exemptions column.

State	Exemption Statute	Exemptions
Alabama	Ala. Code §§ 35-9A-122, 35-9A-601	1. Occupancy under a contract of sale of a dwelling unit or the property of which it is a part, if the occupant is the purchaser or a person who succeeds to the interest of the purchaser. 2. Occupancy by a member of a social organization in the portion of a structure operated for the benefit of the organization. 3. Transient occupancy in a hotel, motel, or lodgings. 4. Occupancy by an employee of a landlord whose right to occupancy is conditional upon employment at the premises. 5. Occupancy under a rental agreement covering premises rented by the occupant primarily for agricultural purposes. 6. Continuation of occupancy by the seller or a member of the seller's family for a period of not more than 36 months after the sale of a dwelling unit or the property of which it is a part. 7. Rental agreements most recently entered into, extended, or renewed before January 1, 2007.
Alaska	Alaska Stat. §§ 34.03.330, 34.03.370	1. Occupancy under a contract of sale of a dwelling unit or the property of which it is a part if the occupant is the purchaser or a person who succeeds to the interest of a purchaser. 2. Occupancy by a member of a social organization in the portion of a structure operated for the benefit of the organization. 3. Transient occupancy in a hotel, motel, lodgings, or other transient facility. 4. Occupancy by an employee of a landlord whose right to occupancy is conditioned upon employment substantially for services, maintenance, or repair to the premises. 5. Occupancy under a rental agreement covering premises used by the occupant primarily for agricultural purposes. 6. Occupancy under a rental agreement covering premises used as part of a transitional or supportive housing program that is sponsored or operated by a public corporation or by a nonprofit corporation and that provides shelter and related support service. 7. Any rental agreement, lease, or tenancy most recently entered into, extended, or renewed before March 19, 1974.
Arizona	Ariz. Rev. Stat. § 33-1308	1. Occupancy under a contract of sale of a dwelling unit or the property of which it is a part, if the occupant is the purchaser or a person who succeeds to the purchaser's interest. 2. Occupancy by a member of a social organization in the portion of a structure operated for the benefit of the organization. 3. Transient occupancy in a hotel, motel, or recreational lodging. 4. Occupancy by an employee of a landlord as a manager or custodian whose right to occupancy is conditional upon employment at the premises. 5. Occupancy in or operation of public housing as authorized, provided, or conducted under or pursuant to any federal law or regulation.

State Landlord-Tenant Exemption Statutes (continued)

State	Exemption Statute	Exemption
Arkansas	Ark. Code § 18-17-202	1. Occupancy under a contract of sale of a dwelling unit or the property of which it is a part, if the occupant is the purchaser or a person who succeeds to the purchaser's interest. 2. Occupancy by a member of a social organization in the portion of a structure operated for the benefit of the organization. 3. Transient occupancy in a hotel, motel, or other accommodations subject to any sales tax on lodging. 4. Occupancy by an employee of a landlord whose right to occupancy is conditional upon employment in and about the premises. 5. Occupancy under a rental agreement covering the premises used by the occupant primarily for agricultural purposes. 6. Residence, whether temporary or not, at a public or private charitable or emergency protective shelter.
California	Cal. Civ. Code § 1940	1. Transient occupancy in a hotel, motel, residence club, or other facility. 2. Occupancy at a hotel or motel where the innkeeper retains a right of access to and control of the dwelling unit and the hotel or motel provides or offers certain services.
Colorado	Colo. Rev. Stat. § 38-12-511	1. Occupancy under a contract of sale of a dwelling unit or the property of which it is a part, if the occupant is the purchaser, seller, or a person who succeeds to the purchaser's or seller's interest. 2. Occupancy by a member of a social organization in the portion of a structure operated for the benefit of the organization. 3. Transient occupancy in a hotel or motel that lasts less than 30 days. 4. Occupancy by an employee or independent contractor whose right to occupancy is conditional upon performance of services for an employer or contractor. 5. Occupancy in a structure that is located within an unincorporated area of a county, does not receive water, heat, and sewer services from a public entity, and is rented for recreational purposes, such as a hunting cabin, yurt, hut, or other similar structure. 6. Occupancy under rental agreement covering a residential premises used by the occupant primarily for agricultural purpose. 7. Any relationship between the owner of a mobile home park and the owner of a mobile home situated in the park.
Connecticut	Conn. Gen. Stat. § 47a-2	1. Occupancy under a contract of sale of a dwelling unit or the property of which such unit is a part, if the occupant is the purchaser or a person who succeeds to the purchaser's interest. 2. Occupancy by a member of a social organization in the portion of a structure operated for the benefit of such organization. 3. Transient occupancy in a hotel, motel, or similar lodging. 4. Occupancy by a personal care assistant or other person who is employed by a person with a disability to assist and support such disabled person with daily living activities or housekeeping chores and is provided dwelling space in the personal residence of such disabled person as a benefit or condition of such employment.
Delaware	Del. Code tit. 25, §§ 5101, 5102	1. Residence at an institution where such residence is merely incidental to detention or to the provision of medical, geriatric, educational, counseling, religious, or similar services. 2. Residence by a member of a fraternal organization in a structure operated for the benefit of the organization. 3. Residence in a hotel, motel, cubicle hotel, or other similar lodgings

State Landlord-Tenant Exemption Statutes (continued)

State	Exemption Statute	Exemption
Delaware (continued)		4. Nonrenewable rental agreements of 120 days or less for any calendar year for a dwelling located within the boundaries of Broadkill Hundred, Lewes-Rehoboth Hundred, Indian River Hundred, Baltimore Hundred, and Cedar Creek Hundred. 5. Rental agreements for ground upon which improvements were constructed or installed by the tenant and used as a dwelling, where the tenant retains ownership or title thereto, or obtains title to existing improvement on the property. 6. Residence in a certified recovery house.
District of Columbia	D.C. Code § 42-3502.05	1. Rental units operated by a foreign government as a residence for diplomatic personnel. 2. Rental units in an establishment that has as its primary purpose providing diagnostic care and treatment of diseases. 3. Dormitories. Also: Following a determination by the Rent Administrator, any rental intended for use as long-term temporary housing by families with 1 or more members that satisfies each of the following requirements: A. the rental is occupied by families that, at the time of their initial occupancy, have had incomes at or below 50% of the District median income for families of the size in question for the immediately preceding 12 months B. the provider of the rental is a nonprofit charitable organization that operates the rental on a strictly not-for-profit basis; and C. the housing provider offers a comprehensive social services program to resident families.
Florida	Fla. Stat. § 83.42	1. Occupancy under a contract of sale of a dwelling unit or the property of which it is a part in which the buyer has paid at least 12 months' rent or in which the buyer has paid at least 1 month's rent and a deposit of at least 5 percent of the purchase price of the property. 2. Transient occupancy in a hotel, condominium, motel, roominghouse, or similar public lodging, or transient occupancy in a mobile home park.
Georgia	No statute	
Hawaii	Haw. Rev. Stat. § 521-7	1. Residence in a structure directly controlled and managed by: A. the University of Hawaii or any other university or college in the State for housing its own students or faculty or residence in a structure erected on land leased from the university or college by a nonprofit corporation for the exclusive purpose of housing students or faculty of the college or university; or B. a private dorm management company that offers a minimum of 50 beds to students of any college, university, or other institution of higher education in the State. 2. Occupancy under a bona fide contract of sale of the dwelling unit or the property of which it is a part where the tenant is, or succeeds to the interest of, the purchaser. 3. Residence by a member of a fraternal organization in a structure operated without profit for the benefit of the organization. 4. Transient occupancy on a day-to-day basis in a hotel or motel. 5. Occupancy by an employee of the owner or landlord whose right to occupancy is conditional upon that employment for a period of up to four years, pursuant to a plan for the transfer of the dwelling unit or the property of which it is a part to the occupant. 6. A lease of improved residential land for a term of 15 years or more. 7. Occupancy by the prospective purchaser after an accepted offer to purchase and prior to the actual transfer of the owner's right. 8. Occupancy by the seller of residential real property after the transfer of the seller's ownership rights.
Idaho	No statute	

State Landlord-Tenant Exemption Statutes (continued)		
State	**Exemption Statute**	**Exemption**
Illinois	No statute	
Indiana	Ind. Code § 32-31-2.9-4	1. Occupancy under a contract of sale of a rental unit or the property of which the rental unit is a part if the occupant is the purchaser or a person who succeeds to the purchaser's interest. 2. Occupancy by a member of a social organization in the part of a structure operated for the benefit of the organization. 3. Transient occupancy in a hotel, motel, or other lodging. 4. Occupancy by an employee of a landlord whose right to occupancy is conditional upon employment at the premises. 5. Rental agreements covering property used by the occupant primarily for agricultural purposes.
Iowa	Iowa Code §§ 562A.5, 562A.37	1. Occupancy under a contract of sale of a dwelling unit or the property of which it is a part, if the occupant is the purchaser or a person who succeeds to the purchaser's interest. 2. Occupancy by a member of a social organization in the portion of a structure operated for the benefit of the organization. 3. Transient occupancy in a hotel, motel, or other similar lodgings. 4. Occupancy by an employee of a landlord whose right to occupancy is conditional upon employment at the premises. 5. Rental agreements covering premises used by the occupant primarily for agricultural purposes. 6. Rental agreements most recently entered into, extended, or renewed on or before January 1, 1979.
Kansas	Kan. Stat. §§ 58-2541, 58-2573	1. Occupancy under a contract of sale of a dwelling unit or the property of which it is a part, if the occupant is the purchaser or a person who succeeds to the purchaser's interest. 2. Occupancy by a member of a social organization in the portion of a structure operated for the benefit of the organization. 3. Transient occupancy in a hotel, motel, or roominghouse. 4. Occupancy by an employee of a landlord whose right to occupancy is conditional upon employment at the premises. 5. Occupancy under a rental agreement covering premises used by the occupant primarily for agricultural purposes. 6. Any rental agreement most recently entered into, extended, or modified before July 1, 1975.
Kentucky	Ky. Rev. Stat. § 383.535	1. Occupancy under a contract of sale of a dwelling unit or the property of which it is a part, if the occupant is the purchaser or a person who succeeds to the purchaser's interest. 2. Occupancy by a member of a social organization in the portion of a structure operated for the benefit of the organization. 3. Transient occupancy in a hotel, or motel, or lodgings subject to state transient lodgings or room occupancy excise tax act. 4. Occupancy by an employee of a landlord whose right to occupancy is conditional upon employment at the premises. 5. Occupancy of a dwelling located on land devoted to the production of livestock, livestock products, poultry, poultry products, or the growing of tobacco or other crops.
Louisiana	No statute	
Maine	No statute	

State Landlord-Tenant Exemption Statutes (continued)

State	Exemption Statute	Exemption
Maryland	Md. Code Real Prop. § 8-201	Tenancies arising after the sale of owner-occupied residential property where the seller and purchaser agree that the seller may remain in possession of the property for a period of not more than 60 days after the settlement.
Massachusetts	No statute	
Michigan	Mich. Comp. Laws § 554.601	1. Occupancy in a motel, motor home, or other tourist accommodation, when used as a temporary accommodation for guests or tourists.
	Mich. Comp. Laws § 554.632	2. Premises used as the principal place of residence of the owner and rented occasionally during temporary absences.
Minnesota	No statute	
Mississippi	Miss. Code § 89-8-3	1. Occupancy under a contract of sale of a dwelling unit or the property of which it is a part, if the occupant is the purchaser or a person who succeeds to the purchaser's interest.
		2. Occupancy by a member of a social organization in the portion of a structure operated for the benefit of the organization.
		3. Transient occupancy in a hotel, motel, or lodgings.
		4. Occupancy under a rental agreement covering premises used by the occupant primarily for agricultural purposes.
		5. Occupancy when the occupant is performing agricultural labor for the owner and such premises are rented for less than fair rental value.
		6. Any rental agreement entered into before July 1, 1991.
Missouri	No statute	
Montana	Mont. Code § 70-24-104	1. Occupancy under a contract of sale of a dwelling unit or the property of which it is a part if the occupant is the purchaser or a person who succeeds to the purchaser's interest.
		2. Occupancy by a member of a social organization in the portion of a structure operated for the benefit of the organization.
		3. Transient occupancy in a hotel or motel.
		4. Occupancy under a rental agreement covering premises used by the occupant primarily for commercial or agricultural purposes.
		5. Occupancy by an employee of a landlord whose right to occupancy is conditional upon employment at the premises.
		6. Occupancy outside a municipality under a rental agreement that includes hunting, fishing, or agricultural privileges, along with the use of the dwelling unit.
Nebraska	Neb. Rev. Stat. §§ 76-1408, 76-1448	1. Occupancy under a contract of sale of a dwelling unit or the property of which it is a part, if the occupant is the purchaser or a person who succeeds to the purchaser's interest.
		2. Occupancy by a member of a social organization in the portion of a structure operated for the benefit of the organization.
		3. Transient occupancy in a hotel or motel.
		4. Occupancy by an employee of a landlord whose right to occupancy is conditional upon employment at the premises.
		5. Occupancy under a rental agreement covering premises used by the occupant primarily for agricultural purposes.
		6. A lease of improved or unimproved residential land for a term of five years or more.
		7. Rental agreements most recently entered into, extended, or renewed on or before July 1, 1975.

State Landlord-Tenant Exemption Statutes (continued)

State	Exemption Statute	Exemption
Nevada	Nev. Rev. Stat. §§ 118A.180, 118A.530	1. Rental agreements for manufactured homes. 2. Occupancy under a contract of sale of a dwelling unit or the property of which it is a part, if the occupant is the purchaser or successor to the purchaser's interest. 3. Occupancy by a member of a social organization in the portion of a structure operated for the benefit of the organization. 4. Occupancy in a hotel or motel for less than 30 consecutive days unless the occupant clearly manifests an intent to remain for a longer continuous period. 5. Occupancy by an employee of a landlord whose right to occupancy is solely conditional upon employment at the premises. 6. Occupancy under a rental agreement covering premises used by the occupant primarily for agricultural purposes. 7. Occupancy by a person who is guilty of a forcible entry or forcible detainer. 8. Rental agreements most recently entered into, extended, or renewed before July 1, 1977. 9. Occupancy under an agreement for the purchase and sale of a dwelling unit or the property of which it is a part for a period not to exceed 90 days, if the occupant is the seller or his or her successor in interest.
New Hampshire	N.H. Rev. Stat. § 540:1-a	1. Rooms in rooming or boarding houses that are rented to transient guests for fewer than 90 consecutive days. 2. Rooms in hotels, motels, inns, tourist homes, and other dwellings rented for recreational or vacation use. 3. Single-family homes in which the occupant has no lease, which is the primary and usual residence of the owner. 4. Shared residential facilities (properties with separate sleeping areas for each occupant and in which each occupant has access to and shares with the owner one or more areas of the property). 5. Vacation or recreational rentals. 6. Residential units leased by a member of a social organization that provides student housing for a postsecondary institution in a structure owned and operated by the social organization. 7. Occupancies in which the occupant is hired to provide care or assistance for a person with disabilities.
New Jersey	N.J. Stat. § 46:8-9.12	1. Seasonal rentals (does not include use or rental of living quarters for seasonal, temporary or migrant farm workers in connection with any work or place where work is being performed).
	N.J. Stat. § 46:8-44	2. Dwelling units in rentals containing not more than two such units. 3. Owner-occupied premises of not more than three dwelling units. 4. Hotels, motels, or other guest houses serving transient or seasonal guests.
New Mexico	N.M. Stat. §§ 47-8-9, 47-8-51	1. Occupancy under a contract of sale of a dwelling unit or the property of which it is part, if the occupant is the purchaser or a person who succeeds to the purchaser's interest. 2. Occupancy by a member of a social organization in the portion of a structure operated for the benefit of the organization. 3. Transient occupancy in a hotel or motel. 4. Occupancy by an employee of an owner pursuant to a written rental or employment agreement that specifies the employee's right to occupancy is conditional upon employment at the premises. 5. Occupancy under a rental agreement covering premises used by the occupant primarily for agricultural purposes. 6. Rental agreements most recently entered into, extended, or renewed on or before July 1, 1975.

State Landlord-Tenant Exemption Statutes (continued)

State	Exemption Statute	Exemption
New York	N.Y. Mult. Dwell. Law §§ 3, 4, 8, 9, 13, 14	1. Rentals in cities with a population of less than 325,00. 2. Rentals occupied by fewer than three families living independently of each other.
	N.Y. Mult. Resid. Law §§ 3, 4, 9	1. Rentals in cities with a population equal to or greater than 325,000. 2. Rentals occupied by fewer than three families living independently of each other.
	N.Y. Gen. Oblig. Law § 7-108	Seasonal use dwelling units are exempt from the security deposit limit under N.Y. Gen. Oblig. Law § 7-108(1-a)(a).
North Carolina	N.C. Gen. Stat. §§ 42-14.6, 42-39	1. Transient occupancy in an inn, hotel, motel, recreational vehicle park, campground, or similar lodging for fewer than 90 days. 2. Vacation rentals. 3. Dwellings provided without charge or rent.
North Dakota	No statute	
Ohio	Ohio Rev. Code § 5321.01	1. Tourist homes, hotels, motels, recreational vehicle parks, recreation camps, combined park-camps, temporary park-camps, and other similar facilities where circumstances indicate a transient occupancy. 2. Farm residences furnished in connection with the rental of land of a minimum of two acres for production of agricultural products by one or more of the occupants. 3. Manufactured home parks, marinas, and agricultural labor camps. 4. Occupancy in hotels and single room occupancy facilities.
Oklahoma	Okla. Stat. tit. 41, § 104	1. Occupancy under a contract of sale or contract for deed of a dwelling unit or of the property of which it is a part, if the occupant is the purchaser or a person who succeeds to the purchaser's interest. 2. Occupancy by a member of a social organization in a structure operated for the benefit of the organization. 3. Transient occupancy in a hotel, motel, or other similar lodging, regardless of the length of stay. 4. Occupancy under a rental agreement covering premises used by the occupant primarily for agricultural purposes.
Oregon	Or. Rev. Stat. §§ 90.110, 90.113, 90.120	1. Occupancy of a dwelling unit for no more than 90 days by a purchaser prior to the scheduled closing of a real estate sale or by a seller following the closing of a sale, in either case as permitted under the terms of an agreement for sale of the property. 2. Occupancy by a member of a social organization in the portion of a structure operated for the benefit of the organization. 3. Transient occupancy in a hotel or motel. 4. Occupancy by a squatter. 5. Vacation occupancy. 6. Occupancy by an employee of a landlord whose right to occupancy is conditional upon employment at the premises. 7. Occupancy under a rental agreement covering premises used by the occupant primarily for agricultural purposes. Note that different rules might apply to occupancy of manufactured dwellings, floating homes, and recreational vehicles.
Pennsylvania	No statute	

State Landlord-Tenant Exemption Statutes (continued)

State	Exemption Statute	Exemption
Rhode Island	R.I. Gen. Laws § 34-18-8	Unless the parties expressly agree to be governed by them, the following occupancies are exempted from the residential landlord-tenant statutes: 1. Occupancy under a contract of sale of a dwelling unit or the property of which it is a part, if the occupant is the purchaser or a person who succeeds to the purchaser's interest. 2. Occupancy by a member of a social organization in the portion of a structure operated for the benefit of the organization. 3. Transient occupancy in a hotel, motel, or other lodging. 4. Occupancy by a paid employee of a landlord, whose right to occupancy is conditional upon employment substantially for services, maintenance, or repair of premises containing more than 11 units. 5. Residence at a transitional housing facility.
South Carolina	S.C. Code § 27-40-120	1. Occupancy under a contract of sale of a dwelling unit or the property of which it is a part, if the occupant is the purchaser or a person who succeeds to the purchaser's interest. 2. Occupancy by a member of a social organization in the portion of a structure operated for the benefit of the organization. 3. Transient occupancy in a hotel, motel, or other accommodations subject to the sales tax on accommodations. 4. Occupancy by an employee of a landlord whose right to occupancy is conditional upon employment at the premises. 5. Occupancy under a rental agreement covering the premises used by the occupant primarily for agricultural purposes. 6. Occupancy under a rental agreement for a vacation time share.
South Dakota	No statute	
Tennessee	Tenn. Code § 66-28-102	1. Rentals in counties with a population of less than 75,000, according to the 2010 federal census. 2. Rental agreements most recently entered into, extended, or renewed before July 1, 1975. 3. Occupancy under a contract of sale of a dwelling unit or the property of which it is a part, if the occupant is the purchaser or a person who succeeds to the purchaser's interest. 4. Transient occupancy in a hotel, motel, or lodgings subject to city, state, or transient lodgings laws. 5. Occupancy under a rental agreement covering premises used by the occupant primarily for agricultural purposes.
Texas	No statute	
Utah	Utah Code § 57-22-2	1. Boarding houses or similar facilities. 2. Mobile home lots. 3. Recreational properties rented on an occasional basis.
Vermont	Vt. Stat. tit. 9, § 4452	1. Occupancy under a contract of sale of a dwelling unit or the property of which it is a part, if the occupant is the purchaser or a person who succeeds to the purchaser's interest. 2. Occupancy by a member of a social or religious organization in the portion of a building operated for the benefit of the organization. 3. Transient occupancy in a hotel or motel. 4. Rental of a mobile home lot. 5. Transient residence in seasonal or short-term vacation or recreational properties. 6. Occupancy of a dwelling unit without right or permission by a person who is not a tenant.

State Landlord-Tenant Exemption Statutes (continued)

State	Exemption Statute	Exemption
Virginia	Va. Code § 55.1-1201	1. Occupancy by a member of a social organization in the portion of a structure operated for the benefit of the organization. 2. Occupancy in a campground. 3. Occupancy by a tenant who pays no rent pursuant to a rental agreement. 4. Occupancy in a recovery residence. 5. Occupancy by an employee of a landlord whose right to occupancy in a multifamily dwelling unit is conditioned upon employment at the premises or a former employee whose occupancy continues less than 60 days. 6. Occupancy under a contract of sale of a dwelling unit or the property of which it is a part, if the occupant is the purchaser or a person who succeeds to the purchaser's interest. 7. Occupancy in a hotel, motel, extended stay facility, vacation residential facility, timeshare, boardinghouse, or similar transient lodging when the occupancy is not the resident's primary residence, or when the resident uses it as a primary residence for less than 90 days.
Washington	Wash. Rev. Code §§ 59.18.040, 59.18.415, 59.18.430, 59.18.435	1. Occupancy under a bona fide earnest money agreement to purchase or contract of sale of the dwelling unit or the property of which it is a part, where the tenant is, or stands in the place of, the purchaser. 2. Occupancy under a written rental agreement entered into by a seller and buyer of a dwelling unit, for the seller to retain possession of the dwelling unit after closing of the sale of the dwelling unit, if the conditions in (a) through (c) of this subsection are satisfied: a. the rental agreement permits the seller to remain in the dwelling unit for no more than three months after closing, and the buyer does not accept any rent payments from the seller after three months from closing b. at the time of closing of the sale, the dwelling unit was not a distressed home as defined in chapter 61.34 RCW; and c. during negotiation of the purchase agreement or at the time of closing of the sale, the seller was represented by an attorney licensed to practice law in this state or by a real estate broker or managing broker licensed under chapter 18.85 RCW. 3. Residence in a hotel, motel, or other transient lodging whose operation is defined in RCW 19.48.010. 4. Rental agreements entered into pursuant to the provisions of chapter 47.12 RCW where occupancy is by an owner-condemnee and where such agreement does not violate the public policy of this state of ensuring decent, safe, and sanitary housing and is so certified by the consumer protection division of the attorney general's office. 5. Rental agreements for the use of any single-family residence which that are incidental to leases or rentals entered into in connection with a lease of land to be used primarily for agricultural purposes. 6. Rental agreements providing housing for seasonal agricultural employees while provided in conjunction with such employment. 7. Rental agreements with the state of Washington, department of natural resources, on public lands governed by Title 79 RCW. 8. Occupancy by an employee of a landlord whose right to occupy is conditioned upon employment in or about the premises.
West Virginia	No statute	

State Landlord-Tenant Exemption Statutes (continued)		
State	**Exemption Statute**	**Exemption**
Wisconsin	Wis. Admin. Code § ATCP 134.01	1. Occupancy by a member of a fraternal or social organization that operates that dwelling unit. 2. Occupancy under a contract of sale, by the purchaser of the dwelling unit or the purchaser's successor in interest. 3. Occupancy by tourist or transient occupants. 4. Occupancy that the landlord provides free of charge to any person, or that the landlord provides as consideration to a person whom the landlord currently employs to operate or maintain the premises. 5. Occupancy by a tenant who is engaged in commercial agricultural operations on the premises.
Wyoming	No statute	

State Rent Rules

Here are citations for statutes that set out rent rules in each state. When a state has no statute, the space is left blank. (See the State Rules on "Notice Required to Change or Terminate a Month-to-Month Tenancy" chart in this appendix for citations to laws about raising rent.)

State	When Rent Is Due	Grace Period	Where Rent Is Due	Late Fees
Alabama	Ala. Code § 35-9A-161(c)		Ala. Code § 35-9A-161(c)	
Alaska	Alaska Stat. § 34.03.020(c)		Alaska Stat. § 34.03.020(c)	
Arizona	Ariz. Rev. Stat. §§ 33-1314(C), 33-1368(B)		Ariz. Rev. Stat. § 33-1314(C)	Ariz. Rev. Stat. § 33-1368(B) [1]
Arkansas	Ark. Code § 18-17-401	Ark. Code §§ 18-17-701, 18-17-901	Ark. Code § 18-17-401	
California	Cal. Civ. Code § 1947		Cal. Civ. Code § 1962	*Orozco v. Casimiro*, 121 Cal. App.4th Supp. 7 (2004) [2]
Colorado		Colo. Rev. Stat. § 38-12-105		Colo. Rev. Stat. § 38-12-105 [3]
Connecticut	Conn. Gen. Stat. § 47a-3a	Conn. Gen. Stat. § 47a-15a	Conn. Gen. Stat. § 47a-3a	Conn. Gen. Stat. §§ 47a-4(a)(8), 47a-15a [4]
Delaware	Del. Code tit. 25, § 5501(b)		Del. Code tit. 25, § 5501(b)	Del. Code tit. 25, § 5501(d) [5]
D.C.		D.C. Code § 42-3505.31		D.C. Code § 42-3505.31 [6]
Florida	Fla. Stat. § 83.46(1)			
Georgia [7]				
Hawaii	Haw. Rev. Stat. § 521-21(b)		Haw. Rev. Stat. § 521-21(b)	Haw. Rev. Stat. § 521-21(f) [8]
Idaho				
Illinois	735 Ill. Comp. Stat. § 5/9-218		735 Ill. Comp. Stat. § 5/9-218	
Indiana	*Watson v. Penn*, 8 N.E. 636 (Ind. 1886)			
Iowa	Iowa Code § 562A.9(3)		Iowa Code § 562A.9(3)	Iowa Code § 562A.9(4) [9]
Kansas	Kan. Stat. § 58-2545(c)		Kan. Stat. § 58-2545(c)	
Kentucky	Ky. Rev. Stat. § 383.565(2)		Ky. Rev. Stat. § 383.565(2)	
Louisiana	La. Civ. Code art. 2703		La. Civ. Code art. 2703	
Maine		Me. Rev. Stat. tit. 14, § 6002		Me. Rev. Stat. tit. 14, § 6028 [10]

[1] Late fees must be set forth in a written rental agreement and be reasonable. (Arizona)

[2] Late fees must reflect landlord's actual damages; courts likely won't enforce a preset fee (liquidated damages clause). (California)

[3] Landlord can't charge tenant a late fee unless the rent payment is late by at least 7 calendar days. Late fee can't exceed the greater of $50 or 5% of the amount past due, and landlords must disclose late fees in lease or rental agreement. Landlord can't impose a late fee on any portion of the rent that a rent subsidy provider is paying. A late fee can be imposed more than once only if the total amount doesn't exceed the limit. Late fees can't be taken out of rent payments, and landlord can't charge interest on late fees. Landlord must provide the tenant with written notice of the late fee within 180 days after the date the rent payment was due. (Colorado)

[4] Landlords may not charge a late fee until 9 days after rent is due (4 days for weekly tenancy), and may assess a charge only once per each late rent payment. Late fee limit is $5/day, up to $50 maximum; or 5% of the delinquent rent payment, whichever is greater; if tenancy is subsidized, 5% of the tenant's share. (Connecticut)

[5] To charge a late fee, landlord must maintain an office in the county where the rental unit is located at which tenants can pay rent. If a landlord doesn't have a local office for this purpose, tenant has 3 extra days (beyond the due date) to pay rent before the landlord can charge a late fee. Late fee cannot exceed 5% of rent and cannot be imposed until the rent is more than 5 days late. (Delaware)

[6] Fee policy (including a statement of the maximum amount of late fees that may be charged) must be stated in the lease, and cannot exceed 5% of rent due or be imposed until rent is five days late (or later, if lease so provides). Landlord cannot evict for failure to pay late fee (may deduct unpaid fees from security deposit at end of tenancy). (District of Columbia)

[7] Although there is no specific statute regarding late fees, Georgia law states that all contracts for rent bear interest from the time rent is due. (Georgia)

[8] Late charge cannot exceed 8% of the amount of rent due. (Hawaii)

[9] When rent is $700 per month or less, late fees cannot exceed $12 per day, or a total amount of $60 per month; when rent is more than $700 per month, fees cannot exceed $20 per day or a total amount of $100 per month. (Iowa)

[10] Late fees cannot exceed 4% of the amount due for 30 days. Landlord must notify tenants, in writing, of any late fee at the start of the tenancy, and cannot impose it until rent is 15 days late. (Maine)

State	When Rent Is Due	Grace Period	Where Rent Is Due	Late Fees
State Rent Rules (continued)				
Maryland				Md. Code Real Prop. § 8-208(d)(3) [11]
Massachusetts		Mass. Gen. Laws ch. 186, § 15B(1)(c); ch. 239, § 8A		Mass. Gen. Laws ch. 186, § 15B(1)(c) [12]
Michigan	*Hilsendegen v. Scheich,* 21 N.W. 894 (Mich. 1885)			
Minnesota				Minn. Stat. § 504B.177 [13]
Mississippi				
Missouri	Mo. Rev. Stat. § 535.060			
Montana	Mont. Code § 70-24-201(2)(c)		Mont. Code § 70-24-201(2)(b)	
Nebraska	Neb. Rev. Stat. § 76-1414(3)		Neb. Rev. Stat. § 76-1414(3)	
Nevada	Nev. Rev. Stat. § 118A.210		Nev. Rev. Stat. § 118A.200	Nev. Rev. Stat. §§ 118A.200, 118A.210(4) [14]
New Hampshire				N.H. Rev. Stat. § 540:8 [15]
New Jersey		N.J. Stat. § 2A:42-6.1	N.J. Stat. § 2A:42-6.1	N.J. Stat. § 2A:42-6.1 [16]
New Mexico	N.M. Stat. § 47-8-15(B)		N.M. Stat. § 47-8-15(B)	N.M. Stat. § 47-8-15(D) [17]
New York		N.Y. Real Prop. Law § 238-a		N.Y. Real Prop. Law § 238-a [18]
North Carolina		N.C. Gen Stat. § 42-46		N.C. Gen. Stat. § 42-46 [19]
North Dakota	N.D. Cent. Code § 47-16-20			
Ohio				*Campus Village Toledo Univ. Park, LLC v. Mowrer,* 68 N.E.3d 219 (Ohio App. 2016); Ohio Rev. Code § 5321.14 [20]
Oklahoma	Okla. Stat. tit. 41, § 109		Okla. Stat. tit. 41, § 109	*Sun Ridge Investors, Ltd. v. Parker,* 956 P.2d 876 (1998) [21]
Oregon	Or. Rev. Stat. § 90.220	Or. Rev. Stat. § 90.260	Or. Rev. Stat. § 90.220	Or. Rev. Stat. § 90.260 [22]
Pennsylvania				

[11] Late fees cannot exceed 5% of the rent due. (Maryland)

[12] Late fees, including interest on late rent, may not be imposed until the rent is 30 days late. (Massachusetts)

[13] Late fee policy must be agreed to in writing, and may not exceed 8% of the overdue rent payment. The "due date" for late fee purposes does not include a date earlier than the usual rent due date, by which date a tenant earns a discount. (Minnesota)

[14] A court will presume that there's no late fee provision unless it's included in a written rental agreement, but the landlord can offer evidence to overcome that presumption. Landlord may charge a reasonable late fee as set forth in the rental agreement, but it cannot exceed 5% of the amount of the periodic rent, and the maximum amount of the late fee must not be increased based upon a late fee that was previously imposed. For tenancies that are longer than week-to-week, landlords can't charge a late fee until at least three calendar days after the rent due date.(Nevada)

[15] Landlord cannot demand an amount greater than the the whole rent in arrears when rent is late. (New Hampshire)

[16] Landlord must wait 5 business days before charging a late fee, but only when the premises are rented or leased by senior citizens receiving Social Security Old Age Pensions, Railroad Retirement Pensions, or other governmental pensions in lieu of Social Security Old Age Pensions; or when rented by recipients of Social Security Disability Benefits, Supplemental Security Income, or benefits under Work First New Jersey. (New Jersey)

[17] Late fee policy must be in the lease or rental agreement and may not exceed 10% of the rent specified per rental period. Landlord must notify the tenant of the landlord's intent to impose the charge no later than the last day of the next rental period immediately following the period in which the default occurred. (New Mexico)

[18] Landlord must wait five days after the rent due date before imposing a late fee. A late fee may not be more than $50 or 5% of the rent, whichever is less. (New York)

[19] Late fee when rent is due monthly cannot be higher than $15 or 5% of the rental payment, whichever is greater (when rent is due weekly, may not be higher than $4.00 or 5% of the rent, whichever is greater); and may not be imposed until the rent is 5 days late. A late fee may be imposed only one time for each late rental payment. A late fee for a specific late rental payment may not be deducted from a subsequent rental payment so as to cause the subsequent rental payment to be in default. (North Carolina)

[20] Late fees won't be enforced if a court finds that they are an "unconscionable penalty." (Ohio)

[21] Reasonable late fees are allowed, but "per-day" or similar charges intended as penalties—rather than actual expenses—are invalid. (Oklahoma)

[22] Landlord must wait 4 days after the rent due date before imposing a late fee, and must disclose the late fee policy in the rental agreement. A flat fee must be "reasonable." A daily late fee may not be more than 6% of a reasonable flat fee, and cannot add up to more than 5% of the monthly rent. (Oregon)

State Rent Rules (continued)

State	When Rent Is Due	Grace Period	Where Rent Is Due	Late Fees
Rhode Island	R.I. Gen. Laws § 34-18-15(c)	R.I. Gen. Laws § 34-18-35	R.I. Gen. Laws § 34-18-15(c)	
South Carolina	S.C. Code § 27-40-310(c)		S.C. Code § 27-40-310(c)	
South Dakota	S.D. Codified Laws § 43-32-12			
Tennessee	Tenn. Code § 66-28-201(c)	Tenn. Code § 66-28-201(d)	Tenn. Code § 66-28-201(c)	Tenn. Code § 66-28-201(d) [23]
Texas		Tex. Prop. Code § 92.019		Tex. Prop. Code §§ 92.019, 92.0191 [24]
Utah				Utah Code § 57-22-4(5) [25]
Vermont	Vt. Stat. tit. 9, § 4455			
Virginia	Va. Code § 55.1-1204	Va. Code § 55.1-1204	Va. Code § 55.1-1204	Va. Code § 55.1-1204 [26]
Washington		Wash. Rev. Code Ann. § 59.18.170		Wash. Rev. Code Ann. § 59.18.285 [27]
West Virginia				
Wisconsin				Wis. Admin. Code § ATCP 134.09(8) [28]
Wyoming				

[23] Landlord can't charge a late fee until the rent is 5 days late (the day rent is due is counted as the first day). If day five is a Sunday or legal holiday, landlord cannot impose a fee if the rent is paid on the next business day. Fee can't exceed 10% of the amount past due. (Tennessee)

[24] Late fee provision must be included in a written lease and cannot be imposed until the rent remains unpaid two full days after the date it is due. The fee must be reasonable: For properties that have four or fewer units, it cannot be more than 12% of the rent; for properties that have more than four units, it cannot be more than 10% of the rent; OR it must be related to the late payment of rent (such as expenses, costs, and overhead associated with the collection of late payment). Landlord may charge an initial fee and a daily fee for each day the rent is late—the combined fees are considered a single late fee. Tenants can ask landlords to provide statement of whether they owe late fees. (Texas)

[25] Late fees can't exceed the greater of 10% of the rent agreed to in the lease or rental agreement, or $75. The fee must be disclosed in the lease or rental agreement unless the lease or rental agreement is month-to-month and the landlord provides the renter a 15-day notice of the charge. (Utah)

[26] Landlords cannot charge a tenant a late fee unless it is provided for in a written rental agreement or lease. No late charge shall exceed the lesser of 10% of the periodic rent or 10% of the remaining balance due and owed by the tenant. (Virginia)

[27] Nonrefundable fees must be described in lease or rental agreement; otherwise, they will be considered to be deposits. Landlords may not impose late fees until the rent is more than five days late. The fee may commence as of the first day the rent is overdue, and landlords may serve a notice to pay rent or quit as soon as the rent is overdue. If tenants can demonstrate in writing that their primary source of income is a regular, monthly source of governmental assistance that is not received until after the date rent is due in the rental agreement, landlords must adjust rental due date (to no more than five days after the date specified in the rental agreement). (Washington)

[28] Late fee policy must be in the rental agreement, landlord must first apply any prepaid rent (such as last month's rent) to the unpaid rent, and landlord may not charge a fee or impose a penalty for failure to pay the late rent fee. (Wisconsin)

State Rent Control Laws

Rent control (also known as "rent stabilization") limits the amount of rent landlords can charge. Rent control laws vary by state. A few states have statewide rent control, noted with a "Yes" in the "Is There Statewide Rent Control?" column. Most rent control laws, though, are local—passed and enforced by county or city governments. While some states specifically allow local rent control laws— noted with "Yes" in the "Is Local Rent Control Permitted?" column—most states specifically prohibit them; these states have a "No" in the "Is Local Rent Control Permitted?" column. When a state has neither specifically allowed nor prohibited local rent control, you'll see "No statute or case law" in the "Is Local Rent Control Permitted?" column.

Some states require landlords to have "just cause"—good reason—for terminating a tenancy. In other words, a landlord cannot require a tenant to leave or refuse to renew a lease without having a reason specified by state statute. States with just cause statutes are noted with a "Yes" in the "Just Cause Required for Termination?" column. We've noted the applicable statutes or cases for both rent control laws and just cause laws—if any—in the "Legal Authority" column.

State	Is There Statewide Rent Control?	Is Local Rent Control Permitted?	Just Cause Required for Termination?	Legal Authority
Alabama	No	No	No	Ala. Code § 11-80-8.1
Alaska	No	No statute or case law	No	N/A
Arizona	No	No	No	Ariz. Rev. Stat. § 33-1329
Arkansas	No	No	No	Ark. Code §§ 14-16-601, 14-54-1409
California	Yes	Yes	Yes	Cal. Civ. Code §§ 1946.2; 1947.12 to 1947.13; 1954.50 to 1954.535
Colorado	No, but landlords are limited in how much more they can charge when a tenant has a pet: landlord may increase the rent by $35 or 0.05% of the monthly rent, whichever is greater.	No	No	Colo. Rev. Stat. §§ 38-12-106; 38-12-301 to 38-12-302
Connecticut	No	No. But cities may enact some control over local rents.	Yes, but only for tenants in buildings of 5 or more units, who are 62 or older (or live permanently with specified family member who is 62 or older), or who are disabled (or live permanently with specified family member who is disabled and whose disability will last for at least 12 months or result in death).	Conn. Gen. Stat. §§ 7-148b, 47a-23c

State Rent Control Laws (continued)

State	Is There Statewide Rent Control?	Is Local Rent Control Permitted?	Just Cause Required for Termination?	Legal Authority
Delaware	No	No statute or case law	No	N/A
District of Columbia	Yes (District-wide)	N/A	Yes	D.C. Code §§ 42-3502.01 to 42.3509.10 (D.C. Code § 42-3505.01 is just cause statute)
Florida	No	No	No	Fla. Stat. §§ 83.425, 125.0103
Georgia	No	No	No	Ga. Code § 44-7-19
Hawaii	No	No statute or case law	No	N/A
Idaho	No	No	No	Idaho Code § 55-307
Illinois	No	No	No	50 Ill. Comp. Stat. 825/1 to 825/99
Indiana	No	No, unless authorized by an act of the general assembly	No	Ind. Code § 32-31-1-20
Iowa	No	No	No	Iowa Code §§ 331.304, 364.3
Kansas	No	No	No	Kan. Stat. § 12-16,120
Kentucky	No	No	No	Ky. Rev. Stat. § 65.875
Louisiana	No	No	No	La. Stat. Ann. § 9:3258; *Javers v. Council of City of New Orleans*, 351 So. 2d 247 (La. Ct. App. 1977), writ denied, 354 So. 2d 200 (La. 1978)
Maine	No, but landlords are prohibited from raising rent when the rental is in violation of the warranty of habitability.	No statute or case law	No	Me. Rev. Stat. tit. 14, § 6016
Maryland	No	Yes	No	*Heubeck v. City of Baltimore*, 205 Md. 203, 107 A.2d 99 (1954); *Westchester West No. 2 Ltd. Partnership v. Montgomery County*, 276 Md. 448, 348 A.2d 856 (1975); *Hardy v. Housing Management Co.*, 293 Md. 394, 444 A.2nd 457 (1982)
Massachusetts	No	No	No	Mass. Gen. Laws ch. 40P, §§ 1 to 5
Michigan	No	No	No	Mich. Comp. Laws § 123.411
Minnesota	No	No, unless approved in a general election.	No	Minn. Stat. § 471.9996
Mississippi	No	No	No	Miss. Code. § 21-17-5
Missouri	No	No	No	Mo. Stat. § 441.043
Montana	No	No	No	Mont. Code § 7-1-111
Nebraska	No	No statute or case law	No	N/A
Nevada	No	No statute or case law	No	N/A
New Hampshire	No	No	Yes (if the rental is a "restricted property")	N.H. Rev. Stat. §§ 540:1-a, 540:2; *Girard v. Town of Allenstown*, 121 N.H. 268, 428 A.2d 488 (1981)

State Rent Control Laws (continued)			
State	**Is There Statewide Rent Control?**	**Is Local Rent Control Permitted?**	**Just Cause Required for Termination?**	**Legal Authority**
New Jersey	No	Yes	Yes	N.J. Stat. § 2A:18-61.1; *Inganamort v. Borough of Fort Lee*, 62 N.J. 521, 303 A.2d 298 (1973)
New Mexico	No	No	No	N.M. Stat. § 47-8A-1
New York	Yes	Yes	Yes	N.Y. Unconsol. Law §§ 26-401 to 26-530 (NYC only); N.Y. Unconsol. Law §§ 8581 to 8634 (NY state only, excludes NYC); N.Y. Real Prop. Law § 226-c
North Carolina	No	No	No	N.C. Gen. Stat. § 42-14.1
North Dakota	No	No	No	N.D. Cent. Code § 47-16-02.1
Ohio	No	No	No	Ohio Rev. Code § 5321.19
Oklahoma	No	No	No	Okla. Stat. tit. 11, § 14-101.1
Oregon	Yes	No	Yes	Or. Rev. Stat. §§ 90.100, 90.220, 90.323, 90.324, 90.427, 91.225
Pennsylvania	No	No statute or case law	No	N/A
Rhode Island	No	No statute or case law	No	N/A
South Carolina	No	No	No	S.C. Code § 27-39-60
South Dakota	No	No	No	S.D. Codified Laws § 6-1-13
Tennessee	No	No	No	Tenn. Code § 66-35-102
Texas	No	No. But municipalities may enact local rent control following a housing emergency caused by a natural or manmade disaster, such as fire, flood, epidemic, air contamination, and extreme heat, among others. The governor must approve the legislation, and the rent control can last only as long as the housing emergency lasts.	No	Tex. Loc. Gov't Code § 214.902
Utah	No	No	No	Utah Code § 57-20-1
Vermont	No	No statute or case law	No	N/A
Virginia	No	No statute or case law	No	N/A
Washington	No	No	Yes	Wash. Rev. Code §§ 35.21.830, 59.18.650
West Virginia	No	No statute or case law	No	N/A
Wisconsin	No	No	No	Wis. Stat. § 66.1015
Wyoming	No	No statute or case law	No	N/A

State Rules on Notice Required to Change or Terminate a Month-to-Month Tenancy

Except where noted, the amount of notice a landlord must give to increase rent or change another term of the rental agreement in a month-to-month tenancy is the same as that required to end a month-to-month tenancy. Be sure to check state and local rent control laws, which might have different notice requirements.

State	Tenant	Landlord	Statute	Comments
Alabama	30 days	30 days	Ala. Code §§ 35-9A-302, 35-9A-441	A rule or regulation that substantially modifies the tenant's use of the rental isn't valid unless the tenant consents to it in writing.
Alaska	30 days	30 days	Alaska Stat. §§ 34.03.130, 34.03.290(b)	After giving reasonable notice, landlords may adopt new rules and regulations that don't substantially modify the rental agreement.
Arizona	30 days	30 days	Ariz. Rev. Stat. §§ 33-1342, 33-1375	After giving the tenant 30 days' notice, landlords may adopt new rules and regulations that don't substantially modify the rental agreement.
Arkansas	30 days	30 days	Ark. Code § 18-17-704	No state statute on the amount of notice required to change rent or other terms.
California	30 days	30 days to terminate if tenant has lived in property for under 12 months; if 12 months or longer, the landlord must have just cause to terminate. 30-90 days to change terms or increase rent, depending on size of increase.	Cal. Civ. Code §§ 827, 1946, 1946.2	At least 30 days' notice to change rental terms, but if the change is a proposed rent increase of more than 10% of the rental amount charged to that tenant at any time during the 12 months prior to the effective date of the increase, either in and of itself or when combined with any other rent increases for the 12 months prior to the effective date of the increase, then an additional 60 days' notice is required.
Colorado	21 days	21 days	Colo. Rev. Stat. §§ 13-40-107, 38-12-701, 38-12-702	No state statute on the amount of notice required to change rent or other terms, unless there is no written agreement, in which case the landlord must give 60 days' notice of a rent increase. For all tenancies, the landlord can increase the rent only once within any 12-month period of consecutive tenancy.
Connecticut		3 days	Conn. Gen. Stat. §§ 47a-9, 47a-23	Landlord must provide 3 days' notice to terminate tenancy. Landlord is not required to give a particular amount of notice of a proposed rent increase unless prior notice was previously agreed upon. If landlord makes a new rule or regulation resulting in a substantial modification of the rental agreement, it is not valid unless tenant agrees to it in writing.
Delaware	60 days	60 days	Del. Code tit. 25, §§ 5106, 5107	For termination, the 60-day notice period begins on the first day of the month following the day of actual notice. For change of terms, upon receiving notice of landlord's proposed change of terms tenant has 15 days to notify landlord of rejection of those terms and intent to terminate the lease. Otherwise, changes will take effect as announced.

State Rules on Notice Required to Change or Terminate a Month-to-Month Tenancy (continued)

State	Tenant	Landlord	Statute	Comments
District of Columbia	30 days	30-120 days, depending on reason for terminating the tenancy	D.C. Code §§ 42-3202, 42-3505.01, 42-3509.04(b)	No rent increases shall be effective until the first day on which rent is normally paid occurring more than 30 days after notice of the increase is given to the tenant. Landlords must have good reason (just cause) to terminate a month-to-month tenancy so long as the tenant is still paying rent.
Florida	30 days	30 days	Fla. Stat. § 83.57	No state statute on the amount of notice required to change rent or other terms.
Georgia	30 days	60 days	Ga. Code §§ 44-7-6, 44-7-7	No state statute on the amount of notice required to change rent or other terms.
Hawaii	28 days	45 days	Haw. Rev. Stat. §§ 521-21(d), 521-71	Landlord shall not increase rent without written notice given 45 consecutive days prior to the effective date of the increase. The landlord may terminate the rental agreement by notifying the tenant, in writing, at least 45 days in advance of the anticipated termination. The tenant may terminate the rental agreement by notifying the landlord, in writing, at least 28 days in advance of the anticipated termination.
Idaho	One month	One month to terminate; 15 or 30 days to change terms of tenancy.	Idaho Code §§ 55-208, 55-307, 55-314	A "month" means a calendar month. For landlords: 30 days' notice to increase rent, end tenancy, or make changes regarding fees, fines, assessments, interest, or other costs. 15 days' notice to change other terms.
Illinois	30 days	30 days	735 Ill. Comp. Stat. § 5/9-207	No state statute on the amount of notice required to change terms of lease other than rent.
Indiana	One month	One month	Ind. Code §§ 32-31-1-1, 32-31-5-4	Unless agreement states otherwise, landlord must give 30 days' written notice to modify written rental agreement.
Iowa	30 days	30 days	Iowa Code §§ 562A.13(5), 562A.34	To end or change a month-to-month agreement, landlord must give written notice at least 30 days before the next time rent is due (not including any grace period). Each tenant shall be notified, in writing, of any rent increase at least 30 days before the effective date. Such effective date shall not be sooner than the expiration date of original rental agreement or any renewal or extension thereof.
Kansas	30 days	30 days	Kan. Stat. §§ 58-2556, 58-2570	After the tenant enters into the rental agreement, if a rule or regulation that effects a substantial modification of the rental agreement is adopted, such rule or regulation isn't enforceable against the tenant unless the tenant consents to it in writing.
Kentucky	30 days	30 days	Ky. Rev. Stat. §§ 383.610, 383.695	If a rule or regulation is adopted after the tenant enters into the rental agreement that works a substantial modification of the bargain, it is not valid unless the tenant consents to it in writing.
Louisiana	10 days	10 days	La. Civ. Code Art. 2728	No state statute on the amount of notice required to change rent or other terms.
Maine	30 days	30 days	Me. Rev. Stat. tit. 14 §§ 6002, 6015	Landlord must provide 45 days' written notice to increase rent; and 75 days' notice if the increase is 10% or more or when the sum of more than one increase within a 12-month period adds up to 10% or more.
Maryland	30 days	60 days	Md. Code Real Prop., §§ 8-209, 8-402	Before increasing the rent, landlords must give 90 days' notice for tenancies lasting more than a month, 60 days' notice for tenancy terms of one week to one month, and 7 days' notice if the parties have a written lease (21 days if no written lease). These rules do not apply in Baltimore City.

State Rules on Notice Required to Change or Terminate a Month-to-Month Tenancy (continued)

State	Tenant	Landlord	Statute	Comments
Massachusetts	See comments	See comments	Mass. Gen. Laws ch. 186, § 12	Interval between days of payment or 30 days, whichever is longer.
Michigan	One month	One month	Mich. Comp. Laws § 554.134	No state statute on the amount of notice required to change rent or other terms.
Minnesota	See comments	See comments	Minn. Stat. §§ 504B.135, 504B.147	For terminations, notice period must be the interval between time rent is due or three months, whichever is less. If the lease provides a notice period for the landlord to end the tenancy that's different from the notice required by the tenant, the tenant can use either time period. The landlord can't give a notice to end the tenancy or raise the rent that is shorter than the time period for the tenant to give notice to end the tenancy.
Mississippi	30 days	30 days	Miss. Code §§ 89-8-11, 89-8-19	No state statute on the amount of notice required to change rent or other terms. A rule or regulation added or changed after the tenancy began is enforceable only if it does not substantially alter the terms of the tenancy and only when the landlord has given reasonable notice.
Missouri	One month	One month	Mo. Rev. Stat. § 441.060	No state statute on the amount of notice required to change rent or other terms.
Montana	30 days	30 days	Mont. Code § 70-24-441, 70-26-109	Landlord may change terms of tenancy with 15 days' notice.
Nebraska	30 days	30 days	Neb. Rev. Stat. §§ 76-1422, 76-1437	A rule or regulation adopted after the tenant enters into the rental agreement is enforceable if the landlord gives reasonable notice to tenant of its adoption and if it doesn't substantially modify the rental agreement.
Nevada	30 days	30 days	Nev. Rev. Stat. §§ 40.251, 118A.300	Landlords must provide 60 days' notice to increase rent. Tenants 60 years old or older, or physically or mentally disabled, may request an additional 30 days of possession, but only if they have complied with basic tenant obligations as set forth in Nev. Rev. Stat. Chapter 118A (termination notices must include this information).
New Hampshire	30 days	30 days	N.H. Rev. Stat. §§ 540:2, 540:3, 540:11	Landlord may terminate only for just cause. Tenant's termination: If the date of termination given in the notice does not coincide with the rent due date, tenant is responsible for the rent for the entire month in which the notice expires, up to the next rent due date, unless the terms of the rental agreement provide otherwise.
New Jersey	One month	One month	N.J. Stat. §§ 2A:18-56, 2A:18-61.1	Landlord may terminate only for just cause. The landlord may increase the rent only at the beginning of the term of the agreement. The landlord cannot increase the rent while an agreement exists. The landlord must offer the tenant the option of entering into a new agreement, at the increased rental rate, after the old agreement expires. If the tenant doesn't sign the new agreement and doesn't move at the expiration of the old agreement, and has been given a valid notice to quit and notice of rent increase, a new tenancy is automatically created at the increased rental rate. New Jersey landlords should check local ordinances, as they might have different rules regarding rent increase notice.

State Rules on Notice Required to Change or Terminate a Month-to-Month Tenancy (continued)

State	Tenant	Landlord	Statute	Comments
New Mexico	30 days	30 days	N.M. Stat. §§ 47-8-23, 47-8-37, 47-8-15(F)	Landlord must deliver rent increase notice at least 30 days before rent due date. Landlord can change a rule or regulation in force when the tenancy began only after the landlord has given notice. Rules or regulations added after the tenancy began are enforceable only if they do not substantially alter the terms of the tenancy and only when the landlord has given notice.
New York	One month, within NYC and statewide	Within NYC and statewide, 30 to 90 days for terminations and rent increases of 5% or more	N.Y. Real Prop. Law §§ 226-c, 232-b	Terminations and rent increases of 5% over existing rent: Tenants occupying for a year or having a lease of at least one year: 30 days' notice. Tenants occupying from one to two years and lease holders of one- to two-year leases: 60 days' notice. Tenants occupying more than two years or having leases of two years or more: 90 days' notice.
North Carolina	7 days	7 days	N.C. Gen. Stat. § 42-14	No state statute on the amount of notice required to change rent or other terms.
North Dakota	One calendar month	One calendar month	N.D. Cent. Code §§ 47-16-07, 47-16-15	Landlord may change the terms of the lease to take effect at the expiration of the month upon giving notice in writing at least 30 days before the expiration of the month. Tenant may terminate with 25 days' notice if landlord has changed the terms of the agreement.
Ohio	30 days	30 days	Ohio Rev. Code § 5321.17	No state statute on the amount of notice required to change rent or other terms.
Oklahoma	30 days	30 days	Okla. Stat. tit. 41, §§ 111, 126	No state statute on the amount of notice required to change rent or other terms. Rules and regulations adopted after the start of the tenancy that substantially modify the terms of the rental are not valid or enforceable unless the tenant agrees in writing.
Oregon	30 days, or 72 hours (lack of bedroom exit only)	Termination: 30 days within the first year (except Portland and Milwaukie, which require a 90-day notice); 90 days after that, only for cause. A landlord with five or more residential dwelling units must also pay tenants the equivalent of one month's rent. Rent increase: See comments. Rules and regulations adopted after the start of the tenancy that substantially modify the terms of the rental are not valid or enforceable unless the tenant agrees in writing.	Or. Rev. Stat. §§ 90.262, 90.275, 90.323, 90.427, 90.460, 91.070	When the rental is in the same building or on the same property as the landlord's residence, and the property has no more than two dwelling units, unique termination periods and notice requirements apply. Temporary occupants are not entitled to notice. Rent cannot be increased during the first year of the tenancy. After that, the landlord must give at least 90 days' notice of an increase in rent, and the rent cannot be increased more than 10% or 7% plus the September annual 12–month average change in the Consumer Price Index for All Urban Consumers, West Region. Rent cannot be increased more than once in a 12-month period. A landlord is exempt from the 7%+ CPI increase limit if either: The unit's first certificate of occupancy was issued less than 15 years from the date of the rent increase notice, or the landlord accepts reduced rent as part of a federal, state, or local program or subsidy.

State Rules on Notice Required to Change or Terminate a Month-to-Month Tenancy (continued)

State	Tenant	Landlord	Statute	Comments
Pennsylvania		15 days	68 Pa. Stat. § 250.501	At the end of the term or due to a breach of the lease landlord must give 15 days' notice to terminate. If notice to terminate is due to tenant's failure to pay rent, notice required is 10 days.
Rhode Island	30 days	30 days	R.I. Gen. Laws §§ 34-18-16.1, 34-18-25, 34-18-37	Landlord must provide 30 days' notice to increase rent if tenant is age 62 or younger; if tenant is over 62 years old, landlord must provide 60 days' notice. Rules and regulations adopted after the start of the tenancy that substantially modify the terms of the rental are not valid or enforceable unless the tenant agrees in writing.
South Carolina	30 days	30 days	S.C. Code §§ 27-40-520, 27-40-770	Rules or regulations adopted after a tenant enters into a rental agreement do not apply to a tenant if the rules or regulations substantially modify the tenant's agreement with landlord and, after receiving notice upon adoption of the right to object, the tenant objects in writing to the landlord within 30 days after the rules are made.
South Dakota	One month	One month	S.D. Codified Laws §§ 43-8-8, 43-32-13	If tenant (or spouse or minor child) is in active duty in the military, landlord must give two months' notice (unless there is tenant misconduct, a sale of the property, or the property has passed into the landlord's estate). Landlord must give at least 30 days' notice to modify lease (including rent amount). Tenant may terminate lease within 15 days of receipt of the notice of modification.
Tennessee	30 days	30 days	Tenn. Code §§ 66-28-402, 66-28-512	A rule or regulation adopted after the tenant enters into the rental agreement is enforceable against the tenant if reasonable notice of its adoption is given to the tenant and it does not work a substantial modification of the rental agreement.
Texas	One month	One month	Tex. Prop. Code §§ 91.001, 92.013	Landlord and tenant may agree in writing to different notice periods, or none at all. No state statute on the amount of notice required to change rent or other terms. A landlord shall give prior written notice to a tenant regarding a landlord rule or policy change that is not included in the lease agreement and that will affect any personal property owned by the tenant that is located outside the tenant's dwelling.
Utah		15 days	Utah Code § 78B-6-802	No state statute on the amount of notice required to change rent or other terms.
Vermont	One rental period, unless written lease says otherwise	30 days	Vt. Code tit. 9, §§ 4456(d), 4467	If there is no written rental agreement, for tenants who have continuously resided in the unit for two years or less, 60 days' notice to terminate; for those who have resided longer than two years, 90 days. If there is a written rental agreement, for tenants who have lived continuously in the unit for two years or less, 30 days; for those who have lived there longer than two years, 60 days.

State Rules on Notice Required to Change or Terminate a Month-to-Month Tenancy (continued)

State	Tenant	Landlord	Statute	Comments
Virginia	30 days	30 days	Va. Code §§ 55.1-1204, 55.1-1228, 55.1-1253	Rental agreement may provide for a different notice period. When a month-to-month tenant doesn't have a written lease, the law states that the lease is for 12 months by default, and its terms and conditions can be changed only by agreement of the parties. Rules and regulations changed or added after the start of the tenancy are valid only after landlord has given reasonable notice and they do not substantially modify the terms of the tenancy (substantial modifications are enforceable only after tenant has agreed in writing). Terminations of monthly tenancies in a multi-family property: 60 days, notice when landlord seeks to terminate 20 or more or 50% of the tenancies within a consecutive 30-day period (does not apply to termination for rent nonpayment).
Washington	20 days before the end of the "rental period" (the rental period ends the day before rent is due); tenants who are members of the armed forces (as well as their spouses and dependents) may give less than 20 days' notice if they receive permanent change of station or deployment orders that don't allow a 20-day written notice.	Landlord must have a just cause, as enumerated in state law, to terminate a month-to-month tenancy, including one that has resulted from a lease-holding tenant remaining with the consent of the landlord (as a month-to-month tenant). Tenants whose leases are for 6 to 12 months may be terminated upon 60 days' notice in advance of the tenancy end date.	Wash. Rev. Code §§ 59.18.140, 59.18.200, 59.18.650	Landlord must give 60 days' notice to change rent, and any increase in rent may not become effective before the end of the term of the rental agreement, but if the rental is a subsidized tenancy, landlord can give 30 days' notice. If the landlord plans to change rental agreement to exclude children, the landlord shall give tenant at least 90 days' notice. All other changes require 30 days' written notice.
West Virginia	One month	One month	W.Va. Code § 37-6-5	No state statute on the amount of notice required to change rent or other terms.
Wisconsin	28 days	28 days	Wis. Stat. § 704.19	No state statute on the amount of notice required to change rent or other terms.
Wyoming			No statute	

State Security Deposit Rules

Here are the statutes and rules that govern a landlord's collection and retention of security deposits. Many states require landlords to disclose, at or near the time they collect the deposit, information about how deposits may be used, as noted in the Disclosure or Requirement section. (Required disclosures of other issues, such as a property's history of flooding, are in the chart, "Required Landlord Disclosures.")

Alabama

Ala. Code § 35-9A-201

Limit: One month's rent, except for pet deposits, deposits to cover undoing tenant's alterations, and deposits to cover tenant activities that pose increased liability risks.

Deadline for Landlord to Itemize and Return Deposit: 60 days after termination of tenancy and delivery of possession.

Alaska

Alaska Stat. § 34.03.070

Limit: Two months' rent, unless rent exceeds $2,000 per month. Landlord may ask for an additional month's rent as deposit for a pet that is not a service animal, but may use it only to remedy pet damage.

Disclosure or Requirement: Orally or in writing, landlord must disclose the conditions under which landlord may withhold all or part of the deposit.

Separate Account: Required (but may commingle prepaid rent with security deposits).

Advance Notice of Deduction: Not required.

Deadline for Landlord to Itemize and Return Deposit: 14 days if the tenant gives proper notice to terminate tenancy; 30 days if the tenant does not give proper notice or if landlord has deducted amounts needed to remedy damage caused by tenant's failure to maintain the property (Alaska Stat. § 34.03.120).

Arizona

Ariz. Rev. Stat. § 33-1321

Limit: One and one-half months' rent.

Disclosure or Requirement: If landlord collects a nonrefundable fee, its purpose must be stated in writing. All fees not designated as nonrefundable are refundable.

Advance Notice of Deduction: Not required.

Deadline for Landlord to Itemize and Return Deposit: 14 days; tenant has the right to be present at final inspection.

Arkansas

Ark. Code §§ 18-16-301 to 18-16-305

Exemption: Security deposit rules do not apply to landlords who own five or fewer units unless the management of the rental (including rent collection) is performed by a third party for a fee.

Limit: Two months' rent, but this limit does not apply to landlords who own 5 or fewer properties, unless the landlord has hired a third party to manage the property.

Advance Notice of Deduction: Not required.

Deadline for Landlord to Itemize and Return Deposit: 60 days.

California

Cal. Civ. Code §§ 1940.5(g), 1950.5

Limit: Until July 1, 2024: Two months' rent (unfurnished); three months' rent (furnished). If the tenant is an active service member, no more than one month's rent (unfurnished) or two months' rent (furnished). Add extra one-half month's rent for waterbed.

On and after July 1, 2024: If the landlord is an individual or an LLC whose members are all individuals AND the landlord owns no more than two residential properties that collectively include no more than four dwelling units for rent, the landlord can collect a maximum of two months' rent. All other landlords can collect a maximum of one month's rent. However, all landlords can collect only one month's rent from active service members. Add extra one-half month's rent for waterbed.

Advance Notice of Deduction: Required.

Deadline for Landlord to Itemize and Return Deposit: 21 days.

Colorado

Colo. Rev. Stat. §§ 35-80-102; 38-12-102 to 38-12-106

Limit: Two months' rent. In addition to the security deposit, a landlord may impose a refundable deposit of up to $300 for a pet (any animal kept as a household pet, except livestock or working animals on a ranch or farm). As an alternative to the pet deposit, a landlord can charge an additional 1.5% more rent or $35 per month, whichever is greater.

State Security Deposit Rules (continued)

Advance Notice of Deduction: Not required.

Deadline for Landlord to Itemize and Return Deposit: One month, unless lease agreement specifies longer period of time (which may be no more than 60 days); 72 hours (not counting weekends or holidays) if a hazardous condition involving gas equipment requires tenant to vacate.

Connecticut

Conn. Gen. Stat. § 47a-21

Limit: Two months' rent (tenant under 62 years of age); one month's rent (tenant 62 years of age or older). Tenants who paid a deposit in excess of one month's rent, who then turn 62 years old, are entitled, upon request, to a refund of the amount that exceeds one month's rent.

Separate Account: Required.

Interest Payment: Interest payments must be made annually (or credited toward rent, at the landlord's option) and no later than 30 days after termination of tenancy. The interest rate must be equal to the average rate paid on savings deposits by insured commercial banks, rounded to the nearest 0.1%, as published by the Federal Reserve Board Bulletin.

Advance Notice of Deduction: Not required.

Deadline for Landlord to Itemize and Return Deposit: 21 days, or within 15 days of receiving tenant's forwarding address, whichever is later.

Delaware

Del. Code tit. 25, §§ 5311, 5514

Limit: One month's rent on leases for one year or more. For month-to-month tenancies, no limit for the first year, but after that, the limit is one month's rent (at the expiration of one year, landlord must give tenant a credit for any deposit held by the landlord that is in excess of one month's rent). No limit for furnished units. Tenant may offer to supply a surety bond in lieu of or in conjunction with a deposit, which landlord may elect to receive.

Separate Account: Required. Orally or in writing, the landlord must disclose to the tenant the location of the security deposit account.

Advance Notice of Deduction: Not required.

Deadline for Landlord to Itemize and Return Deposit: 20 days.

District of Columbia

D.C. Code § 42-3502.17; D.C. Mun. Regs. tit. 14, §§ 308 to 311

Exemption: Landlords cannot demand or receive a security deposit from a tenant in a rental unit occupied by the tenant as of July 17, 1985, when no security deposit had been required prior to that date.

Limit: One month's rent.

Disclosure or Requirement: In the lease, rental agreement, or receipt, landlord must state the terms and conditions under which the security deposit was collected (to secure tenant's obligations under the lease or rental agreement).

Separate Account: Required.

Interest Payment: Interest payments at the prevailing statement savings rate must be made at termination of tenancy.

Advance Notice of Deduction: Not required.

Deadline for Landlord to Itemize and Return Deposit: 45 days.

Florida

Fla. Stat. §§ 83.43(13), 83.49, 83.491

Limit: No statutory limit. Landlords may offer to let tenants pay a nonrefundable, recurring fee in place of a security deposit. Landlords must give fee-paying tenants a written disclosure that includes, among other provisions, that they can discontinue at any time and pay a security deposit instead; and that the tenant's default in paying the fee will not be reported to a credit reporting agency.

Disclosure or Requirement: Within 30 days of receiving the security deposit, the landlord must disclose in writing whether it will be held in an interest- or non-interest-bearing account; the name of the account depository; and the rate and time of interest payments. Landlord who collects a deposit must include in the lease the disclosure statement contained in Florida Statutes § 83.49.

Separate Account: Landlord may post a security bond securing all tenants' deposits instead.

Interest Payment: Interest payments, if any (account need not be interest-bearing) must be made annually and at termination of tenancy. However, no interest is due a tenant who wrongfully terminates the tenancy before the end of the rental term.

State Security Deposit Rules (continued)

Advance Notice of Deduction: Required.

Deadline for Landlord to Itemize and Return Deposit: 15 to 60 days depending on whether tenant disputes deductions.

Georgia

Ga. Code §§ 44-7-30 to 44-7-37

Exemption: Landlord who owns ten or fewer rental units, unless these units are managed by an outside party, need not supply written list of preexisting damage, nor place deposit in an escrow account. Rules for returning the deposit still apply.

Limit: No statutory limit.

Disclosure or Requirement: Landlord must give tenant a written list of preexisting damage to the rental before collecting a security deposit.

Separate Account: Required. Landlord must place the deposit in an escrow account in a state- or federally regulated depository, and must inform the tenant of the location of this account. Landlord may post a security bond securing all tenants' deposits instead.

Advance Notice of Deduction: Required.

Deadline for Landlord to Itemize and Return Deposit: 30 days.

Hawaii

Haw. Rev. Stat. § 521-44

Limit: One month's rent. Landlord may require an additional one month's rent as security deposit for tenants who keep a pet.

Advance Notice of Deduction: Not required.

Deadline for Landlord to Itemize and Return Deposit: 14 days.

Idaho

Idaho Code § 6-321

Limit: No statutory limit.

Separate Account: Security deposits for rentals that are managed by a third-party property manager must be held in a separate account at a federally insured financial institution. The account must be separate from the operating account. (These rules don't apply to managers who are owners, who have a real estate license, or who are nonprofit entities.)

Advance Notice of Deduction: Not required.

Deadline for Landlord to Itemize and Return Deposit: 21 days, or up to 30 days if landlord and tenant agree.

Illinois

420 Ill. Comp. Stat. 46/20; 765 Ill. Comp. Stat. 710/1; 715/1 to 715/3

Limit: No statutory limit.

Disclosure or Requirement: If a lease specifies the cost for repair, cleaning, or replacement of any part of the leased premises; or the cleaning or repair of any component of the building or common area that will not be replaced, the landlord may withhold the dollar amount specified in the lease. Landlord's itemized statement must reference the specified dollar amount(s) and include a copy of the lease clause. Landlord may not deduct for the cost of radon testing or mediation, but if tenant installed a mitigation system without consent and it was not properly installed by a radon contractor, landlord may deduct for the cost of properly installing the system.

Interest Payment: Landlords who rent 25 or more units in either a single building or a complex located on contiguous properties must pay interest on deposits held for more than six months. The interest rate is the rate paid for minimum deposit savings accounts by the largest commercial bank in the state, as of December 31 of the calendar year immediately preceding the start of the tenancy. Within 30 days after the end of each 12-month period, landlord must pay any interest that has accumulated to an amount of $5 or more, by cash or credit applied to rent due, except when the tenant is in default under the terms of the lease. Landlord must pay all interest that has accumulated and remains unpaid, regardless of the amount, upon termination of the tenancy.

Advance Notice of Deduction: Not required.

Deadline for Landlord to Itemize and Return Deposit: 30 days after the tenant has vacated or when the tenant's right to possession ended, whichever is later. If landlord does not return the deposit in full but fails to provide an itemized damage statement with repair costs and receipts, landlord must return the full deposit within 45 days of tenant's vacating the rental.

State Security Deposit Rules (continued)

Indiana

Ind. Code §§ 32-31-3-1.1 to 32-31-3-19

Exemption: Does not apply to rental agreements entered into before July 1, 1989.

Limit: No statutory limit.

Advance Notice of Deduction: Not required.

Deadline for Landlord to Itemize and Return Deposit: 45 days.

Iowa

Iowa Code § 562A.12

Limit: Two months' rent.

Separate Account: Required.

Interest Payment: Interest payment, if any (account need not be interest-bearing) must be made at termination of tenancy. Interest earned during first five years of tenancy belongs to landlord.

Advance Notice of Deduction: Not required.

Deadline for Landlord to Itemize and Return Deposit: 30 days.

Kansas

Kan. Stat. §§ 58-2548, 58-2550

Limit: One month's rent (unfurnished); one and one-half months' rent (furnished); for pets, add extra one-half month's rent.

Advance Notice of Deduction: Not required.

Deadline for Landlord to Itemize and Return Deposit: 14 days after the determination of the amount of any deductions, but in no event longer than 30 days after the end of the tenancy.

Kentucky

Ky. Rev. Stat. § 383.580

Limit: No statutory limit.

Disclosure or Requirement: Orally or in writing, landlord must disclose where the security deposit is being held and the account number. Before accepting a security deposit, landlords must give tenants a list of preexisting damage that would justify a charge against the deposit, including the amount of the charge. Tenants have the right to inspect before taking possession. Both parties must sign the list, and if tenants disagree with its accuracy, they must state in writing the basis for their disagreement and sign the statement of dissent. A mutually signed listing is conclusive proof of the listed defects, but not as to latent (unobservable) defects.

Separate Account: Required.

Advance Notice of Deduction: Required.

Deadline for Landlord to Itemize and Return Deposit: 30 to 60 days depending on whether tenant disputes deductions.

Louisiana

La. Rev. Stat. § 9:3251

Limit: No statutory limit.

Advance Notice of Deduction: Not required.

Deadline for Landlord to Itemize and Return Deposit: One month.

Maine

Me. Rev. Stat. tit. 14, §§ 6022, 6031 to 6038

Exemption: Entire security deposit law does not apply to rental unit that is part of structure with five or fewer units, one of which is occupied by landlord.

Limit: Two months' rent.

Disclosure or Requirement: Upon request by the tenant, landlord must disclose orally or in writing the account number and the name of the institution where the security deposit is being held. Landlord must provide tenant with a receipt for security deposits that are paid at least partially in cash.

Separate Account: Required.

Advance Notice of Deduction: Not required.

Deadline for Landlord to Itemize and Return Deposit: 30 days (if written rental agreement) or 21 days (if tenancy at will).

Maryland

Md. Code Real Prop., §§ 8-203, 8-203.1, 8-208

Exemptions: Security deposit statutes do not apply to a tenancy arising after the sale of owner-occupied residential property where the seller and purchaser agree that the seller may remain in possession of the property for not more than 60 days after the settlement.

Limit: Two months' rent.

State Security Deposit Rules (continued)

Disclosure or Requirement: Landlord must provide a receipt that describes tenant's rights to move-in and move-out inspections (and to be present at each), and right to receive itemization of deposit deductions and balance, if any; and penalties for landlord's failure to comply. Landlord must include this information in the lease.

Separate Account: Required. Landlord may hold all tenants' deposits in secured certificates of deposit, or in securities issued by the federal government or the State of Maryland.

Interest Payment: For security deposits of $50 or more, when landlord has held the deposit for at least six months: Within 45 days of termination of tenancy, interest must be paid at the daily U.S. Treasury yield curve rate for 1 year, as of the first business day of each year, or 1.5% a year, whichever is greater, less any damages rightfully withheld. Interest accrues monthly but is not compounded, and no interest is due for any period less than one month. (See the Department of Housing and Community Development website for a calculator.) Deposit must be held in a Maryland banking institution.

Advance Notice of Deduction: Required.

Deadline for Landlord to Itemize and Return Deposit: 45 days.

Massachusetts

Mass. Gen. Laws ch. 186, § 15B

Limit: One month's rent.

Disclosure or Requirement: At the time of receiving a security deposit, landlord must furnish a receipt indicating the amount of the deposit; the name of the person receiving it and, if received by a property manager, the name of the lessor for whom the security deposit is received; the date on which it is received; and a description of the premises leased or rented. The receipt must be signed by the person receiving the security deposit.

Separate Account: Required. Within 30 days of receiving security deposit, landlord must disclose the name and location of the bank in which the security deposit has been deposited, and the amount and account number of the deposit.

Interest Payment: Landlord must pay tenant 5% interest per year or the amount received from the bank (which must be in Massachusetts) that holds the deposit.

Interest should be paid yearly, and within 30 days of termination date. Interest will not accrue for the last month for which rent was paid in advance.

Advance Notice of Deduction: Not required.

Deadline for Landlord to Itemize and Return Deposit: 30 days.

Michigan

Mich. Comp. Laws §§ 554.602 to 554.616

Limit: One and one-half months' rent.

Disclosure or Requirement: Within 14 days of tenant's taking possession of the rental, landlord must furnish in writing the landlord's name and address for receipt of communications, the name and address of the financial institution or surety where the deposit will be held, and the tenant's obligation to provide in writing a forwarding mailing address to the landlord within 4 days after termination of occupancy. The notice shall include the following statement in 12-point boldface type that is at least 4 points larger than the body of the notice or lease agreement: "You must notify your landlord in writing within 4 days after you move of a forwarding address where you can be reached and where you will receive mail; otherwise your landlord shall be relieved of sending you an itemized list of damages and the penalties adherent to that failure."

Separate Account: Required. Landlord must place deposits in a regulated financial institution, and may use the deposits as long as the landlord deposits with the secretary of state a cash or surety bond.

Advance Notice of Deduction: Required. Not a typical advance notice provision: Tenants must dispute the landlord's stated deductions within 7 days of receiving the itemized list and balance, if any, or give up any right to dispute them.

Deadline for Landlord to Itemize and Return Deposit: 30 days.

Minnesota

Minn. Stat. §§ 504B.151, 504B.175, 504B.178, 504B.182, 504B.195

Limit: No statutory limit. If landlord collects a "prelease deposit" and subsequently rents to tenant, landlord must apply the prelease deposit to the security deposit.

State Security Deposit Rules (continued)

Disclosure or Requirement: Before collecting rent or a security deposit, landlord must provide a copy of all outstanding inspection orders for which a citation has been issued, pertaining to a rental unit or common area, specifying code violations that threaten the health or safety of the tenant, and all outstanding condemnation orders and declarations that the premises are unfit for human habitation. Citations for violations that do not involve threats to tenant health or safety must be summarized and posted in an obvious place. With some exceptions, landlord who has received notice of a contract for deed cancellation or notice of a mortgage foreclosure sale must so disclose before entering into a lease, accepting rent, or accepting a security deposit; and must furnish the date on which the contract cancellation period or the mortgagor's redemption period ends.

Interest Payment: Landlord must pay 1% simple, non-compounded interest per year. (Deposits collected before 8/1/03 earn interest at 3%, up to 8/1/03, then begin earning at 1%.) Any interest amount less than $1 is excluded.

Advance Notice of Deduction: Required.

Deadline for Landlord to Itemize and Return Deposit: Three weeks after tenant leaves and landlord receives forwarding address; five days if tenant must leave due to building condemnation.

Mississippi

Miss. Code § 89-8-21

Limit: No statutory limit.

Advance Notice of Deduction: Not required.

Deadline for Landlord to Itemize and Return Deposit: 45 days.

Missouri

Mo. Stat. § 535.300

Limit: Two months' rent.

Advance Notice of Deduction: Not required.

Deadline for Landlord to Itemize and Return Deposit: 30 days.

Montana

Mont. Code §§ 70-25-101 to 70-25-206

Limit: No statutory limit.

Disclosure or Requirement: Before signing a lease, landlords must give tenants a signed statement of the physical condition of the premises, including a statement (if applicable) that the premises have never been leased. Upon request, landlords must furnish a separate written statement of the damage and cleaning charges of the departing tenants. Landlords who fail to comply may not deduct any sums for damage or cleaning unless the landlord can establish by "clear and convincing evidence" that the tenant, tenant's family, licensees, or invitees were responsible.

Advance Notice of Deduction: Required. Tenant is entitled to advance notice of cleaning charges, but only if such cleaning is required as a result of tenant's negligence and is not part of the landlord's cyclical cleaning program.

Deadline for Landlord to Itemize and Return Deposit: 30 days; 10 days if no deductions. Landlord need not return the deposit if the tenancy was terminated pursuant to Mont. Code §§ 70-24-427 or 70-33-427 (eviction with a claim for rent and damages), and landlord has a pending claim in court for actual damages.

Nebraska

Neb. Rev. Stat. § 76-1416

Limit: One month's rent (no pets); one and one-quarter months' rent (pets).

Advance Notice of Deduction: Not required.

Deadline for Landlord to Itemize and Return Deposit: 14 days.

Nevada

Nev. Rev. Stat. §§ 118A.240 to 118A.250

Exemption: Security deposit rules do not apply to the following, among others: (1) Occupancy under a contract of sale of a dwelling unit or the property of which it is a part, if the occupant is the purchaser or a person who succeeds to the purchaser's interest; (2) Occupancy by an employee of a landlord whose right to occupancy is conditional upon employment in and about the premises; (3) Occupancy by a person who is guilty of a forcible entry or forcible detainer.

Limit: Three months' rent; if both landlord and tenant agree, tenant may use a surety bond for all or part of the deposit.

Disclosure or Requirement: Lease or rental agreement must explain the conditions under which the landlord will refund the deposit.

State Security Deposit Rules (continued)

Advance Notice of Deduction: Not required.

Deadline for Landlord to Itemize and Return Deposit: 30 days.

New Hampshire

N.H. Rev. Stat. §§ 540-A:5 to 540-A:8; 540-B:10

Exemption: Entire security deposit law does not apply to landlord who leases a single-family residence and owns no other rental property, or landlord who leases rental units in an owner-occupied building of five units or fewer (exemption does not apply to any individual unit in owner-occupied building that is occupied by a person 60 years of age or older).

Limit: One month's rent or $100, whichever is greater; when landlord and tenant share facilities, no statutory limit.

Disclosure or Requirement: Unless tenant has paid the deposit by personal or bank check, or by a check issued by a government agency, landlord must provide a receipt stating the amount of the deposit and the institution where it will be held. Regardless of whether a receipt is required, landlord must inform tenant that if tenant finds any conditions in the rental in need of repair, tenant may note them on the receipt or other written instrument, and return either within five days.

Separate Account: Required. Upon request, landlord must disclose the account number, the amount on deposit, and the interest rate. Landlord may post a bond covering all deposits instead of putting deposits in a separate account.

Interest Payment: Landlord who holds a security deposit for a year or longer must pay interest at a rate equal to the rate paid on regular savings accounts in the New Hampshire bank, savings & loan, or credit union where it's deposited. If a landlord mingles security deposits in a single account, the landlord must pay the actual interest earned proportionately to each tenant. A tenant may request the interest accrued every three years, 30 days before that year's tenancy expires. The landlord must comply with the request within 15 days of the expiration of that year's tenancy.

Advance Notice of Deduction: Not required.

Deadline for Landlord to Itemize and Return Deposit: 30 days; for shared facilities, if the deposit is more than 30 days' rent, landlord must provide written agreement acknowledging receipt and specifying when deposit will be returned—if no written agreement, 20 days after tenant vacates.

New Jersey

N.J. Stat. §§ 46:8-19 to 46:8-26

Exemption: Security deposit law does not apply to owner-occupied buildings with not more than two rental units where the tenant has failed to provide 30 days' written notice to the landlord invoking the law.

Limit: One and one-half months' rent. Any additional security deposit, collected annually, may be no greater than 10% of the current security deposit.

Separate Account: Required. Within 30 days of receiving the deposit and every time the landlord pays the tenant interest, landlord must disclose the name and address of the banking organization where the deposit is being held, the type of account, current rate of interest, and the amount of the deposit.

Interest Payment: Landlord with 10 or more units must invest deposits as specified by statute or place deposit in an insured money market fund account, or in another account that pays quarterly interest at a rate comparable to the money market fund. Landlords with fewer than 10 units may place deposit in an interest-bearing account in any New Jersey financial institution insured by the FDIC. All landlords may pay tenants interest earned on account annually or credit toward payment of rent due.

Advance Notice of Deduction: Not required.

Deadline for Landlord to Itemize and Return Deposit: 30 days; within five days if tenant has to move out due to fire, flood, condemnation, or evacuation.

New Mexico

N.M. Stat. § 47-8-18

Exemption: Security deposit rules do not apply to the following, among others: (1) Occupancy under a contract of sale of a dwelling unit or the property of which it is a part, if the occupant is the purchaser or a person who succeeds to the purchaser's interest; (2) Occupancy by an employee of an owner pursuant to a written rental or employment agreement that specifies the employee's right to occupancy is conditional upon employment in and about the premises.

State Security Deposit Rules (continued)

Limit: One month's rent (for rental agreement of less than one year); no limit for leases of one year or more.

Interest Payment: Landlord who collects a deposit larger than than one month's rent on a year's lease must pay interest, on an annual basis, equal to the passbook interest.

Advance Notice of Deduction: Not required.

Deadline for Landlord to Itemize and Return Deposit: 30 days.

New York

N.Y. Gen. Oblig. Law §§ 7-103 to 7-108

Limit: One month's rent for units other than those subject to the City Rent and Rehabilitation Law or the Emergency Housing Rent Control Law.

Disclosure or Requirement: If deposit is placed in a bank, landlord must disclose the name and address of the banking organization where the deposit is being held, and the amount of such deposit.

Separate Account: Required. Statute requires that deposits not be commingled with landlord's personal assets, but does not explicitly require placement in a banking institution (however, deposits collected in buildings of six or more units must be placed in New York bank accounts).

Interest Payment: Landlord who rents out nonregulated units in buildings with five or fewer units need not pay interest. Interest must be paid at the "prevailing rate" on deposits received from tenants who rent units in buildings containing six or more units. The landlord in every rental situation may retain an administrative fee of 1% per year on the sum deposited. Interest can be subtracted from the rent, paid at the end of the year, or paid at the end of the tenancy according to the tenant's choice.

Advance Notice of Deduction: Yes.

Deadline for Landlord to Itemize and Return Deposit: 14 days.

North Carolina

N.C. Gen. Stat. §§ 42-50 to 42-56

Exemption: Not applicable to rentals of single rooms.

Limit: One and one-half months' rent for month-to-month rental agreements; two months' rent if term is longer than two months; may also charge a reasonable, nonrefundable pet deposit.

Disclosure or Requirement: Within 30 days of the beginning of the lease term, landlord must disclose the name and address of the banking institution where the deposit is located or the name of the insurance company providing the bond.

Separate Account: Required. The landlord may choose to furnish a bond from an insurance company licensed to do business in N.C. rather than deposit the security deposit in a trust account.

Advance Notice of Deduction: Not required.

Deadline for Landlord to Itemize and Return Deposit: 30 days; if landlord's claim against the deposit cannot be finalized within that time, landlord may send an interim accounting and a final accounting within 60 days of the tenancy's termination.

North Dakota

N.D. Cent. Code § 47-16-07.1

Limit: One month's rent. If tenant has a pet, an additional pet deposit of up to $2,500 or two months' rent, whichever is greater. To encourage renting to persons with records of felony convictions, landlords may charge these applicants up to two months' rent as security. Applicants who have had court judgments entered against them "for violating the terms of a previous rental agreement" can also be charged up to two months' rent (this appears to refer to prior evictions and might not apply to evictions based on conduct not prohibited by the rental agreement).

Separate Account: Required.

Interest Payment: Landlord must pay interest if the period of occupancy is at least nine months. Money must be held in a federally insured interest-bearing savings or checking account for benefit of the tenant. Interest must be paid upon termination of the lease.

Advance Notice of Deduction: Not required.

Deadline for Landlord to Itemize and Return Deposit: 30 days.

Ohio

Ohio Rev. Code § 5321.16

Limit: No statutory limit.

Interest Payment: Any deposit in excess of $50 or one month's rent, whichever is greater, must bear interest on the excess at the rate of 5% per annum if the tenant stays

State Security Deposit Rules (continued)

for six months or more. Interest must be paid annually and upon termination of tenancy.

Advance Notice of Deduction: Not required.

Deadline for Landlord to Itemize and Return Deposit: 30 days.

Oklahoma

Okla. Stat. tit. 41, § 115

Limit: No statutory limit.

Separate Account: Required.

Advance Notice of Deduction: Not required.

Deadline for Landlord to Itemize and Return Deposit: 45 days.

Oregon

Or. Rev. Stat. § 90.300

Exemption: Security deposit rules do not apply to the following, among others: (1) Occupancy of a unit for no more than 90 days by a purchaser prior to the scheduled closing of a real estate sale or by a seller following the closing of a sale, in either case as permitted under the terms of an agreement for sale of a dwelling unit or the property of which it is a part (a tenant who holds but has not exercised an option to purchase the unit does not qualify for this exemption); (2) Vacation occupancy; (3) Occupancy by an employee of a landlord whose right to occupancy is conditional upon employment in and about the premises.

Limit: No statutory limit. Landlord may not impose or increase deposit within first year unless parties agree to modify the rental agreement to allow for a pet or other cause, and the imposition or increase relates to that modification.

Disclosure or Requirement: Landlord must provide a receipt for any security deposit the tenant pays.

Advance Notice of Deduction: Not required.

Deadline for Landlord to Itemize and Return Deposit: 31 days.

Pennsylvania

68 Pa. Cons. Stat. §§ 250.511a to 250.512

Limit: Two months' rent for first year of renting; one month's rent during second and subsequent years of renting.

Disclosure or Requirement: For deposits over $100, landlord must deposit them in a federally or state-regulated institution, and give tenant the name and address of the banking institution and the amount of the deposit.

Separate Account: Required. Instead of placing deposits in a separate account, landlord may purchase a bond issued by a bonding company authorized to do business in the state.

Interest Payment: Tenant who occupies rental unit for two or more years is entitled to interest beginning with the 25th month of occupancy. Landlord must pay tenant interest (minus 1% fee) at the end of the third and subsequent years of the tenancy.

Advance Notice of Deduction: Not required.

Deadline for Landlord to Itemize and Return Deposit: 30 days.

Rhode Island

R.I. Gen. Laws § 34-18-19

Exemption: Security deposit rules do not apply to the following, among others: (1) Occupancy under a contract of sale of a dwelling unit or the property of which it is a part, if the occupant is the purchaser or a person who succeeds to the purchaser's interest; (2) Occupancy by a paid employee of a landlord, whose right to occupancy is conditional upon employment substantially for services, maintenance, or repair of premises containing more than 11 units.

Limit: One month's rent (unfurnished); if furnished, separate furniture security deposit up to one month's rent if furnishings' replacement value at the start of the tenancy is $5,000 or more.

Advance Notice of Deduction: Not required.

Deadline for Landlord to Itemize and Return Deposit: 20 days.

South Carolina

S.C. Code § 27-40-410

Exemption: Security deposit rules do not apply to the following, among others: (1) Occupancy under a contract of sale of a dwelling unit or the property of which it is a part, if the occupant is the purchaser or a person who succeeds to the purchaser's interest; (2) Occupancy by an employee of a landlord whose right to occupancy is conditional upon employment in and about the premises; (3) Certain vacation rentals.

Limit: No statutory limit.

Advance Notice of Deduction: Not required.

Deadline for Landlord to Itemize and Return Deposit: 30 days.

State Security Deposit Rules (continued)

South Dakota

S.D. Codified Laws §§ 43.32-6.1, 43-32-24

Limit: One month's rent (higher deposit may be charged if special conditions pose a danger to maintenance of the premises).

Advance Notice of Deduction: Not required.

Deadline for Landlord to Itemize and Return Deposit: Two weeks and must supply reasons if withholding any portion; 45 days for a written, itemized accounting, if tenant requests it.

Tennessee

Tenn. Code § 66-28-301

Limit: No statutory limit.

Separate Account: Required. Orally or in writing, landlord must disclose the location of the separate account (but not the account number) used by landlord for the deposit.

Advance Notice of Deduction: Required.

Deadline for Landlord to Itemize and Return Deposit: No statutory deadline for returning security deposit, but landlord must send notification to the tenant's last known address of the amount of any refund due. If the landlord doesn't receive a response from the tenant within 60 days of sending the notification, the landlord may retain the deposit.

Texas

Tex. Prop. Code §§ 92.101 to 92.111

Limit: No statutory limit. Landlord may choose to offer the tenant the option to pay a nonrefundable fee in lieu of a security deposit. See Tex. Prop. Code § 92.111.

Disclosure or Requirement: If a security deposit isn't required by the lease or rental agreement, but the tenant is liable for damage or rent when they leave, the landlord must notify the tenant in writing about the claim before reporting the claim. Landlords who don't provide notice forfeit the right to collect damages and charges from the tenant.

Advance Notice of Deduction: Not required.

Deadline for Landlord to Itemize and Return Deposit: 30 days. Landlord need not refund deposit until the tenant gives the landlord a forwarding address. If landlord wants to condition the refund of the security deposit on the tenant's giving advance notice of surrender, landlord

must put this condition in the lease, and it must be either underlined or printed in conspicuous bold print.

Utah

Utah Code §§ 57-17-1 to 57-17-5

Limit: No statutory limit.

Disclosure or Requirement: For written leases or rental agreements only, if part of the deposit is nonrefundable, landlord must disclose this feature.

Advance Notice of Deduction: Not required.

Deadline for Landlord to Itemize and Return Deposit: 30 days.

Vermont

Vt. Stat. tit. 9, § 4461

Exemption: Security deposit rules do not apply to the following, among others: (1) Occupancy under a contract of sale of a dwelling unit or the property of which it is a part, if the occupant is the purchaser or a person who succeeds to the purchaser's interest; (2) Occupancy of a dwelling unit without right or permission by a person who is not a tenant.

Limit: No statutory limit.

Advance Notice of Deduction: Not required.

Deadline for Landlord to Itemize and Return Deposit: 14 days; 60 days if the rental is seasonal and not intended as the tenant's primary residence.

Virginia

Va. Code §§ 55.1-1204, 55.1-1206, 55.1-1208, 55.1-1226, 55.1-1234.1

Limit: Two months' rent. Alternatively, landlord may permit a tenant to provide damage insurance coverage in an amount not more than two months' rent in lieu of the payment of a security deposit. The damage insurance coverage must meet the requirements listed in Virginia Code Annotated sections 55.1-1226(I)-(K).

Advance Notice of Deduction: Not required.

Deadline for Landlord to Itemize and Return Deposit: 45 days after termination date or the date the tenant vacates, whichever occurs last; 30 days to itemize any deductions to be made during the course of the tenancy (60 days if the deductions exceed the amount of the security deposit). Lease can provide for expedited processing at the end of the tenancy and specify an

State Security Deposit Rules (continued)

administrative fee for such processing, which will apply only if tenant requests it with a separate written document. Landlord must give tenant written notice of tenant's right to be present at a final inspection. If tenant finds the unit uninhabitable within 7 days of move-in, tenant may terminate and vacate; landlord must return the deposit within 15 days of receipt of the termination notice or tenant's vacating the unit, whichever is later.

Washington

Wash. Rev. Code §§ 59.18.260 to 59.18.285; 59.18.610; 59.18.670

Limit: Landlords must allow tenants to pay the deposit and fees in installments (does not apply if the deposit and any nonrefundable fees are less than 25% of the monthly rent, or the landlord has not demanded the last month's rent). Tenants with tenancies of three months or more may pay in three equal and consecutive installments, beginning at the start of the tenancy; two installments for shorter tenancies. Installment schedules must be written and signed. Does not apply to holding deposits (which may not be more than 25% of the first month's rent). Landlord may offer to waive the security deposit and instead collect a monthly fee, but cannot require tenant to opt for the fee. Landlord cannot consider tenants choice when deciding whether to approve or deny tenants rental application. Tenant may opt to pay a deposit during the tenancy. Various written disclosures concerning insurance and tenants liability for damage must be made.

Disclosure or Requirement: In the lease, landlord must disclose the circumstances under which all or part of the deposit may be withheld. No deposit may be collected unless the rental agreement is in writing and a written checklist or statement specifically describing the condition and cleanliness of or existing damages to the premises and furnishings is provided to the tenant at the start of the tenancy. The landlord must provide tenant with a written receipt for the deposit and provide the name, address, and location of where the deposit will be kept; if location changes, landlord must notify tenant. Nonrefundable fees must be identified as such in a written rental agreement. If landlords fail to provide a written agreement, tenants are entitled to the return of the fee.

If the written agreement does not specify that the fee is refundable, it must be treated as a refundable deposit.

Separate Account: Required.

Advance Notice of Deduction: Not required.

Deadline for Landlord to Itemize and Return Deposit: 30 days, but if landlord retains the deposit for reasons unrelated to damages (such as for rent or other unpaid charges), landlord need not comply with checklist and documentation requirements.

West Virginia

W. Va. Code §§ 37-6A-1 to 37-6A-6

Exemption: Agreements for the payment of security deposits entered into before June 10, 2011.

Limit: No statutory limit.

Deadline for Landlord to Itemize and Return Deposit: 60 days from the date the tenancy has terminated, or within 45 days of the occupancy of a subsequent tenant, whichever is shorter. If the damage exceeds the amount of the security deposit and the landlord has to hire a contractor to fix it, the notice period is extended 15 days.

Wisconsin

Wis. Admin. Code § ATCP 134.04, 134.06; Wis. Stat. § 704.28

Exemption: Security deposit rules do not apply to the following, among others: (1) A dwelling unit occupied, under a contract of sale, by the purchaser of the dwelling unit or the purchaser's successor in interest; (2) A dwelling unit that the landlord provides free of charge to any person; (3) A dwelling unit that the landlord provides as consideration to a person whom the landlord currently employs to operate or maintain the premises.

Limit: No statutory limit.

Disclosure or Requirement: Before accepting the deposit, landlord must inform tenant of tenant's inspection rights, disclose all habitability defects, and show tenant any outstanding building and housing code violations, inform tenant of the means by which shared utilities will be billed, and inform tenant if utilities are not paid for by landlord.

Advance Notice of Deduction: Not required.

Deadline for Landlord to Itemize and Return Deposit: 21 days.

State Security Deposit Rules (continued)

Wyoming

Wyo. Stat. §§ 1-21-1207, 1-21-1208

Limit: No statutory limit.

Disclosure or Requirement: Lease or rental agreement must state whether any portion of a deposit is non-refundable, and landlord must give tenant written notice of this fact when collecting the deposit.

Advance Notice of Deduction: Not required.

Deadline for Landlord to Itemize and Return Deposit: 30 days, when applying it to unpaid rent (or within 15 days of receiving tenant's forwarding address, whichever is later); additional 30 days allowed for deductions due to damage.

Required Landlord Disclosures

Many states require landlords to inform tenants of important state laws or individual landlord policies, either in the lease or rental agreement or in another writing. Common disclosures include a landlord's imposition of nonrefundable fees (where permitted), tenants' rights to move-in checklists, and the identity of the landlord or landlord's agent or manager. Disclosures concerning the security deposit are in the chart, "State Security Deposit Rules." Also, keep in mind that landlords in all states must disclose information about lead-based paint to tenants if the building they are renting was built before 1978.

Alabama

Owner or agent identity: Landlord must disclose to the tenant in writing at or before the commencement of the tenancy the name and address of the person authorized to manage the premises, and an owner of the premises or a person authorized to act for and on behalf of the owner for the purpose of service of process and for the purpose of receiving notices and demands. (Exception: does not apply to resident purchaser under a contract of sale (but does apply to a resident who has an option to buy), nor to the continuation of occupancy by the seller or a member of the seller's family for a period of not more than 36 months after the sale of a dwelling unit or the property of which it is a part.) (Ala. Code § 35-9A-202)

Alaska

Owner or agent identity: Landlord must disclose to the tenant in writing at or before the commencement of the tenancy the name and address of the person authorized to manage the premises, and an owner of the premises or a person authorized to act for and on behalf of the owner for the purpose of service of process and for the purpose of receiving notices and demands. (Alaska Stat. § 34.03.080)

Extended absence: The rental agreement must require that the tenant notify the landlord of an anticipated extended absence from the premises in excess of seven days; however, the notice may be given as soon as reasonably possible after the tenant knows the absence will exceed seven days. (Alaska Stat. § 34.03.150)

Arizona

Nonrefundable fees permitted? Yes. The purpose of all nonrefundable fees or deposits must be stated in writing.

Any fee or deposit not designated as nonrefundable is refundable. (Ariz. Rev. Stat. § 33-1321)

Move-in checklist required? Yes. Tenants also have the right to be present at a move-out inspection. (Ariz. Rev. Stat. § 33-1321)

Separate utility charges: If landlord charges separately for gas, water, wastewater, solid waste removal, or electricity by installing a submetering system, landlord may recover the charges imposed on the landlord by the utility provider, plus an administrative fee for the landlord for actual administrative costs only, and must disclose separate billing and fee in the rental agreement. If landlord uses a ratio utility billing system, the rental agreement must contain a specific description of the ratio utility billing method used to allocate utility costs. (Ariz. Rev. Stat. § 33-1314.01)

Owner or agent identity: Landlord must disclose to the tenant in writing at or before the commencement of the tenancy the name and address of the person authorized to manage the premises, and an owner of the premises or a person authorized to act for and on behalf of the owner for the purpose of service of process and for the purpose of receiving notices and demands. (Ariz. Rev. Stat. § 33-1322)

Business tax pass-through: Until January 1, 2025: If the landlord pays a local tax based on rent and that tax increases, landlord may pass through the increase by increasing the rent upon 30 days' notice (but not before the new tax is effective), but only if the landlord's right to adjust the rent is disclosed in the rental agreement. (Ariz. Rev. Stat. § 33-1314)

Availability of Landlord and Tenant Act: Landlord must inform tenant in writing that the Residential Landlord and Tenant Act is available on the Arizona Department of Housing's website. (Ariz. Rev. Stat. § 33-1322)

Bed bug information: Landlords must provide existing and new tenants with educational materials on bed bugs, including information and physical descriptions, prevention and control measures, behavioral attraction risk factors, information from federal, state, and local centers for disease control and prevention, health or housing agencies, nonprofit housing organizations, or information developed by the landlord. (Ariz. Rev. Stat. § 33-1319)

Required Landlord Disclosures (continued)

Smoke detectors: Landlords must install smoke detectors and give tenant written notification of tenant's responsibilities (tenant must maintain it unless tenant gives written notification to the landlord of its malfunction, at which point landlord must maintain it). (Ariz. Rev. Stat. § 36-1637)

Arkansas

Move-in checklist required? Yes. To show compliance with the law of implied warranty of habitability, landlord must provide tenant with a written form in which the tenant can note any habitability-related defects. The landlord is deemed to be in compliance if the tenant signs and returns the form without noting any defects or fails to return the form within two business days. Applies to leases and rental agreements entered into or renewed after November 1, 2021. (Ark. Code § 18-17-502)

Must checklist rights be stated in the lease? No.

California

Nonrefundable fees permitted? No. (Cal. Civ. Code § 1950.5(m))

Move-in checklist required? No.

Must fee policy be stated in the rental agreement? N/A

Registered sexual offender database: Landlords must include this notice in every lease or rental agreement: "Notice: Pursuant to Section 290.46 of the Penal Code, information about specified registered sex offenders is made available to the public via an Internet Web site maintained by the Department of Justice at www. meganslaw.ca.gov. Depending on an offender's criminal history, this information will include either the address at which the offender resides or the community of residence and ZIP Code in which the offender resides." (Cal. Civ. Code § 2079.10a)

Tenant paying for others' utilities: Prior to signing a rental agreement, landlord must disclose whether gas or electric service to tenant's unit also serves other areas, and must disclose the manner by which costs will be fairly allocated. (Cal. Civ. Code § 1940.9)

Ordnance locations: Prior to signing a lease, landlord must disclose known locations of former federal or state ordnance in the neighborhood (within one mile of rental). (Cal. Civ. Code § 1940.7)

Mold: Prior to signing a rental agreement, landlord must provide written disclosure when landlord knows, or has reason to know, that mold exceeds permissible exposure limits or poses a health threat. Landlords must distribute a consumer handbook, developed by the State Department of Health Services, describing the potential health risks from mold. (Cal. Health & Safety Code §§ 26147, 26148)

Pest control service: When the rental agreement is signed, landlord must provide tenant with any pest control company disclosure landlord has received, which describes the pest to be controlled, pesticides used and their active ingredients, a warning that pesticides are toxic, and the frequency of treatment under any contract for periodic service. (Cal. Civ. Code § 1940.8; Cal. Bus. & Prof. Code § 8538)

Intention to demolish rental unit: Landlords or their agents who have applied for a permit to demolish a rental unit must give written notice of this fact to prospective tenants, before accepting any deposits or screening fees. (Cal. Civ. Code § 1940.6)

No-smoking policy: For leases and rental agreements signed after January 1, 2012: If the landlord prohibits or limits the smoking of tobacco products on the rental property, the lease or rental agreement must include a clause describing the areas where smoking is limited or prohibited (does not apply if the tenant has previously occupied the dwelling unit). For leases and rental agreements signed before January 1, 2012: A newly adopted policy limiting or prohibiting smoking is a change in the terms of the tenancy (will not apply to lease-holding tenants until they renew their leases; tenants renting month-to-month must be given 30 days' written notice). Does not preempt any local ordinances prohibiting smoking in effect on January 1, 2012. (Cal. Civ. Code § 1947.5)

Flooding: In leases or rental agreements signed after July 1, 2018, landlord must disclose, in at least eight-point type, that the property is in a special flood hazard area or an area of potential flooding if the landlord has actual knowledge of this fact. Actual knowledge includes receipt from a public agency so identifying the property; the fact that the owner carries flood insurance; or that the property is in an area in which the owner's mortgage

Required Landlord Disclosures (continued)

holder requires the owner to carry flood insurance. Disclosure must advise tenant that additional information can be had at the Office of Emergency Services' website, and must include the internet address for the MYHazards tool maintained by the Office. Disclosure must advise tenant that owner's insurance will not cover loss to tenant's property, and must recommend that tenant consider purchasing renter's insurance that will cover loss due to fire, flood, or other risk of loss. Disclosure must note that the owner is not required to provide additional information. (Cal. Gov't. Code § 8589.45)

Bed bug information: Before signing a lease or rental agreement, landlord must give potential tenants information about bed bugs, including information about their behavior and biology, the importance of cooperation for prevention and treatment, and the importance of prompt written reporting of suspected infestations to the landlord. (Cal. Civ. Code § 1954.603)

Methamphetamine or fentanyl: If a property has been contaminated and is subject to a remediation order, landlord must provide written notice of and a copy of the order to all prospective tenants who have submitted an application. The tenant has to acknowledge receipt of the notice in writing before signing a rental agreement, and the landlord must attach the notice to the rental agreement. If a landlord fails to provide this notice, the prospective tenant can void the rental agreement.

For the rental of mobile homes and manufactured homes, the landlord must notify prospective tenants, in writing, of all methamphetamine or fentanyl laboratory activities that have taken place in the mobile home or manufactured home, and any remediation of the home or vehicle, and the property can't be rented until the prospective tenant is provided with a copy of the order. If there is already a tenant, the landlord must attach the notice and order to the rental agreement. (Cal. Health & Safety Code § 25400.28)

Death on the premises within the past three years: If an occupant died on the property within three years of the landlord's offer to rent, the landlord must disclose this fact. Landlords are not required to disclose that an occupant of that property was living with human immunodeficiency virus (HIV) or died from AIDS-related complications. (Cal. Civ. Code § 1710.2)

Single-family tenancies subject to the Tenant Protection Act of 2019. Landlords of single-family rentals that are not subject to the Tenant Protection Act of 2019 must put the following notice in the lease or rental agreement: "This property is not subject to the rent limits imposed by Section 1947.12 of the Civil Code and is not subject to the just cause requirements of Section 1946.2 of the Civil Code. This property meets the requirements of Sections 1947.12 (d)(5) and 1946.2 (e)(8) of the Civil Code and the owner is not any of the following: (1) a real estate investment trust, as defined by Section 856 of the Internal Revenue Code; (2) a corporation; or (3) a limited liability company in which at least one member is a corporation." (Cal. Civ. Code §§ 1946.2(e)(8), 1947.12)

Single-family tenancies subject to the Tenant Protection Act of 2019, owner move-in. For tenancies subject to the Tenant Protection Act, landlord may terminate the lease in order to move in the owner or the owners spouse, domestic partner, children, grandchildren, parents, or grandparents. If the lease was entered into on or after July 1, 2020, though, the landlord can terminate the lease for this reason only when the tenant agrees in writing OR when the lease specifies that the owner can terminate the lease for this reason. (Cal. Civ. Code § 1946.2(b)(2)(A)))

Tenancies subject to the Tenant Protection Act of 2019. Owners of rentals subject to the Tenant Protection Act of 2019 must provide the following as a written notice to tenants or include it in the written lease or rental agreement: "California law limits the amount your rent can be increased. See Section 1947.12 of the Civil Code for more information. California law also provides that after all of the tenants have continuously and lawfully occupied the property for 12 months or more or at least one of the tenants has continuously and lawfully occupied the property for 24 months or more, a landlord must provide a statement of cause in any notice to terminate a tenancy. See Section 1946.2 of the Civil Code for more information." The notice must be in at least 12-point type. (Cal. Civ. Code § 1946.2(f))

Colorado

Nonrefundable fees permitted? Yes. (Colo. Rev. Stat. § 38-12-801)

Must fee policy be stated in the rental agreement? Yes.

Required Landlord Disclosures (continued)

Landlords can require tenants to pay a fee markup for a service for which the landlord is billed by a third party only when the written rental agreement states that the tenant must pay the markup or fee, and that the markup or fee will be no more than $10 per month or 2% of the amount the landlord was billed—but not both.

Landlords cannot charge a fee for a tenant's failure to provide notice of nonrenewal of a lease, but can charge tenants actual losses incurred as a result of the tenant's failure to provide notice if notice is required under the lease.

Disclosure of landlord: Written rental agreements and leases must include a statement of the name and address of the person who is the landlord or the landlord's authorized agent. If this person's identity changes, the tenants must be notified of the new contact person within one business day after the change, and the landlord must post the identity of the new landlord or authorized agent in a conspicuous location on the rental premises. (Colo. Rev. Stat. § 38-12-801)

Bed bugs: Upon request from prospective tenants, landlords must disclose whether the unit for rent contained bed bugs within the previous eight months. If requested, landlords must also disclose the last date (if any) the unit being rented was inspected for, and found to be free of, bed bugs. (Colo. Rev. Stat. § 38-12-1005)

Rental application fee: Landlords who collect a rental application fee must disclose the anticipated expenses for which the fee will be used or itemize the actual expenses incurred. When landlords charge application fees based on the average cost of processing rental applications, they must explain how they determined the average rental application fee. (Colo. Rev. Stat. § 38-12-903)

Notification of right to use portable screening report: Before a landlord takes any action that might incur an application fee, the landlord must advise the prospective tenant that (1) they have the right to provide the landlord with a portable tenant screening report and (2) if they provide the landlord with a portable tenant screening report, the landlord cant charge an application fee or charge a fee to access or use the report. The notice must be provided in a location and using a method reasonably likely to reach prospective tenants–see statute for specific requirements. (Colo. Rev. Stat. § 38-12-904)

Rental application denial: Landlords who deny rental applications must give rejected applicants a written notice of the denial that states the reasons for the denial. If a landlord cannot site the specific screening criteria because of the use of a proprietary screening system, the landlord must instead provide the rejected applicant with a copy of the report from the screening company. Landlords can provide electronic versions of the denial notice, but must provide a paper denial notice upon request. Landlords must make a good-faith effort to provide the notice within 20 calendar days of the denial. (Colo. Rev. Stat. § 38-12-904)

Source of income nondiscrimination statement: Written lease must include a statement that Colo. Rev. Stat. § 24-34-502(1) prohibits source of income discrimination and requires a non-exempt landlord to accept any lawful and verifiable source of money paid to the landlord directly, indirectly, or on behalf of a person. These sources include income derived from any lawful profession or occupation, and income or rental payments derived from any government or private assistance, grant, or loan program (does not apply to a landlord with five or fewer single-family rental homes and no more than five total rental units, including any single-family homes). (Colo. Rev. Stat. § 38-12-801)

Radon. Before signing a lease, landlords must disclose in writing a notice about radon from the Colorado Department of Public Health, which advises tenants of the risks of radon and recommends testing and remediation. Landlords must disclose any knowledge the landlord has of the property's radon concentrations, and provide a copy of the most recent brochure published by the department of public health and environment that provides advice about radon in real estate transactions. The tenant must sign the notice to acknowledge receipt. Check the statute for the full text of the language required in the notice. (Colo. Rev. Stat. § 38-12-803)

Connecticut

Move-in checklist required? Yes. 2023 Conn. Legis. Serv. P.A. 23-207 (S.B. 998) creates two new landlord-tenant statutes (see sections 4 and 6). The checklist rule is in section 4. At this time, the new rule has not yet been codified.

Must checklist rights be stated in the lease? No.

Required Landlord Disclosures (continued)

Common interest community: When rental is in a common interest community, landlord must give tenant written notice before signing a lease. (Conn. Gen. Stat. § 47a-3e)

Owner or agent identity: Before the beginning of the tenancy, landlord must disclose the name and address of the person authorized to manage the premises and the person who is authorized to receive all notices, demands, and service of process. (Conn. Gen. Stat. § 47a-6)

Bed bug information: Landlords may not advertise a unit that the landlord knows or reasonably suspects is infested with bed bugs. Before signing a lease, landlords must tell prospective tenants whether the unit (or any contiguous unit owned or subleased by the landlord) is infested. If asked by tenants or prospective tenants, landlords must disclose the last date on which the rental unit was inspected for bed bugs and found to be free of any infestation. (Conn. Gen. Stat. § 47a-7a)

Fire system information: When renting a dwelling unit in a building required to be equipped with a fire sprinkler system pursuant to any statute or regulation, the landlord of such dwelling unit must include notice in the rental agreement as to the existence or nonexistence of an operative fire sprinkler system in such building, and such notice shall be printed in not less than twelve-point boldface type of uniform font. If there is an operative fire sprinkler system in the building, the rental agreement will also state the last date of maintenance and inspection, in not less than twelve-point boldface type of uniform font. (Conn. Gen. Stat. § 47a-3f)

Well water testing: If the premises uses water from a private or semiprivate well constructed after October 1, 2022, landlord must submit water quality tests to the Department of Public Health and tell applicants about the availability of literature on the Department's website. Tenant's leasing agent or landlord (if tenant has no agent) must give tenant copies of the Department's recommendations for testing. (Conn. Gen. Stat. § 19a-37)

Just cause eviction protection and rent increase limits: In buildings of five or more units, landlords must give tenants the notice prepared by the Commissioner of Housing, advising tenants of their just cause eviction protections and the requirement that any rent increase be fair and equitable, as defined by statute. (Conn. Gen. Stat. § 47a-23c)

Delaware

Nonrefundable fees permitted? No, except for an optional service fee for actual services rendered, such as a pool fee or tennis court fee. Tenant may elect, subject to the landlord's acceptance, to purchase an optional surety bond instead of or in combination with a security deposit. (*Stoltz Management Co. v. Phillip,* 593 A.2d 583 (1990); Del. Code tit. 25, § 5311)

Owner or agent identity: On each written rental agreement, the landlord must prominently disclose the names and usual business addresses of all persons who are owners of the rental unit or the property of which the rental unit is a part, or the names and business addresses of their appointed resident agents. (Del. Code tit. 25, § 5105)

Summary of Landlord-Tenant Law: A summary of the Landlord-Tenant Code, as prepared by the Consumer Protection Unit of the Attorney General's Office or its successor agency, must be given to the new tenant at the beginning of the rental term. If the landlord fails to provide the summary, the tenant may plead ignorance of the law as a defense. (Del. Code tit. 25, § 5118)

Bed bug information: Before showing or renting a unit, landlords must inspect rentals for evidence of bed bugs and may not show or rent units that the landlord knows or has reason to know are infested. Landlords must tell prospective tenants whether adjacent units are infested with or are being treated for an infestation. (Del. Code tit. 25, § 5317)

Separate utility metering: Landlords may install meters for the purposes of separately charging individual units for utility services, but can only bill tenants according to these measurements if the rental agreement discloses the existence and use of meters. (Del. Code tit. 25, § 5312)

Right to counsel: Landlords must provide tenants with informational materials that explain tenants rights to legal representation in evictions and other landlord-tenant proceedings. The materials must be provided: when signing a lease or entering into an oral tenancy, on the first renewal or modification of a rental agreement, when the landlord provides any other notices regarding the right to counsel, or when the tenant receives notice of the termination of a housing subsidy. (Del. Code tit. 25, § 5606)

Required Landlord Disclosures (continued)

District of Columbia

Nonrefundable fees permitted? Yes. (D.C. Code § 42-3502.22

Must fee policy be stated in the rental agreement? Yes.

General disclosures: Upon receiving a rental application, landlords must provide on a disclosure form published by the Rent Administrator (or in another suitable format until a form is published) along with supporting documents each of the following : (a) the unit's rental rate; (b) any pending petitions filed that could affect the rental unit, including petitions for rent increases during the following 12 months; (c) any surcharges on the rent (including capital improvement surcharges) and the date they expire; (d) the frequency of possible rent increases; (e) the rent-controlled or exempt status of the rental, its business license, and a copy of the registration or claim of exemption (and any recent related filings) ; (f) all copies of code violation reports for the rental within the last 12 months, or previously issued reports for violations that have not been abated; (g) the Rent Administrator's pamphlet that explains rent increases and petitions that can be filed; (h) the amount of any nonrefundable application fee; (i) the amount of the security deposit, the interest rate on the security deposit, and how the security deposit will be returned when the tenant vacates the unit; (j) ownership information; (k) information about the presence of mold in the rental unit or common areas in the previous three years, unless the mold has been remediated by certified and licensed indoor mold remediation professional; (l) the voter registration packet developed by the D.C. Board of Elections (this packet should be part of the Rent Administrator's disclosure form, but if it has not been included in the form, the landlord should provide the packet if one exists); and (m) a copy of the current Tenant Bill of Rights published by the Office of the Tenant Advocate.

Landlords must give written notice to each tenant, on a form published by the Rent Administrator (or in another suitable format until a form is published), that the disclosure forms and documents for the tenants rental unit are available for inspection. The written notice must include the location of the disclosure forms and a table of contents laying out the categories of information included in the disclosure forms.

Upon a tenant's written request not more than once per calendar year, the landlord, within 10 business days of the request, must also disclose the amount of, and the basis for, each rent increase for the prior three years. If applicable, the disclosure must identify any substantially identical rental unit on which a vacancy increase was based. (D.C. Code § 42-3502.22)

Rental regulations: At the start of every new tenancy, landlord must give tenant a copy of the District of Columbia Municipal Regulations, CDCR Title 14, Housing, Chapter 3, Landlord and Tenant; and a copy of Title 14, Housing, Chapter 1, § 101 (Civil Enforcement Policy) and Chapter 1, § 106 (Notification of Tenants Concerning Violations). (14 D.C. Mun. Regs. § 300)

Late fees: Landlords can charge late rent fees only if the maximum amount of the late fee that may be charged is disclosed in the written lease or rental agreement. (D.C. Code § 42-3505.31)

Fire alarms: In buildings with four or more rental, rooming, or sleeping units (including condominium or cooperative units), owners must conspicuously post (and give to each tenant) written information on the following: How to operate manual alarm boxes, how to respond when smoke detectors activate (including abandoning the dwelling unit, closing its door, and activating the nearest alarm box), information on whether the building is monitored by a supervising station, and instructions on calling 911. (12 D.C. Mun. Regs. § PM-704G)

Fees and data: Before requesting information or fees from applicants, landlords must disclose amount and purpose of fees or deposits, whether mandatory or voluntary, and whether refundable. Must describe the types of information requested, the landlord's automatic and optional denial criteria, and the tenant's right to specified information about any credit or consumer report. Landlords must furnish data on the number of units that will become available over a specified time (or, if such data is not available, the number of units available over the prior fiscal year). Must tell applicants that the landlord will approve or deny their application within a stated number of days after receiving it. Tenants must be told of their right to dispute a decision allegedly based on inaccurate information or the landlords use of prohibited criteria (landlords must respond); and of their

Required Landlord Disclosures (continued)

right to file a complaint with the Office of Human Rights or the Superior Court, if they think the landlord has violated these provisions. (D.C. Code § 42-3505.10)

Bed bug information: Landlords may not offer rentals that they know or have reason to know contain bed bugs. If the building has had an infestation within the previous 120 days, before signing a rental agreement the landlord must give tenants the Department of Buildings form, on which specified information must be disclosed. (D.C. Code § 42-3551.02)

Florida

Nonrefundable fees permitted? Yes, allowed by custom, although there is no statute.

Landlord identity: The landlord, or a person authorized to enter into a rental agreement on the landlord's behalf, must disclose in writing to the tenant, at or before the commencement of the tenancy, the name and address of the landlord or a person authorized to receive notices and demands on the landlord's behalf. (Fla. Stat. § 83.50)

Radon: In all leases, landlord must include this warning: "RADON GAS: Radon is a naturally occurring radioactive gas that, when it has accumulated in a building in sufficient quantities, may present health risks to persons who are exposed to it over time. Levels of radon that exceed federal and state guidelines have been found in buildings in Florida. Additional information regarding radon and radon testing may be obtained from your county health department." (Fla. Stat. § 404.056)

Fee in lieu of security deposit: When a tenant chooses to pay a fee in lieu of a security deposit, there must be a written agreement to collect the fee that's signed by the landlord and the tenant. The agreement must specify (1) the amount of the fee; (2) how and when the fee will be collected; (3) the process and timeframe during which the tenant must pay a security deposit if the tenant defaults on paying the fee (and that the default won't affect the tenant's credit rating if the tenant timely pays the security deposit); (4) that the agreement can be terminated at any time as long as the tenant pays the security deposit specified in the rental agreement; and (5) that if the tenant pays the amount of the security deposit specified in the rental agreement, the tenant's default

on paying the fee or termination of the agreement won't adversely affect the tenant's credit report. The agreement must also include specific language that can be found in the statute. (Fla. Stat. § 83.491)

Georgia

Nonrefundable fees permitted? Yes. Landlord and tenant may agree that certain prepaid sums, covering future rent or services or utilities supplied to the tenant, will not be returned to the tenant at the end of the tenancy. (Ga. Code § 44-7-30)

Move-in checklist required? Yes. Landlords cannot collect a security deposit unless they have given tenants a list of preexisting damages. Landlord must provide tenant with a comprehensive list of any existing damage to the premises before the tenant gives landlord a security deposit. (Ga. Code § 44-7-33)

Flooding: Before signing a lease, if the living space or attachments have been damaged by flooding three or more times within the past five years, landlord must so disclose in writing. (Ga. Code § 44-7-20)

Owner or agent identity: When or before a tenancy begins, landlord must disclose in writing the names and addresses of the owner of record (or a person authorized to act for the owner) for purposes of service of process and receiving and receipting demands and notices; and the person authorized to manage the premises. If such information changes during the tenancy, landlord must advise tenant within 30 days in writing or by posting a notice in a conspicuous place. (Ga. Code § 44-7-3)

Former residents, crimes: Unless asked by a prospective tenant, landlord does not have to disclose whether the rental was the site of a homicide or other felony, or a suicide or a death by accidental or natural causes; or whether it was occupied by a person who was infected with a virus or any other disease that has been determined by medical evidence as being highly unlikely to be transmitted through the occupancy of a dwelling place presently or previously occupied by such an infected person. However, if a prospective tenant asks about any of these things, landlord must answer truthfully to the best of the landlord's individual knowledge. (Ga. Code § 44-1-16)

Required Landlord Disclosures (continued)

Hawaii

Nonrefundable fees permitted? No.

Must fee policy be stated in the rental agreement? No.

Other fees: The landlord may not require or receive from or on behalf of a tenant at the beginning of a rental agreement any money other than the money for the first month's rent and a security deposit as provided in this section. (Haw. Rev. Stat. § 521-44)

Owner or agent identity: Landlord must disclose name of owner or agent; if owner lives in another state or on another island, landlord must disclose name of agent on the island. (Haw. Rev. Stat. § 521-43)

Move-in checklist required? Yes. (Haw. Rev. Stat. § 541-42)

Tax excise number: Landlord must furnish its tax excise number so that tenant can file for a low-income tax credit. (Haw. Rev. Stat. § 521-43)

Idaho

No disclosure statutes.

Illinois

Utilities: Where tenant pays a portion of a master metered utility, landlord must give tenant a copy in writing either as part of the lease or another written agreement of the formula used by the landlord for allocating the public utility payments among the tenants. (765 Ill. Comp. Stat. § 740/5)

Rent concessions: Any rent concessions must be described in the lease, in letters not less than one-half inch in height consisting of the words "Concession Granted," including a memorandum on the margin or across the face of the lease stating the amount or extent and nature of each such concession. Failure to comply is a misdemeanor. (765 Ill. Comp. Stat. §§ 730/0.01 to 730/6)

Radon: Landlords are not required to test for radon, but must provide tenants with the Illinois "Radon Guide for Tenants," copies of any records that indicate a radon hazard to the tenant, and the Disclosure of Information on Radon Hazards to Tenants form (see the language in the statute). These disclosures must be made at the time of application, before a lease is entered into, or at any time during the leasing period upon request. (420 Ill. Comp. Stat. § 46/26)

Smoke detectors: Landlord must give one tenant per dwelling written information about smoke detector testing and maintenance. (425 Ill. Comp. Stat. § 60/3(d))

Carbon monoxide alarms: Landlord must give one tenant per dwelling written information regarding CO alarm testing and maintenance. (430 Ill. Comp. Stat. § 135/10(c))

Indiana

Agent identity: Landlord's agent must disclose in writing the name and address of a person living in Indiana who is authorized to manage the property and to act as the owner's agent. (Ind. Code § 32-31-3-18)

Smoke detectors: Landlord must require the tenant to acknowledge in writing that the rental unit is equipped with a functional smoke detector. (Ind. Code § 32-31-5-7)

Floodplain disclosures: If the lowest floor of a rental structure (including a basement) is at or below the 100-year frequency flood elevation, the landlord must disclose in the lease that the structure is located in a floodplain. (Ind. Code § 32-31-1-21)

Water or sewage disposal services: A landlord who pays for water, sewage disposal, or both, and who passes the costs on to tenants must describe the following in the lease, the tenants' first bill, or in a writing before signing the lease: A description of the water or sewage disposal services to be provided, and an itemized statement of the fees that will be charged. The disclosure must be printed using a font that is at least as large as the largest font used in the document in which the disclosure is included. The disclosure must include a description of the water or sewage disposal services to be provided, an itemized statement of the fees that will be charged, and this statement: "If you believe you are being charged in violation of this disclosure or if you believe you are being billed in excess of the utility services provided to you as described in this disclosure, you have a right under Indiana law to file a complaint with the Indiana Utility Regulatory Commission. You may contact the Commission at (insert phone number for the tenant to contact the Commission)." (Ind. Code § 8-1-2-1.2)

Required Landlord Disclosures (continued)

Iowa

Owner or agent identity: Landlord must disclose to the tenant in writing at or before the commencement of the tenancy the name and address of the person authorized to manage the premises, and an owner of the premises or a person authorized to act for and on behalf of the owner for the purpose of service of process and for the purpose of receiving notices and demands. (Iowa Code § 562A.13)

Utilities: For shared utilities, landlord must fully explain utility rates, charges, and services to the prospective tenant before the rental agreement is signed. (Iowa Code § 562A.13)

Contamination: The landlord or a person authorized to enter into a rental agreement on behalf of the landlord must disclose to each tenant, in writing before the commencement of the tenancy, whether the property is listed in the comprehensive environmental response compensation and liability information system maintained by the federal Environmental Protection Agency. (Iowa Code § 562A.13)

Kansas

Move-in checklist required? Yes. Within 5 days of move-in, landlord and tenant must jointly inventory the rental. (Kan. Stat. § 58-2548)

Must checklist rights be stated in the lease? No.

Owner or agent identity: Landlord must disclose to the tenant in writing at or before the commencement of the tenancy the name and address of the person authorized to manage the premises, and an owner of the premises or a person authorized to act for and on behalf of the owner for the purpose of service of process and for the purpose of receiving notices and demands. (Kan. Stat. § 58-2551)

Kentucky

Move-in checklist required? Yes. Landlord and tenant must complete a checklist before landlord can collect a security deposit. (Ky. Rev. Stat. § 383.580)

Owner or agent identity: Landlord must disclose to the tenant in writing at or before the commencement of the tenancy the name and address of the person authorized to manage the premises, and an owner of the premises or a person authorized to act for and on behalf of the owner for the purpose of service of process and for the purpose of receiving notices and demands. (Ky. Rev. Stat. § 383.585)

Methamphetamine contamination disclosure: An owner of contaminated property who rents a property where the local health department has posted a methamphetamine contamination notice must disclose in writing to potential tenants that the property is contaminated and has not been decontaminated pursuant to the state's requirements. The disclosure must contain the physical address of the property, the location within the posted property that was used in the production of methamphetamine, and a copy of the Notice of Methamphetamine Contamination. If a prospective tenant asks, the owner must provide a copy of any documents related to the methamphetamine contamination provided to the owner by law enforcement, the Energy and Environment Cabinet, the Department for Public Health, or the local health department. (Ky. Rev. Stat. § 224.1-410; 902 Ky. Admin. Regs. 47:200)

Louisiana

Application fee: Landlords can't charge an application fee unless they give applicants a written notice of (1) the amount of the fee (2) whether the landlord will consider credit scores, employment history, criminal history, or eviction records in deciding whether to rent to the applicant; and (3) permission for the applicant to provide a statement of 200 words or less explaining that the applicant has experienced financial hardship resulting from a state or federally declared disaster or emergency and how that hardship impacted the applicant's credit, employment, or rental history (the landlord must reference COVID-19 and hurricanes). (La. Rev. Stat. § 9:3258.1)

Foreclosure: Before entering into a lease or rental agreement, landlord must disclose to potential tenants their right to receive notification of any future foreclosure action. If the premises are currently subject to a foreclosure action, landlord must also disclose this in writing. (La. Rev. Stat. § 9:3260.1)

Required Landlord Disclosures (continued)

Maine

Application fee: Landlords can't charge application fees. (Me. Rev. Stat. tit. 14, § 6030-H)

Utilities: No landlord may lease or offer to lease a dwelling unit in a multiunit residential building where the expense of furnishing electricity to the common areas or other area not within the unit is the sole responsibility of the tenant in that unit, unless both parties to the lease have agreed in writing that the tenant will pay for such costs in return for a stated reduction in rent or other specified fair consideration that approximates the actual cost of electricity to the common areas. (Me. Rev. Stat. tit. 14, § 6024)

Energy efficiency: Landlord must provide to potential tenants who will pay for energy costs (or upon request from others) a residential energy efficiency disclosure statement in accordance with Title 35-A, section 10117, subsection 1 that includes, but is not limited to, information about the energy efficiency of the property. Before a tenant enters into a contract or pays a deposit to rent or lease a property, the landlord must provide the statement to the tenant, obtain the tenant's signature on the statement, and sign the statement. The landlord must retain the signed statement for at least 3 years. Alternatively, the landlord may include in the application for the residential property the name of each supplier of energy that previously supplied the unit, if known, and the following statement: "You have the right to obtain a 12-month history of energy consumption and the cost of that consumption from the energy supplier." (Me. Rev. Stat. tit. 14, § 6030-C)

Radon: Unless a mitigation system has been installed, starting in 2014 and every 10 years after when requested by a tenant, the landlord shall test for radon in the rental. If the building was constructed after March 1, 2014, the landlord shall test for radon within 12 months of the occupancy of the building by a tenant. Within 30 days of receiving test results, the landlord shall provide written notice to existing tenants that includes the date of the test, the results, whether mitigation has been performed, the risk associated with radon, and notice that the tenant has the right to conduct a test. The same written notice must also be given to any new tenants before they sign

a lease or pay a deposit to rent. The notice must include an acknowledgment that the tenant has received the disclosure. (Me. Rev. Stat. tit. 14, § 6030-D)

Bed bugs: Before renting a dwelling unit, landlord must disclose to a prospective tenant if an adjacent unit or units are currently infested with or are being treated for bed bugs. Upon request from a tenant or prospective tenant, landlord must disclose the last date that the dwelling unit the landlord seeks to rent or an adjacent unit or units were inspected for a bed bug infestation and found to be free of a bed bug infestation. (Me. Rev. Stat. tit. 14, § 6021-A)

Smoking policy: Landlord must give tenant written disclosure stating whether smoking is prohibited on the premises, allowed on the entire premises, or allowed in limited areas of the premises. If the landlord allows smoking in limited areas on the premises, the notice must identify the areas on the premises where smoking is allowed. Disclosure must be in the lease or separate written notice, landlord must disclose before tenant signs a lease or pays a deposit, and must obtain a written acknowledgment of notification from the tenant. (Me. Rev. Stat. tit. 14, § 6030-E)

Fees at time of application: Although landlords can't charge application fees, they can require applicants to pay the actual cost of a background check, a credit check, or another screening process. A landlord can't charge these fees unless they've notified the applicant that the landlord is required by law to provide the applicant a complete copy of the information obtained pursuant to the background check, credit check, or other screening process. (Me. Rev. Stat. tit. 14, § 6030-H)

Maryland

Move-in checklist required? Yes. Before collecting a deposit, landlord must supply a receipt with details on move-in and move-out inspections, and the receipt must be part of the lease. (Md. Code Real Prop., § 8-203.1)

Must checklist rights be stated in the lease? No.

Habitation: A lease must include a statement that the premises will be made available in a condition permitting habitation, with reasonable safety, if that is the agreement, or if that is not the agreement, a statement of the agreement concerning the condition of

Required Landlord Disclosures (continued)

the premises; and the landlord's and the tenant's specific obligations as to heat, gas, electricity, water, and repair of the premises. (Md. Code Real Prop., § 8-208)

Owner or agent identity: The landlord must include in a lease or post the name and address of the landlord; or the person, if any, authorized to accept notice or service of process on behalf of the landlord. (Md. Code Real Prop., § 8-210)

Montgomery County: Before a prospective tenant signs a lease for 125 days or more, the landlord of a rental within a condominium or development must provide to the prospective tenant, if applicable, a copy of the rules, declaration, and recorded covenants and restrictions that limit or affect the use and occupancy of the property or common areas and to which the owner of the rental is obligated. The written lease must, if applicable, include a statement that the obligations of the owner that limit or affect the use and occupancy of the property are enforceable against the tenant. (Md. Code Real Prop., § 8-210)

Reusable tenant screening reports: Landlords must notify prospective tenants about whether the landlord accepts reusable tenant screening reports (reports generated by a consumer reporting agency within the previous 30 days that the tenant provides to the landlord and for which the landlord doesn't charge an additional fee). Notice must be made in writing or by posting in a conspicuous manner. (Md. Code Real Prop., § 8-218)

Ratio billing systems: Landlords who use a "ratio billing system" must disclose to prospective tenants the utilities that are covered, the landlords method of allocation, and any administrative fees; and copies of the last two statements for each utility and average monthly usage information. Landlords must tell tenants of their rights to inspect records and provide them with a citation to this legal rule. Failure to disclose as required makes the lease unenforceable. (Md. Code Real Prop., § 8-212.4)

Department of agriculture fact sheet: If the landlord knows that the tenant has a domesticated dog or cat, the lease must include a link to the fact sheet from the Department of Agriculture, which will include information on local resources (shelters and rescue organizations) that the tenant can access in the event of termination or eviction. (Md. Code Real Prop., §§ 14-803, 14-804)

Massachusetts

Move-in checklist required? Yes, if landlord collects a security deposit. (Mass. Gen. Laws ch. 186, § 15B(2)(c))

Insurance: Upon tenant's request and within 15 days, landlord must furnish the name of the company insuring the property against loss or damage by fire and the amount of insurance provided by each such company and the name of any person who would receive payment for a loss covered by such insurance. (Mass. Gen. Laws ch. 186, § 21)

Tax escalation: If real estate taxes increase, landlord may pass on a proportionate share of the increase to the tenant only if the lease discloses that in the event of an increase, the tenant will be required to pay only the proportion of the increase as the tenant's leased unit bears to the property being taxed (that proportion must be disclosed in the lease). In addition, the lease must state that if the landlord receives a tax abatement, landlord will refund a proportionate share of the abatement, minus reasonable attorneys' fees. (Mass. Gen. Laws ch. 186, § 15C)

Utilities: Landlord may not charge for water unless the lease specifies the charge and the details of the water submetering and billing arrangement. (Mass. Gen. Laws ch. 186, § 22(f))

Michigan

Move-in checklist required? Yes. (Mich. Comp. Laws § 554.608)

Must checklist rights be stated in the lease? No.

May landlord charge nonrefundable fees? Yes. (*Stutelberg v. Practical Management Co.*, 245 N.W.2d 737 (1976))

Owner or agent identity: A rental agreement must include the name and address at which notice can be given to the landlord. (Mich. Comp. Laws § 554.634)

Truth in Renting Act: A rental agreement must also state in a prominent place in type not smaller than the size of 12-point type, or in legible print with letters not smaller than 1/8 inch, a notice in substantially the following form: "NOTICE: Michigan law establishes rights and obligations for parties to rental agreements. This agreement is required to comply with the Truth in Renting Act. If you have a question about the interpretation or legality

Required Landlord Disclosures (continued)

of a provision of this agreement, you may want to seek assistance from a lawyer or other qualified person." (Mich. Comp. Laws § 554.634)

Rights of domestic violence victims: A rental agreement or lease may contain a provision stating, "A tenant who has a reasonable apprehension of present danger to him or her or his or her child from domestic violence, sexual assault, or stalking may have special statutory rights to seek a release of rental obligation under MCL 554.601b." If the rental agreement or lease does not contain such a provision, the landlord must post an identical written notice visible to a reasonable person in the landlord's property management office, or deliver written notice to the tenant when the lease or rental agreement is signed. (Mich. Comp. Laws § 554.601b)

Minnesota

Move-in checklist required? Yes. (Minn. Stat. § 504B.182)

Must checklist rights be stated in the lease? No.

Owner or agent identity: Landlord must disclose to the tenant in writing at or before the commencement of the tenancy the name and address of the person authorized to manage the premises, and an owner of the premises or a person authorized to act for and on behalf of the owner for the purpose of service of process and for the purpose of receiving notices and demands. (Minn. Stat. § 504B.181)

Outstanding inspection orders, condemnation orders, or declarations that the property is unfit: The landlord must disclose the existence of any such orders or declarations before the tenant signs a lease or pays a security deposit. (Minn. Stat. § 504B.195)

Buildings in financial distress: Once a landlord has received notice of a deed cancellation or notice of foreclosure, landlord may not enter into a periodic tenancy where the tenancy term is more than two months, or a lease where the lease extends beyond the redemption period (other restrictions may apply). (Minn. Stat. § 504B.151)

Landlord and tenant mutual promises: This mutual promise must appear in every lease or rental agreement: "Landlord and tenant promise that neither will unlawfully allow within the premises, common areas, or curtilage of the premises (property boundaries): controlled sub-stances, prostitution or prostitution-related activity; stolen property or property obtained by robbery; or an act of domestic abuse, criminal sexual conduct, or harassment, as defined by MN Statute Section 504B.206(1)(a), against a tenant, licensee, or any authorized occupant. They further promise that the aforementioned areas will not be used by themselves or anyone acting under their control to manufacture, sell, give away, barter, deliver, exchange, distribute, purchase, or possess a controlled substance in violation of any criminal provision of chapter 152." (Minn. Stat. § 504B.171)

Screening fee: Before accepting an applicant's screening fee, landlords must disclose in writing: The name, address, and phone number of the tenant screening service (if landlord uses such a service), and the landlord's acceptance criteria. Landlords must notify rejected applicants within 14 days, identifying the criteria the applicant did not meet. (Minn. Stat. § 504B.173)

"Nonoptions fees": The sum of all nonoptional fees must be described as the "Total Monthly Payment" on the first page of the lease, and included in any ad or posting. In the lease and any ad, landlord must disclose whether utilities are included in the rent. (Minn. Stat. § 504B.120)

Initial inspection right: The landlord must notify the tenant (at either the beginning of the tenancy or within 14 days of moving in) of their option to request an initial inspection. (Minn. Stat. § 504B.182)

Move-out inspection right: Within a reasonable time after notification of either the landlords or tenants intent to end the tenancy (or before the end of the lease term), the landlord must notify the tenant in writing of the tenants option to request a move-out inspection and of the tenants right to be present at the inspection. (Minn. Stat. § 504B.182)

Mississippi

No disclosure statutes.

Missouri

Methamphetamine: Landlord who knows that the premises were used to produce methamphetamine must disclose this fact to prospective tenants, regardless of whether the people involved in the production were convicted for such production. (Mo. Rev. Stat. § 441.236)

Required Landlord Disclosures (continued)

Owner or agent identity: Landlord must disclose to the tenant in writing at or before the commencement of the tenancy the name and address of the person authorized to manage the premises, and an owner of the premises or a person authorized to act for and on behalf of the owner for the purpose of service of process and for the purpose of receiving notices and demands. (Mo. Rev. Stat. § 535.185)

Radioactive or hazardous material: Landlords who know that the rental property is or was contaminated with radioactive or other hazardous material must disclose this fact to prospective tenants. Landlords have knowledge when they've received a report stating that the property is or was contaminated. Failure to disclose when required is a Class A misdemeanor. (Mo. Rev. Stat. § 442.055)

Montana

Nonrefundable fees permitted? No. A fee or charge for cleaning and damages, no matter how designated, is presumed to be a security deposit. (Not a clear statement that such a fee isn't nonrefundable, but by implication it must be.) (Mont. Code § 70-25-101(4))

Must fee policy be stated in the rental agreement? Yes.

Move-in checklists required? Yes, checklists are required when landlords collect a security deposit. (Mont. Code § 70-25-206)

Owner or agent identity: Landlords or people authorized to enter into a rental agreement on their behalf shall disclose to the tenant in writing at or before the commencement of the tenancy the name and address of the person authorized to manage the premises; and the owner of the premises or a person authorized to act for the owner for the purpose of service of process and receiving notices and demands. (Mont. Code § 70-24-301)

Mold: Before signing a lease, if a landlord has knowledge that mold is present in the rental, the landlord must disclose its presence; and if the landlord knows that the building has been tested for mold, the landlord must advise the tenant that testing has occurred and provide a copy of the results (if available), as well as any evidence of subsequent treatment. Landlords can avoid liability for damages resulting from mold if they comply with these rules, provide tenants with a mold disclosure statement in the form prescribed by statute, and obtain the tenants' written acknowledgment of receipt of the statement. (Mont. Code § 70-16-703)

Methamphetamine contamination: Before signing a lease or rental agreement, a landlord who knows that the property has been contaminated from smoke from the use of meth or was used as a meth lab must disclose this history to a potential tenant. Disclosure is not required if the property has been remediated to the states standards by a contractor who is certified by the state. Landlords who themselves did not cause the contamination, and who have obtained documentation of decontamination that they have provided to tenants, will not be liable in a tenant's lawsuit for damages. (Mont. Code § 75-10-1305)

Nebraska

Owner or agent identity: The landlord or any person authorized to enter into a rental agreement on his or her behalf shall disclose to the tenant in writing at or before the commencement of the tenancy the name and address of the person authorized to manage the premises; and an owner of the premises or a person authorized to act for and on behalf of the owner for the purpose of service of process receiving notices and demands. (Neb. Rev. Stat. § 76-1417)

Nevada

Nonrefundable fees permitted? Yes. Lease must explain fees that are required and the purposes for which they are required. (Nev. Rev. Stat. § 118A.200)

Must fee policy be stated in the rental agreement? Yes.

Move-in checklist required? Yes. Lease must include tenants' rights to a checklist and a signed record of the inventory and condition of the premises under the exclusive custody and control of the tenant. (Nev. Rev. Stat. § 118A.200)

Must checklist rights be stated in the lease? Yes.

Nuisance and flying the flag: Lease must include a summary of the provisions of NRS 202.470 (penalties for permitting or maintaining a nuisance); information regarding the procedure a tenant may use to report to the appropriate authorities a nuisance, a violation of a building, safety, or health code or regulation; and information regarding the right of the tenant to engage in the display of the flag of the United States, as set forth in NRS 118A.325. (Nev. Rev. Stat. § 118A.200)

Required Landlord Disclosures (continued)

Foreclosure proceedings: Landlord must disclose to any prospective tenant, in writing, whether the premises to be rented is the subject of a foreclosure proceeding (disclosure need not be in the lease). (Nev. Rev. Stat. § 118A.275)

Lease signed by an agent of the landlord who does not hold a property management permit: In single-family rentals only, unless the lease is signed by an authorized agent of the landlord who holds a current property management permit, the top of the first page of the lease must state, in font that is at least twice the size of any other size in the agreement, that the tenant might not have valid occupancy unless the lease is notarized or signed by an authorized agent of the owner who holds a management permit. The notice must give the current address and phone number of the landlord. In addition, it must state that even if the foregoing has not been provided, the agreement is enforceable against the landlord. (Nev. Rev. Stat. § 118A.200)

New Hampshire

Move-in checklist required? Yes. Landlord must inform tenant that if tenant finds any conditions in the rental in need of repair, tenant may note them on the security deposit receipt or other writing (not a true checklist). (N.H. Rev. Stat. § 540-A:6)

Must checklist rights be stated in the lease? No.

Methamphetamine: If methamphetamine was produced on a property and the department of environmental sciences has not determined that the property meets remediation cleanup standards, the landlord must disclose in writing to the tenant that methamphetamine production has occurred. (N.H. Rev. Stat. § 477:4-g)

New Jersey

Flood zone: Before signing or renewing a lease, landlords must notify tenants in writing whether the property is in a 100-year floodplain or a 500-year floodplain and whether the landlord has actual knowledge of the rental or any portion of the parking area having flooded in the past. The notice must be signed by the tenant. If disclosure is done as part of the lease, it must be a separate rider, individually signed or otherwise acknowledged by the tenant, and written in not less than 12–point typeface. Landlords may instead use the Department of Community Affairs model flood risk notice. (N.J. Stat. § 46:8-50)

Flood insurance: Leases must contain the following notice: "Flood insurance may be available to renters through FEMA's National Flood Insurance Program to cover your personal property and contents in the event of a flood. A standard renter's insurance policy does not typically cover flood damage. You are encouraged to examine your policy to determine whether you are covered." (N.J. Stat. § 46:8-50)

Truth in Renting Act: Except in buildings of two or fewer units, and owner-occupied premises of three or fewer units, landlord must distribute to new tenants at or prior to move-in the Department of Community Affairs' statement of legal rights and responsibilities of tenants and landlords of rental dwelling units (Spanish also). (N.J. Stat. §§ 46:8-44, 46:8-45, 46:8-46.)

Child protection windowguards: Landlords of multi-family properties must include information in the lease about tenants' rights to request window guards. The Legislature's Model Lease and Notice clause reads as follows: "The owner (landlord) is required by law to provide, install and maintain window guards in the apartment if a child or children 10 years of age or younger is, or will be, living in the apartment or is, or will be, regularly present there for a substantial period of time if the tenant gives the owner (landlord) a written request that the window guards be installed. The owner (landlord) is also required, upon the written request of the tenant, to provide, install and maintain window guards in the hallways to which persons in the tenant's unit have access without having to go out of the building. If the building is a condominium, cooperative or mutual housing building, the owner (landlord) of the apartment is responsible for installing and maintaining window guards in the apartment and the association is responsible for installing and maintaining window guards in hallway windows. Window guards are only required to be provided in first floor windows where the window sill is more than six feet above grade or there are other hazardous conditions that make installation of window guards necessary to protect the safety of children." The notice must be conspicuous and in boldface type. Also, certain multi-family landlords must offer a window guard orientation program, and must post notice of the program in appropriate common

Required Landlord Disclosures (continued)

areas of the building at least two weeks before the date of the program. (N.J. Stat. § 55:13A-7.14; N.J. Admin. Code §§ 5:10-27.1, 5:10-27 App. 27A)

Water quality: Owners of multifamily properties who must prepare a Consumer Confidence Report, or who receive such a report from a public community water system, must post the report in every routinely used common area (if the property has no such area, owners must give copies to each rental unit). Owners of multifamily properties who supply water, who are not required to prepare a Consumer Confidence Report, but who must test its water, must post a chart containing the results of the tests. Charts must be posted in every routinely used common area (if the property has no such area, owners must give copies to each rental unit). (N.J. Stat. § 55:13A-7.18)

Application fee: Landlords cannot collect application fees without first disclosing in writing to the applicant whether the landlord will review and consider criminal history and a statement that the applicant may provide evidence demonstrating inaccuracies within the applicant's criminal record or evidence of rehabilitation or other mitigating factors. (N.J. Stat. § 46:8-55)

Postings in multiple dwellings: Landlords of tenant-occupied multiple dwellings must post in a conspicuous area where likely to be seen by tenants the following information in both English and Spanish: (1) emergency contact info for the owner or managing agent (2) instructions on how to access and use the comprehensive social services information toll-free telephone hotline. The information must also be posted on the website of any management company that manages a tenant-occupied multiple dwelling. (N.J. Stat. § 55:13A-7.19(1)(a))

Multiple dwellings lease disclosure: Every lease offered to a tenant in a multiple dwelling must include in both English and Spanish: (1) the website address of the management company and (2) instructions on how to access and use the comprehensive social services information toll-free telephone hotline. (N.J. Stat. § 55:13A-7.19(1)(b))

New Mexico

Owner or agent identity: Landlord must disclose to the tenant in writing at or before the commencement of the tenancy the name and address of the person authorized

to manage the premises, and an owner of the premises or a person authorized to act for and on behalf of the owner for the purpose of service of process and for the purpose of receiving notices and demands. (N.M. Stat. § 47-8-19)

Illegal drug lab on premises: Landlord cannot rent a property where controlled substances were manufactured or located unless landlord provides written notice to tenant of these facts. The tenant must acknowledge receipt of the notice in writing, and the landlord must provide a copy of the notice and acknowledgement to the New Mexico environment department. (N.M. Admin. Code § 20.4.5.13)

New York

Nonrefundable fees permitted? No. (N.Y. Gen. Oblig. Laws § 7-108)

Must fee policy be stated in the rental agreement? No.

Move-in checklist required? Yes. Tenants are entitled to a pre-move out inspection unless tenant terminates with less than two weeks' notice. (N.Y. Gen. Oblig. Laws § 7-108)

Must checklist rights be stated in the lease? No.

Air contamination: Landlord who receives a government report showing that air in the building has, or may have, concentrations of volatile organic compounds (VOCs) that exceed governmental guidelines must give written notice to prospective and current tenants. The notice must appear in at least 12-point bold face type on the first page of the lease or rental agreement. It must read as follows: "NOTIFICATION OF TEST RESULTS The property has been tested, for contamination of indoor air: test results and additional information are available upon request." (N.Y. Envtl. Conserv. Law § 27-2405)

Certificate of occupancy: In structures with three or fewer dwelling units, where a certificate of occupancy is required by law, landlords must provide prospective tenants proof of a current certificate prior to signing a lease or rental agreement. Landlords may provide prospective tenants with a copy of the actual certificate, or provide notice of said certificate in boldface type. Waivers of this requirement are void. (N.Y. Real Prop. Law § 235-bb)

Smoke detectors: In most multifamily buildings of three or more units, condominiums, and cooperatives throughout the state, landlords must notify tenants in writing, individually or by posting a notice in a common

Required Landlord Disclosures (continued)

area, of owners' and tenants' duties regarding smoke detectors. Check state and local laws for the exact requirement that applies to your unit. (See, e.g., N.Y. Mult. Res. Law §§ 3, 4, 15; N.Y. Mult. Dwell. Law §§ 3, 4, 68.)

Reasonable accommodation: Landlords must give all tenants and prospective tenants a written notice of their right to request reasonable modifications and accommodations for their disability. The notice must be posted in all vacant available rentals and given to all current tenants within 30 days of the beginning of their tenancy. The law, 9 NYCRR Section 466.15(e), provides the wording for the required notice, which landlords may copy and distribute.

Flood disclosures: Every lease must disclose whether any or all of the premises are within a FEMA flood plain, a Special Flood Hazard Area or 100-year floodplain, a Moderate Risk Flood Hazard Area or 500-year floodplain, and whether the premises has been flooded due to a natural flood event. The lease must include this notice: "Flood insurance is available to renters through the Federal Emergency Management Agency's (FEMA's) National Flood Insurance Program (NFIP) to cover your personal property and contents in the event of a flood. A standard renter's insurance policy does not typically cover flood damage. You are encouraged to examine your policy to determine whether you are covered." (N.Y. Real Prop. Law § 231-b)

North Carolina

Nonrefundable fees permitted? Landlord may collect only one of the following, when specific conditions are met: Complaint filing fee, court appearance fee, and second trial fee. Failure to pay the fees cannot support a termination notice. (N.C. Gen. Stat. § 42-46)

Must fee policy be stated in the rental agreement? Yes.

Eviction fees: If landlords wish to collect fees relating to eviction, they must specify certain types of fees in a written lease. Landlords must disclose their right to collect reasonable attorneys' fees, which cannot exceed 15% of the amount owed by the tenant, or 15% of the monthly rent stated in the lease if the eviction is based on a default other than the nonpayment of rent. Landlords must also disclose the fees they will charge for filing a complaint, to appear in court, and for their

second trial (landlord can charge and retain only one of these fees). (N.C. Gen. Stat. § 42-46)

Attorneys' fees and costs: Landlords cannot charge tenants for attorneys' fees and costs without making certain disclosures.

North Dakota

Move-in checklist required? Yes. Landlord must give tenant a statement describing the condition of the premises when tenant signs the rental agreement. Both parties must sign the statement. (N.D. Cent. Code § 47-16-07.2)

Must checklist rights be stated in the lease? No.

Ohio

Owner or agent identity: Every written rental agreement must contain the name and address of the owner and the name and address of the owner's agent, if any. If the owner or the owner's agent is a corporation, partnership, limited partnership, association, trust, or other entity, the address must be the principal place of business in the county in which the residential property is situated. If there is no place of business in such county, then its principal place of business in this state must be disclosed, including the name of the person in charge thereof. (Ohio Rev. Code § 5321.18)

Oklahoma

Flooding: If the premises to be rented has been flooded within the past five (5) years and such fact is known to the landlord, the landlord shall include such information prominently and in writing as part of any written rental agreements. (Okla. Stat. tit. 41, § 113a)

Owner information: As a part of any rental agreement the lessor shall prominently and in writing identify what person at what address is entitled to accept service or notice under this act. Landlord must disclose to the tenant in writing at or before the commencement of the tenancy the name and address of the person authorized to manage the premises, and an owner of the premises or a person authorized to act for and on behalf of the owner for the purpose of service of process and receiving notices and demands. (Okla. Stat. tit. 41, § 116)

Smoke detectors: Landlord must explain to tenant how to test the smoke detector to ensure that it is in working order. (Okla. Stat. tit. 74, § 324.11a)

Required Landlord Disclosures (continued)

Methamphetamine: Before signing a rental agreement, if the landlord knows or has reason to know that the unit or any part of the premises was used in the manufacture of methamphetamine, the landlord must disclose this information to a prospective tenant. Does not apply when the landlord has tested the unit or premises and the results show that the level of contamination is less than 0.1 mcg per 100cm2 of surface materials in the affected part. (Okla. Stat. tit. 41, § 118)

Tenant repairs, maintenance, alterations or remodeling: When landlord and tenant agree that the tenant will perform specified repairs, maintenance tasks, alterations, or remodeling, they must put this agreement in writing, independent of the rental agreement, and presented in a manner that will make it hard to overlook (using ample font size, for example). (Okla. Stat. tit. 41, § 118)

Oregon

Nonrefundable fees permitted? No. (Or. Rev. Stat. § 90.302)

Must fee policy be stated in the rental agreement? Yes.

Other fees? Landlords' written rules may not provide for tenant fees, except for specified events as they arise, including a late rent payment; tenant's late payment of a utility or service charge; a dishonored check, pursuant to Or. Rev. Stat. § 30.701(5); failure to clean up pet waste in areas other than tenant's unit; failure to clean up garbage and rubbish (outside tenant's dwelling unit); failure to clean pet waste of a service or companion animal from areas other than the dwelling unit; parking violations and improper use of vehicles within the premises; smoking in a designated nonsmoking area; keeping an unauthorized pet capable of inflicting damage on persons or property; and tampering or disabling a smoke detector.

Owner or agent identity: Landlord must disclose to the tenant in writing at or before the commencement of the tenancy the name and address of the person authorized to manage the premises, and an owner of the premises or a person authorized to act for and on behalf of the owner for the purpose of service of process and for the purpose of receiving notices and demands. (Or. Rev. Stat. § 90.305)

Legal proceedings: If at the time of the execution of a rental agreement for a dwelling unit in premises containing no more than four dwelling units the premises are subject to any of the following circumstances, the landlord must disclose that circumstance to the tenant in writing before the execution of the rental agreement:

a. Any outstanding notice of default under a trust deed, mortgage, or contract of sale, or notice of trustee's sale under a trust deed

b. Any pending suit to foreclose a mortgage, trust deed, or vendor's lien under a contract of sale

c. Any pending declaration of forfeiture or suit for specific performance of a contract of sale; or

d. Any pending proceeding to foreclose a tax lien.

(Or. Rev. Stat. § 90.310)

Utilities: The landlord must disclose to the tenant in writing at or before the commencement of the tenancy any utility or service that the tenant pays directly to a utility or service provider that directly benefits the landlord or other tenants. A tenant's payment for a given utility or service benefits the landlord or other tenants if the utility or service is delivered to any area other than the tenant's dwelling unit.

A landlord may require a tenant to pay to the landlord a utility or service charge that has been billed by a utility or service provider to the landlord for utility or service provided directly to the tenant's dwelling unit or to a common area available to the tenant as part of the tenancy. A utility or service charge that shall be assessed to a tenant for a common area must be described in the written rental agreement separately and distinctly from such a charge for the tenant's dwelling unit. Unless the method of allocating the charges to the tenant is described in the tenant's written rental agreement, the tenant may require that the landlord give the tenant a copy of the provider's bill as a condition of paying the charges. (Or. Rev. Stat. § 90.315)

Recycling: In a city or the county within the urban growth boundary of a city that has implemented multifamily recycling service, a landlord who has five or more residential dwelling units on a single premises must notify new tenants at the time of entering into a rental agreement of the opportunity to recycle. (Or. Rev. Stat. § 90.318)

Smoking policy: Landlord must disclose the smoking policy for the premises, by stating whether smoking is prohibited on the premises, allowed on the entire

Required Landlord Disclosures (continued)

premises, or allowed in limited areas. If landlord allows smoking in limited areas, the disclosure must identify those areas. (Or. Rev. Stat. § 90.220)

Carbon monoxide alarm instructions: If rental contains a CO source (a heater, fireplace, appliance, or cooking source that uses coal, kerosene, petroleum products, wood, or other fuels that emit carbon monoxide as a by product of combustion; or an attached garage with an opening that communicates directly with a living space), landlord must install one or more CO monitors and give tenant written instructions for testing the alarm(s), before tenant takes possession. (Or. Rev. Stat. §§ 90.316, 90.317)

Smoke alarm or smoke detector: When tenant moves in, landlord must give tenant written instructions for testing smoke alarms and smoke detectors. (Or. Rev. Stat. § 479.270)

Flood zone: If a dwelling unit is located in a 100-year floodplain, the landlord must provide notice in the dwelling unit rental agreement that the dwelling unit is located within the floodplain. If a landlord fails to provide a notice as required under this section, and the tenant of the dwelling unit suffers an uninsured loss due to flooding, the tenant may recover from the landlord the lesser of the actual damages for the uninsured loss or two months' rent. (Or. Rev. Stat. § 90.228)

Renters' insurance: Landlord may require tenants to maintain liability insurance (certain low-income and subsidized tenancies excepted), but only if the landlord obtains and maintains comparable liability insurance and provides documentation to any tenant who requests the documentation, orally or in writing. The landlord may provide documentation to a tenant in person, by mail, or by posting in a common area or office. The documentation may consist of a current certificate of coverage. Any landlord who requires tenants to obtain renters' insurance must disclose the requirement and amount in writing prior to entering into a new tenancy, and may require the tenant to provide documentation before the tenancy begins. (Or. Rev. Stat. § 90.222)

Homeowner assessments: If landlord wants to pass on homeowners' association assessments that are imposed on anyone moving into or out of the unit, the written rental agreement must include this requirement. Landlord must give tenants a copy of each assessment before charging the tenant. (Or. Rev. Stat. § 90.302)

Applicant screening fees: Before accepting application fees, landlords must, among other things, disclose in writing to the applicant (1) the amount of the screening charge (2) the landlord's criteria for selection (3) the screening process and considerations (4) the applicant's right to dispute information in a screening report (5) required nondiscrimination policies (6) the amount of rent and deposits, and (7) whether the landlord requires renters' insurance (and how much). After each screening, the landlord must provide the applicant with a confirmation of the screening along with a copy of the receipt for the screening. (Or. Rev. Stat. § 90.295)

Receipt of notices via email: Official notices from either the landlord or the tenant may be sent by email only if a written addendum to the rental agreement specifies the email addresses for the tenant and landlord, is signed by each party after the tenancy begins and the tenant has moved in, allows the landlord or tenant to terminate the ability to send notices by email, and contains a statutory notice about receiving written notices (see statute for language). (Or. Rev. Stat. § 90.155)

Pennsylvania

No disclosure statutes.

Rhode Island

Owner disclosure: Landlord must disclose to the tenant in writing at or before the commencement of the tenancy the name and address of the person authorized to manage the premises, and an owner of the premises or a person authorized to act for and on behalf of the owner for the purpose of service of process and for the purpose of receiving notices and demands. (R.I. Gen. Laws § 34-18-20)

Code violations: Before entering into any residential rental agreement, landlord must inform a prospective tenant of any outstanding minimum housing code violations that exist on the building that is the subject of the rental agreement. (R.I. Gen. Laws § 34-18-22.1)

Notice of foreclosure: A landlord who becomes delinquent on a mortgage securing real estate upon which the rental is located for a period of 120 days must notify the tenant that the property may be subject to foreclosure; and until the foreclosure occurs, the tenant must continue to pay rent to the landlord as provided under the rental agreement. (R.I. Gen. Laws § 34-18-20)

Required Landlord Disclosures (continued)

General liability insurance policy: Landlords must provide a copy of the declaration page from the landlord's general liability policy with the lease, and must provide tenants with a new copy each time the policy is renewed. (R.I. Gen. Laws § 34-18-22)

South Carolina

Owner or agent identity: Landlord must disclose to the tenant in writing at or before the commencement of the tenancy the name and address of the person authorized to manage the premises, and an owner of the premises or a person authorized to act for and on behalf of the owner for the purpose of service of process and for the purpose of receiving notices and demands. (S.C. Code § 27-40-420)

Unequal security deposits: If landlord rents five or more adjoining units on the premises, and imposes different standards for calculating deposits required of tenants, landlord must, before a tenancy begins, post in a conspicuous place a statement explaining the standards by which the various deposits are calculated (or, landlord may give the tenant the written statement). (S.C. Code § 27-40-410)

Smoke detectors: When tenant moves in, owner must give tenant written or verbal instructions, or both, for testing the detectors and replacing batteries in battery-powered detectors. (S.C. Code § 5-25-1330)

South Dakota

Methamphetamine: Landlord who has actual knowledge of the existence of any prior manufacturing of methamphetamines on the premises must disclose that information to any lessee or any person who may become a lessee. If the residential premises consists of two or more housing units, the disclosure requirements apply only to the unit where there is knowledge of the existence of any prior manufacturing of methamphetamines. (S.D. Codified Laws § 43-32-30)

Tennessee

Owner or agent identity: The landlord or any person authorized to enter into a rental agreement on the landlord's behalf must disclose to the tenant in writing at or before the commencement of the tenancy the name and address of the agent authorized to manage the premises, and an owner of the premises or a person or agent authorized to act for and on behalf of the owner for the acceptance of service of process and for receipt of notices and demands. (Tenn. Code § 66-28-302)

Showing rental to prospective tenants: Landlord may enter to show the premises to prospective renters during the final 30 days of a tenancy (with 24 hours' notice), but only if this right of access is set forth in the rental agreement or lease. (Tenn. Code § 66-28-403)

Texas

Nonrefundable fees permitted? Yes. (*Holmes v. Canlen Management Corp.*, 542 S.W.2d 199 (1976).) Landlords cannot collect late fees unless notice of the fee is included in a written lease. (Tex. Prop. Code § 92.019)

Must fee policy be stated in the rental agreement? Yes.

Owner or agent identity: In the lease, other writing, or posted on the property, landlord must disclose the name and address of the property's owner and, if an entity located off-site from the dwelling is primarily responsible for managing the dwelling, the name and street address of the management company. (Tex. Prop. Code § 92.201)

Emergency contact information: Landlords must provide tenants with an emergency phone number to call when there is a condition affecting physical health or safety of tenant. (Tex. Prop. Code § 92.020)

Security device requests: If landlord wants tenant requests concerning security devices to be in writing, this requirement must be in the lease in boldface type or underlined. (Tex. Prop. Code § 92.159)

Return of security deposit: A requirement that a tenant give advance notice of moving out as a condition for refunding the security deposit is effective only if the requirement is in the lease, underlined or printed in conspicuous bold print. (Tex. Prop. Code § 92.103)

Domestic violence victims' rights: Victims of sexual abuse or assault on the premises may break a lease, after complying with specified procedures, without responsibility for future rent. Tenants will be responsible for any unpaid back rent, but only if the lease includes the following statement, or one substantially like it: "Tenants may have special statutory rights to terminate the lease early in certain situations involving family violence or a military deployment or transfer." (Tex. Prop. Code § 92.016)

Required Landlord Disclosures (continued)

Tenant's rights when landlord fails to repair: A lease must contain language in underlined or bold print that informs the tenant of the remedies available when the landlord fails to repair a problem that materially affects the physical health or safety of an ordinary tenant. These rights include the right to: repair and deduct; terminate the lease; and obtain a judicial order that the landlord make the repair, reduce the rent, pay the tenant damages (including a civil penalty), and pay the tenant's court and attorneys' fees. (Tex. Prop. Code § 92.056)

Landlord's towing or parking rules and policies: For tenants in multiunit properties, if the landlord has vehicle towing or parking rules or policies that apply to the tenant, the landlord must give the tenant a copy of the rules or policies before the lease agreement is signed. The copy must be signed by the tenant, included in the lease or rental agreement, or be made an attachment to either. If included, the clause must be titled "Parking" or "Parking Rules" and be capitalized, underlined, or printed in bold print (Tex. Prop. Code § 92.0131)

Electric service interruption: Landlord who submeters electric service, or who allocates master metered electricity according to a prorated system, may interrupt tenant's electricity service if tenant fails to pay the bill, but only after specific notice and according to a complex procedure. Exceptions for ill tenants and during extreme weather. (Tex. Prop. Code § 92.008(h))

Selection criteria for applicants: At the time landlords provide prospective tenants with applications, they must also provide printed notice of their tenant selection criteria, including reasons why applications may be denied. The notice must contain certain acknowledgment language that the applicant must sign. (Tex. Prop. Code § 92.3515)

Floodplain disclosure: Landlords must provide tenants with written notice stating the substantial equivalent of: "Landlord ( ) is or ( ) is not aware that the dwelling you are renting is located in a 100-year floodplain. If neither box is checked, you should assume the dwelling is in a 100-year floodplain. Even if the dwelling is not in a 100-year floodplain, the dwelling may still be susceptible to flooding. The Federal Emergency Management Agency (FEMA) maintains a flood map on its Internet website that is searchable by address, at no cost, to determine if a dwelling is located in a flood hazard area. Most ten-

ant insurance policies do not cover damages or loss incurred in a flood. You should seek insurance coverage that would cover losses caused by a flood." If the landlord knows that flooding has damaged any portion of a dwelling at least once during the five-year period immediately preceding the effective date of the lease, the landlord shall provide a written notice to tenant that's substantially equivalent to: "Landlord ( ) is or ( ) is not aware that the dwelling you are renting has flooded at least once within the last five years." These notices must be given to the tenant in a separate written document at or before the execution of the lease. (Tex. Prop. Code § 92.0135)

Utah

Nonrefundable fees permitted? Yes. All fees, fines, assessments, interest, or other costs must be included in the lease or rental agreement, unless the rental agreement is on a month-to-month basis and the landlord provides the renter a 15-day notice of the charge. (Utah Code § 57-22-4)

If there's a written agreement and if any part of the deposit is to be made nonrefundable, the landlord must put this in writing at the time the deposit is collected. (Utah Code § 57-17-2)

Must fee policy be stated in the rental agreement? Yes.

Move-in checklists required? Yes. Landlords must give prospective renters a written inventory of the condition of the residential rental unit (excluding ordinary wear and tear); give the renter a form to document the condition of the residential rental and allow the resident a reasonable time after the renter's occupancy of the unit to complete and return the form; or provide the prospective renter an opportunity to conduct a walk-through inspection of the rental. (Utah Code § 57-22-4)

Must checklist rights be stated in the lease? No.

Applicant Disclosures: Before accepting an application fee or any other payment from a prospective renter, the landlord must disclose in writing: (1) a good faith estimate of the rent and each fixed, non-rent expense that's part of the lease or rental agreement (2) the type of each use-based, non-rent expense that's part of the lease or rental agreement (3) the day that the rental will be available (4) the criteria the landlord will use to determine

Required Landlord Disclosures (continued)

whether to rent to the applicant; and (5) how the applicant can recover any payments made if the good-faith rent or expense estimates were incorrect. (Utah Code § 57-22-4)

Disclosure of management: Before the tenancy begins, the landlord must disclose in writing the owner's name, address, and telephone number or the name, address, and telephone number of any person authorized to manage the rental or act on behalf of the owner and receive notices. (Utah Code § 57-22-4)

Disclosure of rules: Before the tenancy begins, the landlord must provide the renter with a copy of any rules and regulations applicable to the rental. The landlord must also provide a signed copy of the written lease or rental agreement. (Utah Code § 57-22-4)

Methamphetamine contamination: If landlord has actual knowledge that the property is currently contaminated from the use, storage, or manufacture of methamphetamine, the landlord must disclose that the property is contaminated in the lease. (Utah Code § 57-27-201)

Vermont

No disclosure statutes.

Virginia

Move-in checklist required? Yes. Within five days of move-in, landlord or tenant or both together must prepare a written report detailing the condition of the premises. Landlord must disclose within this report the known presence of mold. (Va. Code § 55.1-1214)

Must checklist rights be stated in the lease? No.

Tenant rights and responsibilities: Landlords shall offer prospective tenants a written lease or rental agreement that contains the terms of the tenancy and provide with it the statement of tenant rights and responsibilities developed by the Department of Housing and Community Development. (Va. Code § 55.1-1204)

Renters' insurance: If the lease or rental agreement doesn't require the tenant to obtain renters' insurance, the landlord must provide a written notice to the tenant before signing the lease or rental agreement stating that (1) the landlord isn't responsible for the tenant's personal property (2) the landlord's insurance doesn't cover the tenant's personal property (3) if the tenant wishes to

protect personal property, the tenant should purchase renter's insurance; and (4) that any renters' insurance obtained by tenant won't cover flood damage and the renter should find out whether the property is in a special flood hazard area. (Va. Code § 55.1-1206)

Owner or agent identity: Landlord must disclose to the tenant in writing at or before the commencement of the tenancy the name and address of the person authorized to manage the premises, and an owner of the premises or a person authorized to act for and on behalf of the owner for the purpose of service of process and for the purpose of receiving notices and demands. (Va. Code § 55.1-1216)

Sale plans: In the event of the sale of the premises, the landlord must notify tenants of the sale and disclose to tenants the name and address of the purchaser and a telephone number for contacting the purchaser. (Va. Code § 55.1-1216)

Military zone: The landlord of property in any locality in which a military air installation is located, or any person authorized to enter into a rental agreement on landlord's behalf, must provide to a prospective tenant a written disclosure that the property is located in a noise zone or accident potential zone, or both, as designated by the locality on its official zoning map. (Va. Code § 55.1-1217)

Mold: Move-in inspection report must include whether there is any visible evidence of mold (deemed correct unless tenant objects within five days); if evidence is present, tenant may terminate or not move in. If tenant stays, landlord must remediate the mold condition within five business days, reinspect, and issue a new report indicating that there is no evidence of mold. (Va. Code § 55.1-1215)

Ratio utility billing: Landlords who use a ratio utility billing service or who intend to collect monthly billing and other administrative and late fees, must disclose these fees in a written rental agreement. (Va. Code § 55.1-1212)

Condominium plans: If an application for registration as a condominium or cooperative has been filed with the Real Estate Board, or if there is within six months an existing plan for tenant displacement resulting from demolition or substantial rehabilitation of the property, or conversion of the rental property to office, hotel, or

Required Landlord Disclosures (continued)

motel use or planned unit development, the landlord or any person authorized to enter into a rental agreement on his behalf must disclose that information in writing to any prospective tenant. (Va. Code § 55.1-1216)

Defective drywall: Landlords who know of the presence of unrepaired defective drywall in the rental must disclose this before the tenant signs a lease or rental agreement. (Va. Code § 55.1-1218)

Methamphetamine: When the landlord knows that the unit was used to manufacture methamphetamine, landlord must give the tenant a written disclosure of this use before the tenant signs a lease, if the unit hasn't been mitigated as required by law. (Va. Code § 55.1-1219)

Insecticide/pesticide application: Landlords must give tenants written notice no less than 48 hours prior to applying an insecticide or pesticide in the tenant's dwelling unit unless the tenant agrees to a shorter notification period. If a tenant requests the application of the insecticide or pesticide, the 48-hour notice is not required. Tenants who have concerns about specific insecticides or pesticides must notify the landlord in writing no less than 24 hours before the scheduled insecticide or pesticide application. The tenant shall prepare the dwelling unit for the application of insecticides or pesticides in accordance with any written instructions of the landlord and, if insects or pests are found to be present, follow any written instructions of the landlord to eliminate the insects or pests following the application of insecticides or pesticides. In addition, landlords must post notice of all insecticide or pesticide applications in areas of the rental other than the dwelling units. Such notice shall consist of conspicuous signs placed in or upon the rental where the insecticide or pesticide will be applied at least 48 hours prior to the application. (Va. Code § 55.1-1223)

Washington

Move-in checklists required? Yes. Checklists are required when landlords collect a security deposit. If landlord fails to provide checklist, landlord is liable to the tenant for the amount of the deposit. (Wash. Rev. Code § 59.18.260)

Nonrefundable fees permitted? Yes. If landlord collects a nonrefundable fee, the rental document must clearly specify that it is nonrefundable. Landlords cannot collect

fees to put a prospective tenant on a wait list for a rental. (Wash. Rev. Code § 59.18.285)

Must fee policy be stated in the rental agreement? Yes.

Fire protection: At the time the lease is signed, landlord must provide fire protection and safety information, including whether the building has a smoking policy, an emergency notification plan, or an evacuation plan. (Wash. Rev. Code § 59.18.060)

Owner or agent identity: In the rental document or posted conspicuously on the premises, landlord must designate to the tenant the name and address of the person who is the landlord by a statement on the rental agreement or by a notice conspicuously posted on the premises. If the person designated does not reside in Washington, landlord must also designate a person who resides in the county to act as an agent for the purposes of service of notices and process. (Wash. Rev. Code § 59.18.060)

Mold: At the time the lease is signed, landlord must provide tenant with information provided or approved by the department of health about the health hazards associated with exposure to indoor mold. (Wash. Rev. Code § 59.18.060)

Screening criteria: Before obtaining any information about an applicant, landlord must provide (in writing or by posting) the type of information to be accessed, criteria to be used to evaluate the application, and (for consumer reports) the name and address of the consumer reporting agency to be used, including the applicant's rights to obtain a free copy of the report and dispute its accuracy. Landlord must advise tenants whether landlord will accept a comprehensive reusable tenant screening report done by a consumer reporting agency (in which case the landlord may not charge the tenant a fee for a screening report). If landlord maintains a website that advertises residential rentals, the home page must include this information. (Wash. Rev. Code § 59.18.257)

Tenant screening fee: Landlords who do their own screening may charge a fee for time and costs to obtain background information, but only if they provide the information explained in "Screening criteria," above. (Wash. Rev. Code § 59.18.257)

Required Landlord Disclosures (continued)

Holding deposits: Fees or deposits to hold a rental cannot exceed 25% of the first months rent. Upon receipt of the fee or deposit, landlords must issue a receipt and a written statement of the conditions, if any, under which the fee or deposit may be retained. (Wash. Rev. Code § 59.18.253)

West Virginia

Nonrefundable fees permitted? Yes. Nonrefundable fee must be expressly agreed to in writing. (W.Va. Code § 37-6A-1(14))

Must fee policy be stated in the rental agreement? No.

Carbon monoxide (CO): Anyone who installs a CO detector in a rental unit must inform either the owner, landlord, or resident of the dangers of CO poisoning, and must supply instructions on how to operate the detector. When landlords work on fuel-burning heating or cooking equipment or a units venting system, they must inform tenants of the dangers of CO poisoning and recommend the purchase of a CO detector.

Any landlord who performs repair or maintenance work on a fuel-burning heating or cooking source or a venting system in a rental unit must inform the tenant of the dangers of carbon monoxide poisoning and recommend the installation of a carbon monoxide detector. (W.Va. Code § 15A-10-12)

Methamphetamine: Landlord who has received a remediation completion certificate from the West Virginia Department of Health and Human Resources must disclose it to prospective tenants. If work is ongoing, landlord must disclose the location of the drug lab, remediation plans, and law enforcement actions. (W. Va. Code R. § 64-92-7)

Wisconsin

Move-in checklist required? Yes. Tenant has a right to inspect the rental and give landlord a list of defects, and to receive a list of damages charged to the prior tenant. Tenant has seven days after start of the tenancy to return the list to the landlord. (Wis. Admin. Code § 134.06; Wis. Stat. § 704.08)

Must checklist rights be stated in the lease? No.

Owner or agent identity: Landlord must disclose to the tenant in writing, at or before the time a rental agreement is signed, the name and address of: the person or persons authorized to collect or receive rent and manage and maintain the premises, and who can readily be contacted by the tenant; and the owner of the premises or other person authorized to accept service of legal process and other notices and demands on behalf of the owner. The address must be an address within the state at which service of process can be made in person. (Wis. Admin. Code § 134.04)

Nonstandard rental provisions: If landlord wants to enter premises for reasons not specified by law, landlord must disclose the provision in a separate written document entitled "NONSTANDARD RENTAL PROVISIONS" before the rental agreement is signed. (Wis. Admin. Code § 134.09)

Habitability deficiencies: Landlord must disclose serious problems that affect the rental unit's habitability. (Wis. Admin. Code § 134.04)

Utility charges: If charges for water, heat, or electricity are not included in the rent, the landlord must disclose this fact to the tenant before entering into a rental agreement or accepting any earnest money or security deposit from the prospective tenant. If individual dwelling units and common areas are not separately metered, and if the charges are not included in the rent, the landlord must disclose the basis on which charges for utility services will be allocated among individual dwelling units. (Wis. Admin. Code § 134.04)

Uncorrected code violations: Before signing a rental contract or accepting a security deposit, the landlord must disclose to the tenant any uncorrected code violation of which the landlord is actually aware, that affects the dwelling unit or a common area and poses a significant threat to the tenant's health or safety. "Disclosure" consists of showing prospective tenants the portions of the building affected, as well as the notices themselves. (Wis. Stat. § 704.07(2)(bm); Wis. Admin. Code § 134.04)

Disposing of abandoned property: If landlord intends to immediately dispose of any tenant property left behind after move-out, landlord must notify tenant at the time lease is signed. (But landlord must hold prescription medications and medical equipment for seven days,

Required Landlord Disclosures (continued)

and must give notice before disposing of vehicles or manufactured homes to owner and any known secured party.) (Wis. Stat. § 704.05(5))

Notice of domestic abuse violations: Landlords must include the following notice in the rental agreement or in an addendum to the agreement: "NOTICE OF DOMESTIC ABUSE PROTECTIONS

(1) As provided in section 106.50(5m)(dm) of the Wisconsin statutes, a tenant has a defense to an eviction action if the tenant can prove that the landlord knew, or should have known, the tenant is a victim of domestic abuse, sexual assault, or stalking and that the eviction action is based on conduct related to domestic abuse, sexual assault, or stalking committed by either of the following:

(a) A person who was not the tenant's invit§ed guest.

(b) A person who was the tenant's invited guest, but the tenant has done either of the following:

1. Sought an injunction barring the person from the premises.

2. Provided a written statement to the landlord stating that the person will no longer be an invited guest of the tenant and the tenant has not subsequently invited the person to be the tenant's guest.

(2) A tenant who is a victim of domestic abuse, sexual assault, or stalking may have the right to terminate the rental agreement in certain limited situations, as provided in section 704.16 of the Wisconsin statutes. If the tenant has safety concerns, the tenant should contact a local victim service provider or law enforcement agency.

(3) A tenant is advised that this notice is only a summary of the tenant's rights and the specific language of the statutes governs in all instances." (Wis. Stat. § 704.14)

Wyoming

Nonrefundable fees permitted? Yes. If any portion of the deposit is not refundable, rental agreement must include this information and tenant must be told before paying a deposit. (Wyo. Stat. § 1-21-1207)

Must fee policy be stated in the rental agreement? Yes.

State Laws in Domestic Violence Situations

State	Statute	State	Statute
Alabama	No statute	**Massachusetts**	Mass. Gen. Laws ch. 186, §§ 24, 25, 26, and 28; ch. 239, § 2A
Alaska	No statute	**Michigan**	Mich. Comp. Laws § 554.601b
Arizona	Ariz. Rev. Stat. §§ 33-1315, 33-1318, 33-1414	**Minnesota**	Minn. Stat. §§ 504B.171, 504B.205, 504B.206
Arkansas	Ark. Code § 18-16-112	**Mississippi**	No statute
California	Cal. Civ. Code §§ 1941.5, 1941.6, 1946.7; Cal. Civ. Proc. Code §§ 1161, 1161.3, 1174.27; Cal. Gov't Code § 53165.1	**Missouri**	Mo. Rev. Stat. § 441.920
Colorado	Colo. Rev. Stat. §§ 13-40-104 (4), 13-40-107.5 (5), 38-12-401, 38-12-402, 38-12-503	**Montana**	No statute
Connecticut	Conn. Gen. Stat. § 47a-11e	**Nebraska**	Neb. Rev. Stat. §§ 76-1431, 76-1431.01
Delaware	Del. Code tit. 25, §§ 5141 (7), 5314 (b), 5316	**Nevada**	Nev. Rev. Stat. §§ 118A.345, 118A.347, 118A.510
District of Columbia	D.C. Code §§ 2-1401.02, 2-1402.21, 42-3505.07, 42-3505.08	**New Hampshire**	N.H. Rev. Stat. § 540:2(VII)
Florida	No statute	**New Jersey**	N.J. Stat. §§ 46:8-9.5 through 46:8-9.12
Georgia	Ga. Code § 44-7-23	**New Mexico**	N.M. Stat. § 47-8-33(J)
Hawaii	Haw. Rev. Stat. §§ 521-80 to 521-82	**New York**	N.Y. Real Prop. Law §§ 227-c(2) and 227–d; N.Y. Real Prop. Acts. Law § 744; N.Y. Crim. Proc. Law § 530.13(1); N.Y. Dom. Rel. Law § 240(3); N.Y. Exec. Law § 296
Idaho	No statute	**North Carolina**	N.C. Gen. Stat. §§ 42-40, 42-42.2, 42-42.3, 42-45.1
Illinois	735 Ill. Comp. Stat. 5/9-106.2; 765 Ill. Comp. Stat. 750/1 through 750/35	**North Dakota**	N.D. Cent. Code § 47-16-17.1
Indiana	Ind. Code §§ 32-31-9-1 through 32-31-9-15	**Ohio**	No statute
Iowa	Iowa Code §§ 562A.27A, 562A.27B, 562B.25A (3)	**Oklahoma**	Okla. Stat. tit. 41, § 113.3
Kansas	Kan. Stat. § 58-25,137	**Oregon**	Or. Rev. Stat. §§ 90.449, 90.453, 90.456, 90.459
Kentucky	Ky. Rev. Stat. §§ 383.300, 383.302	**Pennsylvania**	53 Pa. Cons. Stat. § 304; 246 Pa. Code Rule 514.1
Louisiana	La. Rev. Stat. § 9:3261.1 (domestic violence); La. Rev. Stat. § 9:3261.2 (sexual assault)	**Rhode Island**	R.I. Gen. Laws §§ 34-37-1 through 34-37-4
Maine	Me. Rev. Stat. tit. 14, §§ 6000, 6001, 6002, 6025	**South Carolina**	No statute
Maryland	Md. Code Real Prop. §§ 8-208, 8-208.1; 8-5A-01 through 8-5A-06; 14-126	**South Dakota**	S.D. Codified Laws §§ 43-32-18.1, 43-32-19.1

State Laws in Domestic Violence Situations (continued)			
State	**Statute**	**State**	**Statute**
Tennessee	Tenn. Code §§ 66-7-109(e), 66-7-112, 66-28-205, 66-28-517(g)	**Washington**	Wash. Rev. Code §§ 59.18.130(8)(b)(ii), 59.18.352, 59.18.570, 59.18.575, 59.18.580, 59.18.585
Texas	Tex. Prop. Code §§ 92.015, 92.016, 92.0161	**West Virginia**	No statute
Utah	Utah Code § 57-22-5.1	**Wisconsin**	Wis. Stat. §§ 106.50, 704.14, 704.16
Vermont	15 Vt. Stat. § 1103(c)(2)(B); 9 Vt. Stat. §§ 4471 through 4475	**Wyoming**	Wy. Stat. §§ 1-21-1301 through 1-21-1304
Virginia	Va. Code §§ 55.1-1203, 55.1-1208, 55.1-1230, 55.1-1236		

State Laws on Rent Withholding and Repair and Deduct Remedies

This chart lists the statutes and cases in each state that address whether tenants have the right to withhold rent or repair and deduct when their landlord fails to provide housing that is in good repair and that meets basic structural, health, and safety standards (see the discussion in Chapter 8 for details). Just because a statute or case is listed below does not mean that the state allows the remedy. Although these remedies can get results when used properly, tenants who misuse these remedies or who don't follow the law precisely can face drastic consequences, including eviction. If you think you might be in a position to use one of these remedies, we recommend consulting with a lawyer or legal aid before you take action.

State	Statute or case on rent withholding	Statute or case on repair and deduct
Alabama	Ala. Code § 35-9A-164	Ala. Code § 35-9A-164
Alaska	Alaska Stat. §§ 34.03.100, 34.03.180(a)(3), 34.03.190	Alaska Stat. §§ 34.03.100, 34.03.180
Arizona	Ariz. Rev. Stat. §§ 33-1364, 33-1365	Ariz. Rev. Stat. §§ 33-1363, 1364
Arkansas	Ark. Code § 18-17-502. Statute prohibits tenants from withholding or offsetting rent for alleged violations of state habitability law.	No statute
California	Cal. Civ. Proc. Code § 1174.2; *Green v. Superior Court*, 10 Cal. 3d 616 (1974)	Cal. Civ. Code § 1942
Colorado	Colo. Rev. Stat. § 38-12-507	Colo. Rev. Stat. § 38-12-507
Connecticut	Conn. Gen. Stat. §§ 47a-13 to 47a-14h	Conn. Gen. Stat. § 47a-13
Delaware	Del. Code tit. 25, § 5308	Del. Code tit. 25, §§ 5307, 5308
District of Columbia	D.C. Mun. Regs. § 14-4303; *Javins v. First Natl Realty Corp.*, 428 F.2d 1071 (D.C. Cir. 1970)	No statute
Florida	Fla. Stat. § 83.60	Fla. Stat. § 83.60
Georgia	No statute	Not addressed by statute, but Georgia courts recognize a tenant's right to this remedy. See *Georgia Landlord Tenant Handbook*, 2021, Georgia Department of Community Affairs; and see *Abrams v. Joel*, 108 Ga. App. 662, 134 S.E.2d 480 (1963).
Hawaii	Haw. Rev. Stat. § 521-78	Haw. Rev. Stat. § 521-64
Idaho	No statute	No statute on repair and deduct generally, but if a landlord won't make repairs, tenant's remedy is to provide landlord with a written notice with a list of violations. Landlord then has three days to fix; failure to repair allows the tenant to sue the landlord to force compliance. (Idaho Code § 6-320.) Repair and deduct is available specifically (and only) for failure to install and/or maintain smoke detectors. (Idaho Code § 6-320(a)(6).)
Illinois	765 Ill. Comp. Stat. §§ 735/2, 735/2.2 (applies only when a court has appointed a receiver to collect rents, following landlord's failure to pay for utilities)	765 Ill. Comp. Stat. § 742/5
Indiana	No statute	No statute on repair and deduct, but once tenant gives landlord notice of landlord's need to repair, landlord has reasonable amount of time to remedy. If landlord doesn't remedy, tenant can sue for enforcement and might obtain actual and consequential damages, as well as attorneys' fees and court costs. (Ind. Code Ann. § 32-31-8-6.)

State Laws on Rent Withholding and Repair and Deduct Remedies (continued)

State	Statute or case on rent withholding	Statute or case on repair and deduct
Iowa	Iowa Code § 562A.24	Iowa Code § 562A.23
Kansas	Kan. Stat. § 58-2561	No statute
Kentucky	Ky. Rev. Stat. § 383.645	Ky. Rev. Stat. §§ 383.635, 383.640
Louisiana	No statute	La. Civ. Code art. 2694
Maine	Me. Rev. Stat. tit. 14, § 6021	Me. Rev. Stat. tit. 14, § 6026
Maryland	Md. Code Real Prop., §§ 8-211, 8-211.1	No statute
Massachusetts	Mass. Gen. Laws ch. 239, § 8A; ch. 111, § 127F	Mass. Gen. Laws ch. 111, § 127L
Michigan	Mich. Comp. Laws § 125.530	*Rome v. Walker*, 198 N.W.2d 850 (1972); Mich. Comp. Laws § 554.139
Minnesota	Minn. Stat. §§ 504B.215(3)(d), 504B.385	Minn. Stat. § 504B.425
Mississippi	No statute	Miss. Code § 89-8-15
Missouri	Mo. Stat. §§ 441.570, 441.580; *Kohner Properties, Inc. v. Johnson*, 553 S.W.3d 280 (Mo. Sup. Ct. 2018)	Mo. Stat. § 441.234
Montana	Mont. Code § 70-24-421	Mont. Code §§ 70-24-406 to 70-24-408
Nebraska	Neb. Rev. Stat. § 76-1428	Neb. Rev. Stat. § 76-1427
Nevada	Nev. Rev. Stat. § 118A.490	Nev. Rev. Stat. §§ 118A.360, 118A.380
New Hampshire	N.H. Rev. Stat. § 540:13-d	No statute
New Jersey	*Berzito v. Gambino*, 63 N.J. 460 (1973)	*Marini v. Ireland*, 265 A.2d 526 (1970)
New Mexico	N.M. Stat. § 47-8-27.2	No statute
New York	N.Y. Real Prop. Law § 235-b; N.Y. Mult. Dwell. Law § 302-a (applies to all cities with populations of 400,000 or more); N.Y. Mult. Res. Law § 305-a (applies to cities with populations of less than 500,000 and all towns and villages); *Semans Family Ltd. Partnership v. Kennedy*, 675 N.Y.S.2d 489 (N.Y. City Civ. Ct.,1998) As with many areas of law in New York, it's important to check your local laws and procedures. Specifically, the laws in New York City and the counties of Nassau, Suffolk, Rockland, and Westchester often differ from state law.	For emergency repairs (such as broken door lock) only: N.Y. Real Prop. Law § 235-b; *Jangla Realty Co. v. Gravagna*, 447 N.Y.S. 2d 338 (Civ. Ct., Queens County, 1981) As with many areas of law in New York, it's important to check your local laws and procedures. Specifically, the laws in New York City and the counties of Nassau, Suffolk, Rockland, and Westchester often differ from state law.
North Carolina	No statute, but tenants can sue in small claims court, asking a judge to order repairs, to reduce rent while repairs are being made, and for a retroactive rent abatement for the time during which repairs were not made. See, "Landlord's Maintenance and Repair Duties: Your Rights as a Residential Tenant in North Carolina," North Carolina Attorney General publication.	No statute, but tenants can repair the problem and sue in small claims court for reimbursement. See, "Landlord's Maintenance and Repair Duties: Your Rights as a Residential Tenant in North Carolina," North Carolina Attorney General publication.

State	Statute or case on rent withholding	Statute or case on repair and deduct
North Dakota	No statute	N.D. Cent. Code §§ 47-16-13, 47-16-13.1
Ohio	Ohio Rev. Code § 5321.07 (does not apply to student tenants; or when landlord owns three or fewer rental units, as long as landlord has given written notice to tenant)	No statute
Oklahoma	Okla. Stat. tit. 41, § 121	Okla. Stat. tit. 41, § 121
Oregon	Or. Rev. Stat. § 90.365	Or. Rev. Stat. § 90.365
Pennsylvania	68 Pa. Cons. Stat. § 250.206; 35 Pa. Cons. Stat. § 1700-1	*Pugh v. Holmes*, 405 A.2d 897 (1979)
Rhode Island	R.I. Gen. Laws § 34-18-32	R.I. Gen. Laws §§ 34-18-30 to 34-18-31
South Carolina	S.C. Code § 27-40-640	S.C. Code § 27-40-630
South Dakota	S.D. Codified Laws § 43-32-9	S.D. Codified Laws § 43-32-9
Tennessee	Tenn. Code § 68-111-104	Tenn. Code § 66-28-502
Texas	No statute	Tex. Prop. Code §§ 92.056, 92.0561
Utah	No statute	Utah Code § 57-22-6
Vermont	Vt. Stat. tit. 9, § 4458	Vt. Stat. tit. 9, § 4459
Virginia	Va. Code § 55.1-1244	Va. Code § 55.1-1244.1
Washington	Wash. Rev. Code §§ 59.18.060, 59.18.110, 59.18.115	Wash. Rev. Code §§ 59.18.060, 59.18.100, 59.18.110
West Virginia	*Teller v. McCoy*, 253 S.E.2d 114 (W.Va. 1978)	*Teller v. McCoy*, 253 S.E.2d 114 (W.Va. 1978)
Wisconsin	Wis. Stat. § 704.07(4)	No statute
Wyoming	Wyo. Stat. § 1-21-1206	No statute

State Laws on Rent Withholding and Repair and Deduct Remedies (continued)

State Laws on Landlord's Access to Rental Property

In all states, even in the absence of a statute, landlords may enter to deal with a true emergency (an imminent and serious threat to health, safety, or property); and when the tenant has abandoned the property (left for good). Most states specify non-emergency circumstances that justify entry, and some explicitly include abandonment and "extended absence" (temporary but prolonged absence, which allows a landlord to enter when necessary to protect the property). But even when the statute doesn't mention "extended absence," landlords may enter when it's necessary to avert serious property damage (an emergency situation).

State	State Law Citation	Amount of Notice Required in Nonemergency Situations	Form of Notice	To Deal With an Emergency	To Inspect the Premises	To Make Repairs, Alterations, or Improvements	To Show Property to Prospective Tenants or Purchasers	During Tenant's Extended Absence	When Tenant Has Abandoned the Property
				Reasons Landlord May Enter					
Alabama	Ala. Code §§ 35-9A-303, 35-9A-423	Two days	Not specified	✓	✓	✓	✓	✓	✓
Alaska	Alaska Stat. §§ 34.03.140, 34.03.230	24 hours	Not specified	✓	✓	✓	✓	✓	✓
Arizona	Ariz. Rev. Stat. § 33-1343	Two days; notice period does not apply, and tenant's consent is assumed, if entry is pursuant to tenant's request for maintenance as prescribed in Ariz. Rev. Stat. § 33-1341, paragraph 8.	Not specified	✓	✓	✓	✓		✓
Arkansas	Ark. Code § 18-17-602	No notice specified	Not specified		✓	✓	✓		
California	Cal. Civ. Code §§ 1950.5, 1954	Reasonable notice; 24 hours is presumed reasonable (48 hours for initial move-out inspection)	Written notice required, but oral notice is sufficient if the entry is to show the property to prospective or actual purchasers, but only if the landlord has given written notice within the previous 120 days, telling the tenant that the property is for sale and such oral notice might be given (24 hours' notice is presumed reasonable; landlord must leave a note when leaving).	✓	✓	✓	✓		✓
Colorado	Colo. Rev. Stat. § 38-12-1004	Notice statute relates only to access for inspecting for or treating a bed bug infestation. 48 hours' notice required unless lease says otherwise.	Not specified, unless the access is related to a possible or actual bed bug infestation, in which case notice must be electronic or written.						
Connecticut	Conn. Gen. Stat. §§ 47a-16 to 47a-16a	Reasonable notice	Written or oral	✓	✓	✓	✓	✓	✓

State Laws on Landlord's Access to Rental Property (continued)

State	State Law Citation	Amount of Notice Required in Nonemergency Situations	Form of Notice	Reasons Landlord May Enter					
				To Deal With an Emergency	To Inspect the Premises	To Make Repairs, Alterations, or Improvements	To Show Property to Prospective Tenants or Purchasers	During Tenant's Extended Absence	When Tenant Has Abandoned the Property
Delaware	Del. Code tit. 25, §§ 5113, 5507, 5509, 5510	48 hours	Written, by giving a copy to an adult who resides at the rental unit or at the tenant's usual residence (if it's not the rental) or by mailing via registered or certified mail or first class mail as evidenced by a certificate of mailing postage-prepaid, addressed to the tenant at the rental. The notice can also be posted at the rental unit when it's combined with a return receipt of a certificate of mailing.	✓	✓	✓	✓	✓	
D.C.	D.C. Code § 42-3505.51	48 hours	Written and electronic (including email and mobile text messaging), but if the tenant doesn't provide an acknowledgment of the electronic notice in writing, the landlord must provide a paper notice.	✓	✓	✓	✓		
Florida	Fla. Stat. § 83.53	24 hours for repairs; landlord may enter "when necessary" in an emergency, when a tenant unreasonably withholds consent, or when the tenant is gone (without notifying the landlord) for a period of time equal to one-half the time for periodic rental payments.	Not specified	✓	✓	✓	✓	✓	
Georgia	No statute								
Hawaii	Haw. Rev. Stat. §§ 521-53, 521-70(b)	Two days	Not specified	✓	✓	✓	✓	✓	✓
Idaho	No statute								
Illinois	No statute								
Indiana	Ind. Code § 32-31-5-6	Reasonable notice	Written or oral	✓	✓	✓	✓		✓

				Reasons Landlord May Enter					
State	State Law Citation	Amount of Notice Required in Nonemergency Situations	Form of Notice	To Deal With an Emergency	To Inspect the Premises	To Make Repairs, Alterations, or Improvements	To Show Property to Prospective Tenants or Purchasers	During Tenant's Extended Absence	When Tenant Has Abandoned the Property
Iowa	Iowa Code §§ 562A.19, 562A.28, 562A.29	24 hours	Not specified	✓	✓	✓	✓	✓	✓
Kansas	Kan. Stat. §§ 58-2557, 58-2565	Reasonable notice	Not specified	✓	✓	✓	✓	✓	✓
Kentucky	Ky. Rev. Stat. §§ 383.615, 383.670	Two days	Not specified	✓	✓	✓	✓	✓	✓
Louisiana	La. Civ. Code art. 2693	No notice specified	Not specified				✓		
Maine	Me. Rev. Stat. tit. 14, § 6025	24 hours; no notice if the welfare of an animal is at risk.	Not specified	✓	✓	✓	✓		
Maryland	No statute								
Massachusetts	Mass. Gen. Laws ch. 186, § 15B(1)(a)	No notice specified	Not specified		✓	✓	✓		✓
Michigan	No statute								
Minnesota	Minn. Stat. § 504B.211	24 hours	Not specified	✓	✓	✓	✓		
Mississippi	Miss. Code § 89-7-49	When a landlord believes tenant has abandoned property, and the tenant owes rent, the landlord may request the constable of the county to go onto the premises to ascertain abandonment and leave a notice.	Written notice						✓
Missouri	No statute								
Montana	Mont. Code §§ 70-24-108, 70-24-312, 70-24-426	24 hours	Email (if email is provided in the lease or rental agreement), hand delivery, mail with a certificate of mailing or by certified mail, or a post on the main entry door of the dwelling unit.	✓	✓	✓	✓	✓	✓
Nebraska	Neb. Rev. Stat. §§ 76-1423, 76-1432	24 hours	Not specified	✓	✓	✓	✓	✓	✓
Nevada	Nev. Rev. Stat. § 118A.330	24 hours	Not specified	✓	✓	✓	✓		✓

State Laws on Landlord's Access to Rental Property (continued)

State	State Law Citation	Amount of Notice Required in Nonemergency Situations	Form of Notice	To Deal With an Emergency	To Inspect the Premises	To Make Repairs, Alterations, or Improvements	To Show Property to Prospective Tenants or Purchasers	During Tenant's Extended Absence	When Tenant Has Abandoned the Property
New Hampshire	N.H. Rev. Stat. § 540-A:3	Notice that is adequate under the circumstances; however, 48 hours' notice when entering after receiving notice of a bed bug infestation in an adjacent unit	Not specified, but 48 hours when entering to evaluate a possible or actual bed bug infestation.	✓	✓	✓	✓		
New Jersey	N.J. Stat. § 2A:39-1; N.J.A.C. 5:10-5.1 (for buildings with more than one unit)	In buildings with fewer than three units: Landlords can enter only when they have the tenant's permission or a court order. In buildings with three or more units: Landlords have a right to access the unit to inspect it, make repairs or perform maintenance, and deal with emergencies, but must give reasonable notice (one day under ordinary circum-stances) before entering.	Not specified						
New Mexico	N.M. Stat. §§ 47-8-24, 47-8-34	24 hours	Written notice	✓	✓	✓	✓	✓	✓
New York	No statute								
North Carolina	No statute								
North Dakota	N.D. Cent. Code § 47-16-07.3	Reasonable notice	Not specified	✓	✓	✓	✓		✓
Ohio	Ohio Rev. Code §§ 5321.04(A) (8), 5321.05(B)	24 hours	Not specified	✓	✓	✓	✓		
Oklahoma	Okla. Stat. tit. 41, § 128	One day	Not specified	✓	✓	✓	✓		✓
Oregon	Or. Rev. Stat. §§ 90.322, 90.410	24 hours	Not specified	✓	✓	✓	✓	✓	✓
Pennsylvania	No statute								
Rhode Island	R.I. Gen. Laws § 34-18-26	Two days	Not specified	✓	✓	✓	✓	✓	✓
South Carolina	S.C. Code §§ 27-40-530, 27-40-730	24 hours	Not specified	✓	✓	✓	✓		✓
South Dakota	No statute								

State Laws on Landlord's Access to Rental Property (continued)

State	State Law Citation	Amount of Notice Required in Nonemergency Situations	Form of Notice	Reasons Landlord May Enter					
				To Deal With an Emergency	To Inspect the Premises	To Make Repairs, Alterations, or Improvements	To Show Property to Prospective Tenants or Purchasers	During Tenant's Extended Absence	When Tenant Has Abandoned the Property
Tennessee	Tenn. Code §§ 66-28-403, 66-28-507	24 hours (applies only within the final 30 days of the rental agreement term, when landlord intends to show the premises to prospective renters and this right of access is set forth in the rental agreement)	Not specified	✓	✓	✓	✓	✓	✓
Texas	No statute								
Utah	Utah Code §§ 57-22-4, 57-22-5(2)(c)	24 hours, unless rental agreement specifies otherwise	Not specified			✓			
Vermont	Vt. Stat. tit. 9, § 4460	48 hours	Not specified	✓	✓	✓	✓		
Virginia	Va. Code §§ 55.1-1229, 55.1-1249	For routine maintenance only: 72 hours, but no notice needed if entry follows tenant's request for maintenance	Not specified	✓	✓	✓	✓	✓	✓
Washington	Wash. Rev. Code § 59.18.150	Two days; one day to show property to actual or prospective tenants or buyers	Written notice, unless it is impracticable to do so.	✓	✓	✓	✓		✓
West Virginia	No statute								
Wisconsin	Wis. Stat. § 704.05(2); Wis. Adm. Code § ATCP 134.09(2)	With 12 hours' advance notice, landlords may enter at reasonable times. Landlords and tenants may sign a separate "Nonstandard Rental Provision" agreement, in which they provide for entry for reasons not enumerated in this chart.	Not specified	✓	✓	✓	✓	✓	✓
Wyoming	No statute								

State Laws on Handling Abandoned Property

Most states regulate the way landlords must handle property left behind by departed tenants. Many set notice requirements as to how landlords must contact tenants regarding abandoned property. States might also regulate how landlords must store abandoned property and dispose of it when tenants do not claim their belongings. For details, check your state statute, listed in this chart. Keep in mind that court cases not mentioned here might also describe proper procedures in your state.

State	Statute	State	Statute
Alabama	Ala. Code § 35-9A-423	Missouri	Mo. Rev. Stat. § 441.065
Alaska	Alaska Stat. § 34.03.260	Montana	Mont. Code § 70-24-430
Arizona	Ariz. Rev. Stat. §§ 33-1314, 33-1370	Nebraska	Neb. Rev. Stat. §§ 69-2302 to 69-2314
Arkansas	Ark. Code § 18-16-108	Nevada	Nev. Rev. Stat. §§ 118A.450, 118A.460
California	Cal. Civ. Code §§ 1965, 1980 to 1991	New Hampshire	N.H. Rev. Stat. § 540-A:3(VII)
Colorado	Colo. Rev. Stat. §§ 38-20-116, 13-40-122	New Jersey	N.J. Stat. §§ 2A:18-72 to 2A:18-84
Connecticut	Conn. Gen. Stat. § 47a-11b, § 47a-42	New Mexico	N.M. Stat. § 47-8-34.1
Delaware	Del. Code tit. 25, §§ 5507, 5715	New York	No statute
D.C.	D.C. Code §§ 42-32101.01, 42-3505.01a	North Carolina	N.C. Gen. Stat. §§ 42-25.9, 42-36.2
Florida	Fla. Stat. §§ 83.67; 715.10 to 715.111	North Dakota	N.D. Cent. Code § 47-16-30.1
Georgia	Ga. Code § 44-7-55	Ohio	*Ringler v. Sias*, 428 N.E.2d 869 (Ohio Ct. App. 1980)
Hawaii	Haw. Rev. Stat. § 521-56	Oklahoma	Okla. Stat. tit. 41, § 130
Idaho	Idaho Code § 6-316	Oregon	Or. Rev. Stat. §§ 90.425, 105.165
Illinois	735 Ill. Comp. Stat. § 5/9-318	Pennsylvania	68 Pa. Cons. Stat. § 250.505a
Indiana	Ind. Code §§ 32-31-4-1 to 32-31-4-5, 32-31-5-5	Rhode Island	R.I. Gen. Laws § 34-18-50
		South Carolina	S.C. Code §§ 27-40-710(D), 27-40-730
Iowa	*Khan v. Heritage Prop. Mgmt.*, 584 N.W.2d 725, 730 (Iowa Ct. App. 1998)	South Dakota	S.D. Codified Laws §§ 43-32-25, 43-32-26
Kansas	Kan. Stat. § 58-2565	Tennessee	Tenn. Code § 66-28-405
Kentucky	No statute	Texas	Tex. Prop. Code § 92.014
Louisiana	La. Civ. Code § 2707, La. Civ. Proc. § 4705	Utah	Utah Code § 78B-6-816
Maine	Me. Rev. Stat. tit. 14, §§ 6005, 6013, 6025-A	Vermont	Vt. Stat. tit. 9, § 4462; Vt. Stat. tit. 12, § 4854a
Maryland	Md. Code Real Prop., §§ 8-208, 14-806	Virginia	Va. Code §§ 55.1-1249, 55.1-1254 to 55.1-1256
Massachusetts	Mass. Gen. Laws ch. 186, § 30; Mass. Gen. Laws ch. 239, §§ 4, 14	Washington	Wash. Rev. Code §§ 59.18.310, 59.18.312, 59.18.595
Michigan	No statute	West Virginia	W. Va. Code §§ 37-6-6, 55-3A-3
Minnesota	Minn. Stat. § 504B.271	Wisconsin	Wis. Stat. § 704.05(5)
Mississippi	Miss. Code §§ 89-7-31, 89-7-35, 89-8-13, 89-8-39	Wyoming	Wyo. Stat. § 1-21-1210

State Laws Prohibiting Landlord Retaliation

State	Statute	Tenant's Complaint to Landlord or Government Agency	Tenant's Involvement in Tenants' Organization	Tenant's Exercise of Legal Right	Retaliation Is Presumed If Negative Reaction by Landlord Within Specified Time of Tenant's Act
Alabama	Ala. Code § 35-9A-501	✓	✓		
Alaska	Alaska Stat. § 34.03.310	✓	✓	✓	
Arizona	Ariz. Rev. Stat. § 33-1381	✓	✓		6 months
Arkansas [1]	Ark. Code § 20-27-608	✓			
California [2]	Cal. Civ. Code §§ 1940.35, 1942.5	✓	✓	✓	180 days
Colorado [3]	Colo. Rev. Stat. §§ 38-12-509, 38-12-1203, 38-12-1205	✓	✓		
Connecticut	Conn. Gen. Stat. §§ 47a-20, 47a-33	✓		✓	6 months
Delaware	Del. Code tit. 25, § 5516	✓	✓	✓	90 days
D.C.	D.C. Code §§ 42-3505.02, 42-3505.06	✓	✓	✓	6 months
Florida [4]	Fla. Stat. § 83.64	✓	✓	✓	
Georgia	Ga. Code § 44-7-24	✓	✓	✓	3 months
Hawaii	Haw. Rev. Stat. § 521-74	✓		✓	
Idaho [5]	No statute				
Illinois	765 Ill. Comp. Stat. § 720/1	✓			
Indiana	Ind. Code §§ 32-31-8.5-0.5–32-31-8.5-6	✓	✓	✓	
Iowa	Iowa Code § 562A.36	✓	✓		1 year
Kansas	Kan. Stat. § 58-2572	✓	✓		
Kentucky	Ky. Rev. Stat. § 383.705	✓	✓		1 year
Louisiana	No statute				
Maine [6]	Me. Rev. Stat. tit. 14, §§ 6001, 6021-A	✓	✓	✓	6 months

[1] Only prohibits retaliation by landlord who has received notice of lead hazards. (Arkansas)

[2] Applies when a retaliatory eviction follows a court case or administrative hearing concerning the tenant's underlying complaint, membership in a tenant organization, or exercise of a legal right. In this situation, a tenant may claim the benefit of the antiretaliation presumption only if the eviction falls within six months of the final determination of the court case or administrative hearing. (California and Massachusetts) Landlord cannot disclose or threaten to disclose to any government authority information regarding tenants' or occupants' immigration or citizenship status for the purpose of retaliating. (California)

[3] Landlords are prohibited from retaliating by increasing rent, decreasing services, terminating a tenancy without written consent of the tenant (unless for reasons provided by law, such as not paying rent), bringing or threatening an eviction suit, or taking action that in any manner intimidates, threatens, discriminates, or retaliates against the tenant. When a landlord illegally retaliates, tenants may terminate rental agreement and recover either three months' rent or three times their actual damages, whichever is greater, plus attorneys' fees and costs. Also specifies that if a landlord replaces an appliance with a substantially similar one (presumably in response to a complaint), there is no presumption of retaliation. Landlords cannot retaliate against tenants for exercising their rights under or opposing any conduct prohibited under the Immigrant Tenant Protection Act. (Colorado)

[4] Statute lists retaliatory acts as illustrative, not exhaustive, and includes retaliation after the tenant has paid rent to a condominium, cooperative, or homeowners' association after demand from the association in order to pay the landlord's obligation to the association; when the tenant is a servicemember who legally terminates the tenancy; and when the tenant has exercised his or her rights under state, local, or federal fair housing laws. (Florida)

[5] No statute, but Idaho courts have recognized retaliation as a defense to evictions. *Wright v. Brady*, 889 P.2d 105 (Idaho App. 1995). (Idaho)

[6] Also presumption of retaliation when tenant has complained to a fair housing agency; has informed landlord that the tenant or tenant's child is a victim of domestic violence, sexual assault or stalking; or has communicated to the landlord about or has filed a complaint about the landlord's or landlord's agent's act of sexual harassment. Retaliation is also presumed if tenant is served with an eviction notice within 6 months of tenant's exercise of rights regarding bed bug infestations (does not apply to eviction for nonpayment or for causing substantial damage); or if tenant has asserted their rights pursuant to Me. Rev. Stat. tit. 14, §§ 6015 and 6016, regarding the illegality of a rent increase when the rental is in violation of the warranty of habitability (but not if the tenant has caused the habitability violation). (Maine)

State Laws Prohibiting Landlord Retaliation (continued)

State	Statute	Tenant's Complaint to Landlord or Government Agency	Tenant's Involvement in Tenants' Organization	Tenant's Exercise of Legal Right	Retaliation Is Presumed If Negative Reaction by Landlord Within Specified Time of Tenant's Act
Maryland [7]	Md. Code Real Prop., §§ 8-208.1, 8-208.2	✓	✓		6 months
Massachusetts [2]	Mass. Laws ch. 239, § 2A; ch. 186, § 18	✓	✓	✓	6 months
Michigan [8]	Mich. Comp. Laws § 600.5720	✓	✓	✓	90 days
Minnesota	Minn. Stat. §§ 504B.285, 504B.441	✓		✓	90 days
Mississippi [9]	Miss. Code §§ 89-8-9, 89-8-17			✓	
Missouri	No statute				
Montana	Mont. Code § 70-24-431	✓	✓		6 months
Nebraska	Neb. Rev. Stat. § 76-1439	✓	✓		
Nevada [10]	Nev. Rev. Stat. § 118A.510	✓	✓	✓	
New Hampshire	N.H. Rev. Stat. §§ 540:13-a, 540:13-b	✓	✓		6 months
New Jersey [11]	N.J. Stat. §§ 2A:42-10.10, 2A:42-10.12	✓	✓	✓	
New Mexico	N.M. Stat. § 47-8-39	✓	✓	✓	6 months
New York [12]	N.Y. Real Prop. Law § 223-b	✓	✓	✓	One year
North Carolina	N.C. Gen. Stat. § 42-37.1	✓	✓	✓	12 months
North Dakota	No statute				
Ohio	Ohio Rev. Code § 5321.02	✓	✓		
Oklahoma [13]	No statute				
Oregon [14]	Or. Rev. Stat. § 90.385	✓	✓	✓	
Pennsylvania	68 Pa. Cons. Stat. §§ 250.205, 250.504-A, and 399.11		✓	✓	6 months (for exercise of legal rights connected with utility service)
Rhode Island	R.I. Gen. Laws §§ 34-18-46, 34-20-10, and 34-20-11	✓	✓	✓	6 months
South Carolina	S.C. Code § 27-40-910	✓			

7 Landlords may not retaliate against tenants who provide information to the landlord regarding the state's lead hazard reduction program, or after the tenant (or another person) has summoned the help of law enforcement or emergency services. (Maryland)

8 If landlord tries to increase tenant's obligations under the lease as a penalty for asserting rights, and the tenant doesn't perform these additional obligations, the tenant can use the retaliation as a defense against eviction for failure to perform under the lease. (Michigan)

9 Mississippi law specifically requires that landlords exercise good faith when they terminate or don't renew a lease. This could expand the categories of behavior that are considered prohibited retaliation. (Mississippi)

10 Statute protects tenants or tenants' guests who reasonably request emergency assistance. Local government cannot deem the request itself to be a "nuisance." Landlord may, however, take appropriate adverse actions based on information supplied by emergency responders, as can local governments with regard to declaring a nuisance. Federal, state, and tribal employees, and their household members, have broad anti-eviction rights during a government shutdown; landlord must not retaliate against them for exercising these rights. (Nevada)

11 If a tenant fails to request a renewal of a lease or tenancy within 90 days of the tenancy's expiration (or by the renewal date specified in the lease if longer than 90 days), a landlord may terminate or not renew without a presumption of retaliation. (New Jersey)

12 Landlord also cannot retaliate for tenant's attempt to enforce the warranty of habitability, nor evict when tenant objects to a new lease with an "unreasonable" rent increase. Presumption of retaliation applies to nonpayment evictions as well as holdovers. (New York)

13 Oklahoma law specifically requires that landlords exercise good faith in their performance under the Oklahoma Residential Landlord and Tenant Act. An argument could perhaps be made that terminating a tenancy or otherwise retaliating against a tenant for taking certain legal measures could be in bad faith. (Oklahoma)

14 Landlord may not retaliate against tenant if the tenant uses, intends to use, or attempts to use the rental as a family child care home (in compliance with applicable laws) (Oregon)

State	Statute	Tenant's Complaint to Landlord or Government Agency	Tenant's Involvement in Tenants' Organization	Tenant's Exercise of Legal Right	Retaliation Is Presumed If Negative Reaction by Landlord Within Specified Time of Tenant's Act
South Dakota	S.D. Codified Laws §§ 43-32-27, 43-32-28	✓	✓		180 days
Tennessee	Tenn. Code §§ 66-28-514, 68-111-105	✓		✓	
Texas	Tex. Prop. Code § 92.331	✓	✓	✓	6 months
Utah	Building Monitoring Sys. v. Paxton, 905 P.2d 1215 (Utah 1995)	✓			
Vermont 15	Vt. Stat. tit. 9, § 4465	✓	✓		90 days
Virginia 16	Va. Code §§ 55.1-1258, 55.1-1259	✓	✓	✓	
Washington	Wash. Rev. Code §§ 59.18.240, 59.18.250	✓		✓	90 days
West Virginia	Imperial Colliery Co. v. Fout, 373 S.E.2d 489 (1988); Murphy v. Smallridge, 468 S.E.2d 167 (W. Va. 1996)	✓		✓	
Wisconsin	Wis. Stat. § 704.45; Wis. Admin. Code § ATCP 134.09(5)	✓	✓	✓	
Wyoming	No statute				

State Laws Prohibiting Landlord Retaliation (continued)

15 Retaliation presumed only when landlord terminates for reasons other than rent nonpayment, after tenant has filed complaint with a governmental entity alleging noncompliance with health or safety regulations. (Vermont)

16 Tenants can sue for damages and injunction. (Virginia)

State Laws on Termination for Nonpayment of Rent

When a tenant is late with the rent, in most states the landlord cannot immediately file for eviction. Instead, the landlord must give the tenant written notice that the tenant has a specified number of days in which to pay up or move. If the tenant does neither, the landlord can file for eviction. In some states, the landlord must wait a few days after the rent is due before giving the tenant the notice; other states allow the landlord to file for eviction immediately. The following rules might be tempered in domestic violence situations, depending on state law (see "State Laws in Domestic Violence Situations" chart in this appendix).

State	Statute	Time Tenant Has to Pay Rent or Move Before Landlord Can File for Eviction	Legal Late Period: How Long Landlord Must Wait Before Giving Notice to Pay or Quit
Alabama	Ala. Code § 35-9A-421	7 business days	
Alaska	Alaska Stat. §§ 09.45.090, 34.03.220	7 days	
Arizona	Ariz. Rev. Stat. § 33-1368	5 days	
Arkansas [1]	Ark. Code §§ 18-16-101, 18-17-701, 18-60-304	3 days if landlord is filing a civil eviction ("unlawful detainer"); 10 days if landlord is filing a criminal eviction ("failure to vacate") under Ark. Code § 18-16-101.	5 days
California	Cal. Civ. Proc. Code § 1161(2)	3 days, excluding Saturdays, Sundays, and other judicial holidays	
Colorado [2]	Colo. Rev. Stat. §§ 13-40-104(1)(d), (5)(b)	10 days, 5 for single-family houses being rented under an "exempt residential agreement."	
Connecticut	Conn. Gen. Stat. §§ 47a-23, 47a-15a	9 days	Unconditional quit notice cannot be delivered until the rent is 9 days late.
Delaware	Del. Code tit. 25, §§ 5501(d), 5502	5 days	If rental agreement provides for a late charge, but landlord does not maintain an office in the county in which the rental unit is located, due date for the rent is extended 3 days; thereafter, landlord can serve a 5-day notice.
District of Columbia [3]	D.C. Code § 42-3505.01	At least 30 days before filing, the landlord must provide the tenant with written notice of the intent to file for eviction. The landlord can't provide this notice unless the tenant has failed to pay $600 or more of rent. A tenant might be able to further prevent an eviction and obtain funds to pay the rent by filing an Emergency Rental Assistance Program application.	
Florida	Fla. Stat. § 83.56(3)	3 days, excluding Saturdays, Sundays, and legal holidays	
Georgia	Ga. Code §§ 44-7-50, 44-7-52	Landlord can demand the rent as soon as it is due and, if not paid, can file for eviction. Tenant then has 7 days to pay to avoid eviction.	

[1] Arkansas uses unconditional quit notices (tenant does not have the opportunity to pay rent owed). Tenants who are evicted under the criminal failure to vacate statute are guilty of a misdemeanor and can be fined no more than $25 for each day the tenant remains in the rental after the notice has expired. (Arkansas)

[2] Landlords who own five or fewer single-family rental homes may state in the lease or rental agreement for a single-family home that only five days' notice to pay rent or quit is required. (Colorado)

[3] Before filing a complaint for nonpayment of rent (eviction), landlord must send the tenant a notice of past due rent that contains language specified by D.C. Code § 42-3505.01(a-1)(2). (District of Columbia)

State Laws on Termination for Nonpayment of Rent (continued)

State	Statute	Time Tenant Has to Pay Rent or Move Before Landlord Can File for Eviction	Legal Late Period: How Long Landlord Must Wait Before Giving Notice to Pay or Quit
Hawaii	Haw. Rev. Stat. § 521-68	5 days	
Idaho	Idaho Code § 6-303(2)	3 days	
Illinois	735 Ill. Comp. Stat. § 5/9-209	5 days	
Indiana	Ind. Code § 32-31-1-6	10 days	
Iowa	Iowa Code § 562A.27(2)	3 days	
Kansas	Kan. Stat. § 58-2564(b)	3 days (if notice is delivered by mailing, add two days from date of mailing)	
Kentucky	Ky. Rev. Stat. § 383.660(2)	7 days	
Louisiana	La. Civ. Proc. Code art. 4701	Landlord can terminate with an unconditional quit notice.	
Maine	Me. Rev. Stat. tit. 14, § 6002	7 days	Notice cannot be delivered until the rent is 7 days late, and landlord must tell tenant that tenant can contest the termination in court (failure to so advise prohibits entry of a default judgment).
Maryland	Md. Code Real Prop., § 8-401	10 days	
Massachusetts 4	Mass. Gen. Laws ch. 186, §§ 11, 11A, 12	Tenants with rental agreements or leases: Whatever amount of time is specified in agreement or lease, but if not addressed in the agreement, 14 days' notice in writing (but tenant can avoid by paying rent and costs on or before day the answer is due). Holdover tenants (tenants at sufferance): No specific time for notice to quit, but landlord must give them a reasonable period of time to remove themselves and property from the premises.	
Michigan	Mich. Comp. Laws § 554.134(2)	Landlord may terminate immediately with 7-day notice.	
Minnesota	Minn. Stat. §§ 504B.291, 504B.321	14 days' notice or 30 days' notice for leases with a term of more than 20 years	
Mississippi	Miss. Code § 89-8-13	3 days. Tenant may stay if rent and costs are paid prior to removal.	
Missouri	Mo. Rev. Stat. § 535.010	Landlord can terminate with an unconditional quit notice.	
Montana	Mont. Code § 70-24-422(2)	3 days	
Nebraska	Neb. Rev. Stat. § 76-1431(2)	7 days	
Nevada 5	Nev. Rev. Stat. §§ 40.2512, 40.253	7 days	

4 For tenants at will who have not received notices in the preceding 12 months, 10 days to pay, 4 more to quit (unless notice is insufficient, then 14 days to pay). (Massachusetts)

5 Under Nevada's "summary eviction" procedures, after a landlord serves the tenant with a notice to pay rent or quit, the tenant must go to court within seven days of notice to contest the notice. If the tenant doesn't, the landlord can file a complaint for eviction in court and get an order for law enforcement to remove the tenant within 24-36 hours of the order. (Nevada)

	State Laws on Termination for Nonpayment of Rent (continued)		
State	**Statute**	**Time Tenant Has to Pay Rent or Move Before Landlord Can File for Eviction**	**Legal Late Period: How Long Landlord Must Wait Before Giving Notice to Pay or Quit**
New Hampshire 6	N.H. Rev. Stat. §§ 540:2, 540:3, 540:9	7 days	
New Jersey	N.J. Stat. §§ 2A:18-53, 2A:18-61.1, 2A:18-61.2, 2A:42-9	Landlord can terminate with an unconditional quit notice.	
New Mexico	N.M. Stat. § 47-8-33(D)	3 days	
New York 7	N.Y. Real Prop. Law § 235-e(d); N.Y. Real Prop. Acts. Law § 711(2)	14 days	Landlords must send written notice (via certified mail) to tenants who are five days late paying rent. Failure to provide this written notice of nonpayment of rent can be used by tenant as a defense to an eviction suit.
North Carolina	N.C. Gen. Stat. § 42-3	10 days	
North Dakota	N.D. Cent. Code § 47-32-01	Landlord can file for eviction when rent is 3 days overdue and can terminate with an unconditional quit notice.	
Ohio	Ohio Rev. Code § 1923.02(A)(9)	Landlord can terminate with an unconditional quit notice.	
Oklahoma	Okla. Stat. tit. 41, § 131	5 days	
Oregon 8	Or. Rev. Stat. §§ 90.394(2)(a), 90.394(2)(b)	10 days	Notice cannot be delivered until the rent is 8 days late.
	Or. Rev. Stat. § 90.394(2)(b)	13 days	Notice cannot be delivered until the rent is 5 days late.
Pennsylvania	68 Pa. Stat. § 250.501(b)	10 days	
Rhode Island	R.I. Gen. Laws § 34-18-35	5 days. Tenants can stay if they pay rent prior to commencement of suit. If tenants haven't received a pay or quit notice for nonpayment of rent within past 6 months, they can stay if they pay rent and costs prior to eviction hearing.	15 days
South Carolina	S.C. Code §§ 27-37-10(B), 27-40-710(B)	5 days. If there is a written lease or rental agreement that specifies in bold, conspicuous type that landlord may file for eviction as soon as tenant is 5 days late (or if there is a month-to-month tenancy following such an agreement), landlord may do so without further notice to tenant. If there is no such written agreement, landlord must give tenant 5 days' written notice before filing for eviction.	
South Dakota	S.D. Codified Laws §§ 21-16-1(4), 21-16-2	Landlord must give a 3-day notice to quit (unconditional quit notice) before filing for eviction.	3 days

6 If the tenant pays all rent due, all other lawful charges contained in the lease, $15 liquidated damages, and any filing fee and service charges the landlord incurs, the court will dismiss the eviction action if the landlord files a receipt of the payments to the court before the scheduled hearing date. If the tenant pays but the landlord doesn't submit a receipt, the hearing on the action will happen, but if the tenant proves payment in full the court will dismiss the case. A tenant can have the eviction dismissed in this manner no more than three times in a 12-month period.. (New Hampshire)

7 If tenant offers landlord full amount of past due rent at any time before the eviction hearing, landlord must accept it and the eviction proceeding will not take place. (New York)

8 Landlord has a choice: Serve pay or quit notice after rent is 8 days late (tenant has 10 days to pay or quit), or serve the notice earlier, after rent is overdue 5 days (tenant has longer, 13 days, to pay or quit). (Oregon)

State Laws on Termination for Nonpayment of Rent (continued)

State	Statute	Time Tenant Has to Pay Rent or Move Before Landlord Can File for Eviction	Legal Late Period: How Long Landlord Must Wait Before Giving Notice to Pay or Quit
Tennessee	Tenn. Code § 66-28-505 (in counties with a population of more than 75,000 according to the 2010 census); Tenn. Code § 66-7-109 (in counties with a population with fewer than 75,000)	14 days	
Texas	Tex. Prop. Code § 24.005	3 days' notice to move (lease may specify a shorter or longer time).	
Utah	Utah Code § 78B-6-802	3 business days	
Vermont	Vt. Stat. tit. 9, § 4467(a)	14 days	
Virginia	Va. Code §§ 55.1-1245, 55.1-1250	5 days. After landlord has filed and before the date tenant must answer, tenant who offers to pay rent, costs, interest, and reasonable attorneys' fees has 10 days to do so, after which the lawsuit will be dismissed (if tenant doesn't make the payment, the landlord gets a judgment for possession and all amounts due). Post-judgment, the case will be dismissed if tenant pays all amounts due, including late fees, civil recoveries, and sheriff fees within two days of the scheduled eviction.	
Washington	Wash. Rev. Code §§ 59.12.030(3), 59.18.057, 59.18.650	14 days	
West Virginia	W.Va. Code § 55-3A-1	Landlord can file for eviction immediately, no notice required, no opportunity to cure.	
Wisconsin	Wis. Stat. § 704.17	Month-to-month tenants: 5 days; landlord can use an unconditional quit notice with 14 days' notice. Tenants with a lease less than one year, and year-to-year tenants: 5 days (cannot use unconditional quit notice). Tenants with a lease longer than one year: 30 days (cannot use unconditional quit notice).	
Wyoming	Wyo. Stat. §§ 1-21-1002 to 1-21-1003	Landlord must give a 3-day notice to quit (unconditional quit notice) before filing for eviction.	3 days

State Laws on Termination for Violation of Lease

Many states give the tenant a specified amount of time to cure or cease the lease or rental agreement violation or move before the landlord can file for eviction. In some states, if the tenant has not ceased or cured the violation at the end of that period, the tenant gets additional time to move before the landlord can file; in others, the tenant must move as soon as the cure period expires. And some states allow the landlord to terminate with an unconditional quit notice, without giving the tenant a chance to cure or cease the violation. The following rules might be tempered in domestic violence situations, depending on state law (see "State Laws in Domestic Violence Situations" chart in this appendix).

State	Statute	Time Tenant Has to Cure the Violation or Move Before Landlord Can File for Eviction
Alabama	Ala. Code § 35-9A-421	7 business days
Alaska	Alaska Stat. §§ 09.45.090, 34.03.220	10 days for violations of agreement materially affecting health and safety. If the notice is because of the tenant's failure to pay utility bills that has resulted in a shut-off, the landlord can serve the tenant with a 5-day notice to quit. The tenant has 3 days from the date of the notice to reinstate service and reimburse landlord for any costs. If the tenant doesn't cure in those 3 days, they have the remaining 2 days of the 5-day notice to move out.
Arizona	Ariz. Rev. Stat. § 33-1368	5 days for violations materially affecting health and safety; 10 days for other violations of the lease terms. If there's an additional act of noncompliance during the same lease term, the landlord can give a 10-day notice to quit (no chance to cure). If the violation is material, irreparable, and relates to health and safety (or is a criminal act), the landlord can give tenant a notice to quit immediately.
Arkansas	Ark. Stat. §§ 18-17-701, 18-17-702	Tenant has 14 days to cure a remediable violation. If violation materially affects tenant's health and safety, tenant must remedy as promptly as conditions require in case of emergency (or within 14 days after written notice by the landlord if it is not an emergency); failure entitles landlord to terminate the tenancy.
California	Cal. Civ. Proc. Code § 1161(3)	3 days, excluding Saturdays, Sundays, and other judicial holidays
Colorado	Colo. Rev. Stat. §§ 13-40-104(1)(d.5)-(e), (5)(b); 13-40-107.5	10 days to cure a nonsubstantial lease violation, unless the property is leased under an "exempt residential agreement" (in which case it's 5 days to cure). Landlords who own five or fewer single-family rental homes may state in the lease or rental agreement for a single-family home that only 5 days' notice to cure is required. (Colo. Rev. Stat. §§ 13-40-104(1)(e), (5)(b).) No opportunity to cure substantial lease violations, landlords must give 3 days' notice to move. (Colo. Rev. Stat. §§ 13-40-104(1)(d.5), 13-40-107.5.)
Connecticut	Conn. Gen. Stat. § 47a-15	15 days; no right to cure for serious nuisance.
Delaware	Del. Code tit. 25, § 5513(a)	7 days
District of Columbia	D.C. Code § 42-3505.01	30 days
Florida	Fla. Stat. § 83.56(2)	7 days (no cure for certain substantial violations).
Georgia	Ga. Code § 44-7-50	Although statute doesn't specifically mention lease violations as grounds for eviction, Georgia courts allow lease violation as a ground for an unconditional quit notice under the statute.
Hawaii	Haw. Rev. Stat. §§ 521-72, 666-3	10 days' notice to cure, landlord must file for eviction within 30 days' if the violation hasn't been cured by the deadline in the notice. For a nuisance, 24 hours to cease the nuisance. If the nuisance hasn't stopped within 24 hours, the landlord can terminate with a written 5-day notice.
Idaho	Idaho Code § 6-303	3 days
Illinois	735 Ill. Comp. Stat. 5/9-210	10 days
Indiana	Ind. Code § 32-31-1-8	Landlord can terminate with an unconditional quit notice.

State Laws on Termination for Violation of Lease (continued)

State	Statute	Time Tenant Has to Cure the Violation or Move Before Landlord Can File for Eviction
Iowa	Iowa Code § 562A.27(1)	7 days
Kansas	Kan. Stat. § 58-2564(a)	14 days to cure and an additional 16 to vacate. If there's a repeat violation, no opportunity to cure and landlord can file eviction suit after 30 days' notice.
Kentucky	Ky. Rev. Stat. § 383.660(1)	15 days to cure. If there's a repeat violation within 6 months, the landlord can give an unconditional 14-day notice to quit.
Louisiana	La. Civ. Proc. art. 4701	5 days, no opportunity to cure necessary.
Maine	Me. Rev. Stat. tit. 14 § 6002	7 days
Maryland	Md. Code Real Prop., § 8-402.1	30 days unless breach poses clear and imminent danger, then 14 days (no cure).
Massachusetts	Mass. Gen. Laws ch. 186, § 12	Landlord can terminate with 30 days' notice or one full rental period in advance of termination date, whichever is longer.
Michigan	Mich. Comp. Laws § 600.5714	For causing serious, continuous health hazards or damage to the premises: 7 days after receiving notice to restore or repair or quit (domestic violence victims excepted).
Minnesota	Minn. Stat. §§ 504B.171 (Subd. 2), 504B.285 (Subd.4)	Landlord can immediately file for eviction.
Mississippi	Miss. Code § 89-8-13	14 days. If there's a repeat violation within six months, no opportunity to cure is necessary.
Missouri	Mo. Rev. Stat. § 441.040	10 days' unconditional notice to quit.
Montana	Mont. Code § 70-24-422	14 days; 3 days if unauthorized pet or person on premises, or if the noncompliance is from verbal abuse of the landlord by a tenant.
Nebraska	Neb. Rev. Stat. § 76-1431	14 days to cure, 16 additional days to vacate if not cured within 14 days. If substantially the same violation recurs within six months, the landlord can terminate without opportunity to cure with 14 days' notice.
Nevada	Nev. Rev. Stat. § 40.2516	5 days to cure
New Hampshire	N.H. Rev. Stat. §§ 540:2, 540:3	30 days; 7 days if there's substantial damage to the premises by the tenant or tenant poses a risk to health or safety of other tenants or the landlord.
New Jersey	N.J. Stat. §§ 2A:18-53(c), 2A:18-61.1(e) (1)	3 days; lease must specify which violations will result in eviction. (Some courts have ruled that the tenant be given an opportunity to cure the violation or condition any time up to the entry of judgment in favor of the landlord.)
New Mexico	N.M. Stat. § 47-8-33(A)	7 days
New York	N.Y. Real Prop. Acts Law §§ 711, 753(4)[NYC]	Regulated units: 10 days or as set by applicable rent regulation. Nonregulated units: No statute. Lease sets applicable cure and/or termination notice periods. State-wide: When eviction is based on violation of lease, court must grant a 30-day stay of the eviction warrant to give tenant an opportunity to cure the breach.
North Carolina	No statute	Landlord can terminate with an unconditional quit notice if lease specifies termination for violation.
North Dakota	N.D. Cent. Code § 47-32-02	3 days
Ohio	Ohio Rev. Code §§ 1923.02(A)(9) and 1923.041	3 days
Oklahoma	Okla. Stat. tit. 41, § 132(A), (B)	10 days to cure, additional 5 days to vacate.
Oregon	Or. Rev. Stat. §§ 90.392, 90.405	14 days to cure, additional 16 days to vacate; 10 days to remove an illegal pet.

State Laws on Termination for Violation of Lease (continued)

State	Statute	Time Tenant Has to Cure the Violation or Move Before Landlord Can File for Eviction
Pennsylvania	68 Pa. Con. Stat. § 250.501	15 days if the lease is for one year or less; 30 days if lease is for more than a year.
Rhode Island	R.I. Gen. Laws § 34-18-36	20 days for material noncompliance.
South Carolina	S.C. Code § 27-40-710(A)	14 days
South Dakota	S.D. Codified Laws §§ 21-16-1(7), 21-16-2	Landlord must give tenant 3 days' notice to quit (no opportunity to cure) before filing for eviction, in specified situations. Other situations require no notice.
Tennessee	Tenn. Code § 66-28-505(a)(3)	14 days
Texas	Tex. Prop. Code § 24.005	3 days
Utah	Utah Code § 78B-6-802	3 days
Vermont	Vt. Stat. tit. 9 § 4467(b)(1)	30 days; 14 days for criminal activity, drug activity, or acts of violence.
Virginia	Va. Code § 55.1-1245	21 days to cure, additional 9 to quit; 30 if violation can't be cured.
Washington	Wash. Rev. Code §§ 59.12.030(4), 59.18.650	10 days; 3 days if tenant commits or permits waste or nuisance, engages in unlawful activity, or other substantial or repeated and unreasonable interference with the use and enjoyment of the premises by the landlord or neighbors.
West Virginia	W. Va. Code § 55-3A-1	Landlord can immediately file for eviction; no notice is required.
Wisconsin	Wis. Stat. § 704.17	5 days, no opportunity to cure for public housing tenants who have committed drug-related violations. If it's a repeat violation, 14 days with no opportunity to cure.
Wyoming	Wyo. Stat. §§ 1-21-1002, 1-21-1003	3 days

State Laws on Unconditional Quit Terminations

An unconditional quit notice is one that tells the tenant they must move out by the deadline stated in the notice. The tenant won't have an opportunity to fix the problem that led to their receiving the notice (such as having a pet in violation of a no-pets policy). The following rules might be tempered in domestic violence situations, depending on state law (see "State Laws in Domestic Violence Situations" in this appendix).

State	Statute	Time to Move Out Before Landlord Can File For Eviction	When Unconditional Quit Notice Can Be Used
Alabama	Ala. Code § 35-9A-421	7 business days	Intentional misrepresentation of a material fact in a rental application or rental agreement; possession or use of illegal drugs in the rental or common areas; illegal use, possession, discharge of a firearm on the premises (some exceptions); criminal assault of a tenant or guest on the premises (some exceptions); any breach for substantially the same acts or omissions for which a notice to terminate has previously been provided for by the landlord and cured by the tenant within the past six months.
Alaska	Alaska Stat. § 34.03.220(a)(1)(2)	5 days	Tenant repeats a violation of the lease or other violation of law within 6 months.
	Alaska Stat. §§ 09.45.090(a)(2)(G), 34.03.310(c)(3)	5 days	Tenant is committing waste or nuisance, is using the rental for an illegal purpose, or is using the rental for purposes other than living or dwelling (in violation of the lease or rental agreement).
	Alaska Stat. §§ 09.45.090(a)(2)(G), 34.03.120(b), 34.03.220(a)(1), and 34.03.310(c)(3)	24 hours to 5 days	Tenant or guest intentionally inflicts "substantial damage" (damage greater than $400) to the premises; or engages in prostitution, an illegal activity involving a place of prostitution, an illegal activity involving alcoholic beverages, an illegal activity involving gambling or promoting gambling, an illegal activity involving a controlled substance, or an illegal activity involving an imitation controlled substance, or knowingly permitting others in the premises to engage in one or more of those activities at the rental premises.
	Alaska Stat. § 34.03.220(e)	3 days	Failure to pay utility bills that resulted in service termination twice within six months. Refusal to allow the landlord to enter.
	Alaska Stat. § 34.03.300(a)	10 days	Refusal to allow the landlord to enter.
Arizona	Ariz. Rev. Stat. § 33-1368	10 days	Material misrepresentation of criminal record, current criminal activity, or prior eviction record; additional act of noncompliance of same or similar nature after a previous remedy of noncompliance.
		Immediately	Discharging a weapon; homicide, prostitution, criminal street gang activity; use or sale of illegal drugs, assaults, acts constituting a nuisance or breach of the rental agreement that threaten harm to others.
Arkansas	Ark. Stat. §§ 18-16-101, 18-17-701,	5 days	Noncompliance by the tenant with the rental agreement when the violation is not remediable; using (or allowing another person to use) the premises in a way constituting a common nuisance, or permitting/conducting specified criminal offenses; rent unpaid within five days of rent due date. If rent is unpaid within ten days of due date, tenant may be charged with a misdemeanor (fine only).
California	Cal. Civ. Proc. Code § 1161(4)	3 days	Assigning or subletting without permission, committing waste or a nuisance, illegal activity on the premises.

State Laws on Unconditional Quit Terminations (continued)

State	Statute	Time to Move Out Before Landlord Can File For Eviction	When Unconditional Quit Notice Can Be Used
Colorado	Colo. Rev. Stat. §§ 13-40-104(1)(d.5), (1)(e.5), (5)(b); 13-40-107.5	3 days for substantial violations. (Colo. Rev. Stat. § 13-40-107.5.)	When tenant has substantially violated lease clause. (Colo. Rev. Stat. §§ 13-40104(1)(d.5), 13-40-107.5.)
		10 days for repeated violation of lease clause, except that landlords who own five or fewer single-family rental homes may provide in their lease or rental agreement for a single-family home (an "exempt residential agreement") that only five days' notice is required. (Colo. Rev. Stat. §§ 13-40-104(1) (e.5), (5)(b).)	Any repeated violation of a lease clause (Colo. Rev. Stat. § 13-40104(1)(e.5).)
Connecticut	Conn. Gen. Stat. §§ 47a-15, 47a-23, 47a-23b	3 days (or 10 days if the tenant is not a resident of the state)	Nonpayment of rent, serious nuisance, violation of the rental agreement, same violation within 6 months relating to health and safety or materially affecting physical premises, rental agreement has terminated (by lapse of time, stipulation, violation of lease, nonpayment of rent after grace period, serious nuisance, occupancy by someone who never had the right to occupy), when summary eviction is justified (refusal to a fair and equitable increase, intent of the landlord to use as a principal residence, removal of the unit from the housing market), domestic or farm worker who does not vacate upon cessation of employment and tenancy.
	Conn. Gen. Stat. § 47a-31	Immediately	Conviction for prostitution or gambling that occurred at the rental.
Delaware	Del. Code tit. 25, § 5513	7 days	Violation of a lease provision that also constitutes violation of municipal, county, or state code or statute; or a violation of a material lease provision repeated within 12 months of a substantially similar previous violation.
		Immediately	Violation of law or breach of the rental agreement that causes or threatens to cause irreparable harm to the landlord's property or to other tenants.
District of Columbia	D.C. Code § 42-3505.01(c)	30 days	Court determination that an illegal act was performed within the rental unit.
Florida	Fla. Stat. § 83.56(2)(a)	7 days	Intentional destruction of the rental property or other tenants' property or unreasonable disturbances; for destruction, damage, or misuse of the landlord's or other tenants' property by intentional act or a subsequent or continued unreasonable disturbance (after written warning within previous 12 months); a subsequent or continuing noncompliance within 12 months of a written warning by the landlord of a similar violation.
Georgia	Ga. Code §§ 44-7-50, 44-7-52	Immediately	Nonpayment of rent more than once within 12 months; holding over.

State Laws on Unconditional Quit Terminations (continued)

State	Statute	Time to Move Out Before Landlord Can File For Eviction	When Unconditional Quit Notice Can Be Used
Hawaii	Haw. Rev. Stat. §§ 521-69, 521-71, 521-72	Immediately	Tenant fails to use the property according to law and the failure causes or threatens to cause damage to any person, certain property, or constitutes a violation of certain codes; tenant fails to maintain unit according to law, and the failure causes or threatens to cause irremediable damage to any person or property. When tenant continues in possession after the agreed date of termination without the landlord's consent, the landlord can give unconditional notice to quit immediately within the first 60 days of holdover.
	Haw. Rev. Stat. § 666-3	5 days	Second failure to abate a nuisance within 24 hours of receiving notice.
Idaho	Idaho Code § 6-303	Immediately	Using, delivering, or producing a controlled substance on the property at any time during the lease term.
		3 days	Assigning or subletting without the consent of the landlord or causing serious damage to the property.
Illinois	735 Ill. Comp. Stat. § 5/9-210	10 days	Failure to abide by any term of the lease.
	740 Ill. Comp. Stat. § 40/11	5 days	Unlawful use or sale of any controlled substance.
Indiana	Ind. Code § 32-31-1-8	Immediately	Tenants with lease: holding over. Tenants without lease: committing waste.
Iowa	Iowa Code § 562A.27	7 days	Repeating same violation of lease within 6 months that affects health and safety.
	Iowa Code § 562A.27A	3 days	Creating a clear and present danger to the health or safety of the landlord, tenants, or neighbors within 1,000 feet of the property boundaries.
Kansas	Kan. Stat. § 58-2564(a)	30 days	Second similar material violation of the lease after first violation was corrected.
Kentucky	Ky. Rev. Stat. § 383.660(1)	14 days	Repeating the same material violation of the lease within 6 months of being given a first cure or quit notice.
Louisiana	La. Civ. Code art. 2686; La. Code Civ. Proc. art. 4701	5 days	Failure to pay rent, using dwelling for purpose other than the intended purpose (lease may specify shorter or longer notice, or eliminate requirement of notice) or upon termination of the lease for any reason.
Maine	Me. Rev. Stat. tit. 14, §§ 6001, 6002, 6025	7 days	Holdover tenants if notice is served within 7 days of the end of the original term; substantial and unrepaired damage to the premises; causing, permitting, or maintaining a nuisance; tenant is a perpetrator of domestic violence, sexual assault, or stalking and the victim is also a tenant; tenant or tenant's guest is a perpetrator of violence, a threat of violence, or sexual assault against certain others; the person occupying the premises is not an authorized occupant of the premises. Landlord can also terminate when a tenant changes the lock and refuses to provide landlord with a duplicate key.
Maryland	Md. Code Real Prop., § 8-402.1(a)	14 days	Breaching lease by behaving in a manner that presents a clear and imminent danger to the tenant themself, other tenants, guests, the landlord, or the landlord's property, lease provides for termination for violation of lease clause, and landlord has given 14 days' notice.
	Md. Code Real Prop., § 8-401	10 days	When tenant hasn't paid rent and has had 3 judgments of possession entered for rent due and unpaid in the 12 months prior.
Massachusetts	Mass. Laws ch. 186, § 12	14 days	Tenant at will receiving second notice to pay rent or quit within 12 months.

State Laws on Unconditional Quit Terminations (continued)

State	Statute	Time to Move Out Before Landlord Can File For Eviction	When Unconditional Quit Notice Can Be Used
Michigan	Mich. Comp. Laws § 600.5714(d) and (e)	7 days	Failure to pay rent, causing or threatening physical injury to an individual (landlord must have filed a police report).
	Mich. Comp. Laws § 554.134	24 hours	Manufacture, dealing, or possession of illegal drugs on leased premises (landlord must first file a police report).
Minnesota	Minn. Stat. §§ 504B.135, 504B.321(1a)	14 days for termination based on unpaid rent or other monetary obligation. For other terminations, the notice period must be at least as long as the interval between when rent is due or three months, whichever is less.	Tenant at will who fails to pay rent or other monetary obligation when due.
Mississippi	Miss. Code § 89-8-13	14 days	Repeating the same act—which constituted a lease violation and for which notice was given—within 6 months; nonremediable violation of lease or obligations imposed by statute.
Missouri	Mo. Stat. §§ 441.020, 441.030, 441.040	10 days	Using the premises for gambling, prostitution, or possession, sale, or distribution of controlled substances; assigning or subletting without consent; seriously damaging the premises or violating the lease.
Montana	Mont. Code. § 70-24-422(1)(e)	5 days	Repeating the same act (that constituted a lease violation and for which notice was given) within 6 months.
	Mont. Code § 70-24-422	3 days	Unauthorized pet or person living on premises; destroying or removing any part of the premises; creating a reasonable potential that the premises might be damaged or destroyed, or that neighboring tenants might be injured, due to tenant's drug, or gang-related, or other illegal activity.
	Mont. Code § 70-24-422(1)(d)	14 days	Any other noncompliance with rental agreement that can't be remedied or repaired.
Nebraska	Neb. Rev. Stat. § 76-1431(1)	14 days	Repeating the same act (that constituted a lease violation and for which notice was given) within 6 months.
	Neb. Rev. Stat. § 76-1431(4)	5 days	When tenant or guest engages in violent criminal activity or sells a controlled substance on the premises, or acts in a way that threatens the health or safety of other tenants, landlord, landlord's employees or agents.
Nevada	Nev. Rev. Stat. § 40.2514	3 days	Assigning or subletting in violation of the lease; substantial damage to the property; conducting an unlawful business; permitting or creating a nuisance; causing injury and damage to other tenants or occupants of the property or adjacent buildings or structures; unlawful possession for sale, manufacture, or distribution of illegal drugs.
	Nev. Rev. Stat. § 40.2516	Immediately	Violation of lease term that cannot be cured.

State Laws on Unconditional Quit Terminations (continued)

State	Statute	Time to Move Out Before Landlord Can File For Eviction	When Unconditional Quit Notice Can Be Used
New Hampshire	N.H. Rev. Stat. § 540:1-a		Different rules apply depending on whether the property is "restricted" (most residential property) or "nonrestricted" (single-family houses, if the owner of such a house does not own more than 3 single-family houses at any one time; rental units in an owner-occupied building containing a total of 4 dwelling units or fewer; and single-family houses acquired by banks or other mortgagees through foreclosure).
	N.H. Rev. Stat. § 540:2, 540:3	7 days	Restricted property: Neglect or refusal to pay rent due and in arrears, upon demand; fourth instance within a 12-month period in which the rent has been in arrears; substantial damage to the premises; failure to comply with a material term of the lease; behavior of the tenant or members of their family that adversely affects the health or safety of the other tenants or the landlord or landlord's representatives; failure of the tenant to accept suitable temporary relocation required by lead-based paint hazard abatement; other good cause. Nonrestricted: Neglect or refusal to pay rent due and in arrears, upon demand; substantial damage to the premises; behavior of the tenant or members of tenant's family that adversely affects the health or safety of the other tenants or the landlord or landlord's representatives; failure of the tenant to accept suitable temporary relocation required by lead-based paint hazard abatement; failure to prepare unit for insect (including bed bug) remediation.
		30 days	Nonrestricted only: For any legal reason other than those specified just above (for which 7 days' notice is required).
New Jersey	N.J. Stat. §§ 2A:18-53(c), 2A:18-61.2(a), 2A:19-61.1	3 days	Disorderly conduct; willful or grossly negligent destruction of landlord's property; assaults upon or threats against the landlord; termination of tenant's employment as a building manager, janitor, or other employee of the landlord; conviction for use, possession, or manufacture of an illegal drug either on the property or adjacent to it within the last two years, unless the tenant has entered a rehabilitation program (includes harboring anyone so convicted); conviction or civil liability for assault or terroristic threats against the landlord, landlord's family, or landlord's employee within the last two years (includes harboring); liability in a civil action for theft from landlord, landlord's family, landlord's employee, or another tenant; committing or harboring human trafficking.
	N.J. Stat. §§ 2A:18-61.1, 2A:18-61.2(b)	One month	Habitual failure to pay rent after written notice; continued violations, despite repeated warnings, of the landlord's reasonable rules and regulations; at the termination of a lease, refusal to accept reasonable changes of substance in the terms and conditions of the lease, including specifically any change in the term thereof.
New Mexico	N.M. Stat. § 47-8-33(I)	3 days	Substantial violation of the lease.
	N.M. Stat. § 47-8-33(B) & (C)	7 days	Repeated violation of a term of the rental agreement within 6 months.

State Laws on Unconditional Quit Terminations (continued)

State	Statute	Time to Move Out Before Landlord Can File For Eviction	When Unconditional Quit Notice Can Be Used
New York	N.Y. Real Prop. Acts. § 711	Immediately	When there is a landlord-tenant relationship, the landlord can begin a special proceeding to remove the tenant when tenant: Holds over after the lease has expired; has a lease for a term of three years or less and has (during the tenancy) taken the benefit of an insolvency statute or been declared bankrupt; or uses the rental as a "bawdy-house," for prostitution, or other illegal business. Other rules will apply to properties subject to statewide rent control/rent stabilization laws or NYC rent control/rent stabilization laws. Contact a local attorney or rent control organization for more information.
North Carolina	N.C. Gen. Stat. § 42-26(a)	Immediately	Violation of a lease term that specifies that eviction will result from noncompliance or holdover of tenancy.
North Dakota	N.D. Cent. Code § 47-32-01	No notice required	Entering by force, intimidation, fraud, or stealth; committing acts of force, threats, or menacing conduct; retaining possession by menacing and threats of violence; unreasonably disturbing other tenants' peaceful enjoyment of the premises.
	N.D. Cent. Code §§ 47-32-01 and 47-32-02	3 days	Holding over after the lease has expired; holding over after a sale or any judicial process ending the tenancy; violating a material term of the lease; using the property in a manner contrary to the agreement of the parties; using the property in a manner that unreasonably disturbs other tenants' peaceful enjoyment.
	N.D. Cent. Code § 47-16-07.6	No notice required	Making a false claim of a legal disability, in an attempt to obtain an accommodation (waiver of landlord's no pets rule); or knowingly providing fraudulent documentation in connection with such a claim. Each violation is an infraction and entitles the landlord to evict and demand a damage fee of up to $1,000.
Ohio	Ohio Rev. Code §§ 1923.02 to 1923.04, 5321.17	3 days	Nonpayment of rent; violation of a written lease or rental agreement; when the landlord has "reasonable cause to believe" that the tenant has used, sold, or manufactured an illegal drug on the premises (conviction or arrest not required).
Oklahoma	Okla. Stat. tit. 41, § 132	Immediately	Criminal or drug-related activity or repeated violation of the lease.
Oregon	Or. Rev. Stat. §§ 90.396, 90.398, 90.403	24 hours	Violence or threats of violence by tenant or a guest; intentionally causing substantial property damage; giving false information on an application within the past year regarding a criminal conviction (landlord must terminate within 30 days of discovering the falsity); committing any act "outrageous in the extreme" (see statute); intentionally or recklessly injuring someone (or placing them in fear of imminent danger) because of the tenant's perception of the person's race, color, religion, national origin, or sexual orientation; second failure to remove a pet that has caused substantial damage; a repeat within six months of a prior drug or alcohol violation of which notice was given.
Pennsylvania	68 Pa. Cons. Stat. § 250.501(b) and (d)	10 days	Nonpayment of rent.
		15 days (lease 1 year or less or lease of unspecified time)	Violations of the terms of the lease.
		30 days (lease more than 1 year)	Violations of the terms of the lease.
	68 Pa. Cons. Stat. § 250.505-A	10 days (any tenancy)	First conviction for illegal sale, manufacture, or distribution of an illegal drug; repeated use of an illegal drug; seizure by law enforcement of an illegal drug within the leased premises.

State Laws on Unconditional Quit Terminations (continued)

State	Statute	Time to Move Out Before Landlord Can File For Eviction	When Unconditional Quit Notice Can Be Used
Rhode Island	R.I. Gen. Laws § 34-18-36(e)	20 days	Repeating an act that violates the lease or rental agreement or affects health or safety twice within 6 months (notice must have been given for the first violation).
	R.I. Gen. Laws §§ 34-18-24, 34-18-36(f)	Immediately	Any tenant who possesses, uses, or sells illegal drugs or who commits or attempts to commit any crime of violence on the premises or in any public space adjacent; "seasonal tenant" whose lease runs between May 1 to October 15 or from September 1 to June 1 of the next year, with no right of extension or renewal, who has been charged with violating a local occupancy ordinance, making excessive noise, or disturbing the peace.
South Carolina	S.C. Code § 27-40-710	Immediately	Nonpayment of rent after receiving one notification during the tenancy or allowing illegal activities on the property.
South Dakota	S.D. Cod. Laws §§ 21-16-1, 21-16-2	Immediately	Forceful or violent detainer of the property, substantial damage to the property.
		3 days	Nonpayment of rent for three days after due date or holdover.
Tennessee	Tenn. Code §§ 66-28-406, 66-28-505, 66-28-517 (applies only in counties having a population of more than 75,000 residents, as measured in the 2010 federal census)	3 days	3 days when tenant or guest willfully or intentionally commits a violent act, threatens health, safety, or welfare or life or property of others on premises, or is an unauthorized subtenant or occupant who refuses to leave. (Tenn. Code § 66-28-517)
		14 days	14 days when tenant materially violates the lease or rental agreement or engages in acts that materially affect health and safety, and the action is not remediable. (Tenn. Code § 66-28-505(a)(3))
		7 days	7 days when tenant repeats within six months a violation of being late with rent or damaging property. (Tenn. Code § 66-28-505(a)(2)(B))
		Immediately	Immediately when tenant misrepresents a disability or disability-related need for the use of a service or support animal or provides false documentation stating that an animal is a service or support animal. (Tenn. Code §§ 66-28-505(f) and 66-28-406(f))
	Tenn. Code §§ 66-7-109, 66-7-111 (applies only in counties with fewer than 75,000 residents, as measured in the 2010 federal census)	14 days	14 days when tenant willfully or intentionally commits a violent act or threatens health, safety, or welfare of property or people; but if the tenant is in a housing authority or is not mentally or physically disabled, the landlord can give only 3 days' notice. (Tenn. Code § 66-7-109(a)(1) and (d))
		14 days	14 days if repeats within six months a violation of being late with rent or damaging property. (Tenn. Code § 66-7-109(a)(2))
		30 days	30 days when tenant violates lease agreement in another way. (Tenn. Code § 66-7-109(b))
		3 days	3 days when tenant engages in any drug-related criminal activity. (Tenn. Code § 66-7-109(d)(2))
		3 days	3 days when the landlord seeks to remove an unauthorized subtenant or occupant. (Tenn. Code § 66-7-109(f))
		Immediately	Immediately when tenant misrepresents a disability or disability-related need for the use of a service or support animal or provides false documentation stating that an animal is a service or support animal. (Tenn. Code § 66-7-111)

State Laws on Unconditional Quit Terminations (continued)

State	Statute	Time to Move Out Before Landlord Can File For Eviction	When Unconditional Quit Notice Can Be Used
Texas	Tex. Prop. Code § 24.005	3 days (lease may specify a shorter or longer time)	Nonpayment of rent or holdover.
Utah	Utah Code § 78B-6-802	3 days	Holdover, assigning or subletting without permission, substantial damage to the property, carrying on an unlawful business on the premises, maintaining a nuisance, committing a criminal act on the premises.
Vermont	Vt. Stat. tit. 9, § 4467	30 days (for material breach of lease or rental agreement)	Violation of a material term of the lease; failure to comply with state's landlord-tenant law.
		14 days (for criminal activity, illegal drug activity, or acts of violence)	14 days' notice applies for termination based on criminal activity, illegal drug activity, or acts of violence that threaten the health or safety of other residents.
Virginia	Va. Stat. § 55.1-1245	30 days	30-day unconditional quit notice used when: (a) tenant commits an unremediable breach; or (b) tenant repeats a violation of lease (after earlier violation was cured and tenant intentionally commits another breach similar to the first).
		Immediately	Immediate unconditional quit notice used when tenant breaches the lease or rental agreement by committing a willful or criminal act that is a threat to the health or safety of others.
Washington	Wash. Rev. Code §§ 59.12.030, 59.18.650	3 days	Holdover, serious damage to the property, carrying on an unlawful business, maintaining a nuisance, trespasser, or gang-related activity.
West Virginia	W.Va. Code § 55-3A-1	Immediately	Failure to pay rent, violation of any lease provision, or damage to the property.
Wisconsin	Wis. Stat. § 704.17	14 days (month-to-month tenants)	Failing to pay rent, violating the rental agreement, or causing substantial damage to the property.
		14 days (tenants with a lease of less than one year, or year-to-year tenants)	Failing to pay the rent on time, causing substantial property damage, or violating any lease provision more than once within one year (must have received proper notice for the first violation).
		5 days (all tenants)	Causing a nuisance on the property (landlord must have written notice from a law enforcement agency regarding the nuisance).
Wyoming	Wyo. Stat. §§ 1-21-1002, 1-21-1003	3 days	Nonpayment of rent, holdover, damage to premises, interference with another's enjoyment, denying access to landlord, or violating duties defined by statute (such as maintaining unit, complying with lease, disposing of garbage, etc.).

State Small Claims Court Limits

State	Statutes	Dollar limit	Can Hear Eviction Suits?	Court Website
Alabama	Ala. Code §§ 6-3-2; 6-3-7; 12-12-30; 12-12-31; 12-12-70; 12-12-71	$6,000	No.	http://judicial.alabama.gov/library/SmallClaimsRules
Alaska	Alaska Stat. §§ 22.15.040; 22.15.050	$10,000	No.	https://public.courts.alaska.gov/web/forms/docs/sc-100.pdf
Arizona 1	Ariz. Rev. Stat. §§ 22-501 to 22-524	$3,500	No.	www.azcourts.gov/selfservicecenter/Small-Claims
Arkansas	Ark. Const. amend. 80, § 7; Ark. Code § 16-17-706	$5,000	No.	https://arkansasag.gov/arkansass-lawyer/legal-resources/guide-to-small-claims-court
California	Cal. Civ. Proc. Code §§ 116.110 to 116.950	$12,500 for individuals, except that a plaintiff may not file a claim over $2,500 more than twice a year. Limit for local public entity or for businesses is $6,250. $8,125 is the limit in suits by an individual against a guarantor that charges for its guarantor or surety services. Until October 1, 2025, court may hear claims for COVID-related rental debt of any amount (limit of two filings per year does not apply to such actions).	No.	https://selfhelp.courts.ca.gov/small-claims-california
Colorado	Colo. Rev. Stat. §§ 13-6-401 to 13-6-417	$7,500	No.	www.courts.state.co.us/Self_Help/smallclaims
Connecticut	Conn. Gen. Stat. §§ 51-15; 51-345; 52-259	$5,000 (except you might be able to get more in landlord-tenant security deposit claims)	No.	www.jud.ct.gov/SmallClaims.htm
Delaware	Del. Code tit. 10, §§ 9301 to 9640	$25,000	Yes.	https://courts.delaware.gov/jpcourt
District of Columbia	D.C. Code §§ 11-1301 to 11-1323; 16-3901 to 16-3910; 17-301 to 17-307	$10,000	No.	www.dccourts.gov/services/civil-matters/requesting-10k-or-less
Florida	Fla. Sm. Cl. Rule 7.010 to 7.230; Fla. Sm. Cl. Form 7.300 to 7.353	$8,000	Yes.	https://help.flcourts.org/Other-Resources/Small-Claims
Georgia	Ga. Code §§ 15-10-1; 15-10-2; 15-10-40 to 15-10-54; 15-10-80; 15-10-87	$15,000 (no limit in eviction cases)	Yes.	https://consumer.georgia.gov/resolve-your-dispute/other-options-resolving-your-dispute
Hawaii	Haw. Rev. Stat. §§ 604-5; 633-27 to 633-36	$5,000; no limit in landlord-tenant residential security deposit cases. For return of leased or rented personal property, the property must not be worth more than $5,000.	No.	www.courts.state.hi.us/self-help/small_claims/small_claims

1 Justice Courts, similar to small claims court but with more procedures, have a limit of $10,000. Rules can be found at Ariz. Rev. Stat. §§ 22-201 to 22-284. (Arizona)

State Small Claims Court Limits (continued)

State	Statutes	Dollar limit	Can Hear Eviction Suits?	Court Website
Idaho	Idaho Code §§ 1-2301 to 1-2315	$5,000	No.	https://courtselfhelp.idaho.gov/Forms/claims
Illinois 2	735 Ill. Comp. Stat. §§ 5/2-101 to 5/2-208; 705 Ill. Comp. Stat. § 205/11	$10,000	Check with clerk of local circuit court, because court rules vary.	www.illinoiscourts.gov/self-help/rss-feeds/small-claims
Indiana 3	Ind. Code §§ 33-28-3-2 to 33-28-3-10 (circuit court); 33-29-2-1 to 33-29-2-10 (superior court); 33-34-3-1 to 33-34-3-15 (Marion County Small Claims Court)	$10,000 (limit might be different in Marion County)	Yes, if total rent due does not exceed $10,000.	www.in.gov/courts/publications/small-claims-manual
Iowa	Iowa Code §§ 631.1 to 631.17	$6,500	Yes.	www.iowacourts.gov/for-the-public/representing-yourself/small-claims
Kansas	Kan. Stat. §§ 61-2701 to 61-2714	$4,000	No.	www.kscourts.org/Public/Small-Claims
Kentucky 4	Ky. Rev. Stat. §§ 24A.200 to 24A.360	$2,500	Yes.	www.kycourts.gov/Legal-Help/Documents/P6SmallClaimsHandbookweb.pdf
Louisiana	La. Rev. Stat. §§ 13:5200 to 13:5211 (city court); La. Code Civ. Proc., Art. 4831, 4832, 4845, 4901 to 4925, and Art. 42 (Justice of the Peace Courts)	$5,000 (city court); $5,000 (justice of the peace, but no limit in eviction cases)	Available in Justice of the Peace courts only.	www.lsba.org/Public/CourtStructure.aspx www.brla.gov/150/City-Court
Maine	Me. Rev. Stat. tit. 14, §§ 7481 to 7487	$6,000	No.	www.courts.maine.gov/help/small-claims/index.html
Maryland	Md. Code Cts. & Jud. Proc., §§ 4-405; 6-403	$5,000	Yes, as long as the rent claimed does not exceed $5,000.	www.mdcourts.gov/legalhelp/smallclaims
Massachusetts 5	Mass. Gen. Laws ch. 218, §§ 21 to 25; ch. 93A, § 9 (consumer complaints)	$7,000	No.	www.mass.gov/small-claims

2 An alternative procedure exists for claims of $3,000 or less in Cook County's Pro Se Court. Plaintiffs represent themselves, and lawyers are allowed for defendants. (Illinois)

3 Tenants who are the object of a self-help eviction or its attempt, who suffer or are at risk of suffering serious harm, may ask the small claims court for an order directing the landlord to stop and return possession of the rental if needed. When a tenant commits or threatens to commit waste to the rental unit, landlords may ask the small claims court for an emergency order directing the tenant to return possession of the rental to the landlord, refrain from committing waste, or both. (Indiana)

4 Professional moneylenders and collection agents cannot sue in small claims court. (Kentucky)

5 Might be entitled to attorneys' fees above and beyond the $7,000 limit. (Massachusetts)

State Small Claims Court Limits (continued)

State	Statutes	Dollar limit	Can Hear Eviction Suits?	Court Website
Michigan	Mich. Comp. Laws §§ 600.8401 to 600.8427	$7,000	No.	www.courts.michigan.gov/SCAO-forms/small-claims
Minnesota	Minn. Stat. §§ 491A.01 to 491A.03	$15,000	No.	www.mncourts.gov/Help-Topics/Conciliation-Court.aspx
Mississippi	Miss. Code §§ 9-11-9 to 9-11-33; 11-9-101 to 11-9-147; 11-25-1; 11-51-85	$3,500	Yes.	www.courts.ms.gov/trialcourts/justicecourt/justicecourt.php
Missouri	Mo. Rev. Stat. §§ 482.300 to 482.365	$5,000	No.	www.mo.gov/government/judicial-branch
Montana	Mont. Code §§ 3-10-1001 to 3-10-1004	$7,000	No.	https://dojmt.gov/consumer/guide-to-small-claims-court
Nebraska 6	Neb. Rev. Stat. §§ 25-505.1; 25-2801 to 25-2807	$3,900 from July 1, 2020, through June 30, 2025 (adjusted every five years based on the Consumer Price Index)	No.	https://supremecourt.nebraska.gov/self-help/small-claims
Nevada	Nev. Rev. Stat. §§ 73.010 to 73.060	$10,000	No.	www.civillawselfhelpcenter.org/self-help/small-claims
New Hampshire	N.H. Rev. Stat. §§ 503:1 to 503:11	$10,000	No.	www.courts.nh.gov/our-courts/circuit-court/district-division/small-claims
New Jersey 7	N.J. Ct. R. 6:1-2	$5,000	No.	www.njcourts.gov/self-help/small-claims-court
New Mexico	N.M. Stat. §§ 34-8A-1 to 34-8A-10 (metropolitan court); 35-3-3, 35-3-5, 35-8-1 and 35-8-2 (magistrate court); 35-11-2, 35-13-1 to 35-13-3 (appeals)	$10,000	Yes.	www.nmcourts.gov/self-help/self-help-guide
New York 8	N.Y. City Civ. Ct. Act §§ 1801 to 1815, 1801-a to 1814-a; N.Y. Uniform City Ct. Act §§ 1801 to 1815, 1801-a to 1814-a, 2300; N.Y. Uniform Dist. Ct. Act §§ 1801 to 1815, 1801-a to 1814-a, 2300; Village, Town and District Courts in N.Y. § 1:12; N.Y. Uniform Justice Court Act §§ 1801 to 1815, 2300; N.Y. Dist. Ct. Act §§ 1801 to 1815	$10,000 in New York City; $5,000 in Nassau County, Western Suffolk County, and City Courts (excluding NYC); $3,000 in Eastern Suffolk County, Town Courts, and Village Courts.	No.	www.nycourts.gov/courthelp/SmallClaims/index.shtml https://ww2.nycourts.gov/lawlibraries/nycodes statutes.shtml (state statutes) www.courts.state.ny.us/courthelp/pdfs/SmallClaimsHandbook.pdf www.nycourts.gov/COURTS/nyc/smallclaims/pdfs/smallclaims.pdf

6 Check this website for any changes to jurisdictional limit after June 30, 2020: https://supremecourt.nebraska.gov/self-help/small-claims. (Nebraska)

7 The Special Civil Part, like the small claims court but with more procedures, has a limit of $20,000. See www.njcourts.gov/self-help/special-civil-court. (New Jersey)

8 Corporations and partnerships cannot sue in small claims court, but may appear as defendants. (Does not apply to municipal and public benefit corporations and school districts.) Instead, they can bring commercial claims, which have similar rules to small claims courts but are subject to these additional restrictions: (1) Same limits and procedures as regular small claims except claim is brought by corporation, partnership, or association. Business must have principal office in N.Y. state; Defendant must reside, be employed, or have a business office in the county where suit is brought. (New York)

State Small Claims Court Limits (continued)

State	Statutes	Dollar limit	Can Hear Eviction Suits?	Court Website
North Carolina	N. C. Gen. Stat. §§ 7A-210 to 7A-232; 42-29	Varies from $5,000 to $10,000. Call clerk of court in your county to find out limit.	Yes.	www.nccourts.gov/courts/small-claims-court
North Dakota [9]	N. D. Cent. Code §§ 27-08.1-01 to 27-08.1-08	$15,000	No.	www.ndcourts.gov/legal-self-help/small-claims
Ohio	Ohio Rev. Code §§ 1925.01 to 1925.18	$6,000	No.	www.supremecourt.ohio.gov/courts/services-to-courts/court-services/access-to-justice-resources
Oklahoma [10]	Okla. Stat. tit. 12, §§ 131 to 141; 1751 to 1773	$10,000	Yes.	https://oklacountyjudges.org/small-claims
Oregon	Or. Rev. Stat. §§ 46.405 to 46.570; 55.011 to 55.140	$10,000	No.	www.courts.oregon.gov/forms/Pages/small-claims.aspx
Pennsylvania	42 Pa. Cons. Stat. §§ 1123; 1515	$12,000	Yes.	www.pacourts.us/courts/minor-courts
Rhode Island	R.I. Gen. Laws §§ 10-16-1 to 10-16-16; 9-4-3; 9-4-4; 9-12-10 (appeals)	$5,000	No.	www.courts.ri.gov/Courts/districtcourt/Pages/smallclaims.aspx
South Carolina	S.C. Code §§ 22-3-10 to 22-3-320; 15-7-30; 18-7-10 to 18-7-30	$7,500	Yes.	www.sccourts.org/selfHelp
South Dakota	S.D. Codified Laws §§ 15-39-45 to 15-39-78; 16-12B-6; 16-12B-12; 16-12B-16; 16-12C-8; 16-12C-13 to 16-12C-15	$12,000	No.	https://ujs.sd.gov/Small_Claims
Tennessee [11]	Tenn. Code §§ 16-15-501 to 16-15-505; 16-15-710 to 16-15-735; 16-15-901 to 16-15-905; 20-4-101; 20-4-103	$25,000. No limit in eviction suits or suits to recover personal property.	Yes.	http://tncourts.gov/programs/self-help-center
Texas	Tex. Gov't. Code §§ 27.031, 27.060	$20,000	Separate small claims courts have been abolished as of August 2013; both small claims cases and evictions are heard in Justice Court. Evictions cases are governed by Rules 500-507 and 510 of Part V of the Rules of Civil Procedure.	https://guides.sll.texas.gov/small-claims
Utah	Utah Code §§ 78A-8-101 to 78A-8-109	$15,000 through December 31, 2024; $20,000 as of January 1, 2025.	No.	www.utcourts.gov/en/self-help/case-categories/consumer/small-claims.html
Vermont	Vt. Stat. tit. 12, §§ 5531 to 5541; 402	$10,000	No.	www.vermontjudiciary.org/self-help/debt-collection-small-claims

9 Plaintiff may not discontinue once small claims process is begun; if plaintiff seeks to discontinue, claim will be dismissed with prejudice (plaintiff cannot refile claim). (North Dakota)

10 Collection agencies may not sue in small claims court. (Oklahoma)

11 Tennessee has no actual small claims system, but trials in General Sessions Court are normally conducted with informal rules. (Tennessee)

State Small Claims Court Limits (continued)

State	Statutes	Dollar limit	Can Hear Eviction Suits?	Court Website
Virginia [12]	Va. Code §§ 8.01-262; 16.1-76; 16.1-77; 16.1-106; 16.1-113; 16.1-122.1 to 16.1-122.7	$5,000	No.	www.courts.state.va.us/resources/small_claims_court_procedures.pdf; www.courts.state.va.us/courts/gd/home.html
Washington	Wash. Rev. Code §§ 12.36.010 to 12.40.120; 3.66.040	$10,000 if brought by natural person; $5,000 all other cases.	No.	www.courts.wa.gov/newsinfo/resources/?fa=newsinfo_jury.scc&altMenu=smal
West Virginia	W.Va. Code §§ 50-2-1 to 50-6-3; 56-1-1	$10,000	Yes.	www.courtswv.gov/lower-courts
Wisconsin	Wis. Stat. §§ 799.01 to 799.445; 421.401; 801.50; 808.03	$10,000. No limit in eviction suits.	Yes.	www.wicourts.gov/services/public/selfhelp/smallclaims.htm
Wyoming	Wyo. Stat. §§ 1-21-201 to 1-21-205; 5-9-128; 5-9-136	$6,000	No.	www.courts.state.wy.us/court_rule/rules-and-forms-governing-small-claims-cases

[12] General district courts, similar to small claims court but with more procedures, have exclusive jurisdiction of cases where the claim doesn't exceed $4,500, and it shares jurisdiction with the circuit courts for cases where $4,500 to $25,000 is in controversy. (See Va. Code §§ 16.1-77 to 16.1-80.)(Virginia)

Landlord's Duty to Rerent

State	Legal authority	Must make reasonable efforts to rerent	Has no duty to look for or rent to a new tenant	Law is unclear or courts are divided on the issue
Alabama	Ala. Code §§ 35-9A-105, 35-9A-423	✓ [1]		
Alaska	Alaska Stat. § 34.03.230(c)	✓		
Arizona	Ariz. Rev. Stat. § 33-1370	✓		
Arkansas	*Grayson v. Mixon*, 5 S.W.2d 312 (Ark. 1928)		✓	
California	Cal. Civ. Code §§ 1951.2, 1951.4	✓	✓ [2]	
Colorado	*Schneiker v. Gordon*, 732 P.2d 603 (Colo. 1987)	✓ [3]		
Connecticut	Conn. Gen. Stat. § 47a-11a	✓		
Delaware	25 Del. Code § 5507(d)(2)	✓		
District of Columbia	D.C. Code § 42-3505.52	✓		
Florida	Fla. Stat. § 83.595		✓ [4]	
Georgia	Ga. Code § 44-7-34; *Peterson v. Midas Realty Corp.*, 287 S.E.2d 61 (Ga. Ct. App. 1981)		✓	✓ [5]
Hawaii	Haw. Rev. Stat. § 521-70(d)	✓ [6]		
Idaho	*Consol. Ag v. Rangen, Inc.*, 128 Idaho 228 (Idaho 1996)	✓		
Illinois	735 Ill. Comp. Stat. § 5/9-213.1	✓		
Indiana	*Nylen v. Park Doral Apartments*, 535 N.E.2d 178 (Ind. Ct. App. 1989)	✓		
Iowa	Iowa Code § 562A.29(3)	✓		
Kansas	Kan. Stat. § 58-2565(c)	✓		
Kentucky	Ky. Rev. Stat. § 383.670	✓		
Louisiana	La. Civ. Code § 2002; *Easterling v. Halter Marine, Inc.*, 470 So.2d 221 (La. Ct. App. 4 1985); *Gray v. Kanavel*, 508 So.2d 970 (La. Ct. App. 1987)			✓
Maine	Me. Rev. Stat. tit. 14, § 6010-A	✓		
Maryland	Md. Code Real Prop., § 8-207	✓		

1 Landlord can prioritize renting other vacant units first. (Alabama)

2 Landlord must make reasonable efforts to rerent. However, landlord may keep the lease in effect and recover rent as it becomes due provided possession is not retaken and the lease states the tenant has the right to sublet or assign, subject only to landlord's reasonable limitations. (California)

3 Case law favors mitigation. (Colorado)

4 Landlord can rerent; do nothing (tenant remains liable for rent as it comes due); or invoke any liquidated damages or early termination provision(s). The latter two remedies are available only if the lease includes a liquidated damages addendum, or addition, that provides for no more than two months' damages and requires tenant to give no more than 60 days' notice. Liquidated damages provision must substantially include the language specified in Fla. Stat. § 83.595. (Florida)

5 Ga. Code § 44-7-34 states that nothing precludes landlords from retaining the security deposit for rent and other damages provided the landlord attempts to mitigate the actual damages. However, a Georgia court has held that a landlord could keep the rental vacant and sue for rent as it becomes due in spite of this statute. *Kimber v. Towne Hills Dev. Co.*, 274 S.E.2d 620 (Ga. Ct. App. 1980). (Georgia)

6 The statute implies that the landlord has a duty to rerent: When a tenant breaks the lease, the landlord is entitled to the lesser of (1) the entire rent due for the remainder of the term, or (2) the amount of rent accrued during the period reasonably necessary to rerent at a fair rent plus the difference between fair rent and the rent under the lease, as well as a commission for the renting of the unit. The landlord is entitled to the lesser of these two even if the landlord doesn't actually rerent the unit. (Hawaii)

Landlord's Duty to Rerent (continued)

State	Legal authority	Must make reasonable efforts to rerent	Has no duty to look for or rent to a new tenant	Law is unclear or courts are divided on the issue
Massachusetts	*Edmands v. Rust & Richardson Drug Co.*, 191 Mass. 123, 128 (1906).	✓ [7]		✓ [8]
Michigan	*Fox v. Roethlisberger*, 85 N.W.2d 73 (Mich. 1957)	✓		
Minnesota	*Control Data Corp. v. Metro Office Parks Co.*, 296 Minn. 302 (Minn. 1973)		✓	
Mississippi	*Alsup v. Banks*, 9 So. 895 (Miss. 1891)		✓	
Missouri	*Rhoden Inv. Co. v. Sears, Roebuck & Co.*, 499 S.W.2d 375 (Mo. 1973), Mo. Rev. Stat. § 535.300	✓ [9]		
Montana	Mont. Code § 70-24-426	✓		
Nebraska	Neb. Rev. Stat. § 76-1432	✓		
Nevada	Nev. Rev. Stat. § 118.175	✓		
New Hampshire	*Wen v. Arlen's, Inc.*, 103 A.2d 86 (N.H. 1954); *Modular Mfg., Inc. v. Dernham Co.*, 65 B.R. 856 (Bankr. D. N.H. 1986)			✓
New Jersey	*Sommer v. Kridel*, 378 A.2d 767 (N.J. 1977)	✓		
New Mexico	N.M. Stat. § 47-8-6	✓		
New York	N.Y. Real Prop. Law § 227-e	✓		
North Carolina	*Isbey v. Crews*, 284 S.E.2d 534 (N.C. Ct. App. 1981)	✓		
North Dakota	N.D. Cent. Code § 47-16-13.5	✓		
Ohio	*Stern v. Taft*, 361 N.E.2d 279 (Ohio Ct. App. 1976); *Dennis v. Morgan*, 732 N.E.2d 391 (Ohio 2000)	✓ [10]		
Oklahoma	Okla. Stat. Ann. tit. 41, § 129	✓		
Oregon	Or. Rev. Stat. § 90.410	✓		
Pennsylvania	*Stonehedge Square Ltd. P'ship v. Movie Merchs.*, 715 A.2d 1082 (Pa. 1998)		✓	
Rhode Island	R.I. Gen. Laws § 34-18-40	✓		
South Carolina	S.C. Code § 27-40-730(c)	✓		

7 From www.masslegalhelp.org/housing/lt1-chapter-11-moving-out.pdf: For various statements of the landlord's requirement to mitigate damages, see *Edmands v. Rust & Richardson Drug Co.*, 191 Mass. 123, 128 (1906). The Massachusetts Supreme Court found that the "[landlord] owed to the [tenant] the duty to use reasonable diligence and to make the loss or damage to the [tenant] as light as [the landlord] reasonably could." *Woodbury v. Sparrell Print*, 198 Mass. 1, 8 (1908). See also *Loitherstein v. International Business Mach. Corp.*, 11 Mass. App. Ct. 91, 95 and n. 3 (1980), rev. denied 441 N.E.2d 1042 (1981); *Cantor v. Van Noorden Co.*, 4 Mass. App. Ct. 819 (1976). But see *Fifty Assocs. v. Berger Dry Goods Co. Inc.*, 275 Mass. 509, 514 (1931). Note that the Boston Housing Court has at least twice found a clear obligation to mitigate. *Bridges v. Palmer*, Boston Housing Court, 07326 (May 24, 1979); *Grumman v. Barres*, Boston Housing Court, 06334 (March 1, 1979). See also *Gagne v. Kreinest*, Hampden Housing Court, 91SC1569 (December 6, 1991), where the judge found that a landlord who did not advertise a vacant unit in the newspaper had not mitigated her damages. (Massachusetts)

8 Although case law seems to accept a duty to mitigate, there is no definitive statement of the law and the issue remains unsettled. (Massachusetts)

9 Landlord must mitigate only if intending to use tenant's security deposit to cover future unpaid rent. (Missouri)

10 Duty to mitigate applies in absence of any clause that purports to relieve the landlord of this duty (courts might enforce such a clause). (Ohio)

		Must make reasonable efforts to rerent	Has no duty to look for or rent to a new tenant	Law is unclear or courts are divided on the issue
State	**Legal authority**			
South Dakota	No cases or statutes in South Dakota discuss this issue for residential tenancies.			✓ [11]
Tennessee	Tenn. Code § 66-28-507(c)	✓ [12]		
Texas	Tex. Prop. Code § 91.006	✓		
Utah	Utah Code § 78B-6-816; *Reid v. Mutual of Omaha Ins. Co.*, 776 P.2d 896 (Utah 1989)	✓		
Vermont	Vt. Stat. tit. 9, § 4462		✓	
Virginia	Va. Code § 55.1-1251	✓		
Washington	Wash. Rev. Code §§ 59.18.310, 59.18.595	✓ [13]		
West Virginia	W.Va. Code § 37-6-7; *Teller v. McCoy*, 253 S.E.2d 114 (W.Va. 1978)	✓		
Wisconsin	Wis. Stat. § 704.29	✓		
Wyoming	*Goodwin v. Upper Crust, Inc.*, 624 P.2d 1192 (1981)	✓		

Table title: **Landlord's Duty to Rerent (continued)**

[11] However, it is likely that a S.D. court would require a landlord to mitigate damages. The S.D. Supreme Court has found that "[t]he breaching party has the burden of proving damages would have been lessened by the exercise of reasonable diligence on the part of the non-breaching party." (Ducheneaux v. Miller, 488 N.W.2d 902, 918 (S.D. Sup. Ct. 1992).) Also see Peska Properties, Inc. v. Northern Rental Corp., 976 N.W.2d 749 (S.D. 2022), where the court noted that a commercial landlord must make "commercially reasonable efforts to mitigate its damages. (South Dakota)

[12] Applies only in counties having a population of more than 75,000, according to the 2010 federal census. (See Tenn. Code § 66-28-102.) (Tennessee)

[13] Tenant's death: Detailed procedures must be followed when premises are vacant due to tenant's death. (See Wash. Rev. Code § 59.18.595.) (Washington)

Consequences of Self-Help Evictions

State	Amount Tenant Can Sue For	Statute Provides for Tenant's Court Costs & Attorneys' Fees	Statute Gives Tenant the Right to Stay	Statute or Legal Authority
Alabama	Three months' rent or actual damages, whichever is greater. If tenant elects to terminate the lease, landlord must return entire security deposit and all unearned prepaid rent.	Yes	Yes	Ala. Code § 35-9A-407
Alaska	One-and-one-half times the actual damages. If tenant elects to terminate the lease, landlord must return all prepaid rent and security deposits. Tenant can sue for attorneys' fees but not court costs.	Yes	Yes	Alaska Stat. §§ 34.03.210; 34.03.350
Arizona	Two months' rent or twice the actual damages, whichever is greater. If tenant elects to terminate the lease, landlord must return all security deposit and prepaid rent.	Yes	Yes	Ariz. Rev. Stat. §§ 33-1364; 33-1367
Arkansas	Self-help evictions are not allowed, but it's up to the court to determine damages.	N/A	N/A	*Gorman v. Ratliff*, 712 S.W. 2d 888 (1986)
California	Actual damages plus $100 per day of violation ($250 minimum). Tenant may ask for an injunction prohibiting any further violation during the court action.	Yes	Yes	Cal. Civ. Code § 789.3
Colorado	Tenant may bring a civil action to prevent further violations and to recover damages, costs, and reasonable attorneys' fees. If a violation is found, the tenant will receive an award of their actual damages, costs, and attorneys' fees, plus the higher amount of either 3 times the monthly rent or $5,000.	Yes	Yes	Colo. Rev. Stat. § 38-12-510
Connecticut	Double actual damages. Landlord may also be prosecuted for a misdemeanor.	Yes	Yes	Conn. Gen. Stat. §§ 47a-43, 47a-46, 53a-214
Delaware	Triple damages or three times per diem rent for time excluded, whichever is greater. Tenant may recover court costs, but not attorneys' fees.	Yes	Yes	Del. Code tit. 25, § 5313
District of Columbia	Actual and punitive damages.	N/A	N/A	*Mendes v. Johnson*, 389 A.2d 781 (D.C. 1978)
Florida	Actual damages or three months' rent, whichever is greater.	Yes	No	Fla. Stat. § 83.67
Georgia	Landlord may not resort to self-help evictions. Damages are determined by the court.	N/A	N/A	*Forrest v. Peacock*, 363 S.E. 2d 581 (1987), reversed on other grounds, 368 S.E.2d 519 (1988)
Hawaii	Two months' rent or free occupancy for two months (tenant must have been excluded "overnight"). If tenant elects to terminate the lease, landlord must return the security deposit in accordance with Haw. Rev. Stat. § 521-44(c). Court may order landlord to stop illegal conduct.	Yes	Yes	Haw. Rev. Stat. § 521-63(c)

	Consequences of Self-Help Evictions (continued)			
State	**Amount Tenant Can Sue For**	**Statute Provides for Tenant's Court Costs & Attorneys' Fees**	**Statute Gives Tenant the Right to Stay**	**Statute or Legal Authority**
Idaho	Three times the amount of actual damages.	Yes	N/A	*Schlegel v. Hansen*, 570 P.2d 292 (Idaho Sup. Ct. 1977); *Riverside Dev. Co. v. Ritchie*, 650 P.2d 657 (Idaho Sup. Ct. 1982); Idaho Code §§ 6-317 and 6-324
Illinois	One month's rent for every month without utility service (partial months prorated), plus consequential damages. If termination resulted from deliberate or reckless indifference or disregard for tenant's rights, or bad faith, court may award each tenant $300 or (when multiple tenants have been affected), the sum of $5,000 divided by the number of affected tenants, whichever is less.	No	Yes	735 Ill. Comp. Stat. §§ 1.4, 2.1; *U.S. v. White*, 541 F.Supp. 1181 (N.D. Ill. 1982) (held that a tenant who has been subject to a self-help eviction remains entitled to possession of the premises)
Indiana	Statute doesn't specify damages.	No	No	Ind. Code § 32-31-5-6
Iowa	Actual damages, plus punitive damages up to twice the monthly rent and attorneys' fees. If tenant elects to terminate the lease, landlord must return all prepaid rent and security deposits.	Yes	Yes	Iowa Code § 562A.26
Kansas	Actual damages or one-and-one-half months' rent, whichever is greater. If the rental agreement is terminated, the tenant is entitled to the return of security deposit.	No	Yes	Kan. Stat. § 58-2563
Kentucky	Three months' rent. Tenant may also recover reasonable attorneys' fees. If tenancy is terminated, the landlord must return prepaid rent.	Yes	Yes	Ky. Rev. Stat. § 383.655
Louisiana	Landlord may not resort to self-help evictions. Damages are determined by the court.	N/A	N/A	*Weber v. McMillan*, 285 So.2d 349 (1973)
Maine	Actual damages or $250, whichever is greater. The court may award costs and fees to landlord if it finds that the tenant brought a frivolous court lawsuit or one intended to harass.	Yes	No	Me. Rev. Stat. tit. 14, § 6014
Maryland	Actual damages, reasonable attorneys' fees and costs.	Yes	No	Md. Code Real Prop., § 8-216
Massachusetts	Three months' rent or three times the actual damages.	Yes	Yes	Mass. Gen. Laws ch. 186, § 15F
Michigan	Up to three times actual damages or $200, whichever is greater.	No	Yes	Mich. Comp. Laws § 600.2918
Minnesota	Treble damages or $500, whichever is greater, and reasonable attorneys' fees. Landlord might also be found guilty of a misdemeanor.	Yes	Yes	Minn. Stat. §§ 504B.225; 504B.231; 504B.375
Mississippi	Landlord may not resort to self-help evictions unless lease gives landlord the right to remove the tenant and take possession of the premises without notice.	N/A	N/A	*Bender v. North Meridian Mobile Home Park*, 636 So.2d 385 (Miss. Sup. Ct. 1994)

	Consequences of Self-Help Evictions (continued)			
State	**Amount Tenant Can Sue For**	**Statute Provides for Tenant's Court Costs & Attorneys' Fees**	**Statute Gives Tenant the Right to Stay**	**Statute or Legal Authority**
Missouri	A landlord who wrongfully removes a tenant or tenant's property from rental, or who changes the locks, is guilty of forcible entry and detainer. Court will determine damages.	N/A	N/A	*Steinke v. Leight*, 235 S.W.2d 115 (1950); Mo. Stat. § 441.233
Montana	Three months' rent or three times the actual damages, whichever is greater, along with all security deposits and prepaid rent recoverable.	Yes	Yes	Mont. Code §§ 70-24-411; 70-24-442
Nebraska	Up to three months' rent and reasonable attorneys' fees. If tenancy is terminated landlord shall return all recoverable security deposit and prepaid rent.	Yes	Yes	Neb. Rev. Stat. § 76-1430
Nevada	Actual damages, an amount up to $2,500 to be fixed by the court, or both. If tenant elects to terminate rental agreement or lease, landlord must return all prepaid rent and any security deposit that is recoverable under law. Tenant might be entitled to court costs.	Yes	Yes	Nev. Rev. Stat. § 118A.390
New Hampshire	Actual damages or $1,000, whichever is greater; if court finds that landlord knowingly or willingly broke the law, two to three times this amount. (Amount might also vary depending on the situation.) Each day that a violation continues is a separate violation. Court may order a tenant who brings a frivolous suit or one intended to harass to pay landlord's costs and fees.	Yes	Yes	N.H. Rev. Stat. §§ 540-A:3, 540-A:4, 358-A:10
New Jersey	Self-help is prohibited, and landlord who engages in self-help is a "disorderly person," a criminal offense that subjects the landlord to up to six months in jail.	No	No	N.J. Stat. §§ 2A:39-1, 2C:43-8
New Mexico	A prorated share of the rent for each day of violation, actual damages, and civil penalty of twice the monthly rent.	Yes	Yes	N.M. Stat. § 47-8-36
New York	Three times the actual damages. Violations are misdemeanors, and landlords are subject to civil penalties of $1,000 to up to $10,000.	No	Yes	N.Y. Real Prop. Acts. Law §§ 768, 853
North Carolina	Actual damages.	No	Yes	N.C. Gen. Stat. § 42-25.9
North Dakota	Triple damages.	No	No	N.D. Cent. Code § 32-03-29
Ohio	Actual damages. Tenant can sue for attorneys' fees but not court costs.	Yes	No	Ohio Rev. Code § 5321.15
Oklahoma	Twice the average monthly rental or twice the actual damages, whichever is greater. If tenant elects to terminate the rental agreement, landlord must return all prepaid and unearned rent, and return deposits in accordance with Okla. Stat. tit. 41, § 115.	No	Yes	Okla. Stat. tit. 41, § 123
Oregon	Two months' rent or twice the actual damages, whichever is greater. If the rental agreement is terminated, the landlord shall return all security deposits and prepaid rent recoverable under the state security deposit law.	No	Yes	Or. Rev. Stat. § 90.375

Consequences of Self-Help Evictions (continued)

State	Amount Tenant Can Sue For	Statute Provides for Tenant's Court Costs & Attorneys' Fees	Statute Gives Tenant the Right to Stay	Statute or Legal Authority
Pennsylvania	Self-help evictions are not allowed, but no specific penalties are provided (it's up to the court to determine damages).	N/A	N/A	*Wofford v. Vavreck*, 22 Pa. D. & C.3d 444 (1981); *Kuriger v. Cramer*, 498 A.2d 1331 (1985)
Rhode Island	Three months' rent or three times the actual damages, whichever is greater. Tenant can sue for attorneys' fees but not court costs. If the rental agreement is terminated the landlord must return all prepaid rent and security deposit recoverable under state security deposit law.	Yes	Yes	R.I. Gen. Laws § 34-18-34
South Carolina	Three months' rent or twice the actual damages, whichever is greater. If tenant chooses to terminate the rental agreement, landlord must return the security as specified under S.C. Code § 27-40-410. Tenant can sue for attorneys' fees but not court costs.	Yes	Yes	S.C. Code § 27-40-660
South Dakota	Two months' rent. If tenant elects to terminate the lease, landlord must return entire security deposit.	No	Yes	S.D. Codified Laws § 43-32-6
Tennessee	Actual and punitive damages. If tenant elects to terminate the lease, landlord must return entire security deposit and any prepaid rent. Tenant can sue for attorneys' fees but not court costs.	Yes	Yes	Tenn. Code § 66-28-504
Texas	A civil penalty of one month's rent plus $1,000, actual damages, court costs, and reasonable attorneys' fees.	Yes	Yes	Tex. Prop. Code §§ 92.008, 92.0081, 92.009
Utah	Self-help evictions are not allowed, but no specific penalties are provided.	No	No	Utah Code § 78B-6-814
Vermont	Unspecified damages, plus court costs and attorneys' fees. Court may award costs and attorneys' fees to landlord if the court finds that the tenant brought a frivolous lawsuit or one intended to harass.	Yes	Yes	Vt. Stat. tit. 9, §§ 4463, 4464
Virginia	Actual damages, reasonable attorneys' fees, and the greater of either $5,000 or 4 month's rent.	Yes	Yes	Va. Code § 55.1-1243.1
Washington	Actual damages. For utility shut-offs only, actual damages and up to $100 per day of no service. Court may award costs and fees to the prevailing party.	Yes	Yes	Wash. Rev. Code §§ 59.18.290, 59.18.300
West Virginia				No cases or statutes on point, but see Renters' Rights Brochure from the Office of the West Virginia Attorney General.
Wisconsin	Self-help evictions are prohibited. The court will determine damages.	No	No	Wis. Admin. Code ATCP § 134.09(7)
Wyoming				

How to Use the Downloadable Forms on the Nolo Website

This book comes with downloadable files that you can access online at:

www.nolo.com/back-of-book/EVTEN.html

You can open, edit, print, and save these RTF (Rich Text Format) form files with most word processing programs such as Microsoft *Word*, Windows *WordPad*, and recent versions of *WordPerfect*. On a Mac, you can use Apple *TextEdit* or Apple *Pages*. You can also work with the forms thorough a word processing app such as Google Docs (www.docs.google.com).

Editing RTFs

Here are some general instructions about editing RTF forms in your word processing program. Refer to the form instructions in this book for help about what should go in each blank.

- **Blank lines.** Blank lines indicate where to enter information. After filling in the needed text, delete the line.
- **Bracketed and italicized text.** Bracketed and italicized text indicates instructions. Be sure to remove all instructional text before you finalize your document.
- **Optional text.** Optional text gives you the choice to include or exclude text. Delete any optional text you don't want to use. Renumber numbered items, if necessary.
- **Alternative text.** Alternative text gives you the choice between two or more text options. Delete those options you don't want to use. Renumber numbered items, if necessary.
- **Signature lines.** Signature lines should appear on a page with at least some text from the document itself.

Every word processing program uses different commands to open, format, save, and print documents, so refer to your software's help documents for help using your program. Nolo cannot provide technical support for questions about how to use your computer or your software.

> **CAUTION**
> **In accordance with U.S. copyright laws, the forms provided by this book are for your personal use only.**

List of Forms Available on the Nolo Website

The following forms are available as RTF files at: **www.nolo.com/back-of-book/EVTEN.html**

Form Title	File Name
Rental Priorities Worksheet	Priorities.rtf
Rental Application	Application.rtf
Consent to Background and Reference Check	CheckConsent.rtf
Receipt and Holding Deposit Agreement	Receipt.rtf
Landlord-Tenant Checklist	Checklist.rtf
Agreement Regarding Tenant Improvements to Rental Unit	Alteration.rtf
Amendment to Lease or Rental Agreement	Amendment.rtf
Tenant's Notice of Intent to Move Out	MoveNotice.rtf
Landlord-Tenant Agreement to Terminate Lease	Terminate.rtf
Consent to Assignment of Lease	AssignConsent.rtf
Demand for Return of Security Deposit	DepositReturn.rtf

Index

deadlines for receipt of, 281

Demand for Partial Return of Security Deposit, and sample, 294

Demand for Return of Security Deposit, and sample, 292–294

disputes, how to handle, 296–302

documenting condition of the unit, 290

eviction and, 317

and inspection, final (pre–move-out), 280–281, 290–292

and Landlord-Tenant Checklist, 112, 289, 290, 291, 292, 300

lawsuit against landlord for, 281, 290, 291, 292, 296, 297, 298–301

Letter #1: Tenant's Cleaning Plans, sample, 287

Letter #2: Tenant's Cleaning Plans, sample, 289

mediation, 297, 298

Request to be Present at Inspection, sample, 291

Request to Clean Further, sample, 291

to roommates (cotenants), 295–296

Second Demand for Return of Security Deposit, and sample, 296, 297

state statutes summarized, 379–390

written demand for, second, 297

in written rental documents, 43–44, 83

written request for, first, 292–294

written request for, second, 296, 297

written requests, sent by mail or delivery service (with proof of delivery) as best practice, 122–123, 146, 147, 280

See also Security deposits, deductions from

Self-employment, and rental applications, 17

See also Home office or business

Self-help evictions, illegal, 186, 321, 452–455

Self-help remedies. *See* Repairs and maintenance (major): remedies when landlord refuses to make

Senior citizens housing, 89, 213

Service animals, 50, 96, 97, 99

Sex discrimination (gender), 29, 89, 100, 132

Sex offenders, 16

Sexual assault by landlord, 186

Sexual harassment, 100–101, 104–105, 186, 200

lawyer for, finding, 343

Sexual orientation, discrimination based on (now federally protected), 89, 101

Shepard's, 351

Short-term hosting (Airbnb, Vrbo, etc.)

overview, 138

landlord permission for, 138

in multi-unit buildings, as factor in choosing a rental, 16

neighbor complaints and, 138

as option while seeking housing, 13

and "primary residence" requirement, 40

renters' insurance/liability coverage and, 138

written agreement with landlord for, 138

zoning laws and, 138

Short-term rentals

exempt from lead regulations, 213

as option while seeking housing, 4, 12–13

university housing offices and publications as source for, 12

Single-family residences

and bed bugs, 232, 234

carbon monoxide monitors and, 223

and delegation of repair and maintenance responsibilities to tenant, 45, 47, 145, 162, 164, 224

exempt from antidiscrimination laws, 89–90

exempt from random municipal inspections, 184

leases as common with, 36

mold investigation in, 228–229

and rent control, 64

security and, 244

Slumlords, and rent control, 65

Small claims court

overview, 298–301, 335

arrival and presence in court, 301

clerk or advisor for help with, 300, 335

compared to regular trial courts, 321–322

cost of filing, 298

evidence for, 299–300, 335

evidence, written communication sent by mail or delivery service (with proof of delivery) as best practice for, 122–123, 146, 147

frequency of landlord in, 77

if person being sued doesn't show up, 301, 302

lawyers and, 301, 335

legal problems suitable for, 335

limiting your claim to the maximum allowed, to avoid civil court, 336

limits on claims allowed in, 299, 335–336, 444–448

mediation as prerequisite to, 298

names for, in various states, 298

photography or videography of unit prior to move-in and at move-out, 120, 290, 291, 299, 326

practicing your presentation, 300–301

presenting your case in, suggestions for, 300–301

relevant laws, reading, 299

resource for, 336

rules for, 335

self-representation in, 335

tenants' groups using, 243, 336, 339

time for process of, 298

time to file, 299

witnesses in, 299, 300, 335

See also Courts; Eviction lawsuits (unlawful detainer); Lawsuits; Small claims court situations

Small claims court situations

abandoned property, retrieval of, 306

asbestos exposures, temporary housing costs, 211

credit bureau will not correct error on your credit report, 26

eviction lawsuits (unlawful retainer), 322

excessive late fee, 71

finder's fees, fraudulent, 29

hold-over tenants, 51

holding deposit refund, 31

landlord suing for broken lease, 273–274

landlord suing when deposit doesn't cover what tenant owes, 302

lead exposure, 220, 221

neighbor groups targeting drug houses, 243

"not ready" apartment, 51

privacy invasions by landlord, 185, 188–189

repairs landlord refuses to make, 157–158, 167–169

retaliatory rent increases, 77

roommates, departing, 135

security deposit disputes, 298–301

security issues, 243, 249

Smoke detectors, 120, 143

tenant disabling, 198

Smoking

marijuana smoke, 52

nonsmoking/smoke-free rentals, 52

policies on, as permissible reason to reject tenant, 28

and radon, 221

Social media, finding a rental with, 9